THE LEGEND OF John Brown

THE LEGEND OF
John Brown

A Biography and a History

RICHARD O. BOYER

ALFRED A. KNOPF *New York*

1 9 7 3

THIS IS A BORZOI BOOK
PUBLISHED BY ALFRED A. KNOPF, INC.

Library of Congress Cataloging in Publication Data

Boyer, Richard Owen   The Legend of John Brown.
Includes bibliographical references.
1. Brown, John, 1800–1859. I. Title.
E451.B77 973.6'8'0924 [B] 69–10672
ISBN 0-394-46124-X

Manufactured in the United States of America

FIRST EDITION

TO

Sophia A. Boyer

CONTENTS

PART THREE

FREE AT LAST
1850–1855

Illustrations

INFLUENCES, PLACES,
PEOPLE, AND EVENTS

FOLLOWING PAGE 264

PARTISANS, NORTH AND SOUTH

FOLLOWING PAGE 488

FOREWORD

"It Takes an Epoch...
the Whole of a Society..."

I

John Brown was born in Connecticut in 1800 and executed in Virginia in 1859 for his abortive attempt to destroy American slavery by force of arms. However harsh and single-minded his struggle for black freedom, it is a root story of American history concerned with that crucial issue which had its origin even before the nation's beginning and is perhaps still central to its fate. Because, whatever his faults, he acted at the very center of the greatest American crisis, losing his life in an effort to solve it, because thousands of Americans were later to die as part of that crisis, John Brown has become an American legend, a symbol of the struggle for full freedom to all Americans, white and black.

His life, writes John Jay Chapman, is an example "of the symbolism inherent in human nature and in human society. . . . Everyone living at the time takes some part in the episode; and thereafter, the story remains . . . an epitome of the national and religious idea, which was born through the crisis. . . . It takes an epoch, it takes the whole of a society, it takes a national and religious birthpang" to produce such a one as John Brown, Chapman writes, and adds that "the story of him is an immortal legend—perhaps the only one in our history." [1]

A legend is often defined as the popular if unverifiable story of a hero coming down from the past. But in this narrative we prefer Chapman's insight with his insistence that a major legend of a people involves, however symbolically, everyone living at a time of national crisis. It involves opponents of the protagonist as well as his supporters, for it is their clash which shapes the action and development of all concerned. A legend in this sense is the story of a people at a time of peril. Its central figure is transformed and shaped by the experiences of his generation and in turn transforms it. It is not necessary that he be good or bad but it is necessary that he be representative, however oversized his actions. The hopes and deeds of thousands create both him and his legend, which influences other thousands because it contains their inner aspirations if not their outward actions.

A legend is at once less verifiable and more complete than more measurable facts because it encompasses not only the heart of epic action but also such subtle intangibles as obscure visions and cloudy dreams and hungry hopes and all that unpredictable, unarticulated human yearning that gives to man and history not only meaning but something more poignant. But if legend has elements of strangeness, if it is more inclusive than verifiable statistics or dates, it is nonetheless more than a dream or a story told by a fireside. It is also fact. It springs from a specific historical situation, as Chapman recognized when he said that neither Brown nor his legend could be accounted for except in terms of an epoch in which the whole of a society was caught in a crisis increasingly threatening its destruction. It is this whole of a society in an epoch of developing crisis that this inquiry into a time and a man tries to suggest, for it was that society and that crisis which brought into being the legend of an American whose dust, if one may vary an old song, still marches.

2

It is this solid historical base which must be indicated unless John Brown is to remain in the vacuum which makes of all his acts only idiosyncrasy or psychosis, unless he is to remain one of the great enigmas of American history. There are two different ways of viewing John Brown. They are the way he was regarded by many during his lifetime and the way he has been seen by most since. Before one can understand the passionate admiration he evoked in the thousands who mourned his death, one must experience something of the long cold war between South and North over slavery that created John Brown, as well as his supporters and antagonists, however anemic the contrast between print and the agony of actuality.

It was a time whose pressures were sufficient to unite the nonresistant Thoreau with the gun-bearing John Brown in defense of the latter's invasion of Virginia. This foray against slavery resulted in a peculiar violence, as Thoreau pointed out, and if it often had the sanction of the saintly, this can only be explained, as John Brown can only be explained, by what happened to Americans everywhere during the long years preceding the assault on Virginia's slavery. "What sort of violence is that," Thoreau wrote in his journal on October 22, 1859, of John Brown's invasion a few days before, "which is encouraged not by soldiers but by citizens, not so much by laymen as by ministers of the Gospel, not so much by fighting sects as by Quakers, and not so much by Quaker men as Quaker women?" [2] The question suggests that there are more peculiarities to American history of this period than those possessed by John Brown.

3

This book concerns the time and its temper, the long cold war over slavery between South and North, the large and violent land steeped in almost permanent crisis that formed John Brown and his contemporaries. It concerns, too, the first fifty-five years of John Brown's life (he had only four more to live), a story complete in itself in that it describes the development necessary both within him and the country before either he or it could give reality to his bloody crusade. It is the slow transformation of the American people under the impress of slavery that is important, for out of that, and as a part of that, came the slow transformation of John Brown. This part of the story ends with zero hour, with John Brown, transformed at last, arriving in Kansas as the two sides face each other in a momentary pause just before the real beginning of the American Civil War. And how men came to that point is no small part of this narrative.

Our story begins where it will end on another level and in another book; begins as John Brown's life nears its end, for his execution was the common climax of many distinguished lives, North and South, some trying to use his hanging to advance secession and civil war, others risking all they had in his defense as a patriot and martyr; some fleeing the results of the conspiracy he headed, others trying to rescue him from the gallows, some of his associates torturing themselves into breakdown or insanity. Thus from the very first his full story is indicated. Only beginning so can the modern reader see John Brown from the start as his contemporaries saw him then in that blaze of horror and heroism as he burst upon the country after the Raid at Harper's Ferry.

What gives him his significance is that he became a part of the lives of so many Americans at a point of climax both in their years and in their country's life. Without the framework of that significance from the very beginning neither his life, nor a book about it, can contain much meaning.

Only after something of the terrific impact upon the country of John Brown's invasion of Virginia is indicated, only after time and place and the extraordinary Dramatis Personae of John Brown's life are posited, as well as his own portrait presented, does his chronological story begin, because only then is it clear that this is more the story of a time than a man. Even when his years are outlined chronologically, the lives of those who acted with him or against him or who influenced him are synchronized with his own development. Perhaps this story resembles to a degree some crowded American mural, revealing the great tide of events that swept the American land and the central figures involved, but also showing in the background other figures, some less important but equally compelling, who had significant roles in the immense drama involving a good deal more than John Brown.

4

And yet of course John Brown is the center of our story. He is the Ahab of our history, pursuing with single-minded passion during the last years of his life the great leviathan of slavery; and if he is wrecked at last, the ship of his expedition South going down with all hands, he strikes his antagonist, even as he dies, a mighty blow. But he was an Ahab with a difference, an Ahab who was not alone but supported by many of the most distinguished Americans of his time. If he was strange so was the period. If he was violent what of the many eminent Americans who supported him?

If his character remains dubious in the eyes of some, a battleground of strength and weakness, if he was a Dostoyevskian Yankee Puritan, as filled with violence as with benevolence, it is also true that the triumphs of the stainless are not as appealing as the more human victories of the flawed. History has seldom been forwarded by the unsullied, the uncompromised. Its great movements are more often made up of Melville's "kingly commons," of the spotted and stained average containing within them, despite every excess, an esssential human goodness.

The careful writer will be the last to deny any ill of his protagonist; rather, he will accord him the last full measure of his perversity, treasuring every desperate larceny, every lacerating self-betrayal, every bloody brutality, for only by knowing the full extent of failure can one celebrate the overcoming of it, however partially. And yet whatever John Brown's shortcomings, there is one aspect of his character that has never been convincingly challenged and that is his compelling identification with what he called "the great family of man." [3] Few, after all, have ever denied that however mistaken his methods, he was an American who gave his life that millions of other Americans might be free. It is true enough that the sacrificing of his life may have been a final egotism; but that does not impeach an act which forwarded liberty; it only makes it human.

In a country where millions of Americans still press for the full redemption of the Declaration of Independence; in a world where whole continents contain "His despised poor," [4] for whom John Brown tried to act; at a time when the species of man is one in its vulnerability to a common and massive disaster, the vision and commitment of John Brown to "the great family of man" perhaps offers a peculiar treasure upon which Americans may be again ready to draw. It is not his violence but his complete commitment to the point of life itself, to his country, and to man that is John Brown's bequest to the American people. Thoreau drew upon this bequest, as did Emerson and Theodore Parker, Frederick Douglass and Walt Whitman, and thousands of America's best in its greatest crisis. It is possible that we are neither richer nor wiser than they.

PART ONE

OF TIME
AND PLACE
AND
THOSE WHO
FOUGHT

1859 AND BEFORE

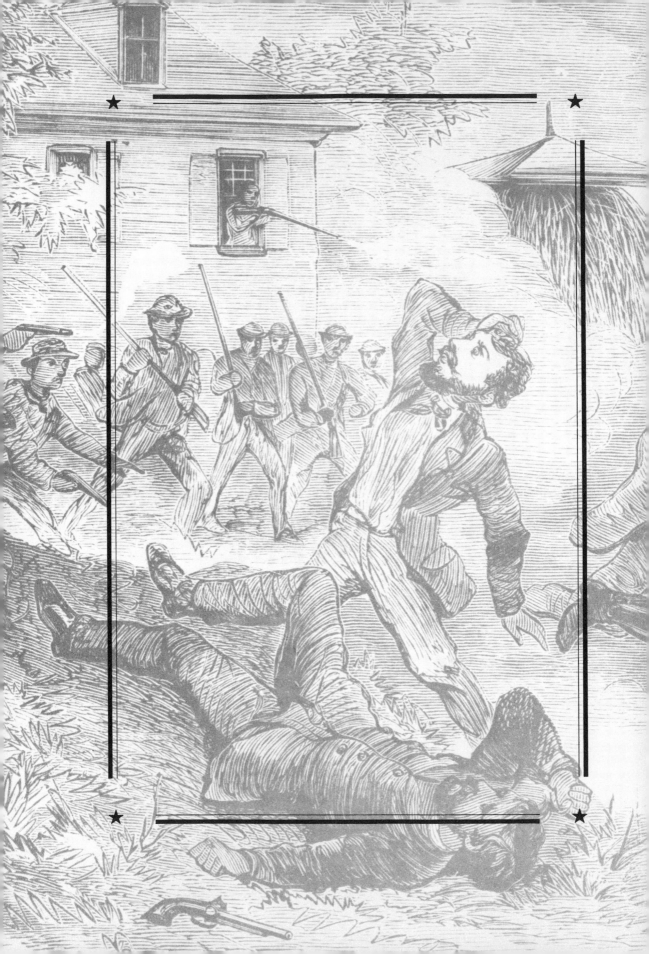

I

On the Success of Being Hanged

ALTHOUGH THOREAU was to call John Brown "an angel of light," and Emerson to describe him as a hero of "simple, artless goodness," Old Brown, as he liked to call himself, had more than innocence. He was brave enough in word and act to make men gasp, but he also had a talent for disguise and alias, a liking for such resounding *noms de guerre* as Shubel Morgan and Nelson Hawkins, a certain aptitude for the devious in which he did not let his left hand know the actions of his right. A monument of principle, giving his life for it in the end, the exigencies of revolutionary conspiracy had sometimes made him prone to the quick, defensive lie, to the half-truth which conceals as much as it reveals. Slim and sinewy of figure, with an imperious slant of nose, the dim discomfort of mortality simmering within and making his features bleak, he had a hard granitic angularity that suggested little of the angelic.

Convinced that the American nation would be killed if slavery were not, he justified his methods by the holiness of his cause, by his belief that both ends and means came from the Lord God Almighty whose servant he was. As ascetic as a desert anchorite, he also had a broad streak of the romantic in which he saw himself as the leading figure in some florid historical canvas, one hand comforting the oppressed, the other receiving the surrendered sword of the tyrant. He could on occasion react with the suddenness of a coiled spring but there were times when his high, thin mind was a little cloudy, when he seemed poised on some dead center of paralysis, incapable of action.

Such had been the case in his last warfare against slavery when, after all his campaigns in Kansas, some old guilt or some passionate discursive urge for self-justification had placed him in a vacuum, separate, apart, and remote from the battle swirling around him at Harper's Ferry. As his two sons fell at his side, as others of his young men died, he failed them by a fatal indecision while he debated with the slaveholders who were his prisoners about the metaphysics of guilt, the justification of force against those who held almost four million Americans in slavery.[1]

THE MILITARY DEACON

I

If public sentiment in the North in 1859 was such that John Brown could not doubt that he was winning some measure of success by being hanged for treason for his bungled attack on slavery on October 16, 17, and 18 at Harper's Ferry, Virginia, none knew better than he that it had taken more than artlessness to achieve. Rather than the angelic, it had required a willingness to kill for victory, an aptitude for building fame and power on his Kansas battles of 1856, an ability to raise cash through those euphemisms for war which stirred without disturbing. After all, unusual talents are required to make a success of being hanged. Simple innocence, he had found, was not enough to raise a secret army, however small, for an insurrectionary war, however holy.

Viewing men and events as divinely predestined, he had nevertheless left little to the Lord as he dodged about the country during the three years beginning in 1857, federal marshals sometimes in pursuit, Navy colts in his waistband, bowie knives in his boots; endlessly begging funds for his war against slavery, ceaselessly patching up the tenuous logistics of his shadowy little army, which at its largest was composed of twenty-one young men, black and white. Occasionally "jocuse and mirthful,"[2] cackling about with prim country witticisms, Captain Brown, as he was usually called, was often bleak enough for days on end, but always under the bitterest bludgeonings of circumstance he had a vein of sour enjoyment. Believing himself the center of a Providential plan, he felt a sense of cosmic significance which touched all his acts with ardent drama whether he was pursuing a barrel of mackerel or the freedom of a people. There were times when he seemed to some only a dour, obdurate farmer, others when he appeared as an impressive man of affairs, or some overpowering military deacon, and still others when he had all the projective force of an actor or a consummate medicine man, able to bring even the greatest under the hypnotic sway of his will.

Then, queerly martial in his deaconish suit of brown kerseymere, its tails flapping over his thin rump, his face, when full-bearded, that of a Yankee Moses, he may have reminded some of a holy confidence man as he stood in the parlors of the rich and respectable, separating them from their money while he charmed their wives and excited their children with stories of his battles in Kansas. Nor did he confine his appeals for funds to attack slavery to the mansions of the wealthy, making a series of one-night stands that dotted the North, appearing in little Negro churches, in lyceums and town halls, standing in the pulpit or behind the lectern, joining in hymns, passing the hat, at once a hero and increasingly under the cloud that shadowed his life whether in business or in battle.

2

There were times as the weeks and months progressed, as postponements and delays of his invasion of the South followed one on another, that even his own closest supporters wondered where the money went and if the blow would ever be struck.[3] On one occasion, unbearably frustrated by a series of mishaps he could not control, the Old Man wept;[4] but usually he was cheerful enough, particularly when, hiding out from the federal marshals, he found himself in the imposingly comfortable homes of such of his adherents as Gerrit Smith, or Judge Thomas Russell, or George Luther Stearns. He often affected to be a little uneasy about all the soft luxury around him, refusing butter, for example, not confessing that he had never liked it, but declaring with the merest hint of Puritan flourish that it did not become the harsh fare of a soldier.

With the women of the household hovering adoringly about, he liked to discuss fine points of theology as he loaded and cleaned his revolvers, blowing down the barrels, once expressing the hope that he would not be forced to bloody the carpets while battling against capture.[5] At such moments, his stories punctuated by little exclamations of awe and horror, he might display his aptitude for Old Testament cadence, using perhaps phrases that he had used before and telling of how when he and his men were faint from hunger amid the warfare of bleeding Kansas in 1856 they had successfully trusted to "Him who feeds the young ravens when they cry," and of how he and his little band had been cared for while dwelling "like David of Old . . . with the serpents of the rocks and the wild beasts of the wilderness." [6]

Something of the gallant impression he made at such times is suggested by Mrs. Mary E. Stearns, the wife of one of his wealthiest and most generous Boston supporters, who felt that he had an air of "singular refinement." In describing her first meeting with him, she writes,

When I entered the parlor he was sitting near the hearth, where glowed a bright open fire. He rose to meet me, stepping forward with such an erect military bearing, such a fine courtesy of demeanor and grave earnestness that he seemed to my instant thought some old Cromwellian hero suddenly dropped down before me. . . .[7]

Although Mrs. Stearns's parlor was crowded at the time with men of character and prominence, she had eyes for none but John Brown. It was not only that he was the victor of Kansas but that he had impact, an uncanny ability at playing a role, at seizing the center of the stage, of controlling a given moment, and whether he was dour in mood or magnetizing himself into attractiveness, people usually turned to look at him when passing on the street. Not the least of his roles was that of failure, having a decent sense of pride in his opponent, the Lord God Himself, who had justly sent it. He was capable of really impressive heights as he wallowed in his afflictions, sending up bootless, self-accusing cries to Heaven with all the abandon of Job. If to others his diverse roles occasionally seemed contradictory and impeaching, he knew they were given unity and coherence by the overwhelming reality of John Brown, whether as the high-minded chivalric *Mayflower* descendant in Boston, the ragged desperate border chieftain in Kansas who would not hesitate to kill, or the simple old wool merchant in Springfield, Massachusetts, so benign that some called him Uncle John.

All were true because they were facets of himself played with the intensity of profound self-belief, including the air of "singular refinement" seen by Mrs. Stearns and "the iron man that few would like to sail into" described by Artemus Ward in reporting a public meeting in Cleveland where Uncle John, in trying to raise money, had indicated something of his bloody exploits in Kansas. Ward perceived little "fine courtesy of demeanor" but rather saw in John Brown one who although "rising sixty" could "lick a yard full of wild cats before breakfast and without taking off his coat." [8]

THE PUBLIC CONSPIRACY

☆

Since it was to become impossible for John Brown to doubt either himself or his mission, it was also difficult for others. It was this, or partly this, that made him and his cause compelling to the young men he drew to their deaths in Virginia, to the wealthy and distinguished he enlisted in his crusade and brought to visions of the hangman's noose.

When one of his young men, soon to be executed in Virginia, was asked why he and his fellows had followed the Old Man to the death, he replied, "Ah, you gentlemen don't know Captain Brown. When he calls us, we never think of refusing to come." [9] When John A. Andrew, later the wartime Governor of Massachusetts, was asked why he contributed $25 to John Brown just before he invaded Virginia, he said Old Brown had somehow made him ashamed of never having suffered in the fight against slavery. "He was . . . a very magnetic person," he said, "and I felt very much impressed by him." [10]

But it was not John Brown's magnetism alone that made him compelling. It was also the time and its temper. To understand his acceptance by men of God and men of letters, by women of charm and sensibility and some of the foremost Americans of his day, one must apprehend the long cold war between North and South. Although the conflict was never entirely sectional, a fact to which we shall recur, that did not detract from its intensity. By the 1850's the issue of slavery was like a steadily ticking time bomb, excruciating men's nerves into an almost permanent tautness as they waited day by day and year by year for the all-enveloping explosion.

After the Kansas civil war, intensity was further heightened by the general conviction that it was high noon, that a time of decision was arriving when it would be made clear once and for all whether the country would become all slave or all free. It was becoming a political commonplace to say as did Abraham Lincoln that the country could not long endure half-slave and half-free, that one or the other must triumph,[11] or to declare as did Senator William H. Seward of New York that sooner or later either slavery or the free labor system must control the whole country.[12] In addition, many were losing faith in the electoral process as a means of destroying slavery—the Civil War was to prove them right—while some were increasingly inclined to believe that John Brown's projected invasion was one of the many proposals for slavery's destruction that must be tried.[13]

Nor were the rescues of fugitive slaves, involving riots and jail breaks and the flouting of federal law in the North, calculated to soothe the public temper. It was the dominant period of the so-called Higher Law, whose proponents maintained, as John Brown maintained, that the role of conscience and the law of God made it mandatory for the righteous to violate any man-made law furthering slavery.* If John Brown was exceptional it was only in degree. In basic philosophy he was typical of radical anti-slavery opinion above the Ohio. It was a time in which a good many more than he favored slave insurrections, in which better-known men than he had proposed armed invasions of slave states by guerrilla forces as a means of destroying slavery.

It was, as a matter of fact, a rather common proposal, as if ideas are socially derived rather than born in lonely isolation. Dr. Samuel Gridley Howe, for example, one of Boston's foremost citizens whom we shall have frequent opportunity to meet, had "proposed some movement of actual force . . . against slavery" in the South as early as 1844.[14] The Reverend Thomas Wentworth Higginson, a Worcester clergyman of impeccable ancestry and refined pugnacity, had proposed a private army in 1856 to be used against United States troops in Kansas and elsewhere in the fight against slavery.[15] Jabez Hammond, lawyer and reformer of Cherry Valley, New York, had twice urged armed invasions of the South for the destruction of slavery; the first proposal on May 18, 1839, in a letter to Gerrit Smith, the wealthy philanthropist who never turned a man or a good cause from his door in Peterboro, New York, the second also in a letter to Smith on February 28, 1852.[16] Smith himself, for all his benevolence and charity, had advocated publicly the raising of a private army of one thousand men and $1 million to finance it in an armed invasion of the slave state of Missouri.[17] Lysander Spooner, well-known Boston attorney, had proposed in a widely circulated and widely praised brochure an armed invasion of the South for the razing of slavery and the raising of slave insurrections, sending a copy of the plan to Higginson on November 28, 1858.[18] There were other similar plans and if John Brown's was unique it was only because he was willing to sacrifice his own life, and the lives of many others, to make it a reality.

Perhaps his greater readiness for action stemmed from his more accurate appraisal of the temper of the times. If Mrs. Stearns, and others of Boston's

---

* The *New York Herald*, on October 29, 1859, said editorially, "So accustomed have thousands of our citizens become to sit under and follow the 'higher law' . . . that many have forgotten their paramount duty to their country. . . ."

most cultivated women, could glory in the battles that John Brown had fought in Kansas, or even in the men he had killed there, it was because the American people were already in a virtual state of civil war. That conflict began only formally at Charleston and Fort Sumter at 2:30 A.M., April 12, 1861. If the first battle between North and South is a proper criterion it had actually begun, at least in a sense, on June 2, 1856, when John Brown and his followers had met and defeated a pro-slavery company at the Battle of Black Jack in Kansas.[19]

At any rate it was because much of the North was imbued with a war psychology that John Brown by 1859 could publicly disclose his purpose of attacking the South's slavery by force of arms, asking and receiving contributions to bring his plan into actuality at a good many public meetings, some of which were widely attended. If his plot was a conspiracy, and it was one of the strangest in American annals, it was also perhaps the most public conspiracy in the history of the United States. In whole communities, from Ohio to Iowa to Massachusetts, his purpose was general knowledge months before he attacked Harper's Ferry, Virginia, with his little army of white and black.* One of his most intimate confederates estimated that as many as a thousand knew in advance of John Brown's purpose, if not the time and place of his attack, and it may have been a good many more.[20]

Another of Brown's admirers, in recalling his public disclosures, wrote, ". . . he did not withhold even from public assemblies, the avowal of his determination to attack, wherever slavery was vulnerable, and to take property, or even life, if it were necessary. . . ."[21] Joshua R. Giddings, representative in Congress for twenty-one years from Ohio's Western Reserve, testified that John Brown during the summer of 1859 had appeared at public meetings throughout the Western Reserve, asking and receiving public contributions for his plan.[22] A sign of the times was revealed in the fact that Garrisonian

---

* Knowledge of John Brown's general plan to invade the South was widespread in such communities as Ashtabula County, Ohio, where he had a staging area for men and supplies in 1858 and 1859; in Hudson, Ohio, where he had lived and addressed public meetings; in Springdale, Iowa, where he had a training school for his military company; in Concord, Massachusetts, where he spoke; and probably also in a good many other communities. See Chester Lampson, *John Brown and Ashtabula County*, typescript, Western Reserve Libraries, Cleveland; Cleveland *Plain Dealer*, Oct. 8, 1899; MS. Reminiscences of Mrs. Edwin King, Cherry Valley, Ashtabula County, Villard Collection, Columbia University; Benjamin Kent Waite, interview with K. Mayo, December 26, 27, 1908, in which he said "many people in Hudson knew of the Harper's Ferry raid in advance," Villard Collection; MS. Reminiscences of George B. Gill, mentioning the extent of knowledge of John Brown's plans in Springdale, Iowa, Hinton Collection, Kansas State Historical Society; and C. B. Galbraith, "Edwin Coppoc," *Ohio Archaeological and Historical Quarterly* (October 1921), in which he says it was general knowledge in Springdale that Brown intended to overthrow slavery by force of arms.

abolitionists, for almost thirty years champions of nonviolence, were finding ways and means of celebrating the forcible liberation of slaves and even of contributing to John Brown. *The Liberator* declared that many abolitionists "in different parts of the country" had contributed funds to John Brown in the belief that he would soon liberate slaves, who would be delivered to Canada "under his instrumentality." [23]

Bronson Alcott, the transcendentalist philosopher of Concord, wrote in his journal on May 8, 1859, after hearing John Brown speak at a crowded Concord meeting, ". . . he does not conceal his hatred of slavery, nor his readiness to strike a blow for freedom at the proper moment. . . . I think him equal to anything he dares, the man to do the deed if it must be done, and with the martyr's temper and purpose." In the same entry he recorded of the meeting, "Our best people listen to his words—Emerson, Thoreau, Judge Hoar, my wife—and some of them contribute something in aid of his plans without asking particulars, such confidence does he inspire with his integrity and abilities. . . ." [24]

THE SECOND AMERICAN REVOLUTION

I

This fact of so many knowing of his purpose, if not the time and place of his incursion, of so many contributing sums large and small to forward his design, knowing and waiting silently until the invasion of Harper's Ferry burst upon the nation, may in itself indicate something of the time's temper. Perhaps the tolerance, if not active approval of John Brown, was because so many of the North's respectable were themselves violating the law as a matter of principle. Too many had undertaken violence, as will presently appear, in opposing the Fugitive Slave Law of 1850 for them to be shocked by other violence against slavery.

Too many had practiced war themselves, at least to the extent of collecting funds and guns for the guerrilla armies in Kansas fighting to prevent that Territory from entering the Union as a slave state—a policy favored by the national administration of President Franklin Pierce—for them to be dismayed by other warfare against slavery. But, above all, John Brown had wider support in the North than is usually portrayed because the 1850's were a revolutionary age in which increasing thousands were struggling to overthrow or contain a slavery authorized by the federal Constitution and defended by the central government, struggling to extend the freedom won in the first American Revolution to black as well as white.

Even as mild a sage as Emerson was predicting in 1856 a second American Revolution, this one against slavery.[25] The terms and mood of revolution were more and more a part of the North's vocabulary. Emerson's protégé, that tall young Harvard graduate Franklin Benjamin Sanborn, was writing John Brown in 1857 that the pro-slavery rulers of Kansas "must be immediately seized and hung" if they foisted a pro-slavery constitution on the people of Kansas.[26] At about the same time he was reproving the Reverend Thomas Wentworth Higginson, another Harvard graduate, for complaining that John Brown was not revolutionary enough, declaring that John Brown was "as ready for revolution as any other man." [27] As early as 1849, Thoreau had declared that it "is not too soon for honest men to rebel and revolutionize," [28] and if he felt then that a pro-slavery government might be checked by civil disobedience, the time would soon come when he would envision himself either killing or being killed in the fight against slavery.[29]

William Lloyd Garrison, a founding father of American abolition, was calling for revolution, however he reconciled it with his nonresistance, as he urged the free states to declare their independence from a pro-slavery national government as the colonies had declared their independence from Great Britain in 1776.[30] If it seems that such sentiments were only the strophes of dilettantes, the figures of speech of visionaries, then the words of Jefferson Davis, Secretary of War, ordering Army officers in Kansas to use "the military power of the United States" against Free State forces in suppressing "insurrection" and "revolutionary and lawless proceedings," [31] the telegram of President Pierce authorizing the use of federal troops in Boston to enforce the Fugitive Slave Act,[32] and the words of that complete professional, Senator Seward, may be more convincing. "I know and you know," Seward said, "that a revolution has begun. I know, and all the world knows, that revolutions never go backward." [33]

2

Seward's words were soon to be corroborated by events. The most powerful class in the country, the slaveholders, long dominant on the national scene through the North's acquiescence to slavery and the degree of slaveholder control of the Democratic Party, was ousted, smashed, and expropriated by the force and violence of the Civil War. An old class was violently overthrown and replaced by a new one. The new Republican Party, representing a rising industrial class allied with the West's farmers, and destined to the revolutionary expropriation of $2 billion of private property in slaves, was increasingly impelled, by the slaveholders' determination to rule or ruin, to the smashing of slavery's power both political and economic.[34]

Forced by events as often as by conscious, predetermined policy, for men do not always control or even quite understand the tides they ride, the Republican Party objectively became the vehicle of revolution. Conservative men, not given to attacking private property or expropriation, were brought against their will into a death grapple with the slaveholders impeding their progress and development. Some men, such as Senator Seward, saw it as a revolutionary clash of economic systems, a new and developing class against an old and outmoded one.

Most Republicans were scarcely interested in the destruction of slavery, although there were some who believed themselves entirely animated by humanitarian impulse for the slave. But both combined in the end, driven by a dynamic so terrible that individual choice became almost a fancy, to defeat and dispossess the slave aristocracy. The causes of the conflict may have been complex and multiple, however primary slavery was as an issue, but the result was clear. Whatever the degree of consciousness or men's control of events, the slaveholders were smashed in a war liberating four million Americans from chattel bondage. Not every event is a simple equation and it may finally appear possible that in the complex that made for revolution an old man, one John Brown, was the tinder, the spark, the human will, that ignited the fire that at length consumed slavery.

3

The situation, North and South, was explosive enough in 1859, the Civil War less than three years away, when John Brown traversed the country above the Ohio asking publicly for money and support of his projected invasion. If he had a talent for disguise and alias he also had an urge to proclaim and a need to divulge. A hero cannot thrive in anonymity nor can money or recruits be easily gained while in hiding. Still his ruses and stratagems, such as living in the mansion of a respected judge or residing with a brave black too anonymous for suspicion, not only served the purpose of outwitting the federal marshals on his trail but also added to his romance and mystery when he surfaced from hiding to address public meetings. Then he was apt to say, in a characteristically dry and understated manner, if any wished to arrest him they would settle the matter on the spot, speaking as suggestively as if flourishing a revolver and making his meaning as clear.[35]

He appeared twice at public meetings in March of 1859 in Cleveland where, reporters said, posters were prominently displayed offering rewards for his capture. He had just completed a well-publicized rehearsal of his coming invasion of Virginia, invading the slave state of Missouri, liberating eleven slaves, capturing their masters whom he later released after killing one who had resisted. Not only did he lecture on his exploit but on one occasion asked and received a vote of confidence from an audience approving his Missouri invasion.*

Not the least of John Brown's accomplishments as he spoke in 1859 was the beginning of his own legend. For generations the legend of his opponent, the figure of the gallant slaveholder, had flourished, that hard rider, hard drinker, hard fighter, as graceful in the cotillion as he was dauntless on the field of honor, as lavishly hospitable in his white-columned mansion as he was irresistible in battle. It was he who had furnished the country's foremost Presidents, its most victorious generals, he who had won the slave empire of Texas, he who had extended slavery across the continent from Maryland to the Rio Grande. It was largely his valor, or so he said, which had defeated Mexico in 1846 and ripped from her half of the defeated country's territory, an expanse of western wilderness that many feared before 1850 might become slave soil.† Already the gallant slaveholder was irretrievably embedded in the American imagination, a picture of power, dash, and charm, often as attractive to the New York longshoreman or the Illinois merchant as he was to himself.

As John Brown told of his victories in Kansas and Missouri over this hitherto invincible figure, it was almost as if he were simultaneously creating in himself and with himself an answering legend to that of the gallant slaveholder, the legend of the Bible-reading, hymn-singing Puritan, fierce throwback to Cromwell's Ironsides of two centuries before who had defeated the cavaliers of King Charles as Brown would defeat the slaveholders of the

---

* One reason for the sentiment favoring John Brown may have been the fact that when he spoke in Cleveland thirty-seven men, black and white, some of them prominent and including the professor of moral philosophy at Oberlin College, were on trial there for violation of the Fugitive Slave Law. They had refused bail and there was a good deal of talk of a forcible jail delivery.

† The Wilmot Proviso expressed the North's fear that conquered Mexican soil would become slave territory. The legislatures of New York, Massachusetts, Michigan, and Vermont passed resolutions backing the Wilmot Proviso, a congressional proposal banning slavery from the seized territory. Although the proviso had wide backing in the North, it never became law.

South. If he never characterized himself thus, he did not need to. The circumstances of his life and ancestry had combined to so suspend him in time, to so keep him in the Puritan ethic of the seventeenth century, or so his admirers felt and said, that they instantly recognized him as an almost exact reincarnation of Cromwell's warriors. Like them, the rhythms of the Old Testament beat within him, offering him succor and strength on the day of battle, and the psalms of David they had sung or recited around campfires two centuries distant were a part of the very core of John Brown. Sanborn was typical in his reaction to Brown when, in an address to Concord schoolchildren in March 1857, he said,

I have lately met a person who so well illustrates in himself the Puritan of Cromwell's time that he seems to me worth describing. . . . I refer to the justly famous Captain Brown of Kansas, otherwise known as "Old Brown" and "Osawatomie Brown" of whom you have no doubt heard something in connection with recent events in Kansas.[36]

It might have puzzled those who saw John Brown as a latter-day Cromwell, as well as a good many other of his contemporaries, had they known that his role in history was later to be described only as that of a solitary fanatic. To them it seemed as if he were in the mainstream, the victor of Kansas, at the very center of the country's greatest crisis, the man who could act when others only spoke, the man who could wield the authority of the gun when most of his admirers, "not men with fists," as Theodore Parker called them, had only the power of rhetoric.[37]

"A REMARKABLE CHEERFULNESS"

☆

Wherever or however John Brown was, in Emerson's Concord home, or discussing Kansas with Thoreau, or addressing a committee of the Massachusetts legislature, or only in his own family, he had a compelling necessity for taking charge. He usually succeeded in doing so whether rallying his neighbors in the defense of Osawatomie when that Kansas town was under attack, or inducing men of means to finance and back his assault on slavery in Virginia. Despite his habit of command, as involuntary as the hiccoughs, he had never amounted to much until the Kansas civil war brought him not only success of a kind but peace within himself, attained after considerable delay and torment by the meshing of his professions with his actions. For years he had planned to attack slavery by force of arms, speaking of it so frequently to so many, while he made no move, that some were inclined to regard him as only a harmless eccentric.

Perhaps he had been beguiled, as his father feared, by the hope of wealth and position; [38] but by 1858, when he was fully engaged in his great crusade, it was often evident that he was enjoying himself more than he ever had before. Particularly when surrounded by the ladies, displaying a kind of ecclesiastical bonhomie as he buttressed his arguments by alternately quoting Scripture and the Declaration of Independence, he was apt to reveal all the happy release of a man who had possessed small aptitude for private life, having tried unsuccessfully all the small chicaneries of commerce, and thankful he was at last delivered of it.

For thirty years, most of them spent as an Ohio sheep farmer and tanner —although he also lived in western Pennsylvania, Springfield, Massachusetts, and North Elba, New York—his days had been narrowed to the support of his family, which first and last included twenty-three mouths to feed, forced to sweat for every precarious meal, for fodder for the stock and shoes for the children, a drama he found intense enough but a little parochial for one who felt destiny repressed within him. At length he had been liberated from necessity's limitations to the wider stage for which he had yearned and which the Lord had suddenly opened to him and thousands of others who during the Kansas civil war had begun to fight against slavery or, more affirmatively, for what John Brown liked to call the harvest. "I felt for a number of years in earlier life a steady strong desire to die," he wrote in appraising his new role, "but since I saw any prospect of becoming a 'reaper' in the great harvest, I have not only felt quite willing to live, but have enjoyed life much." [39]

This sense of acute enjoyment, of incredible Providential success after the disaster at Harper's Ferry, swelled within him as he awaited his execution, savoring while still he lived the fervid eulogies paid him at a series of public meetings in the North, enjoying the tributes voiced by a long list of notables, some of whom still rank among the foremost of Americans. "I have enjoyed *remarkable cheerfulness and composure of mind* ever since my confinement," he wrote, underlining his words with his usual random emphasis, "and it is great comfort to *feel assured* that *I am permitted* to die (for a *cause*) not merely to pay the debt of nature (as all must)." [40] And he had previously written from his death cell to his family, "I cannot remember a night so dark as to have hindered the coming day, nor a storm so furious and dreadful as to prevent the return of warm sunshine and a cloudless sky." [41]

DEEPER AND MORE DANGEROUS

I

Long years of conflict over slavery were necessary before it seemed to many in the South as if John Brown were the embodiment of all they wished to kill in the North; before thousands in the North were to see something of themselves standing beside John Brown when he mounted the gallows. His Raid on Harper's Ferry inflicted a national trauma deeper and more dangerous than any ever experienced by the American people. Everywhere men and women were raised to a pitch of unbelievable, desperate drama that would have seemed impossible but a few short days before.

As John Brown waited in his cell for hanging on December 2, 1859, the Reverend Thomas Wentworth Higginson, graduate of the Harvard Divinity School and one of the most distinguished Americans who had helped John Brown mount his attack on the South's slavery, was organizing an expeditionary force to storm the jail at Charlestown, Virginia, and rescue him.[42] At the same time Lysander Spooner, prominent Boston attorney, who had called off his own plan for invasion of the South when he heard of John Brown's, was enlisting men and money to kidnap at pistol point Governor Henry A. Wise of Virginia from the executive mansion at Richmond, spirit him to a waiting tug, and hold him as a hostage off the Atlantic coast, his life to be taken if John Brown were executed.[43]

As Old Brown, fetters on his feet, his bayonet wounds and saber thrusts still bleeding, was poring over his Bible in the dim light of his cell, seven survivors of the Raid were groping their way through the Pennsylvania mountains, pursued by posses, hiding by day, traveling by night, half-starved, exhausted, almost despairing of escape to life and freedom.[44] Two would be captured and returned to death in Virginia, while Henry Thoreau, aiding one of the escaping five to Canada, would become an accessory after the fact of Harper's Ferry.[45] In Ohio's Ashtabula County, where a secret anti-slavery, semi-military organization had been organized by John Brown, his eldest son, and others, scores were under arms determined to protect from arrest those leading citizens of their community who had known of John Brown's invasion or helped prepare it.[46] In Iowa at Springdale, where John Brown's company had drilled, an armed organization similar to that in Ashtabula was patrolling the roads, its members intent on preventing the arrest of any of its citizens.[47]

In Peterboro, New York, John Brown's wealthy associate Gerrit Smith, who had helped finance the attack, was lurking in his home, moaning and exclaiming that he was responsible for the deaths at Harper's Ferry. Soon he was to be led off to a New York asylum, waving his arms and calling out that he was going to Virginia to suffer with John Brown.[48] In Boston, Dr. Samuel Gridley Howe, America's foremost humanitarian and internationally known as a pioneer in the education of the blind, the deaf, and the mute, was presently fleeing to Canada, unmanned by the fear that his distinguished career might terminate at the end of a Virginia rope as another who had helped prepare John Brown's attack.[49]

In Italy, where the Reverend Theodore Parker lay dying in Rome, he hailed John Brown as an American saint and wrote that "The road to heaven is as short from the gallows as from a throne." [50] One of the most widely known Americans of his day, and himself considered an American saint by his admirers, Parker had done as much as any man in helping John Brown toward Harper's Ferry. In Concord, Massachusetts, handsome 6 foot 3 Franklin B. Sanborn, another who had helped plot and finance the invasion and another Harvard graduate, was soon resisting the arrest of federal marshals long enough and stoutly enough to permit cultured Concord to raise a mob that rescued him.[51]

At Niagara Falls, the respected George Luther Stearns, who to the casual eye was the most conservative and stodgy of men, a successful Boston manufacturer of lead pipe, was also a fugitive, "listening to the dirge of the cataract," glad that he had helped supply John Brown with arms and money, and repeating his vow "to devote the rest of his life and fortune to the liberation of the slave." [52] Frederick Douglass, one step ahead of pursuing officers, and as an escaped slave and the foremost leader of the black people in the North more liable to hanging in Virginia than others who had also helped John Brown, was on the deck of the steamer *Scottia* in the North Atlantic bound for England and safety.[53]

In New York, German veterans of the Revolution of 1848, meeting on November 22, agreed to join with others from Boston and Ohio in invading Charlestown with bombs and hand grenades on the day of the execution to rescue Brown as he approached the gallows guarded by fifteen hundred federal and Virginia troops.[54] In Ashtabula County, which had been a staging center for recruits and arms for the little army's invasion, the slim and pretty Jennie Dunbar was soon to leave for Richmond to plead with the Virginia Governor for the life of Aaron Dwight Stevens, one of John Brown's chief lieutenants, so badly wounded it was feared for a time by his Virginia antagonists that he would not live to be hanged.[55]

Another beauty was being urged to speed from Kansas to Virginia, there to use her pulchritude to charm her way into John Brown's cell, where, while kissing the Old Man, she would slip into his mouth a paper outlining plans for his rescue.[56] Before this could be done, a twenty-one-year-old lawyer from Athol, Massachusetts, George H. Hoyt, left for the trial of John Brown, his ostensible purpose to help defend him, his real intent to survey the jail for possibilities of escape and gain John Brown's consent to plans for rescue.[57] Judge Thomas Russell, of Boston, who with Mrs. Russell visited John Brown in the Charlestown prison, looked at a huge chimney opening into the jail and exclaimed: "Two good Yankees could get these men out and away so easily!" [58]

But Old Brown refused any part of the rescue plans, as far as his own rescue was concerned, saying, "I am worth now infinitely more to die than to live." [59] He was not to be returned to the risks of life now that he could foresee the triumph he was winning for himself and his cause by being hanged. As a result, the plans for his rescue and the kidnapping of Governor Wise, although money had been raised and men enlisted and a tug was being chartered, had to be abandoned; but the attempt to rescue his followers continued. New York Germans, Boston intellectuals, and Kansas guerrilla fighters, under the famed guerrilla leader Captain James Montgomery, were converging on Harrisburg, Pennsylvania, taking up headquarters at a drover's inn and masquerading as cattle buyers.[60] One of those from Kansas, Charles Lenhart, a printer and himself one of the fiercest of Kansas guerrilla chieftains, contrived to enlist in a Virginia company guarding the jail and almost succeeded in engineering the escape of two of John Brown's young men, just before they were hanged.[61] Another Kansas guerrilla fighter, Silas Soule, later gained access to the prison itself by feigning drunkenness and informed the last two surviving prisoners of the plan to rescue them.[62]

2

All over the country every edition of every paper contained reports almost more astonishing than the Raid itself. From Virginia to Georgia, from Alabama to Texas, rumors of slave insurrections fomented by mysterious white invaders from the North multiplied daily, while Vigilance Committees were everywhere organized in the South in the conviction that almost any stranger might be an abolitionist agent of Old John Brown.[63] In New York it was alleged in the *Herald*, and not without a measure of substance, that such Republican stalwarts as Horace Greeley, owner and editor of the *New York Tribune;* Senator William H. Seward of New York; Senator Henry Wilson and Senator Charles Sumner, both of Massachusetts; Senator John P. Hale of New Hampshire; and Governor Salmon P. Chase of Ohio, among a good many others, not all Republicans, had been told of John Brown's approaching invasion a full year before it happened without informing authorities.[64]

Unmentioned by the press and unsought by federal or Virginia officials were the many black Americans, men and women from Canada to Michigan to Ohio to Massachusetts to Pennsylvania, most escaped slaves and many influential leaders, who had indeed known of John Brown's plan long before it happened, but who were now protected by being part of a race and a world that seemed invisible to most whites. Among them were Harriet Tubman, the black woman who had led hundreds to freedom from the South's bondage; Bishop J. W. Loguen, of Syracuse; Lewis Hayden, of Boston; William Still, of Philadelphia, who had helped set up the Underground Railroad route which was to deliver slaves liberated by John Brown in Virginia through Pennsylvania; the Reverend Henry Highland Garnet, of Troy, New York; Dr. J. N. Gloucester and his wife, of Brooklyn; and Dr. Stephen Smith, of Philadelphia. In addition, there were the thirty-four black men —including Martin R. Delany, one of the leading black figures of his time— who had approved of John Brown's plan after hearing him describe it at a two-day conference on May 8 and 10, 1858, at Chatham, Canada West, now Ontario.[65]

As a matter of fact, so many knew about the coming invasion in so many parts of the country that how it had ever been launched before detection, before apprehension of its participants, seemed increasingly a mystery. The Secretary of War, John B. Floyd of Virginia, had been warned of it in August, less than two months before it happened, even as to approximate place and date, by two brothers and their cousin who had never met John Brown but were visiting near Springdale, Iowa, where knowledge of it was so widespread that they received a remarkably accurate picture of John Brown's plan. They described it in two anonymous letters to the Secretary of War, one of which he received, read, "Laid . . . away in my trunk," and ignored.[66]

A book, freely circulated, on sale at many bookstores, and advocating Negro insurrection aided by white armed allies from the North, had been published five months before the invasion of Virginia, dedicated to John Brown. With little of indirection but rather with flamboyant bravado, it gave clear notice of some armed movement against Southern slavery. Apostrophizing John Brown's belief in revolution for black as well as white, his conviction that slavery must be destroyed if the nation were to be saved, the author, James Redpath, also privy to the Old Man's plans, addressed him thus in the dedication: "You, Old Hero! believe that the slave should be aided and urged to insurrection and hence do I lay this tribute at your feet." [67]

3

All over the North women were writing John Brown, some entreating that they be allowed to come to him in his cell, there to nurse him of his wounds, undeterred by reports of violence and mobs. Mrs. Lydia Maria Child, that passionate crusader for the slave, wrote from her home in Wayland, Massachusetts, asking Brown's permission to come to him but he replied that it would be better if she would help in seeing to it that his impoverished wife and surviving children did not suffer want.[68] Mrs. Marcus Spring, of Perth Amboy, New Jersey, did succeed in reaching him in his Charlestown prison.[69] And Mrs. Thomas Russell, of Boston, accompanied by her husband, the well-known jurist who had sheltered John Brown in his home when he was threatened with arrest, also journeyed to his cell where Mrs. Russell contrived to have his bloody clothing cleaned. They, too, had almost certainly known of his plan and contributed to it. "At last," recalled Mrs. Russell, "we had to take our leave. I kissed him, weeping. His mouth trembled, ever so little, but he only said, 'Now go.' " [70]

Walt Whitman, a little later, was to imagine himself standing beside John Brown on the gallows "when cool and indifferent, but trembling with age and your unheal'd wounds you mounted the scaffold," * [71] as Herman Melville was writing of John Brown "hanging from the beam . . . slowly swaying" while "hidden in the cap is the anguish none can draw." [72] The still young and unknown William Dean Howells saw John Brown as an "Old Lion, tangled in the net . . . A captive, but a lion yet. . . ." [73]

A torrent of less distinguished poetry, of dirges and hymns, was pouring forth in the North, soon to appear in newspapers or to be sung or recited at services on December 2, the day of the execution. A Boston sculptor, Edwin A. Brackett, determined that John Brown should be immortalized in marble and equally intent on drawing a plan of his jail for use in a possible escape,

---

* Whitman wrote in part, "I would now sing how an old man, tall, with white hair, mounted the scaffold in Virginia / (I was at hand, silent I stood with teeth shut close, I watched / I stood very near you old man when cool and indifferent, / but trembling with age and your unheal'd wounds / you mounted the scaffold)."

made his way with some difficulty to the prisoner's cell door, where he made sketches of him for a bust.[74] John Brown himself was being engulfed by sympathetic letters from above the Ohio and when not reading his Bible was writing replies of a queer, old-fashioned dignity, made more appealing perhaps by his occasional mistakes in spelling and grammar.

While John Brown still lived, Wendell Phillips, one of the greatest anti-slavery figures, who himself had prior knowledge of Brown's plan, was comparing him to Huss and Wycliffe, martyrs of the Reformation, "who died violent deaths for breaking the laws of Rome," as well as to George Washington, who, "had he been caught before 1783 would have died on the gibbet, for breaking the laws of his sovereign." [75] And in Kansas, William A. Phillips, another who was privy to the plot, one of the foremost newspaper correspondents of his day and later a soldier and congressman of distinction, was soon declaring that the best of an epoch and its men were combined in John Brown.[76] It was during these days of waiting that Emerson said that if John Brown were hanged he would "make the gallows as glorious as the cross," [77] while Victor Hugo, writing from his exile in Guernsey, was pleading for the life of John Brown, declaring that for Americans to take it was like "Washington slaying Spartacus." [78]

To some this time of waiting before the execution was like a fever or a sickness in which the patient could not sleep, or if he did sleep might dream of visiting John Brown in his cell, as did Sarah Grimké, the South Carolina aristocrat who had deserted a fortune in slaves and slavery for abolition.[79] Mrs. Child was another who complained of sleepless nights, when eyes staring into the blackness could see nothing but chained John Brown in his Virginia prison, and she wrote as if such nights were a widespread affliction.[80] In the South, where John Brown was being often declared the inevitable result of the abolitionist movement and the newly formed Republican Party, there was sleeplessness too, for there his Raid meant the heightened possibility of slave uprisings in which to be white might mean to be slain.[81]

AN AMERICAN LEGEND

I

When Henry Thoreau in Concord could not sleep for thoughts of John Brown—and he said if there were any getting their usual night's allowance he would guarantee them to fatten easily under any circumstances—he kept paper and pencil under his pillow and wrote in the dark of John Brown's fate with a fury that seemed to suggest a personal as well as a national crisis.[82] Perhaps it was during these nights of sleeplessness, twisting and turning in his bed, sitting up and groping for his paper and pencil in the dark as he thought of John Brown and the fight against slavery, that the non-resistant Thoreau wrote his great reversal: "I do not wish to kill or be killed but I can foresee circumstances in which both of these things would be by me unavoidable." [83]

By October 21 he had read, as had most in the North, John Brown's replies when, slashed by saber thrusts and pierced by bayonet wounds, he lay on the floor in a puddle of his own blood, answering the questions of those who held him captive. With his replies more an indictment of slavery than a defense of himself, many who had been appalled by the Raid found themselves profoundly moved and more than half-convinced by John Brown's words of the essential rightness of his position. He had come to free the slave, he said, and only that, and if his death, soon to follow, he presumed, would help in the destruction of slavery he was well content.

His words were singularly eloquent and singularly effective because of the scene, the prone old man, his white beard red with blood, surrounded by all the pride and power of a triumphant Virginia, as far as it could be mustered for the occasion, the bodies of his slain young men and sons still lying in the village streets, hogs rooting at their wounds, dogs lapping their cold congealing blood. "You may dispose of me very easily," he said. "I am nearly disposed of now: but this question is still to be settled—this Negro question, I mean—the end of that is not yet." [84]

His replies were the beginning of a steadily increasing sentiment favoring him until by December 6 Thoreau was to write, "Most Northern men, and a few Southern ones, have been wonderfully stirred by Brown's behavior and words." Only a minority in the North, he said, were without strong sympathy for the Old Man.[85] Willing enough to defend John Brown's use of arms, Thoreau was particularly moved by Brown's victory after arms had been struck from his hands and all he had of strength was the power of his own spirit. It was this power, expressed in his letters and in his speech before sentence of death was passed on him, that so impressed thousands in the North that his body had scarcely been cut from the gallows before many of the foremost figures above the Ohio were declaring his story would live forever in American history.

2

In a formal sense the memorial services held all over the North on the day of execution were the beginning, in Chapman's words, of "an immortal legend—perhaps the only one in our history." More basically, the legend derived from the fact that John Brown was central to the most anguished and most significant of all American experience, to a continuing crisis in which many more than he would ultimately die. He was, too, the climax of a long agony, the latest of many anti-slavery martyrs killed or imprisoned, including Elijah Lovejoy and Charles Torrey and Reuben Crandall, Seth Concklin and John Fairfield and Calvin Fairbank, Richard Dillingham and William Chaplin and Daniel Drayton, as well as the six white Mississippians hanged, as John Brown was hanged, for fomenting a slave rebellion; an agony including "General" Gabriel and Denmark Vesey and Nathaniel Turner, the black insurrectionist slaves hanged, as John Brown was hanged, for organizing Negro slave revolts, as well as the hundreds of nameless slaves who over two hundred years had been killed, maimed, or flogged for fighting against their bondage.

As Thoreau said in writing of John Brown, "Men have been hung in the South before for attempting to rescue slaves and the North was not much stirred by it. Whence, then, this wonderful difference?" [86] The difference was the long years behind the condemned man, in which so many others had suffered and fought as he had suffered and fought, finally reaching a climax when those living through them saw John Brown standing on the gallows. More than John Brown stood there. The difference was that when the trap was sprung and the bayonet-scarred, work-worn body of Old Brown swung in the mild Virginia air, there was something of him left. He had become more than a man because of his cause.

As hymn and dirge and psalm swelled at services for John Brown all over the North on December 2, the mourners were distraught and tense. Most felt they were solemnly marking a bloody end and perhaps a bloodier beginning. As they listened to the words that ranged the long history of martyrdom from the earliest times, something may have stirred within them, going back perhaps to the most ancient and shadowy of man's concepts as to sacrifice and redemption. To a generation believing on Christ crucified and Christ risen, it was inevitable that an American parallel should haunt the mind, and others than Thoreau spoke something as he had when he said:

"Some eighteen hundred years ago Christ was crucified; this morning, perchance, Captain Brown was hung. These are the two ends of a chain which is not without its links. He is not Old Brown any longer; he is an angel of light." [87]

It was inevitable, too, that with the advent of war John Brown should quit his grave to fight once more against slavery, if only in a song that said his soul was marching on with the Union armies. As Thoreau had written before the Old Man's hanging, "It is in vain to kill him. He died lately in the time of Cromwell and he reappeared here." [88] He was to reappear again after his hanging when Thoreau expressed what many felt. "I meet him at every turn. He is more alive than he ever was. . . . He is no longer working in secret. He works in public and in the clearest light that shines on this land."[89]

3

Whether John Brown did in fact gain success by being hanged for treason, even though it was merely to the Commonwealth of Virginia, may be answered in part by this account of his time, his contemporaries, and his own slow evolution from a man of peace to a man of war. Whatever the degree of triumph attending his execution, however, he could never have accomplished it alone. If he had taken the center of the stage, there were many others black and white who helped place him there. They included the extraordinary Dramatis Personae of his life, the actors from the South as well as the North, his young men slain in battle or executed, their brides and sweethearts who had consented to their going to Harper's Ferry, the blacks who had revolted again and again against slavery, the conductors and engineers of the Underground Railroad, the slaveholders plotting treason even as they hanged the Old Man for it, the thousands in the anti-slavery movement of which John Brown, however singular or strange, was the product and the climax.

II

Dramatis Personae

WITH THE PASSAGE of the Fugitive Slave Act of 1850, designed for the swifter and more certain return of those who had escaped from bondage, the struggle over slavery hit a new height of deadliness not to be exceeded until four years later when the crisis broke into actual if undeclared war after the passage of the Kansas-Nebraska Act.

But the quarrel over the Fugitive Slave Act, a part of the Compromise of 1850, was deadly enough. It was sharper than anything preceding it; more bitter by far than the dispute over Missouri's entry into the Union as the first trans-Mississippi slave state in 1820–1; more envenomed than the long fight for the right of petition and free speech in the House of Representatives, both denied for almost a decade by congressional pro-slavery forces intent on silencing criticism of the peculiar institution; more intense than the conflict over the annexation of Texas between 1836 and 1845 which carried slavery to the Rio Grande; or even the struggle over the Mexican War which Conscience Whigs, dissident Democrats, Free Soilers, and abolitionists feared might increase slavery's domain by more than 1 million square miles through a war of conquest.

It was this qualitative jump in bitterness and intensity in the struggle for and against the Fugitive Slave Act which made Americans increasingly ready, South and North, for Kansas and Harper's Ferry. It was in this atmosphere of widespread forcible resistance to the law of 1850 that the supporters of John Brown were conditioned to violence; through it they were educated, acclimated, and brought together, before they ever met John Brown, these leading citizens, Harvard graduates, men of wealth, eminent preachers, and notable writers who, in aiding or defending John Brown, included the most impeccably improbable group of conspirators, the most distinguished advocates of servile insurrection in all of history.

MR. PARKER AND MR. EMERSON

I

When Theodore Parker, in Emerson's view one of the three greatest Americans of his day, and perhaps the time's foremost preacher and scholar, armed himself for resistance to the Fugitive Slave Act of 1850, he felt within himself not only excited determination but occasionally a wistful regret that affairs had come to so sharp an issue. As he gazed at the sword on his desk, at the loaded pistol near it, wondering whether he would soon use them in defense of the escaped slaves who were now his parishioners in Boston, he had a sense of awe and strangeness at his own contemplation of himself, the scholar with a gun, the churchman ready to kill.

This future confederate of John Brown—and we shall here introduce others of the Dramatis Personae of John Brown's story—had not planned it this way. Being an orderly man who plotted both his sermons and his years in logical sequence, the Reverend Mr. Parker may have resented the fact that his life was being driven by events which had disrupted the carefully cogitated progression he had charted. Like Emerson he was inclined toward concern with the universal, and with the specific and the partial only as they exemplified entirety. He had always pictured himself as the promulgator of first principles, of great religious truths, of basic social relationships in which even slavery was only a facet that shed light on the whole. As he waited in late October of 1850 to repel a possible attack of federal officials seeking fugitive slaves in his Boston home on Essex Place, he thought a little sadly that his life had been mortgaged before he was born; that if he had not been native to Lexington in Massachusetts, if his grandfather had not made him a direct inheritor of man's fight for liberty by beginning the American Revolution on Lexington Green, he might have been able to remain the peaceful scholar, depending on the exposition of universal truth for progress instead of sword and gun.

As instinctively combative as a bulldog, with a square pugnacious face soon to be winnowed by fatal illness, he nevertheless preferred to regard himself as a man of peace and prudence. "You know that I do not like fight-ing," he said in an impromptu talk on the Fugitive Slave Act, speaking a trifle defensively and referring to the weapons he was to become increas-ingly ready to use. "But what could I do? I was born in the little town where the fight and the bloodshed of the Revolution began. . . . My grand-father drew the first sword in the Revolution; my fathers fired the first shot. . . ." [1]

If events had at last forced him into the thick of the anti-slavery fight, his somewhat late and reluctant appearance was not because of fear. From his early youth he had felt it incumbent on himself to begin at the begin-ning—where else would a logical man begin?—by discovering and enunciat-ing the essence of true religion whose absence was basically responsible for all the many evils of society including slavery. First things first, he said, believing it ineffective to attack the result of an evil and not its cause, to assail a problem before presenting its solution, which was always the applica-tion of the great truths of rational religion.

A slight man despite the thick shoulders and muscular arms which revealed his boyhood on a Lexington farm, his body overweighed by the great bald dome of his large Socratic head, he had the capability of constant delight in the commonplace. He gained intense enjoyment from such small things as rain on the roof, the benign faces of cows, the smells of dark and dusty barns, the sound of sleigh bells in the winter night, now faint and far away, now loud, clear, and present, and then fading, like a memory too precious to hold, into the dark distance. His favorite word, in fact, was "delight." He drew sustenance from piety, his term for that state resulting from constant communion with God, and once declared, "I have swum in clear, sweet waters all my days." Sometimes he said that all his life had been sheer content, asserting there was no moment of his past that had not "left me honey in the hive of memory that I now feed on for present de-light." [2] But still he had always yearned after beautiful women with an ardor at once proper and painful, had always mourned that his marriage had been childless. And once he had gone weeping through Boston's streets, desperate with loneliness and despair.

2

If Parker's slim body was overbalanced by his great bald cranium, his spirit, eager and generous, was overweighed, too, by his never-ceasing passionate drive for more and more study. Later, when ill, he said it made his "flesh creep to think how I used to work." He knew so many languages it was absurd, his pursuit of them resembling some esoteric disease which compelled him on and on, not only Greek, Latin, Hebrew, German, French, Spanish, Italian, but Arabic, strange Slavonic dialects, the Icelandic, archaic middle European usages; and he could not hear of a grammar in any language without lusting for it.

Equally passionate for philosophy, particularly that of Immanuel Kant, for science, especially botany, for comparative religion and above all German biblical criticism, he was not only an authority on American politics and early English law, specializing in the great English state trials, but on the feudal codes of the Middle Ages, including the Salic, the Burgundian, and the Ripuarian. He had an uncanny memory for the position of some specific book among the thousands of the largest Boston libraries, a useful attribute in the days before precise catalogues, and could tell an inquirer, for example, to go to the second room off the main hall and on the third shelf along the east wall, perhaps twentieth from the right end as he faced the books, he would find the volume sought. Possessing a thirst for statistics and government reports, he was constantly harrying his friends in Congress for virtually every government document issued, pleading that they be sent immediately. With all his other work as a preacher, and later as an editor, a lyceum speaker, writer, and agitator, he habitually studied from twelve to seventeen hours a day for his "great omniverous, hungry intellect must have food—new languages, new statistics, new scientific discoveries, new systems of scriptural exegesis." [3]

He was, in fact, like some aggressive walking fifty-volumed universal encyclopedia, and he never touched a subject without exhausting it, showing its origin, its history, its relationships, drawing up section after section which he liked to divide into subsections labeled one, two, three, and onward; when he scheduled his future years he organized them, too, with an equally precise numerical progression. In his plan for himself and his ministry he had determined first on revivifying basic religious principles and, that done, their application. If religion, the foundation, had degenerated into mere formalism and superstition, even his own Unitarianism, how could the world be put aright with its very foundation moldering and out of plumb? So, upon his ordination as a minister in 1837, at the age of twenty-seven, and just after his graduation from the Harvard Divinity School, he had determined on no less than the discovery and formulation—based on impeccable scholarship, historicity, and psychological truth—of the great basic human and historical facts on which a true and rational religion could be erected.

It had taken him eight years of Herculean labor to erect the foundation of the new religion; to replace the twin Calvinistic errors of man's utter depravity and the Lord's penchant for the burning of sinners in everlasting Hell with the two basic tenets of his reformed religion, the lovingness and utter perfection of God and the adequacy of man for all his functions. By 1845, he was ready to apply his pious rationality—he had always despised any division between belief and action—planning first to attack poverty, or rather its causes, and then, successively, drunkenness and ignorance, particularly among the poor denied opportunities for education, progressing to the attack on prostitution and the penal system which made criminals instead of curing them.[4]

And now in 1850, his attack on Boston's evils only begun, the carefully planned one, two, three of his life was being disrupted by the Fugitive Slave Act, events rather than logic taking the initiative from him. Now, he reported, he was writing his sermons "with my sword in an open drawer under my inkstand and a pistol in the flap of my desk, loaded and ready," sworn to protect human beings he had grown to like and respect as members of his church but who might be seized and returned to slavery. He was filled then with a kind of permanent tension, not entirely unpleasant for he enjoyed danger but it was tinged with pain. One of his most treasured projects—it was to have been the climax and the monument to a life of quiet scholarship—long had been the writing of a multi-volume history of the development of religion from man's earliest infancy, a work that was to be evolutionary in theme; but it was increasingly doubtful as the times sharpened if he would ever be able to do it. Like Emerson, who had led him into transcendentalism with his address before the Harvard Divinity School in 1837, Parker had thought that others could attack slavery since his mission was broader and more all-inclusive. But apparently it was not to be.[5]

3

Yet under the time's pressure even Emerson was wondering if he could summon sufficient resolve to face danger on behalf of the fugitive slave, although the very thought, he wrote, made him tremble. An essentially timid man for all his public character, his tall, slim distinction, Emerson was a gentleman in the full sense of that designation, both invidious and admirable; but if he hated violence he loved principle more. In moments of fatuity, he liked to think he had all the gallantry of the Cid, of Sidney, or of Raleigh, or so his journal indicates, but in later reaction usually realized that his chivalry was ordinarily confined to the literary. Occasionally he felt annoyed at the strident insistence of the abolitionists upon black freedom, once advising them "never varnish your hard, uncharitable ambition with this incredible tenderness for black folk a thousand miles off." [6] And yet the years would bring him, despite all retreat and hesitation, to the facing of a pro-slavery mob and contributing a small amount to John Brown's cause in 1859, at least according to the suggestion of Bronson Alcott, Emerson's Concord neighbor, when it was clear to Alcott, and surely to Emerson, too, that Brown was planning an armed attack on slavery. [7] And later Emerson collected money for Brown's defense at his trial in Virginia.

Still Emerson had not come easily to the anti-slavery fight. "I waked at night," he wrote in his journal in 1852, "and bemoaned myself because I had not thrown myself into this deplorable question of slavery. . . . But then in hours of sanity I recover myself. . . . I have quite other slaves to free than those negroes, to wit, imprisoned spirits, imprisoned thoughts far back in the brain of man. . . ." [8] But as conflict and riot increased in the North with efforts to enforce the Fugitive Slave Law, he was writing again that he must act although he trembled at the thought. "I am here to represent humanity," he wrote. "It is by no means necessary that I should live, but it is by all means necessary that I should act rightly. If there is danger I must face it. I tremble. What of that? So did he who said, 'It is my body trembles, out of knowing into what dangers my spirit will carry it.' " [9]

And gunfire was faced by those who trembled, by such as Emerson, by men without fists, as Parker would call them, who often led the mobs from Boston to Syracuse to the Western Reserve in battles to free captured slaves. It might have seemed unlikely to some that the mere passage of federal law, providing for the swift and expeditious return to bondage of Americans escaped from slavery, could have spurred so dramatic a change in the character of those usually extraordinarily mild in conduct and temperament. Scholars such as Parker were to find that the time became so increasingly strange that even men of piety and learning might find themselves running through the streets beneath the moon, the sound of footsteps clattering all around, the breath whistling with the efforts of middle age, as portly men rushed to a courthouse whose massive strength, composed of brick, timbers, bars, and men with guns, their elderly bodies were to assail and reduce that a black within might be freed.

It was a time of ever-growing peculiarity when customarily peaceful professors, pedantic philosophers, proper preachers, and law-abiding lawyers, a controlled panic within their breasts and revolvers sometimes in their pockets, thronged into hotels containing slaveholders seeking their escaped chattels in the North; trying to project from themselves so much of fierce hostility that the slaveholders would depart in frightened retreat and strangely enough sometimes succeeding.* It was a time when the very flower of communities, at least under certain criteria, gathered at secret meetings, guards at doors, passwords agreed upon, conspiring to break the law, some bracing themselves for prison, others signing over property so they could not be effectively sued for civil damages under the Fugitive Slave Act. It was a period when such scholars as Theodore Parker, aching only to work on his history of religion, worked instead on the writing of resolutions or incendiary handbills intended to incite to civil tumult, and when the righteous, unable to sleep, suffered through the long night hours by rehearsing speeches of defense they might have to give before juries called to try them for treason.

All of this and more came about through the Fugitive Slave Law, precipitating the most provocative of crises at a time when crisis had piled upon crisis from the annexation of Texas to the Mexican War, forcing the breakup of the old political parties in the North and the formation of new political anti-slavery efforts. This law goaded Northerners into action who had hitherto been passive enough when slavery involved only the South or possible expansion into the West. But the new Fugitive Slave Act brought slavery into their own backyards. It flouted their own state laws, the so-called personal liberty laws designed to prevent illegal seizure of fugitives; it made a mockery of their most dearly held Revolutionary traditions concerning all men's sacred right to freedom; it made their streets scenes in which desperately struggling fugitives, clawing at every wall and tree to stay their return to slavery, shrieked for help from free men who themselves were arrested if they gave it.

The law was regarded by increasing numbers as proof positive that the federal government was owned by the slave power, as a penetration and offensive of slavery into the very vitals of the North; an invasion which

---

* As in the case of the fugitive slaves William and Ellen Craft, in Boston in 1850 when Parker and sixty others frightened the slaveholders out of town after visiting their hotel; and in Oberlin, Ohio, in 1858 when Oberlin professors, preachers, lawyers, and other leading citizens were indicted for the rescue of John Price, a fugitive slave, from slaveholders and their agents. Other leading cases in the 1850's thwarting the Fugitive Slave Law, in which force was sometimes used in rescues, included the Christiana, Pennsylvania, affair where a slaveholder was killed by black fugitives resisting capture, with the result that two Quakers were indicted for treason for failure to aid in the attempted seizure; the Jerry rescue in Syracuse, New York; several rescues in Chicago; the Shadrach rescue in Boston; and the Joshua Glover rescue in Milwaukee, Wisconsin.

leaped the Ohio and the Mason-Dixon line, bringing the slave catcher into Boston, Philadelphia, into the Western Reserve and Cleveland, into Milwaukee and Chicago, and particularly into the border communities of Ohio and Pennsylvania. But worse than this invasion was the law's stipulation that any Northerner anywhere could be forced to help slave catchers pursue and subdue poor human beings whose only crime was efforts for their own freedom.

The penalty for refusal to so help might be six months in prison and a $1,000 fine, although those captured were sometimes bona fide Northern citizens who happened to be black, the heads of long-established homes, the mothers of children, and even the children themselves, for the kidnapping of legally free Negroes for sale into slavery was far from unknown. It was a statute, moreover, which set aside the writ of habeas corpus, admitted *ex parte* testimony, denied trial by jury or any testimony at all from the victim being sent into slavery, a law which gave United States Commissioners $10 if they gave over the seized individual into slavery but only $5 if they discharged him to freedom.

4

Few labored so long and passionately to thwart this law as the Reverend Theodore Parker. As he wrote, with his hands so near the sword and revolver on his desk, he was beginning to elaborate his moral and political thesis—long before his association with John Brown—that any American had the right and duty to kill any other American, official or otherwise, who was stealing a man's most precious possession, his liberty, on the grounds of his color or birth or previous condition of servitude. Almost as soon as the Fugitive Slave Act became law he had preached a sermon declaring, "The man who attacks me to reduce me to slavery, in that moment of attack alienates his right to life, and if I were the fugitive, and could escape in no other way, I would kill him with as little compunction as I would drive a mosquito from my face." In the same sermon he said it was the "natural duty" of all Americans to rescue fugitives being returned to slavery by federal officials "peaceably if they can, forcibly if they must, but by all means to do it." [10] He progressively extended the principle of the right of resistance until by 1859, in defending the justness of John Brown's attack on slavery in Virginia, he suggested that it might be the duty of all white Americans to help slaves recover their freedom, even to invading the South and the slaying of the slaveowners who held them.[11]

It was not just any man who was thus advising his fellow citizens to kill, if necessary, in their opposition to Negro slavery. By the 1850's Parker was one of the most influential of American leaders. It was as if, at a later day, Woodrow Wilson, or Nicholas Murray Butler, or William Jennings Bryan had taken gun in hand and advised others to follow him in meeting with gunfire any officer who tried to enforce a law considered tyrannic discrimination against a minority. Parker had made the entire North above the Ohio as much his province as his own parish, traveling so constantly, speaking so continually, that it was finally permanently to exhaust him. Anti-slavery members of Congress were his special wards to be advised and encouraged by almost daily letters. Some of John Brown's young men were to read his books, lectures, and tracts, a torrential flood of unceasing publication. William R. Herndon, the law partner of a rising political figure in Springfield, Illinois, was one of his many correspondents, a diverse and widespread group, covering the North, whose members looked to Parker for guidance in the anti-slavery fight.

Something of his widespread activity may be seen from his letter from Boston, April 17, 1856, to Herndon, Lincoln's partner, in which he wrote:

I did not answer before for I had no time—and a hundred letters now lie before me not replied to. When I tell you that I have lectured 84 times since Nov. 1, and preached at home every Sunday but 2 when I was in Ohio—and never an old sermon, and have had 6 meetings a month at my own house—and have written more than 1000 letters—besides doing a variety of other work belonging to a Minister and a Scholar—you may judge that I must economize minutes and often neglect a much valued friend.[12]

His sermons were also circularized through the North in pamphlet form after being delivered in the Boston Music Hall where each Sabbath he was heard by some three thousand. Increasingly they concerned slavery, Miltonic in their sweep and majesty, terrible in their indictment of the North's numerous and powerful conservatives, called Hunkers in the language of the day and whom Parker declared profited from slavery as much as the South's plantation owners through their textile mills, loans, and commercial connections with the South. Those who heard his denunciation of Daniel Webster for his March 7 speech in 1850 advocating the Compromise of 1850, including the Fugitive Slave Act, never forgot it. It was more memorable in that Webster had just died. Uniting the slaveholders and Northern conservatives into the single monster of Hunkerism, declaring that the North had been joined to the South's fifteen slave states through the Fugitive Slave Act, Parker said:

Slavery, the most hideous snake which Southern regions breed, with fifteen un-equal feet, came crawling North, fold on fold, and ring on ring, and coil on coil, the venomed monster came; then Avarice the foulest worm which Northern cities gender in their heat, went crawling South; with many a wriggling curl it wound along its way. At length they met and twisting up in their obscene embrace, the twain became one monster, Hunkerism; theme unattempted yet in prose or song; there was no North, no South, they were one poison . . . Northward and South-ward wormed the thing along its track, leaving the stain of its breath in the peo-ple's face; and its hissing against the Lord rings yet in many a speech. . . . Then what a shrinking there was of great consciences, and hearts, and minds! [13]

If his sermons were dramatic so were his actions, which he could also make preach a sermon. When he married William and Ellen Craft, young fugitives from Georgia's slavery, Parker had a Bible and a sword on the table before him. After testing the poignard and "finding the blade had a good temper, stiff enough and yet springy withal; the point was sharp," he gave it to the groom with instructions to kill if necessary any United States officer or slaveowner who tried to return either his bride or himself to slavery. " 'With this sword, I thee wed,' " he wrote of the ceremony, "suited the circumstances of that bridal." [14]

MR. HIGGINSON AND MR. SMITH

I

But Theodore Parker was not one to be content with symbolism, however menacing. Soon he and his associates were planning the storming of a court-house and the delivery of one Anthony Burns, a black being returned to slavery, an event which played its part in bringing important allies to John Brown. The assault was led by the Reverend Higginson, a young man so excessively handsome and exquisitely cultured that few could associate him with raw courage and real ability; or could have believed, before the fact, that he was to be one of the most effective members of John Brown's con-spiracy and the colonel of the first regular army regiment of blacks during the Civil War.

As permeated by the literature of chivalry and derring-do as any in the South, where it held a special sway, this tall, slim young man of thirty-one liked to speak, quite disarmingly, of ancestors so near to royalty that they called Queen Elizabeth "Cousin Betsy Tudor," but also of his patriot grandfather who had been a member of the Continental Congress.[15] He had entered Harvard at the age of thirteen and when he later described himself as "a child of the College," he was accurate. A lover of Greek and Latin, of Chaucer and Spenser, a persistent and overly charming writer who worshipped good taste above all, he nevertheless had believed from an early age that if liberty were to be saved it would have to be fought for.

Now as he moved in the thickening dusk of a May evening in 1854 before the Boston courthouse among the company which had been organized for the attack in Worcester, some 40 miles west of Boston, where he was pastor of the Free Unitarian Church, he was only thankful that the chance for action had come once more. As he gave his men instructions to remain concealed so that those defending the courthouse could not see them, distributing axes among them that he had previously bought nearby, his manner, others later recalled, was easy and even debonair. He had flair in everything he did but he knew how to hold it to the casual. If he was an indubitable aristocrat, he was also a natural athlete, almost always tingling with animal spirits and restless energy. If he was dedicated to God and reform, he was conscious that too much solemnity made for the ridiculous. Usually he tried for an easy, offhand manner which did not always quite come off. An admirer of the common man, he had a tendency, one suspects, to offend him by addressing him as "My good fellow."

IIe had never read, he once confessed, of a brave deed, of an intrepid explorer, or a feat of endurance, or a gallant gesture in the face of peril, without wishing to emulate it and without confidence that he could. Even as a child he had yearned for burning buildings so that he might rescue their occupants. Already he was a veteran in the anti-slavery fight, having participated in the attempted rescue of the fugitive Sims, run unsuccessfully for Congress on the Free State ticket in 1848 and as a result lost his pastorate in Newburyport, where his congregation included wealthy shipowners who did not wish slavery attacked.

Born in 1823, the abolitionist movement had been at its height under Garrison in Boston when he was still a boy. Although he came under its influence early enough, there had been a time as a callow youth when he had been more interested in himself than anti-slavery and perhaps, in a sense, he always remained so. When he was seventeen and a senior at Harvard, he visited cousins in Virginia and found their life attractive. He found defending it attractive, too, almost iconoclastic, for already in certain restricted circles in Boston and Cambridge anti-slavery had something of the orthodox.[16] This was a momentary impulse, for he soon became engaged to Mary

Channing, herself and her father abolitionists. It was but a matter of time until he became much more militant than they. He never did anything by halves when he saw an opportunity for notoriety and heroism.

Nevertheless, the time, however early it had begun to work on him, had transformed him too, changing one destined to be little more than a charming aristocrat into a clergyman leading a mob. Despite his fitness for the task, it had not been planned that he was to have sole responsibility for leading the attack to rescue Burns. But then nothing had happened as planned after a mixup of signals at a Faneuil Hall protest meeting. It was this failure of communication which prevented Parker, Dr. Samuel Gridley Howe, and Wendell Phillips from leading the audience to the courthouse to join the attack.

Waiting in the dark before the Boston courthouse for reinforcements that did not come, and for the approaching impact of assault, young Mr. Higginson was perhaps glad that he was in such perfect physical condition; that for all his love of belles-lettres, his occasional composition of poetry, he was an expert in gymnastics and tumbling, hardened by rowing and boxing. The moments of waiting seemed endless, Higginson later recalled, but presently there was "a rush of running figures, like the sweep of a wave," and the clergyman felt for a moment that the great audience at Faneuil Hall was swarming to the attack; but a single glance, he said, "brought the conviction of disappointment. We had the froth and scum of the meeting, the fringe of idlers on its edge. The men on the platform, the real nucleus of the great gathering, were far in the rear, perhaps were still clogged in the hall." [17]

But the defenders of the courthouse had been alerted and the attack had to be made instantly or abandoned. With Higginson at their head, a group, including his friend Martin Stowell, seized a heavy beam that had been brought to the scene. Mounting the courthouse steps to the west door, they managed to stagger forward and smash the beam twice against the portals, springing the hinges awry before a burst of gunfire sent most of the attackers fleeing.

Angered by their flight, Higginson called after them, "You cowards, will you desert us now?" Almost alone he and two companions turned and pressed through the hanging door, a huge black man squeezing through before him, Stowell following, and in the sudden boil of fighting inside the courthouse a deputy sank to the floor fatally wounded.

As the young clergyman charged into the melee, he wondered as police clubs beat about his head why the blows did not hurt. Blood was running down his throat from a saber-slashed chin but he did not feel the wound. Slowly, he and his black friend were forced to retreat and they might have been captured if Lewis Hayden, another black who was to be the instrument of giving important help to John Brown, had not fired a shot to cover their escape.

Outside, panting and exhausted, and still not knowing he had been wounded, Higginson saw the gentle and bumbling philosopher Bronson Alcott, a cane in his hand, attempting to rally the crowd, walking alone up the courthouse steps and turning to say to those who hesitated to face the government guns, "Why are we not within?" [18]

2

As Mr. Higginson was being educated in Massachusetts for the use of force and violence in connection with John Brown, an equally impeccable personage was being similarly conditioned in New York. In Syracuse, the handsome Gerrit Smith, always intent on expiating the guilt of his vast inherited wealth and described by an acquaintance as one of the time's "finest specimens of a Man, physically, morally and intellectually," [19] had led a band of refined but earnest preachers, free Negroes, anti-slavery workers, and farmers who had rescued Jerry McHenry, another fugitive being returned to slavery. Although Smith was finally to break under the unbearable tension and real danger consequent to his association with John Brown, he showed no sign of weakness on this day of attack. Rather, he was in the vanguard as the mob stormed the police station imprisoning McHenry, blowing out its windows as shots were fired and holding the police captive until the liberators had succeeded in spiriting McHenry away.[20]

The most conscientious of philanthropists and the most persistent of hypochondriacs, Smith, who had given three thousand farms to three thousand blacks, many of whom were escaped slaves, was elected to Congress shortly after the Jerry rescue, as it was called, where he was perhaps the richest member. Before the Fugitive Slave Act, he had been "a peace man and a non-resistant," renowned for an unctuous, well-bred spirituality, a kind of Christian Mycenas. If over his lifetime he vacillated in his opposition to slavery between nonresistance, violence, and political action, between believing that the Constitution was a pro-slavery instrument and that it was not, thousands of others, black and white, were also shifting in their views with a constantly changing situation. And he was one of the very first to participate in the earliest independent political action which eventuated finally in the Republican Party. Whatever his changes, he always tried hard to be the perfect gentleman and most agreed that he was.

Even a Southern woman who had felt that as an abolitionist Gerrit Smith would resemble a monster, found, she wrote upon meeting him, that he was "a gentleman possessing every lordly grace of presence, manner and dignity." [21] To see his lordly grace of presence, all 6 feet and 200 pounds of it, at the head of a mob assaulting a police station was startling indeed to those who had known him only as the charmingly cultivated host of his estate at Peterboro, not far from Syracuse. There he occasionally entertained his many guests, including John Brown, by singing "uncommon well" such Scottish ballads as "Come Under My Pleadie." [22] There was nothing then to suggest that presently he would be led off to an asylum, wildly waving his hands and calling out that he was going to Virginia to suffer with John Brown.[23]

THOREAU, DOUGLASS, AND UNCLE JOHN

I

These transformations of character, these changes of the peaceful into firebrands, were not uncommon in the North then, nor were they confined to Gerrit Smith or Parker or Higginson, or without occurrence in the South where in a different way men were changing too. The spirit of resistance above the Ohio, to confine it for a moment, was a force penetrating into the most remote and quiet of places, even into Emerson's study, into Thoreau's most distant meadow and furthest swamp. Thoreau had complained that Concord's most slovenly nonentities called him patronizingly by his first name and it was true that few of that town could perceive in him the distinction that later ages saw nor see in his homely familiarity a certain elegance.

They could not understand his daily search for reality, an actual search leading through the woods and fields, and wondered why he did not work as ordinary men. Even Emerson said that Thoreau could have been a great engineer but remained instead the captain of a huckleberry party. A short-legged, long-nosed, long-torsoed man of thirty-seven in 1854, with prim interior pressures, an obstinate expression, and a great yearning for a great friend, Thoreau had nonetheless been the possessor of an occasional and unique happiness; but now he was beginning to feel within himself a distressing division he had felt once before with the Mexican War.

He had dedicated his life to seeing what most men never see, to hearing what to most is inaudible, to savoring the changing continents of the sky, the slow circle of the earth with its slow turn of seasons. But in 1854 as he went about his great project of recording all the change and movement, not only of each day and night but of the equinox and the years, not only of the quick and live but also of the inanimate, he found his happiness being compromised by that outside world he had tried to ignore.

When almost four million of his fellow Americans were being held in slavery, how could he continue to attend only to his private pursuits, silent and alone on Concord's hills, trying to hear, he wrote, what was in the wind that he might carry it express? If Massachusetts, his beloved commonwealth, was giving up its citizens to slave catchers, it was destroying, too, he said, the serenity gained from such fulfilling pleasures as watering the sand cherry, the red huckleberry, and the nettle tree, which, he recorded, might have perished from drought without his care.

On June 16, 1854, he wrote in his journal:

I had never respected this government, but I had foolishly thought that I might manage to live here, attending to my private affairs and forget it. For my part, my old and worthiest pursuits have lost, I cannot say how much of their attraction, and I feel that my investment in life here is worth many per cent less since Massachusetts last deliberately and forcibly restored an innocent man Anthony Burns to slavery. . . . It is not an era of repose. If we would save our lives we must fight for them. . . .

There is a fine ripple and sparkle on the pond, seen through the mist. But what signifies the beauty of nature when men are base? We walk to lakes to see our serenity reflected in them. When we are not serene, we go not to them. Who can be serene in a country where both rulers and ruled are without principle? The remembrance of the baseness of politicians spoils my walks. My thoughts are murder to the State; I endeavor in vain to observe nature; my thoughts involuntarily go plotting against the State. I trust that all just men will conspire.[24]

2

As Thoreau went to nearby Framingham, forced to what he could not help but feel at times was the indignity of public political address, but forced, too, to speak out on the Burns case, Frederick Douglass, thirty-seven in 1854 as was Thoreau, was also speaking out and on the same case. He agreed with Parker that to slay the kidnapper of a man was a patriotic act, declaring that those who killed the officer in the attempted rescue of Burns must continue to be honored, or so he wrote, until the fight for liberty at Bunker Hill was forgotten, until the nation "ceases to glory in the deeds of Hancock, Adams and Warren." [25] If Thoreau and Douglass were similar in age and in intensity of reaction to the plight of Anthony Burns, they were about as different as two men could be in most other respects, destined to have in the future only one other similarity and that connected with an old man who formed the common climax of their lives.

While Thoreau in his youth had the peace of Concord's fields and streams for the scene of his own peculiar struggles, Douglass's struggles were a little more hot and physical, their setting a little less pastoral. While Thoreau, in a sense, was his own foe, the victim of those inner tensions that made him alternate between ecstasy and uneasy endurance, Douglass's struggle, however inner, too, was more importantly fought against a society seeking to enslave him. While Thoreau was attending Harvard College and later serving Emerson as a handyman, writing poetry under his roof, Douglass was fighting a slave breaker for his life; fighting his way free from slavery, fighting a gang of white ship calkers who did not intend to stand the competition of a black, later fighting a train crew trying to eject him from a coach, ripping three seats from the floor in the brawl; and later still, fighting a mob in Indiana until he was beaten unconscious.[26]

It was not that Douglass was less complicated than Thoreau, for he was a subtle man of sufficient range to be confronted with a variety of choices, and he, too, at times could know the torture of indecision; but circumstances forced on him a certain unanimity of self. He fought not because he liked to fight but because he was forced to and at a moment of crisis in his life he was to decide, as we shall see, and perhaps quite properly, that the better part of valor was to flee, and that far and promptly, if he was to live to fight further. By 1854 he was fast becoming one of the great men of his generation and he looked the part, a darkly regal giant, an escaped slave whose protean abilities were conquering one field after another, that of orator, editor, publisher, anti-slavery agitator, politician, man-of-the-world, and valued friend of many of the earth's great, particularly among the public figures of England.

It was this development that an elderly deacon-like gentleman of Springfield, Massachusetts, a wool merchant there who had once been a farmer in Ohio, was to ask Douglass to give up in favor of a venture that might include violent death. Under the impetus of the Fugitive Slave Act, Douglass may have found himself thinking again of Uncle John, as John Brown was occasionally called in Springfield—not out of relationship to those who called him so, but perhaps because the stern archaic rectitude he affected reminded them of vanished kinsmen of a Puritan past. He had talked so persistently to Douglass, since first he met him in 1847, of attacking slavery by force of arms, drawing up plans for rude wilderness fortifications in the Southern Appalachians on a drafting board night after night until, Douglass writes, "I confess it began to be something of a bore to me." The Negro leader "paid but little attention" to the Old Man's constant discussion of his plan, apparently thinking it would never become an actuality.[27] But a pressing and distressing invitation was to prove Douglass wrong.

THE KNIGHTLY DR. HOWE

I

In Boston, Uncle John's future associates, Parker, Higginson, and Wendell Phillips, that blue-blood who called himself a nonresistant and had once been the boxing champion of Harvard, were among seven being indicted in connection with the attempted rescue of Burns. The knightly Dr. Samuel Gridley Howe, a tart, tortured prima donna constantly predicting his own imminent demise, was somehow missed by the authorities and not indicted although up to his neck in the Burns affair.

An editor as well as a physician, a hater of politics, who had forced himself to enter them to fight slavery, Howe acted as a kind of unofficial manager for his best friend, Senator Charles Sumner—elected in 1851 by an anti-slavery coalition as senator from Massachusetts—handling his affairs in Boston while Sumner was in Washington, trying for example, under Sumner's confidential guidance, to lure some notable Southern fire-eater to Boston for a public lecture so that Sumner and others could proclaim that a slaveholder could be heard in the North while an abolitionist would be lynched if he spoke in the South.[28] But Howe hated these chores, he said, much preferring direct action in the field and at the head of a column of well-armed men. As early as 1843, as we have seen, he had said that he would like to lead a military expedition South to free the slaves and none could have been more astonished than himself at his reaction when he was accused of aiding one who did.[29]

He had long been accustomed to regarding himself as a hero, perhaps because he had been one once when as a young man he fought for six long years for the independence of Greece and suffered prison in Berlin for aiding Polish patriots. But that had been before the reckless generosity of youth was eroded by the increasing sobriety of middle age. His friend Wendell Phillips confessed that he enjoyed the time's excitement, writing of "the long evening sessions—debates about secret escapes—plans to evade where we can't resist—the doors watched that no spy may enter. . . ." [30] But Dr. Howe was too victimized by his tensions to enjoy it much.

A nervous, trim martinet, who contrived to give something of the dashing and military even to his civilian attire, he had an energy that gave him neither peace nor rest, a fondness for riding mettlesome horses, an imposingly barbered beard and occasional bouts of migraine, neuralgia, and melancholia, perhaps not unconnected with his ardent wish that his wealthy wife, the gifted Julia Ward Howe, would pay a little less attention to herself and more to him. He, however, liked to attribute his bodily ills to the hardships he had suffered in Greece, while his friends thought that the origin, at least of his melancholia, might be found in the solitary confinement he had suffered in Berlin.

Known the country over for his appearances before state legislatures on behalf of the blind, Dr. Howe was the founder of one of the nation's first schools for the blind, the Perkins Institute. Here he had rescued from dark and silence, through pioneer labor almost incredible in its persistence and ingenuity, Laura Bridgman, the deaf and blind mute, who was the Helen Keller of her time. Gaining an international reputation for his work with the blind, it seemed but to divide him further. He was no provincial, no demagogue, but a physician and a man of science as well known in England and France as he was in the United States. His letters from abroad, liberally interspersed with Latin and French, were both worldly and moral, pessimistic as to himself and confident as to man. On the one hand he yearned for the seemly, appropriate to his professional dignity, but on the other he had insisted on becoming known as a man who, if he saw injustice, would attack it and probably by force of arms.

2

If it had not been for John Brown and the institution of slavery, so manifestly and overwhelmingly an injustice in Dr. Howe's eyes above all, he might have remained a spotless model of professional virtue with his derring-do in Greece and Poland only a testimonial to the ardor of youth. It was risky but still not entirely without the pale to attack slavery by words and political action. But in assaulting the great wrong by backing John Brown, he had not quite reckoned upon ignoble fiasco with little of the seemly to be found in young men's brains splattered on the walls of an unknown village. Squalid ugliness, homely failure—particularly after his part in it was publicly exposed—he could not endure, nor did his picture of himself include the possibility of hanging as a criminal.

His own image of himself was rather reflected by the fact that he had been called the "Chevalier" (shortened to just "Chev" by such intimates as Parker, Henry Wadsworth Longfellow, and Senator Sumner) throughout the years following 1835 when he had been created a Chevalier of the Order of St. Savior by the King of Greece for his help in liberating Greece from Turkey.[31] Perhaps he was also called so, one admirer wrote, because he suggested "Sir Philip Sidney or Chevalier Bayard or Coeur de Lion." [32] It was this knightly image that remained intact both to Howe and his friends until the doctor became convinced, late in 1859, after his part in the Harper's Ferry Raid had become public knowledge, that Southern fire-eaters were intent on capturing him and either handing him over to a mob or hanging him as an accessory to murder. Then his character cracked in a manner as unexpected to himself as to his admirers.

It had begun to crack in 1858 under the peculiar tortures of a peculiar Englishman, one Hugh Forbes, known as Colonel Forbes, who had fought under Garibaldi in Italy and had joined John Brown as drill master and military expert for Brown's little army. Quickly he had learned of the Old Man's plans and almost as quickly he began to blackmail Howe, demanding money with the threat that if it were not forthcoming he would expose Howe and others implicated with Brown to the whole world. When Howe refused, Forbes did his best to carry out his threat. It was he who had revealed something of the plan for the attack on the South's slavery, a full year before it happened, to Senator William H. Seward of New York; Senator Henry Wilson of Massachusetts; Senator John P. Hale of New Hampshire; Horace Greeley, editor and owner of the *New York Tribune;* and such other Republican stalwarts, according to Forbes and the *New York Herald*, as Senator Sumner of Massachusetts and Governor Salmon P. Chase of Ohio, later to be Secretary of the Treasury under Lincoln and Chief Justice of the United States Supreme Court.* [33]

---

* Despite the allegations of the *Herald* and Forbes, it is virtually certain that neither Sumner nor

It was not only the fact that the plan to attack slavery in Virginia had been jeopardized by the Forbes betrayal that Dr. Howe deplored. But he personally, the country's foremost humanitarian, scientific philanthropist of international position, a man of judgment and dignity, had been revealed to some of the country's greatest men as an associate of wildly questionable characters, at least in the eyes of the respectable, in a wildly questionable plan which might end in bloodshed. Still, he was not a man to be bullied. He had a sense of his own worth and it did not include knuckling under to such as Forbes. He had not cracked yet. When John Brown's assault against slavery was postponed a year because of the Forbes disclosures, Dr. Howe was against the postponement. He remained active in supporting and advocating the deferred expedition. Yet he may have continued to wonder if he were embarked upon the kind of dignified action he was increasingly preferring when he learned that the preposterous Forbes, a fencing master as well as a military expert, was supposedly being shadowed under John Brown's order by one of the Old Man's men, the equally implausible Englishman Richard Realf, an alcoholic poet and former protégé of Lady Byron.

Chase had prior knowledge of Brown's plan. Senators Seward and Wilson testified before the Senate Committee inquiring into the Harper's Ferry Raid that Forbes had told them something of Brown's plans in the spring of 1858.

III

The Cast

in the South

As JOHN BROWN was gathering his forces in Maryland near Virginia during that summer of 1859, Jefferson Davis was not far away escaping from Washington's heat in the Maryland mountains after another of his periodic breakdowns.[1] Of all the opponents of the anti-slavery movement none was more a principal than he and, as a member of the Senate investigating committee inquiring into the Harper's Ferry invasion, none was to know more of the nationwide ramifications of John Brown's plot for liberty. He had probably first heard of John Brown in 1856 as Secretary of War under President Pierce, when he had directed the Army against Free State forces in Kansas and had been a powerful advocate of pro-slavery expansion whether in the West, the Caribbean, or Mexico. Wounded hero of the Battle of Buena Vista in the Mexican War, in 1859 senator from Mississippi and foremost leader of pro-slavery forces in Washington, he seemed to some representative of slaveholders at their very best with even his weaknesses partaking of a certain bravery.

A tall, slim man of fifty-one, impatient with himself and the collapse which had forced him to his bed in the cottage at Oakland in Maryland's Allegany County, he had always driven his ailing body as relentlessly as if it had belonged to an enemy. He was strong enough, as his military exploits in

Mexico had proven, but it was a strength that came in bursts and wore him out. It was as if his thin frame were too frail for the energy it carried. Upon his arrival in Maryland during the last week in July after two wearing trips to the family plantations in Warren County, Mississippi, first fighting the spring floods and then repairing their ravages, he was so completely exhausted that remaining quietly in bed was his only recourse no matter how humiliating.

THE GALLANT SLAVEHOLDER

I

As Jefferson Davis lay back on his pillows, his wife moving solicitously about, Varina Howell Davis may have admired her husband's classic profile, for in later years she wrote at length of his striking appearance. His features were regular, composed, and strong, if often, according to his opponents, a little disdainful in expression, and only a vulnerable mouth indicated a sensitivity usually hidden. Like Howe, his temperament was too intense to make for either peace of mind or health of body. Like most slaveholders, and perhaps most men, he had such a genius for partisanship that he could conceive neither himself wrong nor an opponent right. Not even with his utmost effort could he understand how any could be so dense as to disagree with him, or so his wife reported, after he had been good enough to explain his views.[2]

Filled with a kind of innocent vanity, he was proud, for example, of his well-shaped, well-shod feet, his iron certitude compensated for nerves which were often ragged and raw. Never was he more courteous than when suffering from a recurring facial neuralgia, his face wrapped in a disfiguring bandage, and such was his dignity and control that he could address the Senate bandaged so and still remain impressive. He suffered periodically, too, from a painful eye disease, when the slightest light was excruciating, and then his code forced him to a cheeriness, thin and ghastly above his agony.

Always considerate with those whom he led, whether it was a slave working in the field or President Pierce in the White House, he was quietly conscious of his superiority over Negro or Yankee, but was not one to be histrionic in its display. *Noblesse oblige.* A graduate of West Point, he regarded himself as a professional soldier, even after a dozen years in politics, and as such all things were clear in a world which superiors should direct while inferiors obeyed.[3]

As his wife moved in and out of his bedroom in the Maryland cottage, the younger Davis children sometimes following her, her husband may have discussed the alarming state of the country. When speaking similarly in the Senate corridors, his was always the quiet assumption that men who were gentlemen would naturally agree with him, and other Northerners than President Pierce found both his views and his manner attractive. Even Horace Greeley in the *New York Tribune* confessed that Jefferson Davis was impressive. He had the impregnable confidence of a perfect case. It rested on the uncontestable fact that slavery had been authorized by the Constitution and that even Northern states had threatened secession when it advanced their interests. None could deny, in his opinion, that slaves were property and that the Constitution protected property. And no one was kinder to his slaves than Davis or more determined to keep them so.

He and his brother, Joseph, owned scores of slaves and hundreds of acres on Davis Bend, a peninsula jutting into the Mississippi River where it was said that their property was valued at almost $1 million. Never did Jefferson Davis publicly mention that if the slaves were freed he and his class would be impoverished but always said instead that the sectional conflict was a constitutional question. He was fighting, he said, not primarily to own men but for a way of life, for states' rights, against the aggrandizement of a growing federal power, for a strict construction of the national charter against the doctrine of implied powers, for the right of states to abrogate and terminate a Constitution which had been freely entered into and could be as freely dissolved for cause at the will of the contracting parties.

Unbothered by any ideas but his own, he was utterly and completely sincere. Since he knew his own virtue, he knew that when he advocated secession he was a patriot and when opponents agitated against slavery they were traitors to the Constitution which approved it. Moreover, he was not an extremist pressing always for secession. He favored secession only when the slaveholders did not control the national government. When they did, they could use all that government's power to forward their ends and it was no purpose of Davis's to divide or betray a national government forwarding slavery. He was not for secession under the pro-slavery administrations of Polk, Pierce, or Buchanan, although he had favored it before and after the Compromise of 1850 and would do so again with the election of Lincoln.

It was as clear to him as that the Mississippi flowed south that slaves as constitutionally protected property could not be banned from any territory held by the United States in the West or anywhere else, that Cuba should be seized if it could not be purchased, Nicaragua conquered for slavery, Mexico again reduced and more territory taken including Yucatan, and that the international slave trade banned in 1808 should be reopened so that the South's supply of slaves might be increased. It was equally clear that the South had the right and the duty to secede, opposing the federal government by force of arms on the field of battle should that be necessary, if the Republicans won either the presidential election of 1856 or 1860.

2

As the days in his Maryland retreat progressed into Indian summer, Jefferson Davis regained his strength. He and his family had returned to Washington when the news arrived from Harper's Ferry. As he read of John Brown chained in his cell he reflected that the Raid was an inevitable result of Republican teachings, but one can be certain that he had no inkling of himself as he was soon to be, also in a cell and ironed and handcuffed on charges of treason after being physically subdued. Despite his own plans for what some would call treason, he could see no similarities between himself and a John Brown charged with treason to the Commonwealth of Virginia. There was an inescapable difference between the actions of men of breeding and property and the actions of desperadoes, the scourings of the Kansas border.

None could have been more certain of the difference between the criminals of Harper's Ferry and her husband than Varina Howell Davis. To his wife Jefferson Davis's life was a romance of which he was the hero. He was the perfect exemplar of the Southern Gentleman, gallant, courteous, and learned, and how he could ride, and how handsome he looked riding off to war on his black stallion, Tartar, and what a center of unpretentious culture and social charm were the Davis plantations—Brierfield, and the adjacent Hurricane, the mansion of his elder brother Joseph.

In writing his life, she described him riding away to his first Army assignment as a fledgling second lieutenant after his graduation from West Point, accompanied by the friend who was perhaps closer to him than any other man. He was his slave, James Pemberton, about the same age, fully as handsome and equally dignified, who nursed him when he was ill and sustained him during the eight dark years that followed the death of Knox Taylor, Jefferson's first wife, daughter of a Colonel Zachary Taylor who was to be a President of the United States.

She did not write much of Colonel Taylor's strange aversion to his future son-in-law, or of how he forbade the marriage, or mention the report that the desperate young officer had once considered challenging his intractable future father-in-law to a duel. But she did describe how bride and groom became desperately ill of malaria in the Louisiana home of Jefferson's sister shortly after their marriage, told how he had heard his bride singing in a weak small voice some pretty ballad of long ago, and had dragged himself to his wife's bedroom where he had heard her song end as the singer died.

Varina liked to remember her husband's way with the slaves and how proud he was of their accomplishments. None was ever lashed or flogged on the Davis plantations except after trial by their peers, Jefferson or Joseph rocking back and forth on the verandah overseeing a justice often described as benevolent. Jefferson was particularly proud of James Pemberton, who ran Brierfield, buying other slaves for his master, superintending the crops, and directing the slaves in their work.

He was proud, too, of the Montgomerys, also slaves of the Davis's, who were far more able than most whites, the father a self-taught civil engineer, devising his own instruments, singularly proficient at erecting the levees that kept the Mississippi from the Davis acres; his two sons keeping the Davis accounts, all of their records and books, and writing their business letters. She knew her husband would have freed them as well as the other slaves had it not been for his sense of responsibility. Despite exceptions they were not fit for freedom, he said, their inferiority being a divine decree. It was all the result of Noah's curse on Shem, he said, and all Shem's descendants, who were the Negroes, after Shem had looked upon Noah's nakedness when Noah was asleep, drunk with wine.[4]

THE SOUTHERN GENTLEMAN

I

It was not that Varina Davis could not see her husband's weaknesses. She felt, for example, that he was dominated by his elder brother, Joseph, and was indignant that the title to Brierfield, although Jefferson owned the slaves that worked it, and with James Pemberton directed it, remained in his brother's name. But whatever small weaknesses he had, she believed that her husband's qualities made him all in all the superior representative of a superior class, the Southern Gentleman, who in all his various guises, whether he took the shape of Robert Barnwell Rhett of South Carolina or Senator James M. Mason of Virginia or William Lowndes Yancey of Alabama, was the foremost opponent of the anti-slavery movement and John Brown. As such he is an important member of our Dramatis Personae. At his best he was, of course, a slaveholder; and to Varina Davis he was also, however maligned in the North, essentially a benevolent patriarch, open-handed and open-hearted, impetuous, generous, and daring, caring for his people, as he liked to call his slaves, in good times and bad.

And there can be no doubt that the slaveholder, as conceived by himself and occasionally in fact, was exceedingly attractive. Whatever his individual variation, he was fond of presenting himself as a member of an aristocracy with certain well-defined characteristics. He was the careless outdoor sportsman, or so it was generally agreed, who was apt to know his Horace and his constitutional law as well as he knew his thoroughbreds and guns. Hospitable and gracious behind the columns of his mansion, where candlelight shone in burnished mahogany as violin and spinet sent loveliness through the flowered night, he liked at such times to talk with his neighbors of foxes and hounds or perhaps affairs of state. At such moments, according to the accepted legend, white-haired Old Cato, not so much a slave, sir, as a member of the family, bowed low as he presented his tray to the high-toned quality whose members might endure anything save a slur on honor.

So, at any rate, did many plantation owners see themselves, often finding that their virtues stemmed from a slavery which gave to men a habit of command while giving lovely Southern womanhood the responsibility of tenderly caring for the family retainers, offering their sweetness hourly and without stint to the poor creatures, really just children, whom they loved and who loved them. Sitting on the verandah, their eyes misty, their kind voices faltering, members of the quality sometimes liked to regale each other with tales of the extraordinary devotion of these simple black folk; perhaps telling on occasion of how the slave of Mrs. Jackson, wife of the President-elect of the United States, weeping and wailing, had tried to throw herself into the grave of her dead mistress so that she might be buried with her; of how the stern and mourning Andrew Jackson had said to those who tried to quiet her, "Let that faithful servant weep for her best friend and loved mistress; she has the right and cause to mourn . . . and her grief is sweet to me." [5]

But it is doubtful if they mentioned at such a time Andrew Jackson's advertisement of a $50 reward he offered for the capture of a man he owned who had escaped, "and ten dollars extra for every hundred lashes any person will give him up to the amount of three hundred." [6] The gentle talk on the verandah may have occasionally concerned the subtly spun metaphysics of the great John Caldwell Calhoun, senator and statesman from South Carolina, and then the owners might well have spoken admiringly of the Calhoun theories of interposition, nullification, concurrent majorities, and other of his semantics which comforted slavery's beneficiaries by reducing that institution to only a question of constitutional checks and balances. But it is unlikely that the Chivalry dwelled as long on Calhoun's more practical words on slavery. Referring to one of his runaways, he wrote, "I wish you would have him lodged in jail for one week, to be fed on bread and water and to employ someone for me to give him 30 lashes well laid on. . . ." [7]

2

Neither President Jackson nor Calhoun were unkind masters. Quite the contrary. Their instructions merely revealed the normal practice of the most humane of owners. Nor was the fact that their slaves had run away unusual. Hundreds were constantly being forced to advertise in the press for the recalcitrant, for runaway slaves whose brandings, croppings of ears, lashed backs, and various scars and wounds were carefully described as an aid to identification, along with the various ingenious irons, collars, prongs, handcuffs, metal masks, and leg irons that had been fastened to them as punishment or to impede flight. Such advertisements read:

RANAWAY, my negro man Richard. A reward of $25 will be paid for his apprehension DEAD or ALIVE.

RANAWAY, a negro woman and two children. A few days before she went off I burnt her with a hot iron on the left side of her face. I tried to make the letter M.

RANAWAY, a negro woman, named Maria, some scars on her back occasioned by the whip.[8]

Similar insertions, almost as stylized as a sonnet, "RANAWAY," "scarred by the whip," "branded on the left thigh," "DEAD or ALIVE," were carried by the thousands over the years in all the Southern press. In the Charlestown *Mercury*, the Mobile *Register*, the Vicksburg *Sentinel*, and the New Orleans *Crescent*, in weeklies in every corner of the South from Kentucky and North Carolina to Georgia and Texas, the columns of advertisements regularly added to this long-continued story of flight and pursuit. Sometimes the pursued took on something of character as he appeared each week in a series of advertisements until he was finally captured or killed, or succeeded in fighting his way out of a trap, perhaps suffering new wounds duly described in a new advertisement. Usually, however, he was only an ill-defined shadow, a man in trouble, his only personality his scars, "A mulatto fellow, his back showing lasting impressions of the whip," or plain Ben Fox and "a negro by the name of Rigdon," whose owner promised a $200 reward for their capture, "or for the KILLING OF THEM SO THAT I CAN SEE THEM." [9]

A more pleasant topic of conversation among owners was the carefree happiness of the well-cared-for slave; but more intriguing still was the subject of how slavery made for leadership in politics and war and all the social graces of polite society. "Slavery established in the South a peculiar and noble type of civilization," wrote a Virginian of the time, adding that the institution "inculcated notions of chivalry, polished the manners and produced many noble and generous virtues." [10] Perhaps its noblest triumph, however, was the creation of the Southern Gentleman, who was thus described by one of them:

> Besides being of faultless pedigree, the Southern Gentleman is usually possessed of an equally faultless physical development. His average height is about six feet, yet he is rarely gawky in his movements, or in the least clumsily put together; and his entire *physique* conveys to the mind the impression of firmness united to flexibility.
>
> . . . [We] may attribute the good size and graceful carriage of the Southern Gentleman, to his out-of-doors and a-horseback mode of living. . . . By the time he is five years of age he rides well; and in a little while thereafter has a fowling piece put into his hands . . . and so accoutred he sallies forth into the fields and pastures in search of adventure. . . .
>
> But of all things, he is most enamoured by politics and the Army; and it is owing to this cause that the South has furnished us with all our great generals, from Washington to Scott, as well as most of our leading statesmen, from Jefferson to Calhoun. . . .[11]

Another aspect of the Southern Gentleman, or so another of them proclaimed in verse, was his "gallant bearing and reckless daring." [12] He loved "the Hero's glorious life," still another sang, only asking that his be "the sword whose flashes bright are foremost in the thick'ning fight." [13] As the sectional contest between North and South stimulated the South's martial propensity to an ever-higher degree, it became clear to some Southerners, or so they declared, that the North, as well as Mexico, Central America, and Cuba, would have to be conquered and mastered for its own well-being.

Fortunately, the Southern Gentleman had been trained in handling his inferiors and was thus ideally equipped for Northern conquest. "Naturally generous," one of them wrote, "Southerners exercise much forebearance till the question of honor is raised and then they rush to the sword. . . . Fierce and fearless in a contest, yet just, and generous in command they possess every quality to rule the Northern people." [14]

3

By the 1850's, the Southerners were not only praising themselves as paragons of cavalier grace but finding that their sectional opponents of the North were money-grubbing hypocrites "hardly fit for association with the southern gentleman's body servant," [15] unfeeling boors who somehow contrived to obtain most of the profits of the Southern planter, too hospitable and generous for his own good and obviously no match for the tight-fisted Yankee banker. The North's quality, insofar as it had any, "smelled of trade," and felt when viewing the South's slaveholders, " a sneaky sense of its own inferiority." [16]

It was both the Chivalry's strength and weakness that its members believed implicitly, and even ardently, in the legend they had woven about themselves and their opponents. Their virtues, according to the legend, were not so much the result of effort as of blood, as decisive in a man as in a racehorse. Blood would tell and high worth was inevitable through that straight descent so many planters claimed from the Norman nobility which had conquered England, from the cavaliers who had opposed the regicide Cromwell before fleeing to Virginia. From there, the aristocrats had replenished the earth so effectively that men claiming the bluest of blood were likely to be found at any crossroads widening in Arkansas, at any log cabin plantation in the wilderness of Alabama, as ready to defend their honor as the most punctilious aristocrat of Old Virginny, whether by shooting from the hip on sight at some surprised offender on Main Street or upon the more formal fields of the duello.

This tenet of high-born descent was among the most ubiquitous and most fallacious of all the several aspects of the Southern legend, for the great preponderance of those who viewed themselves as of the Chivalry derived from the middle classes and peasants of England, Scotland, Wales, and Northern Ireland and even from the German Palatinate.[17] Nevertheless, the gentry, as they held their tournaments, wearing the colors of their beloved, and tilting with lances at county fairs as if they were knights from the pages of the admired Scott, held firmly to the belief that they were of finer clay than most more humbly descended, and saw their various circles as congregations of unbelievable charm and nobility, whether the locus was Virginia's Tidelands or Alabama's rude canebrake region.

So Henry Wise, Governor of Virginia and John Brown's final and most generous opponent, viewed his colleagues whose plantations ranged between

Virginia's York and James as they flowed toward the Chesapeake Bay. Seldom in all of history, he believed, had so much of bravery and worth and grace been gathered in so small an area. "It was settled by a race, or rather stock, of families, the like of which will be rarely seen again," he wrote, "so manly, so refined, so intelligent, so spirited, proud, self-reliant, independent, strong, so fresh and so free." As if the mere mention of the families living there would prove his point, he lists the slaveholders of the region, the Armisteads, Bollings, Byrds, Blairs, Burwells, Amblers, Carters, Cloptons, Christians, Carys, Dandridges, Digges, Fontaines, Gregorys, Randolphs, Pages, Nelsons, Tuckers, Tylers, Tazewells, and Lightfoots, and on and on, Barrons, Sclaters, Shields, and Dudleys, but with never a word of the thousands of human beings who did their work and formed their wealth.[18]

Instead, he writes of the "packs of hounds" and of "the bugles for horn music of frosty mornings," of aristocrats who were "genial in intercourse and profuse in hospitality," "of gentle graces and of manly bearing," happy and prosperous in their "boundless broad acres, fair and fertile." Yet despite such lyricism as that of Wise, the South's slaveholders knew, of course, or some of them knew, however unwillingly, that the columbine and wisteria, the avenue of moss-festooned oaks leading to the Great House shining whitely in the sunlight were only a facade concealing a massive crime; that however dainty the gesture or gallant the word or exquisite the sentiment or sweet the horn music or swift the hound, there was something of sweat, blood, and torture in the background.

4

This knowledge of an always implicit violence may have heightened the aristocratic posturing, made the voice a little more suavely firm as it defended slavery as an institution of purely patriarchal love, or increased its kindness to the amiable old servitor—"Sir, he would give his life for me"—while lashings went on daily amid the field hands perhaps scarcely a mile away. For no authority has ever denied that floggings were a regular and inevitable part of large-scale cotton and tobacco, sugar and rice production, however minimized they have sometimes been in the total picture of the South.

For all of the Southern legend's elements of truth and power, it was as much a development, a product of slavery and sectional conflict as abolition itself, its rococo extravaganzas extolling war and honor completely absent from the mild rationality of earlier slaveholders such as Washington and Jefferson, Madison and Monroe. Its base, posited on the inherent, predestined, eternal, God-given inferiority of some men, who were and should be slaves, and on the divinely decreed superiority of others, who were justly their masters forever, was so unsound that everything based upon it leaned crazily askew. Every generous attribute was tinged with its opposite as a result of the slaveholders' belief that some were born with saddles on their backs and others booted and spurred to ride them and that it was as much in the order of nature for men to enslave each other as that other animals should prey on each other. This was the essence of the professional Southern apologist for slavery, from Senator James H. Hammond of South Carolina to President Thomas R. Dew of William and Mary, to George Fitzhugh of Virginia and Chancellor William Harper of the Supreme Court of South Carolina.

For all of its moonlight and roses and sabers ringing in the dawn, the rustle of crinolines and the pounding hooves of charging horses, the legend was built on need, designed to serve utilitarian political and economic ends as well as to comfort and inspire. In a sense Eli Whitney's cotton gin, invented in 1793, turned out Southern honor as fast as it did ginned cotton. The South's peculiar legend burgeoned with the swelling of the Cotton Kingdom, intensified as plantations, fortunes, and slaves increased, rising in militance almost in ratio with the rise of its great cash crop. It became increasingly frenetic as its colossal property in slaves was threatened when many in the North and in much of the world condemned the slavery upon which the South lived. And it was then that charges of mass cruelty were countered by pictures of the kind and loving slaveholder who cared not for worldly wealth but only for his honor.

If some slaveholders lived in a state of almost perpetual indignation at the worldwide condemnation of slavery, their anger can be easily understood. They had been born into the system of slavery, accepting it from infancy as inevitably as a young Yankee accepted the society in which he lived. As the Southerner grew older he learned that most of the world, for most of history, had honored slavery, that Plato and Aristotle thought it vital to an ordered society, that Athenian democracy had rested upon it as had the mighty power of Rome. He learned that God Himself as revealed in the Bible approved of slavery and that wherever there had been grace and learning and culture there had also been that slavery without which such attributes were impossible. Even when he knew of slavery's cruelty, he regarded it as a necessary part of a greater good, as another might justify the lives lost in a necessary war. As for living off unearned profit, living off the labor of slaves, it seemed to him no different than the Northern capitalist who lived off the dividends of his stocks, often working as little in the factory whence he received his dividends as the great Southern slaveholder worked in the fields with his slaves. Each had invested his capital in the work of others, the capitalist through investing in stocks, the Southern planter through investing in slaves. He was as genuinely aghast at any proposal to deprive him of his slaves as any Northern entrepreneur would have been at a proposal to seize his stocks and bonds.

5

Yet there were many differences between the two systems, not all of which were spoken of in the South. The very essence of that region was the unspoken and unadmitted, a great silence with which the well-bred covered much that was painful. If the white women of the South seldom mentioned the institution of concubinage, in which their menfolk, pausing for a space in their ceaseless tributes to the purity and loveliness of white womanhood, periodically stole off to the embraces of slave mistresses, many Southern wives endured it throughout lives embittered by it. There was a massive and unmentioned linkage of white and black blood in which many an aristocrat, impressive on his pillared portico, sold his own son or daughter at a price to himself never articulated—a mere formless something in the back of his mind. Of course, there were many who went to great lengths to free and provide for their slave children, or even the mistresses to whom they had given an equivocal loyalty over the years; but at best it was a sorry business, perhaps the only great social, political, and economic problem in American history which included sex and heartbreak and even love, however painful and peculiar.

"God forgive us," wrote one Southern lady in an oft-quoted passage,

but ours is a monstrous system, a wrong and iniquity! Like the patriarchs of old, our men live all in one house with their wives and their concubines; and the mulattoes in every family partly resemble the white children. Any lady is ready to tell you who is the father of all the mulatto children in everybody's household but her own. Those, she seems to think, drop from the clouds. My disgust sometimes is boiling over.[19]

But Mrs. Mary Boykin Chesnut, who penned this bitter lament, had no word of sympathy for the women slaves, bred as cows are bred for the increase and profit of their owners, and whose submission to the Chivalry was sometimes a part of rape, nor did she mention the anguish of the black men who loved them.

There was in truth a great deal going on behind the South's moonlight and roses which could not well be mentioned in polite society, not only the illicit affairs of the institution that was miscegenation, but occasionally events that were a little more psychotic. Letters and journals of the time, the testimony of fled slaves, are punctuated with references to the sadistic; to the strange antics of solitary men and women on lonely plantations forced by the torment of their own starved lives to try for some relief by torturing the helpless whom they controlled. Mrs. Chesnut, for example, writes of one whom she describes as "a slaveholder and a savage. He put Negroes into hogsheads with nails driven in all around, and rolled the poor things down hill." [20] There were alcoholics such as Liliburne Lewis, Thomas Jefferson's nephew, who with his brother once slowly dismembered a Negro boy with a hatchet for dropping a vase, and the sadist "Madame Lalaurie, of New Orleans, who tortured her slaves for her own amusement." [21] Such peculiar carryings-on were by no means uncommon in the South. But it was the ordinary severity of hired overseers, intent on speed-up and increased production per acre, particularly when cotton was high and in danger of falling in price, that made those Southerners who gave their whole lives trying to improve the lot of those they owned say so frequently and disapprovingly of a neighbor or one more distant, "I hear he does not treat his people well."

6

While there were always some white men and women in the South willing actively to oppose slavery, even at the risk of death, imprisonment, or ostracism, their numbers steadily decreased as the Civil War neared with the fire-eaters imposing an ever more stringent dictatorship over all public opinion. As early as 1804 a judge for the eastern district of Georgia, one George Jabez Brown, Jr., in a charge to a grand jury declared that if the Georgia legislature did not abolish slavery immediately "he would put himself at the head of the Negroes, and effect it, though at the expense of the lives of every white inhabitant of the state." [22]

But even then, when sentiment was not nearly as intense as it later became, Judge Brown was dismissed from office and imprisoned on a charge of inciting servile insurrection. By the 1850's, however, Southern opponents of slavery, often ill-starred, sensitive men plagued by guilt, unsuccessful in the harsh business of forcing slaves to turn out profitable crops, were voiceless and without power when compared with slavery's champions who declared it a positive good that must expand if not into the North itself, then surely into the new West, into Cuba, Mexico, and Central America.

A Virginian was not untypical of these lonely slaveholding dissenters from slavery when he declared in his will that he was freeing his chattels in the belief "that slavery in all its forms . . . is inconsistent with republican principles . . . a violation of the bill of rights . . . repugnant to the spirit of the gospel." [23] But there were more who suffered the burden of slavery while condemning it, while predicting often enough that the South was pursuing tragedy by insisting that its vices were virtues. There were hundreds almost daily revolted by the auctions which everywhere disposed of men and women, forcing them to show their teeth and reveal their persons, purchasers running practiced hands over legs and prodding their muscles as they spat tobacco and barked their bids, while the auctioneer praised a human being up for sale in such words as these:

There's a cotton nigger for you! Genuine! Look at his toes! Look at his fingers! There's a pair of legs for you! If you have the right sile and the right sort of overseer, buy him, and put your trust in Providence! He's just as good for ten bales [a crop] as I am for a julep at eleven o'clock.[24]

It was such scenes that forced a good many more than one, in the privacy of home or friendship, to exclaim as did the South Carolinian who said in honest anguish, "We may shut our eyes and avert our faces, if we please, but there it is, the dark and growing evil at our doors; and meet the question we must at no distant day. . . . What is to be done? Oh! My God, I do not know, but something must be done." [25]

But John Brown at last would not shut his eyes or avert his face. For he, too, had come to feel, after some delay and considerable travail, "Oh! My God . . . something must be done."

THE GOVERNOR AND THE FARMER

I

Governor Wise was too brightly romantic a character to care to dwell on such darkly distressing aspects of the Southland. A cheerful man, he preferred the more conventional tributes to the South's brave men and lovely women. Writing of the latter, or at least of their higher echelons in Virginia's mansions between the York and James, he describes them as "pure, refined, chaste, delicate and modest . . . queenly, high, commanding and stately." [26] As for the men, what horsemen they were! How quick to resent insult, how implacable in the duel which Wise frequently declared was the very crux of civilized conduct.

"Every boy had his horse," he wrote, in recalling the glad days of slavery, "and lived in the saddle: there were riders in those days. Thus minds and bodies . . . were trained to the nerve tunes of health and strength and burly freshness: and manners and morals were brought in all gentleness to make a glad, social and glorious political state." [27]

Such was the proclaimed type of the gallant slaveholder; but Governor Wise of Virginia was the specific, improbable fact. No one desired more than he to be the *compleat cavalier* nor failed more narrowly. His private character, as aristocratic as that of most slaveholders, was at length lost in the tobacco-chewing, backslapping politician. If he had the recklessness proper to the Southern Gentleman, always ready to give or receive a challenge, always insistent that one Southerner could whip ten Yankees, he had, too, a certain unacceptable unpredictability, as when he praised John Brown as brave and sane, or came out against secession, just before the Civil War, and for fighting the North while remaining in the Union.

He had many gifts but gentility was not one of them. Yet he admired it in others and could only regret that his impetuous and original nature prevented him from having very much of his own. No man in the state could swear as long without repetition nor pray more fervently, a consequence of his being both "pious and profane at one and the same time." [28] He was an expert whittler, habitually attracting crowds around some crossroads general store where his virtuoso skill with the knife impressed Virginia's rural voters. Although he did not drink, neither did he shrink from places and occasions where men did, and once saved Webster from being brained when he caught the arm of a drunken congressman just as he was attempting to throw a bottle at point-blank range at the "God-like Daniel." [29] He was fond of the bowie knife, if not for his own use then as a sectional asset, claiming that the South could overcome the North's superior armament if it had to, by the bowie knife alone. It was better, he said, than the bayonet.[30]

Eccentricity erupted from him as if it were a rash and his temperament plagued him persistently, sometimes forcing him into challenges to duels he really did not want to fight. But eccentricity and temperament helped make him the most entertaining stump speaker in the state. His forte was appealing to his constituents not as the slaveholder he was, but as if he were some poor old broken-down farmer. Although he ardently admired the aristocrats of the

Tidelands, as his writings sufficiently attest, he himself had been reared on the salt-water farms of Accomack County on Virginia's eastern shore, a sandy spit of land extending into the Atlantic and perhaps resembling the rocky slaveless farms of Virginia's west more than the lush plantations between the York and James. The slaveless farmers of the state's west loved him and helped elect him Governor in 1855. If he admired their rivals, the owners of the slave plantations of the Tidelands, he also knew the plantation owner could never be secure until some measure of political equality was given to the poor farmers in the west of Virginia's mountains. They had long been shortchanged as to political power through the allotting of representation in the state legislature on the basis of property including slaves. In 1860 Virginia had almost 500,000 slaves—more slaves than any single state of the fifteen slave states—most of whom were bred for sale to the lower South.

Wise was a brave, unpredictable man with a shrill voice and the attitude of a Shakespearian tragedian when engaged in declamation, often thrusting a foot forward while raising one hand and one finger above his head and pointing heavenward. Slim but not tall, his complexion almost the color of rigor mortis, he possessed that kind of attractive ugliness that borders on the handsome. He had entered political life by both defeating in an election and later wounding in a duel his opponent for Congress in 1833.[31] The climax of his ten years in the House of Representatives came in 1838 when, as a second to William Graves, representative of Kentucky, he insisted that a duel between Graves and Jonathan Cilley, member from Maine, continue after an initial harmless exchange of shots had satisfied the usual requirements of honor. It did continue until Cilley was killed.[32]

Old John Quincy Adams, the former President, who almost daily received assassination threats from the South as he led anti-slavery forces in the House of Representatives from 1836 to 1848, charged in open debate, while referring to Cilley's slaying, that Wise had entered the House with "his hands reeking with the blood of murder."[33] And yet Wise was not a ruffian. He had ability and even generosity and favored the duel, in his own mind at least, only as a method of keeping the peace and an honorable decorum. Throughout his later political life, he suffered from the itch of presidential ambition and if he did not become President, he at least dominated one and made another, controlling President John Tyler at a point of crisis, as shall presently appear, and assuring the Democratic nomination in 1856, or so he liked to think, of President James Buchanan.[34] He left the Union with reluctance for it was his plan to save it, and slavery too, perhaps, as President of the United States. Not the least of the casualties of Harper's Ferry and the Civil War in

Wise's mind may have been his long-cherished hope of residence in the White House.[35]

2

For Edmund Ruffin, that individualistic prototype of the Southern fire-eater, Harper's Ferry was not an end, however, but a beginning. A crusty devotee of the South and slavery, an ailing little man of sixty-five in 1859, with long strands of white hair hanging over his shoulders, he weighed a frail 130 pounds, was but 5 feet 8 inches tall, and was as pronounced a rustic, as militant an eccentric, in his own way, as John Brown himself.[36] Despite his years and silver ringlets, Ruffin contrived to gain a temporary admission to the corps of the Virginia Military Institute on the day of John Brown's hanging that he might witness a scene reserved only for the military out in force to prevent a possible rescue. As queer an apparition as the Ancient Mariner, old Ruffin stood shouldering his musket among the fresh-faced scions of Virginia's aristocracy, wearing their uniform of scarlet flannel shirt, criss-crossed with white bandoliers, and a long gray overcoat, undisturbed, he wrote, by the fact that "the young men found my position was very amusing and perhaps ludicrous," permitting nothing to detract from the triumph of hanging one, who was, in Ruffin's eyes, the North's leading abolitionist.[37]

For twenty years, the Virginian had been the South's foremost exponent of scientific agriculture. If John Brown had won a good many prizes for his cattle and sheep at state and county fairs, Edmund Ruffin had won even more honors for his demonstrations as to the efficacy of marl as fertilizer. He might have remained as one whose chief claim to fame derived from his accomplishments in agriculture, but the same forces that shaped John Brown, ruined Wise's presidential hopes, and deprived Parker of the pleasure of writing his history of religion had changed Ruffin by 1850 into one of the South's leading advocates of secession. Whatever their uniquely personal quality, the fine flair of their separate stance and being, Howe and Higginson, Thoreau, Douglass, Davis, and Ruffin had the common experience with other thousands of being propelled in large degree, whether forward or backward, by the nation's struggle over slavery.

As John Brown mounted the scaffold, Edmund Ruffin could see plainly enough that the execution meant the advance of the cause of secession but he could not perceive at all that it meant, too, the end of slavery, nor that he also would presently die a grimmer, more hopeless death than John Brown's and one not unconnected with it. Nevertheless, he noted in his journal of his antagonist, so like himself and so different, too: "He is as thorough a fanatic as ever suffered martyrdom and a very brave and able man. . . . It is impossible for me not to respect his thorough devotion to his bad cause and the undaunted courage with which he has sustained it through all losses and hazards." [38]

IV

Of Time
and Temperament

JOHN BROWN was as much a product of his time and its temperament as any Southern bravo facing his foe with pistols at twenty paces. Each was something of a warrior and each was equally willing to bring affairs to what was called "a bloody issue." If the Southern planter liked to imagine himself as a knight defending white Southern womanhood from a fate worse than death, John Brown preferred to regard himself as a gallant soldier, terrible to his slaveholder foe, but irresistible to the beautiful belles of the South who would be quite overcome by his soldierly chivalry. Writing in 1858 of his coming invasion of the South, he said he meant to treat all his prisoners kindly but especially the women. "Females," he wrote, perhaps a bit hopefully, "are susceptible of being carried away entirely by the kindness of an intrepid and magnanimous soldier even when his name was but a terror the day previous." [1]

If the Southern Gentleman could order the flogging of a field hand while regarding Old Cato as a member of the family, John Brown could execute five pro-slavery settlers in Kansas and yet while at home in Ohio tuck his old father tenderly into bed each night. Both were sentimental, the slaveholder's eyes perhaps misting with tears as he drank a Christmas toast "To our people," a common designation for the slaves, while John Brown, as lethal as a knife on occasion, could weep upon hearing some pretty ditty or when on his knees praying with a sinner.[2] But whatever the kinship between the antagonists resulting from a common country and a common time, there was one monumental difference between them. One fought to destroy slavery, the other to perpetuate it.

A MAN OF HIS TIMES

I

It is in the Kansas civil war that John Brown makes one of his first formal appearances in American history when he is interviewed on the morning of Friday, May 30, 1856, by James Redpath, a newspaper reporter.[3] Already he is in hiding for the Pottawatomie executions, the reprisal slayings of five pro-slavery settlers, undertaken when the Free State cause is reeling in defeat. With him are four of his seven sons, his son-in-law, and a half-dozen other young men, encamped in a grove of oaks on Ottawa Creek in eastern Kansas, seeking to avoid pursuing federal cavalry and pro-slavery militia companies which have captured his two oldest sons, John, Jr., and Jason.

As he leans over a campfire roasting a pig, his dusty toes sticking through the ends of boots almost completely worn away, John Brown suggests neither the prosperous bank director he once was nor the significant figure he is to become. His bristly reddish brown mat of hair streaked with gray has been queerly mangled by some home-trained barber. Invincibly rustic in appearance, he is wearing an old-fashioned floppy starched collar, without stock or cravat, its points turning limply away from an unshaven bristly jut of chin, a gold collar button gleaming nudely beneath his Adam's apple.

His scrawny turkey neck extends leanly from his crumpled collar, and his face, creviced and wrinkled about the nose and mouth by the elements and the years, has a kind of peaked severity. As devoid of belly, as slimly concave as any boy, his nose "hawked and thin," his eyes sky blue in a brick red face, he has on this bright May morning in Kansas that moldy, creaky aspect common to those who have been for days without shelter, as subject to wind and rain as some old tree.

As he straightens from the fire and glances around the camp, at the string of horses, saddled as if to be ready for instant flight, at the young men who have gathered around him to fight the pro-slavery forces, he has for a moment the air of one listening for an approaching enemy. His mouth is bitter, a thin wide slit turning bleakly downward, his eyes truculently steady in their gaze and yet with something unsated and lonely in them, too.[4]

He is 5 feet 10 inches in height, with no more hips than a rope, his shoulders somewhat narrow and a little stooped, his weight about 150 pounds. Fifty-six years old that very May, but appearing older, he has a stringy muscularity about him, a kind of whipcord tension that marks him primarily as a product of the frontier farm. Occasionally he retires from the camp on the Ottawa into the thickets along the creek where, according to Redpath, "he wrestles with His God in secret prayer,"[5] hoping, as to the executions of the five at Pottawatomie, that "He who sees not as men see, does not lay the guilt of innocent blood to our charge."[6] Occasionally, too, he skulks through the brush like some old gray wolf trailing the cavalry that hold his two sons prisoner. Held prisoner with them are many other Free State men.

With Lawrence, the Free State center, invaded, bombarded, and looted by pro-slavery forces but a few days past; with most of the Free State leaders either fleeing or imprisoned on charges of treason, it seems to most, and even to the Old Man at times, as if slavery has triumphed in Kansas. Yet frequently he gathers his young men around the campfire, insisting that they must fight on even if their little camp is all that remains in Kansas of the fight against slavery.

"Many and various were the instructions he gave us," one of the young men recalled.

He expressed himself to us that we should never allow ourselves to be tempted by any consideration to acknowledge laws and institutions to exist as of right if our conscience and our reason condemned them. He admonished us not to care whether a majority, no matter how large, opposed our principles and opinions, the largest majorities being sometime only organized mobs whose howlings never changed black to white or night into day. . . . While it was true that the pro-slavery people had the upper hand at present, and the Free State organization had dwindled to a handful in the bush, nevertheless we ought to be of good cheer and start the ball rolling at the first opportunity, no matter whether its starting motion would even crush us to death.[7]

2

John Brown was born in Torrington, Connecticut, in 1800. When he was five years old he had moved with his family to "the Ohio forest primeval," which the settlers "were to destroy with great labor, driving wolves, panthers and bears from their rude cabin doors."[8] He had been shaped, perhaps a bit sparsely, but ruggedly enough, by the clearing of land, the felling of trees, by wrestling with stumps, hauling rocks, building vats and tanneries, cabins and barns, roads, churches, and schools. As a surveyor, he had trudged hundreds of miles, his compass his guide, measuring the wilderness. A 400-mile journey by horseback and the Erie Canal, driving cattle from Ohio to the Eastern market, was not unusual for him. Drought and flood, crop failure and business failure, typhoid fever and dying children, had fashioned a man more than a little different from softer men of a later day.

His nose was sufficiently commanding to cause an admirer to remark that the Old Man looked like an eagle, to which one of the Brown sons replied, "Yes, or some other carniverous bird."[9] Another son, chuckling a little, and speaking of his father years later, said, "He looked like a meat axe, didn't he?" and then told how his father had frightened a pro-slavery judge in Kansas by merely looking into his courtroom.[10]

But it was not only John Brown's grimness that may have frightened the judge. He had a kind of jaunty challenge often somehow emphasized by being understated. His utterance was usually sparse enough but occasionally it had a quality that echoed a little on the air after he had spoken, as if his bright blue eyes in his red hatchet face had italicized his words into an afterlife. Even at his most deadly his sentences were apt to scan a bit, as when he was asked what he would have done if he had captured a Kansas pro-slavery judge. "If the Lord had put Judge Lecompte into my hands," he said, "I think it would have taken the Lord to get him out again."[11] With one son already killed and the bullets hailing around at the Kansas Battle of Osawatomie in 1856, his instructions to a young man at his side had the same queer swing as he said, "Take more care to end life well than to live long."[12]

John Brown's supporters in New England doted on the neat pithy balance with which he described his battles. But he did not always speak so. He was a man of more than one role and more than one subject. He was as likely to describe his ideas on farming as to describe his warfare. When he spoke in Concord in February of 1857, for example, his toes were not protruding from his boots nor were his eyes truculent. If he had been an actor he could not have been costumed more fittingly. Wearing "a military surtout and a patent leather stock," such as Marine officers often wore then, as well as his deaconish suit of brown kerseymere, he was so religious in his bearing and so strongly suggested the soldier-churchman, in Sanborn's opinion, that "Cotton Mather would have rejoiced in him and Miles Standish owned him as a brother in the Lord."[13] If he spoke of war, he also liked to speak of his way with a little lamb until his auditors scarce knew which to admire most, his bravery or his gentleness.

"He had 3000 sheep in Ohio," he told his Concord audience on this occasion, according to Emerson,

and would instantly detect a strange sheep in his flock. A cow can tell its calf by secret signal, he thinks, by the eye, to run away or lie down and hide itself. He always makes friends with his horse or mule (or with the deer that visit his Ohio farm), and when he sleeps on his horse, as he does as readily as in his bed, his horse does not start or endanger him.[14]

So he charmed his audience by stories of himself in battle and as the tender keeper of the sheep, and in either role they found him moving. In some strange way he was able to strike all the changes demanded by a time that was both savage and sentimental. It was an age in which tears flowed freely at florid tributes to home and mother, when the most prominent of public men blazed away at point-blank range on some dusty Main Street at some fancied insult or slur on their honor, when young men, as John Brown's young men, wrote poetry to love and liberty before going into battle or even before stepping on the gallows. It was a time perfectly shaped for Old John Brown in which he sometimes felt quite at home.

ON STYLE AND FACING THE ULTIMATE

I

The common premise of a man made by and emerging from his time has not often been accorded to John Brown. Rather, he has been presented as a figure whose pressures came not from an historical situation but from himself, whether hero or psychotic; presented in an historical vacuum as if all the drama of his days came only from his own peculiar nature. Yet he was not the only American of his day as intractable in his views as he was in his actions nor the only one who could face finality with something of enjoyment.

If he valued his convictions to the point of dying for them, it was not entirely unusual in that time of anti-slavery mobs and hair-triggered pistols. In temperament, at any rate, there was little difference between Andrew Jackson, the slaveholder President, ready if necessary to face down the world over the barrel of a gun, and John Brown the farmer abolitionist, ready to gun down slavery and almost by himself.[15]

It has been suggested, in fact, that the American temperament, unrestrained by ancient and accepted institutions and stimulated by an excess of frontier democracy, was sufficiently intense during the thirty years before the Civil War to have been a factor in precipitating it.[16] However that may be, it is true enough that the American male, if white, Protestant, and native born, often had a rich dramatic sense of his own value, a conviction that his was a sacred manhood in whose defense he would risk all.

Many actually had then, as this narrative may indicate, a consummate ability to face the ultimate in fortune or life, whether on the turn of a card, or a cavalry charge, whether by facing mobs as abolitionists or bullets on the field of honor or the gallows as traitors. And they did it all with a high, wide, and handsome gesture. The content would inevitably vary, of course, between the magnificently uncompromising anti-slavery declarations of Boston's great abolitionist, William Lloyd Garrison, often made in the face of peril, and the even more florid periods of the Alabama fire-eater, William Lowndes Yancey, who shot and killed his wife's uncle in a family quarrel, but not the sweeping, go-to-hell grandiloquence of their attitude.

The abolitionists, particularly, valued the flair of their own individualities, and could strike an attitude as dramatic in facing martyrdom as that achieved by any Southern fire-eater facing an insult to his honor. Great manly bursts of weeping were not without favor, indicating that well of strong and passionate feeling that was the birthright of every American; and men, deadly enough on occasion, interchanged terms of epistolary endearment—"thine forever," or "my dear, dear boy"—with an innocence completely devoid of the innuendo and snickering of a later day.

"Three times yesterday I wept like a child," Charles Sumner, admired by John Brown, confessed on November 26, 1851, the occasion his departure from Boston to Washington after his election as a senator from Massachusetts.[17] The manly Samuel Gridley Howe confided in a letter to Sumner that he was equally prone to tears, describing an occasion in which he had been barely able to gain the privacy of his chamber before "letting down the floodgates of the eye to the flow of tears."[18] Elijah P. Lovejoy, an important influence in John Brown's career, almost won his life when, weeping himself in proud defiance, he reduced to general blubbering the members of the very Illinois mob which would kill him for his anti-slavery stand four days later.[19]

There was a great deal of mass community weeping when sinners, "Some overcome with emotion and lying on the floor, some applying camphor to prevent their fainting," [20] repented and were born again amid the sobs and hymns of the revivals which were a constant during John Brown's years; and orators, if they did not actually break down, were often determined that their auditors should. It was as manly to weep under proper circumstances, or to start back in anger or dismay, as it was to send or receive a challenge to a duel in Mississippi or California, because each revealed the quivering sensitivity that was the mark of the high-toned.

There was everywhere a certain manly excess and when those indulging in it suffered disappointment they were apt to "fear for reason," or "know not where to turn unless the grave." Breakdowns, mental or otherwise, were not a disgrace but evidence of stress suffered by one not stone. The grave itself was highly regarded, at least as an object of literary sentiment. Death had a sweetly mournful allure, the novels of the time often depicting the heroine's life ebbing with the tide, the hero expiring with the last rays of the setting sun, and mourning scenes, either painted or embroidered and depicting weeping willows, funeral urns, and the lovely departed above some elegiac verse, were on the walls of American parlors from Natchez to Detroit.

Actual deathbed scenes when conventional were at once heart-rending and histrionic. When the twenty-six-year-old Jane Ruffin Dupuy, Edmund Ruffin's daughter, lay dying in her Virginia home on July 24, 1855, she called her large family around her and with her last strength urged each to embrace God and meet her in Heaven. As she spoke hymns were softly sung and prayers, punctuated by gasping sobs, were uttered while downstairs there was the sweet tremolo of the melodeon on which someone was playing "I will arise and go to my Father." [21] The dying often tried hard for an appropriate ending as in the case of the great Webster, who, rallying from unconsciousness, observed, "I still live," and uttered lines on the immortality of the soul before asking with final pride, "Have I—wife, son, doctor, friends, are you all here—have I, on this occasion, said anything unworthy of Daniel Webster?" [22]

It was a romantic age in the western world from Byron in Greece, to the later Garibaldi in Italy, to the scenes created by Dickens, artfully contrived to bring scalding tears. But in the United States this *Weltanschauung* of conduct, this code of behavior, however sentimental, had, in addition, its own peculiar deadliness, a frequent willingness to bring almost any issue, political or personal, to a mortal encounter, which many have attributed, at least in part, to the institution of slavery.[23] The political and economic scene, moreover, stimulated that violence of personality which seemed to become a uniquely American phenomenon as clashes, duels, and mobs increased in ratio to the steady rise of the struggle over slavery.

And the human material involved in the contest, with which we are here particularly concerned, was peculiarly combustible with the very mores of the day a kind of tinder, the whole style of feeling and action too grandiose for avoiding conflict. While there were many exceptions, it is true enough that the dominant types who placed their imprint upon the age were, first, the Southerner who was white, by God, and proud of it, who would not stand for the slightest affront to his honor, and who felt that it was not only manifest destiny but manifest benevolence for such as himself to control lesser breeds whether they were on his own plantation or beneath the palm trees of the Caribbean; and secondly, the Northerner, who had been born again at the mercy seat, who said with Isaiah, "proclaim liberty to the captives, and the opening of the prison to *them that are* bound"; who because of slavery spoke occasionally of even Concord and Lexington and all the glory of the American Revolution in terms of shame, and proposed to follow in Christ's footsteps, Hallelujah!, even though it led to death.

It was the clash of these archetypes that dominated John Brown's years as well as the lives of his countrymen.

2

If it was a histrionic age in which the grand gesture was seldom foregone, its actors, whatever the peril of their conduct, had at least the facility of enjoying their lines and their actions as much as their warmest admirers. Even the most modest and brave of abolitionists, Theodore Dwight Weld, savored the drama of his years, endlessly fascinated by the complex mystery of his own personality, perpetually intrigued by his appearance, his sinfulness, and a long list of self-confessed eccentricities. To himself, he and his cause were the most significant and absorbing of dramas.[24]

Abolitionists during the 1830's were mobbed or stoned more often than not (even in the North, indeed, particularly there) when attempting to speak against slavery, and it was Weld's custom to announce, as the brickbats flew around him, that his howling audience would either have to kill or listen to him. Occasionally he returned to the site of a mobbing each night for as many as ten, boos and bricks continuing to assail him as he stood with his arms folded, proud and dark, his nose a little awry from a previous fracture, sometimes staggering under the impact of an accurate missile, until there was sufficient silence to make himself heard. Such was his power that at such a time he often persuaded some of those who had come so persistently to mob him to enlist instead in the anti-slavery cause.

No one appreciated his bravery more than Weld, nor for that matter, the whole peculiar range of his diverse abilities. He drew almost as much pleasure from his absent-mindedness as from his courage and he was entranced by the many bone fractures he had suffered as well as his manner of exercise, which was to leap and contort about in the early dawning beneath God's sky as he uttered little cries of ecstasy. He was intrigued, too, by the bleak severity of his mien, which he said was as grim as that of a pirate and so menacing as to make little children cry when they saw him. Writing to his betrothed, Angelina Grimké, South Carolina aristocrat, who with her sister Sarah gave up slaves and pre-eminent social position in Charleston to fight for abolition, he described his nature with a determination, he said, that she should know the worst, but with such a fascinated fondness for his faults that his words seemed to transform them into heroic virtues.

"Of my weaknesses," he wrote to his beloved from New York City, "you know but little. You will find me an untamed spirit—wild as the winds," he continued, declaring he would begin "the sickening catalogue of my shameful defects" by describing his utter selfishness, which he succeeded in making singularly attractive. Next of his sins was pride, but that, too, seemed to partake of virtue as he wrote:

I am too proud to be *ambitious*, too proud to seek applause, too proud to tolerate it when lavished on me, proud as Lucifer that I can and do scorn applause and spurn flattery . . . too proud to betray emotions, too proud ever for an instant to loose my self possession whatever the peril, too proud ever to move a hair for personal interest, too proud ever to defend my character when assailed or my motives when impeached, too proud ever to *wince* when the hot iron enters my soul and passes thro it. . . .

As for his appearance, he wrote, one friend later confessed that upon first seeing him, he was struck "with the *moveless* severity of his countenance mingled with a *deep wild gloom*." Another said that at first glance he was reminded of the chief torturer of the Inquisition, while a woman, Weld recalled, exclaimed after a single sight she hoped he would never marry because he would break his wife's heart. "A few years ago," he continued, apparently reluctant to leave the subject of his appearance, "travelling in the country, I stopped at an Inn for breakfast. A girl of ten with a little sister of perhaps four came into the room. The moment I looked at the child, she screamed in terror and ran to her sister, clung to her and hid her face behind her apron and cried out—'take man away, take man away.' . . ."[25]

"Besides the moral defects already mentioned to you," Weld resumed with evident relish in another letter to his betrothed ten days later,

I have many *mental* defects, probably unknown to you, but which will doubtless occasion you daily and hourly vexation. . . . Many times when sitting in my room I have got up and gone to the window to determine by the face of nature what season of the year it was, whether spring, summer, autumn or winter. . . . I often look all over for my pen when it is [in] my mouth perhaps, or for my knife when it is in my hand. . . . I pare an apple and throw the apple into the street or the fire and hold fast to the parings.

Another sin, tempting God Himself, he continued, was his adventurous spirit, as fierce as any buccaneer's, a reckless daring. "I have always had a dash of personal recklessness in my structure," he wrote. "The love of daring is a perfect passion." After detailing the lacerations, fractures, and contusions he had suffered during his "tornado boyhood," he declared that even to this day he was habitually daring to the point of near self-destruction, constantly climbing trees and leaping from them, "wrestling, leaping fences and chasms, standing on my head, jumping and diving into deep water from the limbs of overhanging trees or from rocks high above the tide." He knew, he wrote, he was tempting God by his presumptuous daring, adding, "I could sob to think how much anxiety it will cause you," but nevertheless concluding firmly, "*I must cut capers.*" He would not blame her, he said, if with this full confession of his sins before her, she would spurn him from her as utterly vile. "True," he wrote, "it would break my heart, *I know it!* and I can have my heart broken and if I cannot survive the shock CAN DIE. . . ."[26]

3

If Weld was the hero of many in the abolitionist movement in the North, Sergeant S. Prentiss, of Mississippi, was equally the prototype of the Southern fire-eater, the wan and careless aristocrat, ever ready for a fight or a frolic, as graceful in an affair of honor as he was in gallant compliment to the fair. He was as "generous as a prince of the blood royal and chivalrous as a knight templar," an admiring associate, Joseph G. Baldwin, wrote of him, declaring he would go surety for any number of his friends' promissory notes without even deigning to look at a note's face to determine the amount.

"Sent to jail for fighting in the court-house," Baldwin continued, Prentiss, who was a lawyer, "made the walls of the prison resound with unaccustomed shouts of merriment and revelry. Starting to fight a duel, he laid down his hand at poker, to resume it with a smile when he returned, and went on the field laughing with his friends, as to a picnic." In his gambling, he "bet thousands on the turn of a card, and witnessed the success or failure of the wager with the nonchalance of a Mexican monte-player," and he awed the

JOHN BROWN
AND HIS SUPPORTERS

1. John Brown.
From a life-sized oil portrait by Nathan B. Onthank,
which he painted on an enlarged photograph of John Brown
taken in Boston by J. W. Black in May 1859

2. *John Brown taking an oath in Springfield, 1846 or 1847. The occasion for the oath is unknown. This is one of the earliest pictures of him*

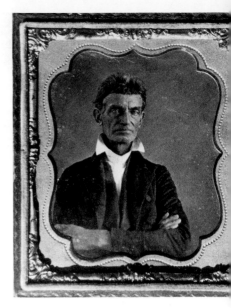

3. *A daguerreotype taken in Kansas in 1856*

4. *Another early picture of John Brown in Springfield in 1846 or 1847*

5. Ralph Waldo Emerson

6. F. B. Sanborn

7. Gerrit Smith

8. *Harriet Tubman*

9. *Lydia Maria Child*

10. *Lucretia Mott*

11. Frederick Douglass   *12. Samuel Gridley Howe*

13. Henry David Thoreau.
Copy of an engraving
from a crayon portrait
by Samuel Worcester Rowse

14. Henry Highland Garnet

15. Lewis Hayden

16. George Luther Stearns

17. Martin R. Delany

18. *J. W. Loguen*

19. *William Still*

20. *William A. Phillips*

21. *Theodore Parker.*
Copy of an engraved portrait

22. Wendell Phillips

23. Bronson Alcott

24. Thomas Wentworth Higginson

veteran dealer of a crooked faro game into honesty "by the glance of his strong and steady eye."

To Mississippians he was Henry Hotspur and brooding Hamlet, he was bluff Prince Hal and the Byron of Vicksburg even to his handsome profile and his limp from a crippled leg. "There was much about him," writes Baldwin, "to remind you of Byron: the cast of head—the classic features— the fiery and restive nature. . . ." He had an air of pale doom, an aura of impending tragedy so carelessly worn that it would have been attractive without the value that such a mien had everywhere in a romantic age but in the South particularly. Another of his attractions was the magnetism of moral frailty. He drew men to him by his flaws as well as by his virtues, being "as lofty in chivalric bearing as the heroes of romance," but with "vices of habit and mind," writes his eulogist, which his "fascinating graces rendered doubly dangerous." He was the prototype admired by many of John Brown's adversaries whether in Kansas or in Virginia.

But it was in his oratory, particularly in his successful campaign to represent Mississippi in the House of Representatives in 1838, that Prentiss seemed to the South to portray to a transcendent degree, both in the substance of his rhetoric and in his own being, that understanding of past chivalry which was thought somehow to describe the ante-bellum South itself. "He had lingered spellbound among the scenes of medieval chivalry," Baldwin wrote, trying to account for his unusual talent in identifying the South with knighthood. "His spirit had dwelt, almost naturalized, in the mystic dream-land they peopled—among paladins, and crusaders, and knights-templars; with Monmouth and Percy—with Bois-Gilbert and Ivanhoe, and the bold McGregor—with the cavaliers of Rupert and the iron enthusiasts of Fairfax." And it was among Sir Walter Scott's paladins and crusaders, with Bois-Gilbert and Ivanhoe, that many Southerners saw themselves; they loved Prentiss for a genius that made their lives with Monmouth and Percy glow with the reality of oratory if not of truth.[27]

EVEN WOMEN, EVEN NEGRO SLAVES

I

Perhaps the time's temper, as suggested by the eulogist of Prentiss and many others, did derive something, however peripheral, from the fact that the noble gallant knight of Scott's novels drew the hearts of men and women as the exemplar of all the American male should be, whether in galluses or high hat, with Bible in hand, or tobacco bulging the cheek. The legend became so compelling, if not through Scott then through bombastic oratory and the example of aristocrats, that there was scarce a common brawler in the South, but elsewhere also, who did not see himself, as he bit off a nose or gouged out an eye, as one animated only by gentlemanly sensitivity to his honor.

In the higher circles of the South, among the Chivalry, as the slaveholders were accustomed to designating themselves, the most benevolent of men were forced to live by the *Code Duello* if they wished to be accepted by their peers. Young Jennings Wise, fond of rare books, frequent prayer, and quiet study, as slim and deadly pallored as his father, Henry A. Wise, that Virginia politician who was one of the chief actors in John Brown's story, forced himself to challenge and meet any he heard questioning his father's integrity during Virginia's uninhibited campaigns. "If you do not bow down to and worship Wise," a critic complained, "the son will challenge you instanter." The editor of the Richmond *Enquirer*, young Wise was one of the worst shots and most inveterate duelists of the Old Dominion. If he suffered repeated and exquisite torture as he waited through the long nights of his many affairs of honor, he miraculously survived them all to be killed in battle during the Civil War.[28]

Senators and representatives, if they desired re-election, were often forced to stand their ground under fire, as in the duels of Henry Clay against John Randolph, William J. Graves against Jonathan Cilley, Thomas L. Clingman against William L. Yancey, and many others. Men who had never fired a gun, particularly if politicians, were sometimes forced to the field by professionals intent on murdering them according to the code of honor, as in the case of Senator David C. Broderick, of California, fatally wounded in a duel with a dead-shot Southern bravo, David S. Terry. Senator Broderick, ill when he accepted the challenge and almost unable to aim his pistol, said as he died, "They have killed me because I was opposed to the extension of slavery."[29]

And at least one President of the United States, as figuratively hair-triggered in temperament as were his dueling pistols in fact, was seldom slow in firing to kill whether on the field of honor or in less formal combat. When William Lloyd Garrison, the Boston abolitionist, was dragged toward the Common, a rope around his neck, by a mob attempting to lynch him in 1835, the President was that doughty Tennessee slaveholder Andrew Jackson, whose popularity had not been diminished by his killing his opponent in a duel. Nor had it been lessened by the affray in which the future President and his friends had blasted away at point-blank range on a Nashville street, before closing with bowie knives, at Thomas Hart Benton, later a distinguished United States senator, and his brother, receiving and returning fire with a recklessness not seen again until the time of Chicago's gangsters.

On December 7, 1835, President Jackson, sixty-eight years old, his lanky attenuated body still carrying the bullet of one of his opponents, his silver hair shooting upward like the crest of a kingfisher, was forced to view as a national menace young Mr. Garrison, that prematurely bald and primly radiant nonresistant who could not see without his spectacles. In a message to Congress, President Jackson proposed that such organs as Garrison's *Liberator*, the anti-slavery weekly founded on January 1, 1831, as well as other abolitionist literature, be barred from the mails as so incendiary that it might incite slaves to revolt.[30] The President was right in viewing as a menace this godly young man who aspired to complete moral perfection and who loved to turn the other cheek so that it might also be struck.

Yet no Southern fire-eater ever achieved a note of more happy abandon as to his personal safety than the nearsighted, hymn-singing Garrison when, at the beginning of his career and already in a Baltimore prison for verbally pillorying a Massachusetts slave trader, he demanded further suffering for himself with the words: "A few white victims must be sacrificed to open the eyes of the nation, and to show the tyranny of our laws. I expect, and am willing, to be persecuted, imprisoned and bound, for advocating African rights; and I should deserve to be a slave myself if I shrunk from that duty or danger."[31] When his opponents took him at his word through the attempted lynching in Boston, he said that as the mob clawed and hauled at him seeking his life he felt only a supreme happiness that he seemed about to die as Christ had died for His despised poor. As his clothing was ripped from him by those intent on lynching him, he said, "I felt perfectly calm, nay, very happy. Death did not present one repulsive feature. The promises of God sustained my soul, so that it was not only divested of fear but ready to sing aloud for joy."[32]

If young Mr. Wise of Virginia was morbidly ready for death on the field of honor, young Mr. Stephen Symonds Foster, a sparse and angular abolitionist from New Hampshire, was equally prepared for a singular martyrdom, making a profession of offering his inert and nonresisting body to maddened church congregations. Few were as proficient as Foster—a carpenter and a printer before he became a follower of Garrison—in goading others to violence while he himself refrained from it. He could raise more hell with nonresistance than another man might with an ax. It was his custom each Sunday, and often at Wednesday night prayer meetings, to disrupt church services by calling out that the pastor and congregation were "a den of thieves," were "man stealers," because of their failure to oppose the slavery in which slaveowners stole the labor and the bodies of their human chattels. Frequently he was injured as his limp and unprotesting form was hurled from the church by Foster-crazed Christians but if he was still conscious, and not yet arrested, he would run back into the church and again shout out his accusation. So he passed his years, never lifting his hand in violence, but always living in the midst of it, his sense of honor more individual, perhaps, but as incessantly insatiable as that of the most sensitive Southern Gentleman.[33]

2

The time's proud posturing, often false enough, but often, too, a stance taken in the face of peril, was too deeply entrenched a social attitude to be held only to the white, Protestant male. Even women, even Negro slaves, were to prove themselves not only susceptible to the gallant gesture but capable of making it themselves in the face of death and danger. Just before the same mob that attacked Garrison broke up a ladies' abolitionist meeting, the Mayor of Boston appeared before it, saying that the women must disperse if they wished to avoid "a scene of bloodshed and confusion," since the authorities could not protect them. As the members of the mob rushed up the stairway to the second-floor meeting place at 46 Washington Street, ripping down a partition and "hurling missiles at the lady presiding," the beautiful and imperious Maria Weston Chapman replied to the Mayor's warning with the words, "If this is to be the last bulwark of freedom, we may as well die here as anywhere!" and for a few moments it may have seemed to some of the women as if they might.[34]

The attack on the ladies' anti-slavery meeting occurred a few minutes before the attempted lynching of Garrison on October 21, 1835. The mob, frequently described as led by gentlemen of property and standing and numbering into the thousands, greeted the women with a roar of rage and contempt when they left their meeting place, walking two by two, each black woman accompanied by a white companion, through the hostile crowd. None of the women was injured.

And Prudence Crandall, a plain young woman in Quaker costume, but too pleasant to suggest an iron will, revealed sufficient of gallantry when assailed by Connecticut mobs which during 1833 and 1834 tried to close her school for Negro girls at Canterbury by attacking it with crowbars and axes, by poisoning her well, by attempting to prevent the delivery of food and water, and by setting the school on fire. So intense and widespread was public sentiment against her that the Connecticut legislature passed a law making it a crime to operate a school for black children who did not reside in the state, since most of the fifteen girls in Miss Crandall's school came from Massachusetts, Rhode Island, and New York. Upon the law's passage, Miss Crandall was arrested and thrown into a cell but recently quitted by one Watson, a murderer on the way to his execution. Miss Crandall's serene and happy features framed by the bars of her cell aroused the sheriff who had arrested her to such a pitch that he pleaded with her to accept the bail which she had refused for a time in order that the world might know Connecticut provided prison for those who taught black children.

Nor were the girls themselves, ranging between ten and seventeen years of age, any less gallant than Miss Crandall, who had to perform prodigies of emergency organization to get the food and water denied her by Canterbury's citizens as well as to mount guard each night against possible attack. The girls continued to hold classes under siege, even maintaining their studies after they were threatened with arrest for vagrancy under an old Connecticut law which provided flogging "on the naked body not exceeding ten stripes" for any so convicted. A warrant was actually served on Eliza Ann Hammond, "a fine girl from Providence, age seventeen years," according to the Reverend Samuel J. May, an abolitionist, who was one of the few to defend Miss Crandall and her students. "I visited them repeatedly," he wrote, "and always found teacher and pupils both calm and resolute. They evidently felt that it was given them to maintain one of the fundamental, inalienable rights of man." Writing of Miss Hammond, threatened with ten stripes upon the naked body, he said, "I found her ready for the emergency, animated by the spirit of a martyr." [35]

Not long before Prudence Crandall's ordeal in Connecticut, as we shall see, a Negro slave likened his approaching execution in Virginia for leading a slave insurrection to Christ's crucifixion, while another slave in a similar position had said his fate was only what Washington's would have been had he been captured by the British. The hero's gesture somehow could not be quite confined to the white quality. Sojurner Truth, a black woman who was an advocate of both abolitionism and woman's rights, faced many a mob with scorn and daring. Charles Caldwell, another example, was a slave in Mississippi, serving his owner as a blacksmith. He had been well enough schooled in the honor due to a man and a gentleman, even if indirectly, by the Southern Chivalry all about him during the twenty years before the Civil War to demand at last that such honor be accorded to himself. When later in the fight for black freedom Caldwell was riddled with bullets by a mob, he staggered to his feet and, drawing his coat about him, contrived to hold himself erect as he faced his murderers. Standing so, and with a proud glance to left and right, he said with his last breath, "Remember when you kill me, you kill a gentleman and a brave man." [36]

3

Even the high-flown speech demanding liberty or death, a bedrock staple of the time's culture whether in Congress or the town square, could not be held as applying only to the white male. Women, most of them active in the abolitionist movement, such as the Grimké sisters, Lucretia Mott, Elizabeth Cady Stanton, and Abby Kelley, whom John Brown admired, were soon demanding freedom for themselves through suffrage—as at the Seneca Falls convention of 1848 in New York, where they adopted a resounding Declaration of Independence. Frequently, black leaders such as Henry Highland Garnet and David Walker urged America's slaves to die rather than submit, to strike for liberty (John Brown combining the two appeals and publishing them as a single pamphlet in 1848).[37] And frequently, too, as in the Negro slave revolts and attempted revolts led by Gabriel, Vesey, Turner, and others, such advice had been taken.

These exhortations to black resistance had a familiar if embarrassing accent to white ears, echoing as they did Spartacus to the gladiators, the words of Arnold Winkelreid as he cast himself upon the spears of Switzerland's oppressors, or the periods of Robert Emmet and Patrick Henry as they spoke for liberty, all classic favorites of American declamation during the 1840's and 1850's.

Beginning in 1836, McGuffey's Readers increasingly became an institution in the North where public schools were rapidly multiplying. These schoolbooks, and others, such as the earlier *Columbian Orator*, made resistance to tyranny part of the very fabric of the sensitive and generous young, including some of John Brown's young men, who were raised on such fare as "Make Way for Liberty," by James Montgomery, concerning the legendary Swiss patriot Arnold Winkelreid:

"Make way for Liberty!" he cried
Made way for liberty and died! . . .

"Make way for Liberty!" he cried:
Then ran, with arms extended wide,
As if his dearest friend to clasp;
Ten spears he swept within his grasp:

"Make way for Liberty!" he cried,
Their keen points met from side to side:
He bowed among them like a tree,
And thus made way for Liberty . . .

Another favorite was Fritz-Greene Halleck's "Marco Bozzaris," about a Greek patriot's fight against the oppression of the Turks:

"Strike—till the last armed foe expires;
Strike—for your altars and your fires;
Strike—for the green graves of your sires;
God—and your native land! . . ." [38]

Such set pieces, almost the heart of American popular culture and recited by thousands of schoolchildren both as entertainment and inspiration, played their part, along with such biblical injunctions as that God "hath made of one blood all nations of men" and the Declaration of Independence, in contributing to that national schizophrenia induced by the persistent and simultaneous celebration of liberty and slavery.

V

The Large
and Varied Land

IT WAS A PERIOD of painful change, as what period is not, with Emerson and Thoreau frequently commenting in their journals on the new miles of telegraph wire, on the increasing number of steam cars, the expanding acres of textile mills in Lowell and Lawrence, the replacing of the old Puritan values by new business standards which Emerson declared had "grown selfish to the borders of theft, and supple to the borders (if not beyond the borders) of fraud." [1] The old was mixed with the new, as any traveler might find on any considerable journey, when he might be forced to horseback, the jolting stage, the new cars and steamboats, as well as mule-drawn canal boats, sailing packets, and his own two feet before completing it.

Although there were the great depressions of 1837 and 1857 it was a millennial, confident age, too, despite the country's division, and Utopia seemed near, if only to some and only above the Ohio, whether from the Lord's imminent advent still awaited by some of the Millerites, or by the progressive rationality of man himself helped to improvement by cold water therapy, Graham bread, phrenology, mesmerism, and spiritualism.

The Come-Outers, anti-slavery adherents withdrawing from Northern churches approving slavery, still continued during the 1850's to cry with St. John: "Come out of her, my people, that ye be not partakers of her sins," while each year in the great Anniversary Weeks, usually held in May in New York and Boston, there were widely attended simultaneous convocations of able reformers who succeeded in helping many other causes as well as abolition. Many were great organizers and knew how to harness politics to the achieving of a moral end. They were successful, to some extent, in forwarding public education, prison reform, more humane treatment for the insane, better education for the blind, the mute, and the deaf, while laboring for a host of other causes including woman suffrage and international peace.

NORTHERN SOUTHERNERS AND VICE VERSA

I

However diverse the interests of the reformers, the two most significant developments in the country were an increasing slavery in the South and a growing industry in the North. Yet the struggle over slavery was far less sectional and far more complex than it is usually portrayed, with thousands in the North favoring the peculiar institution and almost equal numbers in the South during the 1850's if not against slavery at least against the plans of slavery's leaders for secession from the Union. The six Alabama hill counties in that state's north were enclaves of Union sentiment even after the Civil War began. The same was true of eastern Tennessee and parts of Kentucky. Western Virginia was such a citadel of pro-Union sentiment that it seceded from Virginia to fight with the North during the Civil War. While thousands in southern and western Missouri favored the Confederacy, the majority of the state's population, which lived in its eastern sections, were vociferously anti-slavery and militantly pro-Union. Southern Whigs, their influence diminishing to the vanishing point during the 1850's, were usually reluctant to back secession, while poor farmers of the transmontane Atlantic slave states were often restive under slavery and hostile to the planter aristocracy of the Tidewater regions.

There were no more than ten thousand large slaveholders by 1860 in the South, which then had a population, free and slave, of some twelve million. Of the eight million whites in the slave states, more than three-quarters owned not a single slave. However, 385,000 did own slaves, if often no more than one or two.[2] But it was the ten thousand who owned fifty or more who formed the planter aristocracy which ran the South and often the country, too, however precariously and with whatever difficulty until the election of Lincoln.[3] Aided and abetted by the 375,000 smaller slaveholders, they had gone far by the 1850's in dominating a nation of thirty million through their controlling role in politics and the ownership of those millions of Americans who formed a privately owned labor force. Through this labor, they had secured a stranglehold, or so many including themselves believed, on the nation's economy by the production of cotton and other staples whose value was more than one-half of the nation's exports and a vital element in the North's prosperity.

If the slaveholders had important allies in the North, the anti-slavery movement above the Ohio had outstanding leaders from the South. Some of the foremost abolitionists were former slaveholders, such as James Gillespie Birney, Edward Coles, William Brisbane, William Dunlop, Alexander Campbell, or the famous Kentucky knife fighter, Cassius M. Clay; or were the sons or daughters of slaveholders, such as James Thome or the Grimké sisters; [4] and even at the apex of crisis during the Kansas civil war, many of the best Free State adherents had come from the South to avoid the slavery they hated.[5]

It was equally true that some of the leading Southern militants were of Northern birth, as in Mississippi where its Governor, John A. Quitman, born in New York, was an ardent exponent of secession and slavery's expansion by the armed conquest of all of Mexico, Central America, Cuba, and the Caribbean. Similarly expansionist was the suave and slippery Senator John Slidell of Louisiana, also born in New York and whose name was turned into the adjective "Slidellian," meaning shifty or crooked. Marrying into the élite of the New Orleans aristocracy, a brother-in-law of the Creole gallant General Pierre Gustave Toutant de Beauregard, Slidell acquired something of Creole grace but he did not permit the softer culture to enervate him entirely. Although he spoke only French in his home, assuming Gallic mannerisms seldom found in his native New York, he stole elections, bribed voters, and stuffed ballot boxes with the skill of a Tammany boss and such massive success that he became one of slavery's foremost political leaders in the Deep South.[6]

This presence of Northern Southerners below the Ohio and Northern men with Southern principles above was natural enough. With the great Mississippi and Ohio valleys and the Atlantic littoral a single country geographically, with no important natural boundaries, the rival sections were bound together by history, language, commercial ties, easy communication, and often by marriage between the foremost families of each region. If slaves could escape North, thousands of adventurous young Northerners, particularly amid the boom times of expanding cotton production in the 1820's and 1830's, could and did escape to the South, such as Peter Lawrence Van Alen, professional Southern duelist, also from New York, and the Reverend J. H. Ingraham, Georgia ecclesiastic from Maine, who never entered a pulpit without a pistol concealed in his surplice, or without being prepared to defend the South's cause as well as himself from any irate parishioner.

Even John Quincy Adams as a young man before he too was changed by the struggle against slavery considered emigrating to the South and becoming a cotton planter. Sergeant S. Prentiss, the very prototype of the Southern fire-eater, the idol of Mississippi's youth whom every young blade tried to imitate, had not been born in the South. He had only fallen in love with it. As a matter of fact, he was neither an aristocrat nor a Southerner, coming from Maine and a plain Yankee family; but he became a professional Southerner, applying himself to every facet of his endeavor with all the ardor of a gifted nature until it was everywhere conceded that the accident of birth should be forgiven and forgotten. But at the same time that Prentiss was becoming the beau ideal of Mississippi's young bloods, six white Mississippians, presumably native, were being hanged for aiding an attempted Negro slave revolt.[7]

Such sectional contradictions could be advanced almost endlessly. Edward Coles, the wealthy Virginian slaveholder, friend of Jefferson, and secretary to President Madison, freed his slaves in 1818, moving with them to Illinois where he became Governor, defeating a plot that almost succeeded in making Illinois a slave state by constitutional amendment. But the senator from the nominally free state of Indiana in 1851 was Jesse D. Bright, the owner of slaves and land in Kentucky and as militantly for slavery as the South's great John C. Calhoun of South Carolina.

2

Above and beyond individuals, however, was the fact that the Democratic Party with hundreds of thousands of voters in the North was a pro-slavery party electing as Presidents in the 1850's two Northern men with Southern principles, Franklin Pierce of New Hampshire and James Buchanan of Pennsylvania. Both were frankly pro-slavery and frankly expansionist, with Pierce advocating the acquisition of Cuba and Buchanan more of Mexico than had been gained by the war against her. Every Democratic platform since 1840, although dependent on the more populous North for translation into reality, had been a pro-slavery document, condemning agitation against slavery, demanding loyal adherence to the Constitution's provisions authorizing it, denying the power of Congress to oppose or regulate it in states or territories, backing the strict construction of the Constitution favored by the planters, against internal improvements and a protective tariff and including virtually every other tenet of slaveholder advocacy.[8]

If both old parties were beginning to disintegrate in the North in the growing belief that they were pro-slavery, party regulars still greatly out-numbered dissidents, both parties retaining huge accretions of popular strength, exemplified by the Webster Whigs and their successors in Massachusetts, representing bankers, merchants, and textile interests, and by the Hunker Democrats and Tammany in New York, many of whose members retained their pro-slavery feelings even into the Civil War. Such powerful Northern Democrats as Senator Stephen A. Douglas of Illinois, Senator Lewis Cass of Michigan, Asa Bigler, the Democratic boss of Pennsylvania, Buchanan of that state, John A. Dix, Horatio Seymour, and Fernando Wood of New York, Caleb Cushing and the Democratic machine of Massachusetts, Isaac Toucey of Connecticut, and many others more often than not supported pro-slavery policies in the interests of party unity if not from conviction.

If pro-slavery politicians were often elected in the North it was because they fairly represented the almost unanimous anti-Negro feeling of that section, perhaps even more virulent in certain ways than that which obtained below the Ohio. It was at least the fashion in the South to say one loved the slaves, for their faithfulness, quaintness, their humor. They loved the good nigger and they killed the bad one. But in the North, save for the abolitionists and a few others, there was no circumstance however repressive or unfair that called for any show of benevolence. Virtually every Northern state had black codes, or their equivalents, that denigrated and penalized the Negro, some demanding that he put up bail before he could enter their precincts, others that he be flogged if he overstayed a stipulated period, almost all deny-ing the vote and all other privileges of citizenship save taxation. If the North was often subservient to the South and its slavery it was because its citizens, for the most part (although there was a steadily increasing number of excep-tions) wholeheartedly agreed with the South's concept of white supremacy.

Discussing this subject of the North's subserviency to slavery, Charles Francis Adams, no radical or incendiary, said,

Around it [slavery] have been arrayed, for its protection, alike the conservative and the destructive elements of society in the free states—the richest and the poorest class, the best citizens and the worst; the former from an instinctive dread of anything that looks like an attack upon prescriptive rights to property; the latter from an adhesion to the superiority of caste, the more tenacious by reason of the sense of self-degradation in every other particular.[9]

Basic, of course, to the South's influence in the North was its economic strength. Cotton production had steadily ascended over the years from 171,000 bales in 1810, 731,000 bales in 1830, 2,133,000 in 1850, to more than double that amount nine years later with 5,387,000 bales. One Negro slave in Texas in 1853 could bring a net profit of $300 per season to his owner, after his maintenance had been deducted from the sale of the ten bales of cotton per season that such a slave was expected to produce. All during the 1850's both before and after the depression of 1857, the South was booming, particularly its so-called Cotton Kingdom, extending a thousand miles west from South Carolina to near San Antonio, Texas, varying in breadth from north to south between 200 and 600 miles, a region enclosing some 400,000 square miles and some two million slaves. In 1850, the South's cotton brought $102 million, its sugar $14 million, its rice $2.6 million, for a total of $118,600,000. In 1860, three-fourths of the world's cotton came from the Southern states, Great Britain receiving 2,344,000 bales, continental Europe 1,069,000, and the North nearly 943,000 bales.[10]

It was not only the Northwest's (now the Midwest) farmers shipping grain and pork, or the East's manufacturers selling everything from spades to shoes to the South's plantations, or the textile magnates, owners of the largest industry of the country, who profited from slavery. There was scarce a Northern town of any size whose inhabitants did not have commercial ties to the South. From Alton, Illinois, to Northampton, Massachusetts, there was a network of connections, Alton's merchants living largely by its downriver trade to plantations on the Mississippi, Northampton even as early as 1838 having a score of prominent citizens with connections to slavery through investments, or other business, through marriage, or other family ties.[11] New York City, it was said, "was as dependent on Southern slavery as Charleston, itself." One-third of every dollar paid cotton planters, according to an Alabama legislative inquiry, made its way to New York merchants, brokers, and bankers in the form of carrying charges, insurance interest, and payment for merchandise; a sum which in 1859 was estimated at $131 million. Without slavery, declared James Dunbar De Bow, New York's "ships would rot at her docks, grass would grow in Wall Street and Broadway, and the glory of New York, like that of Babylon and Rome, would be numbered with the things of the past."[12]

3

New York's dependence on slavery and cotton was so fundamental to the city's economy that as the Civil War approached a considerable portion of its merchants participated in an abortive plot to take the metropolis out of the Union, to secede as a free city and become the Republic of New York, that she might continue, war or no war, to trade with the South.[13] This feeling of complete dependence on cotton and slavery was exemplified as early as 1835 when a prominent New York merchant sought out the Reverend Samuel J. May as he was attending an abolition convention being held in New York City.

"Mr. May," he said,

we are not such great fools as not to know that slavery is a great evil, a great wrong. But it was consented to by the founders of our Republic. It was provided for in the Constitution of our Union. A great portion of the property of Southerners is invested under its sanction; and the business of the North, as well as the South, has become adjusted to it.

There are millions upon millions of dollars due from Southerners to the merchants and mechanics of this city alone, the payment of which would be jeopardized by a rupture between North and South. We cannot afford, sir, to let you and your associates succeed in your endeavor to overthrow slavery. . . . We mean, sir . . . to put you Abolitionists down,—by fair means if we can by foul means if we must.[14]

Thousands in the North and South agreed with the New York merchant's warning. To them slavery seemed as necessary to the nation as blood to the body. To most of the press and pulpit, to most manufacturers, merchants, jurists, and politicians, North as well as South, slavery was as sacred as any other private property, justly protected by the Constitution, its expropriation as unthinkable as the expropriation of a factory or a farm. Many years later John Swinton, a former editor of the *New York Times* and a contemporary of John Brown, was thinking of the Old Man and the power and the glory of the institution he attacked at Harper's Ferry. To appreciate John Brown's accomplishment, he said, "It needs that we recall the power of the interests and passions that environed it [slavery], and the subservience or timidity of even its opponents with few exceptions, before we can comprehend the influence of the man who struck through them all, and struck to the heart." [15]

THE UNDERGROUND

I

There was one organization, however, which bound a discordant country together, geographically at any rate, from the bayous of Louisiana to the northernmost stretches of the Great Lakes, even if largely invisible and wholly illegal. That was the Underground Railroad. With its passengers escaping slaves, sometimes in disguise, frequently pursued by posses and bloodhounds, the fugitives were aided by black and white, men and women, Southerners and Northerners who often combined to guide them northward; delivering them from station to station, from house to house, sometimes 40 miles apart, sometimes 10, from concealed chambers in barns and attics to specially outfitted caves and caverns or secluded recesses in remote swamps, moving them forward usually in the nighttime but sometimes in the day when the chase was hot; sometimes by relays of fast horses, sometimes concealed beneath the hay hauled by a plodding team, occasionally hiding them on trains, or lake or river packets, or coastal vessels, until the fugitives arrived at last in safety.[16]

It was the great physical fact of slavery, repeated in almost four million individual cases by the end of the 1850's, the human substance of actual specific fleeing slaves that not only brought the Underground into being but was primary, of course, in creating the whole anti-slavery movement. Long before John Brown and his men headed for Harper's Ferry, Harriet Tubman, that extraordinary black woman who planned to join his expedition; John Fairfield, that reckless ne'er-do-well Virginian who rescued hundreds from Southern plantations; Miss Delia A. Webster, the adventurous Vermont schoolteacher; Calvin Fairbank, who spent seventeen years and four months for his Underground activities in a Kentucky prison where he was flogged almost daily; Seth Concklin, the peculiar New Yorker who died in his last attempt; and scores of others had gone South to rescue slaves, sometimes with arms in hand and sometimes to their deaths. John Brown's plan had its roots in this illegal network of which he himself had long been a member.[17] Many of the black leaders who were to aid him, such as Frederick Douglass, the Reverend J. W. Loguen, and Lewis Hayden, had escaped North on the Underground Railroad. And it was this which may have been a factor in giving the Old Man his high estimate of the black man's will for freedom.

2

Long before the Fugitive Slave Act of 1850, actual fleeing slaves, human beings to whom one talked, to whom one gave food and shelter, kept many in the North aroused. It was the number of fugitives, in fact, that was responsible for the insistence of slaveowners that a new and more stringent fugitive slave act be passed. Frequently, too, escaped slaves, or former slaves who had purchased their liberty by incredible sacrifice, appeared at doors throughout the North begging for funds, one pleading that he be helped "to buy my mother out of slavery," another that he be helped "to buy my wife and children." Bronson Alcott, the transcendentalist philosopher of Concord, saw the fugitive as "an impressive lesson," writing of one whom he had sheltered for a week in February of 1847:

He is scarce thirty years of age, athletic, dextrous, sagacious, and self-relying. He has many of the elements of the hero. His stay with us has given image and name to the dire entity of slavery, and was an impressive lesson to my children, bringing before them the wrongs of the black man and his tale of woes.[18]

If the last shall be first and the first last, as Scripture asserts, it is also true in a measure of American history. It was the Negro and his overwhelming plight, the sentient human base of the nation's economic and political conflict, who was in the last analysis in these years before the Civil War the prime mover of men, the transformer of character, the force for change. Beneath all individual variation, susceptibility, and tendency, it was American slavery, and the actual individuals comprising it, that dark mass of striving, enduring, resisting human beings, that was the fundamental dynamic, forcing such as Emerson or Thoreau, for example, from preferred paths of quiet into courses of risk and peril. It was the struggle of the Negro people, with all its multiple effects, that made John Brown's eminent coadjutors ready for his plan before they ever met him. And John Brown, too, was not a cause but a result.

ON IMPERIAL DESIGN

I

The large and violent land, the homely sprawling time might have seemed too gawky and plain for the tremendously colorful continental conflict over slavery of which it was the scene. If it was a time of rich plenty, for some at least some of the time, the old homestead benign in a soft sun just as depicted in the engravings of Currier and Ives, it was also the time of hogs rooting in the city streets, of fly-specked depots and dirty boarding-houses and gold toothpicks, personal and permanent; of the ague and the fever which gave the shakes to most for too many days of the year.

If God loomed large, Mammon was not far behind, the entrepreneur, the land shark, the go-getter filling a land where the prairies suddenly bloomed with towns which sometimes advanced to cities and sometimes reverted to the wind-blown grass. If some were fevered for a freedom including all Americans, more were fevered for California gold, which in 1849 drew thousands around the Horn or across the isthmus of Panama or Nicaragua or across 2,000 miles of wilderness. If the 1840's and 1850's were a time of tremendous growth in population, in the physical area of the country, in industry, in agriculture generally and cotton production particularly, they were also the years when private armies enlisted for private wars were not uncommon and not all were destined for such plain American precincts as Kansas and Harper's Ferry.*

If it was a day of lovely ladies in crinoline, it was also the time of deftly aimed tobacco arcs splashing into the ubiquitous spittoon; of lyceums bring-ing culture to New England villages and mammoth gang fights in New York's slums; of countless churches and acres of brothels; of spacious man-sions in the South and drunken mayhem at its county seats on every muster day; of professional reformers and professional duelists; of the transcendental-ists of Concord and the vigilantes of California; of religious ecstasy and open sewers and chronic ill-health; of a spreadeagle oratory whose practitioners often saw no discrepancy between praising slavery and hailing liberty as a peculiarly American invention.

It was the day of going West and sometimes going broke, the 1840's

---

* The population of the country grew from 17,069,000 in 1840 to 23,919,000 in 1850, to 31,443,000 in 1860, an increase of 35 per cent during the latter decade. Some 1,193,061 square miles had been added to the national domain as a result of the Mexican War, its organization into terri-tories and then states a matter of dispute as to the admission of slavery during much of the 1850's. In 1859, the value of U.S. industry ($1,885,862,000) exceeded for the first time the value of agricultural products, although cotton production remained crucial to the prosperity of American industry since cotton textile manufacture was the country's first industry as to capital invested, labor employed, and the net value of product. Cotton production in the South had increased from 731,000 bales in 1830 to 2,133,000 in 1850, to 5,387,000 in 1859, while the number of slaves in the same years increased from 2,009,043 to 3,204,313, to 3,953,760 in 1860. (Figures based on U.S. Census and taken from *Encyclopedia of American History*, Richard B. Morris, ed., New York, 1953.)

and 1850's particularly the decades of the long wagon trains, sometimes headed for Kansas and civil war, sometimes for California, sometimes plodding northwest on the Oregon trail toward Fort Laramie on the river Platte—but however far they went they could not always quite escape the issue of slavery. Little puffs of dust ascended upward with each step of the lumbering oxen, of the thin and weary horses, and as the heat danced in the atmosphere, the silt thickening in the throat, men and women from the Atlantic littoral may have thought thirstily of clear cold springs in green damp forests or even of the cool wet heave of the sea breaking on rocks 2,000 miles away.

The wheels continued to keen and lurch over the endless miles of those going beyond Kansas and Nebraska until at last the Rockies, suspected rather than seen—perhaps they were only clouds hanging low over the western edge of the prairie—suddenly loomed incredible and snow-covered, an almost untouched wilderness stretching for a thousand miles on the other side and for the control of which politicians for and against slavery were battling back in Washington. But here in the wagon train the women in their sunbonnets, the barefoot children, the men in cowhide boots, their hats pushed back, stood and gazed at the jagged continental wall, luminous and blue where the sunlight glinted on high and distant snow.

It was the time of steamboat races glowing red in the Mississippi's night as sparks hissed into the broad river, perhaps between the *Eclipse* and the *A. L. Shotwell*, the panting of the engines breathing hoarsely in a stillness punctuated by the sudden jangle of bells; of camp revival meetings in small wilderness clearings, the horses unhitched, their tails switching the flies away, the swelling ecstasy of the Doxology rising into the sky and over the trees. Increasingly in the American night east of the Mississippi there was the long-drawn wail, lonesome and far away, of the locomotive, the rumbling of its cars felt rather than heard, the dogs barking faint and distantly as the train muttered into silence; and increasingly in the day, except in the South and far West, there was the clatter and beat of mushrooming industry, whole communities shaking with the vibration of rudimentary assembly lines, the flap of revolving belts, the whir of speeding wheels creating a new industrial world.

But on Saturday nights, at least in rural areas—and most of the country remained overwhelmingly so—there was the swish and shuffle of dancing feet, often in some cleared hayloft, the fiddle beating out its catgut throb, the horses in the stalls below blowing their lips or nickering or shifting with that peculiar double stomp of equine restlessness while the violin in the loft above curled between the nasal half-rhymed phrases of the dance caller. The boys drank corn liquor behind the barn where they sometimes fought but usually rustic gallantry reigned supreme as the barn shook with the reels and the spirited prancing of the day, with never a thought of Shiloh or Gettysburg.

And yet for all the vigor of the large and varied land there was a kind of muted melancholy behind the unadorned plainness of American life, behind its violence and its boredom and its boasting. It was not only the sometime grieving of the slave, his hymn or spiritual sounding in the night. It was perceived in Lincoln, could be felt clearly enough in the years of John Brown, and even apprehended by the sensitive perhaps behind the classical reserve of the slaveholder Jefferson, crying out against slavery while always the possessor of the painful knowledge that if he was the liberator of man he was also his enslaver. It was found in New England, where Emerson said young men were staying to their rooms, talking of suicide and the emptiness of life, and in the Tennessee mountaineer, his life as solitary as the wail of his fiddle on the still Appalachian air.

This land, to the discerning, accounts for much of John Brown, his urge for wealth, his hymn-singing, and his praying, his homely understated attitude with its echoes of defiance and boasting, his restlessness, the covered wagon that he knew, the posture which combined distinction with rusticity and both with an everlasting search for something perhaps finally found. But so complete was his identification with the large and violent land, so thoroughly was he its product, that the Ohio farmer who was John Brown found no difficulty in communicating with Parker or Higginson, Emerson, Thoreau, or the black man fighting slavery, all of whom were as American and perhaps as permanent, while there is an American consciousness, as the land itself.

2

If Americans had a great fault then, one not entirely overcome, although there have always been exceptions, it was their monumental chauvinism, a fault not unknown in other lands. Occasionally it was a quadruple prejudice, even directed to a degree against all those outside one's own proud and sterling manhood, but ordinarily it was only leveled against those outside one's own state or section, against foreigners in general and nonwhites in particular. There were those, however, ranging from frontier brawlers to statesmen, who could not conceive it possible that they themselves might be personally wrong on anything, and to suggest so might prove a dangerous slur on their honor and their manhood. There were more who felt that the region above or below the Ohio was a precinct of the Devil while their own section, on the contrary, had a definitive corner on patriotism and virtue.

A kind of bullying super-Americanism, a persistent white supremacy, often found in the North as well as the South, was as endemic as the widespread belief that one white American could best ten foreigners whether in a fight or a frolic, a footrace or a turkey shoot. But lastly and over all was the common conviction, common to thousands of native Americans who were not slaves, that a race had evolved here, white and Anglo-Saxon with perhaps a tincture of Protestant Scots-Irish, that was so indisputably superior to all other breeds that it was not only justice but generosity to conquer and lead them. Its peculiarly American glorification of white supremacy stemmed, of course, from the widespread denial that the millions of Americans held in slavery were men as their enslavers were; rather, they were inherently inferior. Even among the abolitionists, largely Protestant old-stock Americans, there were comparatively few who doubted the innate superiority of the so-called Anglo-Saxons over the Negroes; or for that matter, over the Irish-Catholics, arriving in the 1840's and 1850's, along with other immigrants, by the hundreds of thousands.

With American manifest superiority so evident, it was perhaps natural that filibustering was an admired profession, its proclaimed object the extension of American virtue—often including slavery—to lesser breeds of the Caribbean, Mexico, and Central America by force of arms. There were at least seven such expeditions in the 1850's and soon Mississippi and Alabama farm boys were dreaming of luxurious slave empires, of romantic scenes with conquered handmaidens under the Caribbean's palms and moonlight.[19]

3

It was, in short, an era of large imperial design, whether it concerned the selling of town lots, the projection of transcontinental railroads, or armed expeditions to the tropics; a time in which presidents and rural loafers, senators, ambassadors, and swashbuckling privateers combined in these pro-slavery expansionist ventures often backed in the North as well as the South through the pro-slavery policies and power of the Democratic Party, and the widespread feeling that the blessings of American enterprise and democracy should not be denied either Northern entrepreneurs or the blacks, the Indians and Mestizos of Cuba and Central America, even if those blessings had to be forced upon them at the point of a gun. The expeditions were both private and semi-official, both quasi-legal and illegal, sometimes secretly backed by the government and sometimes secretly opposed until officers of the American Army and Navy scarcely knew which private army to round up, for when they did take one into custody they risked ruining their careers by incurring the enmity of powerful pro-slavery forces at Washington.[20]

Americans then had a penchant for the secret and the gaudy, evident even in that political party known as the Know-Nothings which gained more than one million members between 1851 and 1854, in the later year electing seventy-five members to Congress and two years later casting 874,534 votes for the Know-Nothing candidate for President.[21] Its adherents, who were anti-Catholic and anti-foreign, and had an elaborate secret ritual, were officially known as members of the American Party, but gained their popular name from declaring mysteriously when questioned about their party, "I know nothing." Americans everywhere had a fondness, as will become increasingly apparent, for secret military organizations with esoteric recognition signals whereby a man was to know a friend and brother, as if midnight pledges, blood oaths, and mysterious ceremonials might somehow overcome a scene essentially drab, angular, jerry-built, and tobacco-stained.

If the North had its Captain John Brown, the South, as Thoreau pointed out in 1859, had its General William Walker, who just before Brown advanced on Kansas was himself moving with a secret armed expedition to Nicaragua, where, backed by Northern shipping interests profiting from trans-isthmian transportation as well as Southern expansionists, he re-established slavery. The South had, too, its Lopez and its Quitman and their Southern volunteers thrice attempting invasions of Cuba in unsuccessful efforts to expel Spain and place the island and its slavery under the American flag.[22] Above all, it had its General George Washington Lafayette Bickley, that blandly plausible medicine man extraordinary, who sometimes felt himself, and not without cause, on the very verge of bringing to reality through his widespread Knights of the Golden Circle (another secret military organization) his fantastic dream of an American slave empire in the Caribbean, Mexico, Central America, and South America, more grand than the glories of ancient Rome. If the Knights, too, had their gaudy rococo ceremonials that did not necessarily mean, as time was to prove, that they were entirely without menace.[23]

It may occasionally seem strange that John Brown's career has usually been so thoroughly separated from those of his ideological opponents who were also using force and violence for slavery's expansion at the same time John Brown was using it for slavery's destruction. General Bickley, for example, and his Knights of the Golden Circle were meeting in secret conclave in Virginia, plotting to increase slavery's domain, at the very moment that Brown's little band was gathering at the Kennedy farmhouse for their attack on slavery in Virginia. And that "gray-eyed man of destiny," as he liked to be called, William Walker, the minute (5 feet 5 inches in height) journalistic bravo from Tennessee who re-established slavery in Nicaragua before he was executed by a firing squad, might seem deserving of some mention in any account of his Yankee antagonist who was also executed—but for opposing the slavery which Walker fought to extend.

VI

The Great Transformer

FOR ALL THE BRASH CONFIDENCE, the high-flown hyperbole of our large and violent land, its inhabitants, being men, had their share of uncertainty and guilt, of opportunism and sell-out. Even little William Walker imposed slavery on Nicaragua not because he liked slavery—he had in fact once been against it—but because he needed the support of those who did.[1] If Walker was to live and die with his guilt, however faintly he felt it, he was not the only one to do so nor the only one to shift as to slavery, whether for or against it or only into a miserable and paralyzing indecision. If John Brown took some twenty years to be transformed from a man who talked of attacking slavery to one who actually did so in Virginia, such transformations were not uncommon, however differently men experienced them or however varied the result.

"The great and foul stain,"[2] as John Quincy Adams called the slavery that transformed him as radically as any man, tortured others than those it held in bondage and in other ways than flogging. Many white Americans could not travel quite so far that they could well forget it and even when they thought they had, it might move far beneath their lives, a faint controlling uneasiness. When Americans praised liberty, and it was a national avocation, there sounded an unspoken echo. The more they loved freedom, the more slavery corrupted their peace.

It had been so from the first. The very birth of the nation had contained slavery's bar sinister, not only by perpetuating black slavery while fighting for white liberty, but when representatives of South Carolina and Georgia, aided and abetted by Northern allies, had stricken the indictment of the international slave trade from the Declaration of Independence. It had been implanted in the country's fundamental and basic charter with the so-called three-fifths provision of the Constitution, under which the states having the most slaves were rewarded with the most political power—the more slaves at home, the more representatives in Congress.

THE UNDERLYING REALITY

I

It was slavery that edged Jefferson's later years with something approaching despair as he foresaw a civil war, the fight over the Missouri Compromise "like a fire bell in the night," sounding the knell, he feared, for the nation he had helped to found.[3] The slaveholder Washington had felt its inescapable impeachment, as had the slaveholder Franklin whose last public act, long after he had freed his own few slaves, was the defense of the memorial to the first Congress asking that it stretch its power to the utmost toward the liberation of those Americans held in slavery.[4] George Mason, another Revolutionary patriot and one of the largest slaveholders of Virginia, had to live with his belief that the slavery giving him his wealth was a slow poison corrupting individuals and undermining the country he had fought to establish.[5] And Patrick Henry, who was to demand so passionately either liberty or death for himself, was to suffer a painful wonder at the unfeeling paradox of struggling for one's own liberty while enslaving others.[6]

Slavery was the curse which men indicted in their private diaries even while they avoided it or praised it in public life. John Quincy Adams gagged himself for years from the public indictment of the slavery he so frequently condemned when alone with his journal, whatever the violence it did his acerb and combative nature.[7] Accepting and defending slavery changed a man as much as fighting it or favoring it in public while opposing it in private. It was the dominating influence, the former of character South and North, as much the creator of the Southern fire-eater as the Northern abolitionist.

Every American President from Washington to Lincoln, the great majority of whom were slaveholders or what was called "Northern men with Southern principles," was persistently plagued by it. Every presidential aspirant, from Henry Clay to Daniel Webster to Stephen A. Douglas, had to deal with it, often wrecking his hopes however supple his maneuvers in his attempts to reconcile the irreconcilable. It was slavery that was the source of that continued tension, sometimes almost unbearable in its intensity, which marked the life of virtually every public figure, North and South, from Jefferson and John Quincy Adams to Senators Thomas Hart Benton, Sam Houston, and John Caldwell Calhoun, from the Southerners Jefferson Davis, Henry Wise, and Edmund Ruffin, to the Northerners Charles Sumner, Joshua Giddings, and Theodore Parker.

If slavery became the great transformer, finally changing peaceable men in the North into leaders of anti-slavery mobs and conservative slaveholders in the South into those who tried to overthrow the federal government by force and violence, it was because it increasingly became the reality behind most issues, however disguised by the circumlocutions of politics, the euphemisms of constitutional debate. It was the underlying foundation, often concealed but often made explicit enough, at the bottom of every question whether of peace or war, states' rights or the tariff, concurrent majorities or implied powers, free speech or free assembly, the right of petition, the annexation of Texas, foreign expansion into the Caribbean, the territorial powers of Congress, internal improvements, railroads, Indian policy, or public lands.

2

Slavery's very antiquity exacerbated the problem. Modern slavery, as opposed to that of Athens and Rome, antedated the first white settlers on the North American continent, enslavement of Africans by white Christians beginning in the fifteenth century when the slave traffic, the largest commerce in human beings in the history of the world, had its shadowy inception. (And yet the line, however far its starting point, ran straight enough from the Gold Coast of Africa to the battlefield at Gettysburg and considerably beyond.) It was a problem somewhat like original sin, inherited rather than committed, as some preferred to think, bequeathed by the British slave trade to the American land like some primal curse from Adam. But if this American story begins so far back in time as to make its inception dim, the beginning was clear enough to each of the millions of Africans who were shipped to the New World as articles of commerce.

To them the story began on the day they were captured by force, often by African chieftains who sold them to the white man; the day they were ripped from their families and homes and driven through the bush to the slave factories on the coast, there to await shipment across the sea.

Stretched naked and chained to a plank, with the timbers of the overhead almost pressing into the face often scarce 18 inches away, tortured by thirst, defiled by vomit and excrement, amid heat and stench that was almost unbearable, the long, slow voyage west was unique in the lengthy annals of man's ingenuity at torturing man. The ship, creaking and groaning, seesawing ceaselessly up and up and then plunging down, now rolling, now yawing, the manacles endlessly sliding with the ship's motion over the tender flesh, the sickening roll ceased only when the ship was becalmed in the tropic waters. Then in the blackness of a hold, the thick heat almost palpable to the hand, there was no sound save gasping and the horrible choking gurgling of suffocation. With death often nearly halving the cargo, the slaves were periodically forced from the airless stench of the hold to the deck, where they were whipped into staggering dances, the object the exercise of the human cargo. Millions of human beings, men, women, and children, died on such voyages, or shortly after landing, in a commerce so profitable that it formed part of the base of that English capital that brought into being the modern industrial age.[8]

3

It was this slave trade which brought to American colonial shores some 300,000 Africans before the Revolution.[9] By 1790, there were 697,624 American slaves, but despite this increase there were still high hopes that slavery might be contained, through the colonization of American slaves in Africa or elsewhere as proposed by Jefferson as early as 1776; or might even be abolished gradually in the South as it was being gradually abolished in the North in the aftermath of the Revolution. Instead, it multiplied inexorably, particularly after the invention of the cotton gin in 1793 and the expulsion of most of the Indians from what was then the Southwest between 1812 and 1839.

As a physical malignancy spreads and increases, so did the peculiar institution, growing from 2,009,043 Americans held in bondage in 1830 to 2,487,355 in 1840 to 3,204,413 in 1850 and almost four million near the end of that decade. Slowly but relentlessly it spread across the continent from Maryland to Texas, from Virginia to Alabama, from the Delaware River to the Ohio to the Mississippi to the Rio Grande. It seemed to multiply independently of the will of man, or worse than that, as a result of his irrepressible desire for profit, as much a part of his nature as procreation. It was a problem that gave no peace, omnipresent, ubiquitous, always escalating in intensity beneath the surface even when opposing forces seemed to have achieved a precarious equipoise.

Omnipresent as the problem was, there were, of course, millions of Americans who did not think of it, except as one thought of the weather, or any other unchallengeable fact of nature. But consciousness is not necessary to a causal result and their lives, too, were often as changed by slavery as those within whom it consciously festered. It was somewhat irrelevant, in fact, whether or not they thought about it since wherever men and women moved they touched it. A man might go to church and become involved in the struggle which separated congregations and denominations into hostile sects, their crucial difference the defense or condemnation of slavery. Increasingly, it became so involved in the fundamental conditions of American life, in economics, politics, reform, the movement west, the Mexican War, that an American did not require either sympathy for the slave or slaveholder to become involved in the struggle.

In the South, where slavery was a way of life and the source of most of that section's wealth, one did not need to be a slaveholder or even sympathetic to such to fear that abolition might be only a formula for black insurrection and economic destitution. In the North, thousands who were at first unconcerned with the plight of the slave came to the anti-slavery movement, not to aid the Negro but to protect basic American constitutional rights, believing it was the threat to free speech and the right of petition, the insistence of Southern congressmen that slavery not even be discussed, that had moved them into action, and conscious only later that the basic mover had been slavery itself.[10]

And it was not a struggle that one could enter quietly, continuing to live out one's years as before. Women who enlisted in the anti-slavery fight began to think of their own freedom and started the women's rights movement.[11] Men who began by thinking slavery wrong sometimes decided that all society was so, forming utopian communities, and declaring against all government on the ground that it was a conspiracy of force and violence against the God-given rights of the individual.[12] The Southerners who began by planning to overthrow foreign governments, as in Cuba or Nicaragua, to extend or maintain slavery were soon planning to overthrow their own to preserve it. Mild men who decided that God's words provided for freedom were presently following Garrison's and were not so mild. Those who began by helping fugitive slaves in the North sometimes continued until they were invading the South to recruit slaves for escapes.

As in most bitter fights there was a persistent escalation of the struggle.

Slaves, having won their own freedom by escape or purchase, wanted more freedom for more slaves, usually for mothers, wives, children, and friends. Men who began by advocating black slavery continued until they felt that some form of authoritarian subordination of all workers was the essential principle for a good society, North, South, or anywhere else, agreeing with the Virginian George Fitzhugh, who wrote that "slavery is the natural and normal condition of the laboring man, whether white or black." [13] It was a struggle so basic, so pregnant with change, so filled with a dynamic pressing to further extremes that it could not diminish without some all-embracing, resolving crisis.

Where would it all end? As the severity of the struggle ascended year after year, particularly after 1830, men increasingly said that it would never end until the country was all free or all slave. Soon there would come a time when thousands would agree with William H. Seward, senator from New York, in his description of the contest as "an irrepressible conflict between permanent and enduring forces," which would not end until the United States became "entirely a slave-holding nation or entirely a free labor nation." [14] As the conflict steadily became more all-embracing, more absolute, it also increasingly became the great transformer of Americans, changing them slowly and painfully over the years, whether Emerson or John Brown, Abraham Lincoln or Jefferson Davis, all of whom were turning to face what many were beginning to realize they could not escape.

THE LONG COLD WAR

I

Often it seemed during the 1850's as if the first bloodshed of the long threatened civil war would not come on the battlefield but in the halls of Congress, where Senator Henry Wilson of Massachusetts said he never entered without putting his affairs in order as if he would never return.[15] There, members had for years periodically butted about in little swirls of combat, their fingers on revolvers and bowie knives, as they pushed around debaters they said had insulted them or their section, until a general massacre of American statesmen sometimes seemed but a pistol click away.

The decade began in fact with Representative Thomas L. Clingman, of North Carolina, standing up in Congress and declaring that if the Fugitive

Slave Bill of 1850 was not supported by Northern representatives, "blood would flow until there would not be enough members left alive to form a quorum for business." [16] In milder parliamentary interchange, fists and cuspidors were occasionally used as aids to debate, as when Lawrence Keitt, representative from South Carolina, thundered at Galusha Grow of Pennsylvania, on February 5, 1858, "Sir, I will let you know you are a black Republican puppy!" Instantly, statesmen from North and South were rolling in the aisle, clawing, scratching, gouging, one congressman circling the group with a large brass cuspidor in his hand as he sought an appropriate target, others with guns but unable to shoot because of the twisted intermingling of friend and foe.[17]

After Senator Charles Sumner of Massachusetts was almost beaten to death in the Senate by a South Carolina congressman in 1856, most of the legislators who had not carried guns remedied the deficiency until Senator J. W. Grimes, of Iowa, could report, "The members on both sides are mostly armed with deadly weapons, and it is said that the friends of each are armed in the galleries." [18] As the decade neared its end another senator was declaring, "every man in both Houses is armed with a revolver—some with two and a bowie knife," while the *New York Daily Tribune* was asserting that the North should elect to Congress not sensitive men of intellect but men who were dauntless in personal combat, proficient with fists, pistols, and dirks.[19]

Almost always in these affairs, when they did not degenerate into rough-and-tumble combat, the slaveholders, accustomed to the duel and its code and with that fierce imperious temper they said was natural to a slaveowning aristocracy, seemed to emerge with victory and grace. If they were occasionally daunted by Northern congressmen who answered challenges to duels with proposals that the duelists be tied together at the wrist while they battled to the death with cowhide whips or dirks, they scorned such proposals as beneath the dignity of gentlemen.[20] They were aristocrats and they were born to victory as the steadily expanding area of slavery seemed to be proving over the years; and if the census returns showing growing Northern strength, if the disintegration of the Whig and Democratic parties in the North which had long served their purposes gave them pause, it also gave them high resolve to let the trouble come and that quickly.

Yet it could well be said that at least insofar as violence was concerned, Congress was wonderfully representative of the country. With lawlessness as common to the virtuous as the lout, the *New York Daily Tribune* complained, "there ferments in the bosom of our American society a mass of wanton and obstreperous brutality that does not exist elsewhere." [21] Before the end of the 1850's, lynching was fast becoming the civic duty of every fire-eater in the South when confronted by a Yankee who said, or was said to have said, that Negroes should be free. By 1860, the most conservative of Northern drummers, innocent of everything save the desire for a dollar, were panting toward the Ohio, mobs straining behind. [22]

2

If the conflict, antedating the beginning of the nation, was not new, its violent intensity was. Despite occasional crises, and severe ones, an uneasy sectional balance of a kind had been maintained for almost seventy years, with the struggle in the North largely verbal and agitational and the South satisfied to a degree with the constitutional approval of its peculiar institution, with its measure of control over the two main political parties, the Democratic and the Whig, and with the extent of its dominance over the national government.

But with the annexation of Texas and its slavery in 1845 and the resulting Mexican War of 1846, that balance was overturned. It was feared in the North that Texas (until 1836 a part of Mexico), in which slavery had been prohibited, might be divided into four or five slave states which would be added to the Union. In addition, anti-slavery adherents feared that the huge area gained from Mexico by war would be organized into slave states, giving the South permanent control of the national government; while many in the South feared that the new empire, largely won, they said, by Southern valor, would be denied to a slavery which many believed must constantly expand if it were not to die. [23]

It was the contest for this vast and empty land which spurred fundamental changes in American life. New thousands in the North were becoming convinced that the Whigs and the Democrats were creatures of the slave power and with that conviction came the organization of an independent new political party, the Free Soil Party, founded on the ironclad principle of opposition to any further expansion of slavery.

In 1848, when the new Free Soil Party was founded, it received almost 300,000 votes for its presidential ticket,* Martin Van Buren, ex-President and leading Democrat, and Charles Francis Adams, the son and grandson of

---

* Zachary Taylor, who was elected President in 1848 on the Whig ticket, received 1,360,000 votes.

Presidents as well as a dissident Whig. At its founding convention in Buffalo, on August 9 and 10 of 1848, the platform, referring to the belief that the South wished to make slave states of the territory seized from Mexico, declared: "Resolved, That we accept the issue which the slave power has forced upon us; and to their demand for more slave states and more slave territory, our calm but final answer is: no more slave states and no more slave territory." [24]

But this was just a beginning. The whole character of the anti-slavery movement during the ensuing decade was changing with a fresh, new accession of powerful forces, practical, successful, hard-hitting men convinced that slavery must be stopped now or never, many as willing to oppose it by force, as in the case of Kansas and the Fugitive Slave Law, as they were intent on organizing a permanent political party which would prevent its further expansion. Garrison and his agitation of the 1830's, his doctrine of nonresistance and no political opposition to slavery through the vote, were of the past as an effective influence, while the political abolitionists who had broken with Garrison in 1840 and formed the anti-slavery Liberty Party now saw their cause advanced, at least in part, by the hundreds of thousands who were soon to organize the victorious Republicans.

And yet even as they organized for political action it became steadily more apparent that guns were as necessary as ballots in the rising struggle. All during the 1850's slavery and its opponents were increasingly meeting in actual armed conflict, whether in rescues of fugitive slaves, as in Boston, Syracuse, Oberlin, and Milwaukee; in warfare between opposing guerrilla armies, as in Kansas; or as escaped slaves in Christiana, Pennsylvania, resisting by gunfire and pitched battle federal officials and slaveholders seeking to return them to bondage. Each side felt that the other was trying to impose its system not only on the new and immense West but on the whole country, and failing that to dismember it—the abolitionists by expropriating that peculiar private property on which the economy of the South was based; the fire-eaters, intent on rule or ruin, by dismembering the federal government if they could not control it.

Nor was this entirely a contest by any means over humanitarian principle or such legal niceties as states' rights, whatever the battle cries, however deeply they were believed. What was at stake was more material: the protection and extension of billion dollar property interests, whether the North's industry or the South's slaves valued at more than $2 billion by 1860. It was a struggle for the control of American territory, the American economy, the American government, and the American future, "an irrepressible conflict," as Senator William H. Seward of New York called it, between real and enduring forces.*

3

The Compromise of 1850, designed to avert this nation-shaking conflict, instead inflamed it. If Northerners opposed with guns administration efforts to enforce the Fugitive Slave Act, slaveholders were outraged when the law was thwarted, and ever more frequently invaded the North in little parties seeking to recover their human property. Proponents of slavery found it hard to submit to the Compromise provision admitting California as a free state, Jefferson Davis, of Mississippi, and others continuing to struggle either to reverse the decision or, failing that, to divide the state into slave and free states. Both sections were almost equally outraged by the provision forbidding the sale of slaves in the District of Columbia, anti-slavery sentiment exacerbated because slavery was not entirely barred in the nation's capital, the proponents of slavery humiliated by the statutory admission that the sale of slaves was morally reprehensible and fearful that one breach in slavery's defenses would be followed by others.

Increasing thousands in the North were disturbed when the Compromise legalized the unrestricted entry of slaves and slavery into the huge territory of Utah, extending as far to the North as Chicago does and including what is now Nevada, Utah, western Colorado, and part of Wyoming. Slaveholders and slaves were to be admitted without restriction to this immense area with the approval of federal law. If state constitutions later outlawed slavery at the time a territory applied for admission as a state to the Union, then slavery would be abolished in that state. But if enough proponents of slavery emigrated to the West that later nullification might be difficult. Similarly, slavery was admitted, without restraint but subject to later ratification, into what is now New Mexico, Arizona, and a part of Colorado, then the

---

* "The irrepressible conflict" was expressed legislatively by homestead bills affecting everyone going West or planning to, which were blocked by the slave power in Congress throughout the 1850's. Disputes about proposed transcontinental railroads, whether they should follow Northern or Southern routes, be controlled by Northern or Southern capital, prevented their construction until after secession. Internal improvements, road, harbor, and canal construction needed for the development of Northern industry, were successfully opposed by Southern plantation interests. All during the decade Congress was not only in turmoil as to whether the territories of the West should admit or exclude slavery, but was locked in economic conflict, with the North charging that the South was crippling its industry by preventing an adequate protective tariff, the South declaring such a tariff unjust tribute wrung from it by the high prices it placed on manufactured products.

Territory of New Mexico, by a Compromise which brought not peace but deadlier conflict between the sections.* A still sharper crisis came in 1854 with the passage of the Kansas-Nebraska Act, opening to slavery another great new territory in the West from which it had been barred for thirty-three years by the Missouri Compromise. It was the first unexpected spark that changed the long cold war to hot.

4

Although the North by the end of the 1850's was to possess 61 per cent of the population, 75 per cent of the wealth produced, 81 per cent of the country's factories, and 63 per cent of the railroad mileage, the slaveholders during that period dominated two Presidents and their cabinets. The Supreme Court, however fortuitously, tallied with their will in the Dred Scott decision of 1857 legalizing slavery in every inch of every territory, as opposed to states, under the American flag; and they controlled the Senate through most of the decade and the House of Representatives until 1854. If the population of the North Central states was increasing by more than three and a half million in the ten years beginning in 1850, until these states alone had a population larger than the white population of the entire South, the slaveholders had the satisfaction of seeing the regular Democratic organizations of these states, even in the face of revolt, holding firm to pro-slavery candidates and pro-slavery principles in national elections.

But it was not by conspiracy or force that the South's ten thousand largest slaveholders were dominating the nation. It was because so many in the North agreed with them. Although a powerful property interest such as the planters comprised ordinarily has a unanimity denied its foes, it was not through Machiavellian cleverness that the slaveholders were winning. It was

---

* Thousands in the North drew slight comfort from Daniel Webster's assurance in the Senate in his March 7 speech of 1850 that slavery had been forever excluded from such territories as those of Utah and New Mexico, if not by law, then by act of God and the climate. Other Northern apologists for the Compromise of 1850 said that since slavery was fitted only for the gang labor of large plantations it could never be successfully introduced into the West although some Southerners hoped to operate mines with slave labor. As to climate barring slavery, those fearing its penetration into the immense new areas where legislation or court decision had made it legal pointed to the fact that slavery did not depend on weather alone, that it had long existed amid the winter snows of Virginia, Kentucky, Missouri, and Maryland but little different in crops or climate from Pennsylvania, Ohio, Indiana, and Illinois. Other forces than favorable climate impelled slaveholders toward expansion, such as hopes of increasing their political power through the admission of more slave states. As to slavery being suitable only for large plantations, it has often been pointed out that there was scarce an industry or business enterprise in the South that did not use slave labor nor a skill or trade in which slaves were not proficient.

because the rank and file of the Northern Democrats, usually victorious over the crumbling Whigs, loved the dashing legend of the Southern cavalier and hated and feared the despised Negro.*

It was because many in the North were almost as moved by the romance of far-flung conquest, as devoted to Manifest Destiny, as were the slaveholders themselves for more practical reasons. It was because Northern Democratic aspirants for the presidency, always plentiful and often powerful in local machines, knew they could not be nominated without the South's 117 votes in the national Democratic convention, and because the North's richest wanted no threat to any private property. So it was that in 1852 the South was so dominant politically—despite the North's preponderance in population, wealth, and industry—that every state in the Union save four gave a majority to the slaveholder-backed candidate for President, Franklin Pierce, that Democratic Northern man with Southern principles from New Hampshire.[25]

Jefferson Davis, the new Secretary of War, as well as other pro-slavery Democrats, felt that with the election of Pierce all that the South had been cheated of after its victories in the Mexican War might now be regained; that the right of slavery, as with any other private property, to enter any and all territories of the United States (whether in the West or the tropics, or in new territory to be acquired from Mexico) would at last be guaranteed by a Democratic Congress and a complaisant President. Such was the public

---

* Even workingmen, described by slavery's apologists as the white slaves of the North, were often pro-slavery because they were often members of the pro-slavery Democratic Party and because they feared the competition of a flood of freed slaves. Sometimes, too, they had been offended by the anti-labor bias of many abolitionists who could see oppression below the Ohio but were entirely unmoved by starvation wages and killing hours above it. Yet "the platform of many of the labor parties formed in New York state during the early thirties contained planks calling for the abolition of Negro slavery, 'the darkest, foulest blot upon the nation's character.' Included in 'the Workingmen's Prayer' submitted in 1830 by the trades unions of Massachusetts to the State Legislature, was the appeal: 'May the foul stain of slavery be blotted out of our fair escutcheon; and our fellow men, not only declared to be free and equal, but actually enjoy that freedom and equality to which they are entitled by nature.'" (Philip S. Foner, *History of the Labor Movement in the United States*, New York, 1947, vol. i, p. 266.)

It is true that the labor leader George Henry Evans alienated many in the Northern labor movement during the 1850's from opposition to slavery by his stand that land reform and the abolition of wage slavery should precede the end of chattel slavery. But much of his influence was dissipated by early American Marxists, many of them veterans of the European revolutions of 1848, who sought to persuade, and with considerable success, that labor in a white skin could not be free while labor in a black skin was enslaved. They, and native anti-slavery labor leaders, were sufficiently successful in their campaign, that when Lincoln called for volunteers after the firing on Fort Sumter, the entire membership of trade union locals enlisted in single groups, knowing well by that time that there could be no free trade union movement if the slaveholders triumphed. Workers constituted almost half of the Union Army. (Ibid., pp. 308–9.)

temper in the North toward slavery's plans for expansion that President Pierce did not hesitate to proclaim them in his inaugural address. "The policy of my administration," he said, "will not be controlled by any timid forebodings of evil from expansion. Indeed, it is not to be disguised that our attitude as a nation and our position on the globe, render the acquisition of certain possessions, not within our jurisdiction, eminently important for our protection." [26]

The only misjudgment Jefferson Davis was to make, as he himself saw through aftersight, was in backing the Kansas-Nebraska Act, introduced by the Democrat Stephen A. Douglas of Illinois, and in persuading the President to do so. In the first place it was made unnecessary three years later by the Supreme Court's Dred Scott decision, which gave slave interests by judicial decree more than they had gained by the Kansas-Nebraska legislation. More importantly, it precipitated a revolt in the North, involving large numbers of Democrats hitherto loyal to slavery and its expansion, ultimately resulting in a qualitative political change even wider and deeper than that following the Mexican War and the Fugitive Slave Act.

WANTED: A HERO

I

The Kansas-Nebraska Bill aroused Northerners, many of whom had not before been active against slavery, to an unprecedented pitch because it seemed to them to provide for the climax and completion of slavery's triumph in most of the West. If passed, they feared, it would form the capstone of slavery's trans-Mississippi structure, which had been mightily extended in 1845 with the gaining of Texas, and extended again five years later, as we have seen, with slavery's admission into the vast new territories of Utah and New Mexico won through the Mexican War. Now it was proposed in the Kansas-Nebraska Bill to admit slavery into a region extending from Oklahoma to the Canadian border and the Northwest Rocky Mountains, an area which was to later include as states Kansas, Nebraska, South Dakota, North Dakota, Montana, and parts of Colorado and Wyoming.

As in the case of Utah and New Mexico, slaveholders with their human chattels could freely enter the new territories of Kansas and Nebraska and remain and multiply forever if slavery's adherents were able to overcome its opponents through elections and win slavery's authorization in state constitutions when the territories applied for admission as states into the Union. It was this principle, the principle of popular sovereignty, that was proposed in the legislation of 1854 for the organization of the Territory of Kansas and the Territory of Nebraska, the latter not as vulnerable as Kansas to slavery's penetration because it did not share a common border with a slave state, as Kansas did with Missouri to the immediate east. Those against slavery and those for it would compete as to which would control the territories, which jointly comprised some 485,000 square miles, were ten times larger than the State of New York, and larger by 33,000 square miles than the combined area of all the free states east of the Rocky Mountains. The actual settlers of a territory would vote slavery in or out, up or down.*

2

In fighting to prevent passage of the Kansas-Nebraska Bill through Congress, Northern Democrats and Free Soilers, the latter former Whigs, revolted and adopted a declaration terming it "a criminal betrayal of precious rights," a design to convert the West's free land

into a dreary region of despotism inhabited by masters and slaves. . . . It is a bold scheme against American liberty worthy of an accomplished architect of ruin. . . . Let all protest, earnestly and emphatically, by correspondence, through the press, by memorials, by resolutions of public meetings and legislative bodies, and in whatever mode may seem expedient, against this monstrous crime.[27]

And the North did protest earnestly and emphatically. Six Northern legislatures resolved against the bill. "The storm that is rising," wrote Senator Seward to his wife, "is such a one that this country has never yet seen."[28] Protest meetings were so spontaneous, so numerous, and so far-flung, that

---

* The Kansas-Nebraska Act, at least in part, was a by-product of a struggle between politicians and entrepreneurs from both North and South over the route of a proposed continental railroad. Jefferson Davis was proposing a Southern route which would tie Memphis and the lower South with California, and he pushed through the Gadsden Purchase of Mexican soil to give the proposed line a straighter and better route. Stephen A. Douglas, Democratic senator for Illinois, favored a route through Nebraska in which he had at least an indirect monetary interest through extensive property holdings in Minnesota and Chicago; but to build such a project, Indians had to be cleared from the land and the area given the stability of a territorial government. This need for territorial organization was the starting point of the involved maneuvers finally resulting in the Kansas-Nebraska Act and the repeal of the Missouri Compromise which Douglas favored, perhaps not entirely uninfluenced by his need for Southern support if he were to realize his ambition of becoming President. As chairman of the Senate Committee on Territories, Douglas sponsored and led the fight for passage of the Kansas-Nebraska Act.

the *New York Evening Post* declared that if its pages were three times larger and issued three times a day instead of only once, "we still should despair of finding room for anything like full reports of the spontaneous gatherings which are held every day throughout the North and West." [29]

Senator George E. Badger of North Carolina rose in Congress to say that he could not understand the North's indignation. All Southerners wanted, he said, was to take their old Mammies with them when they settled in Kansas. "The Senator entirely mistakes our position," replied Senator Wade of Ohio. "We have not the least objection . . . to the Senator's migrating to Kansas and taking his old 'Mammy' along with him. We only insist that he shall not be empowered to *sell* her after taking her there." [30]

But the majority of Congress agreed with Senator Badger that he should be allowed to emigrate to Kansas with his old Mammy, and in May 1854, the Kansas-Nebraska Bill became law. Its popular sovereignty provisions almost immediately became a legislative formula for civil war. If there were those who had believed that the law was only a provision for popular democracy, permitting the settlers in Kansas to decide through free, open, and peaceful elections whether Kansas should be slave or free, their belief was soon shown to be utopian. While Northerners were raising and equipping parties of emigrants to settle in Kansas and make it free, the slaveowners of Missouri, its border adjacent to Kansas, were sending thousands into the Territory not to settle there but to take possession for slavery by force of arms.

There were four major invasions, the armies of the so-called Border Ruffians of the Missouri frontier ranging from about two to five thousand in number, advancing with revolvers, shotguns, and bowie knives, howitzers, and cannon, most mounted but some riding in wagons, occasionally with bands and music and frequently with flags of strange device bearing slogans extolling slavery, and always, too, with a large supply of whiskey. They had been organized as invading forces, as well as into a secret society known as the Blue Lodges, by the slaveholders of western Missouri, who in 1854 owned some fifty thousand slaves valued at $25 million.[31]

Because the power of the Missourians was so overwhelming, because their numbers were so preponderant, because they were backed by a federal government whose officials were soon declaring that Free State settlers were threatening revolution, it was the general policy of Free State leaders for a time not to oppose the invaders forcibly with arms. Infrequently, usually in the case of individuals or small groups of Free State settlers, they were forced to fight in self-defense; but the basic strategy of their chieftains in Lawrence, the center of the movement and not far from the Missouri border, was to hope that the immense wrongs suffered, that the outrages committed, that the elections seized by fraud and the scale of depredations would produce a national reaction which would prove so strong that President Pierce would be forced to withdraw his support of slaveholder forces while the North became nearly unanimous in supporting the Free State settlers. Their great strength by 1855 was the fact that such settlers, actual bona fide residents of Kansas, greatly outnumbered slavery's partisans living in the Territory, although greatly inferior in numbers to the hosts from Missouri who invaded to fight but not to settle.[32]

The first invasion was on November 29, 1854, when about two thousand Missourians crossed the border into Kansas and seized election polling places, ousting officials at gunpoint while 1,729 of them voted for J. W. Whitfield, the successful pro-slavery candidate for territorial representative to Congress.[33] The second invasion was on March 30, 1855, when five thousand Missourians overwhelmed the election which was to choose the territorial legislature to govern Kansas—where they did not live. Dividing up and terrorizing virtually every election district, according to voluminous evidence before a congressional committee, threatening to hang any who opposed them, shoving bowie knives and revolvers into the midriffs of any who protested, forcing Free State men to mount wagons and make pro-slavery speeches, rocking voting places back and forth on poles, breaking their windows and firing off guns, seizing ballot boxes and carrying them outside where they were stuffed with fraudulent ballots, the Border Ruffians not only enjoyed a great drunken fiesta but completely cowed Free State settlers and illegally set up a pro-slavery territorial government.[34]

3

With accounts of such events filling the North's press, the campaign above the Ohio to relieve "Bleeding Kansas" became almost evangelical in its fervor with old hymns, set to new words concerning Kansas, sung at scores of mass meetings where money, clothing, and recruits were raised after veterans of Kansas told of Free State sufferings. Great crowds escorted companies of men and women bound for the Territory to trains, the emigrants singing as they embarked, to the tune of "Auld Lang Syne," Whittier's "Song of the Kansas Emigrant":

> *We cross the prairies as of old*
> *The Pilgrims crossed the sea,*

To make the West, as they the East,
The household of the free.

The junior class at Yale presented the captain of a New Haven company
with a handsome rifle inscribed *Ultima Ratio Liberarum* (the final argument
of liberty). At an emotional meeting in Plymouth Church, Brooklyn, where
feelings were so intense they seemed to fill an air still echoing with hymns
and prayers, the Reverend Henry Ward Beecher, raising money for Sharps
rifles, new carbines of unusual power, described the weapons as more powerful as a spiritual regenerator in Kansas than the Bible. Ever afterwards the
rifles were known in Kansas as Beecher's Bibles. "There are times," said
Beecher, "when self-defense is a religious duty." [35]

From Boston and Worcester and Bangor, from New Haven, Buffalo,
Cleveland, and Chicago, companies of armed men were departing for Kansas
while women's sewing circles in upstate New York's Burned-Over Region,[36]
on Ohio's Western Reserve, and in New England particularly, patched and
mended and sorted clothing which had been contributed for the settlers. The
most prominent of men, the most conservative citizens, manufacturers such as
Amos A. Lawrence and George Luther Stearns of Boston; merchants such as
George Carter Brown of Providence and Moses Grinnell of New York; well-
known figures such as Horace Greeley, Dr. Samuel Gridley Howe, Theodore
Parker, Frederick Law Olmsted, Dr. Samuel Cabot, Dr. William R. Lawrence, Wendell Phillips, Gerrit Smith, John Bertram, Samuel Hoar, E.
Rockwood Hoar, and hundreds less well known were buying guns for Kansas
or otherwise contributing to the Free State cause.[37]

4

It was at this peak of public excitement that one of anti-slavery's great spokes-
men in the Senate of the United States, Senator Charles Sumner of Massachusetts, was beaten into insensibility while working at his desk in the Senate
Chamber. His assailant was a member of the House of Representatives from
South Carolina, Preston S. Brooks, who was universally acknowledged by
his peers to be an exemplar of the Southern Gentleman, a man whose quick
honor and generous bravery had required that he assault Sumner with a
sturdy gutta-percha cane.

It was everywhere seen by the Chivalry, as approving editorials and
speeches abundantly attested,[38] that Brooks had no other recourse if he were
to retain the name of gentleman. Courteous and somewhat stately, he was
tall and soldierly, with a small and sensitive mouth above a goateed chin, a

victim of the beliefs that had been bred into him, and at the time of test he did not shrink. Not only had his South been insulted in Sumner's speech in the Senate on May 19 and 20, 1856, on "The Crime Against Kansas," but South Carolina's honor had been impugned and, even worse, the honor of his family, of his kinsman Senator Andrew P. Butler, had, Brooks felt, been traduced in Sumner's speech.

So it was that the congressman near noon on Thursday, May 22, his heavy walking stick, which he had carefully selected, he said, because he did not think it would break, in hand strode toward the Massachusetts senator. The latter had many vanities, including a firm belief in his own moral grandeur. Forty-five years old, an extraordinarily handsome man, 6 feet 3 in height and 185 pounds in weight, his great size pinned him securely between his chair and the desk, riveted to the Senate floor, over which he leaned as he wrote.

"Mr. Sumner," Brooks said, "I have read your speech twice over carefully. It is a libel on South Carolina and Mr. Butler who is a relative of mine. . . ." [39] Before the busily writing Sumner quite knew who was facing him, or what the fellow had said, he was dazed by a blow. When he raised his arms to shield his head, Brooks said, he was "compelled to strike him harder" than he had planned. But, the congressman continued, "every lick went where I intended," adding that he struck as hard as he could. [40]

As Sumner struggled to rise, Brooks, reversing his cane and using it as a club, rained a series of full, fast blows on Sumner's head and shoulders. His long legs caught beneath his desk, his large form held as a target by his chair, Sumner could not avoid the cane's crashing downward arc, the blood splattering with each successive impact, each strike resounding with a crunching crack that could be heard all over the Senate. With a great convulsive wrench, actually ripping his riveted desk from the floor, Sumner, blinded by his own blood and already half unconscious, succeeded in gaining his feet, staggering forward in an effort to close with his assailant. But Brooks, the bloodlust on him now that he was actually securing his honor, apparently went wild in an effort to kill the now defenseless Sumner, reeling and slipping in his own blood, his leonine head still the target of blow after blow, each sickening crunch audible yards away, until the stout cane broke, and Brooks, his honor still unsated, continued to beat and stab with the splintered end until Sumner was senseless on the floor. Then Brooks, as befitted a sensitive gentleman, seemed a little appalled and gasped, "I did not intend to kill him. . . ." He had not murdered the Massachusetts senator but it would be a long time before Sumner returned to the Senate. [41]

5

Seldom in all of America's political or criminal annals has there been such overwhelming shock and indignation as swept the North the day after the assault on Sumner. The most conservative of men in Boston were talking of a march on Washington, a taking over by force of the Southern-owned government; and even such a moderate as Edward Everett, not long since the president of Harvard College and who had once declared he would march with the South to put down a slave rebellion, was to report: "When the intelligence of the assault on Mr. Sumner . . . reached Boston, it produced an excitement in the public mind deeper and more dangerous than I have ever witnessed. . . . If a leader daring and reckless enough had presented himself, he might have raised any number of men to march on Washington." [42]

Now the talk of revolution was more prevalent than ever before, revolution against the slaveholder-owned national government which, many Northerners believed, was using violence in Washington as it had in Kansas to subvert on behalf of slavery the most fundamental of American rights, including the right of Senate debate. Sumner had used the terms of Revolution and 1776 in describing the administration's tyranny in Kansas, and Seward had said in so many words "Kansas is today in the very act of revolution against a tyranny of the President of the United States." [43] In Kansas many more than John Brown were declaring, despite the strategy of peace urged by Charles Robinson and other Free State leaders, that only a recourse to the armed Revolutionary resistance of 1776 could save Kansas and the nation.

But as Seward talked, and Sumner spoke, and Free State leaders in Kansas attempted negotiation, the South was acting and the South was winning. Six Free State settlers had been killed by the Border Ruffians and one of the slain had been tortured before he died, lynched by a mob one of whom fractured his skull with a hatchet. [44] The North was growing tired of saintliness, of passive resistance like that of Garrison's, of triumphs of character won by turning the other cheek. They admired Sumner, the martyr, but they longed for victories other than the moral grandeur of physical defeat. As they spoke of charred and looted Lawrence, the Free State center which had been reduced by Missouri's forces, there were those who yearned passionately for a hero who would meet the South on its own ground and on its own terms, for a champion who would oppose the slaveholders not with the purity of superior character but with the strength of superior force. Soon they were to have such a hero. And if his methods were occasionally dubious they were ignored because his victories were bloody, actual, and sorely needed, many felt, at a time when all victories actual and not moral had seemed to belong only to the partisans of slavery.

6

The first Northern victory in Kansas was at the Battle of Black Jack on June 2, 1856. The pro-slavery force was led by a dashing young man, the brave and debonair H. Clay Pate, who had attended the University of Virginia and who was to die gallantly in later battle at the side of J. E. B. Stuart, the South's romantic cavalry leader.[45] Pate was, or aspired to be, an authentic Southern Gentleman who should have been easily the superior in battle to a queer old man in a linen duster who, with revolver shoved into Pate's stomach, had forced him to surrender himself and his company unconditionally.[46]

With the unconditional surrender, anti-slavery Northerners had the hero for whom they had yearned so long, one who could best the Southern Cavalier not by moral principle alone but with a gun. They had eaten of defeat and humiliation for years while the graceful gallants of slavery had challenged them, taunted them, invited them to pistols at twenty paces. Now a gnarled old Yankee farmer—just where did he come from and who was he?—had made a dashing Southern fire-eater crawl, and there were few above the Ohio even remotely against slavery who could suppress some feeling of elation.

VII

Portrait of
the Old Man

JOHN BROWN'S FAME or notoriety began with his victory at Black Jack in Kansas, June 2, 1856.[1]

Thereafter Americans were to read and talk about Old John Brown with an ever-increasing passion, but in the enduring argument that beat about his head, his separate indisputable self was often lost in the scoring of debaters' points. Behind the legends of utter goodness or complete evil, there was an actual man of flesh and blood. It is this specific unique individual we seek, not in costume or on stage, as he is ordinarily presented, but as if glimpsed at night, the hairy calves protruding from his nightdress in summer, or while seeking the icy floor from his bed amid the dark of a winter's dawn before prayers were said, or breakfast had, or the hay thrown down from the loft.

It is this precise person, beyond legend, libel, or superlative, with whom we are concerned, smelling of horses and the barn and the sweat that darkened his shirt, this person with his knobby knees, his ramrod back, his large ears, his pinched and hungry nostrils that could sniff doughnuts frying five miles away.[2] It is this one and only John Brown we wish to apprehend, with his compelling metallic voice, with his own peculiar musings as to God and death, and meaning, as different and as similar to every other man's as the whorls on the thumb of each human hand.

Yet he was not a man easily read by either his contemporaries or later biographers. About all his acts there is the enigmatic, in all his life there are gaps and silences that cannot easily be filled. He wore neither his heart nor his purpose where either could always be seen and although there came a time, however singular and violent, that he would take the whole country into his confidence as to his plans and hopes and the purpose of his years, there still remained something more, as if he had a reserve which even he could not breach.

THE SUCCESSFUL FAILURE

I

Jack-of-all-trades, and master of most, tanner, surveyor, sheepherder, farmer, postmaster, wool merchant, land speculator, the trials of many failures had given John Brown by 1856 a varied experience that he somehow made impressive. His failures had even included his eyes when young, as optic inflammation had forced him to abandon his studies for the ministry. Despite his many pursuits, the common denominator to them all, usually carried on in conjunction with them, was farming, his thoughts in times of peace often running on winter forage for the cattle and whether, come spring, the south 30 acres should be planted in oats or allowed to remain in pasture.

Yet his yeasty discontent, combining with the increasing needs of a growing family and forcing him to branch out in various unsuccessful efforts to make money, had made of him an unusual farmer. He was, for example, a forceful public speaker, having addressed more than one meeting of his assembled creditors as well as more than one meeting of assembled worshippers as unofficial preacher *pro tem* when a regular ordained minister was not available. If he was skillful in controversy this, too, was the result of a dichotomy between the secular and the ecclesiastical, deriving on the one hand from his penchant for theological disputation and on the other from his long experience as a defendant under the hostile cross-examination of attorneys for his business opponents.

Then, too, he had learned to think large through failure, since occasionally his reverses had something of the grandiose. Such was the case when, representing the wool growers of Ohio, southwestern Pennsylvania, and northwestern Virginia as broker and commission merchant at Springfield,

Massachusetts, he had brought a large loss on himself, his partner, and the farmers he was acting for by challenging the powerful wool manufacturers of the East in an unsuccessful effort to get a better price for his product.

Although he always feared the ways of Mammon and the world, he had nevertheless at times lusted for riches with the best, had yearned for success as ardently as any American. Often he seemed on the verge of both, for he was not without ability of a desperate and feverish kind, when he did the work of three men, keeping books, signing promissory notes, and other-wise arranging credit, answering all letters and then copying the answers into his books while he sorted wool or tanned hides and did a little farming on the side, or helped organize the blacks into armed opposition to the Fugitive Slave Act, always trading horses and sheep and land with the persistence if not the shrewdness of a David Harum, and always continuing, of course, to run his family as if it were a small state and he a patriarchal king.

And yet for all of his many-faceted activities, he was a deliberate and methodical man, fond of doing the same thing every day at the same hour. It was his weakness or his strength that he found it well-nigh impossible to change or modify a plan after he had adopted it and would keep calmly plodding on to success or ruin no matter what the warnings or pleas of friends.

As a matter of fact, despite the prevailing tenor of failure marking his years, he had enjoyed comparatively long periods of success and command, some ten years as the head of a tanning venture employing between ten and fifteen men, some four or five years while directing his far-flung adventure in wool. For a time he was even a bank director. During such spaces of prosperity he was usually a community leader, active in securing libraries, churches, roads, and schools, and then he was indeed his brother's keeper, determined that his community should reward the worthy and punish the sinner even if he had to do both himself. For years he regarded himself as a bulwark of law and order, or his concept of it, once ending a letter to an abolitionist newspaper with the sentence, "I forgot to head my remarks, 'Law and Order.'"[3] And if he aspired to be "only a patriot to heaven," he was, too, more conventionally patriotic, insisting on one occasion, "We will ever be true to the flag of our beloved country, always acting under it."[4]

Failure had not diminished his belief in his ultimate importance, although it had seriously weakened it for a time, and when he left for Kansas in 1855 he still enjoyed quoting the careful maxims of Franklin. Soon in fact he was to be introduced at important public meetings in Massachusetts as a man "in whose veins the best blood of the Mayflower runs," and as "a modest vet-eran" of the Kansas war "whom all Massachusetts rises up to honor."[5] He himself, however, was more critical, once declaring that he was "too much disposed to speak in an imperious and dictating way," asserting that he had early become accustomed to being obeyed and recalling that a younger brother had described him as "A King against whom there is no rising up." [6] Now and again he asked himself what manner of man he was, often finding that the Lord Almighty was forcing on him "a bitter cup, indeed," from which he had "drunk deeply," [7] but often finding himself, too, quite satisfactory, once observing approvingly that he *"habitually expected to succeed."* [8] Yet sometimes he recalled the sorrows of his childhood with a grief unreconciled.

2

If Thoreau had "long ago lost a hound, a bay horse and a turtle dove," for which he ever searched, John Brown had long ago lost a yellow stone and a bobtailed squirrel for which he ever grieved. When at fifty-seven he wrote of his loss a half century before on the Ohio frontier, he used the third person in describing himself * and in recalling how "a poor Indian boy" had given him a yellow marble, the first he had ever seen. A lonely little boy, he had treasured the yellow stone, feeling of it in his pocket, perhaps, and regarding it as company of a sort, or as a talisman or charm. He had "kept it a good while; but at last he lost it beyond recovery. It took years to heal the wound & I think," John Brown wrote of himself and his boyhood grief, "he cried at times about it." [9]

As for the little bobtailed squirrel, the boy "almost idolized his pet," the fifty-seven-year-old man recalled. "This, too, he lost . . . and for a year or two John was in mourning and looking at all the squirrels he could see," walking weeping through the woods and calling its name, "to try and discover Bobtail if it was possible." But it was not. The Old Man came to think of the vanished stone, the lost squirrel, as symbols of the inevitability of all human loss, or even as a divine lesson, particularly when he thought of the deaths of his small children, concluding that "the Heavenly father sees it best to take all of the little things out of his hands which he has placed in them." [10]

During most of his years, and not without cause, he suffered periodic bouts of a kind of scriptural melancholy in which he attempted to justify the ways of God against man in general but against John Brown in particular.

---

* The autobiographical quotations given here and in succeeding chapters are from a letter of July 15, 1857, from Red Rock, Iowa, to twelve-year-old Henry L. Stearns, the son of John Brown's Boston supporter.

In 1843, four of his youngest children died, three in a single month, during an epidemic at Richfield, Ohio, where John Brown had a large flock of sheep, or at least their care and supervision, for another man supplied the capital. He had been particularly taken with his son, Charles, only six when he died, who was "very swift and strong, his legs and arms as straight as broomsticks, of sandy complexion, quiet as a cat, but brave as a tiger." And Peter, only three when he died that month at Richfield, had been "the best-looking member of the family." [11]

"They were all children towards whom perhaps we might have felt a little partial," John Brown wrote to his eldest son, his careful restraint curbing his grief, "but they all now lie in a little row together. . . ." He may have paused here in his writing, seeing again the fresh final mounds of earth over what had been life, but then he added, "but still the Lord reigneth and blessed be his great and holy name." [12] Thereafter he spoke more often as he did when he wrote that "this world is not the *Home* of man," and of "the very short season of trial," as swift as the melting of a snowflake, through which man must pass to eternity. He lamented that he could not be more resigned when "smarting under the rod of our Heavenly Father," writing: "My attachments to this world have been very strong, & Divine Providence has been cutting me loose from one Cord after another up to the present time, but notwithstanding that all ties must soon be severed: I am still clinging like those who have hardly taken a single lesson." [13]

3

Although such thoughts were common enough to the Old Man, he could neither long retain them in their full somberness nor ever quite lose them for all their recession. He found the drama of the endurance contest between himself and the Lord painfully absorbing but he knew with quiet confidence that he could outlast Him. "Though He slay me yet will I trust in Him," he wrote, "and bless His name forever!" [14] But the sharp edge of grief usually faded in time to a dull but ever-present background as the ferment of some new plan rose within him, generally accompanied by the sanguine expectation of success. He had, one of his sons said, an ardent and enthusiastic nature.

Occasionally he was cheerfully garrulous, particularly when the young were around, permitting him the gratification of a nature incurably sententious. He liked at such times to give them the benefit of his skills, to instruct them on the proper way to operate a theodolite, run a surveyor's line, build a log cabin, strop a razor, skin a deer, smoke ham, salt pork, make butter, tan a hide, shoot straight, cure a horse of colic or a sheep of foot rot. For that matter he felt equally qualified to instruct on the value of early rising, child training, outdoor exercise, and infant damnation, and was always ready to debate on these and other subjects, preferably with a clergyman.

Once after a debate with a clergyman on predestination, the preacher came to him and said he had heard that Brown had said he was no gentleman.

"I did say you were no gentleman," Brown replied. "I said more than that, sir."

"What did you say?"

"I said, sir, that it would take as many men like you to make a gentleman as it would wrens to make a cock turkey." [15]

By 1849 his failures had been numerous enough to carry him far, even to London and Paris. In that year he had traversed the Atlantic in a futile attempt to sell the wool he would not sell at the price offered by American wool manufacturers. In Europe he must have been considered as strangely American as a tomahawk or a buffalo when he walked city streets, moving "with a long, springing race horse step," as Frederick Douglass, the black abolitionist, described his stride.[16] He must have seemed strange indeed to any blue-smocked Belgian peasant who saw him prowling the battlefield of Waterloo, possessed by the notion that examination of the scene of Napoleon's defeat would somehow help him achieve his long-deferred dream of saving the American nation through the forcible extirpation of slavery. Napoleon's tactics, as well as the Bible's Gideon, he felt, would increase his own military knowledge for the coming battle.

If Frenchmen and Englishmen thought him peculiarly American they were right. He was as typical of his time as the covered wagon in which he had headed West from his native Connecticut to Ohio as a boy, as the Sharps rifle he carried in the Kansas war, as the Bible he read each night and morning and knew almost by heart. His family was at once as plain as an old shoe, and rather distinguished, descended from the earliest settlers of Massachusetts and New York, his father Owen Brown long a trustee of Oberlin College, a cousin the president of Amherst, a brother a somewhat prominent lawyer and editor for a time of the New Orleans *Bee*.

He was not always honest, although he tried hard to be, and once, as we shall see, when harried by bankruptcy and debt and mortgage foreclosure, he appropriated to his own use $7,800, of which $2,800 was advanced to him for the purchase of wool by an Eastern wool company, a fact he sorrowfully admitted and a debt he was still trying to pay back when they hanged him for treason years later.[17] Often he inveighed against debt when lecturing the young and then he would observe mournfully that he had lived all his life under its weight, "like a toad under a harrow." [18]

Although he knew probably as much about sheep, wool, and tanning as any man in the United States, his reputation, such as it was, was parochial and restricted to his various residences and occupations until the political situation brought him to national prominence. The growing conviction in the North that something had to be done to stop the expansion of slavery did more than bring thousands of his fellow citizens into partial agreement with views long held by Brown. It provided the necessary setting, the essential scene, for his own individual renascence, after a critical failure that for some time made him almost incapable of decisive action. It brought him four years of success, of a kind at least, after all his reverses. The fevered political scene, the gathering crisis, seemed to revitalize the Old Man and give his life a force and meaning that it had never had before.

Then what had been growing tentative within him, or at any rate subdued by years of humiliation, became positive again and he liked to give little homilies, instructive lectures to the great, from Emerson to Theodore Parker to rich Gerrit Smith, as he told them what they should do to save the nation. Like most Americans of the period, he was still under the spell of the American Revolution and the words "*All* men are created equal" were to him not a Fourth of July orator's phrase but a fact his grandfather had died to prove in the War for Independence and to which he would similarly attest. Sometimes he enjoyed speaking of the Revolution to the eminent as if it were still going on and then he liked to say, bristling and rearing back and savoring himself a little, that he believed in the Declaration of Independence and the Golden Rule, sir, that he believed they meant the same thing, sir, and that it would be better for a whole generation to pass from the earth, men, women, and children, than that one jot or tittle of either should be lost, adding with an imperious flash, "I mean exactly so, sir." [19]

When he spoke so to Emerson and Thoreau in Concord in 1857, they regarded him with unfeigned admiration. After all, in their view he was the foremost victor of Kansas, the pre-eminent champion against slavery in that Territory's civil war. It was an age of absolutes, and both Thoreau and Emerson were inclined to regard him as spotless. Yet they had every reason for knowing, if they wished to know, of his bloody exploit at Pottawatomie, where he supervised the midnight execution of five pro-slavery settlers in Kansas, since it had been reported in a widely circulated government report.

But in wartime all wickedness is with the enemy, all virtue with ourselves, and we wish to know nothing that would impeach this truth.

Nevertheless, John Brown was not compacted entirely of virtue. The admiring Emerson, so quick to see "the pure idealist, with no by-ends of his own" in Brown, might have been surprised if he had realized that John Brown possessed something of the gambler, not in essaying a venture without adequate planning but in his willingness to stake his life, and the lives of others, on a goal that might be exceedingly risky to all concerned. He had, too, an element of the adventurer, of one ready to incriminate any number in his own private attempts at either personal riches or obtaining the freedom of a people, plausible whether in pyramiding notes for a business venture or in obtaining contributions from the wealthy for his invasion of the South. He also had something of swagger, the more impressive in that it was implied rather than practiced. To the perceptive there was occasionally a note of bravado in his statements, however chaste his speech or temperate his manner. All this was encased in a simple and rather innocent man. In his own view he was animated only by concern for the welfare of man, the relief of the oppressed, and by the fact that he was the servant of the Lord God Almighty. If he was in reality a little more complex than this, those of his admirers who value the infinite contradictions contained in most may be thankful.

But if he impressed Emerson he did not always impress his seven sons, all of whom had grown by 1855 to be larger than he, and softer, too, at least in spirit, great sensitive giants with a kind of brooding excess within them. If six of them followed their father in Kansas, they were also against him in a kind of war between the young and old, a contest of the generations. If they accepted his leadership, it was not entirely because of his force but because they were against slavery, too.

They were brave, even John and Jason were to prove that; they were willing, at least at times, to fight to the death for their convictions. But life had other alternatives more sweet and lovely, for they were not as flint as was the Old Man. None of them believed in the Bible as he did and all were in revolt against his Calvinism. Strange doubts and strange desires, strange at least to their father, although he learned to respect them, sometimes stirred within them and struggle for them was an effort—there were other brighter possibilities—rather than an inevitable duty. Sometimes resentment flared within them, as when Watson Brown said to his father just before he was fatally wounded at Harper's Ferry, "The trouble is, you want your sons to be brave as tigers, and still afraid of you." [20]

4

John Brown was, as we have seen, a devout believer, inclined to clothe even political ideas in scriptural verse, but so did most Americans of his time. To him the Bible was the inspired word of God, of the Lord God Jehovah, who had guided Moses as he led a captive people from out of the bondage of Egypt, who was perfect in all things and all knowledge, and in whom there could be no ignorance either of the past or of what was to come. And might not He who had raised up a deliverer for the Hebrews in their captivity raise up a later American Moses for the delivery of other captives? When John Brown read in the Bible, "Remember them that are in bonds, as bound with them," he remembered the bonds of American slavery, certain that if slavery did not die the American Republic would. Although he once said, "I know no more of grammar than one of your calves," when speaking to Thoreau, the latter took this as a recommendation, adding approvingly of Brown, "He did not go to the college called Harvard; he was not fed on the pap that is there furnished." [21]

Among his many occupations was that of breeder, a breeder of Devon cattle and Saxony sheep which won a number of blue ribbons at county and state fairs in Ohio and New York. He began early in life, he wrote in 1857, "to discover a great liking for fine cattle, sheep & swine." [22] He bred race-horses, too, his favorites sired by a long-legged bay called Count Piper. He was, however, his own best stud, being "naturally fond of females," as he confessed, wearing out his first wife, Dianthe Lusk, whom he once praised as being "remarkably plain," and whose mind during the last years of her life when worn out with work and child-bearing was confused and dark. [23]

5

Dianthe died August 10, 1832, after twelve years of marriage in which she bore her husband seven children. "This woman," John Brown wrote twenty-five years after her death, in the letter in which he referred to himself in the third person,

by her mild, frank, & *more than all else:* by her very consistent conduct acquired; & ever while she lived maintained a most powerful; and good influence over him. Her plain but kind admonitions generally had the right effect; without arousing his haughty obstinate temper. [24]

He always felt her influence near him and in 1859, a few months before his execution, he told his eldest son John, while on the road and lying in bed together in the morning, that he had dreamed of Dianthe Lusk during the night.[25] One day after her death in childbirth in 1832, her infant son dying too, he wrote his father that when the doctor told her she was about to die, "it did not depress her spirits. She made answer 'I thought I might go to rest on God's Sabbath.' At her request the children were brought to her and she with heavenly composure gave faithful advice to each. . . . Tomorrow she is to lay beside our little son." [26]

Within a year John Brown married again, this time one Mary Day, a buxom girl of seventeen, and again the children began to arrive regularly, although from the first Mary Day had the five surviving children of Dianthe for whom to care. She was to have thirteen children of her own. For all of John Brown's restless far wandering, he was the most connubial of men, helping his wife with the housework when he was at home, liking to cook and fanatical about the cleanliness of his kitchen. When he was away, few days passed without a letter home, asking about the children's shoes and spiritual condition, closely advising as to how to obtain a side of beef, or giving detailed specific advice about the haying, or exact instructions on how to insulate the house for winter. A little quaint in a stern, old-fashioned way, he once called his family "his own most familiar acquaintance," saying it gratified him that its members were his friends.[27]

He liked to sing hymns and it was his particular pleasure to rock back and forth, an infant in his arms, using "Blow Ye the Trumpet, Blow" and "Why Should We Start and Fear to Die?" as lullabies.[28] He was, too, an extraordinarily tender nurse, always insisting on sitting up all night with the ill of his family to keep up the fire; and for years, as has been told, when his father was visiting him he would tuck him carefully into bed each night.[29]

After such a demonstration of filial regard, he would occasionally use the Bible to admonish his children to go and do likewise, telling them, "Thou shalt rise up before the hoary head, and honour the face of the old man." [30] He liked to tell them, too, of a man who made a wooden trough through which he humiliated his father by forcing him to eat from it after the old man had dropped and shattered plates from his palsied, work-hardened hands. This unfeeling son was brought to his senses when his own little son asked him, "Father, when you are old will I make a wooden trough for you to eat out of?" [31] He was distressed when "an old man leading an old white ox" sought shelter for the night at the Brown door during a storm while John Brown was away. Mary Brown, alone with the children, told him there was a tavern a few miles down the road.

"Oh dear!" Brown said, when he was told of this on his return, "No doubt he had no money and they turned him off at the tavern and he could get no place to stay and was obliged to travel all night in the rain." He brooded for a time and then he addressed his wife, quoting Scripture again, and a little severely:

"Forget not to entertain strangers for thereby some have entertained angels unaware." [32]

6

This concern for others based on Scripture came at length to provide a background for all his thoughts and sometimes even an indictment of his years. If the Bible was right, and every beat of his heart told him that it was, there was no escape from doing for others what you would have them do for you, no avoiding the truth that all men were sacred and brothers in the eyes of God. Nor did *The Liberator* which he read, along with other journals of the abolitionist press, permit him to forget who was asking the help that he himself would expect if he were a slave or who it was that were his brothers.[33]

Yet, even knowing this he often backslid into routine though he was conscious of a command he was not obeying. He was being called and he was not answering.[34] He seemed a grim, hard man to many, "a sharp character, none of your soft fellows," [35] but behind his flinty exterior there was another life that came to be more vivid than the one more easily seen. As he worked and worried, pitching hay in some distant field, or wheedling loans for his hard-pressed wool company, alternating as was his custom between farming and business, he increasingly saw the plight of the slave with such strong immediacy that it became for him an overpowering personal experience.

"I have talked with many men upon the subject of slavery," Frederick Douglass said, in recalling John Brown in Springfield in 1847, "but I remember no one so deeply excited on the subject. . . . He would walk the room with agitation at the mention of slavery. He saw the evil through no mist, haze or cloud, but in a broad light of infinite brightness, which left no line of its ten thousand horrors, out of sight." [36]

But he was not always so. As a matter of fact, he almost missed being an important part of the fight against slavery because of his romantic and imperious nature. Although he entered the struggle long after most of his generation, when he did become concerned he apparently felt that it was not for John Brown to carry out the orders of others whether in the anti-slavery crusade or his own household. He was the hero of his inner life as he was the ruler of his outer, deciding everything from when hogs should be slaughtered to when wool should be sold to how bread should be baked. Perhaps he could not conceive of John Brown as a rank-and-file member of a mass organization, committed to policies which he himself had not drafted and which he could not carry out as the directing head. At any rate, there is no evidence that he ever joined the American Anti-Slavery Society even when he viewed himself as a nonresistant nor did he ever move against slavery in a project he did not control.

His postponements and delays in fighting slavery before 1855 were almost as numerous as his business failures and not unconnected with them. In either enterprise it was difficult to do well without abandoning the other. In both it had been almost impossible for him to take advice. In each he saw himself as the central figure of a drama in which John Brown fought the world single-handedly. For almost twenty years he was whipsawed between his larger purpose and his private necessity, holding within him the irresistible force of his increasing desire to attack slavery and the immovable object of his family's needs. Occasionally he relieved his tension, whether in Ohio or later in Springfield, Massachusetts, and in North Elba, New York, by skillful and daring work on the Underground Railroad.[37]

It was in 1839, standing before the kitchen fireplace of the old Haymaker house in Franklin, Ohio, where the family then lived, the pots and pans and washing strewn about, that he told its members he had decided to free the slave by invading the South.[38] Facing bankruptcy and nearly forty, a long, lank, lean man with a florid face declaring his personal war against the country's strongest institution, he might have seemed to others than his family only an eccentric compensating for constant failure by fantastic fancies of which he was the hero. But his young sons, his impressed wife, could no more doubt that he would in fact attack slavery than they could doubt his emphatic presence, his hawklike profile bent intently forward, his manner as portentously solemn as if he were not in a farmhouse kitchen speaking to his sons and wife but was instead announcing a world-shaking decision to a world parliament.

Although it took years and a national political upheaval to change his quixotic plan into reality, he did not excuse himself for his tardiness in attacking the South's slavery by mentioning any larger force than himself. As a principal—and he always conceived of himself so—he blamed only John Brown for the delay, feeling that he had refused the Lord's yoke because of his attachment to earthly vanity, telling Frederick Douglass as early as 1847 that "he had already delayed too long and had no room to boast either his zeal or self denial." Like Moses, another who had delayed in answering the Lord's command that he liberate a people, Douglass said later, John Brown "made excuses" but "like Moses his excuses were overruled." [39]

ON MAN'S INSANITY AND HEAVEN'S SENSE

I

More than a rural eccentric, although he was also that, this was the man in whom public concern mounted during the three years beginning in 1856 until his name was a curse or a prayer in the mouth of every American who could read or hear his fellows talk or had any degree of mental sentience. By 1859, John Brown was not only universally known but a national agony dividing the country and it is within this division that his memory, his reputation, and his historic role have always been judged.

Virtually all of the testimony concerning him—save that which precedes his fame and the controversy it aroused—lies within this great national division. In general that testimony, despite many variations, was passionately for John Brown when offered by those who believed that slavery was killing the nation and that any sacrifice or any violence was justified in destroying it. It was equally passionate but vehemently against him when uttered by those favoring slavery, or who felt that civil war was too high a price to pay for its destruction, or that black freedom was not quite worth white men's blood, or that violence against slaves did not excuse John Brown's violence against slaveholders. Judgment usually had more to do with political conviction and political necessity, with sectional sympathy and party affiliation, than it did with the character of John Brown.

Yet if even uncommitted men, both during and after his life, became confused by the diverse pictures of John Brown presented to them, they were scarcely to be blamed. Sometimes John Brown was described as at the Battle of Osawatomie in Kansas when he waded a river under fire, his guns high to keep his powder dry, his blazing blue eyes hot with battle, his linen duster billowing out behind him on a current splattered by bullets, a battered old straw hat on his head; and sometimes he was described as a prophet on horseback, who because of years of thought and prayer saw more clearly than most the American future.

Sometimes he was shown as the bandit chieftain, bleating cattle, proslavery cattle, as he called those seized from Kansas Border Ruffians, being driven through a cloud of dust before him, the Old Man erect and tireless in the saddle, his posture too stiff for him to be a graceful rider but so tenacious that he was seldom thrown; and sometimes he was pictured as saving the life of a frozen lamb by bathing it in restoring warm water with absorbed, passionate concern. Occasionally, in 1859 and after, the public was told of such incidents concerning him as when in Kansas, sleeping up against a tree, a rifle on his knees, the Old Man almost blew off the head of a man who unexpectedly waked him, and then read of how he had gone among the black farmers near his last home at North Elba in New York's Adirondacks administering to them as tenderly as if they were in truth a chosen people and he a benign Moses.

Most men saw in him not his own attributes but their own. "When a noble deed is done, who is likely to appreciate it?" asked Thoreau in defending Brown, and answered, "They who are noble themselves." [40] Those who condemned the Old Man for his deed at Harper's Ferry, Thoreau continued, "have either much flesh, or much office, or much coarseness of some kind"; but perhaps the difference of opinion was more complicated and more basic. It was an enduring argument in which the temperament of the opponents was often more decisive than the facts, a debate between those who hated violence on behalf of the oppressed and those who felt that the real conservers of law and peace were those who broke man-made statutes perpetuating man-made injustice, between those holding that the end never justified the means and those who believed that the great sin was the divorcement of belief from action, was not to act in the face of evil, to become committed only to paralysis on the grounds of high principle. It was a controversy for the generations involving the role of force in social change, as well as questions concerning the nature of treason—whether, for example, it was an absolute, or whether occasionally opposition to the alleged defense was only a defense of the status quo in which one man's treason might be another man's patriotism.

And yet Thoreau was right enough in implying that officeholding and officeseeking were factors in the judgment of John Brown. His act at Harper's Ferry had coincided with the opening moves in what was perhaps to be the most crucial national campaign in the history of the country, that of 1860, in which the newly organized Republicans were being charged by their Democratic opponents with fomenting—by their very principles if not by actual connivance—insurrectionary schemes to destroy slavery. With some of the Republicans' foremost leaders accused of having prior knowledge of

John Brown's plan to attack slavery in the South, the claim that he was insane which followed the Harper's Ferry Raid came as a Republican deliverance, devoutly to be wished and ardently espoused.

Thoreau wrote that it was the immediate response of the cautious and the conservative, uttered almost as soon as they heard the news of Harper's Ferry, that any man who would risk his life to free a people, in the manner John Brown had, must be insane. Later, members of the Brown family in Ohio, determined to save their kinsman from hanging even at the cost of their own reputations, desperately sought affidavits, in the fall of 1859, indicating John Brown's insanity by reason of the alleged insanity of relatives. They scoured the family relationship, frantically urging the revelation of any instance of mental unsoundness as a means of saving Brown's life. They secured nineteen affidavits but John Brown rejected their effort to save him, scorning and forbidding any plea of insanity.

If John Brown's act was psychotic, as was ardently wished by many Republicans, then it was the private product of his own disordered mind; it had no political context, no social background, no careful planning involving prominent citizens and great writers and whole communities and black leaders which had been betrayed in part to Republican stalwarts. If he was insane, he was not representative of anyone but himself. But Southern Democrats would have none of this. John Brown was not only sane, shrewd, and brave, said Governor Wise of Virginia, but representative of militant anti-slavery sentiment in the North.[41] Many other Southerners declared the Raid the inevitable result of abolitionist agitation and the Republican Party's central tenet that slavery was a great evil which should not be permitted to expand.

If John Brown's actions, and the charges of their irrationality, were, to a degree, a product of his time and its politics, he had, nevertheless, sufficient of peculiarity. He did oscillate at times, particularly during his final years when engaged in his fatal effort for black freedom, between the crafty and the credulous, the secretive and the confiding, the shrewd and a Tom Sawyer kind of swashbuckling romance. He did alternate, during this final fight, between a bright and enthusiastic confidence and a dark and gloomy foreboding in which he expected death and defeat, although he might have rationalized both by the changing circumstances around him. If he brought off rather impressive feats of persuasion, endurance, and organization in the face of great difficulties, if he wintered and summered for many years his evolving, changing plans for black freedom, he also suffered periodically from painful mental stress when his whole plan, involving time and space, money and supplies, men, betrayal, and delay, seemed too complex to synchronize into actuality.

It was at such a time that he wrote, "I am much confused in mind and cannot remember what I wish to write." [42] His mind and body were occasionally like a pendulum, swinging between health and sickness, between lifelong recurring bouts of fever and ague, for malaria was endemic then, and unusual vigor and zest for life after recovery; between periods when he acted with the swiftness of a tiger and long spells of indecision, particularly during his last year when, worn by danger and exhausted by complexity, he occasionally could not act decisively because he could not think with the swift precision required.

Still, if the human spirit is complex enough to render dogmatic assertions of sanity or insanity a little tendentious, perhaps it would be less than scientific for us to tick off with certainty the exact mental state of one long dead, his death resulting from passions so general and intense that many were as ready to rob him of his character as they were of his life. "If man's insanity is heaven's sense," as Melville wrote, there is perhaps a larger wisdom occasionally displayed by deeds which seem inexplicable and irrational to the conservative. At any rate, we shall not divest John Brown of his own peculiar strangeness, nor argue for his sanity, nor try to reveal him as a model of normalcy, the wise and moderate citizen, who saved his money, kept his shoes shined, and voted a straight party ticket—although he tried hard for these virtues and had sometimes succeeded for a spell when younger in attaining them.

Rather, it is our purpose to place his apparent strangeness, as well as his actions, within a social framework which may help explain both. Then his alternating spells of hope and discouragement may seem sane enough or at any rate adequately explained by events. As for his touching faith in the Bible, it may seem odd to a later age to believe in this instead of in existentialism or Freud or Marx, or to believe that the determinism of God and Providence may even include oneself and one's actions, or to identify with Moses leading a captive people to freedom; but it was not singular in John Brown's day. Even John Quincy Adams, sixth President of the United States, hoped that God might help him become an American Moses, or so a grandson writes, aiding him in leading the American people to a promised land without slavery. And Garrison regarded himself as an American Isaiah. [43]

Still, to deprive John Brown, or any other man, of that inner fantasy, of that poetic drive which turned his days into significant drama is to rob him, if only in print, of that deep dynamic communion where he conversed with himself and eternity and united, in his own mind at least, with all men and all history, with the earliest of beginnings and the future's latest day. It is to emasculate him, if only in transient prose, from that simmering sustained excitement which marked him off from most and gave him to an extent his great ability to act. To divest any man of whatever peculiarity or poetry is the partial mainspring of his actions may give him a comforting propriety while at the same time distorting him into a colorless automaton. And whatever else he was, John Brown was not that.

2

There is a certain larger-than-life perspective ordinarily given to portraits of John Brown, derived in part from the national crisis which formed him and his generation, but resulting partly, too, from the stark blacks and icy whites with which he is drawn. Both the perspective and the somber strokes often prevent us from seeing him in such placid and pleasant pursuits as enjoying himself before a blazing log fire after the day's work was done.

Wherever he lived, at least for most of his life, there were huge fireplaces, and sometimes more than one, as in the long rambling house he built for himself and family in Randolph, near Meadville, in western Pennsylvania. There, "deer, wolves, turkeys and other game were abundant," and "the 'long howl' of the wolf as he prowled about the sheepfolds and the barns in the darkness of night" could be heard. The house was "of logs and divided into two large rooms in the first story," recalled one who as a boy had gone to school between 1830 and 1835 in John Brown's Randolph home, "and was supplied at each end with large fireplaces. In the north end was the living-room or family room, which served for kitchen, dining room, and other domestic purposes, while the other was used for sitting room, library and school room." [44]

Similarly in the "large livingroom of the old-fashioned house" which was the family home at Hudson, Ohio, where John Brown lived after living in Randolph, there was "a fireplace ten feet long, with huge andirons, and a crane and hooks to hang kettles upon. We boys," Salmon, the sixth son, recalled,

would cut logs two and three feet through for the fireplace and at night, in winter, two great back-logs were covered with ashes to hold fire. Father would sit in front of a lively fire, and take up us children, one, two, or three at a time, and sing until bedtime. We all loved to hear him sing as well as to talk of conditions in the country, over which he seemed worried. [45]

The kitchen fireplace at the north end of the Randolph house, particularly of course on winter evenings, was the center of activity, with the latest of the children playing on the floor before it, the larger boys stomping into the kitchen from the barn, lanterns in their hands, little rivulets of snow melting and running from their boots, after they had bedded down the horses and cattle. John Brown himself, helped by one of his hired men, might be bringing in logs—hemlock, maple, and birch, sometimes 3 or 4 feet in length—which would burn all night. Others of his hired help, often as many as ten or twelve when he was in the tanning business as at Randolph, and who lived with the family, were likely to be sitting before the fire on split-log benches and hand-made chairs, or even lying on the floor, their front sides fevered with heat, their rears conscious of the chill breeze moving levelly over the wide-planked floor, like a steady oneway breathing, an unceasing exhalation from the cold night outside.

Mary Brown, John Brown's second wife and only nineteen in 1835, sixteen years younger than her husband, would have been busy clearing the supper table on such a night as this that year in Randolph. She was a large, plain young woman, given to long silences and hard work, and "built for times of trouble," as was also remarked of her husband and as he later proved. There were seven Brown children in 1835, only two of them her own and these still babies. The older children were John, fourteen, Jason, twelve, Owen, eleven, Ruth, six, and Frederick, five. Ruth, and sometimes even Owen and Frederick, were expected to help with the supper dishes.

Supper would have been plain enough but plentiful. "A favorite dish with us children," one of the Brown boys recalled later,

was corn meal mush cooked the whole afternoon long in a huge iron caldron, and served with rich milk or cream. It left a crust a half-inch thick in the caldron, and tasted, so I affirm to this day, like no other mush ever made. The table was always neatly set, never without a white tablecloth; the food was coarse, hearty farmers' food, always in abundance and always well served. Frugality was observed from a moral standpoint; but one and all, we were a well-fed, well-clad lot. . . .

There were no drones in the Brown hive. Little toddlers unable to help were at least not allowed to hinder; as soon as they had achieved a show of stable control of their uncertain little legs the world of work opened to them. There was no pampering; little petting. The boys could turn a steak or brown a loaf as well as their mother.[46]

A winter evening after supper might well begin with John Brown taking one of the younger children on his lap, both sitting as quietly as if the elder boys and their schoolmates were not pushing and skylarking around, both watching the yellow and blue flames lick from the logs, listening to the drowsy, just-heard flittery-flutter of the fire and sometimes to the hissing of the greener or wetter wood; and a little later perhaps, and a little sleepy too, gazing as if mesmerized far away from all the noise and bustle, from the thud of wooden pails and the steady beat of the churn, into the fire's scarlet embers, quivering and pulsing and shifting into ever-changing depths and shapes. Almost always, for that was nightly ritual, the child would presently rouse itself and ask its father to sing and often he would respond with a hymn about the Bible's year of Jubilee when all the slaves went free, his metallic voice sounding a little like the music of a saw, at once disturbing and melodic.

> *Blow ye the trumpet, blow*
> *The gladly solemn sound;*
> *Let all the nations know,*
> *To earth's remotest bound,*
> *The year of Jubilee is come;*
> *Return, ye ransomed sinners, home.*

As the tuneful wail ebbed into silence, the younger children would start for bed, for the hymn's end was the invariable signal for their retiring. John and Jason and the Delamater children, who went to the school held in John Brown's home, usually instantly stopped their roughhousing, if not because of the warning looks from Miss Sabrina Wright, the teacher hired by Brown and the Delamaters, then as a result of one stern glance from their father. With the smaller children, who like most children in a large family could sleep through an earthquake, gone to bed, John Brown liked to organize debates, encouraging his hired help to participate, perhaps on such favorite subjects of the time as whether Washington or Napoleon was the greater general; or whether personal happiness was best promoted by seeking the welfare of others; or whether predestination, the great fact that God had determined the world's fate, and each man's too, from the beginning of time unto the last trump, should mean any lessening of individual struggle. Often, too, there would be games and trials of strength, as in Indian wrestling which would sometimes degenerate into rougher play with the great thump of a large body flat against the floor. Then John Brown would quiet things down and a silence might momentarily fall with those within the brightness and the warmth listening to the wind in the immense blackness just the other side of the log walls, or to the soprano howl of a wolf, perhaps far away and addressed to the moon, the children permitting themselves little shivers of satisfaction that they were sheltered and not outside in the cold winter night.

John Brown did not like it, one of the Delamater boys recalled, when play became rough. He considered it an affront to his own dignity and to the dignity of his house. The contests, he felt, should not be play but exercises in self-improvement, physical and moral. "He held broad views of physical and mental culture," George B. Delamater later wrote,

and I have witnessed contests of strength and skill . . . upon the floor of the house between various competitors during the winter evenings. I was encouraged to try my hand at these sports or exercises, and have seen Mr. Brown do the same. He held that this was not mere amusement, but also a means of strengthening the muscles, and gaining physical power. For a man of his weight he was very strong; his resolute will gave him an advantage here as well as elsewhere.[47]

During the debates Brown was the leading spirit, George Delamater remembered, and

no matter whether the question was religious, political or one involving a knowledge of a domestic, social or scientific subject, he seemed to be well informed on all and always had a decided opinion on one side or the other. One mode of discussion to which he was accustomed was to propose a series of questions to the person who differed from him, concealing his design till the admission of obvious truths would compel a concession of the point for which he contended.[48]

As the evening wore on, the boys might become more restive and when they misbehaved John Brown called them to him and gave them a smart rap on the head with the handle of his pocket knife. This he called "ringing the bell," since the children said it made their ears ring as if hearing a gong. After solemnly rapping one of the children, he would put his arm around the culprit and talk earnestly about life and conduct.

"He often repeated to us," Delamater wrote,

such maxims as these: "Diligence is the mother of good luck," or "God gives all things to industry,"—"plough deep while sluggards sleep, and you shall have corn to sell and keep," or again, "One today is worth two tomorrows," "If you would have a faithful servant and one you like, serve yourself," "What maintains one vice will set up two children," "A small leak will sink a great ship." "Buy what thou hast no need of and ere long thou wilt have to sell thy necessaries," "A ploughman on his legs is higher than a gentleman on his knees," "God helps those that help themselves" . . . "He that walks with wise men shall be wise also" . . . "One valuable idea in a day will give seven in a week, and at the same rate 365 in a year—many persons do not get so many in a lifetime." [49]

3

John Brown lived in Randolph for the ten years between 1825 and 1835, being twenty-five when he arrived in western Pennsylvania, and thirty-five when he returned to Ohio where he remained for a decade. Even as a young man he had the stamp of authority, and often a solemn air as if it were a burden. Even as a young man he seemed old-fashioned or even archaic as when, unable to curse more conventionally because of his religious beliefs, he shrieked in moments of anger or anguish, "God bless the Duke of Argyle!" [50] Sometimes, however, he succumbed to the necessity of short explosive Anglo-Saxon expletives, the four-letter words that after all were never uncommon in the vocabulary of the American farmer. A compulsion for supervision was always with him, whether it concerned his wife's bread, which he preferred to bake himself; a hired girl's hands, which he said should be washed more often; or, after leaving Randolph, the clothing of his own little girls, one of whom he liked to call "my little chick," and another "my strange Anna!"

He liked to refer slyly to his elder boys' love affairs, when they grew old enough to have them, but they did not encourage him in this direction. There was no denying his strong possessive concern for his own family or its affection for him, for all the stress and strain involved in living under him. He was later to write with a kind of quaint and diffident formality and as if a little surprised, that it was "a source of great comfort" to him "that I retain a warm place" in the "sympathies, affections and confidence of my family. Allow me to say," he concluded, "that a man can hardly get into difficulties too big to be surmounted if he has a firm foothold at home. *Remember that.*" [51]

His foothold at home was firm enough. Even during such pleasant winter evenings as at Randolph and later in a half a dozen other homes, he resembled McGregor, in that, like the Scots chieftain, wherever John Brown sat, there was the head of the table. Sometimes he seemed a trifle apologetic, as if to imply he could not help the authority flowing from him and hoped it would bother no one. In appearance, then, he was a sturdy substantial citizen, as strong and as slim and as neat as a new whitewashed post. "He was tasty in his dress—about washing, bathing, brushing, etc. When he washed him, he pushed his hair back from his forehead."

So his brother-in-law, Dianthe's brother, described Brown in Randolph at about this time, adding, "When I had my controversy with the church in Hudson, he came and prayed with me and shed tears." [52] An employee in his Randolph tannery wrote, "Brown in his personal habits was one of the neatest men I ever knew . . . but he would never wear expensive clothing for the reason that it was a useless waste of money which might better be given to the poor; also he despised anything like foping watch chains, guards, Seals, or any unnecessary finery." [53]

"In politics he was originally an Adams man and after wards a Whig and I believe a Strong one. . . . His food was always plain and simple all luxuries being dispensed with and in the year 1830 he rigidly adopted the tetotal temperance principles and I do not believe he ever tasted liquor of any kind from that time to his death." [54]

But John Brown's conversion to total abstinence was a little more violent and a little less permanent than the calm resolve against intoxicants implied by his employee's recollection. Years after his 1830 vow against liquor we find him enjoying a mug of ale in an English inn and in 1852 giving detailed instructions as to how to bottle and ship wine. Still, his 1830 conversion if not completely permanent was dramatic enough. It came with the suddenness of Saul's conversion to Christianity on the way to Damascus, although Brown was only on the way to a barn-raising near Randolph. In his wagon was a 3-gallon jug of whiskey which was not his. He had bought it at the request and with the money—75 cents—of the man whose barn was being raised. It was intended for the festivities incidental to the occasion but it never arrived. It was a hot day and John Brown always thought that the explanation for his wickedness.

"On the road from Meadville," a son writes,

father became thirsty and began taking "nips" from the jug. He was accustomed to drinking from his own barrel, and did not think the practice wrong. On the way to the barn-raising father realized that the liquor was getting hold of him, and he became alarmed. He afterward spoke of the occurrence frequently. He reasoned that if liquor would lead him to drink from another man's jug it was surely getting control over him—a thing he could not allow.

Coming to a large rock by the roadway, he smashed the jug upon it, vowing that he would not be responsible for his neighbor's drinking at the barn-raising, where accidents might happen. He paid for the liquor, and when he reached home rolled his whiskey barrel into the back yard and smashed it to pieces with an axe. No liquor was allowed about the house afterwards.[55]

4

By nine-thirty on most winter evenings, whether in Ohio or Pennsylvania, Massachusetts or New York, most of John Brown's family, and his employees, too, when he had them, had drifted off to bed. Still up and about for a short space after the others had left were himself, his wife Mary, and the eldest children, Ruth, John, Owen, and Jason, or Jase, as everyone but his father called him.

At such a time, John Brown almost always said to one of the elder children, "Read me one of David's Psalms, won't you?" At morning prayers when he passed out a dozen Bibles to the children and the hired help, he often liked the somber, favoring Ecclesiastes, a daughter remembers, particularly on fast days.[56] Then, the early morning fire rising and falling and throwing a flickering pattern of light and shadow on his face, he frequently intoned, solemnly, sepulchrally, but with intense enjoyment, his favorite last chapter:

> REMEMBER NOW THY CREATOR IN THE DAYS OF THY YOUTH, WHILE THE EVIL DAYS COME NOT, NOR THE YEARS DRAW NIGH, WHEN THOU SHALT SAY, I HAVE NO PLEASURE IN THEM ...
>
> OR EVER THE SILVER CORD BE LOOSED, OR THE GOLDEN BOWL BE BROKEN, OR THE PITCHER BE BROKEN AT THE FOUNTAIN, OR THE WHEEL BROKEN AT THE CISTERN.
>
> THEN SHALL THE DUST RETURN TO THE EARTH AS IT WAS: AND THE SPIRIT SHALL RETURN UNTO GOD WHO GAVE IT.

But at night, like a man taking a glass of milk before retiring, John Brown preferred something mildly comforting, and, after requesting a Psalm, one of his children before they all trooped off to bed might read his favorite Twenty-third:

> THE LORD IS MY SHEPHERD; I SHALL NOT WANT. ... YEA, THOUGH I WALK THROUGH THE VALLEY OF THE SHADOW OF DEATH, I WILL FEAR NO EVIL; FOR THOU ART WITH ME. ...

VIII

The American Moses

As John Brown listened to the Twenty-third Psalm on a winter evening in Randolph, it would have seemed quite impossible to any who knew him then that this unknown tanner in the backwoods of Pennsylvania would one day divide the nation. Few could have been more anonymous than he as he savored the hope that goodness and mercy should mark all the days of his life. But the time would come when thousands would call him saint and more proclaim him mad, with few to say that he may have been something of both and not quite either. The question persists, however, that if John Brown were mad, what were Emerson and Thoreau and Frederick Douglass, Theodore Parker, Wendell Phillips, and other great Americans still honored for significant accomplishment, who gave some of their money and all of their honor not to John Brown's plan alone but also to their belief in his integrity and judgment?

Perhaps more light on John Brown's essential nature, on his innermost essence, can be gained through reading his own words, and the words of others about him, before ever he had a chance to pose before history or others to view him as hero or villain. Perhaps they will reveal that his preoccupation with the Bible, his belief in the literal truth of its words, his conviction that they were a guide to all human conduct, was more than a fanatic's eccentricity. Perhaps his own words on slavery may help decide if his was only a personalized and irrational aggression or if a time of crisis gave something of inevitability—and even of hard necessity and firm wisdom—to his attack on slavery by force of arms.

"DEAR WIFE & CHILDREN EVERY ONE"

I

Although John Brown wrote thousands of letters, fewer than seven hundred survive if his business letters are not included in the count. Of these, many were written before he had consciousness of any destiny other than that of a man trying to earn a living, raise a family, and bring it and himself to Heaven.* It is these letters with which we are here particularly concerned, written outside of history, in a way, and therefore revelatory of the real John Brown and perhaps an aid in determining if he was only a bloodthirsty zealot or perhaps something more or less. The unself-conscious, informal expression of ordinary hours, flowing on as spontaneously as the blood, these letters are revealing enough, for it is difficult to pose for history while discussing the children's diarrhea or the sheeps' foot rot.

Some are addressed to the entire family, with the salutation "Dear Wife & Children Every One," some to "Dear Father," and others to "Dear Son John." They concern such matters as bay horses and Devon cattle and Saxony sheep, or speak of light crops of wheat and heavy falls of rain, of slaughtering hogs and salting pork, of fears for "entire leanness of soul" and hopes for more "correspondence with heaven." They tell of the extension of the railroad from Akron to Cleveland, of the comfort and swiftness of the new steam cars, of Frederick, one of his seven sons, being "very wild again," of county and state fairs and of hopes for blue ribbons, and of homesickness so intense that John Brown writes "when the day comes that will afford me opportunity to return [home] I shall be awake to greet its earliest dawn, if not its midnight birth." †[1]

---

* Many of John Brown's letters were destroyed by men who conspired with him to attack the South's slavery when they feared arrest and prosecution after the Harper's Ferry Raid. Others were destroyed in the Chicago fire of 1871 when private collections went up in flames, and the same thing happened in Boston in 1872. Many were destroyed during the Kansas civil war when the homes of John Brown, Jr., and Jason Brown, his brother, were destroyed by the Border Ruffians. Many undoubtedly have been lost, particularly those of the first fifty-five years of his life when, as one unknown to fame, there was no particular reason for recipients of his letters to keep them. See Boyd B. Stutler, "John Brown: His Hand and Pen," *The New Colophon*, New York, October 1948.

† After John Brown's ten comparatively successful years in Randolph, Pennsylvania, he was frequently away from home and this necessitated many of the letters quoted in this chapter. Sometimes he was driving cattle east for sale in Connecticut from Ohio where he had returned

When John Brown is away from home his wife, Mary, seems to him a perfect woman, without flaw or fault, or so he says in what can only be described as a love letter, while he seems to himself, or so he insists, harsh and hard in his dealings with those he loves. Whether enjoying the fine food and solid comfort of the Massasoit House in Springfield, or pressed about by the warm wooly bodies of his black-nosed sheep in a barge on the Erie Canal, he has always in him, he says, an ache for home. As he contrives to write a quick note to his wife, hunching a shoulder shieldingly to protect his paper from his pushing stock, or writes more comfortably in the room of some temperance hotel in upstate New York, he is usually intent on such subjects as new shoes for the boys, made large enough so they will not soon be discarded by the growth of their feet, or the presenting of raisins and candy to the little girls as a gift from their absent father, or how the children are progressing in their school work.

It is a queer experience reading the letters now, John Brown so intent on prosy problems of a vanished time, on such subjects as the price of beef or how a draft shall be cashed by his family while he is away from home, all unconscious of the years ahead of which we know as we read and he does not know as he writes. He is completely absorbed in the present as he writes that he is in good health "except some soreness occasioned by the running off from a steep high bank, & the consequent upsetting of the stage on the Road." [2] He has no prescience of a future including a noose and glory, or a noose and treason, when he declares, "I want very much to see those little girls and say to them that their Fathers hair begins to need cutting again." [3]

The letters are penned in a strong, strikingly legible handwriting, angular and sharp, correct and grammatical enough in the writer's earlier years, although he was always sufficiently eccentric in his spelling, but growing with the years at once more eloquent and forceful if more misspelled and less literate as his views on slavery became more intense. It was an age of the dash, ampersand, and the semicolon, and better educated persons than John Brown

---

with his family, and then herding sheep back home, often on foot, occasionally driving them through blizzards along the Ohio shore of Lake Erie, after returning to Buffalo on the Erie Canal. By 1846 he was writing his family in Akron from Springfield, Massachusetts, where the firm of Perkins & Brown had the wool depot for the collection, storage, sorting, and sale of wool. Back in Ohio, the Brown family was caring for the large herd of sheep, one of the best herds of the country, owned in partnership with Colonel Simon Perkins of Akron, the controlling partner for Perkins & Brown, for it was the colonel who put up the capital in exchange for John Brown's knowledge of sheep and the work of his family. In 1849, while still carrying on the wool business, John Brown bought a farm of 244 acres at North Elba in New York's Adirondacks from Gerrit Smith, and then letters flowed back and forth between members of the family in Springfield, Akron, and North Elba.

were highly individualistic in grammar, spelling, and punctuation. In his earlier days, before the problem of slavery was an ever-present ferment within him, his letters were spare and factual, usually concerned with immediate matters of business, as this one written from Randolph and devoted to wool and the avoiding of toll charges in the delivery of cattle:

> I should be glad to get of you about 16 lb of common wool & to have it come by the team when it returns. I have engaged that we will furnish Osborn with ten head of good beef cattle per month till the first of November. . . . I think there is a prospect of selling many more. The Cap horned steer weighed 675 lbs in the beef. When cattle are brought in by sending over to Osborn across the bridge the toll may [be] saved.[4]

On one of his first trips to Connecticut from Ohio to sell cattle, he writes his father from Centreville, Allegany County, New York, on April 9, 1839:

> I improve almost the first leisure moment since I left your house to let you know we are yet well, & getting along as well quite as we could expect. Our expences have been as yet much less than we expected, & our Cattle generally bear the journey finely. We have had to leave one horse behind in Pa, sick. The bay mare does well & improves. We have missed three head of cattle, & had one give out.[5]

The letter gives evidence that John Brown, just short of his thirty-ninth birthday but already father of seven children, is filled with a sense of adequate rectitude, despite serious financial and moral losses which we shall later detail, as he adventures into the great world with all its strangely diverse characters and lurid temptations, jogging along day after day behind his cattle, perhaps on the bay mare, through Ohio, through Pennsylvania, through New York, and continuing east clear into distant Connecticut. The endless miles mortally exhaust some of the cattle, which die on the road, but the little group presses steadily on. At his side is Edward, his half brother and only sixteen, whom he is resolved to protect from the sins of Eastern Sodoms and Gomorrahs. As a father himself, he can understand his own father's worry over Edward's first trip from home and as a countryman himself, one who distrusted great cities, he will in the future be devoutly thankful when his own son, John, quits New York City where he lived for a time. Still, Edward may profit from this grand tour, John Brown points out in this letter to his father in which he writes:

> I am not without hopes that Edward will profit by the many different kinds of company and examples he will of necessity meet with. I mean to give him the same kind, & useful hints so far as he will receive them, & I am capable, that I would one of my own dear sons. I well know your feelings on his account. . . .

I kneed not write you my best wishes for I trust you well understand that you ever have them. From your affectionate unworthy son.[6]

Six years later he is on the way home to Ohio from a similar trip, this time on a canal boat on the Erie Canal approaching Buffalo. About him are packed the sheep with which he has lived for the past six days and as he writes his wife he is dreading the thought of

driving [the sheep] up the Lake through mud up to my knees facing the rain, & snow together.

I am just going to try my seventh night in the midship of a canal boat among the sheep, (a shepherd without doubt) wraped up nice in a buffalo skin. I trust the boys will take good care of all at home, and hope to see you all well again shortly. My own health is good and hope you will not be over anxious on my account.[7]

2

In most of his letters he is thinking of his boys and there may be times that he cannot help admiring the inspiring advice he gives them. When his eldest son, John, had his first outside job as the teacher of a little country school and had difficulty in keeping order, his father wrote him a letter of which he may have been proud, one well-turned phrase tripping on another, until his counsel suggests something of incoherent eloquence. "If you cannot now go into a disordered country school," he writes,

and gain its confidence, & esteem, & reduce it to good order, & waken up the energies and the verry soul of every rational being in it, yes, of every mean ill behaved, ill governed, snotty boy & girl that compose it; & secure the good will of the parents, then how how how are you to stimulate Asses to attempt a passage of the Alps.

If you run with footmen & they should we[a]ry you how should you contend with horses. If in the land of peace they have wearied you, then how will you do in the swelling of the Jordan. Shall I answer the question myself. If any man lack wisdom let him ask of God who giveth liberally unto all and upbraideth not. Let me say to you again love them all [the children] & commend them, & yourself to the God to whom Solomon sought in his youth & he shall bring it to pass.

Suddenly turning practical, he continues,

You have heard me tell of dividing a school into two great spelling classes & of its effects, if you should think best and can remember the process you can try it. Let the grand reason that one course is right, & another wrong be kept continueally before your own mind & before your school.[8]

When in 1842 his son John leaves for college, "a knapsack on my back," walking to Grand River Institute in Ashtabula County, Ohio, John Brown writes him, "I well know how to appreciate the feelings of a young person among strangers, and at a distance from home." He has been so busy with tanning, he continues,

that I have in great measure neglected the one thing needful, and pretty much stopped all correspondence with heaven. . . . I would send you some money, but I have not yet received a dollar from any source since you left. I should not be so dry of funds could I but overtake my work: but all is well,—all is well.[9]

Again he writes his son,

Have had a good deal of loss amongst our sheep from grub in the head. Have raised 560 lambs, and have 2700 pounds of wool; have been offered 56 cents per pound for one ton of it. . . . Have not yet done finishing leather, but shall probably get through in a few weeks. The general aspect of our worldly affairs is favorable. Hope we do not entirely forget God. I am extremely ignorant at present of miscellaneous subjects.[10]

Writing his son John he is troubled with drowsiness as he sits before the fire in the kitchen after a hard day's work. "I have gone to sleep a great many times while writing the above," he confesses once, but nevertheless proceeds to give his son advice about a love affair. He should not worry, Brown says, if the object of his affections takes a long time in replying to one of his letters. "If hearing from ANY person," he observes, "prove to be (a verry up stream) business I would advise not to worry at present. Will you let me know how it stands between you & all parties concerned." [11]

Not long later he reports to his son,

We get along in our business as well as we ever have done I think. We loose some sheep but not as many as for two seasons past. . . . I hope that entire leanness of soul may not attend any little success. . . . We are nearly through another yeaning time, & have lost but verry few. Have not yet counted Tails: Think there may be about Four Hundred. Never had a finer or more thrifty lot. Expect to begin washing next week. Have received our medals & Diploma. [Apparently from a state or county fair.] They are splendid toys, & appear to be knock down arguments among the sheep folk who have seen them. . . . Cannot tell you much more now, except it be that we all appear to think a great deal more about this world than about the next which proves that we are still very foolish.[12]

As the children become older he is increasingly apprehensive as to their spiritual state, particularly John, who had been beguiled by the new sciences, for so they were regarded, of phrenology and mesmerism. His pleas for a return to the Rock of Ages run like a refrain through his letters. One written to John from Akron in 1853 begins quietly enough about the wheat crop being "right light" and the "oats very poor." However, he continues: "our sheep and cattle have done well; have raised five hundred and fifty lambs and expect about eighty cents per pound for wool."

At nearby Tallmadge, he says, "there has been for some time an unusual seriousness and attention to future interests," the last words accepted terminology for that conversion assuring a future Heaven. This leads him to John's apostasy and the quoting of some two hundred Bible texts designed to prove that the Old Testament prophets had foretold and experienced such backslidings as John's. It was apparently to have been a major effort but after several pages it peters out and concludes lamely enough with the hope that John and his wife, Wealthy Hotchkiss Brown, will visit them at the time of the county fair. "We have a nice lot of chickens fattening for you, when you come," the letter concludes.[13]

Many of John Brown's letters before he became a national figure begin with some mention of the crops, which usually leads to the weather, which in turn leads to God, sender of the rain and the drought. A typical one from Akron to his daughter Ruth in North Elba in 1852 begins by saying he has been "pretty much laid Up" with ague and has "not been good for much," and then continues:

We are getting nearly through with Haying & Harvest. Our hay crop is most abundant, & we have lately had frequent little Rains which (for the present) relieves us from our fears of a terible drouth. We are much rejoiced to learn that God in mercy has given you some precious showers. It is a great mercy to us that we frequently are made to understand our absolute dependence on a power quite above ourselves. . . . How blessed are all whose Hearts & conduct do not set them at variance with *that* power. Why will not my family endeavour to secure *his* favour, & to effect in the One only way a perfect reconciliation?

The cars have been running regularly from Akron to Cleaveland since July 5th so that there is now Steam conveyance from Akron to Westport [near North Elba]. This is a great comfort as it reduces the journey to such a trifling affair. We are making a little preparation for the Ohio State Fair at Cleaveland on 15th.– 16th–17th Sept next, & think we shall exhibit some Cattle & Sheep. . . .

Turning to the activities of the children at Akron, he reports:

Our Oliver has been speculating for some Months past in Hogs. I think he will probably come out about even, & maybe get the Interest of his money. Fred[k] manages the sheep mostly; & Butchers Mutton for the two families [Brown and Perkins]. Watson operates on the Farm, & Salmon is chief Captain over the Cows, Calves, &c. (& he has them all to shine.) Jason & Owen appear to be getting along with their farming midling well. The prospect now is that the potatoe crop will be midling good.

Anne & Sarah go to School. Anne has become a very correct reader. Sarah goes singing about as easy as an old Shoe. Edward [his half brother] still continues in California. Father [who was eighty-four years old] is carrying on his little Farming on his own Hook still; & seems to succeed very well. I am much gratified to have him able to do so, & he seems to enjoy it quite as much as ever he did. I have now written about all I can well think of for this time.

Your affectionate Father
John Brown [14]

"MR. DANA, MR. JEFFERSON"

I

If letters written before John Brown was widely known suggest milder aspects of his character than those usually contained in the customary picture of him as a wild zealot, perhaps the testimony of one who saw him and recorded his impressions when Brown was as anonymous as any American in the country may also be of value.

Richard Henry Dana, the Boston attorney who wrote *Two Years Before the Mast*, accidentally met John Brown in 1849 after becoming lost in the Adirondack wilderness of New York near North Elba, more than six years before Brown attracted the attention of the American people. Because Dana wrote of his experience in his journal immediately after it happened, it has unusual value. In most instances those who described John Brown, even, for example, at the age of twelve, did so after he became a *cause célèbre*, their impressions colored more by the nation's crisis of 1859 than the facts concerning an Ohio boy in 1812.

In June of 1849, Dana and two friends, a Mr. Metcalf and a Mr. Aikens, ventured on an expedition into the wildly mountainous country extending for miles in all directions about the log farmhouse John Brown had only recently rented and which because of its nearness to Canada and its owner's convictions was a station on the Underground Railroad. "From Keene westward," Dana writes, using his journal of the time as his source, "we began to meet signs of frontier life,—log-cabins, little clearings, bad roads overshadowed by forests, mountain torrents, and the refreshing odor of balsam firs and hemlocks." [15] For some days they lived in the forests, camping without tents or other shelter at night, climbing mountains, hunting and fishing by day, "cooking our trout and venison in the open air"; but one evening between five and six o'clock after passing the first branch of the Au Sable, and while searching for the second, it gradually became clear that they were thoroughly lost. They spent a hungry and anxious night, with no supper in the evening or breakfast in the morning, but before noon of the next day, quite exhausted from their experience, they blundered on a path which led to a road. Rounding a turn after some eighteen hours of aimless wandering and waiting in the night they saw "a log-house and half-cleared farm." The log house and the farm were the residence of John Brown and his family.

2

"Three more worn, wearied, hungry, black-fly bitten travellers seldom came to this humble, hospitable door," Dana continues.

The people received us with cheerful sympathy, and while we lay down on the grass, under the shadow of the house, where a *smutch* kept off the black flies, prepared something for our comfort. The master of the house had gone down to the settlements, and was expected back before dark. His wife was rather an invalid, and we did not see much of her at first.

There were a great many sons and daughters,—I never knew how many; one a bonny, buxom young woman of some twenty summers, with fair skin and red hair, whose name was Ruth, and whose good humor, hearty kindness, good sense and helpfulness quite won our hearts. She would not let us eat much at a time, and cut us resolutely off from the quantities of milk and cool water we were disposed to drink, and persuaded us to wait until something could be cooked for us, more safe and wholesome for faint stomachs; and we were just weak enough to be submissive subjects to this backwoods queen.

A man came along in a wagon, and stopped to water his horses, and they asked him if he had seen anything of Mr. Brown below,—which it seemed was the name of the family. Yes; he had seen him. He would be along in an hour or so. "He has two negroes along with him," said the man in a confidential, significant tone, "a man, and a woman." Ruth smiled, as if she understood him.

Mr. Aikens told us that the country about here belonged to Gerrit Smith; that negro families, mostly fugitive slaves, were largely settled upon it, trying to learn farming; and that this Mr. Brown was a strong abolitionist and a kind of king among them. This neighborhood was thought to be one of the termini of the Underground Railroad.

The farm was a mere recent clearing. The stumps of trees stood out, blackened by burning, and crops were growing among them, and there was a plenty of felled timber. The dwelling was a small log-house of one story in height, and the outbuildings were slight. The whole had the air of a recent enterprise, on a moderate scale, although there were a good many neat cattle and horses. The position was a grand one for a lover of mountain effects; but how good for farming I could not tell. Old White Face, the only exception to the uniform green and brown and black hues of the Adirondack hills, stood plain in view, rising at the head of Lake Placid, its white or pale gray side caused, we were told, by a landslide. All about were the distant highest summits of the Adirondacks.

Late in the afternoon a long buckboard wagon came in sight, and on it were seated a negro man and woman with bundles; while a tall, gaunt, dark-complexioned man walked before, having his theodolite and other surveyor's instruments with him, while a youth followed by the side of the wagon. The team turned in to the sheds, and the man entered the house. This was "father." The sons came out and put up the cattle, and soon we were asked in to the meal. Mr. Brown came forward and received us with kindness; a grave, serious man he seemed, with a marked countenance and a natural dignity of manner—that dignity which is unconscious, and comes from a superior habit of mind.

We were all ranged at a long table, some dozen of us more or less; and these two negroes and one other had their places with us. Mr. Brown said a solemn grace. I observed that he called the negroes by their surnames, with the prefixes of Mr. and Mrs. The man was "Mr. Jefferson," and the woman "Mrs. Wait."

He introduced us to them in due form, "Mr. Dana, Mr. Jefferson," "Mr. Metcalf, Mrs. Wait." It was plain that they had not been so treated or spoken to often before, perhaps never until that day, for they had all the awkwardness of field hands on a plantation; and what to do on the introduction, was quite beyond their experience. There was an unrestricted supply of Ruth's best bread, butter and corncakes, and we had some meat and tea, and a plenty of the best of milk.

We had some talk with Mr. Brown, who interested us very much. He told us he came here from the western part of Massachusetts.

Quoting directly from his journal entry made on the day he met Brown, Thursday, June 28, 1849, Dana continues:

The place belonged to a man named Brown . . . a thin, sinewy, hard-favored, clear-headed, honest-minded man, who had spent all his days as a frontier farmer. On conversing with him, we found him well informed on most subjects, especially in the natural sciences. He had books and had evidently made a diligent use of them. Having acquired some property, he was able to keep a good farm, and had confessedly the best cattle and best farming utensils for miles around. His wife looked superior to the poor place they lived in, which was a cabin, with only four rooms. She appeared to be out of health. He seemed to have an unlimited family of children, from a cheerful, nice, healthy woman of twenty or so, and a full-sized, red-haired son, who seemed to be foreman of the farm, through every grade of boy and girl, to a couple that could hardly speak plain.

3

The next day Dana and his friends were heading back for civilization; passing the Brown farm they stopped to say farewell. He describes the incident in his journal:

June 29, Friday. After breakfast, started for home. . . . We stopped at the Brown's cabin on our way, and took an affectionate leave of the family that had shown us so much kindness. We found them at breakfast, in the patriarchal style. Mr. and Mrs. Brown and their large family of children with the hired men and women, including three negroes, all at the table together. Their meal was neat, substantial and wholesome.

Years later in recalling the chance meeting in the Adirondack wilderness with an unknown man, Dana wrote:

It would have been past belief had we been told that this quiet frontier farmer, already at or beyond middle life, with no noticeable past, would, within ten years, be the central figure of a great tragic scene, gazed upon with wonder, pity, admiration or execration by half a continent! [16]

"AND THE WORD WAS GOD"

I

To Dana, John Brown had no "noticeable past" in 1849, and yet more than a little of his not readily discernible vanished years had been spent in the great if silent adventure of pondering man's fate and God's purpose. Like most Americans of 1850, he felt after prolonged study of the Bible that he understood man's evil and God's anger as far as mortal could understand insoluble mystery. If the explanation was near its fullest with the mere utterance of the word "God," religious Americans, and most were professedly so, were nevertheless armored by it to a degree for all the hardness they were called upon to endure. Sickness and death, theft and lust, covetousness and murder, heartbreaking disgrace and sudden ruin, war, flood, and leaping fire, the inexplicable malice of Providence cutting down the young and generous, slavery and massive cruelty for profit, were all contained within the firm framework of their belief in a world made agonizing by man's stiff-necked obduracy to God's will.

They were yet to be softened by the liberalism of a benevolent scientific evolution forever ascending upward in an inevitable progress. They knew the world was hard and they did not despair. To God all was possible and therefore all was possible to man who appealed to Him and might be answered. For God's was the miracle of predestinating all of history to the smallest rainfall on the briefest day, of deciding with His creation of man who of his number to the earth's last moment should be elect and saved and who should be damned to eternal fire, and yet reserving to man some measure of free will and choice as he battled for a salvation long ago decreed or denied.

From this hard mystery of determinism and volition, from the Scriptures of a pastoral people who wandered a distant wilderness with their cattle and their sheep thousands of years ago seeking the promised land of Judea across the river Jordan, many Americans of the nineteenth century drew a body of principle and aspiration with which they sought their own promised land in the rude new country above the mighty Ohio. From Exodus and Leviticus, from the Moses who sought to free a people, from the prophets Isaiah and Jeremiah and the tribulations of Job and the songs of David and the Gospels of Matthew, Mark, Luke, and John, they fashioned, however selectively, an ideology of liberty against American slavery.

Yet so complex and contradictory were the Scriptures of this ancient people, alternating between a thirst for justice which would include the poor and weak and the celebration of a bloody revenge upon any who had incurred their wrath, and so diverse the desires and interests of Americans appealing to the sacred writings, that it was possible to use them in buttressing almost any act or policy a given individual favored. Subjective desire, often spurred by politics and economic interests, seemed ever to control the use of what was regarded as eternal truth. Thus if John Brown, and many others, found the Lord's stern command to set Israel's captives free from Egypt's bondage an injunction against American slavery, Jefferson Davis, as we have seen, justified slavery as a divine institution because of Noah's curse on the descendants of Ham.

2

It is easy a hundred years after John Brown and Jefferson Davis, when man has arrived at that wisdom which may destroy him, to smile a little patronizingly at their beliefs. Yet those beliefs—however self-serving or debased on occasion—had when elaborated into theology a fullness of metaphysic, a subtlety of shading, an all-inclusiveness of statement as to man's fate and meaning every bit as complete, and perhaps as perceptive poetically, as most of man's intellectual structures. Through this theological synthesis Christians had reconciled man's urge for self-destruction with a chance for his salvation, his evil with his aspirations, the iron boundaries of a restraint he could not leap with his firm determination to do so. Those who espoused these beliefs were not intellectual illiterates. Jonathan Edwards, for example, the American Calvinist of the eighteenth century who was John Brown's theological mentor, might well have held his own in any debate as to necessity and determinism with the very latest of physicists timidly positing God on the basis of the principle of indeterminacy.

There was scarce a facet of John Brown's life uninfluenced by that rich tapestry of early human striving known as the Bible. "With this book," he once wrote of himself, he became "very familiar, & possessed a most unusual memory of its entire contents." [17] But it was not his knowledge of the Bible that was unusual. It was his belief in it. He himself seemed to regard his belief in the Bible as another proof of its validity, since he felt he was so naturally skeptical, so inherently doubtful, that only words that came from the Lord were capable of the miracle of making him believe. But even his credulity might have been unexceptionable had he not tried to merge his biblical beliefs with his daily actions. This effort was the source of both his strengths and weaknesses, as when he sought out the poor and fed them because "Inasmuch as ye did it not to one of the least of these, ye did it not to me," and whipped his boys, the tears running down his face, because "He who spareth the rod hateth his son."

In a sense John Brown believed in the Bible not because he agreed with it but because it agreed with him. When it did not he rejected it, as in those instances wherein it seemed to endorse human slavery. It was upon his own natural feelings that his actions were often based and when there was a coincidence between his actions and the Bible's words it may have been partly the result of the stern, Bible-based Puritan culture in which his family had lived during the centuries following the Reformation.

In a rural age the Bible had a persuasiveness, even a familiarity as of scenes half-remembered, it could never have to later city dwellers. It spoke directly to American farmers within the terms of their experience. If the lives of the patriarchs of old were based on cattle and sheep, if they sought water as if it were gold, and feared the drought and locust as if they were the plague, American farmers of 1850 also knew these fears and knew cattle and sheep, too. If the shepherds of the Old Testament regarded Babylon and Nineveh as sores of iniquity, and cried for relief from the moneylender and those who ground the faces of the poor, the American farmer also knew the fear of city ways with their sharpers and their bankers and their holders of mortgages.

3

And yet perhaps the high prestige and omnipresence of the Bible in American life, particularly during the first half of the nineteenth century, was more primarily based on the human need for story, for color, for tales of man's strife and striving, for the contest of the good guys against the bad. The Bible gave to Americans then the equivalent of the soap opera and the Western of later years but gave it in the form of matchless literature whose sponsor was not beer or gasoline but God. On thousands of lonely farms, in windy log cabins stretched the extent of the whole frontier, the Bible was the only book read, the only written drama experienced, the only source of story and suspense, the only sustained description of the human predicament.

Whatever the reasons for its compelling influence, there was perhaps never a time in history that men tried more ardently to base their lives on the written word. They believed with St. John that "In the beginning was the Word, and the Word was with God and the Word was God." If that Scripture seems a contradictory jumble now, to many Americans then it seemed a body of coherent principle. Never did a scientist try more earnestly to give unity to theory and practice than John Brown tried to unite the truths of Scripture with the actions of life. It was to the word that was God he was referring, however indirectly, when he said, denying that he was motivated by revenge or self-seeking, "I act on principle." It was to the Bible he was referring when he wrote in his last letter to his family that it was "the *Helm* or *Compass*" helping us to avoid the errors of "our own vague theories framed up while our *prejudices* are excited; or our Vanity worked up to its highest pitch." [18]

Still, the Bible may have had a stronger appeal to some than the appeal of morality, individual or social. Much that was strange or exotic in a hard plain American life was found in the Bible. Here were cities whose people were "clothed in fine linen, and purple, and scarlet, and decked with gold, and precious stones, and pearls," the like of which was never to be found in Ohio or even Connecticut. Here were temples and walls garnished with jasper and sapphire and chalcedony and emerald and topaz and amethyst that did not remind of farmhouse or log cabin or even the new county courthouse with its large brass spittoons. In its pages there was never a sunbonnet or bustle but rather the soft seductive loveliness of Solomon's full-breasted maidens:

THY NAVEL IS LIKE A ROUND GOBLET, WHICH WANTETH NOT
LIQUOR: THY BELLY IS LIKE AN HEAP OF WHEAT SET ABOUT WITH
LILIES.

THY TWO BREASTS ARE LIKE TWO YOUNG ROES THAT ARE TWINS.
. . . HOW FAIR AND HOW PLEASANT ART THOU, O LOVE, FOR DE-
LIGHTS!

And in its pages there were great feasts of bullocks and calves and fat lambs and red wine, and stories of fornications and bloody battles and whorings after strange Gods—all lovely forbidden sins not often encountered down by the creek in the north 20 acres or anywhere else in pioneer American farm life.

The Bible was, too, a source of creative imagination, of that heightened inner life which comes to man whether from Shakespeare or Jeremiah as he lives the lives of other men faced with peril and heartbreak and failure after mighty effort. For the Bible is a human story showing Samson's helpless lust for Delilah, his weakness for that snare she baited for him with her own sweet deceitful flesh, as well as his final maddened desperation as with his last strength he crushes himself and his tormentors beneath the falling temple. This was a favorite story of John Brown, and there would come a time when, lamenting the death of his sons at Harper's Ferry, he was as David, the King, weeping for his slain son, Absalom. Absalom too had been slain in battle and the King on hearing of his son's death "went up to the chamber over the gate, and wept: and as he went, thus he said, O my son Absalom, my son, my son Absalom! would God I had died for thee, O Absalom, my son, my son!"

4

All of this, and much more from Genesis to Revelations, had a strange immediacy for John Brown. It determined his occupation as "a practical shepherd," or so he thought, by arousing in him as he read of Judea's patriarchs "a kind of enthusiastic longing" to be of those who like them tended the sheep. And as he read of Israel's young bullocks and rams without blemish and of herds of fine cattle and flocks of numberless sheep and of vineyards and olive trees and "the first fruits of all fruit of all trees" and of offerings of corn, it gave him that "great liking" for farming as a holy calling and for "fine Cattle, Horses, Sheep; & Swine" which never left him.[19]

During his early and middle years, he apparently read the Bible as one who sought primarily personal salvation, who hoped to avoid Hell and gain Heaven; but as the problem dividing the nation, the problem of slavery, increasingly occupied the center of his thoughts and being, the Bible increasingly possessed for him a social as well as individual significance. More and more it became, particularly during his last four years, a preachment for liberty and again and again he studied its words, consciously searching for ammunition in the fight against slavery, marking those verses he felt spoke for justice to the poor and freedom for the enslaved.

Even during his last days in a Virginia jail, his feet fettered and chained, his hair now quite white, he leaned over the Bible, marking the passages which he believed at once justified himself and proclaimed liberty throughout the land. It was then, his old hawk face pressed near pages difficult to see in the dim light of his cell, that he underlined such verses as these:

> AND YE SHALL . . . PROCLAIM LIBERTY THROUGHOUT ALL THE LAND UNTO ALL THE INHABITANTS THEREOF: IT SHALL BE A JUBILE UNTO YOU; AND YE SHALL RETURN EVERY MAN UNTO HIS POSSESSION, AND YE SHALL RETURN EVERY MAN UNTO HIS FAMILY.

> REMEMBER THEM THAT ARE IN BONDS, AS BOUND WITH THEM. . . .

> CRY ALOUD, SPARE NOT, LIFT UP THY VOICE LIKE A TRUMPET, AND SHEW MY PEOPLE THEIR TRANSGRESSION, AND THE HOUSE OF JACOB THEIR SINS.

> IS NOT THIS THE FAST THAT I HAVE CHOSEN? TO LOOSE THE BANDS OF WICKEDNESS, TO UNDO THE HEAVY BURDENS, AND TO LET THE OPPRESSED GO FREE, AND THAT YE BREAK EVERY YOKE?

> WOE UNTO THEM THAT CALL EVIL GOOD, AND GOOD EVIL. . . .

> THE SPIRIT OF THE LORD GOD IS UPON ME; BECAUSE THE LORD HATH ANOINTED ME TO PREACH GOOD TIDINGS UNTO THE MEEK; HE HATH SENT ME TO BIND UP THE BROKENHEARTED, TO PROCLAIM LIBERTY TO THE CAPTIVES, AND THE OPENING OF THE PRISON TO THEM THAT ARE BOUND.[20]

5

As John Brown became more involved in the struggle against slavery he increasingly read the Bible as one who wanted specific help in a specific fight. For that matter, there came a time when he could not glance at a map of the South or read a census report or the life of Marion or Napoleon or Spartacus without thinking of his great plan against slavery and it was small wonder that he sought help, too, from that book which was his staff of life. When he read of Gideon's victorious tactics in his battle against the Midianites in the

Book of Judges, he stored them in his mind for future use, and when he read of Samson he wondered if he too would perish in the crashing pillars if he succeeded in pulling down the temple of slavery.

But of all in the Bible it was Moses, the liberator of the chosen people from Egypt's bondage, whom John Brown loved best and studied most. If he thought the Bible the revealed word of God, not the least of his reasons may have been that the center of the Old Testament, as if by some miracle, concerned the United States of America and slavery, if God's rebuke of human bondage still had relevance and John Brown, for one, had no doubt of that. He yearned for the strength of Moses, and his communion with the Lord God Almighty. Although he always seemed as practical as a horse trader there were times when he would leave his camp in Kansas, his young men nearby, and penetrate further into the wilderness until he was alone. Then he would pray and wrestle with his God even as Moses of old. Despite his matter-of-fact attitude, he sometimes dared to think that perhaps he had been chosen as a liberator, for as he knew of his own purposes he also knew that the enslaved Negro people talked and sang of the bondage of Egypt and of the year of jubilee and the crossing of the Jordan under a new Moses into a new promised land.

"A STRANGELY PROPHETIC LOOK NOW"

I

By many, John Brown is seen only as represented in Curry's portrait, his beard blowing in the wind, his arms outstretched in violent appeal, his mouth wide in battle cry; but there were those of his contemporaries who viewed him not only as a fighter but as one of the time's most perceptive students of American slavery. They saw him not as violence incarnate alone, nor only as the act supreme, but rather as one who had pondered and thought and ruminated on slavery and how to end it for some twenty years before he attacked it in Virginia.

It was because of both the national crisis and his own long thoughts about it that John Brown seemed plausible to such men of affairs and public experience as Theodore Parker, Gerrit Smith, and Samuel Gridley Howe when he outlined his plan to move against slavery. For years he had read every statement concerning slavery whether for or against that he could come by and for years he had pondered its beginning, growth, and expansion on the American continent, just as later, after deciding on instigating and leading a slave insurrection in Virginia, to be followed by guerrilla warfare in the larger South, he read of Marion's guerrilla exploits in the American Revolution, of the Spanish guerrillas acting against Napoleon, and of the servile rebellion of Spartacus against the power of ancient Rome. His was more than only an instinctive striking out against what he hated, if years of reading a remarkable press, Garrison's *Liberator*, the *Anti-Slavery Standard*, the *National Era, Frederick Douglass' Paper*, the *New York Tribune*, and other anti-slavery organs could arm a man with principle as well as facts.[21]

2

Knowing his literacy in the anti-slavery controversy, there were those of John Brown's associates who regarded him as something more than mere personalized aggression. W. A. Phillips, special correspondent of the *New York Tribune* in Kansas, and considered in his time one of the most astute of the nation's newspaper reporters, believed that long and close thought on the subject of slavery had given John Brown an insight into the peculiar institution and the designs of its proponents matched by few Americans. Phillips, later an officer in the Union Army and a member of Congress, felt, moreover, that John Brown's passionate identification with the problem had resulted at last in the gift of prophecy, permitting him to see the future with an accuracy denied to most.

Phillips based his estimate on three separate interviews with John Brown during an association over a three-year period, but particularly on the third interview given him in Lawrence, Kansas, in 1859. Recalling this last interview Phillips writes:

The most important interview, the one that has peculiar historical significance, was the last I ever had with him. It occurred during the same year of the Harper's Ferry affair, although several months before. Now we could hear of him in New England, now in Canada, now in Ohio or Pennsylvania. I had lost track of him, when one day Kagi [one of John Brown's lieutenants] came to my house in Lawrence, and told me that the Old Man had arrived and was at the Whitney House, and wished to see me. At first I refused to go, and sent word by Kagi that as he never took my advice I did not see any use in giving him any. Kagi soon returned, and said that the Old Man must see me; he was going away, and might never see me again.

I found him in a small room at the Whitney House, then one of the Lawrence hotels, down towards the river. He had changed a little. There was in the expression of his face something even more dignified than usual; his eye was brighter, and the absorbing and consuming thoughts that were within him seemed to be growing out all over him. He evinced his customary caution by telling Kagi to go out and close the door, and watch on the outside, for fear that someone should come and listen. Then he began.

He sketched the history of American slavery from its beginnings in the colonies, and referred to the States that were able to shake it off. He recalled many circumstances that I had forgotten, or had never heard of. He said the founders of the republic were all opposed to slavery, and that the whole spirit and genius of the American constitution antagonized it, and contemplated its early overthrow. He said this remained the dominant sentiment for the first quarter of a century of the republic. Afterwards slavery became more profitable, and as it did the desire grew to extend and increase it.

The condition of the enslaved negroes steadily became worse, and the despotic necessities of a more cruel system constantly pressed on the degraded slaves. Rights they at first possessed were taken from them. The little of domestic happiness and independence that had been left them was taken away. The [foreign] slave-trade being ended, it was profitable to breed negroes [domestically] for sale. Gradually the pecuniary interests that rested on slavery seized the power of the government. Public opinion opposed to slavery was placed under ban. The politicians of the South became slavery propagandists, and the politicians of the North trimmers.

When the religious and moral sentiment of the country indicated a desire to check this alarming growth, a threat of secession was uttered, and appeals were made not to risk the perpetuation of this glorious republic by fanatical antislavery-ism. Then began an era of political compromises, and men full of professions of love of country were willing, for peace, to sacrifice everything for which the republic was founded.

"And now," he went on, "we have reached a point where nothing but war can settle the question. Had they succeeded in Kansas, they would have gained a power that would have given them permanently the upper hand, and it would have been the death-knell of republicanism in America. They are checked, but not beaten. They never intend to relinquish the machinery of this government into the hands of the opponents of slavery.

"It has taken them more than half a century to get it, and they know its significance too well to give it up. If the Republican Party elects its President next year, there will be war. The moment they are unable to control they will go out, and as a rival nation alongside they will get the countenance and aid of the European nations, until American republicanism and freedom are overthrown."

I have endeavoured to quote him, but it is quite impossible to quote such a conversation accurately. I well remember all its vital essentials and its outlines. He had been more observant than he had credit for being. The whole powers of his mind (and they were great) had been given to one subject. . . .

3

"All this has a strangely prophetic look to me now," Phillips later wrote. "Then it simply appeared incredible, or the dream and vagary of a man who had allowed one idea to carry him away. I told him he surely was mistaken, and had confounded everyday occurrences with treacherous designs."

"No," he said, and I remember this part distinctly,—"no, the war is not over. It is a treacherous lull before the storm. We are on the eve of one of the greatest wars in history, and I fear slavery will triumph, and there will be an end to all aspirations for human freedom. For my part, I drew my sword in Kansas when they attacked us, and I will never sheathe it until this war is over. Our best people do not understand the danger. They are besotted. They have compromised so long that they think principles of right and wrong have no more any power on this earth."

My impression then was that it was his purpose to carry on incursions on the borders of the free and slave States, and I said to him:

"Let us suppose that all you say is true. If we keep companies on the one side, they will keep them on the other. Trouble will multiply, there will be collision, which will produce the very state of affairs you deprecate. That would lead to war, and to some extent we should be responsible for it. Better trust events. If there is virtue enough in this people to deserve a free government, they will maintain it."

"You forget the fearful wrongs that are carried on in the name of government and law."

The Old Man apparently wished to recruit Phillips to his approaching expedition against slavery in Virginia, if not his personal participation, then his support as a journalist. He turned to servile revolts, spoke of the proven courage of the American slave and then passed to Spartacus and the slave revolt he had unsuccessfully led against Rome. But the newspaperman argued against the Old Man's plan, reminding him, he writes, that the "Roman slaves were warlike people" while "the negroes were a peaceful, inoffensive race," apparently "incapable of resentment or reprisal."

"You have not studied them right," John Brown said, "and you have not studied them long enough. Human nature is the same everywhere."

But Phillips continued to oppose the Old Man's plan, telling him "I feared he would lead the young men with him into some desperate enterprise, where they would be imprisoned and disgraced."

John Brown appeared hurt. "He rose," Phillips writes.

"Well," he said, "I thought I could get you to understand this. I do not wonder at it. The world is very pleasant to you. . . ."

I rose somewhat offended, and said, "Captain, if you thought this, why did you send for me?" and walked to the door.

He followed me and laid his hand on my shoulder, and when I turned to him he took both my hands in his. I could see that tears stood on his hard, bronzed cheeks. "No," he said, "we must not part thus. I wanted to see you and tell you how it appeared to me. With the help of God, I will do what I believe to be best." He held my hands firmly in his stern, hard hands, leaned forward and kissed me on the cheek, and I never saw him again.[22]

HIGH TIDE

I

If the country's style and temperament during the thirty years before the Civil War was in fact sufficiently intense to be a factor in precipitating it, that does not alter the more important fact that gigantic matters of substance were dividing the nation. Still, the exhibitionistic aggression of the period's antagonists was not irrelevant in bringing nearer the approaching conflict. If the time was one of gallant gesture and broad drama, of manly weeping and facing death whether on the field of honor or of martyrdom, of Weld, the proud buccaneer of the Lord, or young Wise, the dauntless duelist for his father's honor, neither Weld nor Wise indicate anything of pose or falsity, for Americans actually had then, as has been suggested, a consummate ability for confronting the ultimate. Rather, the wide and handsome gesture, the unequivocating word so current before the war, should be taken as valid, as evidence of the mettle and temper of an age so aggressively romantic that conflict was not easy to avoid. Even Old John Brown, however savage for the Lord, was at heart a romantic who could take the stance dramatic, his hard bronze cheek wet with tears, his voice a manly tremolo as he said farewell forever, at once the military deacon, the plain old farmer, and the American Moses.

Yet it was, in the last analysis, slavery and not temperament that caused Harvard graduates and eminent divines and men of wealth to assault courthouses, guns in hand, defying all the power of the federal government, as they sought to free and deliver fugitive slaves. It was slavery, and not the legend of the Southland, it was slaves, the actual human property valued by 1860 at an average of $1,000 per adult male worker, that spurred plantation owners to a counterrevolution in defense of their vast human property worth some $2 billion. It was slavery that impelled John Brown, as he traversed the large and varied land, sometimes on foot, sometimes by canalboat or in the new steam cars, looking longingly at the new factories and the new towns that sometimes advanced into cities and sometimes reverted to the windblown grass, it was slavery that finally forced him from the efforts for the conventional success for which he often ached to a success more strange.

For whatever the mores of the time, the huge underlying fact that made for crisis beyond all subjectivity, and finally behind all sectional, economic, and political rivalry, was the four million Americans held in chattel bondage. Years after American slavery had been destroyed by a liberating war, it became somewhat the fashion to say that the Civil War had resulted from a failure in statesmanship and that the peculiar institution could have been, and should have been, compromised out of existence. This diagnosis became popular even though the problem had been compromised in fact and in life for almost a century, for the eighty-five years between 1776 and 1861. Yet slavery grew constantly stronger, always expanding, seeking and expecting its Manifest Destiny in all the territories of the West, in Mexico, Central America, and the islands of the Caribbean. It was compromised for eighty-five years not only in politics but in the minds of Americans everywhere, forced to accept a fatal division between profession and practice, to speak for liberty while acquiescing in slavery, to profess democracy while practicing tyranny, to suffer quietly the agonies of conscience, as Emerson did, because one feared to act.

2

Emerson waked at night, we may recall, bemoaning that he had not thrown himself into the fight against slavery, and there were others than Emerson who could not sleep. Thoreau suffered a lifetime of tension in an effort to believe, and act on the belief, that one might have more pressing goals than the abolition of slavery. But slavery would not let him be. Thrice the issue of slavery impeached and reversed him, forcing him to abandon the personal pursuits whose rights he had defended as primary, and enter instead, at times of great national crisis, upon the public field of battle. John Brown's action, as we shall see, was the transforming climax of Thoreau's life, and Thoreau's defense of Brown, his recognition of him as the greatest of transcendentalists, perhaps another insistence that one must act as well as write in order to transcend. Thoreau had always thought, as Milton had, that a heroic poem could only be written by one who had led a heroic life, but it was not easy to lead such a life in reference to the great issue of slavery.

It was John Brown's stand, of course, that slavery could not be compromised but must be forcibly destroyed. Historically, that is, judging him by what actually happened, which is perhaps as proper a criterion as any, he has been proved right. It was this position, and the conviction of increasing numbers that Brown was right, that gave him by 1858 power over some of the strongest and most influential Americans of his time. It was because they felt him right that the Old Man could gather together at the Kennedy Farm House, where they lurked poised for the attack on Virginia's slavery, the twenty-one generous and high-spirited young men, black as well as white, some of whom feared they were going to their deaths. Even now in the yellowing pages of their letters to long-vanished wives and sweethearts one can hear, scarcely muted despite a century gone, despite brave plans for children who were never born, the heartbreak cry for life of these young men who so wanted to live but felt they had to die if necessary in this attack on slavery. Most of them did die and at last it was as if the Old Man and his struggle were a whirlpool, dragging into the center of his own tragedy, if tragedy it were, half the great of the North and some of the greatest names of the nation. Either because of his own force, or of the imperatives of the crisis that was dividing the country, John Brown, first and last, brought to his cause as friends or allies, enemies or witnesses of his death, not only Emerson, Thoreau, Alcott, Douglass, Higginson, and Phillips; not only the young men who fought and died at his side; but Robert E. Lee, J. E. B. Stuart, Stonewall Jackson, Jefferson Davis, Edmund Ruffin, Senator Mason, and Governor Wise of Virginia, as well as the John Wilkes Booth who was later to kill President Lincoln. As John Brown awaited his execution, Theodore Parker lay dying in Rome, Frederick Douglass was in flight for his life, Gerrit Smith, his large wealth of little power now, was willing himself into insanity as a means of escaping from the responsibility that was his, while the great Howe, the Chevalier, was fleeing to Canada. All of these and many more were involved until at last, when the Civil War erupted, it seemed as if there were not an American, man, woman, or child, who was not somehow involved in the fate of John Brown.

And yet it was not John Brown who was primarily responsible for all this. Changes had gradually matured until they had the force of one of history's tidal waves. John Brown was not the wave. Whatever his singular impact upon his time, he, too, was borne along by it, his ideas or plans having little effect until they were carried by the great, forward-running dynamic. The wave, the surging tidal wave of events, by 1859 had all the strength of thousands, of hundreds of thousands of people, slowly gathering in force and conviction. It had the impersonal strength of a new and growing industrial order, which required the whole country for its fulfillment and could not be dammed up by a social anachronism, the plantation system, barring it from the South and attempting to deny it the great new West. It was composed of conscience and economic force, of the resistance, however passive or violent, of the almost four million Americans held in bondage, of the defiance of the government of the thousands forming the Underground Railroad, of the ardent human desire for opportunity in the great West where opportunity could not live with slavery.

It had begun to roll in the 1830's with such events as the martyrdom of Elijah Lovejoy when John Brown made his first public declaration against slavery, with the long fight of John Quincy Adams in the House of Representatives to restore the right of petition so as to include even the thousands petitioning for the abolition of slavery. But John Brown was not the wave. He was only its crest, breaking against the power of slavery at Harper's Ferry, and still marking for Americans a kind of high tide.

PART TWO

A PILGRIM'S PROGRESS

1800–1850

IX

In the Beginning

WHEN JOHN BROWN WAS BORN at the beginning of the nineteenth century, the United States was only twenty-four years old, if its birth was dated from the Declaration of Independence, only twelve if reckoned from the ratification of the Constitution. The horse, the wheel, and the wind were still almost the only means of transportation and life to most was nearly as innocent of material improvement as in the time of Charlemagne. The Saxon farmers of the eighth century, writes Henry Adams, would have found little in the condition of American farmers at the end of the eighteenth century with which they were unfamiliar.[1] The country in its vast preponderance still belonged to the Indian and the beaver, neither of whom had changed its immemorial ecology.

In 1800, the country's population of five million, almost one million of whom were Negro slaves, clung, for the most part, to the eastern seaboard, the expanse of the continent stretching westward beyond the Appalachians nearly as empty of men as it had been before the coming of Columbus.* But this primitive aspect of the country might have been likened to the calm just before an explosion, a population explosion. Within the lifetime of the infant just born, the number of people in his country would increase by 500 per cent. Communities which were frontier stockades threatened by Indians during John Brown's boyhood were considerable cities at his death, such as

---

* The only considerable exceptions were in Kentucky, whose 180,000 whites and 40,000 slaves made it the largest community west of the Appalachians, and in Tennessee, where some 94,000 whites had settled with their 14,000 Negro slaves.

Chicago, Cleveland, and Detroit. If his life was controlled by the great conflict of his time between slavery and its opponents, a counterpoint to this was the pyramiding of inventions and industries creating the opportunities of wealth for which Brown yearned.

Living from the end of the Revolutionary era to the beginnings of the Civil War, there had been only two Presidents before his birth, Washington and Adams. His years spanned the administrations of Jefferson, Madison, and Monroe, of John Quincy Adams, Andrew Jackson, and Martin Van Buren, of William H. Harrison, John Tyler, and James K. Polk, of Zachary Taylor, Millard Fillmore, Pierce, and Buchanan. But they also included the beginnings of the railroad, the steamship, and the telegraph, the development of McCormick's reaper and Colt's revolver, of Kelly's conversion of pig iron into steel and Drake's Pennsylvania oil wells.

John Brown, no less than most other Americans of his day, admired invention and industrial enterprise. He, too, thirsted for wealth and business success until larger matters at length possessed him. After all, he was the contemporary of the millionaires Commodore Vanderbilt, John D. Rockefeller, and Jay Cooke, as well as of Henry Thoreau, William Lloyd Garrison, and Theodore Parker. The same standards that formed Cooke as a boy on the Western Reserve and marked Rockefeller as a young clerk in Cleveland also left their stamp on their fellow Ohioan, John Brown, although in his case it was not indelible.

A CONNECTICUT YANKEE

I

In 1800 when John Brown was born in Connecticut, that state, whatever the hardships of the limitless wilderness to the west, was an unusually pleasant place. Along and near its coast, at Derby on the Housatonic, at New London, and on the Mystic, there was scarce a cove or inlet that did not contain its busy shipyard. Rather than the fumes of later industry, there was the clean, dusty smell of sawed lumber, the sweet, sharp smell of the sea, damp with salt. Often they became as one in the radiant sunlight of summer days and when it was hot there was added the smell of resin oozing from the baking pines.

Everywhere was the cloppity-clop of jogging horses, the keening of wagon wheels against the gravelly roads; and out on the Sound, there was the blossoming canvas of schooner and sloop, bark and brigantine, great bursts of white sliding over the moving blue with only the wind for power. Everywhere, too, along the coast and near the shipyards, there was the mewling cry of circling gulls, the soprano shriek of the whipsaw, the metallic clang of hammers echoing thinly on the air, with the little double beat on the anvil between each stroke.

It was pleasant, too, away from the coast and in the interior, toward the little state's northwest where the white spires of the meetinghouses reached above the green of elms in Torrington and Litchfield, in Walcottville and Winsted. It was from here that the foothills of the Berkshires, edging down from Massachusetts, a series of hills cleft by granite and thick with pine, could first be seen curving against the sky. But if the region was beautiful, its soil was rocky, farming difficult, and the villages small. Despite the sawmills and the grist mills of the Naugatuck, the area did not have the prosperity of the coast. That may have been why Owen Brown, John Brown's father, who lived in Torrington, was soon to move west to Connecticut's Western Reserve, in Ohio, which was receiving its first settlers even as his son John was being born, on May 9, 1800.

Ordinarily at such times, when a child was born, at least in the settled East, a midwife was sent for. Perhaps, with her arrival, Owen Brown retired to the barn. There, amid its shadows and the smell of hay and straw, the oxen calmly revolving their jaws, their eyes placid and indifferent to Owen Brown's fear, he may have waited for the coming event. It would not of necessity be joyous. Women died frequently in childbirth. Owen Brown may well have felt that death was an outcome he could not endure, for he was to write that in marrying Ruth Mills on February 13, 1793, he had found the beginning of life, or as he phrased it, "that was the beginning of days for me." "I never had any person [with] such an ascendancy over my conduct and my life," he wrote on the same occasion. "This she had without the least appearance of usurpation or dictation, and if I have been respected in the world, I must ascribe it more to her than to any other person." [2]

Waiting uneasily by the side of his oxen, he may have moved after a time to the barn door, looking at the unpainted two-story frame house that contained his wife, its roof slanting sharply at the back over the large kitchen with its fireplace in the wall farthest from the kitchen door. Owen Brown was twenty-nine when his son John was born, a lanky, deep-chested man with long, strong arms and large ears extending from a white, apprehensive face, his eyes a pale blue, and as gentle and benign in their gaze as those of his oxen. Usually reserved, he so enjoyed singing hymns and lifting up his voice in prayer that they might be called his only recreations. Except when addressing

God he had trouble in releasing his words with ordinary swiftness. This tendency often made him hesitate, or try again, or even stutter, a failing he occasionally used purposely to gain a laugh which always astonished those regarding the plain, serious expression carefully held while making his little joke. A tanner, a shoemaker, and a farmer simultaneously rather than alternately, he exuded a kind of solid, responsible benevolence, sometimes a trifle worried when things went well for he knew that God was hard, and tried to rejoice in it.

He had a weakness for the young, the younger the better, and invariably complimented them with the temperance natural to his speech as being "very forward, thrifty children." When his first son Salmon died in 1796, he remembered it for years as "a time of sore trial for us." The house seemed so lonely without the little boy that Owen and Ruth adopted a boy of two, one Levi Blakeslee, whom they raised with their own children. Another son died at birth, but in 1798 a daughter was born. If he was uneasy as he waited on this ninth day of May, the time would come when he had cause to be, when after waiting long hours he was called to the side of a dying wife and her just-born daughter. "All my earthly prospects appeared to be blasted," he later wrote, and if his marriage to Ruth Mills had been "the beginning of days for me," her death appeared to her husband and her children as the end of them.[3]

2

But on this morning in May all went well. Owen was gratified that his son had been born just a hundred years after the birth of the child's great-grandfather, who had also been born in Connecticut and whose name had also been John Brown. Although few warned more persistently against the sin of pride than Owen, at least in later letters to his children, frequently repeating variations of the words of Ecclesiastes, "Vanity of vanities, saith the Preacher, vanity of vanities; all *is* vanity," it is nevertheless possible that he had some quiet pride of family. The first of Owen's kin to arrive in this country, or so he believed, came in the *Mayflower* in 1620.*

---

* Modern genealogists often hold that the Peter Browne who arrived on the *Mayflower* was not the founder of John Brown's family in America, the founder being, they say, a later Peter Browne who arrived in Connecticut about 1650. However, other investigators, such as the Reverend Clarence S. Gee, of Lockport, N.Y., an authority on the Brown family genealogy, believe that the *Mayflower* Peter Browne was John Brown's direct ancestor. George F. Willison, another student of the *Mayflower* and its Pilgrims, declares in *Saints and Strangers* (New York, 1945, p. 133) that Peter Browne of the *Mayflower* was the founder of John Brown's family in America.

His own father, Captain John Brown, as none remembered better than he, had died while in the service of his country in the American Revolution, the captain of Train Band Nine of the Eighteenth Connecticut Regiment. The newborn baby's maternal grandfather, Gideon Mills, had also served in the Revolution as a lieutenant, and now as a man of fifty was emigrating to the Western Reserve where the Brown family would soon follow. The infant's great-grandfather, the Reverend Gideon Mills, was a well-known Connecticut preacher and a graduate of Yale. The Mills family had arrived in Connecticut from Holland during the first half of the seventeenth century, almost as early as the Pilgrims had arrived in Massachusetts.

3

Owen had never forgotten the hardships and hunger his family had endured after his father's death during the War for Independence. "His death," he was to write later to his children, "brought hard times on our family. My mother was left with ten children at the time of my father's death and one soon after making eleven in all. . . . She was the best of mothers, active and sensible, she did all that could be expected of a mother." Most of the younger men had gone to war, and the mother and her children, seven of whom were girls, had to struggle alone with the rocky obdurate earth from which they gained their food. "For want of help we lost our crops," Owen continued, "and then our cattle, and so became poor. . . ."

"I very well remember the dreadful winter of 78 & 79," he continued. He was eight years old that winter.

The snow began to come in November, when the waters were very low and [there was] storm after storm until the snow was very deep. Our hogs and sheep would get buried up and we had to dig them out. Wood could not be drawn with teams and so had to be carried on mens shoulders, they going on snow shoes until paths were made hard enough to draw wood on hand sleds. Milling of grain could not be had only by going a great distance. Our family were driven to the necessity of pounding corn for food. The snow at this time was said to be five feet or more in the woods; we lost almost all of our stock of cattle, hogs and sheep that winter, and were reduced very low.[4]

As he looked at his little son in the cradle, he may well have hoped that he would escape such troubles and yet none knew better than Owen Brown that this world was but a testing.

"HUNG BE THE HEAVENS IN SCARLET!"

I

If Owen Brown sometimes wondered about his son's future, he might, had he been prophetic enough, have perceived something of its direction, and the country's too, in an event which happened in the year of John Brown's birth. That year of 1800 marked the election of Thomas Jefferson as the third President of the United States. But more importantly, perhaps, it was also the year of the Gabriel Slave Rebellion in Henrico County, Virginia, an occurrence which played its part in the slow shaping of men's minds and in placing American development on a course which would eventuate in sectional collision.

The rebellion near Richmond in Mr. Jefferson's Commonwealth gained its name from its leader, one Gabriel, the property of Thomas Prosser, a slave of twenty-four years, 6 feet 2 inches in height and described as "a fellow of courage and intellect above his rank in life." He and his friends had intended, one of them said, "to purchase a piece of silk for a flag, on which they would have written 'death or liberty.' " [5] Jefferson himself had marched behind such a banner.

Some one thousand slaves rallied behind this black revolutionary seeking freedom for his oppressed people, but a great storm, washing out roads and bridges, blocked their advance on Richmond, and, in the confusion, their army of liberation was smashed. Jefferson's protégé, James Monroe, then Governor of Virginia, later to be the fifth President of the United States, interviewed Gabriel in an attempt to get the names of his fellow conspirators. But Gabriel adopted the policy of another slave, in a similar revolt, who said, "Die silent as you shall see me do." On October 7, 1800, Gabriel and fifteen others were hanged. Still more were later executed, one of them declaring to the court when the judge asked him what he had to say for himself:

I have nothing more to offer than what General Washington would have had to offer, had he been taken by the British and put to trial by them. I have adventured my life in endeavouring to obtain the liberty of my countrymen, and am a willing sacrifice to their cause: and I beg, as a favour, that I may be immediately led to execution. I know that you have pre-determined to shed my blood, why then all this mockery of a trial? [6]

The infant in Connecticut came in time, when grown to a man, to ponder such statements in forming his estimate of the black man. But Thomas Jefferson had to face them then, and in doing so he wrote to a friend, "We are truly to be pitied," yet the pity Jefferson asked for has seldom been accorded.[7] To give it would be to face the full implications of his life-long dilemma as to slavery. To proclaim to the world that all men have the inalienable right to rebellion against oppression and to execute those who exercise this right is not a formula for peace of mind.

2

In commenting on such rebellions, Jefferson wrote of his wonder at the American who would fight for his own liberty and "inflict on his fellow men, a bondage, one hour of which is fraught with more misery, than ages of that which he rose in rebellion to oppose." Again, he wrote, "I tremble for my country when I reflect that God is just; that His justice cannot sleep forever. . . . The Almighty has no attribute which can take sides with us in such a contest." But the stubborn, essential dilemma remained, for "as it is," he said, "we have the wolf by the ears, and we can neither hold him, nor safely let him go. Justice is in one scale, and self preservation in the other." [8]

In the President's home at Monticello there was an engraving of the federal armory at Harper's Ferry, where the infant just born far to the north would near the climax of a life not unconnected with the problems that troubled Jefferson. Often Mr. Jefferson, author of a Declaration asserting the equal right of liberty for all men and the owner of some two hundred human beings, would ride the Virginia countryside, and at least once he climbed the height overlooking the junction of the Potomac and the Shenandoah where the Harper's Ferry armory would be built in 1796 and where John Brown's sons would die.[9]

Looking out over the west, seeing, he wrote, "the smooth blue horizon at an infinite distance," Mr. Jefferson may have had, as he sometimes indicates, some prescience of the blood which would crimson the waters beneath him. During almost the whole of his life slavery had been the painful paradox impeaching his years and often he had acted to restrict or end it, but end it he could not.[10] Frequently, he predicted civil war or slave insurrection and he had known the latter.[11] But he could not, of course, have known anything of the child born in Connecticut nor of a later Declaration of Independence, taking the well-known phrases he had used but directing them toward the liberation of a people which had not been included in Jefferson's words. It would end, this new wildly written Declaration of the future, with the prophetic exclamation, "Hung be the Heavens in Scarlet!" [12]

THE ROAD WEST

I

Biographers have remarked on John Brown's restlessness, on his many moves to new places, as if this were a trait peculiar to himself, but his time was almost universally marked by the belief that around the next bend the valley would be more lush, the grass more green than any that lay behind. Many of his generation were formed in part by moving West, their earliest major experience the revolving wheels, the creaking straining of the Conestoga wagon wrenching over rocks and stumps, the yoked oxen plodding ahead until the rhythm of their gait seemed a part of nature itself, as everlasting as the hills.

Among John Brown's earliest memories was the road West, breaking camp at dawn, the long day's trek, the campfire at night, the wolf heard far away, the stir of the wind in the darkness, and then on again in the morning, pushing endlessly forward to the next turn, the next bend, the next mountain top, certain that the land ahead must be better than any seen before, as the land beyond it would be better still. There were times when this feeling seemed a permanent part of John Brown's character, although his moves were not always dictated by restlessness or an everlasting optimism for whatever was the latest of his ventures. He had his depressions, too, and one of them was so critical as almost to rob him of his fame.

2

John Brown was only five years old when he began to experience the excitement of what lay beyond. It was in 1805 that he left Connecticut with his family for Ohio's Western Reserve, a serious little boy cantering along on horseback near the ox-drawn wagon containing his family's goods. It was his duty to help Levi Blakeslee, eleven years old and his adopted brother, to herd the cows and perhaps a stringy steer or two to what was then part of the country's westernmost frontier. He was proud of his task and may have felt mature even beyond the successful meeting of this important responsibility, for already he had known sin and suffered from it and was a better being for the experience.

He had been "tempted by Three Large Brass Pins belonging to a girl who lived in the family & he stole them." But that was years ago before going West, before he had come to the maturity of five and some knowledge of the snares of the Devil. He had been helped to his perception of evil by his mother who, after giving him "a full day to think of the wrong," gave him "a thorough whipping," as he later observed with a satisfaction he perhaps did not feel then.[13]

But his sins, however heinous—and the little boy was terribly conscious of a tendency to lie when he was frightened—were probably forgotten as he jogged along, a tiny figure seeming very high from the ground on his horse, filled with a growing sense of importance at going West to "a wilderness filled with wild beasts and Indians." So capable was he becoming at inducing the cattle westward that he began to think, he later recalled, that he "could accomplish *smart things* in driving cows and riding the horses. Sometimes," he continued, he "met with Rattle Snakes which were very large; & which some of the company generally managed to kill." [14]

3

The Browns were accompanied on their journey West, which took forty-eight days, beginning June 9, 1805, by Benjamin Whedon, a Connecticut schoolmaster, and his wife. Mr. Whedon, whom Owen described as "a very kind and helpful Companion on the Road," also had a wagon and an ox team and perhaps a cow or two.[15] There were nine in the company, the two Whedons and seven Browns: Owen, "out of health" but uncomplaining, who was thirty-four that summer; his wife, Ruth, thirty-three, a baby in her arms; Levi Blakeslee, eleven; Ruth, their daughter, who was seven; John, five; Salmon, three; and the baby, Oliver, who was a year old.

Their route lay through New York and Pennsylvania to Pittsburgh where they crossed the Allegheny River. They pushed on to Ohio by way of Beaver, Pennsylvania, and along the Beaver River to just above its junction with the Mahoning River, the road, if it could be called such, generally following the Mahoning Indian Trail which led from Pennsylvania through the Western Reserve and on to Sandusky and Detroit.* [16] Each evening the party sought high ground, easily drained in case of rain, near a lake or river, creek or spring.

Most nights they talked for a time before the fire, a tiny leaping yellow in the immense darkness enveloping the camp, with the little boy solemnly regarding his father as Owen told of the new land to which they were going. Owen had journeyed to Hudson in Ohio's Western Reserve the year before, partly completing a cabin which was awaiting them in the forest. Hudson had been founded in 1799 by Deacon David Hudson, who with others had bought the township later bearing his name, but then known as Township Four, Range Ten, from the Connecticut Land Company at a price of about 34 cents an acre.[17] There were more Indians, Owen said, than white men in and about the township, and his five-year-old son remembered later how eager he had been to see an Indian. They had often brought venison, wild turkey, and fish to hungry settlers, Owen said, and when they themselves were hard up and asked for meal or grain they were always faithful to return it.[18]

4

The road West had become a way of life to the boy as they approached the Western Reserve, his mother sitting in the front of the wagon, lurching back and forth but somehow contriving to keep her baby comfortable and secure in her arms, his sister by his mother's side, his father with his eternal "Gee" and "Haw" guiding the oxen, walking beside them with his goad. John and Levi usually rode behind, John Brown remembered, endlessly turning from the trail and forcing their horses to block the paths of the meekly stubborn cows, their heads down, their horns uncertainly wavering a moment before yielding to the horses herding them back to the road.

---

* The Western Reserve comprised the northeastern corner of Ohio. It was bounded on the north by Lake Erie, on the south by the parallel of the 41st degree of north latitude, on the east by Pennsylvania, and on the west by the counties of Sandusky and Seneca. Its length, east and west, was 120 miles, its average width, north and south, 50 miles, and it enclosed an area of some 3,800,000 acres.

The land had been claimed by Virginia, New York, Massachusetts, and Connecticut, but by 1789 the title of Connecticut had been established to the area by consent of Congress. That state sold the land to the Connecticut Land Company, a private company, which in turn sold it to settlers largely from Connecticut, Massachusetts, and New York. In 1800, through petition of the Western Reserve's settlers, then numbering about one thousand, Congress accepted the Western Reserve as a part of the United States under the act providing for the organization of the Northwest Territory. In 1803, Ohio, the Western Reserve comprising its northeast portion, became the seventeenth state of the Union.

On the morning of July 27, the company was nearing Hudson, forty-eight days removed from Connecticut, and seldom had the forest seemed more darkly impenetrable. John had seen no houses or other signs of human habitation when suddenly they were there, had arrived at their new home, and if John did not realize it for a moment, it was because the clearing, the little space Owen had cut from the forest the year before, seemed so small. In its center was the tiny unfinished cabin his father had built, dwarfed by the height of the encircling trees.

WORK IN THE WILDERNESS

I

The shaggy-haired, blue eyed boy followed his father out of the cabin one morning shortly after the family's arrival in Hudson. On this day Owen was to begin the clearing of his land, a battle that often lasted for years. If he adhered to the usual practice in clearing land, his son saw Owen advance to the nearest tree of a size that could be readily handled and begin "sounding the ax," as the phrase was then, the muffled cadenced beat echoing through the dark woods as if it were the first sound ever to disturb the silence. Turning where he stood, he felled a similar tree, and then another, careless of how or where they crashed to the ground but careful, as his small son may have noticed, that the falling tree did not lodge in the branches of one still standing.

Such points were vital to boys of John Brown's age on the Western Reserve. Most of John's skills as a pioneer farmer were learned from his father. Owen was his son's teacher in the actual work of life, showing him by example more than words how to use an ax, build a cabin, plow a field, tan a hide, and perhaps giving him more valuable instruction than any he ever received in the little log schoolhouse in the township's center.

Clearing the land was hard, grueling, relentless work and soon Owen Brown would have been breathing hard, the sweat rolling from him; but still the rhythmical stroking would go on, the ax biting deep, the chips flying, the smell of sap and freshly cut timber in the air, the crash of tree after tree resounding in the stillness. Occasionally such sounds were the first notice to a settler perhaps a mile or more away that he had a new neighbor and at such a time he would plunge into the woods, heading toward the steady thud of the ax until presently he emerged, panting and excited, his hand extended.[19]

During the first weeks Owen did not haul away the tumbled confusion of tangled and criss-crossed trunks but let the slashing lie where it had fallen for later burning after it dried out. Then, proceeding to the larger trees, too great in size for him to fell, he showed John and Levi how to gird their trunks, cutting a deep circular groove around and through the bark, killing the tree and causing its leaves to fall, permitting the sunshine to nourish the crops which would soon be planted in the crazily irregular field, punctuated by dead trees, their branches bare above the fresh stumps.

In the autumn, when the fallen timber was dried out to an extent, John and Levi had the excitement of the burning, perhaps on a bright, still day with little wind. The blaze sweeping the tangled mass of prone trees was sometimes almost frightening for a time but usually soon died down because the wood was often still too green for it to be entirely consumed. After his burning, Owen, if he did as other settlers, returned with his ax, perhaps showing his small son how to lop off the limbs that had survived the fire, cutting the trunks of the larger trees into lengths that could be hauled by his oxen and splitting some of the logs for fence rails. Then, with the ground still warm from the fire and ashes, he and the boys probably scratched in some winter wheat, hoping that by next July it would be yellow and ripe around the blackened stumps.

2

All his life John Brown ardently admired his father and it might be difficult to overestimate Owen Brown's influence on his son. His first lessons as to race, involving the Indians of the Western Reserve rather than Negro slavery, were learned from his father, and all the influence of the peculiar community that was Hudson—which honored learning and was to establish a college, a western Yale—was filtered through his father. Among the boy's earliest memories of the Western Reserve was watching with intent absorption each move his father made as he dressed a deer skin.[20] If he followed his father about, and occasionally his mother, too, for that matter, consciously observing and trying to remember all the processes of the varied work they did, this was not unusual in a pioneer age. All the details and all the sweat of living were naked, evident, and necessary, and it was a passive child indeed who was not passionately interested in the building by his father of the cabin in which he was to live or the weaving of wool by his mother to protect him from the below-zero cold, or in the plowing that helped feed him, the tanning that made the leather for his shoes.

So it was a dramatic contest in which Owen was engaged, at least to his young son, as he worked hard on his unfinished cabin, racing against the snow, trying to complete their home even while he was clearing his land. With his small son watching, and perhaps not without excitement, Owen split puncheons from large logs, long smooth slabs from which he made the cabin floor, as well as its door, crossed and criss-crossed by strong timbers. The boy watched carefully—and he would later use his knowledge both in Pennsylvania and in Kansas—as his father cut through the logs forming the cabin walls, almost a foot in diameter, fashioning the cabin windows and making board squares which could slide back and forth to open and shut them. With his wife and children all around, Owen may have done some final plastering around his fireplace, built of cobblehead stones laid up with clay mortar, already in use and occupying almost the entire side at the end of the cabin. After a hard day of chopping and cutting and clearing land, he might glance apprehensively at the sky, as if half expecting snow, and then, though it was almost dark, he would be on the roof that was covered with clapboards of long shingles, securing the weight poles athwart each tier of shingles or swabbing more clay onto the chimney, built of sticks laid crosswise and already plastered with clay inside and out.[21]

Before the first snow, the cabin, probably 14 feet wide and 16 in length, was tight and shipshape, its gaps and crevices plugged with wooden wedges and plastered with clay, its door plumb, hanging on wooden hinges, and secured by a heavy cross bar, a loft and a ladder constructed to make additional sleeping space. The cabin was cluttered and crowded with seven in a single room but cheerful, particularly at night with its burst of warm yellow light from the fire touching everything with softness, even the great loom on which his mother would weave the homespun for the family's clothing seeming less angular, less utilitarian, as it flickered in and out of a corner's darkness.

3

That first winter was a little lean, the kettles hanging from the iron trammel above the fire often enough containing little more than corn meal mush, or Johnny cake made of corn meal mixed with salt and water. The cabin's joists were almost bare, but the time would soon come when from them would hang ears of corn, bunches of dried herbs and fruit, a slab of bacon, a side of jerked venison, or perhaps even a cheese.

Ruth's spinning wheels, the smaller one for flax, the larger for wool, were probably near the fireplace but it is doubtful if she had much of flax or wool to spin that first winter. Owen's rifle, if he placed it as most in Hudson did, may have hung from a pair of deer antlers on the chimney over the fireplace along with his powder horn and bullet pouch. The family worked at night as well as day, Ruth and the children, at least when Owen was stocked up with sheep, sometimes dipping candles. Over and over again they plunged lengths of wicking into a kettle of melted tallow until, after repeated dippings, the filled-out lengths were hung up to harden into candles. Owen, of course, was often working away too, making, it may be, bedsteads from tough dogwood, or three-legged chairs, or puncheon benches, or cupboards with wooden pins.

It was their neighbors, distant as most were, who saw them through that first winter, for they had not arrived in time to put in a crop of corn. There were some twenty or thirty families in the 25 square miles that was the township of Hudson. Owen later recalled "the many tokens of kindness" of which the Browns were the recipients. Their poverty was not because of lack of work, for, as Owen said, "We did not come to a land of idleness; neither did we expect it." [22]

Owen did not like to hunt but he may have had to that first winter when provisions were scarce. One of his Hudson neighbors, a Mr. Chauncey Case, also from Connecticut, kept his family's table "very well supplied with game," his son, a friend of John Brown's, recalled. "The woods abounded with deer, bear, racoon, possum, squirrels, rabbit, turkey, quail, partridge and pigeons," he wrote. "We dressed, stuffed and baked the possum as we do a pig now. The coon we hung before the fire to roast as we do spareribs." The quail and turkey, he reported, were particularly plump and delicious. They also enjoyed, he remembered, the wild pigeons which made a tempting pie. "My father," he later wrote, "caught the pigeons with a large net set with a spring. He baited this with straw and wheat spread thin on the ground. . . . He would catch sixty or seventy with one swoop of the net." [23]

Perhaps it was this kind of making do to which Owen Brown was referring when he later wrote of that first winter, "We had some hardships to undergo but they appear greater in history than they were in reality." [24] The people of Hudson were not glum, whatever the hardships they suffered, and neither was Owen, for all his slow-moving, slow-speaking mildness. He regarded himself, as has been said, as a hymn singer and such singing as a spiritual pursuit, writing in his brief autobiography addressed to his children that "our family became singers" while he was still a boy in Connecticut, and adding that their singing of hymns "brought our family into an association with the better class of people" and was "a great aid to restraining grace." [25] The Cases, and probably the Browns too, frequently sang hymns, all the family joining in as their voices praising Jesus echoed through the woods. [26]

4

With the coming of the first spring, Owen began his wrestling match with the hard stubborn ground, preparatory to putting in his first crop of corn. His antagonists were not only the soil but sometimes his oxen, too, whose recalcitrance may have sometimes tried his soul, and above all the cumbersome plow itself, a huge wedge of wood save for the piece of wrought iron sheathing its share. As he worked with John Brown, now nearly six years old—his birthday being in May—no doubt in on every skirmish with the oxen, on each collision with a stump, his mother was probably planting her first vegetable garden. She was the center of the family, and as the years at Hudson progressed, she became more than ever the hub of all its activities and even the quiet governor of Owen, as he himself always proudly insisted.

She quite literally fed and clothed her family, if she worked as the other women of her time did on the Western Reserve, baking bread, roasting venison, mutton, and beef, spinning flax and wool, sewing, cleaning, washing, knitting, mending, rendering soap, churning butter, dipping candles, tailoring coats, pantaloons, mittens, and hats, weaving linen for sheets and wool for homespun and blankets, planting and weeding her vegetable garden, shelling its peas and stripping its corn, preserving its beans, squash, beets, and pumpkin as well as the blueberries, raspberries, wild cranberries, huckleberries, wild cherry, wild plum, the red and black haw, wild gooseberry, and grapes in which the countryside abounded and which she and others of the family picked.

The first one up in the morning, the fire's cheerful leap the signal that she was about, rousing the boys and seeing to it that they brought in the wood and water from the creek while Owen threw down the hay for the stock and milked the cows, the last in bed at night, the thud of her loom or the whir of her spinning wheel the last sound of the day's work, she was the mainspring of the family's life. John Brown learned many skills from her and was always as proud of his bread and the cleanliness of his kitchen as he was of his ability with the ax and the plow.

But she did more than labor for the flesh; she labored for the spirit also, taught John and the other children to fear God and keep His commandments, taught them the hymns the family sang, her voice so pure and sure beneath Owen's heavier tones. It would not be long before John would read in the only memorial preserving her memory that she was sprightly and loving and tender and kind.

By 1805, Ruth Mills Brown was thirty-three and had had six children in ten years, one of whom had died at birth, a second when two years old. In 1807 in the cabin at Hudson, a seventh child was born, Owen later recording that on February 13 Frederick his sixth son was born. Within a few months she was pregnant again and her health began to fail; yet she continued cheerful and she continued working. But work in the wilderness of that day cost lives.

5

Among the first hides Owen Brown tanned on the Western Reserve was a deer skin used to make his son a pair of buckskin breeches. John Brown never forgot them, thinking them much superior to the prosaic homespun he had worn in Connecticut. If he was occasionally a lonely little boy, tall and gangling with sharp features and a mass of tangled hair, he was solaced by the belief that his breeches made him a part of the frontier, or as he said, "a young Buckskin." Years later he recalled his appearance as a boy in Hudson with a hint of approving nostalgia, describing himself as "barefooted, & bareheaded with Buckskin Breeches suspended with one leather strap over his shoulder but sometimes with Two." [27]

Fond as he was of his costume of the frontier—even Hudson's deacons sometimes wore buckskin breeches to church [28]—he was almost as much intrigued by his father's method of curing the deer skin and by his own close following of the tanning. "He was perhaps rather observing," he noted approvingly of himself fifty years later, when recalling his buckskin breeches, "as he ever after remembered the entire process of Deer skin dressing; so that at any time he could dress his own leather such as Squirel, Racoon, Cat, Wolf or Dog Skins. . . ." [29]

By the age of nine or ten John was beginning to learn the routines of tanning, a trade which would form the business of much of his adult life.

While still a child he was learning which hides would be better for boots and shoes, which were more appropriate for harness or saddles, or when a sheepskin had the quality necessary for a warm coat which would be worn with the unpulled wool inside. As solemnly, as purposefully, as if he knew then that more than twenty years of his life would be spent as a tanner, he learned at once that calf skins and sheep pelts were to be tanned whole, the cowhides to be split into two "sides," as they were called, that the first job was the hard work of "beaming," scraping away the flesh and tissue with a sharp knife, after which the sheep and lamb skins were moistened and packed into piles where they would "sweat," his father said, until the wool loosened so that it could be pulled out. At the same time, the cowhides were being placed in the vats containing a lime solution which loosened the hair.

Although this was only the beginning of the long process of tanning—the hides had to be soaked in the vats, each layer separated by bark, and then dried by hanging from the poles in the loft—the boy felt that the proper tanning of leather was much more important than school. From the first, or so he later remembered, he had a fierce desire to excel at a man's work,[30] apparently thirsting for recognition and approbation. Not for him was the adage that a child should be seen and not heard. He wanted both and it was only his bashfulness that kept him silent. He envied the men who stood about a horse and importantly diagnosed its fine points, speaking knowingly of its flanks or its withers or the deepness of its chest, or bringing their hands along a cow's back as they spoke of its conformation, and talked importantly of in-breeding and milk yield and fodder.

From the first, too, it was as if he instinctively knew that business success was not only the American way but a mark of the Lord's favor. The elect won not only salvation but wealth. Even as a boy he admired Deacon Hudson and Captain Heman Oviatt, the Indian trader, who were combining Godliness with dollars. At the age of six he was a small businessman learning "to make whip lashes" which he sold and which, he recalled, "brought him some change at times." When he was seven or eight years old he had "acquired a kind of ownership to certain animals of some little value," probably a lamb or two or a calf or a hog, but his prosperity was cankered by the fear that some sharper would cheat him of them because "he had come to understand that the title of minors might be a little imperfect." To circumvent the hypothetical cheater of minors, he went through some involved nominal trade in which his property still remained his while appearing to be the possession of an older person, a dodge which he described with pride almost a half century later.[31]

Still the boy, for all his attempt at the thrifty canniness of his elders, seemed to have a periodic need for solitude, although he avoided the woods for a space because "he was for some time rather afraid of the Indians & of their Rifles; but this soon wore off." [32] After that the dark forest did not frighten him. Suddenly wilting under the strain of his premature adulthood, he would plunge into the woods, ranging far, "quite a rambler," he recalled, "in the wild new country, finding birds and squirels & sometimes a wild Turkey's nest." Once, over a period of days, he coaxed a squirrel nearer and nearer to him, tempting it with nuts. Suddenly he snatched out and caught it by the tail, hanging on even when it bit him. With the greatest patience he succeeded in taming it so well that it stayed with him for some months, his friend and his delight.[33]

Frequently, too, he sought out the Indian villages, standing silently around their campfires, listening but saying little, observing much with his sharp blue eyes, and trying silently to form the strange words the Indians spoke, learning, he recalled, "a trifle of their talk." An inarticulate little boy, bashful, as he afterward remembered, to the point of pain, he may have been very lonely as he watched the busy communal life of the Indians. Perhaps that was why he always remembered the Indian boy who became his friend and gave him a yellow marble.

Yet if he was reserved and often silent, trying to act as he fancied an adult would act, as deprived of the acceptance of his elders by the fewness of his years as he was from the Indians by his race, he was, nevertheless, passionate enough in his attachments, whether it was to the lost yellow stone or the little bobtailed squirrel which he would soon seek through the woods, weeping and calling out for Bobtail after it ran away. "You may laugh when you come to read about it," he wrote years later in telling of the yellow marble and the squirrel, "but these were sore trials to John: whose earthly treasures were very few, & *small*." [34]

Later he became "the owner of a little Ewe lamb which did finely till it was about Two Thirds grown; & then sickened & died. This brought another protracted *mourning season*: not that he felt the pecuniary loss so heavily: for that was never his disposition: but so strong & earnest were his attachments." [35]

A LASTING INFLUENCE

I

Much as John loved and needed his mother, as he was soon to find, it was his father who impressed him. It was not only his skill with the ax and the plow, his knowledge of tanning, fine cattle, sheep and swine, but even more it was the esteem in which the people of Hudson held him. As early as 1805, and in the three following years, Owen was a delegate to the Ecclesiastical Convention of New Connecticut, as the Western Reserve was sometimes called, its purpose the strengthening of Calvinism, and the building of churches in the wild new country where Congregationalists as well as Presbyterians were acting in a synod governed by the laws of the Presbyterian Church. Accompanying Owen as delegates from Hudson to the Ecclesiastical Convention were Captain Heman Oviatt, Deacon Stephen Thompson, and Hudson's founder, Deacon David Hudson, the three leading citizens of Hudson, of which Owen was soon to be a fourth.[36]

Owen Brown was in considerable demand as a referee in land disputes, traveling far, he recalled, to settle quarrels over titles, "sometimes 60 or 70 Miles [from] home and be gone some two week[s] and sleep on the ground and that without injery." Perhaps it was Owen's manifest preference for the sacrifice of public affairs rather than the profit of private ventures that attracted men to him for he had come to the Western Reserve, he was to write, with "a determination to help build up and be a help in the seport of religion and civil order." [37]

If Owen had difficulty in spelling, he had no difficulty in attracting the learned and distinguished to his home. Often they were missionaries from the East, graduates of Yale, Williams, or Amherst, bringing the gospel to the Senecas, the Ottawas, the Onondagas, Oneidas, Chippewas, and Mingoes of the Reserve and even to the Ojibways as far to the northwest as Mackinaw. The ardor of their beliefs was attested by the rigor of the hardships they had undergone, their endurance by the miles they had trudged seeking out the hidden nomadic villages of the ever-moving Indians, often through snow and blizzards too much for a horse. Not only had they brought Christ's words to the Indians but they had been the founders of the first churches on the Reserve almost always in the log cabins which served the first settlements as schools as well as churches.

"The company that called on us was of the best kind," Owen remembered with satisfaction, describing his visitors as "Missionaries of the Gospel and leading men travailing through the country. . . ." [38] He welcomed them particularly because of his hunger to talk theology, having lived as a young man with prominent divines in Connecticut, trading his work for their talk of the splendid subtleties of salvation as well as for the more prosaic necessity of board and lodging. Like many others then, he loved sitting about the fire and discussing grace against works and Hell's eternal torment and infant damnation and election, with as much skill and knowingness and downright satisfaction as later Americans displayed while sitting around a hot stove discussing baseball.

2

Among Owen's probable visitors was the Reverend Joseph Badger, who enjoyed the title of "The Apostle of the Western Reserve," won by his ubiquitousness over the years among the Indians of that region. It was said that no tribe was too distant, no settlement too remote that it might not occasionally hear him expounding the mysteries of Calvinism. In 1801 alone, he had ridden 1,700 miles on horseback on the Western Reserve and had preached 150 sermons. A bluff and hearty man, broad of shoulder and muscular of calf, he had graduated from Yale in 1785 and was a veteran of the Revolution. His was the first wagon that ever passed between Buffalo and the Western Reserve. He had organized the first church in Hudson on Saturday, September 4, 1802, at the log schoolhouse in the township's center, as well as the first church on the Western Reserve at Austinborough in 1801. He talked so frequently of the battles of the Revolution that it was said he was as much a man of war as a man of God. [39]

Another visitor at Owen's home was the Reverend David Bacon, who in the autumn of 1804 stopped at Hudson from his mission to the Ojibways at Mackinaw, asking if he might leave his wife and children to the care of the people of Hudson, while he continued on foot "through the winter's snows and floods to report his work to the Missionary Society at Hartford, Connecticut." By spring he had returned as Hudson's minister, his salary about $2.50 a week with the provision that he could leave periodically when the holy spirit moved him to return for a time to the Indians. He was an authority on God's covenant with man, believing as the Pilgrims had that civil government should stem from ecclesiastical authority; presently he was to found such a community at nearby Tallmadge in the township immediately to the west of Hudson where he also helped found a school John Brown was to attend.[40] Perhaps Deacon Elizur Wright, also of Tallmadge, and also a graduate of Yale, was one of Owen's visitors, for they were later associates in the founding of Western Reserve College at Hudson. He was a mild little man with a passion for fluxions or the calculus, a teacher in the Academy at Tallmadge which he had apparently helped the Reverend Bacon establish.[41] Certainly, the Reverend William Hanford was frequently one of Owen's guests when he became the pastor of Hudson's Congregational Church in 1815. He was a graduate of Yale and the Andover Theological Seminary and like his colleagues a learned man.[42]

All were Calvinists, of course, and all deeply steeped in the martyrdom of the English Puritans, having pored from childhood over that record as revealed in Foxe's *Book of Martyrs*. Its lurid prints of tortured, bleeding, burning virtue had been a source of nightmare to generations of New England children, for Foxe's *Martyrs* was one of the most omnipresent books in Puritan libraries. These rugged divines from Yale knew, too, their Greek and Latin, their Homer and Virgil, their Plutarch and Herodotus as well as those more practical works, for the preacher at least, as Henry *On Meekness* and Baxter on *The Saints Everlasting Rest*.*

3

As young John Brown, who already affected to despise the idle chatter of mere children, pushed close to the fireplace, drinking in the talk of the divines, listening, it may be, to the Reverend Mr. Badger tell of the great days of the Revolution, or the Reverend Bacon discuss such matters as the sin against the Holy Ghost and true zeal of spirit, he apparently began to feel around the age of ten some diminution of an earlier aversion to school and books. It was then, as he later recalled it, that he began to enjoy "the company and conversation of old & intelligent persons." [43]

That Plutarch became one of his favorite writers [44] may have been the result of hearing such as the Reverend Hanford, who was to become a special friend, speak perhaps of Miltiades and Themistocles and the valor of the Spartans at Thermopylae. If he heard any mention of the glories of martyrdom as told by Foxe, he may have felt some tingle of admiration or even of desire that he might some day be as brave. A John Brown had been one of those executed martyrs in 1511. But whether he heard these stories of

---

* These two volumes were later special favorites of John Brown.

dying for conscience sake or not, he did undoubtedly hear from these missionaries much of the wrongs suffered by their charges and perhaps it was in connection with the red man, rather than the black, that he first began to ponder the import of that verse in Acts proclaiming God "hath made of one blood all nations of men for to dwell on all the face of the earth."

Assuredly that verse had special meaning for his father. As Owen talked by the fire with the missionaries and preachers, he was always earnest in his speech but particularly so when he spoke of the Indians, declaring them to be useful rather than an injury to the settlers and lamenting that some seemed disposed to quarrel with them.[45] His stand for the Indians was not without risk and John early had an opportunity to learn whether such a man as his father backed his words with his deeds. He did, and at some cost, when he opposed many in the community who had pursued and attacked a band of Indians, killing one and injuring others.[46] Owen was one of a group who swore out warrants for murder against those who had killed the Indian. He was quite unpopular for a time. But there were some who admired Owen's efforts in behalf of a wronged race and it may be that his example, growing and expanding in the mind of his son as the boy grew older, became a lasting influence in his own efforts to help another injured people.

A NEARNESS TO RUIN

I

Both Hudson and John Brown were growing and changing. As for Hudson, new sawmills and grist mills were being built. Bulls, cows, sheep, and swine were being increasingly acquired by the township's farmers, who each year cleared more land and put greater acreage into corn and wheat. Roads and log bridges were being constructed although travel was still in "the plainest kind of ox-carts, sleds, and stone-boats."[47]

Deacon Hudson was putting up Hudson's first frame house, handsome and white and as gracious in its lines as most in Connecticut. The village center, near the little log schoolhouse and not far from the Brown cabin, was beginning to show embryonic traces of the New England-like common it would become and it would not be long before the first lawyer's and doctor's offices, a blacksmith shop, stores, and saloons would begin to appear on the muddy rudimentary streets surrounding what would become the town square.[48]

As for John Brown, he too, according to his own report, was growing fast and also changing. He was even beginning to like school, if not for its lessons, then for its games. When playing his usual somberness deserted him. He seemed seized by a releasing recklessness as he raced about, pushing and shoving his playmates, eager for combat, sometimes, he remembered, snowballing dignified old gentlemen, trying to knock off their "old seedy Wool hats." Yet "he was never quarrelsome," as he recalled it, "but was *excessively* fond of the *hardest & roughest* kind of plays; & could never get enough [of] them.

"Indeed when for a short time he was sometimes sent to School," he continued,

the opportunity it afforded to wrestle, & Snow ball & run, & jump . . . offered to him almost the only compensation for the confinement, & restraints of school. I need not tell you that with such feeling & but little chance of going to school at all, he did not become much of a schollar.[49]

His infrequent spells of school were not entirely his fault, although he says he would "always choose to stay home & work hard rather than be sent to school," for teachers were difficult to come by and sessions were often truncated so that boys and girls could help with the farm work.

2

Owen was doing well with his tannery, glad that he had moved from Connecticut, feeling thankful, he remembered, during 1807 and most of 1808 for

the common blessings of health, peace and prosperity. . . . I had a very pleasant and orderly family untill December 9 1808 when all my earthly prospects appeared to be blasted. My beloved Wife gave birth to an Infant Daughter that died in a few ours [and] as my wife expressed [it] had a short passage through time. My wife followed in a few ours . . . these were days of affliction. I was left with five (or six including Levi Blakesley, my adopted son) small Children. . . . This sean all most makes my heart blead now.[50]

Mother and child were the first to be buried in the Hudson cemetery.

Accustomed life in the little cabin came to a complete stop. What meals there were came from distant neighbors. The smallest children cried for their mother and for a time there was little sleep. Owen was completely demoralized and yet it may have been worse for John as he saw his mother die. He had known loss before, the loss of his marble and his little squirrel and then he had wept, but this was beyond weeping, beyond conceiving. The loss, he was to write years later, was "complete and permanent."

"At Eight years old John was left a Motherless boy," he continued as if still incredulous, adding that even after his father again married

a very estimable woman . . . he *never adopted her in feeling:* but continued to pine after his own Mother for years. This opperated very unfavourably uppon him; as he was both naturally fond of females; & withall extremely diffident; & deprived him of a suitable conne[c]ting link between the different sexes; the want of which might under some circumstances have proved his ruin.[51]

In the opinion of Christian Cackler, who sometimes worked for the Browns as a hired man, it proved his ruin immediately. He became sullen and defiant, playing ever more roughly, knocking off more seedy woolen hats with his snowballs than ever before and making the life of his step-mother, Sally Root Brown, quite miserable. If there ever was a time when he regarded his father with reserve, it was when he married on November 8, 1809, replacing the boy's mother with a stranger. Levi Blakeslee, fifteen when Sally came into the family, joined in the hazing, as did Salmon, John's younger brother, who was only seven.

Levi found Sally, who seems to have been a nice enough woman, too "snappish" for his taste, claiming that she had kicked him when he was lying on the floor and telling with satisfaction how he had caught and held her foot.[52] The boys, according to Cackler and others, planned to blow up the poor harried woman when she was in the outhouse and rigged up an ineffectual device with gunpowder which failed to work. Undiscouraged, they took out some boards in the hayloft where Sally went in search for eggs and when she fell, suffering bruises and fright, poor Owen, who did not like corporal punishment, decided that John should be flogged in the morning. But the boy, according to Cackler, placed a sheep hide under his buckskins and did not feel Owen's lashes with a cowhide, although he "would jump at every blow and howl like a panther."[53]

3

"He doted on being head of the heap," said Milton Lusk, in recalling this part of John's life. He had been the leader, Lusk (who was to be John Brown's brother-in-law) remembered, of a gang of Federalist boys who had daily snowball battles with Democratic boys, or boys whose fathers were Democrats, and he recalled how John, on one occasion, "drove them all before him into their schoolhouse. He did not seem to be angry, but there was such force and mastery in everything he did, that everything gave way before him." [54] But presently the boy seemed to tire of his roughness, putting it aside as if it were the last remnant of childhood. He even began to show something of reserved courtesy to Sally Root Brown, who would become the mother of eight children, half sisters and brothers of John Brown.

Reading, he later felt, had been a factor in his new maturity. It was at the age of ten, as he remembered it, that

an old friend induced him to read a little history: & offered him the free use of a good library; by which he acquired some taste for reading: which formed the principle part of his early education: & diverted him in great measure from bad company. . . . By reading the lives of great, wise & good men their sayings, & writings; he grew to a dislike of vain & frivolous *conversation*, & *persons;* & was often greatly obliged by the kind manner in which older, & more intelligent persons treated him at their houses; & in conversation; which was a great relief on account of his extreme bashfulness.[55]

It was during this period that "he became very strong & large for his age & ambitious to perform the full labour of a man; at almost any kind of hard work." By the time he was twelve, he recalled, he was being "sent off more than a Hundred Miles with companies of cattle & he would have thought his character much injured had he been obliged to be helped in any such job. This was a boyish kind of feeling but characteristic however." [56]

At twelve he quite apparently felt that he was a grown man and he was somber enough for the most strait-laced of adults. Yet he was awkward and lonely, too, set quite apart by his own pretensions from the fun of the other boys—from the sugarings and spelling bees and cabin-raisings and cornhuskings that gave other young people so much enjoyment. He preferred to work in his father's tannery, mourning perhaps the irretrievable losses of a childhood he felt forever gone.

If he still retained anything of grief, his new maturity forbade him to show it. And yet there may have been times, perhaps near the end of the day when the dusk might conceal both him and his grief, when he stole over to the village cemetery to see the new tombstone that had been erected there. It read:

SACRED TO THE MEMORY
OF RUTH, WIFE OF OWEN BROWN
WHO DIED DEC. 9 1808 IN THE
37TH. YEAR OF HER AGE
A DUTIFUL CHILD

A SPRIGHTLY YOUTH

A LOVING WIFE

A TENDER PARENT

A KIND NEIGHBOR

AND AN EXEMPLARY CHRISTIAN

"SWEET IS THE MEMORY OF THE JUST."

Its lines are eroded now by more than a century of wind and weather but they were certainly clear enough then, even in the twilight, even through the tears of a gawky boy standing there alone, for him to read the words that memorialized the death of his mother and marked the end of his childhood.

X

On Growing Older
and Eli Whitney

ALTHOUGH HUDSON'S 202 inhabitants in 1812 had their share of drunks and scandal, they also had those who believed so strongly in their happy resurrection that they greeted death with loud cries of triumph and rejoicing. In describing such a blessed event, a preacher, after mentioning the hallelujahs and exclamations of delight with which some old lady greeted her deliverance, occasionally paraphrased Bunyan by declaring, "So she passed over and all the trumpets sounded for her on the other side!" [1]

It was of such matters that Hudson folk talked in Captain Oviatt's general store, often asking if the dying had shown any evidence of salvation such as seeming to see some of the previously departed on the further shore. They talked, too, of weather and crops, of refreshing rains vouchsafed by Providence, of how a neighbor had suffered a crushed leg when a log fell on it, of how one was down with the ague or another had been injured when dragged by his team or still another hurt when kicked by a rambunctious mare. New roads, new schools, new settlers also occupied them as well as more spicy events such as the murder of the Indian chief, Oguntz, by his adopted son, and the appropriateness of the text used by the Reverend Timothy Bigelow as he stood on the gallows beside the first convicted murderer of the area. He had comforted the man about to die with the text, "O wretched man that I am! who shall deliver me from the body of this death?" [2]

EARLY HOPE

I

But it was the Indians they talked about most. They still liked to recall Brady's leap of a generation or more before when a white man pursued by the Indians leaped across the wide chasm formed by the cliffs high above the Cuyahoga and escaped. Cackler had measured the distance and found it to be 21 feet.[3] They spoke uneasily of ceremonial drunks the Indians sometimes performed in the village itself, directly in front of Captain Oviatt's store, in which they wore a drunk suit made of deer skin and bear claws, each drinker wearing it alternately while he whooped and contorted about until exhausted, when another put it on and went to it.[4] They recalled how the Indians had fired guns at the sun during an eclipse [5] and of how the British were inciting them to use these guns more effectively against the white American settlers.

If the people of Hudson talked little of slavery it was because it was still only a rumor from a land far away. Some were against it when they thought of it but they did not think of it often. The fugitive slaves who were soon to give it an ever-increasing reality were virtually nonexistent until after the War of 1812 and even then they were few for more than a decade. But the lack of interest in slavery before the second war with England was perhaps primarily because most on the frontier, whether above or below the Ohio, were preoccupied with gaining the land east of the Mississippi held by the Indians, land which included much of what was later known as the Deep South and the Middle West.*

---

* The War of 1812 largely shattered Indian capability for successful armed resistance to the white man east of the Mississippi, although the Seminoles were not finally cleared from Florida until 1843, the Cherokees, Creeks, Choctaws, and Chickasaws holding valuable land in Georgia, Alabama, and Mississippi as late as 1836 while the brief Black Hawk War took place in Illinois and Wisconsin in 1832. But effective Indian military power was broken by the Battle of the Thames in the Old Northwest in October 1813, and by the Battle of Horse Shoe Bend in what was then the Southwest in August 1814, during America's second war against the British. Thereafter the Indians, with the exception of the Seminole War and the Black Hawk incident, both small-scale regional conflicts, were usually forced to retire from their ancient lands to the trans-Mississippi plains not by war but by treaty, bribe, induced intoxication, or military threat, and often by a combination of all four. The most famous expulsion was the forcing of the Cherokees from Georgia across the Mississippi to what is now Oklahoma in 1836.

Moreover, the people of Hudson, as well as of the remainder of the nation, were still filled with a kind of original optimism. It stemmed from the growth and advance that began with the victorious American Revolution and embraced the belief that almost nothing was impossible of solution, including slavery. Under the impetus of the Revolutionary era and its ideology of liberty eight Northern states had provided for slavery's abolition, three by outright liberation through judicial decree and constitutional provision, five by programs of gradual emancipation; and for a time, however brief, it seemed to some as if this gradual abolition might spread southward.

2

If there were those in the early 1800's who hoped for slavery's peaceful extinction, their hopes were based on facts. One of the first important acts of the new independent American government had been the passage by Congress of the Ordinance of 1787 prohibiting slavery in what was then the Northwest Territory and later the Middle West, Ohio, Indiana, Illinois, Michigan, Wisconsin, and a part of Minnesota, with slaveholders as well as Northern representatives voting for the measure. Three years before Congress had almost passed a similar act, many slaveholders also voting for it, abolishing slavery in much of the South, from territory which later became in part a foremost bastion of slavery and was to form the states of Alabama, Mississippi, Tennessee, and Kentucky.* American import of slaves from Africa had been banned, the international slave trade being outlawed by Congress in 1808 under the specific authorization of a clause in the Constitution.

During the first decade of American independence slavery was of doubtful economic benefit in Virginia, the Carolinas, and Georgia, the price of tobacco, rice, indigo, land, and slaves having fallen disastrously, there being no great cash crop such as cotton to make slavery profitable. For a time there seemed no overriding reason why these states might not eventually

---

* Jefferson wrote of the defeat of this measure which might have been passed if one man, absent when the vote was taken, had been present and voted for the bill, "The voice of a single individual would have prevented this abominable crime. Heaven will not always be silent; the friends to the rights of human nature will in the end prevail." See Rhodes, *History of the United States from the Compromise of 1850*, vol. I, p. 15. Jefferson as early as 1776 proposed a colonization plan for the transport of American slaves back to Africa, or to some other part of the world equally remote, which he hoped might in the end remove slavery from American soil or at least control its expansion to the west and other parts of the continent.

follow the example of Pennsylvania, New Jersey, New York, Connecticut, Rhode Island, Massachusetts, New Hampshire, and Vermont in providing for slavery's extinction, however gradually.*

What was then known as the Great Southwest, soon to form the states of Mississippi, Alabama, and Louisiana and to become the militant heartland of slavery and the Cotton Kingdom, had yet to come into being, the Indians still in possession of much of the best land, Eli Whitney's cotton gin, the saviour and perpetuator of slavery for a half century, still to demonstrate fully how fortunes could be made through the ownership of men and land. With slavery still unsupported by a strong economic base, it was easy for some to think that since the preponderant spirit of American thought and government was equalitarian in its trend, with the initial document, the Declaration, affirming the equality of all men and with the Constitution's preamble promising to Americans "the Blessings of Liberty," it was virtually inevitable that slavery would gradually disappear in the South as it had begun to disappear in the North.

During and just after the American Revolution, when the inalienable rights of all men to liberty received the added impetus of the world-shaking French Revolution, such arguments as these were irresistible and abolitionists of the period used them with effect in persuading the eight Northern states to move against slavery. They also used the danger of slave insurrection as an argument for emancipation, a point emphasized by Thomas Jefferson and reinforced when the slaves of Santo Domingo under Toussaint L'Ouverture as well as the slaves of Virginia under Gabriel proved that the black man valued his liberty as well as the white and could die for it as valiantly.

---

* Donald L. Robinson in *Slavery in the Structure of American Politics, 1765–1820*, New York, 1971, pp. 50–1, argues that while slavery might have been unprofitable in the south Atlantic states during this period it could not have been abandoned because it served as a system of social control over the blacks in a racist society that feared them. Robinson also believes it a delusion that the Founding Fathers were ever effectively against slavery, although it has long been held that many were against it to some degree and hoped it would be temporary. He believes that most if not all of the Republic's early leaders were racists and enough of them slaveholders to easily overcome any mild objections to slavery held in the North.

William W. Freehling in "The Founding Fathers and Slavery," *The American Historical Review*, February, 1972, pp. 81–93, challenges this view, citing the Northwest Ordinance of 1787 and other restrictions against slavery such as the constitutional provision against the slave trade mentioned above. However, he stresses the profound ambivalence of American statesmen during the Republic's early years when most were usually for slavery and only transiently against it and that usually equivocally. Perhaps it should be said that later political abolitionists and leaders of the new Republican Party always stressed that the Founding Fathers designed to make slavery sectional and freedom national while hoping that the latter policy would ultimately prevail. They always held that the Constitution, rightly interpreted as to its essential purpose, provided for the liberty of all Americans, black and white.

3

But the Revolution's abolitionists were not the country's first. There had probably never been a time in the history of American slavery when it did not have its opponents, if at the very beginning it was only slaves themselves. As early as 1667 there was the Quaker indictment of slavery written by William Edmundson in Rhode Island and as early as 1700 Massachusetts's Samuel Sewall had penned his protest, "The Selling of Joseph."

The two foremost leaders of the anti-slavery movement before the Revolution were the Quakers, Anthony Benezet, a Philadelphia school-teacher, and John Woolman, a tailor in New Jersey. In the South, as we have seen, Jefferson, Patrick Henry, and George Mason, among others, condemned slavery; while a little later in the North, free Negroes led by the wealthy James Forten, a Revolutionary veteran of Philadelphia, and Robert Purvis, a wealthy merchant also of that city, were active against the holding of man as private property. For a time there may have been more abolitionist societies in the South, however decorous and passive their efforts, than there were in the North. But under the impetus of gradual abolition in the North, the banning of the international slave trade from American ports, the pro-hibition of slavery in such huge areas as the Northwest Territory, the support of some slaveholders for anti-slavery measures, and a transient if general feeling that slavery was doomed to gradual disappearance, the first anti-slavery societies, organized during and after the Revolution, sank into dissolution and inactivity.

Yet there were still black slaves in much of the North even as the first abolition groups were falling apart, societies which had been founded a generation earlier by such figures as Benjamin Franklin and Dr. Benjamin Rush of Pennsylvania, both signers of the Declaration of Independence, and John Jay, of New York, another Revolutionary leader and the first Chief Justice of the United States. While gradualism in abolishing slavery was perhaps the only method that could have received public approval in such states as New York and Pennsylvania, still it was true that by retaining slaves for a long time, gradualism also fostered familiarity with the system in the North and even a certain tolerance of it.

In New York there were still 15,017 slaves in 1810 and more than 10,000 in New Jersey, where there were 647 slaves in 1840. Freedom did not come in most Northern states until the children of slave mothers born after a certain date reached a stipulated age. In New York, for example, slave children born after July 4, 1799, were to become free after reaching the age of twenty-eight in the case of men and twenty-five in the case of women. Under this system some slaves continued to be held in the North until the very eve of the Civil War.[6]

4

John Brown's grandmother, long before the North's gradual emancipation, had worked a slave named Sam, a native of Guinea on the African Gold Coast, whom she borrowed from a neighbor in West Simsbury, Connecticut. Owen, then a little boy, adored Sam. "I used to go out in the fields with him," he recalled,

and he used to carry me on his back, and I fell in love with him. He worked but for a few days and went home sick with pleurisy, and died very suddenly. When told that he would die, he said he should go to Guinea and wanted victuals put up for the journey. As I recollect this was the first funeral I ever attended in the days of my youth. There were but three or four slaves in West Simsbury.[7]

Even Owen, although he had been against slavery since the age of nineteen when he read a sermon of Jonathan Edwards, Jr., condemning it, may have hoped, as did many others before the War of 1812, that slavery was on the way out. There can be no doubt that he approved of the war despite his benevolent attitude toward the Indians and he was always proud of his part in it. In his mind it was not against the Indians, whom he said he still favored as neighbors, but against the British, the same hereditary enemy against which his father had fought and died.

"July 1812," Owen wrote,

the war began and this called loudly for action, liberality and courage. This was the most active part of my life. We were then on the frontier, and the people were much alarmed, particularly after the surrender of Hull at Detroit. Our cattle, horses, and provisions were all wanted. Sick soldiers were returning and needed all the assistance that could be given them. There was great sickness in different camps, and the travel was mostly through Hudson which brought sickness into our families. By the first of 1813 there was great mortality in Hudson.[8]

WAR AND A FIRST FAILURE

I

When John Brown went to war at the age of twelve it was as precocious an act, and so considered by his elders, as if he had entered Harvard at that age. In order to do so he had to know a great deal more than the Greek and Latin necessary for college matriculation—if knowing how to survive alone in a hostile wilderness is knowing more. His father was supplying beef and horses to General Hull's army at Detroit. Usually he traveled with his father but on at least one occasion, the boy, unaided and entirely by himself, drove a herd of cattle more than 100 miles west around the Ohio shore of Lake Erie and then northwest into Michigan and to the army of Hull.

If he was frightened at night, and many boys of his time and age in and about Hudson have left records of their fright in the blackness of the wilderness as they heard wolves drawing near,[9] he apparently did not know it. He regarded himself as an adult and demanded of himself such standards as he romantically thought for a time all his elders possessed. Although he was traversing a wilderness whose few settlers lived in daily fear of the Indians, who sided with the British in the War of 1812, he suggests nothing in his autobiographical letter of the feelings that may have been a twelve-year-old boy's as he stood guard over his cattle in a country which was to witness such massacres as that at Fort Dearborn.

But he does insist on the respect and admiration given to him by the few settlers he met on his wartime journeys. On one trip he stayed for a "short time with a very gentlemanly landlord," who, John Brown later wrote, "made a great pet" of him and "brought him to table with his first company; & friends; called their attention to every little smart thing he *said* or did: & to the fact of his being more than a hundred miles from home with a company of cattle alone." [10]

But even while the landlord was praising John Brown, he was striking out with anything that came to hand at a slave boy who was waiting on the table and whom John had to conclude had more of skill and character than he himself had. He stayed only a few days with the admiring landlord yet a quick warm friendship sprang up between the two boys of about the same age, both alone in the world, one only temporarily, but the black boy forever, as far as protecting parents were concerned.[11]

Thinking of it some forty-five years later, John Brown believed that the treatment accorded to his friend while he himself was being so lavishly praised was one of the factors "that in the end made him a most determined Abolitionist," a circumstance that ultimately "led him to declare, or Swear: *Eternal* war with slavery." If the Negro boy had not been so congenial, John Brown felt, he might not have felt his friend's plight so keenly. But the young slave was "so very active and intelligent," treating John with so much "good feeling" and placing him "under considerable obligation for numerous little acts of kindness," that he could not but wince when his friend was "beaten before his eyes with Iron Shovels or any other thing that first came to hand."

He noticed that "the negro boy (who was fully if not more than his equal) was badly clothed, poorly fed: & lodged in cold weather." He was particularly impressed with the fact that the boy had no one to whom he could appeal effectually and "This brought John to reflect," John Brown wrote later in his autobiographical letter to the Stearns boy, "on the wretched, hopeless condition of *Fatherless* & *Motherless* slave children; for such children have neither Fathers or Mothers to protect & provide for them. He would sometimes raise the question: is God their Father?" [12]

This letter written near the very apex of anti-slavery sentiment in the North probably expressed more of John Brown's feelings as to slavery in 1857 than it did of what he felt as a boy in 1812. Then he may have thought more specifically of the plight of his friend than the evils of slavery generally. Whatever his thoughts, he pushed on with his cattle to Hull's army. There, circulating about the camp, he "had some chance to form his own boyish judgment of men & measures" and his own boyish judgment found both at fault, perhaps as a result of becoming "somewhat familiarly acquainted with those who have figured before the country since that time." [13]

He was apparently referring to General Hull, whom he liked, and to Lewis Cass, later Secretary of State under Buchanan, whom he disliked and who was then an officer under Hull. The tall silent boy, rather a pet of the officers as he had been of the landlord, was not thought an impediment to talk or planning as he stood in the background and he heard such officers as Cass, or so he later said, threaten a mutiny which forced Hull's surrender.[14] It was thought by many of Hull's staff after he advanced into Canada that his rear was so threatened that Detroit's inhabitants might suffer an Indian massacre if he did not surrender the town to British protection.[15]

Nor did John Brown at the age of twelve think himself too young to bring war itself to judgment. He was against it. All in all it so repelled him that it made him, in his own eyes at any rate, into something of a nonresistant for many years. The common soldier, he felt, was sound enough but the higher one went in the military hierarchy the more frequent was the tendency to sacrifice lives for politics and jealousy. He did not agree at all with a young man in the South, also a participant in the War of 1812, and who would be a witness to the last event in John Brown's life, Private Edmund Ruffin, who although never in battle, felt that only aristocrats could properly withstand the rigors of the camp.[16] But whatever John Brown's future antagonist thought of war, it so disgusted young Brown with "Military affairs that he would neither train or drill," after his return to Hudson and his arrival at the age of militia service, "but paid fines & got along like a Quaker until his age . . . finally cleared him of Military duty." [17]

2

With the war ended John Brown returned to tanning, more certain of himself and his worth than ever before and already something of a character in Hudson. Owen, feeling a little cramped by the stores and buildings beginning to flank the village green, had moved two miles to the northeast where he bought a larger farm and erected a larger tannery as well as a fine white farmhouse considerably more imposing than the old home back in Connecticut. John was becoming so large and so much of an adult that it seemed natural enough for Owen to make him his foreman.[18] By the age of sixteen he had already reached his full height of 5 feet 10 inches. His chest was deepening, his features were losing some of their youthfulness, his blue eyes bright beneath a mat of brown hair growing low on his forehead, his long jaw becoming more accentuated, the first indications of a reddish brown beard marking its line and extending to his jutting chin.

His manner was at once dogmatic and bluffly hearty as he directed his father's employees. As he, himself, said, his

close attention to business; & success in its management: together with the way he got along with a company of men, & boys; made him quite a favorite with the serious & more intelligent portion of older persons. This was so much the case; & secured for him so many little notices from those he esteemed; that his vanity was much fed by it; & he came forward to manhood quite full of self conceit; & self confident: notwithstanding his *extreme* bashfulness.[19]

And yet he was worried and filled with a strange unease. For all his vanity he did not lack the capacity to see himself objectively and even with a certain severity. It was "during this period," he confessed, "that he found much trouble with some . . . bad habits." In addition, the young man for all his surface sureness "felt a good deal of anxiety to learn." [20] He had perhaps spent as much as two or three winters in the little log schoolhouse, taught for a time by Benjamin Whedon who had come with the Browns from Connecticut and was soon to be treasurer of the new college at Hudson. Later he had attended briefly Tallmadge Academy where Deacon Elizur Wright, the friend of his father's, was a teacher. The deacon's son of the same name, a schoolmate of John Brown,[21] was being prepared for Yale by his father and John Brown began to think also of going East to school.

But he was chiefly worried about his sins, about "his future well being," of which he "had always by turns felt much serious doubt." [22] A certain independence—he remembered himself as being at that time "quite skeptical" about some points of religion—had kept him from formal salvation although many younger than he during the constant revivals, reawakenings, and outpourings of grace that marked Hudson's life had gone to glory from the mercy seat.

Owen was as anxious about his son's unredeemed state as the boy himself and prayed for John's salvation. Presently it came during the summer of his sixteenth year when Hudson's hymns and prayers, the persuasions of the Reverend Mr. Hanford, and his own need brought him release and he made a public profession of repentance and acceptance of Christ in the small log schoolhouse still serving as Hudson's church.[23] Once formally a Christian, and never one to be satisfied with half-measures, he almost immediately began to consider entering the ministry of the Congregationalist Church and the struggle he had hoped would be ended with his acknowledgment of sin continued instead with greater force.

3

To become a preacher was to rise a full notch above the station of tanner. It was to become learned in Greek and Latin instead of grinding bark, to make an exegetical study of the Bible in the original Hebrew instead of minding vats, to be accepted as an interpreter of God Almighty on earth instead of deciding whether hides were better suited for boots than harness. It was not to cure hides but to cure souls. It was to become as his friend the Reverend Mr. Hanford, the spiritual leader of Hudson, to become a graduate of Yale (or some other Eastern college) as Hanford was and as was Deacon Wright, the schoolmaster of Tallmadge.

Yet even as a child John Brown had always insisted that he preferred active work to school and he had always been strongly attracted to business. Moreover, there was something in Hudson's air that placed a premium on success and practical accomplishment in the belief that Godliness need not be sacrificed by the gaining of wealth. It was a growing community, soon to have a population of one thousand, a part of a society such as was afterwards described as an expanding economy, population, production (agricultural and industrial), transportation, and other improvements increasing yearly in the main despite periodic depressions.

There were few in Hudson who were not proud of their part in changing it from what many were fond of calling "a howling wilderness" into a town soon to have a college and a church with as high a steeple as any in Connecticut and a bell that rang as sweetly. Even the failures, or the drunks, could often point with satisfaction to a field they had cleared in some far-off burst of energy or to a barn or a road or a bridge they had helped build where once there had been only forest. They had helped found a town, however little their contribution, and they had advanced the frontier, if only by being there. These were accomplishments as honored in their day as in later times, as praised by the pioneers themselves as by their descendants. From the first there were Founders' Days and Old Settlers' Days, in which the pioneers celebrated their own virtue and heroism by speech and feast and dram.

Religion, too, was an adjunct in this building of self-esteem and one didn't need to be a preacher to enjoy it. At Wednesday night prayer meetings any man might savor his own uniqueness as he stood and raised his voice in public prayer, releasing as much of the strange essence of himself as he deemed fitting. Owen Brown, for example, became another individual at such moments, his stuttering gone, his modesty vanished, his voice dramatic, rich, and personal, whether addressing the Lord or soaring above his rivals in hymns. A church member could feel himself grow by the inch as he got a proper hold on a real good prayer and let it rip. Deacon Kilbourne was a power when he let himself go and Captain Oviatt and Deacon Hudson had a way with a prayer or a hymn that could make the spine tingle. These prayers were editorials, too, in which their makers indicted evil and wrong in the community—there were as yet no newspapers in Hudson—while asking Jehovah to assure that proper action for which they beseeched.

A man might feel something of exaltation, too, during the singing of hymns, even feel the throbbing of his own libido, although he would have called it his soul, as he roared along, the soprano of wives, sweethearts, and mothers shrilling above, while the whole congregation sang of love and the Blood of the Lamb, of "Hosanna to the King," and of how "Broad Is the Path that Leads to Death." John Brown loved these hymns and it is said that he knew most of *Watt's Hymnal* by heart, from "The Man Is Ever Blest Who Shuns the Sinners Ways," to "Sin, Like a Venomous Disease, Infects Our Vital Blood," and "Laden with Guilt, and Full of Fears, I Fly to Thee, My Lord." [24] It was these two aspects of Hudson, the secular and the religious,

God and Mammon, that warred within John Brown as he debated between tanning and the ministry at the age of sixteen. The call to preach may have won out as the hymns soared on a Wednesday night in 1816.

4

Owen may also have helped his son in reaching a decision. He was eager for him to enter the ministry, suggesting that he attend Plainfield Academy at Plainfield, Massachusetts, the headmaster of which was the Reverend Moses Hallock. Then he could go on to Amherst College, where a distant Connecticut kinsman was soon to be president, and there receive his doctorate in divinity. If his son still hesitated it may have been because he knew it was emotionally necessary for him to be first and he would be far from that in a preparatory school in the East studying Latin and Greek with which his younger and smaller classmates would already be familiar.

Although there is some uncertainty as to the date, John Brown, his brother Salmon, and a friend of John's age, Orson M. Oviatt, the son of Captain Oviatt, departed for the East and school probably in the autumn of 1816, perhaps after the fall butchering. After the inflation of the War of 1812, prices had fallen, money was scarce, and the best Owen could do was to outfit his two sons with horses which they would sell after their arrival in Massachusetts as payment for their tuition and board.

If Orson had a horse too, the boys were outfitted uncommonly well, for occasionally as many as four boys went East to college from the Reserve with only one horse among them, as was the case with young Elizur Wright when he departed for Yale. In such an instance they used the method known as "ride and tie." Two would ride, whether horseback or in a buggy, for several miles, tie their horse to a tree near the road, then push on by foot while their two friends, who had been walking, upon reaching the horse would ride until they caught up with their companions, when the procedure would be repeated.[25]

As John Brown jogged along on his horse with his brother and his friend away from Hudson and toward the schooling he had only begun to value of late he may have already been wondering whether so poor a scholar as he had always been could master it. If he had little money in his pockets and scant clothing in his saddlebags they did at least contain a square foot of leather with which he intended to mend his shoes, as well as some tanned sheepskins he hoped might help him earn his way. He knew that help from Owen would scarcely take the form of cash. It was more likely to be cloth or clothing which Owen would gain by bartering his hides, much as Deacon Wright bartered sessions at his school for articles to send his son at Yale. Most boys from the West were outfitted as Deacon Wright outlined in his letter to his son when the obtaining of clothing for a young man at college was almost a community project.

"Dear Son," he had written.

I send you by Mr. Fenn, Homer's Iliad together with two shirts and about four yards of cloth for a coat. The yarn for the cloth was spun by Mrs. McClelland, the cloth was manufactured at Kendal by Mr. Rotch and the pattern delivered by Mr. McClelland. This I consider almost as clear gain. When I was musing in what form I should pay for some other articles for you Mr. Wm. Hart voluntarily offered to pay somewhat in advance for the tuition of his sister—who attends the Academy this summer. With a part I purchased this cloth for your shirt[s]. Miss Marcia Wright made them towards pay for her tuition also.[26]

Similarly, when John Brown received clothing from Hudson it may have made him homesick. As he pulled on his trousers or hauled on his coat he may have seen in his mind's eye more than one familiar face from back home, knowing, as he could have, which of his neighbors had sewn the seams of his clothing, who had planned its pattern, and who had spun the wool. A pair of pants had a personalized history then.

But he had more immediate reasons to yearn for Hudson. Upon entering Plainfield Academy in Massachusetts it was as he had feared. He was like an adult among mere children, boys ranging from ten to fourteen who already knew more than he would ever know of rhetoric, grammar, Latin, Greek, and mathematics. He who had made his elders jump when he spoke back in the tanyard was now a junior in knowledge to boys scarcely longer than one of his legs. Somehow he kept his dignity among the little fellows. He had not come East to fail, having been from very early in life, as he remembered it, "ambitious to excell in doing anything he undertook to perform."[27]

Perhaps because he felt his years he became increasingly parental in his treatment of Salmon, only two years his junior. But however humiliating his position, he could not quit for it was his boast that he always "followed up with tenacity whatever he set about. . . ."[28] For hours each night he pressed his eyes close to his Latin and Greek, the text wavering and uncertain in the light of a flickering candle. His eyes smarted and became inflamed but he persisted.

It was not only his size and difficulty in learning that was embarrassing. He seemed to be regarded as a frontiersman by children and teachers, his square of leather and his sheepskins exciting some comment. Heman Hallock, the youngest son of the headmaster, the Reverend Moses Hallock, never forgot him, recalling him years later and believing him to be almost ten years older than he was in reality when attending Plainfield.

"He was a tall, sedate, dignified young man," he remembered,

from twenty-two to twenty-five years old. He had been a tanner and relinquished a prosperous business for the purpose of intellectual improvement. . . . He brought with him a piece of sole-leather about a foot square which he himself had tanned, for seven years, to resole his boots.

He had also a piece of sheep-skin which he had tanned, and of which he had cut some strips, about an eighth of an inch wide, for other students to pull upon. Father took one string, and winding it around his fingers, said, with a triumphant turn of the eye and mouth, "I shall snap it." The very marked yet kind immovableness of the young man's face, on seeing father's defeat, father's own look, and the position of people and things in the old kitchen, somehow gave me a fixed recollection of this little incident.[29]

But such triumphs as this did nothing to improve his position at Plainfield. Within a few months he had decided to transfer to Morris Academy at Litchfield, Connecticut, where he was to study under the Reverend William R. Weeks and his assistant, young Mr. H. L. Vail. There the theological and the religious were more emphasized and he may have felt that he could more easily hold his own in such sacred subjects. His brother and Orson Oviatt accompanied him to Morris Academy as a matter of course. He may not have been expert in Greek but whither he led they followed. He was in charge.*

An instance of his supervision occurred soon after their arrival in Litchfield. Salmon, a flamboyant youngster of fourteen as glib with his tongue as his brother was careful, committed some breach of school discipline. His

---

* Mr. Vail later described John Brown to a friend as "a godly youth, laboring to recover from his disadvantages of early education, in the hope of entering the ministry." (Sanborn, *John Brown*, p. 591 *n.*) John Brown's scholastic difficulties stemmed from his preference for outdoor work rather than school as a boy, the rudimentary instruction at Hudson's log schoolhouse, and the shortness of his stay at Tallmadge Academy. In his own words, he "learned nothing of Grammar: nor did he get at school so much knowledge of comm[on] Arithmetic as the Four ground rules." (Letter to Henry L. Stearns, July 15, 1857.) Virtually every college required for entrance a sound knowledge of grammar, considerable familiarity with Latin and Greek, and some mathematics. At Western Reserve College in Hudson, for example, the requirements for admission, which were not unusual, included, according to the college catalog of 1831, "A knowledge of Cooper's or Adams' Latin Grammar, and making of Latin, Virgil's Aeneid and Bucolics, eight select orations of Cicero, Vulgar Arithmetic, Elements of Geography, a grammatical knowledge of the English language, Volpy's or Buttman's Greek Grammar, Greek Delectus, Graeca Minora with a part of Nielson's Greek Exercises." (Quoted by F. C. Waite in *Western Reserve University, The Hudson Era*, p. 129.) The subjects required for college probably roughly indicate the courses John Brown studied at Plainfield and Morris academies.

elder brother, upon finding that Mr. Vail was not likely to punish Salmon, gave the young teacher an admonitory lecture. If the teacher did not know his duty, John Brown did. "Mr. Vail," he said, "if Salmon had done this thing at home, father would have punished him. I know he would expect you to punish him now for doing this—and if you don't I shall." Mr. Vail refused, so John Brown did, flogging his brother that night.[30]

Mr. Vail was impressed. There was something about the tall young man that always remained in his mind and more than forty years later he wrote him:

. . . I know you have not forgotten the winter of 1816–17 when yourself and your brother Salmon and Orson M. Oviatt, all then from Hudson, Ohio, were pupils in Morris Academy, Litchfield, South Farms, under the care of the Rev. William R. Weeks, I also being assistant teacher in the same institution; how you boarded at General Woodruff's, since deceased; and how we had meetings for religious conferences and prayers, in which your own voice was so often heard. Why, I remember all these times as though they were the times and scenes of yesterday. . . .[31]

But even his proficiency in prayer did not help John Brown with his studies. Few, perhaps, have ever tried harder. The picture of himself returning to Hudson not as a success or a clergyman but as one who failed because he could not master learning must have been a spur to his efforts. Each night he tackled his books with a resolution that did not dim until his candle spluttered out. His vision became steadily worse until it was difficult for him to read at all. He was suffering, in his own words, from "inflamation of the eyes," which for a time became chronic. It was particularly painful for him to surrender his plans for learning, a friend later explained in describing how John Brown was forced to quit Morris Academy and relinquish his plans for the ministry, because "with him it was one of his *principles*, never to yield a point, or abandon anything he had fixed his purpose upon." [32]

By the end of the winter of 1817 he was on his way home to Hudson. Orson Oviatt and Salmon returned with him. If he did not speak of his failure that did not mean that it did not rankle. Even forty years later when he wrote his long autobiographical letter telling of the death of his mother, his boyhood losses, of the Indians of Hudson, his first meager schooling, his industry, his reading, and his various business successes, he wrote nothing at all of Plainfield Academy or of his experience at Litchfield. Not a single word did he write of his youthful plan to become sufficiently learned to desert the tannery for the pulpit, which had ended, despite the fact that he "habitually expected to succeed," in his first bitter defeat.

HIS BROTHER'S KEEPER

I

When John Brown returned to Hudson from Connecticut, perhaps a little more gaunt and angular from his study and his trouble with his eyes, he did not excuse himself for his failure. If on the surface he was silent and bleak enough for a time, it is probable that he was simmering within, beginning to form that habit of converse with the Lord which was to sustain him for so many years.

In this busy if mute colloquy, he liked to accuse himself in a very luxury of self-abasement, declaring, if this communion resembled his letters, that he had not known God at all as he should, that he was smarting under the rod of his heavenly Father because he was utterly unworthy,* and fearing, it may be, that the failure of his eyes might have resulted from the deeper failure of one flawed and uncalled of God. Presently, however, in this case as in others, his ostentatious, if private, despair was displaced by a vigorous optimism and this despite every effort.

So it was that his glumness did not last long after he became once more his father's foreman in the Hudson tannery. In addition to his work at the tannery, he helped with the spring plowing, pitching hay in June and early July, shocking wheat and oats a little later, flailing the grain on the barn floor during the harvest and even occasionally becoming mirthful or attempting jokes, some of which were later described as "more cutting than cute." [33]

He was always prompt, too, in helping with the chores, bedding down the horses at night and lending a hand with the milking as he talked of the blood lines of the fine cattle and swine he might some day own. Particularly skillful in the handling of his father's sheep, his care of them was almost tender, the result of his romantic affection for the biblical concept of the shepherd as a protector and saviour of the weak and helpless.[34]

But he was restless under his father's eye, impatient of being a subordinate, and sometime within the next year or two, probably in 1818, he and Levi Blakeslee went into business for themselves.[35] They built a cabin and a tannery about a mile northwest of Hudson's center, near the road to Cleve-

---

* Such expressions as these, quite apparently the subject of much of his thought, run like a refrain through many of John Brown's letters from early manhood until his death.

land which was some 26 miles distant. There they kept "Bachelors' Hall," as
John Brown called it, he baking the bread and doing the cooking. From the
first the business prospered and soon they had several employees, making it
impractical for John Brown to continue with his work in the kitchen. He
hired Mrs. Lusk, widow of Captain Lusk, who had died in 1813 after the
siege of Sandusky during the War of 1812, and presently he suggested that
she and her daughter, Dianthe, a year younger than John Brown, then probably eighteen, move into the cabin and do all the housework and the cooking.
It had been enlarged to accommodate the employees.

2

From the first John Brown was attracted to Dianthe, partly, he remembered,
because his father was urging him to marry, but, he adds, he was also "led by
his own inclination." [36] Frequently described as the most masculine of men,
he was at that moment in Hudson at the very peak of youthful energy and
desire. He wanted a family and the full-fledged adulthood he had craved
since a child. Dianthe was small and mild and baked good bread. But man lives
by more than bread alone and the flesh has sweeter demands than nutriment.
In addition to her talents as a baker, Dianthe had that remarkable plainness
of which John Brown always spoke with as much admiration as if he were
describing some unusual seductiveness. Indeed, it may have attracted him more
for he so hated coquetry and show that Dianthe, whom he praised as "a neat
industrious & economical girl of excellent character; earnest piety & good
practical sense," [37] drew him with a power utterly beyond that of any frontier
siren.

His blood was fevered, too, by her way with a hymn and his desire was
whetted when he heard she thought so highly of prayer that she retired for a
time each day to practice it. If Dianthe loved her suitor, and there can be no
question but that she did, her younger brother, Milton Lusk, did not particularly care for him for some years. In recalling his sister's marriage, he said, he
objected to it because of John Brown's bossy ways.

He was afraid that John would be hard on Dianthe, who, he says,

was my guiding star, my guardian angel; she sang beautifully, most always sacred
hymns and tunes; and she had a place in the woods, not far from the house, where
she used to go alone to pray. She took me there sometimes to pray with me. She
was a pleasant cheerful person, but not funny; she never said anything but what
she meant. When mother and Dianthe were keeping house for John Brown at the
old log-cabin where he had his tannery, I was working as a boy at Squire Hudson's

in the village and had no time to go up and see my mother and sister except Sundays. Brown was an austere feller and he didn't like that; one day he said to me, "Milton, I wish you would not make your visits here on the Sabbath." I said, "John, I won't come Sunday or any other day," and I stayed away a long time. When Dianthe was married, I would not go to the wedding.[38]

Even before the wedding John Brown was afire with a new ambition. He would become a surveyor. He bought a copy of Abel Flint's *System of Geometry and Trigonometry Together with a Treatise on Surveying*, writing his name in it and the date, 1820.[39] It was hard going, its tables of logarithms difficult, as were the tables of sines, tangents, and secants, the pages about variations of the compass and the attractions of the needle, and the sections on rectangular surveying or the method of computing areas. But he persisted, for the science of measurement had a peculiar fascination for him and he sometimes referred to the compass as if it were a moral instrument, its needle, despite its waverings, finally indicating the true course. "It wabbles about and is mighty unsteady," he once said, likening it to a weak but well-meaning man, "but it *wants to point to the north*." [40]

3

John Brown and Dianthe Lusk, he twenty and she nineteen, were married on June 21, 1820, probably in the new Congregational Meeting House which had been formally dedicated on March 1 of that year.[41] The wedding may have been as notable to some, including Squire Hudson, for its scene as for its union. It is likely that it was one of the first in the new church, the completion of which was a climax in the life of David Hudson, justice of the peace in Hudson, who had proposed to Hudson's first settlers that the community be governed by the four basic principles of religion, morality, law observance, and education.[42]

But from the first there were those who felt it would be touch and go as to whether the region would become a community of law and order or be dominated by the Indian killers, the drunks, trappers, and ne'er-do-wells who were attracted to the Western Reserve not because law and order were strong but because they were weak. They sought the liberty that the holy described as license. They were tired of the East's authority, particularly ecclesiastical authority and the prying of the righteous. In this struggle, a pious act or an assertion of the law was a civic contribution while hell-raising, in the eyes of others, was a public-spirited blow against repression. Often the issue seemed in doubt, if not always in Hudson, then elsewhere on the Western Reserve, where church services were occasionally assaulted, as at Elyria in Lorain County, by those who discharged their muskets against the doors, blasting them open and shattering all the windows.[43]

John Brown and Dianthe must have been as proud of the new church as Deacon Hudson, who loved its steeple and "the elegant bell which is heard not only in town but in Twinsburg and the neighboring towns." Declaring that only twenty years ago Hudson had been "a howling wilderness far away from the preached gospel," Deacon Hudson wrote, "How applicable are the Scriptures saying 'The wilderness shall bud and blossom like the rose and become vocal with the praise of the Most High God!' " The people of Hudson liked to recall that the new meetinghouse had cost $5,400 to build, but that the bell with its beautiful tone had cost only "a load of cheese sold in Pittsburgh." [44]

4

If Deacon Hudson in founding Hudson and attracting settlers to it had always worried as to whether virtue would triumph, he was soon to find he had a powerful ally in the newly married John Brown. Stimulated by being the head of a household, a freeholder, and a voter when he reached his majority on May 9, 1821, he blossomed into a power for good of such persistent militance that it made the actions of others seem pale and anemic by comparison. Perhaps his help came just in time. In Boston, a few miles to the west, some brothers by the name of Brown were becoming counterfeiters whose exploits were such that they became legend long before the deeds of their righteous neighbor were celebrated. One of them, Jim Brown, was hit by a bolt of lightning in 1825 as he stood in a doorway and knocked to the ground, his clothing ripped from him to his shoes and socks. A man of unusual strength, 6 feet and 2 inches in height, he quickly recovered.[45] Ever after he boasted that no living man could lay him on his back as quick as the Almighty had.

In Akron, twelve miles to the southwest, sinners almost as hardy were beginning to congregate, confidence men, blackmailers, card sharps, and other assorted swindlers, and in such numbers that within ten years they would almost take over the town.[46] The godly were soon declaring that the Western Reserve and Ohio were "Satan's seat," its morals deplorable, its "wolfish men . . . much more to be dreaded" than the wolves of the forest.[47]

It was against all this that John Brown firmly set his face. Like his father before him he came out "in the seport of civil order and religion." Before his first child, John Brown, Jr., was born on July 25, 1821, he was becoming a very virtuoso of righteousness. He liked to catch criminals and then reform them, illustrating at one and the same time his stern sagacity and his capacity for forgiveness. He knew that one should love the sinner and hate the sin and it was his aim to do just that. It was his practice, too, to feed the families of those he had jailed, for he said that the innocent should not suffer with the guilty. Occasionally he even fed those who were unconnected in any way with wrong-doing simply because his ever-inquiring eye searching the community for wrong to expose or good to praise had discovered a family in want.[48]

He did all this not only for his own improvement but for Hudson's, too, and later for Randolph's, as another man might lay a board sidewalk or fill a mudhole. One of his first ventures in law enforcement and reform came at about this time when his uncle, Frederick Brown, then a judge at Wadsworth in nearby Medina County, gave his nephew a warrant for a young horse thief who had escaped to New York. John Brown traveled to upstate New York, arrested the boy, talked to him for days on the way home on God's love and God's forgiveness, persuaded Judge Brown and others involved not to send the boy to the penitentiary, where, he said, his character would be ruined, but to apprentice him to the man whose horse he had stolen. (The youth reformed and died years later, a respectable citizen.) [49]

In the year of John Brown's marriage, James Foreman came to work for him in his Hudson tannery, moving with him to Pennsylvania five years later.[50] Foreman came to admire his employer's "Sigacity in detecting crime and his manner of punishing it." [51] In the summer of 1824, Foreman recalled, Brown was disturbed on finding that "a very choice calf skin" was missing.

Suspecting a young journeyman "from the fact that he was rather opposed to good order and religious habits," Brown watched the backslider closely but could learn nothing of his calf skin. Alerted a few days later when the young man's brother visited him, he ordered two of his employees to hide in the brother's room while he packed. They saw the brother pack the calf skin and brought both to Brown when the apprentice "owned up to the theft" and "cryed like a child under the lecture Brown gave him" when he "told him he would not prosecute him unless he left but if he did he would prosecute him to the end of the law."

The boy agreed to stay and for two months suffered John Brown's peculiar punishment, living in absolute silence, as unnoticed as if he were air, his fellows forbidden to speak a syllable to him; sometimes he himself would speak but no one seemed to hear or see him. If at dinner he asked for the potatoes they were silently proffered as if to empty space. "I think," Foreman observed, "a worse punishment could not have been set upon a poor human being . . . but it reformed him and he afterwards became a useful man." [52]

John Brown would not easily permit any interruption of his crusade. In the fall of 1824, for example, he was riding hard to fetch a doctor for Dianthe, who was about to give birth to her third son, when one and a half miles from Hudson's center "he espied two men tying up two bags of apples" in an orchard which was not theirs "and making ready to put them on their horses." Knowing it more urgent to prevent crime than to help his wife, Brown pulled up, dismounted, tied up his horse, chased and captured the men, made them confess and restore the stolen apples to their rightful owner "before he attended to the case of his wife." [53]

Nor did he weary of doing good. Later, Foreman recalled, a man stole a cow but its owner recovered it and declined to prosecute. Upon hearing of the incident the next day, John Brown insisted that the cow stealer be arrested and committed to jail. The thief was confined to jail for some time while Brown "supplied his family with an abundance of provisions once a week until his release," acting under the principle, Foreman says, that the innocent should not suffer from the acts of the guilty. Once he sent Foreman to spy on a family he heard were destitute but whose husband and father, he feared, was so "high spirited" that he "might let his family suffer before he would make his wants known." The family's condition, Foreman found, was indeed deplorable and John Brown sent food and clothing to their aid.[54]

But he knew that works without faith and acts without grace were not enough. He not only observed the Sabbath, doing little more than breathe and pray, but insisted that his journeymen and apprentices do the same as well as attend Sunday services, both in the morning and afternoon. He imposed an almost motionless silence on his household for the twenty-four hours beginning with sundown Saturday that drove its members, particularly the younger ones, to virtual frenzy and when the time was over they broke from the Brown house like an explosion. But his religion was not only for the Sabbath. "I do not believe," Foreman recalled, "he ever eat a meal of even Potatoes & Salt but he asked a blessing and returned thanks."

It was only a part of God's moral order that a man of such virtue should prosper. His business increased and so did his family. After John's birth in 1821, there was Jason's on January 19, 1823, and Owen's on November 4, 1824. (John Brown's father, Owen, continued to have children almost at the same rate as his son until 1832.) The twenty-four-year-old tanner, with three children and a good many more expected, built a big new farmhouse, which he painted white and which was still standing in Hudson a century later.

He had the praise of Hudson's godly for if his concern for righteousness was a little oversized, if his trust in his judgment of sinners was a bit more dogmatic than most, his essential point of view was typical of the time. Man was his brother's keeper and it was as much his duty to rebuke the sinner as it was to see to his own conduct. The concern for sin, at least in the best circles in and around Hudson, was universal. John Brown's uncle, Gideon Mills, for example, each day went the round of his neighbors, anxiously asking them if they thought they were saved, although sometimes he would take to telling stories and when his wife, aunt Dolly, protested, would say, "Just one more story, Mother, and then I'll talk about their souls."

Deacon Ashbiel Kilbourne used a fallen maple leaf, faded but still bright, to lecture his children about how all things fade here below but become bright and beautiful after they fall from the tree of life. Yet the deacon could be stern, too. When one of his daughters asked him if she could have a flower garden, he said she could if she kept it weeded. But she did not and when she returned from school one day she found her garden destroyed, both flowers and weeds wilted and uprooted.[55]

THE SEEDS OF DIVISION

I

As John Brown occupied himself with the tanning of hides and the practice of virtue in Hudson in 1824, a sick and weary man, whom he had never seen and never would see, was living out the final months of a life which profoundly affected the years of the young man on the Western Reserve as well as the lives of most other Americans. The dying man was an inventor and now in his home near New Haven, Connecticut, even as he was wracked by pain so excruciating that he compared it to the tortures of the Inquisition, he was trying to invent a medical device which would relieve his agony.

Eli Whitney was suffering from a diseased prostate gland, then regarded as a fatal illness. His physician was Dr. Nathan Smith, a graduate of the Harvard Medical School, and one of the most proficient medical men of his time. Another friend, who visited him almost daily, was Professor Benjamin

Silliman, among the foremost of the nation's scientists. Both were singularly impressed with the way in which the dying man used his own pain-wracked body as the basis of his final invention. Despite the eminence of his physician, the patient took charge of his own case, examining "with great care and coolness," Silliman remembered, "the best medical articles on his disease." [56]

With plates of the prostate gland and books on the disease all about him on his bed, shifting with the pain he found hard to bear, he nevertheless carefully designed, after he had mastered all the facts, an instrument, probably a flexible catheter.* On finding it necessary to obtain the needed materials abroad, he procured them from London and Paris, and then directed the construction of the instrument. "Nothing he ever invented," observed Professor Silliman, "not even the cotton gin, discovered a more perfect apprehension of the difficulties to be surmounted, or evinced more efficient ingenuity." [57]

His final invention was successful, lessening his pain for hours at a time. Then, propped up on his pillows, the fifty-nine-year-old man made plans for improving another of his inventions, a giant trip hammer driven by a belt; but there may have been times during his last months when he forgot the practical present for a space and considered the years that he was quitting. He had always exhibited in almost equal proportions an indomitable courage and a strong sense of persecution. His mind had usually been so filled with revolving wheels and cogs, with better and quicker ways of doing things mechanically, that it had space for little else save the plots and conspiracies he found everywhere against him. He could make the cogs and wheels do what he wanted them to do but for years, despite the most ardent pursuit, he could not win that success in wealth and recognition for which he had inordinate need.

Nor had he ever succeeded, although powerfully drawn to her for some thirty years, in winning the lovely Catherine Greene, the widow of the Revolutionary War hero, General Nathanael Greene. Instead, Whitney's best friend and partner, Phineas Miller, had married her. Lying in bed during his final illness he may have even smiled, for he had always derived a grim enjoyment from reviewing the unalloyed quality of his persistent misfortune, as he recalled how his career had opened with his being shipwrecked in the waters of Hell's Gate. When he stepped ashore the first man whose hand he shook was suffering from smallpox. Whitney was forced to interrupt his journey for the hospital where he underwent inoculation.

The shipwreck occurred in New York's waters on his way South from Yale where he had been graduated in 1792. Although from boyhood—he

---

* It probably enabled him to pass the urine blocked by his enlarged prostate.

had been born in Massachusetts in 1765—his bent had been strongly mechanical, he had been engaged as a tutor to the children of a South Carolina planter in Latin, Greek, and mathematics. A conservative young man, occupied with his own plans for private advancement, he was completely uninterested in such social questions as the slavery he was soon to see at first hand; but not on the South Carolina plantation.

Having met Catherine Greene in New York, it was as if he could not leave her, although she regarded him then as only a provincial if attractive young man whom she would like to help. He sailed from New York with her to her Georgia home, accompanied by Phineas Miller, who did not marry Mrs. Greene until later and was then manager of her estate, Mulberry Grove. Whitney stayed on and on at her mansion on the Savannah River, never continuing his journey to South Carolina, and it was with Catherine Greene's encouragement, and almost as if to impress her, that he invented the cotton gin in 1793.

He thought his fortune made with his invention. Instead, the factory and all its equipment that he had designed, constructed, and installed at New Haven to manufacture the gin was completely consumed by fire and he had to begin all over again. In addition, his greed and the greed of his partner, Phineas Miller, resulted in the end in their making almost no money at all from the invention.

They had tried to hold it as a monopoly, refusing to sell or rent a single gin, insisting on two-fifths of what might ultimately approximate the South's entire cotton crop for their payment, or two-fifths of all the cotton cleaned by the gin. As a result the invention was pirated, their patent rights were flouted, hundreds of unauthorized models of the gin made and used, and Whitney's profits minimal. Although Whitney wrote on every aspect of his invention, never once did he mention the slavery whose power the cotton gin was such a decisive factor in increasing.

He was similarly plagued by misfortune when some years later he revolutionized industry by the interchangeable parts system. It seemed to him that the War Department, with which he had a contract for muskets—particularly through the sinister machinations of one Callender Irvine, Commissary General of Purchases—was systematically persecuting him to the point of ruin. Before Whitney's time, muskets, and most other articles, were created by craftsmen, fashioning each part by hand and in terms of the specific object they were making, that is, so as to fit only with the other parts of the one article being wrought. Whitney invented and constructed machines that stamped out thousands of uniform interchangeable parts, any one of which

would fit into any musket being assembled, and in doing so created the beginnings of mass production. Even the conservative, with no wish to do so,
sometimes revolutionize the world.

Although after years of harassment he finally succeeded in gaining the
money and recognition he craved, he was never very happy, wistfully regarding the extraordinary Catherine Greene from afar, writing her over the long
years and never forgetting her. His hopes of winning her may have once been
intense, for he had been a handsome young man, tall and well made, his eyes
black, his features regular, his energy immense, his manner attractive although
his inability to think of anything beyond his private concerns was almost
total. But now as he lay abed late in 1824, his body wasted, his black hair
tinged with white, with only his passion for his own affairs unimpaired, he
possessed little more of what had once been his than his continued courage.

2

Even as Whitney lay dying, the Old Southwest was beginning to boom, the
necessary precondition for its prosperity the availability and widespread use
of his cotton gin. With the price of cotton as high as 33 cents a pound—it
had been as low as 7 and 8 cents not long before—Negroes were worked in
Mississippi's and Alabama's slave gangs from dawn to dark and occasionally
at a desperate pace in the fear that the price of cotton might drop before the
crop was made.

In Kentucky and Virginia, where slaves had usually been confined to
general farm work and the cultivation of tobacco and some hemp, they were
now being bred for sale to the Lower South. As cotton acreage pyramided in
the Gulf States, prices for human stock rising from $300 to more than $1,000
for a prime field hand, the export of human beings steadily increased from
1825 until by the 1850's Kentucky was shipping South, usually in coffles of
men and women bound together by chains and under armed guard, some
3,400 annually while Virginia was similarly exporting about 9,371 human
beings each year.[58]

Although there had been a few slaves escaping from Kentucky across
the Ohio River to the free state on the opposite shore as early as 1815, their
number steadily increased as the use of the cotton gin became widespread
during "The flush times of Alabama and Mississippi,"[59] from about 1825 to
the depression of 1837; and their number would increase again.

It was one of these slaves, escaping with his wife from Kentucky and
fearing sale South, who appeared at John Brown's house in Hudson in 1824

or 1825. "When I was four or five years old," John Brown, Jr., wrote in recalling the incident, "and probably no later than 1825, there came one night a fugitive slave and his wife to father's door. . . ." Declaring that fugitive slaves had been very rare before that time, he continued, "They were the first colored people I had seen; and when the woman took me up on her knee and kissed me, I ran away as quick as I could and rubbed my face 'to get the black off.' . . . Mother gave the poor creatures some supper; but they thought themselves pursued and were uneasy."

Presently father heard the trampling of horses crossing a bridge on one of the main roads, half a mile off; so he took his guests out the back door and down into the swamp near the brook to hide, giving them arms to defend themselves, but returning to the house to await the event. It proved to be a false alarm; the horsemen were people of the neighborhood going to Hudson village. Father then went out into the dark wood—for it was night—and had some difficulty in finding the fugitives; finally he was guided to the spot by the sound of the man's heart throbbing for fear of capture.*

3

John Brown knew little of the slave or slavery until the specific aspect of the Industrial Revolution that was the new textile industry produced such a speedup in the cotton fields that fugitive slaves became frequent on the Western Reserve. If his life was influenced by William Lloyd Garrison and his *Liberator*,[60] by Theodore Weld, Elizur Wright, and other abolitionists of whose exploits he read, it was perhaps even more fundamentally affected by men and events even further removed in time and space, by John Kay's flying shuttle, John Wyatt's roller spinning machine, James Hargreaves's spinning jenny, Arkwright's water frame, and Samuel Crompton's mule.

It was these British inventions of the last half of the eighteenth century, including the harnessing of steam, that created the British and American textile industries, crying for cotton, and ultimately created the new anti-slavery movement, the result of a revivified slavery. But before the South could supply this growing demand for cotton, it needed a machine for plantation

---

* A similar story is told of John Brown by Mrs. Danley Hobart, daughter of Levi Blakeslee. She said that when John Brown and her father were in a partnership for the tanning of leather in Hudson in 1818 they also hid a black fugitive when they heard someone approaching on the road. Again John Brown is quoted as hearing the throbbing of the fugitive's heart when he went out into the night after the danger had passed to take him back into Brown's cabin. See MS. interview with Mrs. Danley Hobart, December 1908, by K. Mayo, Villard Collection. The two stories probably concern the same event, the time and place varying because of the memories of those who told them years later.

use which could separate from its seed the short staple cotton, the only variety which could grow in the continental United States. Without this there could be no great cash crop sustaining slavery.

It was in supplying this need that Whitney had done more to influence the course of John Brown's life, and the lives of all Americans, than William Lloyd Garrison ever did. His invention made it possible to grow short staple cotton profitably, that American variety soon largely to displace in the world market the long staple cotton grown in Egypt, India, and elsewhere, which could be cleaned readily of its seed without a machine. As Whitney's mechanism spread into the Old Southwest, into western Georgia, Mississippi, Alabama, and Louisiana with the great migration there between 1815 and 1830, and later to Arkansas and Texas, the Cotton Kingdom came into being, built on slavery and the gin which could clean fifty times as much short staple cotton from its seed in a single day as could be done before by hand.

It is possible that Whitney still lived when the Negro slave and his wife appeared at John Brown's door, desperate to escape from a land where slaveholders were thriving because of his genius. But Whitney never thought of such matters, untroubled by any premonition that, as far as one man could, he embodied in his own person the economic forces that were to clash in the Civil War. Conscious only of his necessity to fulfill himself, inventing both the gin that built the Cotton Kingdom and the beginnings of the North's mass production which was a powerful factor in defeating it, his life contained the seeds of a tragic national division which apparently never once crossed his mind.

Now as that life neared its end, the pain was so severe that it was utterly beyond the capacity of his catheter to reduce it. On January 7, 1825, the day before he died, he made careful preparations to assure the continuity of production and ownership at his manufactory at Mill Rock near New Haven. Sometimes during the final days he was delirious but once when his mind cleared he asked for his pencil. With death reaching for him, he made one final sketch of a new industrial process that had occurred to him as he lay dying. It depicted a tumbler mill designed to wear smooth by friction the rough edges of the component parts of muskets.

XI

The Drama of Self

A GENERATION, however dissimilar its individuals, often has a common identity, its members bound together, if in no other way, by the crisis shaping and controlling them. Yet each responds differently to the developing peril, some swiftly and almost at once while others cannot be moved from the prison of themselves until after a long smoldering of forces within and without. Even knowing this it may seem strange enough that John Brown, known to history as the foremost of anti-slavery fanatics, should have remained so remote and removed from the fight against slavery when other young men of about his age had room for little in life but thought and action against it. He was always against slavery, almost as a matter of inheritance, but it was a long time before the fight against it was the major purpose of his life.

While others were organizing for a collective struggle against slavery during the early 1830's, John Brown's aspirations were directed toward becoming a kind of backwoods Leonardo da Vinci, early American style, a tanner, a cattle dealer, a surveyor, a postmaster, a community leader, a lay educator, and a lay preacher, if supervising a school in his Randolph home and sometimes preaching there made him either of the last. While those of his contemporaries actively against slavery were becoming professionals, giving their entire time at a salary of $8 a week to organizing meetings and anti-slavery societies, collecting funds, distributing abolitionist literature, and facing mobs, he continued a secluded amateur, occasionally reading in *The Liberator* or otherwise hearing of the exploits of others.

THE HUDSON CONTROVERSY

I

Those of whom John Brown read were concerned with such matters as how to obtain a place to speak at a time when almost all halls and churches were denied them, developing techniques of getting prominent citizens to endorse their meetings, running petition campaigns asking Congress to prohibit slavery in the District of Columbia, evolving methods of silencing mobs so that they could continue with their arguments even when confronted by riots. But John Brown's mind was usually on the price of beef, or on where to sell his leather, or on the reading which was increasingly a part of his search for self-improvement and proper conduct, or concerned with his search of the theological volumes of Jonathan Edwards for additional religious insight as to the proper punishment of disobedient or otherwise sinful children.

His development was peculiarly slow, given the two facts that he was against slavery and that his home town of Hudson was the scene of one of the most bitter of the early anti-slavery controversies, a struggle which involved the recently founded Western Reserve College at Hudson and attracted the attention of the entire country. Although John Brown moved some 85 miles to the east to western Pennsylvania's Crawford County in 1825, several years before the Hudson controversy, his distance from it was not the only reason he reacted so slowly. He was not ignorant of the struggle in which those favoring the immediate abolition of slavery fought unsuccessfully for control of the college, and with some disorder and bloodshed.[1]

On the contrary, he knew all about it through visits and letters and newspapers. His whole family was involved in it and he knew many of its central figures, including Professor Elizur Wright, four years his junior, with whom he had attended school, who had been raised much as he had been, and who within a short time would be secretary of the American Anti-Slavery Society. His father was a participant in the battle, leading a separatist movement in the support of Oberlin College, a rival institution of which Owen Brown became a trustee. Its anti-slavery ideology and policies became so dominant on the Western Reserve as to influence not only John Brown when he returned from Pennsylvania but virtually every other abolitionist of the region.[2] But the controversy's influence had a kind of delayed reaction on John Brown.

During its fiercest years, when it was attracting national attention, he was so immersed in the adventure of himself that the battle cries of friend and foe sounded but dimly in his ears.

2

Western Reserve College was dedicated on April 26, 1826, when the cornerstone was laid and a Latin oration delivered by Caleb Pitkin, president of the Board of Trustees, who may have understood the Latin he was speaking as little as did the admiring farmers who stood about. It had been ghost-written for him by Deacon Elizur Wright, the father of the future professor at the college, who suffered not only from Pitkin's delivery but by the fact it was so garbled when printed in a newspaper at Ravenna, twelve miles distant, that he complained "you could not guess whether it was Mohawk, Cherokee or something else." [3]

But Deacon Hudson, forty years old when he founded Hudson in 1799, and sixty-seven when the cornerstone was dedicated, a rough-hewn, kindly faced man whose hair was now white, wept with happiness throughout the day, nor could Pitkin's Latin lessen his rejoicing in the Lord's bounty. He, Owen Brown, and Deacon Wright, among a good many others, had been active in founding the college. "I asked the Lord for a home in the wilderness," he said later, in explaining his tears, "and He gave it to me. I asked Him for a church and He gave it to me. I asked Him for a school and He gave me that. But the college! The college! I never thought He would give me that. That is the child of my old age." [4]

It was this college, however, sent by God to gladden the Deacon's old age, that well-nigh ruined it. Because of the college, or as one of the first results of its establishment, the whole community was thrown into strife over the subject of slavery. It was all so unexpected. Everyone was delighted with the new faculty, particularly with young Elizur Wright, Jr., professor of mathematics and natural philosophy; the Reverend Beriah Green, professor of religion and sacred literature; and the Reverend Charles Backus Storrs, professor of morals and sacred theology and president of the college.* Until January 1, 1831, the faculty and the Board of Trustees had been as one and such terms as "hypocritical pharisees," applied to the trustees, and "Godless incendiaries," applied to the faculty, would have been without meaning.

---

* The faculty consisted of four, the fourth member, Rufus Nutting, professor of languages, taking no part in the controversy.

Before that date the trustees felt, as did most who took any interest in the subject of slavery at all, that the program of the American Colonization Society was adequate to the evil. It provided for the transportation of free American Negroes, as well as slaves whom their masters would free, to the society's colony of Liberia in Africa. The faculty of Western Reserve, including Storrs, Green, and Wright, agreed, insofar as they gave any thought to the subject at all, that this was the only practical program available to alleviate slavery. All the best people, the foremost American statesmen, and even many slaveholders, backed the society.

But this, of course, was before Professors Wright and Green and President Storrs had read *The Liberator*, whose first issue came out on January 1, 1831. Thereafter they were never the same.[5] It might seem unlikely that a mild young man in Boston who had never seen either Hudson or its college was the spark that lighted the controversy which almost destroyed the college, had not the participants in the quarrel assured us that it was so.[6] It did not surprise William Lloyd Garrison, however. He knew the power of his principles.

3

A slim, prim young man of twenty-six, 5 feet 9 inches, his head already becoming as bald as an egg, his hazel eyes calm behind silver-rimmed spectacles, Garrison had a professional benevolence so overpowering that it offended many as strongly as if he had slapped them. A nonresistant, he flaunted that principle in the face of other men as provocatively as if waving a red flag before a bull. Their fists were not as aggressive as his Godliness.

If he was dogmatic, he was also credulous and soon was to be sitting in many a dark and sleazy room before any number of mediums believing that every rap and knock was a manifestation of the dear departed. He had a faith in almost anything untried, including a wide assortment of patent medicines. A militant fighter for temperance, he nevertheless had his equivalent of grog as he swigged innocently and unknowingly such concoctions as "Dr. C——'s Anti-Scrofulous Panacea," once exclaiming after a pull on this alcoholic remedy that he could feel it "permeating the whole system in the most delightful manner."[7]

Born at Newburyport, Massachusetts, in 1805, his father was an alcoholic seaman who deserted his mother, himself, and his brother James, a sufficiently epic drunk for a book to be made of his alcoholic disasters.[8] As a boy, William had eaten scraps from the tables of Newburyport's rich and had been taunted by other boys as he walked through the streets with a tin pail in which he collected the leftovers from the back doors of the seaport's mansions. Apprenticed to a printer and newspaper proprietor at the age of thirteen, he soon became an expert typesetter and often composed not with a pen or pencil but by directly setting up the type. Before he was out of his teens he had written hundreds of editorials on politics, statecraft, and morality, but best of all he liked to compose sonnets to his own dauntless soul.

He had suffered sufficient of humiliation to give him a consuming drive to be heard, to be seen, to be recognized, whatever the means of his eminence. After a series of youthful editorships, he found himself in Boston, a stranger, unemployed and unknown in 1827 when he was twenty-two years old. With a superb effrontery or overwhelming innocence, he managed to enter a caucus of the city's most prominent Federalists where he tried to upset their agreed-upon plan for the choosing of a nominee for Congress by suggesting a nominee of his own. When he was rebuked and taunted as one without friends or reputation by a politician who said he had even found difficulty in learning the young man's name, Garrison replied,

I sympathize with the gentleman in the difficulty which he found to learn my cognomination. It is true that my acquaintance in this city is limited—I have sought for none. Let me assure him, however, that if my life be spared my name shall one day be known to the world. . . . This, I know, will be deemed excessive vanity—but time shall prove it prophetic.[9]

As he spoke he was not thinking of slavery or any other issue. He was speaking of the ferment within him, which he knew could not be repressed but would explode with a force bound to raise him high. Still he was fortunate. If he had become an editor advocating temperance, spiritualism, or absolute moral perfection, all of which were causes he was to favor, he might well have died nearly unknown to national fame. It was the issue he embraced which irresistibly raised him because it was irresistibly rising in the consciousness of the American people. If he had not met Benjamin Lundy and been recruited by him to the anti-slavery cause; if Lundy had not been transformed from a saddler into an anti-slavery editor when the iron entered his soul, as he himself said, upon seeing the lines of manacled Negro slaves, men and women in unending coffles, passing through Wheeling, Virginia, sold to the new Southwest and the booming plantations, Garrison might well have lived and died in an obscurity that might have goaded him, too, to drink.

4

If Garrison seemed to break on the country with his plan for immediate emancipation now, for the abolition of slavery at once, like some sudden and unexpected storm, it was not only because of the new and dramatic impact of his language. If there was, on the surface, at least, a public calm as to slavery, many were increasingly sensing that it was the supreme question before the American public that could not be much longer ignored. The very fact that many knew the subject to be both pertinent and dangerous made its discussion provocative. It was this uneasy, unacknowledged guilt which combined with Garrison's audacious invective to make him, almost from the first, a public force.

There were times when he did not seem impressive, as when, for example, he lowered his head on his table in his printing office so that his cat might rub itself against his baldness. Nor was he imposing when singing hymns, which he frequently did as a recreation, howling a little dolefully as he picked them out with one finger on an upright piano.[10] He always liked, his children remembered, a pretty face and women were often attracted to him, apparently drawn by the stiff little smile with which he doffed his hat in greeting them, by his prim efforts at puns and jollity, for he wanted to be human as well as a reformer.

Whatever his small embarrassments, he was the possessor of an impregnable self-confidence and was never surprised by adulation whether from man or woman. It was merely his just due. He had only two weapons, he felt, his perfect rectitude and his command of language. The first was unassailable as far as he was concerned and the second was unusual. His enemies reacted to it as strongly as his friends. One could refuse to read Garrison, and many did, but of those who faltered in their refusal and read, there were few who could remain indifferent. His language either maddened or converted.

Almost from the beginning of the Garrisonian movement many people against slavery tried to disassociate themselves from Garrison and his American Anti-Slavery Society, founded in Philadelphia in 1833, whose members were, of course, called abolitionists. The usual formulation was, "Yes, I'm anti-slavery but I'm not an abolitionist." Despite this disclaimer, however, many continued to describe anyone actively against slavery as an abolitionist.

5

It was Garrison's outpouring in *The Liberator* which changed Hudson and Western Reserve College from a place of comparative peace into a site of brickbats and fist fights. There were those who sometimes wondered what would have been the course of affairs if Isaac Israel Bigelow, a student returning from a vacation in his Massachusetts home at the end of January 1831, had not picked up some of the opening issues of *The Liberator* and passed them on to President Storrs.[11] Although Storrs had considered himself a colonizationist until he read these issues, when he looked up after reading he was one no more. He was for immediate emancipation. Within less than three years he was dead, consumed, his friends said, by his battle for the slave against the opposition of the college Board of Trustees, and Whittier was writing of him:

> *Thou hast fallen in thine armor*
> *Thou martyr of the Lord!* [12]

Soon Professors Wright and Green were also reading the first issues of *The Liberator* and the result was irreversible. Others far from Hudson were being moved by Garrison's opening statement. When friends objected to the severity of his language, one of them, the Reverend Samuel J. May, saying, "Why, you are all on fire," Garrison had replied, "Brother May, I have need to be all on fire for I have mountains of ice about me to melt." [13] His tone was similar in his initial issue of *The Liberator* when he wrote:

I will be as harsh as truth, and as uncompromising as justice. On this subject, I do not wish to think, or speak, or write, with moderation. No! no! Tell a man whose house is on fire to give a moderate alarm; tell him to moderately rescue his wife from the hands of the ravisher; tell the mother to gradually extricate her babe from the fire into which it has fallen;—but urge me not to use moderation in a cause like the present. I am in earnest—I will not equivocate—I will not excuse—I will not retreat a single inch—AND I WILL BE HEARD.[14]

Still President Storrs and his two professors did not move at once. They hoped, as did many for a time, that there was nothing inherently antagonistic between immediate emancipation and colonization, that they were only two different methods of attacking the same evil. Moreover, it was natural not to hurl themselves immediately upon destruction. They knew the forces that would be arrayed against them. They knew that attacking the Colonization Society, founded in 1816–17 at the initiation of the Virginia legislature and with the support of Congress, was almost like attacking the Constitution itself. It was built on the Constitution's acceptance of slavery. The society did not attack slavery. Rather, it tried to protect it by syphoning off to Africa the free Negroes whom slaveholders felt by their very existence as free men were an indictment and a threat to the peculiar institution.

Respect for the American Colonization Society was so universal that Garrison himself had originally favored it, even making a speech praising it before establishing *The Liberator*. His reversal had been brought about by the Negroes themselves who, whether slave or free, were often the basic cause behind the actions of white abolitionists. Black men had indicted the American Colonization Society as a slaveholder device to perpetuate slavery almost as soon as the organization came into being, the free blacks of Richmond passing resolves so characterizing it in January 1817, while Philadelphia blacks passed similar resolutions in January and August of the same year.[15] *The Liberator* on October 22, 1831, more than six months before Garrison's publication of his book *Thoughts on African Colonization*, carried an account of the First Annual Negro Convention, held in Philadelphia, which scored the American Colonization Society for pursuing a course perpetuating slavery.

Garrison's book against colonization, published in May, was the signal for the attack on colonization and gradualism in Hudson as well as many other places. It was the catalyst which precipitated many from membership in the society into active opposition against it, transforming Gerrit Smith, for example, its wealthy supporter in upstate New York, into an opponent and changing James Miller McKim, of Philadelphia, from a conservative colonizationist into a radical abolitionist who was to give aid and comfort to John Brown during the hours immediately preceding his hanging.[16] In Hudson, Elizur Wright penned a letter to Garrison on December 11, 1832, saying that the book had completely convinced him of the iniquity of colonization. But a good deal earlier than this letter, on August 2, 1832, he, Storrs, and Green had mounted the attack that nearly closed the college.[17]

Although most of its supporters and all but one of its Board of Trustees were strong colonizationists, or gradualists as they were sometimes called, Wright began a series of nine articles, running weekly in the Hudson *Observer and Telegraph* between August 2 and November 26, proving by Scripture, or so he thought, that the sin of man-stealing which was slavery could not be discontinued gradually any more than the sin of murder should be gradually given up; that one had to give up slavery immediately as one should give up immediately drunkenness, and not say "only one more drink" or "only one more murder," or "only one more slave"; that neither a Christian nor a man of conscience could support colonization, for in doing so they were in reality supporting the sin of sins which was slavery.[18]

This was maddening because while the college owned half of the news-paper, members of the pro-colonizationist Board of Trustees owned most of the other half. But the editor, one Warren Isham, published the attacks on the Colonization Society, either because he was a college employee under the control of President Storrs or because he himself favored the attack on the trustees. While the trustees were being flayed in the college newspaper, Beriah Green was condemning them from the pulpit of the college church, preaching four successive sermons on the monstrous sin of pretending to be against slavery while really favoring it. The trustees, after hearing one of the sermons, refused to attend the others but attendance under the college by-laws was compulsory for the student body.[19]

6

The controversy at Hudson played an important part in bringing to the anti-slavery movement one of its most gifted organizers. In October of 1832, Theodore Dwight Weld, twenty-nine years old and already known as an extraordinary evangel of righteousness, visited Hudson and talked to Wright.[20] Commissioned by Arthur and Lewis Tappan, the merchant-phi-lanthropists of New York City, to find a site for a manual training seminary which could educate ministers to win the battle against the Devil in what Weld liked to call "the great valley of the Mississippi," he was also lecturing throughout the state on temperance and manual training schools.

If ever a man had charisma, that nimbus of attraction drawing others to him, it was the darkly magnetic Weld. He felt the power, the pull, the silent persuasion flowing from him and he was determined to use it only for the glory of the Lord, never for his own advance or aggrandizement. He had about settled on the place for his new manual training establishment, intending to revive and reorganize a shaky institution called Lane Seminary at Cincinnati, but he still had not been drawn to the immediate emancipation of the slaves as an object for which he should do battle.

Although it was Weld who was to become the converter extraordinary to anti-slavery, it was he who was the converted on this occasion. That dis-putatious mathematician Professor Elizur Wright, to be known after the Civil War as "The Father of Life Insurance," persuaded Weld to immediate emancipation on this visit to Hudson.[21] Perhaps it was the circumstances at Hudson that gave Wright the power to move Weld, who was in the habit of moving others. A sparse young man of twenty-eight, slight and small-boned like his father Deacon Wright,[22] Wright's arguments had the forcefulness of one who was risking his livelihood by living them.

The very excitement of the conflict in Hudson may have helped to convince the visitor. Some students were refusing to attend the classes of Professor Nutting, the only member of the faculty not against colonization, while others were boycotting the classes of the three abolitionists. Fights were breaking out between the undergraduates, one of the casualties the young Mr. Bigelow who had brought *The Liberator* to Hudson.[23] His jaw was broken when he was smashed in the face with an iron bar. Other students were cutting classes as they traveled about giving lectures against slavery. The trustees issued a wistful statement in which they said they had "seen with deep regret that a spirit of self-sufficiency, pertness and disrespect to the judgment and feelings of their superiors, prevails to a fearful extent among the young of this College." [24]

The whole region occasionally seemed possessed by the "spirit of self-sufficiency, pertness and disrespect," perhaps as a result of the large amounts of whiskey consumed by its inhabitants. Deacon Wright, quoting from the researches of the Temperance Society of Western Reserve College, reported that there were 692 drunkards in the county drinking 160,000 gallons a year, or the capacity of the county's sixteen distilleries.[25] Later he complained of a Hudson lawyer who "was making too free with other men's wives." When Hudson's husbands passed resolutions against him, sending them to the *Observer and Telegraph*, the lawyer broke into the newspaper and smashed the type with a sledgehammer.[26] Even Owen Brown manifested a little self-sufficient pertness. When he was vainly groping for a word, Professor Nutting, the only member of the faculty not supporting the immediate emancipationists, obligingly supplied it. "I am as well supplied as Balaam," Owen told Professor Nutting, "for when he could not speak an ass spoke for him." [27]

But whiskey, if not philandering, was normal enough and Hudson was mainly occupied with the struggle over slavery. The climax came unexpectedly when President Storrs, already ill and worn by the bitterness of the long controversy, gave an outdoor speech of three hours in cold and rainy weather at Tallmadge on May 8, 1833. Shortly after the last word of his address pleading for immediate emancipation, he collapsed from a pulmonary hemorrhage. He never resumed his duties as president, dying almost five months later on September 15.

With his death the actual conflict was over but not the results, which lingered until the Civil War. The college by-laws had endowed Storrs with

sufficient independence of administration and faculty control to make it difficult to discharge him or his allies. But with his death his two colleagues were
at the mercy of the majority on the Board of Trustees. Green resigned immediately, accepting the presidency of Oneida Institute at Whitesboro, New
York.

But Wright decided to have a little fun before leaving. He wrote a
skit lampooning the Board of Trustees for its stand on colonization and
contrived to get it on the Commencement program, then held in the fall,
where it was enacted before a large crowd, including the trustees. In addition, he created a little disturbance by appearing "in the Commencement
academic procession with a black barber . . . on his arm and led the Negro
onto the Commencement platform, traditionally reserved for trustees, and
faculty. Although many in the audience were incensed at this action, and
some left the auditorium, no one had the temerity to demand the Negro
leave the platform." [28] Then, as Wright wrote, "I threw in my resignation
before it could be requested." [29] Within less than a year he was being assailed by mobs in New York City as secretary of the American Anti-
Slavery Society.

THE SEARCH

I

John Brown knew of all this but neither the Hudson controversy nor the
crusade against slavery gathering strength everywhere about him spurred
him into action. Although he saw *The Liberator* in his frequent visits to his
father's home in Hudson,[30] he did not become involved in the struggle. While
numerous local anti-slavery societies were being organized on the Western
Reserve, in Pennsylvania, New York, and New England, he did not organize
one in the township of Randolph just across the Ohio line in northwest
Pennsylvania. A leading citizen there, he took "great pains to circulate general information among the people, good moral books and papers and to
establish a reading community." [31] He organized a church and a school and
helped establish a post office but not an anti-slavery group.

All around him those of a similar background, raised as he had been
on a frontier farm, reared as he had been in the rigors of Calvinism, were
active in the anti-slavery fight. His own father had helped found the Western

Reserve Anti-Slavery Society in Hudson in 1833, serving as its treasurer,[32] while all over Ohio, in Deer Creek and Gilead and Felicity, farming communities not much larger than Randolph, in Shenango and Northwest and Peter's Creek in Pennsylvania, young men of about John Brown's age, and as hard-pressed by growing families, were helping organize local anti-slavery groups.[33]

His failure to act, as we know, was not because he was unopposed to slavery. It was because he was so passionately concerned with what he did put his hand to, with his private sorrows and his public triumphs, that he had little time for anything else. To some his pursuits might have seemed composed of naught but the commonplace at a rural crossroads, but to John Brown it was high drama of which he was the central figure. Even the smallest of family affairs, chores done or undone, children who obeyed or disobeyed, were matters of momentous significance. Fond of saying that the smallest act, like the widening ripples of a rock cast into the water, might extend on and on even to eternity, he once asked, "Who can tell or comprehend the vast results for good or evil that are to follow the saying of one little word?" [34]

It was these vast results from small actions that gave such exciting import to all his days. He was responsible for whether his sons and daughters went to Heaven or Hell, and what passing terrestrial affair could compare with saving his children from eternal torment? But getting a hogshead of salted pork or a blooded bull that might improve the stock for miles around were almost equally absorbing. If he was appropriately serious under these responsibilities he was not a misanthrope. Rather, in these first years at Randolph, he was experiencing an unusual optimism and it was then that he was described as being frequently jocose and mirthful.[35] In Hudson he had seldom escaped from his father's shadow. There when someone spoke of Mr. Brown they did not mean John Brown; but in Randolph they meant no one else.

One reason why he was comparatively uninfluenced by the Hudson controversy for a time was that he had put Hudson behind him with his move to Randolph, attracted to the new area by its plentiful bark, particularly hemlock, which he would use for tanning. The Hudson struggle was his father's fight and he had struggles of his own. Before slavery could be attacked there was work to be done, just as his father had to build a cabin and clear land and help establish church and school before he would advance to larger concerns. His father and hosts of others over the years had gone West but in doing so the stream of emigration had swirled around and left behind many pockets of wilderness in the East which in 1830 were still less developed than the fast-advancing Western Reserve. The township of Randolph, composed of isolated farms and farmers, without roads, schools, and churches, was such a place.

2

Perhaps John Brown was justified in finding his life absorbing for he was not only founding a family but founding a community. To him the struggle to cure his children of what he called the mean habit of lying, the effort to elevate Randolph morally and intellectually, were pursuits too exacting to permit his primary interest to stray from the township. If a fugitive slave came to Randolph he was prepared to help him just as he helped the poor and pursued horse thieves, for a certain tone had to be set and he was the man to set it.[36] If pro-slavery partisans settled in the township he would oppose them because he wanted only the right kind of folks in Randolph. His opposition to slavery at this point was more a part of personal righteousness than a struggle against an institution.[37] But this opposition to slavery was only one aspect of a quadruple standard that he required from his neighbors. The other requisites, in addition to being against slavery, were observance of the Sabbath, belief in the Gospel, and support of "the common schools." If a new settler met these requirements, John Brown was prepared to accept him; "if not he was looked upon by Brown with suspicion." [38]

Since Boston's Brahmins were later to see him as a man of "that religious elevation which itself is a kind of refinement," [39] as one who had "a natural dignity of manner—that dignity which is unconscious and comes from a superior habit of mind," [40] it was perhaps natural enough that Randolph's farmers were impressed by him. So were Samuel Torbett and David Dick, the two leading citizens of Meadville (the region's largest town some 12 miles away), who signed his bond when he became Randolph's first postmaster on January 7, 1828.[41] The power of his example as he labored for Randolph, not only for roads and schools but "encouraging anything that would have a moral tendency to improve the country," grew so strong that "it became almost a proverb" when "speaking of an enterprising man" to say that "He was as enterprising and as honest as John Brown and as useful to the country." [42]

If John Brown impressed his neighbors, it was partly because he had a kind of quiet exhibitionism. It was not in his speech that he was dramatic but in some quality of bearing. His ideal was plainly the strong silent man who said little with words but much with action. Occasionally, however, garrulity overcame him as he ran on and on, a little too full of himself and a little too sure of himself, on anything from the training of oxen, to breaking horses, to the evils of smoking. Still, he aspired to the temperate and matter-of-fact in both statement and manner and usually achieved it. One of his favorite words came to be "midling," used often in his letters, or when someone asked how things were going or how he felt. It may have been about this time that he formed the habit when talking, particularly when amused or pleased with himself, of extending his hands, palms down, and moving them up and down as he enjoyed some point he was making.[43]

He himself felt his magnetism, both then and later, once saying complacently, "The children always come to me," meaning any children anywhere, and he liked to boast that he could make a dog leave the room by merely looking at it.[44] Feeling himself a man of strong emotion, he doubted neither his anger nor his sorrow when he whipped his children, his attitude such as to make them feel sorry not for themselves but for him. They always recalled the tears that coursed down his cheeks as he brought back his arm, were always quick when telling of such punishment to emphasize his unusual tenderness in nursing them when sick.[45]

3

If there was the drama of punishment and tenderness, there was the drama of work too, of course, and John Brown liked to say that "Everything worthy of being done at all is worthy of being done in good earnest and in the best possible manner." [46] When he came to Randolph in 1825 he hurled himself against 25 acres of boulders and forest, attacking the virgin growth of hemlock, maple, and beech with such fury that his family, regarding his efforts with a kind of awe as he stood panting, wiping his brow before he leaped again to the fray, always remembered that "the task of clearing . . . was heartbreaking." [47] Yet it was not his flesh that yielded but the rocks and trees. It may have seemed to his small sons watching him work that he was harder than the boulders which he not only wrenched from the earth with the aid of chains, crowbars, stoneboat, and oxen but used for the foundation of his tannery, still standing more than a hundred years later. Aided by James Foreman, his apprentice who came with him from Hudson, he built his large, two-story log house with fireplaces at either end, the two-story tannery measuring 26 by 50 feet and having eighteen vats. Although he cleared 25 acres he was the owner then of 200 which he bought for $150 from "Armand Martin and wife," according to the deed registered on November 12, 1825, still extant at the Crawford County Courthouse.[48]

Perhaps it was then that John Brown became convinced, as a result of his own exhausting labor in clearing his Randolph acres and building his home and tannery, that land should belong to the man who worked and improved it. Early in 1826 he visited a group of squatters who were being evicted from their land near Meadville by a large land company, and encouraged them to resist, assuring them that the courts would finally find in their favor. On February 1, 1826, Judah Colt, a land agent, writing from Erie, Pennsylvania, to an official of the company in Philadelphia, said,

I sometimes despair of living to see the time when title legally derived from the State, shall no longer be disturbed by evil and unprincipled men. We have recently had a man by the name of John Brown, traveling about in this country, encouraging the *former actual settlers*, that they will ultimately recover back all their claims and that the Company's Title is of no value. . . . [49]

But John Brown's feeling that possession and improvement should make for ownership proved as wrong in this case as it did in others later involving himself and property he had improved. "Brown's Sattelites are quite chopfal[le]n," [50] Colt wrote, after one of the squatters was arrested and jailed.

The unusual size of Brown's establishment in Randolph's isolated countryside indicated something of the largeness of its owner's ambition and some may have thought it also indicated his folly. The vats and tannery were virtually useless for a time because the area was so sparsely settled that the beef cattle and sheep whose hides were needed for tanning were too few to sustain his business. Even if he could get the hides, he needed a more populous district in which to sell them. With a good deal of initiative, perhaps even before he moved to Randolph, he brought into being an unusual partnership which stretched over some 30 miles between northeastern Ohio and northwestern Pennsylvania and which solved both of his problems.

His partner was Seth B. Thompson, a distant kinsman, of Hartford, Trumbull County, near the Ohio-Pennsylvania line. Thompson was to supply beef cattle to John Brown, who would sell the cattle in his neighborhood, remitting the money, often hard to collect, to Thompson. Then, after tanning the hides, which came to him in the natural course of events since his was the only tannery in the area, he would send part of them to Thompson for sale in more settled Trumbull County. In addition, Thompson himself often sent a considerable quantity of his own hides for John Brown to tan, while Brown frequently bought barrels of salt pork from Thompson as well as buying or securing on option blooded stock which he sold in Craw-ford County.

Their accounts became rather complicated as a result of their involved trading although both men remained satisfied with their arrangement during the ten years of this tanning venture. Sometimes Thompson would advance money to Brown when debts were hard to collect and he needed income to pay his employees. Throughout the years of his Randolph tannery be-tween 1825 and 1835, which included much of the so-called martyr era of the abolition movement, John Brown sought to extend his knowledge during many of his evenings but his days, if his letters to Thompson are evidence, were mainly concerned with such matters as these:

"Sir, I send you by the bearer 156 lb. sole, 38 lb. harness & 8 sides upper. Calf skins I have not on hand now. I will either send or fetch out calf skins and other leather before long if you can find market." [51]

Another time he wrote,

Since our statement of Jan. 29th, 1830, there appears to have been finished of your stock,

leather to the amount of $940.00
Leather sent you $146.00
Cash sent you 36.00
Hides bought by me 147.00
Your share of the above would be . . . . $564.00[52]

Not all of their correspondence was so cheerful. Much of it concerned John Brown's loans from banks, often on promissory notes signed by Seth for between $200 and $300, and which Brown always expected to pay off as soon as he cured his hides and sold his leather. But money was scarce and collections slow and Seth was often in danger of being brought to judgment although his partner usually got the loans extended. On July 23, 1831, for example, Brown wrote Seth, "My own Bank debt should be paid off . . . but no news of the cash I expected . . . as yet & I do not know what shift to make about it. . . ." [53] And on August 20, 1831, probably referring to the same debt, he wrote, "I think I shall be able to raise at least 200 on paying off the Bank debt at the end of sixty days." [54] On January 11, 1833, he said, "I have no means of getting money for my bank debt before sometime in March without borrowing as I have no finished leather on hand. If the bank has made a demand on you, or should make one before the time I mention, please let me know it & I will do all I can towards meeting it." [55]

Such matters and such worries occupied his days, but in the evenings he indulged himself in affairs larger than leather and more pleasant than debt, sometimes enjoying an hour or so of reading, sometimes participating in the debates he organized between his employees. He liked to debate such questions as "What is the great end for which man was created?" and "Does mankind taken collectively answer the end for which it was created?" [56] His penetrating questions during the discussions, as well as his persistent reading, or so both appeared to his employees and the children hanging about, made him seem to them an unflagging searcher for truth, and in his own way he was. Increasingly, he seemed to believe that there was some special power in reading and learning, urging his neighbors in that direction, as he later encouraged his young men in Kansas and near Harper's Ferry toward books and debates.

4

Since John Brown's reading so impressed his Randolph friends, perhaps an effort should be made to see him, his face scrubbed and his hair slicked after a hard day's work, bending over a book on some winter evening when there was no discussion going on before the fireplace. With all the children playing about, he must have had a singular ability at concentration to be able to read at all, even with the firelight reinforced, perhaps, by candles or the illumination of a whale oil lamp. Still, the very fact of a man reading in that backwoods farming country may have been unusual enough to induce a certain quiet, create a little island of privacy and withdrawal, respected even by the children.

There can be little doubt that John Brown expected such regard when reading. It was not only that he was not a man to be lightly interrupted. It was even more that he honored books. Any book might contain an adventure in learning and an advance in wisdom if one only brought to it enough of himself to make it a part of him. If such a feeling was not everywhere evident on the frontier or in the backwoods of Pennsylvania, there were always the thirsty who regarded a good book—for books were rare and hard to come by—as an exciting event like a strange journey, or a sudden inexplicable growth, or meeting unexpectedly a sorely needed friend who comforted the soul and enlarged the mind. Then, more than later, books were lived rather than read.

So it was with John Brown. If his books did not indicate so much of his character and suggest so much of his career they might be dismissed with their listing. The very fact that he had so few, despite the criteria of Randolph, meant that he turned to them again and again throughout his life.

He pored over a biography of Cromwell, Britain's Puritan revolutionary of the seventeenth century, until it became so much a part of him, perhaps because of generations of Puritan conditioning, as to later make it a commonplace, as we have seen, for his admirers to point out that he seemed as "some old Cromwellian hero" come back to life.[57]

Often on a winter night, George Delamater recalled, he told the children the stories of Aesop. He so loved the fables, enjoying them with a kind of innocent childlike affection, particularly those stories showing the shrewdness of animals, that he himself came to endow animals with personality, later telling how he made friends with deer and mules and even certain favorite sheep.[58]

It was at Randolph that he enjoyed particularly the books of Jonathan Edwards and Benjamin Franklin, those nearly exact contemporaries and opposites who expressed the opposites of John Brown's nature, Franklin's practical businessman filled with maxims of thrift and prudence, and Edwards's mystic filled with the urge to commune with a God at once awful and just. He so delighted in Franklin's Poor Richard that in 1839 he would try his hand at something similar to Poor Richard's apothegms for improvement. In a small memorandum book he had bought the year before he wrote, "Deacon Abel Hinsdale left off entirely the use of Tobacco at the age of 66 now 73 & has used none since that time. No ba[d] consequnses have followed. Q[u]ery when will a man become to old to leave off any bad habit." [59]

He read frequently in *Plutarch's Lives*, perhaps liking its sententious moral judgments on the follies and errors of long-vanished Greeks and Romans, but also interested in the account of the slave revolt of Spartacus, when bondsmen and gladiators took to the mountains where they stood off all the power of Rome for some two years, a lesson that would grow in his mind until it became an essential point of the thinking that led to Harper's Ferry.[60] His reading of Napoleon's biography may have ultimately had similar results, however long they took to mature, as he pondered the success of the Spanish guerrillas, using the mountains of the Iberian peninsula in their defeats of Napoleon's veterans.[61]

He enjoyed the works of Josephus—Jewish historian and military commander who lived from A.D. 37 to about A.D. 95—probably because he felt, as most did then, that they offered independent historical judgment of the authenticity of the New Testament. And he read Charles Rollin's *The Ancient History of the Egyptians, Carthaginians, Assyrians, Babylonians, Medes and Persians, Greeks and Macedonians*, perhaps because Rollin, a pious

Frenchman born in 1661, seemed to give historical substantiation to the Old Testament.[62] Another of his favorite books was Bunyan's *The Pilgrim's Progress* and he followed Christian through "the wilderness of this world," across the Slough of Despond and the Gulf of Despair and the Valley of the Shadow of Death to the Celestial City, with such intentness that he mentioned "Bunyan's Pilgrim" when he himself was, as he said, "on the brink of Jordan," just before his hanging.[63]

But aside from the Bible, the book he loved most was *The Saints Everlasting Rest or a Treatise of the Blessed State of the Saints in their enjoyment of God and Glory*. Written by Richard Baxter and first published in London in 1649, it went on for some thousand pages to prove the sureness of everlasting delight for the virtuous and eternal torment for the wicked. Of this book, John Brown said "he could not see how any person could read it carefully through without becoming a Christian." [64]

More and more he appeared to feel that he might find the answer for which he searched not only in a more inspired understanding of the Bible but also in some other book if he could only come upon it. It was not that he did not know the truth, but there was the other truth of living it. That was the wisdom for which he searched. He knew the Word for it was his rock but he also knew that man was fallible, and that his own pursuit of it had often led him down false roads. Later he came to think he could "clearly discover" where he had "wandered from the road," and once felt he could never get back upon it.[65] This mulling over of the right, this searching for the road, whether through the Proverbs of the Bible or Franklin's Poor Richard, through Aesop, Plutarch, or Jonathan Edwards, was the never-ending accompaniment of his days. If a man is what he thinks, this search, this quest and questioning, however Calvinistically limited, was his real vocation as another man's might be the law or singing or carpentry.

CRIME AND PUNISHMENT

I

Many of his letters to his family over the years, most revealing a simple unpretentious goodness which must be reconciled with his harsh peculiarities, dwelt upon this worrisome burden as to how beliefs could be translated into conduct. His lament that he had "wandered from the road" referred to his stern disciplinary attitude toward his children, which he came to believe had been wrong after he found that his whippings in the case of at least two of his sons, Salmon and Oliver, made them more wild and defiant as they grew older until there came a time when they would fight if he attempted to flog them.[66]

Yet when John Brown used corporal punishment against his children he was acting in accordance with the prevailing practice of the day. From Rugby to Hudson, from every English public school to every log cabin classroom, the birch and the rule swished stingingly against bottoms and hands for the slightest infraction and even Thoreau, teaching in Concord, would whip six small students at the demand of a deacon, a member of the school committee, before quitting in protest at the barbarism he was forced to inflict.[67]

John Brown had a similar reluctance, his children liked to believe, but he overcame it and never resigned his duty or expressed his regret at performing it until his children were too large to whip. He was particularly severe when the offense involved lying, a fault which he abhorred because he himself as a boy had been so often guilty of it.[68] His four-year-old son, Jason, suffered his father's righteousness in 1827 when his father and mother interpreted a dream the little boy told as a lie. Even as an old man, Jason could not forget the scene near the large log house at Randolph. It was a bright, lovely morning. He had been away staying at the Delamaters', four miles distant, for a time and, excited at seeing his mother again, he followed her down to the spring house where "she was preparing the butter and about to take it to the house."

He wanted to attract her attention, to impress her, and as he thought of his dream it seemed to him as if it must have really happened.

"Mother," he said, "mother, I picked up a little coon by Mr. Delamater's corn crib and he was so pretty and he did not bite me. He was just like a kitten."

"Is that true?" she asked.

The little boy was silent and confused.

"Yes," he finally said.

"Now think. Is that true?" Dianthe asked again.

"She kept on questioning," Jason said years later, "and finally I said, 'No . . . I guess not.' "

Dianthe rose, the butter in her hands.

"I'm afraid then," she said, "that you have told me a wicked lie."

The little boy followed her as she returned to the house. Presently his father came out and cut a switch from a tree. Jason remembered that old Owen, his grandfather, called such a switch "a limber persuader."

"It was out in front of the house," Jason recalled. "That old iron wash basin stood on the lower step. Father stripped off my trousers—no one wore drawers in those days. He took both my hands in his and held me up in the air and thrashed me. How I danced! How it cut! I was only four. *But Father had tears in his eyes while he did it,* and mother was crying. That was the kind of hard heart he had." [69]

2

John Brown's oldest son and namesake thought that punishing his children upset his father and sent him to the theological volumes of Jonathan Edwards for guidance. It was "the Doctrine of Atonement," or so the boy later thought, that accounted for his father's strange conduct when punishing him, probably in 1831, when John was ten. Christ had atoned for man's sins by dying for him. John Brown proposed to atone for his children's sins— at least in part—by suffering himself for their transgressions, by himself receiving some of the lashes properly due them.

John Brown's one recorded attempt in this direction had its origin in the excruciating boredom suffered by his son while working in the Randolph tannery's grinding mill, shoveling bark into it while an old blind horse went round and round, furnishing the power that ground the bark. "This after months and years," John, Jr., recalled, "became slightly monotonous. While the other children were out at play in the sunshine, where the birds were singing, I used to be tempted to let the old horse have a rather long rest."

His father reproved him for this delinquency but

finally grew tired of these frequent slight admonitions for my laziness and other shortcomings, and concluded to adopt with me, a sort of book account, something like this:—

> John, Jr.
> For disobeying mother . . . . 8 lashes
> For unfaithfulness at work . . . . 3 lashes
>   " telling a lie 8   "

This account he showed me from time to time. On a certain Sunday he invited me to accompany him from the house to the tannery, saying he had concluded it was time for a settlement.

The two retired to "the upper or finishing room" where they had "a long and tearful talk," while John Brown solemnly prepared for use a blue beech switch.

I then paid about one-third of the debt. . . . Then, to my utter astonishment, father stripped off his shirt, and seating himself on a block, gave me the whip and bade me "lay it on" his bare back. I dared not refuse to obey, but at first I did not strike hard. "Harder!" he said, "harder, harder!" until he *received the balance of the account*. Small drops of blood showed on his back where the tip end of the tingling beech cut through. Thus ended the account and settlement, which was also my first practical illustration of the Doctrine of Atonement. I was then too obtuse to perceive how Justice could be served by inflicting penalty upon the back of the innocent instead of the guilty; but at that time I had not read the ponderous volumes of Jonathan Edwards' sermons which father owned.[70]

3

But these episodes were painful climaxes in family life, often clearing the air for a considerable time. Jason, for example, says that during his entire boyhood he was whipped by his father on only two occasions. The boys also remembered shared pleasures, even such simplicities as their father's shave. He made something of a ritual of it, at least at the times when his children stood admiringly about. They remembered him working up an immense lather in a gilded shaving mug, watching as the red of his face was covered with the snowy white foam almost up to the blue eyes peering into the mirror on the wall near the kitchen cistern. The stropping of his Sheffield razor, with its yellow-green handle and an American eagle emblazoned on its blade, was a bravura performance which the boys admired immensely. With a great sweeping cadence, their father played a kind of tattoo, slapping the blade against the strop, each stroke cracking like a bull whip.[71]

There was something almost hypnotic to the children in the steady scrape, scrape of the razor, the dry cracking segments of sound, almost like the echo of a motion, a long sweep of the razor, a long sandpapery scratchiness. As he stood before the mirror at such a time, his eyes now and again caught the children in some misdemeanor they felt safe in attempting behind his back. Once he saw Owen, eight years old in 1832, surreptitiously take up the cat from the floor and steal over to the cradle in which Frederick, two years old, was lying. The eight-year-old cautiously and experimentally lowered the pawing cat close to the baby's face, while his father, his back turned, continued his shaving. "Owen," he said after a time, "now put the cat up to your own face." The little boy just stood there and the scratchy sound continued for a space. "Owen," his father repeated, "put the cat up to your own face," not turning around or pausing in his shaving. Presently, he said again, "Put up the cat, Owen," and slowly the boy lifted the squirming cat to a point near his face. It was a very minor incident but it amused Owen's brothers. Their father's order became one of the family jokes and years later when Owen's brothers thought they had caught him in a mistake and had him in a corner, they would say, "Put up the cat, Owen." [72]

Other norms of family life at Randolph (whose name was later changed to New Richmond) included an almost daily exhibition of John Brown's ostentatious integrity as well as that sequence of pregnancies and births which followed one on another as swiftly as biology allowed. The three eldest children had been born at Hudson but four were born at Randolph and there was always a baby in the cradle, another a little older just learning to walk. And while Dianthe, tired and big with child, struggled with her work John Brown was often inconveniencing his customers out in the tanyard by a display of virtue or prejudice.

He so abhorred hunting and fishing, believing it a sure path to loafing, that he found it almost impossible to hand over a tanned hide to any customer who called for it with a gun on his shoulder. But usually it was his invincible honesty that inconvenienced them. "So strict was he that his leather should be perfectly dry before Sold that a man might come ten miles for five pounds of Sole leather and if the least particle of moisture could be detected in it he must go home without." [73]

While the anti-slavery drive was getting under way in 1830–1, John Brown was much more passionately concerned with the campaign against the masonic order than he was with slavery. This was also true of wide sections of his countrymen, aroused as they had been by charges of ritualistic murders of apostate Masons. Although one of the alleged murders, that of William Morgan in upstate New York, took place as far back as 1826 and the other as far away as Belfast, Ireland, the campaign became so much of a national issue that an Anti-Masonic presidential ticket was put in the field in 1832 with William Wirt of Maryland as its nominee. John Quincy Adams had wanted the nomination and when he failed to get it the ex-President ran in 1833 as the Anti-Masonic candidate for governor of Massachusetts, running second in a field of four with 18,274 votes. [74]

John Brown himself had been a Mason, joining Hudson Lodge No. 68, of which his uncle, old Gideon Mills, was Worshipful Master, on May 11,

1824. But he had resigned within a short time in the belief that its members were putting the order's oaths above the public's law. When the *Crawford Messenger* of Meadville reprinted a pamphlet written by Samuel G. Anderton, of Boston,[75] exposing the alleged murder of the Belfast Mason (by having his throat cut at a ceremonial lodge meeting), John Brown inveighed so vigorously against the order in Meadville that he felt his life in danger. In a letter to his father he wrote, "I have aroused such feeling in Meadville by shewing Anderton's statement as leads me for the present to avoid going about the streets at evening and alone. I have discovered my movements are narrowly watched by some of the worthy brotherhood."[76]

John Brown's eldest son recalled that his father had been almost lynched by a pro-masonic mob in Meadville, escaping through the back door of an inn while the mob clamored at the front. "Father then got a sort of pistol," John Brown, Jr., said, "that was about half rifle, and he became very adept in its use, killing deer with it on several occasions."[77] Apparently on occasion he could overcome his prejudice for hunting if he was the hunter.

XII

A Brief

Calvinistic Euphoria

As JOHN BROWN busied himself about his Randolph tannery in August of 1831, he had not the slightest intimation that his career would ever be crucially joined with the life of a Virginia slave about his age and born on October 2, 1800, in the Old Dominion's Tidewater, the property of Benjamin Turner of Southampton County. Yet if Nat Turner had never lived nor inspired the most famous slave revolt in American history in August 1831, filling Southerners with a kind of hysterical terror and Northerners and Southerners alike with the conviction that the hated abolitionists were somehow responsible, it may be that John Brown might never have attempted his own armed foray against slavery.

Certainly, Turner and his revolt became central to all his thought as he planned his own attack.[1] He came to feel that it proved that such a revolt could shake slavery to its very center; even more importantly, perhaps, it proved to him that those held in slavery could and would fight. But however important Turner came to be in his thoughts—and he was in time to rank him with Washington as a revolutionary liberator [2]—there is no indication that he thought of him so during that hot and dusty summer long ago when both men were about thirty-one years old. A community leader, a man of substance and piety, a fighter for common schools, perhaps even a nonresistant of a peculiar kind,[3] John Brown was then inclined to believe, as we shall presently see, that education of the slaves, if it could be accomplished, was the most effective way of destroying slavery. And yet the day would arrive when hanged Nat Turner was so alive in the mind of John Brown, so much the symbol to him of the character of black men, that he could see in his mind's eye hundreds of them rallying to his cause and theirs, when he invaded Virginia, until his little army had grown to a mighty legion.

"WAS NOT CHRIST CRUCIFIED?"

I

It was the insurrection led by this unknown slave, Nat Turner, that unleashed or stimulated forces resulting in President Jackson's message to Congress recommending the banning of abolitionist material from the mails in the South; that made Garrison and his newly born *Liberator* suddenly famous by charges that its circulation in Virginia had inspired the slaves to revolt; [4] that played its part in raising the possibility, however slight, of gradual emancipation in Virginia which was debated by the Virginia legislature during the session of 1831–2; [5] and that established the country's essential temper as to abolitionists all during the 1830's. In its wake there were rumors of similar insurrection attempts in all parts of the South, a slave revolt in Missouri in the spring of 1836 being averted, for example, when slaves were overheard "communicating their designs to other slaves, and by this means . . . detected before their scheme was ripe for execution. The plan was to murder their masters, take whatever money they could find and make for Canada." [6]

Turner's rebellion was one of the most significant events of the entire ante-bellum period. With aftersight it was perceived that the rebellion, or an event similar to it, should have been expected since during the three years preceding it there had been rising slave unrest all through the South. In 1829, Governor John Forsyth of Georgia appealed to the Secretary of War at Washington for arms "to protect the people of the state in case of slave revolt," and in the same year in a message to the legislature he referred to "the late fires in Augusta and Savannah" set by slaves, as well as to a slave conspiracy in Georgetown, South Carolina.[7]

It was during this period that black David Walker sent forth his

Appeal from Boston calling on the slaves of the South to fight for their liberty. Incandescent with fury, it was the kind of message that cannot be reduced to silence, so eloquent in its indignation that it could reach slaves who could not even read. Smuggled into the South by black seamen, copies of it were presently found from Virginia to South Carolina to New Orleans. If many slaves could not read it, they could hear it read, and if many did not even hear it read, they heard of the legend it created, the great rumor of something about to happen that it stirred.

2

But all of this transpired in a kind of underground, in a shadowy ill-defined underworld, an occurrence about which black never talked to white nor master to slave. On most plantations throughout the South, on the surface at any rate, everything was as before. With the dark anonymous mass of unpaid workers seeming as docile as ever, with the house servants as amiable and obsequious, with the carefree happiness of the slave a chief tenet of slaveholder ideology, it was difficult for the white master to come to grips with his problem. He felt that he was the architect of his fate, not his slaves. They numbered some two million by 1831 in the South, and were like some great restless Caliban beneath the earth whose hidden writhings moved the surface of the land, moved the lives of all those upon it without the slaveholders quite knowing the force that stirred the foundation of their years.

They alternated, in fact, between an uneasy knowledge that their black chattels had all the passions and cunning, and yes, abilities, too, of human beings everywhere, and the more comforting belief that they were loyal innocents, who bowed and scraped and laughed and sang even in slavery because they were not really human. At best they were mere happy children who never grew to normal man's fierce aspirations. It was difficult to endow with humanity property which could be wagered on a horse race or bet in a poker game; which could stand surety for a promissory note or security for a loan; which could be put up for auction along with one's horses and plows to satisfy one's creditors; which could be whipped as readily as a refractory mule or sold as cattle were sold or bought as grain was bought.

Thus when the slaves revealed that essential attribute of humanity, revolt in the face of the unendurable, the slaveholders always gave evidence of an acute ideological wrench. It was more than their persons which were under attack. It was a way of life, a system of values, a code and a set of beliefs, and massacre was more easy to endure than the shaking of the shibboleths by which a society lived. This they could not face. It was not Negro resentment, they declared, that was responsible for slave escapes and insurrections, but outsiders, abolitionists, inducing them by conspiracy to act against their own docile natures.

The planters sometimes also seemed to feel as if the Negroes, through remaining black in color, so unkempt and ragged in appearance, so hat-in-hand while addressing the whites, had assumed an unfair disguise which effectively concealed the desperate adventures they were harboring, occasionally as fierce and well planned as if the blacks had been white. (In addition to the Turner insurrection, there had been the slave revolts of Cato in 1739 and Gabriel in 1800, and the conspiracy of Vesey in 1822.) Insurrection outraged the slaveholders' formal concept of slavery as much as if the hogs of the field had banded together for organized revolution.

How could one perceive, for example, in the appearance of Nat Turner a dauntless leader, disguised as he was as only a slave? At the time of the rebellion, he was described as:

5 feet 6 or 8 inches high, weighs between 150 and 160 pounds, rather bright complexion, but not a mulatto, broad shoulders, large flat nose, broad flat feet, rather knockkneed, walks brisk and active, hair on top of the head very thin, no beard, except on the upper lip and the top of the chin, a scar on one of his temples, also one on the back of his neck, a large knot on one of the bones of his right arm, near the wrist, produced by a blow.[8]

3

Yet under the leadership of this knock-kneed slave with a large flat nose and broad flat feet, seventy black conspirators had killed fifty-seven of their masters and their families with a thorough, implacable dispatch, slaying the child as swiftly as they cut down man or woman, sparing but one white family described as "so wretched as being in all respects on a par" with the revolting slaves.[9] Well mounted and well armed, the slaves galloped furiously to the assault, descending on plantation after plantation, each left the burning pyre of their victims. It was a massacre, a slaughter of those guilty only of being white but guilty too, however inadvertently, of being a part of slavery.

Horrible as was the carnage, there were some in the North who greeted it as a revolutionary Lexington of the black people. Old Deacon Hudson, for example, coming from the post office in the Ohio town to which he had given his name, was seen reading his newspaper, "which seemed to excite him very much." A friend heard him exclaiming as he read, "Thank God for that. I am glad of it. Thank God they have risen at last!" When his friend asked him what the news was the old Calvinist replied, "Why the slaves have risen down in Virginia and are fighting for their liberty as we did for ours. I pray God they may get it." [10]

4

When Turner was captured at last, eight weeks after the rising, the great and near great of Southampton County crowded around him in his cell. Before his capture they had summarily executed scores of slaves, perhaps as many as one hundred, most of whom, it was admitted within a fortnight, had had nothing whatever to do with the insurrection. Just before his own execution, loaded down with chains, handcuffs binding his wrists and shackles on his feet, Turner consented to tell his captors what had animated him in his design. As one of them took down his words they found that he held himself as high and sacred and unique as any aristocrat of the Tidewater. He had, he said with a dignity that moved his captors to preserve his words, been called of God to deliver his people.

"I was thirty-one years of age," he said,

the second of October last and born the property of Benjamin Turner, of this county. In my childhood, a circumstance occurred which made an indelible impression on my mind, and laid the groundwork of that enthusiasm which has terminated so fatally to many, both white and black, and for which I am about to atone on the gallows. It is here necessary to relate this circumstance.

Trifling as it may seem, it was the commencement of that belief which has grown with time; and even now, sir, in this dungeon, helpless and forsaken as I am, I cannot divest myself of it. Being at play with other children, when three or four years old, I was telling them something which, my mother overhearing, said it had happened before I was born. I stuck to my story, however, and related some things which went, in her opinion, to confirm it. Others being called on were greatly astonished, knowing that these things had happened, and caused them to say, in my hearing, I surely would be a prophet, as the Lord had shown me things that had happened before my birth. And my mother and my grandmother strengthened me in this my first impression, saying in my presence, I was intended for some great purpose, which they had always thought from certain marks on my head and breast.....[11]

He had learned to read, he said, with remarkable ease while covertly studying the schoolbooks of white children on his plantation. He said that the blacks in the country around had always had confidence "in my superior judgment," which they believed "was perfected by divine inspira-tion." Having discovered that "to be great" one "must appear so," he had studi-ously avoided "mixing in society, and wrapped myself in mystery, devoting my time to fasting and prayer." [12]

During years of prayer, often in the field beside his plow, he saw visions showing black struggling with white, and heard a voice saying, "Such is your luck, such you are called to see; and let it come rough or smooth, you must surely bear it." And then he looked for a sign telling him when to begin the struggle and thought he had found it when

laboring in the field, I discovered drops of blood on the corn, as though it were dew from heaven . . . and then I found on the leaves in the woods hieroglyphic characters and numbers, with the forms of men in different attitudes, portrayed in blood and representing the figures I had seen in the heavens. . . . It was plain to me that the Saviour was about to lay down the yoke he had borne for the sins of men, and the great day of judgment was at hand.[13]

It was then that he began to gather around him trusted friends and confide in them his plans for insurrection. Once he went to a meeting in the woods, finding there a slave, one Will, whom he had not expected to en-list in the conspiracy. "I saluted them on coming up," he said, "and asked Will how came he there. He answered, his life was worth no more than others, and his liberty as dear to him. I asked him if he thought to obtain it. He said he would or lose his life. This was enough to put him in full confidence." [14]

Before the assault he led on his masters, Turner received other signs. "And on the 12th. of May, 1828," he said, in telling of one,

I heard a loud noise in the heavens, and the Spirit instantly appeared to me and said the Serpent was loosened and Christ had laid down the yoke he had borne for the sins of men, and I should take it on and fight against the Serpent, for the time was fast approaching when the first should be last and the last should be first.

It was at this point that a Tidewater aristocrat, referring to Turner's fast-approaching execution, interrupted to ask, "Do you not find yourself mistaken now?" [15]

Turner paused for a long look at his interrogator. Then he said:

"Was not Christ crucified?"

GRIEF AND ITS RETREAT

I

While Turner died on the scaffold as John Brown himself would die some twenty-eight years later, Randolph's young tanner, as innocent of the present as he was of the future, continued to be beguiled by the various excitements, inner and outer, that insulated him from much that was happening on the national scene. Among other matters, he was absorbed by his increasing prosperity and his unusual generosity.

As to his prosperity, with the tannery's business steadily increasing, he bought 200 more acres for $600 from Thomas Cadwalder, Jr., the deed being recorded on July 19, 1831. A little later, he sold 91 acres, reserving the right to use a stone quarry on it and later still he sold 100 acres for $700.

As to his generosity, on June 4, 1831, he presented a farm to James Foreman "for faithful service during his minority." Most men gave an apprentice when he had finished his service a suit of clothes and perhaps $5. But John Brown gave *his* apprentice 116 acres of land.[16] Still, even Foreman said that his employer had nothing of the softly angelic, writing that for tough aggressiveness, "Gen. Jackson was never more than his equal." [17]

With everything combining toward his well-being, there was little disturbing him early in 1832 until Dianthe, worn out by work and childbirth, became ill. Perhaps partly to relieve Dianthe of the schoolchildren crowding the Brown home, he had supervised the construction of the tax-supported common (or public) school the year before near his home, but the Delamater children still stayed with the Browns during the winter. So there was always an abundance of children requiring Dianthe's care. Frederick, the first child born to Dianthe in Randolph, lived only four years after his birth in 1827. Ruth was born two years later and another son, also named Frederick, was born in 1830, the sixth child since Dianthe's marriage on June 21, 1820. After again becoming pregnant, she suffered from palpitations of the heart and there were times when she seemed also confused in mind. Her husband, the older children remembered, tried to help her as best he could, doing much of the cooking and the housework, although he himself became obscurely ill in mind and body, as if his own health were synchronized with that of his wife.

On August 7, 1832, she gave birth to a son who died within a few hours. On August 11, John Brown wrote to his father,

We are again smarting under the rod of our Heavenly Father. Last night about eleven o'clock my affectionate, dutiful and faithful Dianthe (to use her own words) bade "farewell to Earth." My own health is so poor that I have barely strength to give you a short history of what passed since I last wrote you. Her health, I think I mentioned in my last letter, was very poor, partly owing to her pregnancy but more perhaps to a difficulty about her heart. She however kept about a little. . . .

Our hopes were quite revived for the first twenty-four hours for her recovery. About that time the difficulty of the heart palpitation became so great that we thought her dying for some hours. She however revived but not to gain much strength after. Her reason was unimpaired and her mind composed with the peace of God. . . .[18]

After Dianthe's death, John Brown said he was so numb he could feel nothing.[19] He sat for hours motionless and silent, and did not leave the house for days. He cared nothing, he said, as to whether his tannery continued or failed for he thought he would never work again. He did not seem to care, or even notice much, when James Foreman, married now and working the farm John Brown had given him, came and took away the five children. Perhaps his collapse was partly due to his memories of a tombstone in Hudson with its words that applied to a more recent death, "Sweet is the Memory of the Just." All he knew, he wrote, was that he was indifferent to all around him. He did not ascribe it to unfeelingness, he said, but to the illness he had suffered for some time and which he feared might be consumption.* [20]

Three days after Dianthe's death he wrote to Seth Thompson saying that he was unfit to continue their partnership and asking that Thompson come to Randolph to settle up their accounts. "Dear Sir," he wrote,

I feel it my duty no longer to withhold from you the state of my health as I have done for some time past in expectation of being better soon. I have been called to part from my wife during the last week after an illness of one week of great bodily pain & distress. She had been quite unwell for some weeks with a difficulty at her heart which reduced her strength verry much & was probably the main cause of Child bed fever of which she died. I think I might say with safety that no person ever died more composed or happy in mind. This is a great comfort of mind to me.

---

* A similar feeling of numb indifference was to seize him for some months in 1854–5, as we shall presently see.

Such is the state of my health (& of my mind in consequence), for I am unwilling to ascribe it to any other cause, that I have felt my loss but verry little & can think or write about her, or about disposing of my little children, with as little emotion as of the most common subject. This is a matter of surprise to myself for I loved my wife & had lived verry agreeably with her. . . . I supposed & have always supposed my feelings to be as warm & tender as those of other men.

I think my mind to be in a dead calm. I have been pretty much confined to my house for a number of weeks . . . I find I am still getting more & more unfit for every thing. I give you the statement of my feelings in order to convince you that I was not overcome in my feelings but that I have been growing numb for a good while.[21]

2

No matter how tenaciously grief is held, even when its possessor believes it only an illness, it often slips relentlessly away. So it was with John Brown during the year following Dianthe's death. Almost unwillingly he found his health mending, his step quickening, his eye roving toward possible replacements for poor Dianthe, buried beside her two children beyond the tanyard on the highest part of John Brown's land.

At first her husband could not stand the home they had made together, moving with his five children into James Foreman's home where he paid board. For a few weeks he scarcely moved from Foreman's house but perhaps the confining walls, as well as the needs of his children, hastened his decision that it was impractical to nourish his numbness to the point of closing his tannery. Within three months of Dianthe's death, he is writing Seth Thompson, "I should think I might send you from four to six hundred [pounds] of sole [leather] in the course of the month. . . . My health is improving some. . . ."[22]

By the last month of 1832 he is reverting to the professional worries of tanning, fearing that some twenty-two sides of skirting he has sent Thompson, along with 400 pounds of sole leather, may dry out and crack because he has lacked oil to polish and finish it off properly. "It will be best," he writes Thompson, "to have some care about keeping the grain of the skirting clear. It would get dry in three or four days if hung up at full length should the weather remain cold. Do not let the grain & flesh of the skirting come together."[23]

By the first month of 1833 he is telling Seth about an employee, one Joseph, "who seems to hang on to the Old Maid some yet but does not incline to report progress very often." Still, he says, he thinks Joseph will presently want time off to get married, his intended living some distance away, and that he will let him have it, "although I kneed his work." He concludes by reporting, "We are all in good health." [24]

If John Brown was becoming interested again in the idea of marriage, it was natural enough to a man of thirty-three whose five children between the ages of three and twelve needed the care of a mother. Early in 1833, he moved himself and his children out of the Foreman house and back to the rambling log house where he and Dianthe had lived for seven years. He hired a likely young woman, the daughter of Charles Day, a blacksmith, originally from Whitehall, New York, but then living in nearby Troy Township, and folks of the neighborhood predicted that she would soon become Mrs. Brown. She herself thought so too, according to a niece, and she might have, had not her sixteen-year-old sister been hired several weeks later to help her. She was Mary Day, "a large silent girl of sixteen," "never a whiney, clinging woman," but deep-bosomed, broad-shouldered, and broad-hipped, not very articulate but stanch in work and feeling. [25]

John Brown liked her from the first and now his step really did have a spring. His voice rose as stridently as it ever had during the hymns as the Sunday church services were resumed on the second floor of the tannery. The long log house, dark and deserted for months, again held the Delamater children and Miss Wright during the winter of 1833, and the dusty ashes of the great fireplaces were replaced by leaping fires, particularly at night when the debates and games again made the house noisy and cheerful. The tannery, instead of closing, continued to prosper and it was not long before John Brown was employing between a dozen and fifteen journeymen and apprentices, most of whom found a bunk or a bed in the Brown house or in the barn or tannery.

With eight or nine children members of the household during the school sessions in winter and sometimes with more tannery employees, there were often almost twenty pushing up to the breakfasts, dinners, and suppers at the Brown table. Mary and her older sister, eyeing John Brown expectantly, had enough to do with spinning, for which Mary was responsible, laundry, cleaning, cooking, and a good deal more. The younger, so she said later, also liked John Brown but thought him utterly beyond her in station, dignity, and education. After all, he was the first man of Randolph. [26]

But John Brown, who had an eye for fine points in breeding and character, was studying her closely. That spring as the ice was breaking up and the sap beginning to rise, he decided that Mary Day should become the second Mrs. Brown. Of course she would need more schooling. Education was vital for the wife of a man on the way up. But she was young and that could be easily taken care of. He "approved of her—perhaps saw the staying qualities in her." One evening he wrote out a formal offer of marriage and handed it to Mary Day.[27]

"She was so overcome," a daughter later said, declaring her mother had often told her about it, "that she dared not open it but took it to bed that night and slept with it under her pillow. Next morning she found courage to read it." When she went down to the spring for water for the house, John Brown followed her and she gave him her answer there. Thereafter he sent her to school for a time—but her head was turned and her school "amounted to very little." She could not think of anything, she remembered, but John Brown. The elder sister, who had always fancied herself as the future Mrs. John Brown, "never got over her amazement." [28]

They were married on July 11, 1833, shortly after Mary's seventeenth birthday, perhaps on the second floor of the tannery that served as the local church. It is not known whether John Brown sent his bride-to-be to Miss Sabrina Wright for her schooling or elsewhere. But his insistence on her education before marriage—although it had no real result—was typical enough and could not have surprised his neighbors.

3

Of all John Brown's passions then, that concerning education was foremost. His belief that education was the beginning of all advance, public and private, was not peculiar to himself. In Massachusetts, Horace Mann was agitating for public schools with a power that influenced the entire North. Between 1827 and 1837 in that state, Mann led a campaign, soon to be duplicated in other states, resulting in the building of fifty new public high schools.

This passion for education was not directed solely toward the improvement of the young. All over the North, in villages and towns, in churches and meetinghouses, weekly or monthly lyceums were being held in which the citizens heard authoritative lectures on science and literature and public issues. By 1833 the lyceum movement had three thousand local clubs or forums meeting regularly in fifteen states. The evening debates that John Brown organized in his Randolph home, his own constant efforts at self-improvement through reading, were themselves reflections of this widespread urge above the Ohio.

The growing abolition movement itself was based on the premise of the power of education, on the belief that it would not only change individuals through their education as to the realities of slavery but finally transform the institution through the searchlight of truth. Isolated as John Brown was in Randolph, absorbed as he was in the affairs of family and township, he could not help being touched by these great movements. If he did not organize an anti-slavery society he did build into his barn, beneath the haymow, a carefully concealed, carefully ventilated chamber for the harboring of fugitive slaves.

While his son John recalled, as we have seen, his father helping two fugitive slaves in Hudson escape from their pursuers before the family moved to Pennsylvania, he never mentioned a similar instance in Randolph. And yet the tiny community could have been on the increasingly traveled routes of the Underground since it was near the eastern corner of Lake Erie, a favorite path to Canada's freedom. George Delamater said in 1859, in referring to John Brown and these early years, that "Old Citizens of Richmond and Randolph townships tell of his applications to them to furnish relief and homes for fugitives from slavery." [29]

4

It has been said that Emerson's influence was so overwhelming that even those who never read him were affected by him because his ideas and ideals became so general. This was much more true of Garrison. If John Brown during his Pennsylvania residence seldom saw *The Liberator*, save on his visits to his father in Hudson, its ideas were germinating everywhere. Many newspapers in the North, and in the South too, for that matter, were on Garrison's exchange list, and frequently printed excerpts from *The Liberator*.

In its earlier years, in 1833 and 1834 particularly, *The Liberator* published many stories concerning the education of Negroes, giving column after column to attempts by the Lane Seminary students at Cincinnati and Prudence Crandall's efforts in Connecticut. Perhaps that was partly why John Brown began thinking of establishing a Negro school in Randolph, although he himself said, with a kind of typically enthusiastic exaggeration, that "This has been with me a favorite theme of reflection for years." [30] If it had been he did nothing about it save dream of his idea and of how he and Randolph would lead the way to a great national movement. Not force or armed attack or vulgar agitation, he believed then, would destroy slavery, but education. Perhaps he could see himself standing in the main classroom of the new school, which would put Randolph on the map, lecturing a group of young blacks, endowing them with the wisdom that would save the nation.

At any rate, he took the idea to him and mulled it over and made it an inner excitement as he did with so many other matters large and small. Mary's seventeen years had quickened his thirty-three, and he again enjoyed Randolph's small dramas with a zest that had been missing since Dianthe's death. On September 26, not quite three months after the marriage, he, as clerk of the Randolph Congregational Church, had the satisfaction of issuing a kind of passport in Christianity, or at least in Congregationalism, to Horatio and Hannah Wright, recommending them "to the Christian watch, fellowship and communion of all sister Churches where ever God in his providence shall place them." [31] He was a kind of Johnny Appleseed, too, not in spreading apple trees over Ohio, but in selling blooded bulls to his own profit and the improvement of stock all over northwestern Pennsylvania and the Western Reserve.

"I have disposed of all my bulls for the year," he wrote Seth Thompson in 1834, saying that he had long been thinking over a red bull calf that he had seen at Seth's Hartford farm some time before and that he hoped Seth still had him.[32] Not entirely unconnected with such matters was the fact that on May 11 of that year the first of Mary's thirteen children by John Brown was born, whom they named Sarah. As a conservative businessman and Whig, he was naturally opposed to President Jackson's attack on the United States Bank at Philadelphia, believing it would make for a scarcity of currency. He wrote in 1834, "It is a time of General Jackson darkness here about money." [33]

MOBS AND A BRIEF EUPHORIA

I

It was such absorbing affairs as these that made the Hudson controversy over slavery seem very remote at times. Occasionally John Brown thought that his old neighbors there were naturally contentious and felt sure that matters would never get so at Randolph.[34] His visits to Hudson, as has been said, and his father's letters had kept him informed of the Hudson conflict; but when his brother Frederick, then twenty-seven, visited him in Randolph, probably in October 1834, he heard all the latest news.

They had much to talk about. The Western Reserve Anti-Slavery Society, of which their father was treasurer, was gaining in membership. The clash in the college had graduated to the churches of the Western Reserve, where abolitionists under Owen Brown and others were showing surprising strength. A few days before Frederick had left for Randolph, anti-slavery delegates to that peculiar Calvinist organizational blend of Congregationalist and Presbyterian, the Synod of the Western Reserve, had almost passed a resolution calling for immediate emancipation, failing by only 2 votes, 29 to 27.[35]

Professor Wright, whose boyhood background had been so much like John Brown's and whom everyone in Hudson knew, and whom John and Frederick Brown may have discussed, was having his troubles in New York City where he was employed as secretary of the American Anti-Slavery Society. Soon he was to be the target of a covey of Southern bravos who were also said to be intent on assassinating Arthur Tappan. Wright was presently barricading the doors of his home to protect his wife and children against those described as Southern assassins.[36] The house of Lewis Tappan, also an abolitionist leader and the brother of Arthur, was wrecked by a mob which not long later attacked Arthur Tappan's store.

Lydia Maria Child, writing from New York, told of the perils confronting abolitionists. "I have not ventured into the city," she wrote,

nor does one of us dare to go to church today, so great is the excitement here. 'Tis like the times of the French Revolution when no man dared trust his neighbor. Private assassins from N. Orleans are lurking at the corners of the streets to stab Arthur Tappan; and very large sums are offered for anyone who will convey Mr. Thompson [a British abolitionist] into the slave states. . . . Mr. Wright was yesterday barricading his doors and windows with strong bars and planks an inch thick. Violence, in some form, seems to be generally expected.[37]

Perhaps the brothers talked also of Garrison, who celebrated his adventures each week in *The Liberator*. As he prepared to leave for England in 1833, he was both thrilled and appalled that Southern states and counties were offering rewards for his capture. The Georgia legislature had posted a $5,000 bounty for his apprehension, arrest, and conviction on a charge of sedition.[38] As Garrison was about to make his way from Philadelphia to New York for England, he learned, he wrote, of the formation of "a conspiracy to seize my body . . . and deliver me up to the authorities of Georgia—or in other words to abduct and destroy me."[39] The Southern abductors, he felt, were trailing his every move and to elude them he jumped into a sulky, driven by the Philadelphia Negro Robert Purvis, and made for New York behind the fastest horse that could be obtained, taking back roads and short-cuts and detours, until he arrived at a hiding place near New York.

His mission to England was based on the recognition, held for some years by many American abolitionists, that Great Britain, which had just freed some 800,000 slaves in the British West Indies, had much to teach the United States on the subject of emancipation. But it was not of the British example that Garrison was thinking as he prepared to embark on the *Hibernia.* "I cannot know fear," he wrote to a friend. "I feel that it is impossible for danger to awe me." [40] Earlier he had said in a public meeting, "As for myself, whatever be my fate—whether I fall in the springtime of manhood, or be immured in a Georgia cell, or be permitted to live to a ripe old age—I know that the success of your cause depends nothing on my existence." [41]

Another who was to experience his share of danger at about this time was Theodore Dwight Weld, who was also known in Hudson. His magnetism had drawn students from Oneida Institute in New York when he left there to go to Lane Seminary in Cincinnati. He seemed as able to destroy schools as create them. When Lane Seminary, which had received thousands of dollars, through Weld's influence, from Arthur Tappan, refused to allow the student body to continue a discussion on slavery which had drawn national attention, Weld withdrew the student body, or most of it, and sent it to Oberlin which he with others was reviving on a completely anti-slavery basis. He was also instrumental in withdrawing Tappan's money from Lane and sending it to Oberlin.

Claiming that he could not help the immense attraction he everywhere exerted, he said his sole desire was to remain anonymous. Perhaps that was why he was so elusive when Wright tried to commission him as an anti-slavery agent. He wanted no position, no title. He hated even the thought of attending anti-slavery conventions, or anniversary meetings, where despite himself he might enjoy some personal triumph through some casual eloquence or even through the accidental escape of that rugged charm it was so difficult for him to control. In a letter to Lewis Tappan, he wrote: "The stateliness and Pomp and Circumstance of an anniversary [convention] I loathe in my inmost soul. It seems so like ostentatious display, a mere make believe and mouthing. . . ." [42]

By 1835 Wright had succeeded in overcoming Weld's reservations. In that year he became an agent, the most able the American Anti-Slavery Society ever had. His field was Ohio, where since 1834 mobs had harassed most attempts to hold anti-slavery meetings. Within a few months he was the country's foremost expert in the rough-and-tumble battling, the catch-as-catch-can debate that was then the essence of anti-slavery work in the field. A report to "My dear Brother Wright," from Putnam, Ohio, on March 2, 1835, indicates something of the life of all anti-slavery workers in the 1830's.

"Since my last letter," he writes of his work in Ohio, "I have lectured at Concord, Ross Co., five times, at Oldtown (Frankfort) seven times, at Bloomingburg, Fayette Co., nine times, and at Circleville, Pickaway Co., fourteen times. . . ." [43] At Circleville he had some difficulty while speaking in the vestryroom of the Presbyterian Church.

"At the second lecture," he reports, "the mob gathered and threw eggs and stones through the window. One of the stones was so well aimed that it struck me in the head and for a moment stunned me. Paused a few moments until the dizziness had ceased, and then went on and completed my lecture." [44]

The trustees of the church, fearful that it would be destroyed, forced Weld to change the scene of his next night's lecture to a nearby store. "The next night I lectured there," he continued. "Room full. Stones and clubs flew merrily against the shutters. . . . Next evening same state of things, with increase of violent demonstrations. The next, such was the uproar that a number of gentlemen insisted on forming an escort and seeing me safe to my lodgings, which they did. . . ." [45]

This was a normal night for Weld, a little different from John Brown's night hours before the kitchen fireplace so often concluding with a reading from the Psalms before he and his family went sleepily to bed.

2

In peaceful Randolph the two brothers, Frederick and John Brown, may have discussed some of these events during Frederick's visit in the fall of 1834, particularly those involving Hudson and Lane Seminary, Western Reserve College and Oberlin. Even as they talked the Lane rebels, expelled as a result of their discussion on slavery but still to enroll at Oberlin, were continuing their work among the Negroes at Cincinnati.

They had organized for the blacks a circulating library, a regular evening school, and "a select female school." "About 200 [Negroes] attend school daily," wrote Augustus Wattles, a student who had been converted to anti-slavery by Weld.[46] (Wattles would become one of John Brown's strongest supporters in Kansas.) Perhaps it was the widely reported details of the school for blacks in Cincinnati that revived John Brown's interest in his proposal for his own school in Randolph. Not long after Frederick's departure for home, John Brown writes from Randolph on November 21, 1834:

Dear Brother,—As I have had only one letter from Hudson since you left here, and that some weeks since, I begin to get uneasy and apprehensive that all is not well. I had satisfied my mind about it for some time, in expectation of seeing father here, but I begin to give that up for the present. Since you left me I have been trying to devise some means whereby I might do something in a practical way for my poor fellowmen who are in bondage, and having fully consulted the feelings of my wife and my three boys, we have agreed to get at least one negro boy or youth, and bring him up as we do our own,—viz., give him a good English education, learn him what we can about the history of the world, about business, about general subjects, and, above all, to try to teach him the fear of God.

We think of three ways to obtain one: First, to try to get some Christian slave-holder to release one to us. Second, to get a free one if no one will let us have one that is a slave. Third, if that does not succeed, we have all agreed to submit to considerable privation in order to buy one. This we are now using means in order to effect, in the confident expectation that God is about to bring them all out of the house of bondage.

I will just mention when this subject was first introduced, Jason had gone to bed; but no sooner did he hear the thing hinted, than his warm heart kindled, and he turned out to have a part in the discussion of a subject of such exceeding interest. I have for years been trying to devise some way to get a school a-going here for blacks, and I think that on many accounts it would be a most favorable location. Children here would have no intercourse with vicious people of their own kind, nor with open vicious persons of any kind. There would be no powerful opposition influence against such a thing; and should there be any, I believe the settlement might be so effected in future as to have almost the whole influence of the place in favor of such a school. Write me how you would like to join me, and try to get on from Hudson and thereabouts some first-rate abolitionist families with you. I do honestly believe that our united exertions alone might soon, with the good hand of God upon us, effect it all.

This has been with me a favorite theme of reflection for years. I think that a place which might be in some measure settled with a view to such an object would be much more favorable to such an undertaking than would any such place as Hudson with all its conflicting interests and feelings; and I do think that such advantages ought to be afforded the young blacks, whether they are all immediately to be set free or not. Perhaps we might, under God, in that way do more towards breaking their yoke effectually than in any other.

If the young blacks of our country could once become enlightened, it would most assuredly operate on slavery like firing powder confined in rock, and all slaveholders know it well. Witness their heaven-daring laws against teaching blacks. If once the Christians in the free States would set to work in earnest in teaching the blacks, the people of the slaveholding States would find themselves constitutionally driven to set about the work of emancipation immediately. The laws of this State are now such that the inhabitants of any township may raise by a tax in aid of the State school-fund any amount of money they may choose by a vote, for the purpose of common schools, which any child may have access to by application. If you will join me in this undertaking, I will make with you any arrangement of our temporal concerns that shall be fair. Our health is good, and our prospects about business rather brightening.

Affectionately yours,
John Brown.[47]

If this letter, the first written expression by John Brown against slavery, reveals Jason's "warm heart," it also reveals on the part of his father a quickening generosity, a beginning in the break away from his private pursuits. But nothing ever came of the proposal. No first-rate abolitionist families from Hudson came to Randolph to help in the founding of the school and not one slave boy was received in the Brown family to receive a good English education and learn something of the history of the world.

Instead, John Brown backslid into normalcy, forced to it by necessity and routine, as he was to do so many times again with his anti-slavery plans and resolutions. Presently he was again too busy with the many-faceted life of himself, his family, and Randolph to think of the school and so far as is known he never mentioned it again. His time was spent once more in such matters as pressing Deacon John Andrews for payment of $87, in tanning kips for Seth Thompson, in adventuring at night with Christian as he sought to avoid the snares of Mr. Worldly Wiseman, perhaps worried that John Brown was not avoiding them. During the days he passed a good deal of time surveying projected roads for the township, while in the evening he might return to Athens and Pericles through the pages of Plutarch or ponder the mysteries of salvation with Baxter or admire the wise ravens and shrewd mice of Aesop.

In the ensuing weeks as he regarded the work of his hands, the busy tannery with its twelve employees, his barn filled with hay and his house filled with religion and culture where once was wilderness, he may have felt that he had a right to a proper pride. He was not a man to miss analogies, particularly when biblical and particularly when it was clear that he had been created in God's image, that he had been fruitful and multiplied, had replenished the earth and subdued it, even as the Lord had commanded in Genesis. Perhaps as he looked about and saw the earth that he had tilled and the cattle he had bred and the children, male and female, he had created in his own image with the aid of the women God had given him—although it had taken him a good many more days than six to create all this—he may have felt, however humbly, that "behold, *it was* very good."

As he regarded his accomplishments he saw no reason why his local success should not be repeated on a larger scale. He was not one to believe that he was the first citizen of Randolph only because it was small. Soon he would be considering a return to Ohio, where the Western Reserve was booming with the building of canals, the founding of new towns, the rising price of land, and the multiplication of new industries. It was true that he was richer in honors and accomplishment than in ready money. As a matter of fact he was several hundred dollars in debt but he still owned two farms, one of 104 acres and another of 112 on which was his house and tannery, as well as having perhaps $100 still due him on a farm he had sold in 1832 for $700. If he could sell his two farms and tannery, he could pay off his debts and finance his move back to Ohio. Of course, no one knew better than he who had suffered so often from the Lord's rod that success could not be certain, but one might hope that he was of the elect who would prosper on earth as he would in Heaven.

A man of emotional peaks and valleys, he was at this time on a height of confidence, exalted into that state of *hubris* which precedes downfall. Not for him was the spewing forth of propaganda, the passing of resolutions, the raising of tumults and mobs. If the slave was to be helped it was by education in John Brown's home, even if only one at a time. But it was not to be long until disasters, both public and private, would eject him from his brief Calvinistic euphoria.

XIII

Case History

IT IS SOMETIMES SAID that John Brown suffered from monomania and it is true enough that in 1835 he contracted, along with thousands of other Americans, a peculiar disease connected with the economic boom and bust of that period, in which hope could not easily be distinguished from reality nor cupidity from progress. It was a disease of epidemic proportions, spreading from town to town and state to state, as common in the South as in the North, in the wilderness as in the city, sparing neither rich nor poor, the wise or foolish. The eye of those suffering from the malady became unnaturally bright, the pulse exceedingly rapid at any thought of gain, the fever eroding the mind so completely that almost every American believed that the more he could borrow the richer he would become.

The syndrome often began, at least above the Ohio, with the patient suffering from the illusion that some nearby cornfield, or wild ravine, or rocky pasture was about to be transformed into an industrial site of fabulous value by an expected canal or railroad. Almost any farm might be divided into town lots, streets named and running through stalks of corn blowing in the wind, empty, so-called factory sites edging up to the dry land that would soon be a highway for canalboats slipping through yellow wheat, bright new towns, and endless prosperity. All that was necessary to own such lots were promissory notes for land that was bound to quadruple in value and make the repaying of the loan a mere trifle.

But the malady could begin as easily with plans for tripled cotton production in Alabama where cotton prices were soaring, or hopes for a lead mine in Illinois which would make its stockholders fantastically rich, or the sale of government land to speculators who saw visions of a metropolis amid the cottonwoods and sycamores edging a Western creek because of some rumored railroad. Prosperity was soon identified with patriotism, town lots with progress, and none was so despised as he of little faith who hedged his bets or investments on the future of Franklin, Ohio, or Alton, Illinois, or Vicksburg, Mississippi. It was a kind of treason to the general sickness and as those intoxicated with love like to see others similarly happy, so the boom-time investor liked to see all men similarly committed.

Almost all transactions during the boom of the 1830's were carried out through promissory notes, local wildcat banks printing floods of unsecured greenbacks which they were eager to lend on interest and promises to pay, secured by the property of the borrower as well as that of three or four of his friends. In the South, it was thought insulting to look at the face of a promissory note to determine its amount before signing. So freely were such notes signed, whether North or South, that every man of ambition and drive had signed every similar man's notes in a broad and senseless mutual guarantee of debt, paper which the banks used as collateral for other deals or even as security for more greenbacks. Between 1829 and 1837 state banks, most of them of the wildcat variety, increased from 329 to 788, while their circulation of largely unsecured greenbacks increased from $48 million to $119 million. During the same period loans, mostly on promissory notes, increased from $137 million to $525 million. "They do business in a kind of frenzy, largely on credit," a Virginian reported from Vicksburg in words describing the nation as accurately as Mississippi.

It was this frenzy to which John Brown was exposed after moving back to Ohio following his ten years in Pennsylvania. For a time it seemed as if he might be able to throw off the disease, so stubborn was his constitution and temperament. If there was any one quality in him more prominent than any other it was his passion not only to run others but to run himself. He was opposed to hysteria. Rather, he liked to think of himself as a careful planner who counseled only with God.

But despite all efforts for composure and judgment, John Brown gradually succumbed to the general mania. For a time he was very ill, suffering delusions of great wealth which he fancied he had obtained through borrowing. Sometimes he felt quite confused, unable to understand why he was not sustained by that Providence which kept the elect safe from sin while prospering them.

A MAN MUST BORROW

I

John Brown's middle years were profoundly influenced by the Erie Canal. The success of that waterway, built between 1817 and 1825 and running between Buffalo on Lake Erie and New York City at the mouth of the Hudson, released inflationary tendencies that were partly responsible for the boom and bust that followed within a decade of its construction. It benefited the farmers not only of western New York but of the entire Great Lakes region, by opening up great new markets on the Atlantic and in Europe. The time for freight shipments from Buffalo to New York City was reduced by the canal from twenty to six days, while freight charges decreased from $100 a ton to $8. Wheat, corn, oats, flour, whiskey, lumber, cheese, pot and pearl ashes, which before had a limited local market or had gone to the East by road and turnpike, were now arriving swiftly and cheaply, and in bulk, at the Atlantic tidewater. Shipping on the Great Lakes was tripling and quadrupling, the universal destination Buffalo.

In 1835, only ten years after the canal was completed, some 258,259 barrels of flour were arriving in New York from the western lake states by the new canal while farm prices and land prices throughout the region were rapidly increasing. Flour and wool mills were yearly multiplying in what was later called the Middle West. New York was changing from a market town on the Hudson to the nation's leading port, the country's largest city, while such lake towns as Buffalo, Cleveland, Detroit, Milwaukee, and Chicago were prospering at an unprecedented rate.

The success of the Erie Canal caused a canal boom, particularly in Ohio where canals were needed to tap the state's interior and bring its produce, both agricultural and manufactured, to Lake Erie so as to profit from the Buffalo-New York waterway. The first Ohio canal, a north-south highway running 308 miles from Cleveland on Lake Erie to Portsmouth on the Ohio River, was started in 1825 and completed in 1835. Land prices immediately soared, as at Akron which was on the canal and where land worth at most $11 an acre before the canal was built sold for industrial sites at prices from $2,300 to $7,000 for 10- or 20-acre plots, and increasingly after a mill race was developed from the Little Cuyahoga River which gave extraordinary power to the flour and wool mills soon to be built. The canal not only opened the state's interior to New York and Europe but by way of the Ohio River gave it access to New Orleans, the Lower South, and the Caribbean.

For ten years there had been a project, proposed but never built, to construct an east-west canal across the state, connecting with the Ohio–Lake Erie Canal at Akron and proceeding east to Beaver, Pennsylvania. It was to be known as the Pennsylvania-Ohio Canal, connecting the Western Reserve with the Ohio River below Pittsburgh, giving it access not only to the Mississippi and the South but to New York via Akron and Lake Erie. Franklin township, some six miles from Hudson where John Brown had lived as a boy and where most of his family still lived, was to be on the new canal. It was to this township that Brown moved with his family in May 1835, just as it was announced that construction of the Pennsylvania-Ohio would begin immediately.

2

The uprooting of a man or a plant and placing either in a new soil and a new place often inflicts a trauma from which recovery is difficult. Even before he left Randolph, John Brown's brief Calvinistic euphoria was vanishing, destroyed by his inability to sell his tannery or farms so that he might pay his debts and move to Franklin where he had entered into a partnership with Zenas B. Kent to construct and operate a tannery.[1] After borrowing enough from Mr. Kent to move to Franklin township, a fertile area of farmland bordered by the Cuyahoga River and filled with gangs of Irishmen and Germans working on the canal at 80 cents a day, he soon realized that his role had changed. No longer was he a wilderness king whose spacious log house was often filled with debates and games before the leaping fire. Instead he, his wife, and six children were probably crowded into a small rented house and Randolph's leading citizen was only the junior partner in a tannery not even built. No longer was he habitually "jocose and mirthful when the conversation did not turn on anything profane or vulgar." Instead, a little creased V of worry was beginning to appear on his forehead just above his hooked and predatory nose. It was almost as if a new place had made of him a new person.

His worry was not connected with any plan of speculating in land or buying and selling town lots or industrial sites so that he might profit from the building of the canal. He was too innocent for that. He had borrowed before but it had always been small amounts on his hides, his promise to pay based on curing them into leather and selling his product. As he felt then, a man with a

INFLUENCES, PLACES, PEOPLE, AND EVENTS

*1. Mrs. Mary Day Brown, 35, with Anne Brown, 8, left,
and Sarah Brown, 5, right, in about 1851*

*2. Owen Brown,
John Brown's father*

*3. Abby Kelley in 1846.
She was one of Brown's favorite
abolitionist orators*

4. J. Q. Adams, sixth President
of the United States, whose old age
was spent fighting slavery
in the House of Representatives

5. Elijah P. Lovejoy,
anti-slavery editor,
killed by mob at Alton, Illinois

6. Joshua R. Giddings, for 21 years
the anti-slavery congressman
from the Western Reserve.
He was Brown's favorite politician

7. Theodore Dwight Weld at 41.
He was one of the
greatest abolitionist organizers,
speakers, and writers

8. William Lloyd Garrison

*9. Cinque, African chieftain
who led the mutiny on
the Amistad in 1839*

*10. Nat Turner urging the
slaves to rebellion in
1831 when he headed the
most bloody slave revolt
in American history*

11. *"Flogging The Negro"—an abolitionist view of slavery*

12. *Slave auction at Richmond, Virginia*

13. Slaves arriving at a station on the Underground Railroad

14. Twenty-eight fugitives escaping from the Eastern Shore of Maryland

15. The tannery at Randolph, Crawford County, Pennsylvania

16. The so-called John Brown Cabin at Osawatomie, Kansas.
Though he often visited it, the cabin belonged to his brother-in-law, S. L. Adair,
seen in the chair in this photograph, taken in 1896

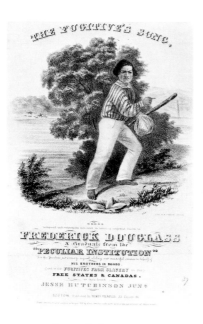

17. *An anti-slavery song dedicated to Douglass with cover showing him escaping from slavery*

18. *John Brown's birthplace in Torrington, Connecticut*

19. *The pro-slavery riot of November 7, 1837, Alton, Illinois. Death of Reverend E. P. Lovejoy*

20. *A slave coffle passing the Capitol*

21. Harper's Ferry before John Brown's invasion

22. "Camp-Meeting"—an early illustration of a nineteenth-century institution

family of six needed a solid business through which to support it and could not indulge in any borrowing on air however substantial the reality of the pyramiding prices of town lots beside the canal. He had been a tanner at Hudson and at Randolph and he intended to remain one at Franklin, his profit from the canal coming only from increased business at his tannery resulting from the community's presumed growth.

It was the tannery and his own position in it which worried him. Mr. Kent, an elderly gentleman, the foremost citizen of Franklin and one of the wealthiest men on the Western Reserve, was ordering him about. To John Brown this was unendurable. As ignorant of vats and hides as a child, Mr. Kent seemed to feel that his money somehow gave him a knowledge of tanning. He insisted on telling his partner, nineteen years a tanner, how the tannery John Brown was building, and he was paying for, should be constructed. When his junior partner ignored him he told his sons that John Brown was so stubborn that nothing short of a mental rebirth could alter him.[2] Each hurt the pride of the other. In John Brown's opinion it was his knowledge that made the partnership effective, while Kent knew there could be no business without his money.

Always disposed, as he himself once wrote, to speak and he might have added to act "in an imperious and dictating way,"[3] John Brown from the first treated Zenas Kent with a high hand. He did not propose to be ordered about, particularly as to tanning, by a mere possessor of money. In one of their first interchanges while Brown was still in Randolph, unable to move because of his inability to sell his property and pay his debts, it was he who ordered Mr. Kent to lend him money and that quickly while rebuking him for not doing it sooner. "Yours of the 14th was received by last mail," he wrote on April 24, 1835. "I was disappointed in the extreme not to obtain the money I expected; & I know of no possible way to get along without it." Declaring he wanted the money "to settle up a number of honorary debts which I could not leave unpaid and come away," he added, "I expect Father [Owen Brown] to come out [to Randolph] for cattle about the first of May and I wish you without fail to send it by him. It is now too late to think of sending it by mail."[4]

Apparently, Mr. Kent obeyed the order and John Brown spent $25 of the sum loaned to buy some shingles in Randolph which he sold at a profit in Franklin as one means of tiding over his family. Almost from the first he felt that Kent was obstructing the building of the tannery, not only by constantly advising on that of which he knew nothing but by withholding money for construction when John Brown ignored his orders.

On October 24, 1835, after almost six months of ineffective activity, Brown wrote Seth Thompson, to whom he owed several hundred dollars:

Mr. Kent's movements are extremely slow & I cannot alter his gait. We have had a quantity of stock [hides] . . . on hand since May last, considerable of which might have been tanned had Mr. Kent got the tannery in readiness as he agreed. I do not in consequence of the unexpected delay I have met with expect that I shall be able to pay you off this season. . . . I think my prospect is that of final success but I have suffered much by delay.[5]

The peculiar dispute between Brown and Kent was carried on, for the most part silently, for neither spoke much, through May, June, July, August, September, October, and November and still the tannery was not complete. In May, as John Brown labored with pick and shovel on the tannery's foundation, hearing those watching his efforts tell how when surveyors appeared in Akron where the canal was to run down Main Street the price of lots had jumped 400 per cent, he may have only thought that ownership of such a lot was an easier way to make money than wielding a pick. In June, when he heard, as he hammered and sawed and sweated, of those who had struck it rich by selling land worth less than $20 an acre before the canal's advent for $1,000 or more a few days past, he may have felt a stir of interest. In July, when he learned that twenty of the leading citizens on the Western Reserve were forming the Franklin Land Company for the development and sale of water power and industrial sites in Franklin township between the Cuyahoga River and the canal, he may have experienced a pang of envy. Everyone said they would make a fortune. Wherever he went, whether general store, post office, or church, people were gasping out stories of incredible riches made by those who bought land cheap, on credit of course, and sold it at quadruple value.

Brown later wrote that he always tried to rejoice in the good fortune of others when he himself was suffering, and now he tried hard as he labored on the tannery to exult in the prosperity of many.[6] It was increasingly difficult. Yet he knew he was doing right in remaining a tanner. After all no one savored the maxims of Benjamin Franklin against debt more than he, or more enjoyed repeating to his children such of Franklin's admonitions as "He that goes a borrowing goes a sorrowing," and "The first vice is running into debt," and "The borrower is the slave of the lender."

His entire Puritan background abhorred and rejected the idea that someone or anyone could prosper without work. But the excitement over riches everywhere evident made him restless. His difficulties with Mr. Kent made him reckless. His great need for money nourished ideas which his mind rejected. Nevertheless in November, as if partly yielding to a mysterious pressure which he neither recognized nor formulated, he suddenly decided to dissolve his partnership with Mr. Kent. He would get a contract for the construction of a part of the canal between Franklin and Akron. At least he would be at the center of activity.

All he needed was a yoke of oxen and a plow, and he may have been surprised at the enthusiasm with which Mr. Kent agreed to the termination of the partnership and loaned him the money for the oxen and the plow. Scores of farmers had short-term construction contracts, scarcely more than contracts for personal labor, and soon John Brown was similarly employed, scooping mud and earth from what was little more than a ditch, 30 feet wide and 4 feet deep, since little more than a ditch would be needed for the flat-boats and scows that would form the canal's traffic. As he sloshed about in the mud, unsnarling his balky oxen when they twisted about in the yoke, he may have been a trifle annoyed by the high-hatted entrepreneurs watching lesser men work while they told innumerable stories, most probably apocryphal, of big Eastern capitalists planning to move to the Western Reserve so as to benefit from the Cuyahoga's power, the new canal's transportation, and of how the shrewd were foregoing chances for investment in Chicago for investment in Franklin as more certain of swift development.

Not much later as he guided his plow and directed his oxen in and out of the cut, he heard more news that should have made him happy for others. The Franklin Land Company, of which Zenas Kent was a director, had purchased of Zenas Kent the water power, mill, and factory sites of Lower Franklin on the Cuyahoga River near the canal, paying Kent $75,000, as well as purchasing the water power and potential factory sites of the firm of Pomeroy & Rhodes at Upper Franklin, also on the river and near the canal, for a sum almost as large. The company had then made a contract with the Pennsylvania-Ohio Canal Company by which the water power of the upper and lower villages was to be combined and concentrated at a point midway between the two villages by means of dams and spillways. This point was Franklin, adjacent to a little settlement called Franklin Mills. Even the most conservative believed that the increased water power there, combined with the easy transportation of the adjacent canal, guaranteed victory in the race with other villages on the canal to attract capital.[7]

Some weeks after the coup of the Franklin Land Company, John Brown visited the site of the future metropolis. As he walked about, a certain natural envy perhaps contesting with his presumed joy over the general good, surveyors were already laying out streets, and plotting the industrial sites edging the Cuyahoga. Already there were rumors of industrial lots being sold for phenomenal prices. He could not have been too content as he watched the activity. After all he had always, as he himself wrote, *"habitually expected to succeed,"* [8] and he was at present little more than an anonymous laborer in the gangs of men working on the canal. Naturally combative, always "ambitious to excel," [9] he must have ached for participation, yearned to compete with those becoming rich as they built what was to be an industrial complex.

As he paced through the winter mud of Franklin—probably in December of 1835—he approached the farm of Frederick Haymaker, in adjacent Franklin Mills, idly examining its 95½ acres, perhaps stooping to scoop a handful of half-frozen dirt, rubbing it between thumb and forefinger in that typical gesture of the inquiring farmer, while gazing over the acres and those working nearby. As he turned full circle, looking at all about, at the Cuyahoga to the north and west, the canal behind him, the future metropolis of Franklin to the immediate west, he may have felt a new idea taking shape within him, slowly and vaguely at first, and then with a rising excitement. It was as if Providential light had shone upon the Haymaker farm, revealing a relationship to which all others had been blind. It immediately adjoined the new town of Franklin, close to the future metropolis at the point where the Cuyahoga's power was being combined and strengthened. Whoever possessed the farm would have all the advantages of the Franklin Land Company without investing in it.

The force of his idea, as if the excitement accompanying it was a catalyst transforming long dormant germs into the pathological, apparently infected him at once with the epidemic now cresting throughout much of Ohio. But he had no awareness of one succumbing to the general economic sickness of boom or bust. He only knew that because of his decision to borrow enough to buy the Haymaker farm, divide it into industrial lots, and become rich by selling them that now he could participate, be a part of the great adventure transforming the countryside, be a leader again as was his natural right, be freed from the embarrassing, harrowing poverty imprisoning himself and his family. As for his fear of borrowing, it, too, had yielded to the pressure long building within him and he saw at once it was a weakness. He had no sense that the dissipation of this fear was also part of the general malady. He was not a statistic of an epidemic but a man of judgment, governed by Providence, which in its own mysterious way had brought him at last to the Haymaker farm.

Years later, looking back on the day he first perceived the possibilities of the Haymaker farm, he saw it also as the beginning of what he later called "my extreme calamity." [10] Speaking to his son John with the sad wisdom of aftersight, he said that all the mistakes he had made started then and "grew out of one root—doing business on credit. Where loans are amply secured," he continued, "the borrower, not the lender, takes the risks and all the contingencies incident to business; while the accumulations of interest and the coming of pay-day are as sure as death. Instead of being thoroughly imbued with the doctrine of *pay as you go*," he had acquired

the idea that nothing could be done without capital, and that a poor man *must* use his credit and borrow; and this pernicious notion has been the rock on which I, as well as so many others, have split. The practical effect of this false doctrine has been to keep me like a toad under a harrow most of my business life. Running into debt includes so much of evil that I hope all my children will shun it as they would a pestilence.[11]

But he saw no evil or pestilence on that December day in 1835. All he saw then was the Haymaker farm shining in the winter sun as if it were the promised land.

3

John Brown began his career of borrowing cautiously enough, but he was soon up to his neck not only in borrowing on promissory notes but in selling land for them. Within a matter of days he owned the Haymaker farm if a small down payment in cash, borrowed from his brother Frederick, made it his own.* His first action was to move his family into the substantial farmhouse included in his purchase and then he was out with compass and chain, laying out streets and dividing the farm into lots, Cuyahoga Street running through sere corn stalks near the river, Haymaker Street bisecting a pasture, Prospect and Franklin Streets on the other side of the canal, extending through the stubble of last year's wheat. As he bent over his compass, waving his hands to right or left to the boy carrying his chain, he was convinced that his land was almost hourly increasing in value, and not en-

---

* This transaction and those ensuing are taken from the largely unused Brown-Thompson correspondence, in the Slaughter Collection, Atlanta University. It differs considerably from the account of these transactions by Villard which he based on an article in the Kent (Ohio) *Courier*, September 14, 1906, apparently valid in some points but incorrect in others. Even that article, however, contradicted Villard's assertion that John Brown was one of twenty-one leading citizens who were the incorporators of the Franklin Land Company. Nor is there any evidence either in the letters or the records of later suits of his assertion that Brown borrowed from Heman Oviatt and Frederick Wadsworth to buy the Haymaker farm.

tirely without evidence. Before he had completed his first rude survey, he counted twelve of his lots as being sold, although probably through promissory notes, to one Wetherell, a Mr. Kilbourne, and Messrs. O'Brien, Hand, and Winkler, according to his map.[12]

It is not known for certain how much John Brown agreed to pay for the Haymaker farm but it may have been as high as $7,000, or almost $74 an acre. He subsequently paid $75 an acre for land adjoining his first purchase. It is known, however, that on January 4, 1836, he wrote his friend and former partner, Seth B. Thompson, of Hartford, Trumbull County, offering him an undivided half of the 95½ acres for $7,000, or the same sum he may have agreed to pay for the whole. In his letter to Thompson he asked him to act fast because the land was going for as high as $900 for a corner lot of three-quarters of an acre. Less desirable lots, he wrote, of less than a half acre were selling for $200.[13] Before the canal a seller would have been lucky to get $20 an acre for the same land.

Thompson was convinced. On January 18 he agreed to buy from Brown the undivided half for $7,000, $1,134 in cash and $1,866 by a note due in five days. He also gave his friend four promissory notes for $1,000 each, payable annually until January 13, 1840.[14] But these notes, in accordance with the practice of the day, were almost as negotiable as currency. John Brown apparently used them in part to retire some of his indebtedness to Haymaker, to repay his brother Frederick, and to make a down payment on a farm and farmhouse three miles from the village of Hudson.

He was learning fast. It was evil neither to lend nor loan. Rather it was a kind of bookkeeping for the solvent or a way of substituting for currency as checks did later. Never had he been more busy and if there was a new excitement within him he tried not to show it. He knew the value of presence, of dignity, of the slow, well-considered reply. When he was not plotting out his industrial lots at Franklin—there would be 150 of them—he was apt to be in his buggy urging his horse toward Hudson, perhaps headed for the Westlands farm in the township of Twinsburg for which he had long lusted, or to Cuyahoga Falls where he was thinking of undertaking another industrial development. Certainly he enjoyed his new dignity, for it was manifest that a promoter, a planner, a developer of industrial sites had a prestige that a tanner had never had.

Folks generally thought he had been right smart in acquiring the use of the Franklin Land Company's increased water power without cost through getting the adjacent Haymaker farm. It was freely predicted that he and

Thompson would make a killing. When it became known that he was considering extending his interests and developmental skills to Cuyahoga Falls, also on the canal and also blessed with phenomenal opportunities through the power of the Cuyahoga, the leading citizens of that little village were eager to induce a man of John Brown's stature to invest in their future. They made him a director of the local bank,[15] and elected him to office in the Cuyahoga Falls Real Estate Association.[16]

Again he was a force for good in the community as he had been at Randolph, a pillar of the Franklin Congregational Church which he attended each Sunday, gleaming with a special Sabbath cleanliness, his red face with its beak of a nose and prowlike chin, sometimes nicked from the closeness of his morning shave. Impressive in his Sunday suit of snuff-colored broadcloth, his white linen shirt with its double ruffles starched and laundered, he wore a black leather stock at his throat, a high beaver hat on his small, compact head. On weekdays his slim, square-shouldered form nearly always suggested the aggressive, but on Sundays he was benign. He could be seen then walking a little importantly at the head of his considerable family on the way to worship, his hands solemnly clasped behind him in a posture that was to become habitual, his head a trifle bowed as if already in that religious meditation appropriate to the Sabbath.

Now when he wanted to borrow $6,000 from the Western Reserve Bank of Warren in 1836, he had no dread of the procedure or consequences. After all, he was a bank director himself. All he had to do was to get six friends to endorse his note, and he scarcely knew whom to choose, so many liked and admired him now that he was successful. In this instance he decided on his brother Frederick, Joshua Stow, Henry, Ogden, and William Wetmore, brothers, and Heman Oviatt, all of whom were glad to guarantee his $6,000 loan. Later there were others who were glad to step up and sign his notes with an affability that did not suggest the law suits of coming years.

With part of the $6,000 borrowed from the Western Reserve Bank, John Brown made a down payment, as one of these suits later revealed, on a second farm near Hudson, called Westlands, for which he always had a peculiar affection. Its contours of pasture land and timber, its flat cultivated fields and its rolling woodlands, a creek winding through the acreage, seemed to him to make it the most perfect farm he had ever seen. It moved him with a desire that was more than acquisitive; it was a thing of beauty and to give it up, as he was to find, was almost more than he could endure.

He had his eye on other farms and if he seemed a man in a hurry as he raced about the country looking them over, it was perhaps because he felt that this might be his only chance for wealth and was resolved to make the most of it. Yet he did not forget the God whose earth was yielding to him its riches, and if it was not in corn or wheat, the produce it did yield, the profit of buying cheap and selling dear, was just as surely from the Lord's bounty. He may have hoped, as he did later at a similar time, that "entire leanness of soul may not attend any little success in business." [17]

4

John Brown, trying for the cautious and moderate, appropriate to a man of judgment, decided to complete the building of his industrial community at Franklin before extending his operations to Cuyahoga Falls. He spent most of his time supervising the erection of a large block building at the corner of what he called Summit and Magadore Streets. It was to contain a hotel, an obvious necessity if the businessmen, investors, and salesmen, presently to be expected, were to be properly sheltered and entertained; but it seemed large and startling in the emptiness of the countryside. It also included a warehouse for the storing of manufactured goods. He continued to lay out the industrial lots of his community which would have residences, too. Its formal title, "Brown & Thompson's Addition to Franklin Village" was modest enough.[18]

Nevertheless it had fine wide avenues and streets 66 feet wide, as indicated by pegs driven in cornfields and pastures, the great lonesome bend of the Cuyahoga River to the north and west, the canal running through the community's center, the streets named—on John Brown's survey—Cuyahoga, Pennsylvania, Bacon, Prospect, Franklin, Hale, Brimfield, Haymaker, and Munroe. He may have felt a little opportunistic in naming the last two streets. He still owed Haymaker perhaps as much as $5,000 but he might not like to foreclose on the land and his chance of immortality by canceling out the broad street which would proclaim his name to future generations.

As to Munroe Street it had been named after Edmund Munroe, a Boston millionaire. Even as John Brown was surveying his own plots, Munroe was laying out another expanse of farmland not far away into what he was sure would be another great manufacturing center. It was on the Cuyahoga River between Tallmadge Center and Stow Corners, and Mr. Munroe, who had some pride of name, called the pasture and woodlands the city of Munroe Falls. It was his idea to manufacture silk there, an idea he promoted so successfully that presently the whole area was seized by what later was called "the silk craze," while investors from the East subscribed $500,000 for the capitalization of the Munroe Falls Manufacturing Company. With an assured market for their produce, farmers of the region began planting mulberry trees by the hundreds and importing silk worms by the thousands which would spin the cocoons, fed by the mulberry leaves, from which the silk was manufactured.[19]

With literally millions expected from the new industry, John Brown may have hoped that if and when Munroe expanded operations he might be attracted to a street bearing his name, or perhaps he only wanted to honor a great man. However, the idea of Franklin, including the Brown & Thompson Addition thereto, as a center of silk manufacture was not exclusive to Brown. As a matter of fact, the Franklin Land Company was being reorganized into the Franklin Silk Company. Its incorporators would continue to sell industrial lots but they would make the major part of their fortunes by manufacturing silk. So certain were the prospects, it seemed natural for the Franklin Silk Company to put out its own currency, a practice not uncommon at the time, the money chiefly secured by its future profits. Its $2, $3, and $10 bills had a handsome engraving on their front showing Benjamin Franklin drawing electricity from the clouds with his kite. The back of the bills depicted a canal scene, plainly Franklin, Ohio, with busy mills in operation, a little fantasy of the certain future. John Brown later wrote Thompson that the currency was well accepted,[20] and there was no reason why it should not have been as sound as that of numerous state banks, issues which were largely unsecured by gold, silver, or anything else.

The situation, as far as sound finance was concerned, was sufficiently obvious for at least a minority to begin to worry a little about over-expansion, about the worth of paper pledges and currency so freely poured forth by companies and banks. But John Brown was still confident. He knew that Providence had always sustained him and so he bought more land adjoining the Brown & Thompson Addition from Chauncey and Harvey Newberry for $75 an acre. It was such a bargain, he wrote Seth Thompson, on February 8, 1836, he could not resist it, although he "could not get it without paying them $500 down and the balance in one year."

5

Marvin Kent, the son of Zenas Kent and destined to be even richer than his father, knew John Brown at this time in Franklin and did not think much of him. He was constitutionally incapable, Kent said, of taking advice. "Brown saw everything large," he continued, "and felt himself the equal of anything. He had such fast, stubborn and strenuous convictions that nothing short of a mental rebirth could ever have altered him." He had no apparent concern as to slavery, Kent said, declaring that all Brown was interested in while in Franklin was the making of money.[21]

It is doubtful, however, if this estimate is entirely correct. Always somewhere beneath his excitement and absorption in his personal affairs—whether as a boy in the War of 1812, or as a young man in Hudson helping a fugitive slave to escape, or as a tanner in Randolph planning to found a school for freed slaves—there was concern for the black and the country enslaving him. Perhaps it was intermittent and it is true enough that he was too busy to dedicate his entire life to the freeing of the slave as increasing numbers were doing; but when opportunity presented itself to defend the rights of Negroes, he took a stand, as he was to do in Franklin in the early summer of 1836.

When a group of blacks, some fugitives and some free, were segregated in the back of the Franklin Congregational Church during an interdenominational revival or protracted meeting, John Brown rose, interrupting a Reverend Avery of Cleveland just as he began his sermon on the text, "Cast ye up, cast ye up! Prepare ye the way of the Lord; make His paths straight!" Raising his strong metallic voice with a harshness that many worshippers found offensive, John Brown said that he was pained to see a discrimination had been made in seating the colored members of the congregation, that God was no respecter of persons but had made of one blood all the nations of men.

The Reverend Avery seemed dazed at the interruption. When neither he nor any of the deacons present nor any of the congregation made any move to rectify the seating, John Brown did it himself. Rising from his pew, he herded his family before him to the rear of the church, and then ushered the Negroes into his own family pew, the only sound in a silence as absolute as it was disapproving the scraping of feet as the whites moved back and the blacks moved forward. Up front, the black faces amid the general sea of white plainly staggered the Reverend Avery. The Browns sat in the rear throughout the service, the head of the family a flinty-faced indictment.

The next day there was considerable indignation in Christian circles. Several deacons came to labor and pray with Brown until he could see the error of his ways. They left rather quickly, never being able to get him down on his knees so they might together beseech the Almighty for guidance. That night and the next, the last of four successive services, John Brown glared from the rear of the church, his family clustered around him, while the blacks sat up front in his pew. It was only an incident, perhaps, but indicated that Brown's new success had not brought "entire leanness of soul." [22]

PROVIDENCE AND PANIC

I

The first indication of approaching panic arrived on July 11, 1836, when the federal government by issuing the Specie Circular gave official notice that it considered worthless not only the promissory notes, mortgages, scrip, and other so-called securities being taken for land but all the nation's paper currency. As far as the national government was concerned, it would take only gold and silver specie in payment for federal government lands after August 15, with a few exceptions having to do with the Virginia Land Company's scrip. It was clear that the Jackson administration, which many thought had wrecked the national economy by refusing to renew the charter of the Bank of the United States, felt that too much land was being sold for prices too high and for an exchange, often the issue of state banks, largely devoid of real value.

If the Specie Circular was intended as a deflationary measure, it was successful. The price of land immediately plunged downward. Frequency of sales dropped drastically all over the country, even including that portion of it known as the Brown & Thompson Addition. Nine days after the government circular, John Brown wrote Thompson that "even the big company," referring to the Franklin Silk Company and its industrial sites, does "not sell any lately. Still," he wrote, "I believe there will be better times before long in some way or other & live in hope." [23]

But Seth Thompson was tired of living in hope. It was with hope of a handsome return that he had paid John Brown $3,000, and notes for $4,000 more, but he had received neither income from the sale of lots at fancy prices, which he had expected, nor even a joint deed to his share of the property. All of the lots sold had been for promises to pay and the notes had been used to buy more land and to finance construction. He wanted out. He asked John Brown for his equity in his investment, asking what assurances he could give that he would get it, and received a letter in reply saying that all Brown could give was advice to "try and trust all with a wise & gracious God." [24]

"As to meeting my engagements (a thing to which you allude)," Brown wrote, "I do not, nor can not, but hope that the same kind Providence that has kept us to this 30th of December will not forget nor forsake us with this year. This is the greatest encouragement I have about our worldly affairs." He admitted, however, that he was beginning to have doubts about the Haymaker venture. The deed was still not recorded in their name nor would it be until 1838. "I do think," Brown conceded in his letter to Thompson,

it is best to sell out if we can come at anything like a fair rate, but I think the time unfavorable. If we have been crazy in getting in, do try & lets exercise a sound mind about the manner of getting out. Let us presume on a merciful Providence (if presumption it be) a little longer. Let us try and trust all with a wise & gracious God & all will be well some way or other.[25]

He continued to beseech Seth to abide by the decrees of Providence rather than act on his own when Thompson offered to sell his undivided half at $1,000 while John Brown was trying to sell half of his undivided half for $8,000. "I have no doubt I shall effect it [the sale] at that price," he wrote, "unless the price you have offered to sell at should come to be known . . . keep your patience with me as much as possible. . . . Hopeing that Providence will appear in your behalf." [26]

2

John Brown kept his own faith in Providence even in the face of the panic of 1837. In fact, he paid it scarcely any mind until he was forced to. His efforts were founded on the Lord's good earth, which was still as good and still as enduring as before the panic began in March of 1837. He was not overly interested in the bank failures which dotted the country. His concern was the canal and the Cuyahoga River, which gave an irreversible value to the land which they endowed with power and transportation now and forever. What did falling stocks and cotton dropping in price in New Orleans and unemployment demonstrations in New York mean to the Brown & Thompson Addition or the Cuyahoga River? Was the first any the less there or did the latter flow any less swiftly?

He may have shared, too, the common American faith in an eternal and expanding prosperity, making it difficult for him to credit reports of panic. Still, he may have felt a twinge of apprehension when he heard the news from Akron. There, loans were being called and mortgages foreclosed. Both in Franklin and Akron, banknotes were almost worthless and citizens were reverting to a system of barter. John Brown's future friend, one Samuel Lane, later to be both the historian and sheriff of Summit County, took forty brass clocks in part payment for a house and then traded the clocks for lumber and labor costs to build another house. Lots on Main Street in Akron which had sold for $1,000 were being sold for less than $100 or even for the payment of back taxes. Eleven out of Akron's fourteen merchants had failed. Ohio law still provided for imprisonment for debt if a creditor would pay a dollar or two a week for a prisoner's board. John Brown may have felt some premonitory shudder when he heard of Charles W. Howard imprisoned in the county jail at Akron. Only yesterday he had been a respected merchant and manufacturer and now he was in a cell as a debtor.[27]

But in the main John Brown kept his faith in the Lord God Almighty and John Brown. As long as the Cuyahoga flowed and the Pennsylvania-Ohio Canal provided cheap and easy transportation, the future was built on unshakable fundamentals, panic or no panic. As long as the silk worm spun, there could be no despair. When he was pressed by creditors—and several were threatening suit—he implored them to trust in God. Everything, he assured them, would come out all right in the end.

Nevertheless, he must have been severely shaken when the construction of the canal was halted in the fall of 1837 for lack of funds because of the panic and Brown & Thompson's Addition no longer had the promise of being connected to the world. The construction had not gone much further, when it halted, than a man could walk in a day. He must have been stunned again when the farmers of the neighborhood, of all the Cuyahoga Valley, in fact, found that Ohio's cold prevented the silk worm from maturing and spinning its cocoon. There would be no silk mills on Brown & Thompson's Addition nor anywhere else on the Cuyahoga, and Edmund Munroe was not a name to praise.

Perhaps it was then that John Brown occasionally suspected, however dimly and however infrequently, a Providential trend in this disaster on disaster. Always beneath his excitement for riches, he had known that his God was a jealous God who had often hurled calamity at those who turned their faces from Him while worshipping the Golden Calf. But he could not really believe it. He did not think that he was worshipping the Golden Calf. If he had foreseen that the time would come when even the Cuyahoga would cease to flow with anything like its old power, he might have feared that perhaps the Lord was smiting a wicked people of which he was one.

But that was in the future and he was cheerful enough when he returned to Hudson with his family in the summer of 1836, driving over to

Franklin some six miles away almost daily until the deepening panic made his presence there unnecessary. He opened a tannery on his farm in the northeast corner of Hudson township. Money was so scarce that he often traded his leather for a side of beef or a barrel of pork. He was not cast down by his reverses, regarding himself as only on a sabbatical from wealth and Franklin. All would be well when construction was resumed on the canal. It was true that he owed some thousands, but he was certain that he could pay his debts and save his farms and the Addition as soon as the panic was over and he again began selling the industrial lots of Brown & Thompson. Still, it may have sometimes seemed strange to him that a man as wealthy as he often did not even have the cash to mail a letter or to pay for one sent collect.

XIV

An Increasing Commitment

Life in Hudson for John Brown was almost as different from that in Franklin as if he had moved to another planet. It was an intellectual center, at least when compared with Franklin, a college town where the oratorios of Handel could be heard in the distance through the night and the elms as sung by the college Handel Society; where addresses on such subjects as the beauties of Dryden were important events scheduled by college literary societies; and where men who knew Greek and Hebrew almost as well as they knew English walked the streets as uninterested in the opportunities of commerce, industrial lots, and the advantages of the canal at Franklin as if such matters were only a distant oddity of the ignorant.

A familiar and impressive figure, passing the hogs lying in Hudson's gutters, oblivious to the hens cackling before him as he paced the trembling board walks, was the ponderous 300-pound George Edmond Pierce, president of Western Reserve College. He was not much interested in slavery and was opposed to militant action against it, but he had an ever-present eagerness to put the college on a sound financial basis. Too heavy to ride a horse without danger of injuring the animal, he drove about the countryside soliciting contributions in a spring buggy. Once when a farmer said he would make a contribution as soon as he sold a calf, at which he pointed, President

Pierce said, "I'll take the calf."[1] Tying the calf's legs, he heaved it under the buggy seat and drove back to Hudson where he sold it to a butcher, turning over the proceeds to the college treasury.

GOD'S COLLEGE

I

However persuasive President Pierce, there were many in Hudson who would not speak to him and would have financed the Devil as soon as contribute to him and his college. For all its pleasant culture, Hudson was a town separated by civil strife, which if not often bloody was always implacable, and it had been so since 1833 when Western Reserve College ousted Professors Beriah Green and Elizur Wright, Jr., after the death of that "Martyr of the Lord," President Storrs, because they fought for the immediate emancipation of all slaves.

In 1836, about a quarter of Hudson's one thousand inhabitants lived only physically in Hudson. Spiritually and intellectually they lived 50 miles away in Oberlin at the Oberlin Collegiate Institute, the anti-slavery college, which was much more than an educational institution. It was a way of thought, a code of conduct, an object of passionate loyalty, *"a noble and potent ism with a college attached,"*[2] in the words of an admirer. It was called "God's College," and all over the Western Reserve men and women were either for or against it and that in no temperate terms. Periodically, at Commencement or other academic or religious festivals, admirers from all over northeast Ohio would flock to its campus where three thousand could be packed into its giant tent, a banner atop it proclaiming "HOLINESS UNTO THE LORD."

When Oberlin was reorganized in 1834–5 as an anti-slavery college, with Owen Brown as one of its trustees, it precipitated a religious and political revolt on the Western Reserve. Within a few years it divided the gradualists in emancipation from the immediate emancipationists and activists on the Underground Railroad—the latter the Oberlinites—and it shattered the Union Plan, the Presbyterian-Congregationalist Synod, that had long been the strongest religious organization on the Western Reserve. It dissolved into a Congregationalist Synod, centering around Oberlin, and a Presbyterian governing body that looked to Western Reserve College for its leadership.

To know something of the stamp of Hudson's dissenters, including the large Brown family and their relatives, one only had to listen to Oberlin's leaders. From the first they had proclaimed what was later known as the Higher Law, that any and every Christian had the right and duty to violate any man-made law he deemed contrary to the law of God. They had no propriety, no temperance, no taste, in the view of President Pierce and Hudson's conservatives. They talked eternally of war, of war against sin, of war against slavery, of war against Satan, of war for peace, of war against intoxicating liquors and atheism and gluttony, but above all of war against slavery. What offended, for the warlike phraseology in a revivalist age was familiar enough, was that they talked as if they really meant to wage war and to win it, not metaphorically but actually.

Their performance proved it. They not only accepted Negroes as students but they actually accepted women. As for the war against sin, it was led by the great Charles Grandison Finney, who had saved thousands in New York in revivals there before he became professor of theology at Oberlin. He had charged about New York's Burned-Over District, shaking his finger in the face of decent men like a prosecuting attorney, calling them a generation of vipers that deserved eternal torture in Hell, warning them to shake the dust of their little village or town from their feet for God was about to destroy it. Only a little less aggressive in Ohio, Finney was tall (6 feet 2 inches), and had a bald head and a baleful hypnotic eye of such power that it could frighten hardheaded and hardhearted reprobates into those whom he described as like "little children before the feet of Jesus." His fierceness, occasionally alternating with a tender sorrow at the coming fate of his auditors, was so overwhelming that they often groaned and moaned, shook, trembled, and cried out. The groaning particularly offended President Pierce and never more so than when Finney said that a man suffering from a deep conviction of sin *had* to groan.

2

As for the war against slavery, Oberlin's students often waged it, and in no figurative or oratorical sense. Some were veterans of the struggle at Lane Seminary under Weld, who gave a course of lectures against slavery in the new half-completed Ladies' Hall at Oberlin, his audience shivering in the wind blowing through the structure's gaps. Many carried the battle to towns and villages where they organized anti-slavery societies. Often when their anti-slavery meetings were assailed by mobs, they joyously charged out and engaged in physical combat, using clubs in one fierce melee.

On Saturday evening, April 28, 1837, Martin L. Brooks, a former student, suddenly appeared at Oberlin with four fugitive slaves in a wagon. They took supper in Oberlin's dining hall and then went to the sitting room, "where crowds of students flocked around them to see and converse with them." On Monday they were taken to Hudson, on their way to Lake Erie and Canada's freedom, guarded by five young men armed with "dirks, butcher knives, pistols, etc.," to fight off their masters who were rumored to be in pursuit.[3] Where they were lodged in Hudson is not known but it would not have been remarkable if it was in the home of the Oberlin trustee, Owen Brown, who was also a stationmaster on the Underground Railroad.

The anti-slavery dissidents in Hudson, led by Owen Brown, formed a dissenting church, sometimes called the Free Church and often the Oberlin Church. They were hated by the majority of the town not only for their activity against slavery but because they had been active in helping persuade six Western Reserve College students to resign and attend Oberlin, including Timothy Hudson, grandson of the Hudson who founded the town and had been one of the founders of the college. Their number also included Samuel Adair, who married John Brown's half sister Florilla, also a student at Oberlin, and who after graduation became a Kansas missionary and a supporter of John Brown.

But most of all they were rejected because they brought the voice of the enemy into Hudson itself. The leaders of Oberlin College frequently appeared in the pulpit of Hudson's Oberlin Church, professors and trustees, perhaps even including President Asa Mahan and the great Finney, who liked to tell how he came to God after three days of wrestling with the Devil in his New York law office. Finally, he said, while sitting before the fire in his office, he "received a mighty baptism of the Holy Ghost. . . .

"The Holy Spirit descended upon me in a manner that seemed to go through me, body and soul," he later wrote, in describing an experience undergone by many of his time.

I could feel the impression, like a wave of electricity, going through and through me. Indeed it seemed to come in waves and waves of liquid love; for I could not express it in any other way. It seemed like the very breath of God. I can recollect distinctly that it seemed to fan me, like immense wings; and it seemed to me, as these waves passed over me, they literally moved my hair like a passing breeze.[4]

Such an experience would not have seemed strange to Owen Brown or John Brown or any other of Hudson's Oberlinites. They, too, had experienced the very breath of God and if it had not literally moved their hair it had otherwise moved them, sometimes to the breaking of the law in the name of the Lord.

CONDUCTORS AND STATIONMASTERS

I

In returning to Hudson, John Brown went back to much that was familiar from boyhood, but he was also living for the first time in an active anti-slavery center. In the eleven years he had been away, Hudson had changed from a village in which American bondage was to the majority little more than an abstraction to a community in which slavery of all public questions was foremost in the minds of most, whether for or against it. For eleven years John Brown had lived in areas somewhat isolated from the struggle, whether in the remoteness of Randolph or the boom atmosphere of Franklin; but now he was subject to all the influences of one who had moved into a focal point of the anti-slavery crusade.

The elms and ivy-covered walls of the college, so far as ten years could give them ivy, were in a sense but a facade for the Underground Railroad, so active in Hudson during the last half of the 1830's that no less than nine of its citizens used their homes, barns, or hidden places in the woods as stations for the harboring of fugitive slaves before forwarding them further on their way to Lake Erie and Canada. Its reputation as a center of the Underground Railroad was sufficiently widespread that someone placed a sign on a road leading to the village on which was painted a smiling black with the words, "Dis de road to Hudson." [5]

Among the number of Hudson's citizens who were stationmasters on the Railroad was, of course, Owen Brown, leader of the Oberlinites, who knew every major anti-slavery figure on the Western Reserve and who was still treasurer of the Western Reserve Anti-Slavery Society. Others who used their property as stations were Deacon Kilbourne, Judge Jesse Dickensen, Sylvester Thompson, Oliver and Fred Brown, Deacon Sanford, and John Brown's friend, Lora Case. Shortly after John Brown's arrival, there was a tenth station in the township's 25 square miles when he built a secret compartment concealed beneath the haymow of his barn in the northeast corner of the township near the Ravenna Road. [6]

The Browns lived about three miles from the center of Hudson in a large white farmhouse, near a great rock covering almost a half acre and nearly as high as the house. From one side of the rock a spring bubbled out, forming a basin and then running off into a creek which John Brown used in his tanning. In the living room was a fireplace 10 feet long which each evening except in summer contained a fire in front of which John Brown would sit with one or two of the smaller children on his lap and sing, as he had at Randolph, "Blow Ye the Trumpet, Blow."

In 1837 he had nine children: John Brown, Jr., sixteen years old; Jason, fourteen; Owen, thirteen; Ruth, eight; Frederick, seven; Sarah, three; Watson, two; Salmon, one; and Charles, only a few months old. Hudson was flooded with Browns and their relatives by blood and marriage, the Mills, Lusks, Bassetts, Rogers, and Merriams, all of whom were violently against slavery and most of whom were strongly marked as to visage and character. Few people then were afraid of eccentricity but rather used it as a form of self-expression and relief for themselves and amusement for others.

John Brown, himself thirty-seven, had two brothers living in Hudson, Oliver, thirty-three, and Frederick, thirty. Both were married and both had three children in 1837. He also had an unmarried sister, Anna Ruth, thirty-nine years old living in Hudson, as well as half brothers and sisters through his father's second marriage, two of whom were younger than many of his own children. His half sister, Sally Marian, was twenty-six and married to Titus S. Hand. They had a two-year-old son whose name was Addison. Another half sister, Florilla, was twenty-one in 1837 and after attending Oberlin would marry in 1841 the Reverend Adair. He also had two half brothers in Hudson, Jeremiah, eighteen in 1837, and Lucien, eight, as well as a half sister, Martha, who was only five.

All of the Browns had a strong sense of family relation. "Blood has always been thick in the Brown family," wrote one of John Brown's sons later. "Family ties were firm, and the tendency has been strong to 'stick together.' "[7] Owen Brown's grandchildren, unusually close among themselves, were brought up to revere and honor him as the patriarch who had founded this family in Ohio. In 1837 Owen was sixty-six—he lived until 1856—and was still very active and strong. He continued farming, taking his part in plowing, haying, and the harvest, visiting Oberlin as often as he could, not only as a trustee but to talk theology with its professors. As an Oberlin trustee he was conscientious in violating the law as often as necessary by delivering escaping fugitives from his home in Hudson to stations at Brecksville or Bedford on the Underground to Cleveland.

Owen still stuttered and had in addition become a little deaf. He subscribed to so many anti-slavery papers and later to so many Free Soil newspapers, most of which attacked the Whigs as a pro-slavery party, that Hudson's Whig postmaster, William Beebe, once protested. After piling journal after journal before Owen, he said, "These are what you are using to kill the grand old Whig party." Owen attempted to answer but stuttered so badly he could not. Beebe said, "Come, come, Squire, you are getting in too heavy a load, let it out."

"I was ju-just con-con-sidering if the game was worth the am-am-ammunition," Owen said.[8] He thought this very funny and so did Hudson's antislavery people when he went around telling about it, carefully stuttering each time as he gave his reply to the postmaster. On another occasion his sons John and Frederick were "discussing some matter and quarreling over it," finally getting so hot about it that they were shouting at the top of their voices. Owen approached the shouting brothers, one hand cupped behind his ear, asking, "What is it you have for to say? Speak a leetle louder."[9]

2

Not only were the Lusks and Mills reputed to be somewhat eccentric but the entire Brown tribe sometimes indulged themselves in any little antic that pleased them. Owen's son Oliver, described as "the most original, perhaps, of them all," and even more gaunt and lanky than his brother John, had a farm in nearby Geagua County on which there was a small church he regarded as his own property because "no deed had ever been made transferring it to the little congregation." Oliver as the owner of the church claimed the right to have abolitionist meetings in it but the congregation was against this sharing.

"One Sunday afternoon," an abolitionist friend of Oliver's later recalled,

we had arranged to have an anti-slavery meeting there, and when we arrived we found the preacher holding forth. Oliver Brown didn't like this, and asked the preacher to vacate, but he wouldn't do it. . . . The preacher announced that he would preach again next Sunday, but Oliver determined he shouldn't.

So during the week he ran a fence around it, a rail fence, not very high, but still high enough to turn stock. Sunday morning he was the first man to get in the church. He took with him a basketful of bowlders and two or three good clubs and prepared to hold the fort. About ten o'clock the congregation began to arrive in their wagons and buggies. When they saw that fence they commenced to get mad, and it wasn't five minutes before it was swept away. But when they got to the door it was locked.

Going around to the window they saw Oliver in there, with hymn book in hand, marching up and down the aisle, singing: "Far from my Thoughts Vain World Begone." They called to him to let them in but he took no notice of them. Then they commenced to batter away at the door, when he with a loud voice warned them to leave him alone, that he was worshiping in his own house and his own way and he would not be disturbed. Still they tried to get in, but he pointed to his armament of clubs and stone, and they stopped for a time.

In the afternoon, however, they got into the church, and that made Oliver so mad he vowed he would burn the pulpit "with fire and brimstone." The next day, toward sunset, I came along there, and sure enough he had loosened the pulpit from the floor and dragged it out in the yard and was just about to set fire to it. Several of the neighbors had gathered, but none of them were willing to have a difficulty with Oliver, and he set it on fire. While it was burning a little old man who felt wrought up by it brought out the pulpit Bible and asked him why he didn't burn it as well. "If you want to burn your Bible, neighbor, just throw it in there," replied Oliver; "but I won't do it, because I have nothing against the Bible. If it will give you any comfort, just throw it on." [10]

Some years later Oliver lost his faith and did have something against the Bible. He collaborated on a manuscript called, "Holy Bible—Old Mother Goose; What's the Difference?" [11]

3

But John Brown never did agree with his brother Oliver on matters theological. Almost immediately on his return to Hudson he began to teach a Men's Bible Class and it was not long until he was considered "about the best Bible teacher in Hudson although we had Professor Nutting of the college, too. He was very well read in the Bible," one of the class recalled, "and was a pretty good talker. He had a pretty good command of language. He held that one man's opinion is just as good as another's on the interpretation of the Scriptures, provided he is naturally as smart a man." [12] Thinking that he was naturally as smart a man as most, John Brown accepted no interpretation of the Bible but his own, nor did he teach any other.

Almost immediately, too, on his return to Hudson, the new Bible teacher began to break the law, habitually and constantly, thus adding to his moral stature, at least in the opinion of his father. If he was the best Bible teacher in Hudson he was soon conceived to be among the best conductors in Hudson on the Underground Railroad. (A conductor actually conveyed escaping slaves from one point to another, usually by wagon or horseback, while a stationmaster gave them shelter. Many of the Underground were both.) If his desire to emulate his father and other of the Oberlinites was one reason for his new role, as well as the opportunity Hudson offered, he probably did not let the fact be known that he was now more active on the Underground Railroad than he had ever been before. Rather, it seemed to those insiders who knew of his midnight work that he had such a gift for subterfuge and swift movement that it must come from long experience.

But very little is known about the details of his work or the work of thousands of others on the Underground, particularly at this period of its history. Its very essence was secrecy and silence. A conductor never said to a stationmaster where he had come from nor where he was bound with the fugitive, if they were continuing on, although the stationmaster might have a good idea of both. If an operator on the Railroad, or a sympathizer with it, woke up to find a horse or horses gone from his stable he made no outcry. Instead he waited, confident that they were being used for a good purpose and would be presently in their stalls again.

Everyone involved on the Railroad concentrated, in fact, on knowing as little as possible about the activities of their colleagues so that if they were arrested they would be unable to involve anyone else. The operators of the Underground were liable to a $500 fine under the federal Fugitive Slave Law of 1793 and a $1,000 fine for each slave aided in escaping from the state under Ohio's Black Laws first passed in 1804 but renewed until 1849.* If they could not or would not pay the fines they went to jail. Negro hunters, men who made a profession of capturing fugitives and returning them to their owners for a reward, or selling them for their own profit, were all over the Western Reserve, eager to inform on members of the Underground since they would receive as high as half of the fines paid in any convictions under state law. Slaveowners and their agents were scouring the state on the track of their property and often offering rewards for the conviction of members of the Underground, or even sub rosa rewards for their abduction or assassination.

Because of these dangers there was not much contemporary comment on the exploits of conductors and stationmasters. Later, many at Hudson testified to John Brown's daring as a conductor and there is scarce a book on the movement that does not refer in general terms to his activity there.[13] Charles S. S. Griffing, a well-known anti-slavery figure on the Western Reserve, said, and in some detail, as we shall soon see, that he was an eyewitness

---

* Early in 1837 John Brown is reported to have addressed a mass meeting of Cleveland black citizens petitioning the Ohio legislature for the repeal of the state's Black Laws. (Edward C. Reilly, *Early Slave Controversy on the Western Reserve*, unpublished Ph.D. thesis, Western Reserve University Library, 1940, p. 240.)

to some of John Brown's exploits on the Underground when he piloted slaves to freedom from the Ohio River.[14]

If John Brown, either while in Hudson or later during the 1840's, while he was still in Ohio, went all the way to the Ohio River region to guide slaves to freedom, his adventures on such an expedition might be almost unbelievable to a later age. He might have gone to a crossing at Marietta, making his way north with one or more fugitives to the village of Barlow, then on to the settlement at Bartlett, both stations on the Underground, thence to the home of Thomas Williams, then to William Colmer's station, on to the farm of I. W. Stansberry, and then to Deavertown, which was a junction point for several Underground routes.[15]

If he took this path, and many did, he might well have been pursued by "the nigger hunters" who lived on the Ohio side of the river, tough adventurous men, who made their livings by capturing runaways, either selling them or gaining rewards from alleged owners, and turning over for arrest or otherwise disposing of those aiding them to escape. Such a man was one Kirby, who lived on Blennerhassett Island near Marietta where he trained a large pack of bloodhounds.[16] He had the swiftest of horses and often was lurking around Deavertown, a favorable site for his business. He boasted that his hounds could trail and catch "a nigger" six days after smelling his clothing and he often came thundering down a road in pursuit of a wagon or a carriage reported to be just ahead.

John Brown, perhaps on horseback, the fugitive he was guiding on a horse beside him, had on occasion, we can be almost certain, galloped through the night, or whipped a team onward in a wagon holding five or six runaways, the thudding hoofbeats of pursuers behind drawing nearer. If he had experienced this, and there is little reason to think he had not, his later career might not seem as inexplicable as it has to many. If the great and good at Oberlin and elsewhere honored those who rescued one man from slavery, then one who rescued thousands must be more honored. If breaking the law to rescue six or seven from slavery was honored by the most distinguished of Western Reserve's citizens, perhaps rescuing a whole people from slavery as was his later intent (although he was far from that purpose while in Hudson) was also virtuous and honorable to one possessing the simple and innocent logic of John Brown. And his experiences on the Underground might account too, in part, for his high estimate of black courage. These fugitives he and others aided were not mere bodies. Often they had traversed innumerable dangers through hundreds of miles of hostile country, sometimes aided by the Underground only after crossing the Ohio. They were not black baggage but companions in a desperate adventure, the stakes of which if they lost might be a prison sentence for one and return to slavery for the other.

4

It was sometimes later said by those in Hudson not too enthusiastic about a war against slavery that if Owen Brown had lived until December 2, 1859, when his son was hanged, he would have died of the disgrace. He might have died out of concern for a favorite son, but it can scarcely be doubted that he would have been proud of him. Because Owen Brown was so well liked, his integrity being universally recognized, it was impossible for many to relate him in any way to what they deemed to be the disgrace of a scaffold.

Yet in view of the letter which John Brown wrote to his father denying he was overly interested in getting rich, one might think that Owen's fear was not that his son would be too involved in the fight against slavery but that he might not be involved enough.[17] It seems certain that his father's views on slavery were the genesis of his own. It seems more certain still that John Brown's activity on the Underground, while primarily determined by the time, had its immediate source in his father's work as a conductor and stationmaster. Until almost the day of his death Owen Brown supported his son and his grandsons in the Kansas civil war, sending them money and words of sympathy and encouragement.[18]

More important was Owen Brown's part in 1836–7 in opening the mind of his son, heretofore immersed for the most part in himself and his adventures in business, to the widening struggle against slavery. Owen, as has been said, subscribed to a number of anti-slavery journals including *The Liberator*, which John Brown now read daily at his father's house before later subscribing to it himself. Owen still liked to talk theology and was particularly intrigued at the time with Oberlin's effort to soften predestination and the certainty of Hell for those not of the elect, its stand that man was more than a stench in the nostrils of the Lord. It had such a wide program for social perfection, including its battle against slavery, war, and sin, that it could not well endorse a theology of determinism which denied man free will. Free will is the essence of individual struggle and Oberlin's theologians were now engaged in drafting formulations as to the possibility of the individual winning moral perfection through his struggles against sin, both personal and social. Owen was interested in the new doctrine but it was not likely he found that his son had an equivalent interest. John always seemed comforted by predestination, flattered and solaced by his belief that the Lord had known of John Brown since time's beginning and had determined then what he would do. It gave him a sponsorship he found comforting.

It was after talks with his father on matters theological that John Brown turned to *The Liberator*. It is likely that in its columns he first read of Elijah Lovejoy, the Illinois anti-slavery editor whose slaying was to be such an important influence in his life. All through 1837 he would have also read in *The Liberator* of the struggle of John Quincy Adams to restore the right of petition to the American people.

Both of these events were among the most important in the history of the anti-slavery movement and both influenced thousands of Americans, including John Brown. A narrative such as this, if it is to be true, cannot be restricted to its protagonist. It must suggest something of the quality of the men and events that moved him toward the climax of his life, however distant their scene from his environs. Lovejoy, whom John Brown never met, may well have influenced him more than any man he knew in the flesh with the single exception of his father.

It is likely, too, that Adams was important in his development. "In politics he was originally an Adams man," being appointed postmaster of Randolph by President Adams as one of the last acts of his administration on January 7, 1828.[19] When Adams later publicly declared that slavery might only be destroyed by the force and violence of a civil war, that statement might not have been lost on one who himself was to use force and violence against slavery and help bring on the civil war to which Adams referred.

THE LIBERATION OF J. Q. ADAMS

I

If John Brown and others were gradually becoming more militant in the fight against slavery, perhaps one of many contributing factors, as has been suggested, was the remarkable second life, the second career of John Quincy Adams, which was to invigorate and broaden the whole anti-slavery movement. After a lifetime of caution as to slavery, the former President, as if suddenly returning to the daring of his Revolutionary youth, became the political leader of the anti-slavery movement, in his own eyes at any rate, in the House of Representatives. Elected to the House when sixty-three years old from the Plymouth District of Massachusetts in 1830, after most of the nation had thought him deep in the retirement of old age, the only former President ever to serve in the House, he was to be re-elected eight times.

His cranium as bald and shiny as a billiard ball, his 5 feet 7 inches of height and 170 pounds remarkably fit—he swam the Potomac's mile width after he was sixty—Adams nevertheless constantly complained in his diary of his weakened state, of inability to work, of depression, disease, and decrepitude until he was rejuvenated by those threats to assassinate or expel him from the House as a traitor that he found so stimulating during his second career. Perhaps it was the heady joy of combat, of the luxury of free speech on the subject of slavery upon which he had forced himself to silence for years, that made the ex-President seem young again. When the fight was at its fiercest, when he was being assailed on every side by the outraged slaveholders of the South, then his joy seemed highest, the boils, carbuncles, sweatings, and tremblings of which he complained in the diary suddenly gone, and he felt as fit as a warhorse.

For a time it seemed during his fight to regain the right of petition to Congress for those Americans petitioning against the entry of Texas into the Union as a slave state and the abolition of slavery in Washington, D.C., as if the whole House, controlled by pro-slavery forces, was on its feet each day in an effort to silence him. The House had passed, and continued to pass for nine years, a so-called gag rule in which no petition against slavery, nor any criticizing it, could be received, considered, circulated, debated, or referred to committee. It was in his fight to have this rule abolished that Adams was so maddening to his opponents. No matter how they roared or objected or called out points of order they were ineffective for he had become expert in making his points between lulls in their uproar. As exhaustion stilled the House, his voice would resume. To every ruling of the chair he would respond with a sentence adding to his argument. He was called traitor, madman, fanatic, senile, incendiary but always he was on his feet resuming his indictment of pro-slavery forces during pauses in the clamor beating against him. Sometimes it seemed, as when almost the whole House was ranged against him, its members shouting, "Order! Order! Order!," that he was about to drive them from their senses.

If he had not enjoyed it so much, it might not have been so maddening. Gone were the usual complaints from his diary. Every anti-slavery man who met him complimented him on the brightness of his eye, the spring in his step, the quickness and force of his mind and his argument, even on the strength of his lungs. In a fight, a friend said, perhaps after seeing him quell some Southern fire-eater, he was like a tiger with an unfailing instinct for the jugular vein. Another said, trying to express some sense of the daring the old man exuded, that he was born for the end of a yardarm during a furious gale on a foundering vessel or at the head of some desperate charge through the breach of a fiercely defended fort.[20]

In the past, pro-slavery congressmen had occasionally silenced any who dared differ from them with insults and the remark, referring to the field of honor, "If the gentleman resents my words he will know where to find me." But Old Man Eloquent, as Adams was being called, said he wanted to hear no more of that kind of talk, and the most doughty of duelists never dared to challenge him.

Even the fiery Henry A. Wise, representative from Accomac in Virginia, who believed in the duel as fervently as he did in slavery, never thought of challenging the old man. Only twenty-eight when he became Adams's chief opponent in Congress, he called him a traitor, a liar, a shame to his ancestry, led a march of Southern members from the floor when an Adams ally rose to speak, and once fainted dead away as he was attacking Adams, the complex form of his emotions as he looked at the maddening old man driving consciousness completely from him.[21] Wise's manner of speaking was so wildly gymnastic that his friends were always afraid he might injure himself, perhaps dislocate an arm or shoulder as he flung himself about, or at the least collapse from exhaustion, for occasionally he spoke as long as four hours. His oratory, however, was widely admired. A cadaverously thin young man wearing a long black bag of a coat and a white cravat, his face paler than the tie beneath it, his hair straw-colored and long, it was said he resembled "a galvanized corpse" when engaged in declamation, which however energetic was eloquent and always entertaining. He permitted himself liberties in describing his character that he would not have permitted another without a challenge, once declaring with a kind of melancholy pride that he was "among the vilest sinners of this House."[22] He was also among the most popular members of the House, filled with high spirits and gaiety when not engaged in duels or debates. He loved his wife but did not even consider giving up the dueling which kept her sick with worry that he would either murder or be murdered in pursuit of his honor.

Young Wise was to do as much as anyone to hang John Brown when Wise became Governor of Virginia some twenty years later, but now if Brown read of him, and his words appeared frequently in *The Liberator*, he knew him only as among the most militant of Southern congressmen, determined to extend slavery by annexing Texas and equally determined that no congressman, under the House gag law, should be allowed to utter a word in slavery's condemnation. Even when Adams called him a murderer, it will be recalled, for his part in the duel in which Representative Cilley of Maine was killed, Wise did not challenge him. It was impossible. Wise, who could order Presidents about, as when he insisted that an unwilling President Tyler appoint Calhoun Secretary of State, could not challenge the whole of American history, and Adams represented that history more clearly than any other living American. He had been the sixth President of the United States and the son of the second, John Adams, who had helped draft the Declaration of Independence. He was virtually the last living remnant of that Revolution which had brought his country into life. Not only had he been President and Secretary of State, a member of the United States Senate, the friend of Washington and Jefferson, American minister to Berlin, Moscow, and London, witness to the wars of the French Revolution and the retreat of Napoleon from Moscow, but he himself had been under British fire when only ten and had seen from afar the Battle of Bunker Hill. To many he seemed the last survivor of a glory departed and even his foes had an uneasy sense that he was a national institution rather than a mere man.

2

Since 1820 Adams had condemned slavery, however secretly, believing long before John Brown that only the force and violence of civil war could extirpate it, but confiding such thoughts to his diary alone. For most of his adult life he had been in the prison of one who longed for the presidency; it was not for such to indulge in the luxury of free speech on the country's most sensitive issue. As one who hoped for the White House, he could not offend the South and its slaveholders. Once in it after his election in 1824, he could say nothing against slavery if he wished for the South's support for administration measures, particularly for internal improvements, a support he never gained.

As a matter of fact, neither he nor most others seemed to consider slavery very seriously until 1820 when it began to threaten the West with the admission of Missouri into the Union as the first trans-Mississippi slave state. As senator from Massachusetts in 1803, he had opposed the bill forbidding the importation of slaves into the huge new Louisiana Territory and had worked against the prohibition of the international slave trade into the United States before 1808 when such action was permitted by the Constitution. It was not only that he was being careful for ambition's sake; like most others, he had a real loyalty to the constitutional compromise permitting slavery that had been framed by the Revolutionary fathers.

But during the crisis over the Missouri Compromise, he began to think, as did many others, that if the years held a shattering of the Union, it would be over slavery. Spurred by the extraordinarily bitter controversy, which was at last compromised by admitting Missouri as a slave state, it will be remembered, in return for the admission of Maine as a free state and the banning of slavery forever from all American territories above 36° 30′ north latitude, he had written in his diary on February 24, 1820:

Slavery is the great and foul stain upon the North American Union, and it is a contemplation worthy of the most exalted soul whether its total abolition is or is not practicable; if practicable by what means it may be effected, and if a choice of means be within the scope of the subject, what would accomplish it at the smallest cost of human sufferance. A dissolution, at least temporary of the Union, as now constituted would be certainly necessary, and the dissolution might be on a point involving the question of slavery, and no other. The Union then might be reorganized on the fundamental principle of emancipation. The subject is vast in its compass, awful in its prospects, sublime and beautiful in its issue.

Then, as if foretelling some future John Brown, he added, "A life devoted to it would be nobly spent or sacrificed." [23]

In similar vein Adams had written on November 29 of that same year:

If slavery is destined to be the sword in the hand of the destroying angel which is to sever the ties of this Union, the same sword will cut in sunder the bonds of slavery itself. A dissolution for the cause of slavery would be followed by a servile war in the slaveholding States, combined with a war between the two severed portions of the Union. It seems to me that the result must be the extirpation of slavery from the whole continent; and calamitous and desolating as this course of events in its progress must be, so glorious would be its final issue, that, as God shall judge me, I dare not say that it is not to be desired.[24]

Perhaps the restraint from public expression of such deeply held views on his country's fate was one source of his tension during his single term in the White House, beginning in 1825. "My eyes complain of inflammation, and my heart is sick," he recorded in his diary. "I wrote this evening with a heavy heart." He complained of "erysipelas, indigestion, inability to perspire in hot weather, a tendency to cramps while swimming the Potomac, catarrh, and uncontrollable dejection of spirits." [25] Even in the White House in 1827, when he wrote a sonnet to his father containing some expressions hostile to slavery, he wrote it in shorthand so only he might know its sentiments. A President, he thought, had to be particularly cautious. It was one of the best

sonnets he ever wrote—he was an inveterate poetaster—but when he placed
it on a tablet in the Adams church at Quincy, he omitted the last two lines
which read:

> *Roll years of promise, rapidly roll around,*
> *Till not a slave on this earth be found.*[26]

He regretted omitting them but a man still ambitious in politics could not
permit himself freedom of expression on such a topic.

3

The anti-slavery movement, before freeing the country's slaves, freed John
Quincy Adams. It was the gigantic petition campaign, organized by the
American Anti-Slavery Society, in which hundreds of thousands of Americans above the Ohio petitioned the House of Representatives for the abolition of slavery in the District of Columbia and the territories while demanding that no new slave state should be admitted to the Union, that first gave
Adams the power of free and public speech on the subject of slavery. If he
was a statesman, he was also a politician and if he was a fighter he did not
aspire to martyrdom. As a politician the first law of life was re-election to the
House he had entered in 1831 after his election the year before. For five
years he was virtually silent on the subject of slavery. It was not until 1836,
and thereafter, when he increasingly knew that hundreds of thousands in the
North, and thousands in his own Plymouth District, would back him that
he availed himself of free speech to the point of attacking slavery. At last
there was a coincidence between his own desire and political practicality.

If the petition campaign and the abolitionists transformed John Quincy
Adams, he did his part in transforming them. There was an intimate relationship between the man and the movement, the latter giving him strength
while his forensic victories, emblazoned in every newspaper, added to the
anti-slavery campaign thousands who had been heretofore indifferent or hostile to the freedom of the slave. The conservative who could not be moved
by Garrison would listen to an Adams, to a former President who was a son
of a President and a survivor of the Revolution. It was his struggle in the
House of Representatives that ever increasingly revealed that while black
freedom was denied, white freedom was endangered, that white Americans
could not enjoy their constitutional rights in the face of slavery, could not
exercise their rights of free speech and petition while the slave interest, intent
on outlawing them, remained in power.

His boldness increased as the flood of petitions increased and as his boldness grew, its results in every newspaper, so did the deluge of petitions. He began by opposing many of the demands of his petitioners, fighting only for their right to ask Congress for a redress of grievances. He was no abolitionist, he said, but he was so completely unable to prevent himself from topping an opponent in argument, to seek a more basic ground than those opposing him, that soon his attack on slavery was more bitter and sweeping than that of many abolitionists.

Soon he often forgot, or deliberately neglected to make, the disclaimer of not being an abolitionist which few in the South believed anyway. More and more, many of his friends, associates, correspondents, and advisers were abolitionists, ranging from Whittier to Benjamin Lundy, from Theodore Weld to Joshua Leavitt. With assassination threats arriving almost daily from the South and the abolitionists writing letters of love and admiration, it was small wonder that he began to respect the only ones who praised him. Presently he was writing in his diary that if being an abolitionist was being willing to lay down one's life for the cause then he surely was one.

The contest changed his most fundamental beliefs. When he entered Congress he was among the country's foremost expansionists. As a young man he had written his mother that he favored "A nation co-extensive with the North American Continent,"[27] presumably including Mexico down through the Isthmus of Panama and so he apparently felt, along with most Americans, until the issue of slavery reversed his opinion after his election to Congress. As senator, diplomat, plenipotentiary, Secretary of State, and President he had ceaselessly worked to increase the American domain. It was a part of the very marrow of his political being, the heart not only of his own policy but of the country's policy since the nation's beginning. Crucial to his entire political life, and the country's life, had been his design to press its sovereignty across the continent to the Pacific.

In negotiations while Secretary of State with Spain and Great Britain, he not only gained Florida for the United States, but laid the basis for American rights to Oregon, forced Great Britain to recognize American sovereignty to land extending between Minnesota and the Rocky Mountains, and gained from Spain recognition of American rights to a huge extent of territory, formerly claimed by Spain—from the Columbia and Missouri rivers on the north to the Sabine and Red rivers on the south, this latter riparian line being extended west to the Pacific along what are now the northern boundaries of California, Nevada, and western Utah. It was the territory north and east of these boundaries and the Sabine and Red rivers to which he gained claim.

While President he had even sought to purchase the Texas whose annexation he was now opposing, but that was before slavery was either present there or so hot an issue in American politics.

Now as petitions against the annexation of Texas poured in by the thousands, as Northern legislatures resolved against the measure, he experienced one of American history's great reversals. It was a genuine reversal, based on his hatred of slavery. In the past he had always thought that in pressing for American expansion he was increasing the area of liberty. Now he was convinced that in annexing Texas, where slavery had been banned by Mexican law, the United States would be usurping land belonging to a neighboring nation and transforming territory once free into slave soil. It was a genuine reversal but public sentiment in the North, as revealed by the petitions, surely helped him in expressing it. He became the country's foremost advocate of no expansion to the South, no annexation of Texas, and no war with Mexico which claimed it, doing more than any single man to delay both annexation and the war against Mexico for almost a decade, declaring that both were only designed to increase the area and power of slavery.

That the fight transformed him can scarcely be denied. Before entering Congress he would as soon have publicly attacked the Holy Spirit as utter a public word against slavery. After the gag forbidding petitions or any expression at all in the House against slavery, scarce a day passed that he did not attack it, ever more vehemently, ever more constantly, ever more skillfully. A master parliamentarian, he circumvented the gag by rising to points of personal privilege, or by attacking slavery under the guise of speaking against an appropriation for the Seminole War in which the United States Army was using bloodhounds to track down slaves who had fled to the Seminoles, fighting for their homeland. Twice he goaded his opponents into trying to vote censure upon him and then all restrictions as to subject matter were virtually gone as he spoke in his own defense, each time speaking so voluminously, holding the floor so long, attacking so fiercely, condemning slavery so unequivocally while all the country listened, that his opponents almost begged him to permit them to abandon their attempts to censure him.

Describing an occasion when Adams was presenting anti-slavery petitions, despite the rule against them, Theodore Weld, who was serving as Adams's research assistant, wrote of him:

Old Nestor [Adams] lifted up his voice like a trumpet; till slaveholding, slave trading and slave breeding absolutely quailed and howled under his dissecting knife. Mr. Adams had said the day before that he should present some petitions that would set them in a blaze, so I took care to be in the house at the time, and such a scene I never witnessed. Lord Morpeth, the English abolitionist of whom you have heard, was present and sat within a few feet of Mr. A., his fine intelligent face beaming with delight as the old man breasted the storm and dealt his blows upon the head of the monster.

Wise of Va., Raynor [Rayner] of N.C., W. C. Johnson of Md., and scores more of slaveholders, striving constantly to stop him by starting questions of order and by every now and then screaming at the top of their voices: "That is false." "I demand, Mr. Speaker, that you *put him down*." "What are we to sit here and endure such insults." "I demand that you shut the mouth of that old harlequin." A perfect uproar like Babel would burst forth every two or three minutes as Mr. A. with his bold surgery would smite his cleaver into the very bones. At least half of the slaveholding members of the house left their seats and gathered in the quarter of the Hall where Mr. Adams stood. Whenever any of them broke out upon him, Mr. Adams would say, "I see where the shoe pinches, Mr. Speaker, it will pinch *more* yet." "I'll deal out to the gentlemen a diet that they'll find hard to digest." "If before I get through every slaveholder, slavetrader and slave breeder on this floor does not get materials for better reflection it shall be no fault of mine." [28]

4

He was sometimes as maddening to his friends as to his foes, outraging his admirers when he presented petitions for the abolition of slavery in Washington, D.C., while declaring that he himself did not favor the petitioners' plea but only their right to make it. Similarly, when petitioners demanded that Florida not be admitted into the Union as a slave state he, when presenting or trying to present their petition, said that he himself was for slavery in Florida because when he negotiated the treaty with Spain for the annexation of Florida he had promised as Secretary of State that there would be no change in existing Florida institutions, which included slavery. And yet, after such a performance he would attack slavery more bitterly and more basically than ever abolitionist attacked it.

Few abolitionists had declared that slavery might be destroyed by the force and violence of a civil war. But Adams said it. At least twice he told the House, legalistically, elliptically, but nevertheless unmistakably, that the annexation of Texas might result in a war with Mexico which could finally eventuate in an American civil war in which Congress, under its war powers, might abolish slavery. Such a prognosis was as unprecedented as it was shocking and each time he made it it seemed to stun the House into a momentary silence. To the slaveholders in Congress it was as if he were predicting, and even rejoicing in it, the end of the world as they had known it, the complete overturn of society and the moral order of the universe. Then they returned to their usual clamor, to their cries for "Order!," pushing around the old man as if they were about to assault him but by then it was too late. The dreadful prophecy had been made and time was to prove it right.

However peculiarly he fought, he was winning. Each year it was getting more difficult for Southern members and their Northern allies to pass the gag law. Each session it became more apparent that in the effort to silence debate on slavery there were more debates as to slavery than ever before or at least more disturbances over the question than ever before. It was apparent to everyone that the anti-slavery cohorts were gaining thousands of new recruits.[29]

Even the schism which divided abolitionists in 1840 into two warring sects, disputing between them about the role of women and politics in anti-slavery ranks, had not diminished the political power of the broader anti-slavery movement. Partly as a result of Adams's struggles, new anti-slavery congressmen were appearing: Joshua R. Giddings, from Ohio's Western Reserve, in 1838;* Francis Jackson Andrews, also from Ohio, in 1839; John Mattocks of Vermont in 1841; Seth Merill Gates of New York in 1839; and Nathaniel Briggs Borden of Massachusetts in 1841. Adams, whatever their views, regarded himself as their leader. All during this fight he had been aided by William Slade, of Vermont, and John Dickson, of New York, both of whom entered the House the same year as he did; but although they fought as bravely as Adams for the right of petition, most of the attention and most of the newspaper stories concerned the former President.

As the years went on, Adams seemed like some natural force, a perpetual motion machine which never tired, or even someone who each year got younger. Through his sixties he fought and on through his seventies and into his eighties. Only when not in combat did he begin to worry, and vacations amid the peace of Quincy seriously upset him. At such times he broke out with pimples, boils, and carbuncles, suffered shortness of breath and dizziness, a catarrhal cough, and once he said he felt as if every inch of his bald head had been stung by bees. When Congress resumed he was always restored to health, on one occasion by the last effort of the House to censure him in the hope he would resign. Instead, he flowered, seeming to become more youthful by the day.

Weld spoke with awe of his energy and endurance during this fight against censure. "The energy with which Mr. A. speaks," he wrote his wife,

---

* Giddings, an important influence in John Brown's life, was converted to abolitionism by Theodore Weld.

is astonishing. Though seventy five years old, his voice is one of the clearest and loudest in the house. And his gestures and bodily action when warmly engaged in speaking are most vigorous and commanding. Last Friday, after he had been sitting in the house from 12 o'clock till 6, and for nearly half that time engaged in speaking with great energy against his ferocious assailants, I called at his house in the evening, and he came to meet me as fresh and elastic as a boy. I told him I was afraid he had tired himself out. "No, not at all," said he, "I am all ready for another heat." He then began and went through with the *main points* which he designed to push in his speech the next day, and with as much rapidity and energy of utterance and gesture as though he had been addressing the house. I tried to stop him, telling him he would need all his strength for the next day, but it was all in vain. He went on for an hour, or very nearly that, in a voice loud enough to be heard by a large audience. Wonderful man! [30]

With such energy at his command, Adams's fight against censure was an unequal struggle. For the second time members of the House begged him to permit them to drop the charges of censure and he graciously consented. Not much later, after Adams for nine years had led the fight against the gag law, the House again recognized the inevitable, wiping the rule, so singularly unsuccessful in gagging Adams, from its books. It was everywhere admitted that Adams in his old age was even more successful than in his prime, that the congressman was a better man than the President had been. If this were true it was because of the liberation of J. Q. Adams, when, with all presidential ambition gone, and with an aroused North behind him, he again gained that right of free speech so often denied Presidents. Even an elderly man grows young when free.

XV

Murder,

the Converter

HOWEVER MUCH John Brown and the North were influenced by J. Q. Adams's struggle against slavery, they were even more moved by the extraordinary travail of Elijah Parish Lovejoy, the anti-slavery editor in Alton, Illinois. To John Brown, and hosts of others, it was a major experience which brought them further along the road of anti-slavery than they had been when first they heard of Lovejoy. That is the nature of a *cause célèbre*—and Lovejoy's plight was followed the world around—the knitting together of thousands in a passionate emotional reaction to what seems to them tragic injustice.

All during the summer of 1837, those who read the abolitionist press were conscious of Lovejoy's danger.[1] They knew that he had been driven from St. Louis after he had protested the burning to death of a black man by a mob, his newspaper office smashed, his home invaded and wrecked, his young and beautiful wife made ill by the violence and persecution directed against her husband and herself. They knew that in Alton, where he had established his newspaper, the Alton *Observer*, in 1836 after fleeing St. Louis, he had been assaulted, threatened, his house attacked, and that his press had been destroyed by mobs three times.

A stalwart, rough-hewn Presbyterian clergyman of thirty-four with black eyes and a snub nose beneath a swirl of hair, Lovejoy was a graduate of Waterville College, later Colby, in Maine and of the Princeton Theological Seminary. An able writer and an extraordinary speaker, he had been the editor of the daily St. Louis *Times* before he became a clergyman. Although he was an unusually aggressive man, he was trying hard to remain a non-resistant after the Garrison mold but his own temperament as well as Alton's atmosphere and customs made it difficult.

It was a free-and-easy boom town of four thousand on the Mississippi River, the slave state of Missouri on the opposite shore, its economic life largely depending on its downriver trade with the South's plantations. Because of its business interests it was a pro-slavery community in the free state of Illinois. It was not a monolith and it had those supporting Lovejoy, but most of its politicians and leading citizens, often from Virginia or Kentucky, were hot for slavery, as eager for Lovejoy's destruction as the rivermen and drunks from Tontine Row, the gamblers, loafers, deckhands, firemen, bawdy-house keepers, rough-and-tumble fighters, pimps, bouncers, and saloon keepers of Alton's Mississippi waterfront who made up the mobs which had repeatedly destroyed Lovejoy's press.

They found his piety, his New England accent—he had been born in Maine—his opposition to intoxicating liquors, his announced purpose of living as Christ had lived, almost as offensive as his attacks against slavery. When insulted, he disobeyed every convention of the Mississippi rivermen, who had both a national reputation for ferocity—ripping off ears and gouging out eyes with a fine abandon—and a strict etiquette for the preliminaries of combat. When Lovejoy was challenged he did not speak of his manhood, nor did he bristle or flush or throw his hat upon the ground, nor say he was damned if he would take such an insult, nor speak of his sacred honor, nor go through any of the rooster-like crowings or dog-like sprangling of the legs that any proper riverman knew were obligatory in such cases.

Rather, he tried for reasoned argument, quoting the Declaration of Independence and the Golden Rule, seeking, mildly enough, to show why slavery should be abolished. They could not know the effort his mildness cost him nor how it concealed a growing urge to break from the path of Garrison and fight. There was little to indicate in the softness of his words the monumental stubbornness that was his. He believed in his own bravery and said more than once that it did not become such a man as himself to flee. And yet he was occasionally tempted to do so. When he saw his wife and little son, his wife confined to bed, sick from the continuing violence in which they lived, he sometimes thought he had no right to pursue a course which might result in her death.

THE TRIALS OF A NONRESISTANT

I

Lovejoy's first press was destroyed in Alton on July 24, 1836, within forty-eight hours of his arrival there. His second was thrown into the Mississippi on August 21, 1837, after a mass meeting had declared that his attacks on slavery were ruining Alton. Slaveholders, it was said, upon whom Alton was economically dependent, were boycotting its trade because of Lovejoy. On that date, August 21, Lovejoy himself was seized by a mob, intent on tarring and feathering him before setting him adrift on the Mississippi. He had faced the mob so bravely, one nonresistant editor against hundreds, that he had escaped harm when the mob's leader said, "Boys, I cannot lay my hands upon as brave and defenseless a man as this." [2]

On September 21, 1837, his third press was destroyed by ten or twelve men whose faces were covered by masks. A few days later his home was assailed by a mob throwing bricks and stones, shattering its windows. Lovejoy himself was away at the time but inside the house was his wife, who was ill, and his one-year-old son. Early in October he and his wife had barely escaped with their lives after a drunken mob had broken into the home of Mrs. Lovejoy's mother at St. Charles, Missouri, where they were visiting. They were forced to flee back to Alton, a doubtful refuge. It was after this that Lovejoy had reluctantly decided he could no longer be a nonresistant. He wrote to Maine asking that his brothers, Owen and Joseph Lovejoy, come to Alton to protect his wife while he was away. They brought muskets, pistols, and ammunition.

His wife was so ill from the violence at St. Charles, Lovejoy wrote, that

what the final result will be for her I know not, but hope for the best. We have no one with us tonight, except the members of our own family. A loaded musket is standing at my bedside, while my two brothers, in an adjoining room, have three others together with pistols, cartridges, etc. And this is the way we live in the city of Alton!

I have had inexpressible reluctance to resort to this method of defense. But dear-bought experience has taught me that there is at present no safety for me, and no defense in this place, either in the laws or the protecting aegis of public sentiment. I feel that I do not walk the streets in safety, and every night when I lie down, it is with the deep settled conviction, that there are those near me and around me, who seek my life. I have resisted this conviction as long as I could, but it has been forced upon me.[3]

2

Within a little more than a fortnight after the incident of the St. Charles mob, during the third week of October, the founding convention of the Illinois State Anti-Slavery Society was held in Alton. Lovejoy had been the central figure in its organization, which increased hostility against him. Pro-slavery forces—led by Usher F. Linder, Attorney General for Illinois, and the Reverend John Hogan, "Honest John" as he called himself, a state senator as well as a merchant and a preacher—gained actual entry into the convention which they took over for a time, even passing a resolution condemning abolition.

On the third day of the convention the real abolitionists, some eighty in number and from all parts of Illinois, retired to a private house and with a mob clamoring outside, succeeded in organizing a statewide anti-slavery society. Their difficulty in the opening sessions had been caused by the Reverend Edward H. Beecher, at once an important acquisition to the abolition movement and a major trial and liability. A graduate of Yale, the son of Lyman Beecher, perhaps the foremost American preacher of the 1830's, the brother of Harriet Beecher Stowe who would write *Uncle Tom's Cabin*, he was the president of Illinois College at nearby Jacksonville. It was his insistence on issuing a call welcoming "all friends of free enquiry" to the abolitionist convention that had almost wrecked it, since many pro-slavery men could and did describe themselves as friends of free inquiry and as such obtained admission to the abolitionist founding convention.[4]

The Reverend Beecher of Illinois was a brave and handsome man, fatally weakened by a bumbling, pretentious rectitude. He liked Lovejoy—they belonged to the same anti-slavery wing of the Presbyterian Church—and he sometimes visited him in Alton where, beside the bed of Mrs. Lovejoy, the two would sink to their knees while Beecher's great preacher's voice beat against the walls, imploring the Lord for wisdom and guidance.

The Reverend Beecher had a profound and innocent faith in words, as though he believed that words were the only reality, somehow laying to rest, if rightly chosen and arranged, the fierce conflicts of men. He felt he could control any public meeting by offering a series of resolutions, as was the custom then, each carrying the meeting a step forward, each a progression that would bring the meeting at last to a unanimously accepted perfect truth.

He ached to get together in Alton a large and representative meeting, certain he could bring it around through a series of successive resolutions to unanimous resolve to protect freedom of the press and Lovejoy. He was working on organizing such an assembly. It would be open, of course, "to all friends of free enquiry."

His fiasco at the anti-slavery convention had not weakened his faith in this principle, nor had Lovejoy been disturbed unduly. After all, the convention had turned out well in the end. It had passed a unanimous resolution advocating the immediate reopening of the Alton *Observer* with Lovejoy as its editor. The new press, Lovejoy's fourth in Alton, for the purchase of which many of those attending the convention had contributed, would soon be on its way from St. Louis. In addition there were those in Alton, not many but an increasing number, not abolitionists but men angered by the repeated attacks on Lovejoy and his press, who were volunteering to help him protect, forcibly if need be, the new press when it arrived.

If it had not been for his wife's illness Lovejoy might have been almost happy at the support and confidence given him in and out of the convention. She seldom left her bed now, seldom spoke, and as her husband saw her lying there he must have asked himself if he had the right to pursue a course that might be killing her. In fact, many of his letters to his family in Maine of late concerned this question. Perhaps as he walked home in the gathering dusk several days later he was thinking of her when he heard a dim roar in the distance which at first he did not quite recognize. His brothers occasionally left the Lovejoy home for a brief space when they believed an attack unlikely. Almost without knowing why he did so he quickened his pace, and then he was running toward his home, a stifling, incredulous indignation within him.

He knew now what the roar was, having heard it before, and as he neared the small two-story white frame house on Huntertown Road sheltering his wife and son, the sound separated into individual shouts, curses, screams. He could see the mob as he drew nearer, see arms rear back, rocks fly, and before he could reach his home, he saw two strange men push their way inside. As he bounded up the steps leading to the front door, the two men, who seemed to be drunk, ran out of the house but Lovejoy paid them no heed as he cried out for his wife. There was no reply. He went from room to room crying her name but there was no answer and no sound save the dull thud of rocks striking against the house, the occasional tinkling crack of breaking glass, and now and again a sudden gust of louder noise from the mob outside.

Now he was going from floor to floor, still shouting her name and still there was no answer until he came at last to the attic. There was his wife, in the attic's very center, as far as she could get from the windows and breaking glass, lying prone, face downward, like a hunted animal, and yet somehow contriving to use her body to protect her little son. "I found her driven to the garret through fear of the mob," Lovejoy later said, as if still incredulous.[5]

That night in his damaged house, glass still splattering the floor and beside the bed of his wife, a rifle in his hands, Lovejoy may have faced himself as never before. Could it be that his own love of his own virtue was the moving force behind the violence that was slowly killing his wife? Whatever his thoughts that night, a few days later, probably on the last of October or November 1, he wrote out an announcement of his decision to resign and quit Alton and took it to the Alton *Telegraph* for publication.[6]

He told a friend of his action, who went to the *Telegraph* and asked for the resignation, declaring that Lovejoy wished to make some corrections. It was never returned to the newspaper. Instead, Lovejoy's friend, shocked by the import of the resignation, took it to the Reverend Beecher and other Lovejoy supporters. They were highly excited and immediately went to Lovejoy's home, where they crowded around the editor. If he fled, they said, he would so encourage mobs everywhere that James G. Birney, the slaveholder turned abolitionist and editor of the anti-slavery *Philanthropist* in Cincinnati which had just been re-established after being wrecked by a mob, would again be threatened. William Lloyd Garrison, almost lynched two years before by a mob in Boston, would again be menaced. The mobs which had attacked abolitionists and abolitionist meetings in Vermont, New Hampshire, Massachusetts, New York, Pennsylvania, Ohio, Kentucky, and Missouri would gain new recruits and deadlier spirit. It was true he was in danger, they said, but he was in the vital breach and he must hold it. He was at a decisive point, one involving the whole abolitionist movement and the freedom of a people, and from it he could not retreat.

Perhaps the Reverend Beecher told Lovejoy then that he had just come from arranging a new meeting which would be attended by all the best citizens of Alton, a meeting to be held on the afternoon of November 2 in the countinghouse of the Reverend "Honest John" Hogan on Market Street. He would submit to these leaders an irresistible array of resolutions, so moderate in tone and compelling in sequence that he was positive no man would ever again in Alton oppose liberty of speech or press.

Some days later, before leaving Alton, and after a temporary triumph of the forces favoring a free press, the Reverend Beecher, with his arm around his brother in Christ, as he liked to call Lovejoy, entered Mrs. Lovejoy's room for prayer. Kneeling beside the bed, his arm still around his brother, the Reverend Beecher lifted up his confident voice to God and presently the room was filled with the magic of his skill and belief. Presently, too, Lovejoy was flooded with his old calm and certitude. The weakness had passed. He could not flee the field of battle that God had given him.

As the two rose from their knees, the Reverend Beecher cheerfully assured Mrs. Lovejoy that all was well. Sentiment in Alton was changing. Soon, he said, she would have health and peace. "As I left her," Beecher wrote, "I cheered her with the hope that her days of trial were nearly over and that more tranquil hours were at hand." [7] There is no record of her reply nor any indication of her husband's feelings as he looked at her lying there, so pale and silent, propped against the pillows of her bed.

DEATH AND CONSEQUENCES

I

The meeting in the Reverend "Honest John" Hogan's countinghouse on November 2 had not turned out at all as Beecher expected. In the first place there were some leading businessmen present but there were more of the publicans and their patrons from Tontine Row. In the second place neither group had been impressed to the slightest degree by his nine resolutions, the last of which provided for the protection of Lovejoy and his fourth press, promising to "maintain him in the free exercise of his rights, to print and publish whatever he pleases. . . ." [8] They did not even vote upon them but referred them to a committee which would report on the whole situation in Alton on the next day at a meeting at 3 P.M. in the Market Street courtroom.

Before 2 P.M. the courtroom was packed to the last inch, the aisles almost impassable, spectators three deep around the walls, some even sitting on the broad window sills, the spittoons so hedged by humanity that tobacco chewers were cruelly inconvenienced. Beyond the windows were glimpses of the Mississippi and of boys in trees, perilously contorting themselves as they stretched to see inside the courtroom.

There was a good deal of banter and bonhomie until a momentary silence marked the entry of the Reverend Beecher. With him was the Reverend

Lovejoy, his youth and vigor contrasting oddly with his clerical black, bowing and smiling to the gamblers and saloon keepers of Tontine Row, as he twisted and pulled himself through their massed numbers with as much good will as if they had been his fellow church members. As he pushed himself toward the front, Lovejoy, a professional orator, was poised for the greatest effort of his life if he was able to get the floor in his own defense. If he was nervous it would have been understandable for Beecher had been insisting that this was his great opportunity for victory, his chance to save his press, his life, his family. He himself was not so sanguine. He was certain that no matter how movingly or logically he spoke the last chance of compromise had gone.

As the Reverend Beecher sat and waited his confidence did not grow. It began to be apparent that as at the abolition convention, he had been mousetrapped again, the pro-slavery forces, "the friends of free enquiry," turning out en masse, the solid citizens upon whom he had depended for support being only a small minority. The meeting was called to order by Cyrus Edwards, Whig candidate for Governor. The chairman's first act, sustained by an almost unanimous vote when Beecher tried to speak, was a ruling that he should not be allowed to vote or address the meeting since he was not a citizen of Alton but a resident of Jacksonville. Although "my dearest interests were involved," Beecher later wrote, "yet by the first vote I was precluded alike from voting and debate. I sat down in silent sadness to await the result." [9]

It was not long in coming. A lengthy committee report, in the form of a series of resolutions, was ready and presented to the meeting for adoption. Although it was described as a "compromise" between those who believed freedom of the press should be protected and those who felt Lovejoy was killing Alton, its content was completely uncompromising. Lovejoy, it said, would have to resign as editor of the *Observer* and leave Alton, or suffer the consequences. It was, Joseph and Owen Lovejoy wrote of the report, "the death warrant of our brother . . . signed and put into the hands of the mob for its execution." [10] Speaker after speaker spoke in favor of the report, addressing Lovejoy in valedictory as if he had already surrendered, as if paying tribute to a sadly mistaken but gallant foe. When he left Alton, they said, they would put no disgrace upon him. After all, one speaker reminded him, he could flee as a Christian even as Paul had fled from Damascus. The report was passed almost unanimously and then there was an expectant pause as if waiting for Lovejoy's acquiescence. He was on his feet now, addressing them, his voice low. Most leaned forward the better to hear and certain the words he was so quietly phrasing would tell of surrender. He had spoken a sentence or two before most realized that he was defying them, that he was throwing their generosity, their statesman-like leniency, back into their faces.

"Mr. Chairman," he was saying, and his voice was louder now,

I do not admit that it is the business of this assembly to decide whether I shall or shall not publish a newspaper in this city. The gentlemen have, as the lawyers say, made a wrong issue. I have the *right* to do it. I know that I have the right freely to speak and publish my sentiments, subject only to the laws of the land for the abuse of that right. This right was given to me by my Maker; and it is solemnly guaranteed to me by the Constitution of the United States and of this state.

What I wish to know of you is whether you will protect me in the exercise of this right; or whether, as heretofore, I am to be subjected to personal indignity and outrage. These resolutions, and the measures proposed by them, are spoken of as a compromise—a compromise between two parties. Mr. Chairman, this is not so. There is but one party here. It is simply a question whether the law shall be enforced, or whether the mob shall be allowed, as they now do, to continue to trample it under their feet, by violating with impunity the rights of an innocent individual. . . .

It has been said here that my hand is against every man, and every man's hand against me. The last part of the declaration is too painfully true. I do indeed find almost every hand lifted against *me;* but against whom in this place has my hand been raised? I appeal to every individual present; whom of you have I injured? Whose character have I traduced? Whose family have I molested? Whose business have I meddled with? If any, let him rise here and testify against me.

He paused. There was only the sound of breathing and Lovejoy waited a long instant before saying: "No one answers.

"You have been exhorted," he continued, "to be lenient and compassionate; and in driving me away to fix no unnecessary disgrace upon me. Sir, I reject all such compassion. You cannot disgrace me. Scandal and falsehood and calumny have already done their worst. My shoulders have borne the burthen till it sits easy upon them."

His manner was almost scornful now as he added,

You may hang me up as the mob hung up the individuals of Vicksburg. You may burn me at the stake as they did McIntosh at St. Louis; or you may tar and feather me, or throw me into the Mississippi as you have often threatened to do; but you cannot disgrace me. I, and I alone, can disgrace myself; and the deepest of all disgrace would be, at a time like this, to deny my Master by forsaking his cause. He died for me; and I were most unworthy to bear his name, should I refuse, if need be, to die for him.

Occasionally he would pause and look around as if savoring the perfect hushed stillness his phrases had evoked. If he was selling his life he was being paid in the only currency the orator values—a complete and absolute attention. "God in his providence—so say all my brethren, and so I think—has devolved upon me the responsibility of maintaining my ground here," he resumed,

and, Mr. Chairman, I am determined to do it. . . . Why should I flee from Alton? Is not this a free state? When assailed by a mob at St. Louis, I came hither, as to the home of freedom and of the laws. The mob has pursued me here, and why should I retreat again? Where can I be safe if not here? Have I not a right to claim the protection of the laws? Sir, the very act of retreating will embolden the mob to follow me wherever I go. No, sir; there is no way to escape the mob but to abandon the path of duty; and that God helping me, I will never do.

It is true, Mr. Chairman, that I am a husband and a father; and this it is that adds the bitterest ingredient to the cup of sorrow I am called to drink. I am made to feel the wisdom of the Apostle's advice, "It is better not to marry." I know, sir, that in this contest I stake not my life only, but that of others also. I do not expect my wife will ever recover the shock received at the awful scenes, through which she was called to pass, at St. Charles. And how was it the other night, on my return to my house? I found her driven to the garret, through fear of the mob who were prowling round my house.

And scarcely had I entered the house ere my windows were broken in by the brickbats of the mob; and she so alarmed that it was impossible for her to sleep or rest that night. I am hunted as a partridge upon the mountains. I am pursued as a felon through your streets; and to the guardian power of the law I look in vain for protection against violence, which even the vilest criminal may claim.[11]

It was at this point that those who were to kill Lovejoy wept at his words. It was a tribute in passing, a graceful irrelevancy that they could well afford since their decision and their course as to his fate were unalterable. Lovejoy's eyes, too, filled with tears, as falling silent for a moment, he regarded those soon to be his murderers, armored by a virtue as implacable as his own. There was not a drunk from Tontine Row who did not believe, even as he wept, that in opposing Lovejoy he was a patriot, defending the Constitution and the country, from one who would destroy both. Those of Alton's businessmen who were present wept too, wept salt tears that did not dissolve their conviction that Lovejoy, having sowed the whirlwind, should be forced to reap it.

"I am not unhappy," the young man was saying in this queer farewell.

I have counted the cost, and stand prepared freely to offer up my all in the service of God. Yes sir, I am fully aware of all the sacrifice I make in here pledging myself to continue this contest to the last. (Forgive these tears—I had not intended to shed them—and they flow not for myself but others.) But I am commanded to forsake father and mother and wife and children for Jesus' sake: and as his professed disciple I stand prepared to do it. The time for fulfilling this pledge in my case, it seems to me, has come.

Sir, I dare not flee away from Alton. Should I attempt it, I should feel that the angel of the Lord with his flaming sword was pursuing me wherever I went. It is because I fear God that I am not afraid of all who oppose me in this city. No sir, the contest has commenced here; and here it must be finished. Before God, and you all, I here pledge myself to continue it, if need be, till death. If I fall, my grave shall be made in Alton.[12]

Now the tears were almost general. He had not convinced his auditors; that they later proved. They may have wondered at their quick and passing grief. Perhaps it was only gratitude for poignant entertainment, testimonial to the art of the orator who had so skillfully touched the old chords, his rendering of threatened womanhood, of the hero standing firm as death approaches. But perhaps, too, art commenting as it does, if only by implication, on the fate of every man, they may have had some sense of all the sentient doomed to dust. It was a strange strain Lovejoy had loosed and perhaps it was for themselves they wept.

"Many a hard face did I see wet with tears," wrote the Reverend Beecher in describing the meeting, "as Lovejoy struck the chords of feeling to which God made the soul respond. Even his bitter enemies wept. As for me I could not endure it. I laid down my head and gave way to my feelings without control." [13]

2

Lovejoy was shot and killed, a musket in his hands while defending his last press, on November 7, 1837, by men who had shed tears at his words four days before. They assaulted the warehouse in which the press was stored, set it afire, and routed the armed company of twenty who had gathered with Lovejoy to defend his press. It is probable that no event in American history between the end of the Revolution and the beginning of the Civil War so stirred the American people as the murder of Lovejoy, with the exception of the news that came from Harper's Ferry in 1859—and these two were not unconnected. It sent, according to J. Q. Adams, "a shock as of an earthquake throughout this continent," [14] and Abraham Lincoln wrote that it was "the most important single event that ever happened in the new world." [15] Some were as moved by Lovejoy's bravery as by the significance of his fate. "The brave Lovejoy," Emerson wrote in his journal on November 24, "has given his breast to the bullet . . . and has died when it was better not to live. There are always men enough ready to die for the silliest punctilio;

to die like dogs . . . but I sternly rejoice that one was bound to die for humanity and the rights of free speech and opinion." [16]

From one end of the North to the other people instantly divided, some mourning Lovejoy's death as a blow to freedom, more declaring in words that became popular for a time that he had "died as the fool dieth." Many in looking back and some at the time thought of the event as the first clear augury of civil war. The nonresistant Sarah Grimké wrote in a letter to a friend on November 23, 1837, that she now had little hope that an end to "the evil of slavery will be brought about by peaceful means. The blood spilled at Alton will be the seed of future discord. . . ." [17] Wendell Phillips wrote later, "I can never forget the quick, sharp agony of that hour which brought us the news of Lovejoy's death. The gun fired at Lovejoy was like that of Sumter—it scattered a world of dreams." [18] And Senator Henry Wilson of Massachusetts was to write,

No previous event had so startled, alarmed, and fixed the attention . . . of the country. Nothing had so clearly indicated to anti-slavery men the nature of the conflict in which they were engaged, the desperate character of the foe with which they were grappling. . . . They saw that the conflict was not to be the bloodless encounter of ideas. . . . As a legitimate result large accessions were made to the ranks of the pronounced and avowed Abolitionists.[19]

When the news of Elijah Lovejoy's death was received in Boston on the morning of November 19—there was as yet no telegraph—men wept on the streets, particularly those who had known of his plight but had made no move to aid him. If Lovejoy's mother wept when she heard the news in Maine, she also said, "Tis well! I would rather that my son had fallen a martyr to his cause than that he had proved recreant to his principles." [20] Garrison in an editorial wrote, "In destroying his press, the enemies of freedom have compelled a thousand to speak out in its stead." [21] Preachers, heretofore lukewarm to the cause of abolition, announced from their pulpits, as did the Reverend Edward B. Hall of Providence, that Lovejoy's murder had transformed them into abolitionists. Distinguished men who had avoided anti-slavery, as was the case with Edmund Quincy, son of Josiah Quincy, president of Harvard College, proclaimed their adhesion to the cause in Lovejoy's name.[22]

Perhaps the most effective accession to the struggle against slavery because of Lovejoy's death was that of his brother Owen, who had been an abolitionist in name but whose militance and usefulness were soon to reach a new level. He had sworn beside the still bloody body of his brother that he would continue his fight and when he was elected to Congress from Illinois there was in the House as implacable a voice against slavery as ever Elijah's had been. When accused on the floor of Congress of being a "nigger stealer," one who aided slaves in escaping, he said he gloried in the term. "Proclaim it upon the housetops," he said, "write it on every leaf that trembles in the forest, make it blaze from the sun at high noon. . . . Owen Lovejoy lives at Princeton, Illinois, three-quarters of a mile east of the village, and he aids every fugitive that comes to his door." And to the Southern congressman who had called him a "nigger stealer," he said, "I bid you defiance in the name of God!" [23]

Although many were converted to abolition as a result of Lovejoy's struggle—William Herndon, later Lincoln's law partner, was one—the generalized, unorganized anti-slavery movement gained more recruits than abolition. As Adams had drawn into hostility against slavery those who feared free speech was being endangered by the slaveholder's gag rule in the House, now thousands who did not like to pronounce for liberty for the slave were willing enough and quick enough to pronounce for liberty of the press, however inextricably the two issues were intermingled at Alton and elsewhere. Thousands who had never advocated abolition now attended great meetings at Boston, New York, and Philadelphia protesting Lovejoy's slaying for advocating abolition, as well as at hundreds of smaller meetings throughout the North, as in Bangor, Maine; Salem, Ohio; Susquehanna, Pennsylvania; Plymouth, Massachusetts; and Washington County, New York. In Negro churches special services were held, as in New York City where a collection was taken up for Mrs. Lovejoy and her son.

3

The meeting at Hudson was not as large as those at Boston, New York, and Philadelphia, of course, but perhaps it was more important. It was here that John Brown made what is usually regarded as his first public statement as to slavery. It was only a single sentence, a little strange when he uttered it at the Congregational Church in Hudson, but gaining in significance through the years. Two who heard it, Edward Brown, John Brown's cousin, then a student at Western Reserve College, and Lora Case, the friend to whom he wrote on the day he was hanged, thought that Lovejoy's slaying and John Brown's declaration resulting from it at the Hudson protest meeting late in November 1837 were the first steps on the road that led to Harper's Ferry.[24]

The meeting was called by Laurens P. Hickok, professor of theology at Western Reserve College. Before Lovejoy's death, he had been little interested in slavery and against immediate emancipation. Reading of the slaying spurred him into a kind of public activity in which he had never before engaged. Mounting his horse, he rode all over Hudson township, calling at every house, inviting everyone to a protest meeting the next day in the Congregational Church.

At the meeting, held on a Thursday afternoon, and one of the largest ever held in the church, he astonished the abolitionists, who had always regarded him as a conservative on the subject of slavery, by declaring,

The crisis has come. The question now before the American citizens is no longer alone, "Can the slaves be made free?" but "Are we free or are we slaves under Southern mob law?" I propose that we take measures to procure another press and another editor. If a like fate attends him, send another till the whole country is aroused; and if you can find no better man for the first victim send me.[25]

Other speakers were as emotional in a meeting that lasted all afternoon. Owen Brown, stammering badly, told of Lovejoy's last days, his cool ignoring of his own painful speech, as if it were irrelevant in the face of so much tragedy, somehow making the recital more impressive. John Brown sat in the back of the church, his cousin Edward Brown, nearby watching him. As Owen Brown, tears running down his cheeks, told of Lovejoy's last public words—"If I fall my grave must be in Alton," John Brown, his stony face held high, did not weep although many others did.[26]

It may be that the recital contained something of indictment to John Brown. While he was seeking riches without any risk but to his soul, Lovejoy had been fighting for the poor in bondage. Whatever his thoughts as he listened, it was just before the meeting's end that John Brown made his first declaration at a public meeting against slavery. He apparently did not intend to be mistaken for just another speaker but to be recognized as a man with more important business. Standing alone in the back of the church, he raised his right hand as if taking a solemn oath, and uttered a single sentence that some at least found strangely moving.

"Here before God," he said slowly, "in the presence of these witnesses, I consecrate my life to the destruction of slavery." [27]

The meeting ended with a prayer by Owen Brown. "When John the Baptist was beheaded," he began, "the disciples took up his body and laid it in a tomb and went and told Jesus. Let us now go to Jesus and tell him." [28] Then he made a great prayer, weeping unashamedly, for he was a copious weeper on occasion, but not stammering.

The prayer and the meeting over, John Brown left quickly. Not long after there began to stir within him the first long thoughts as to the possibility that something more forcible and direct than education might be needed for the abolition of slavery. There had been a time when he had "got along like a Quaker" against war, refusing to train or drill in the militia as a matter of principle but paying fines instead. Only three years before he had advocated the founding of a school for blacks as an important means of liberating them. But after Lovejoy, education and nonresistance seemed academic as weapons against those who would kill to maintain slavery.

If Lovejoy was a factor in the transformation of John Brown, if Brown, too, saw more clearly in the glare of Alton's tragedy, then Lovejoy did not die as the fool dieth. Rather, the effect of his martyrdom was mighty; continuing on through the years and an enduring part of the convulsion which was to free a people and a nation of chattel slavery. John Brown never forgot Lovejoy. Years later he used his name in rallying fugitive slaves to resistance. And Lovejoy was present at Harper's Ferry, if only a ghost, still more alive than many of the quick.

XVI

The Backslider

DURING THE NEXT FEW YEARS there was little to indicate outwardly that John Brown had consecrated his life to the destruction of slavery. He seemed almost entirely absorbed in avoiding his own destruction and not without occasional excitement and even enjoyment. Ten suits, most on promissory notes due but unpaid, were being filed against him in the Court of Common Pleas at nearby Ravenna. It was not, of course, that he liked to be sued and threatened with the loss of his three farms, including the Haymaker farm now transformed into the Brown & Thompson Addition at Franklin; but he could not help responding to challenge with some rising of the spirit. It meant exciting trips far away, for example, seeking the money that would save him from ruin. He could derive drama even from despair, as he was soon to prove, and never was he as strong in virtue as when condemning his own lack of it.

In July of 1838 he moved from Hudson back to Franklin on hearing well-founded reports that the state of Ohio was about to subscribe $420,000 for the completion of the Pennsylvania-Ohio Canal. The appropriation enabled construction of the canal to be resumed in the winter of 1838–9 and that was enough to restore for a time his usual optimism. It was clear that the Providence in which he had always trusted was again about to rescue him. With the canal soon to be an actuality he was once more certain that the sale of the industrial lots of Brown & Thompson's Addition would make him rich. Then he could settle the suits, but in the meantime he needed some thousands of dollars to satisfy the most pressing of his creditors and hold onto his farms and the Addition at Franklin. He was sure that the potential of Brown

& Thompson was great enough to warrant a loan that would solve all his troubles.

On the last of his two trips East he sometimes felt as if some malign force, or inner weakness of which he had not known, were pushing him into courses which shocked and dismayed him. But to the outward eye his feelings of guilt were not discernible, nor did he lose his dignity even when forced into actions that no one condemned more feelingly than he did. Whether thief, which he tried not to be, or servant of the Lord, which he strove to be, he was John Brown, a man for whom he had an abiding respect.

THE HONEST THIEF

I

John Brown could seldom resist a joyful lifting of the heart when he threw his leg astride a horse at the beginning of some long journey. If he could not forget his home, wondering whether the cellar door had been fixed or if the apples had been sorted as he had ordered, he nevertheless enjoyed escape to the open road, writing once of the many different kinds of men and interesting examples one met when traveling to far places.[1] It was to become his habit, as we shall see, to pull up his horse, take out a little notebook, and record some fact which had just impressed him, his handwriting occasionally unsteady as his horse shied a little and skittered sideways with quick small steps.

When he left Franklin in November 1838, mounted on a lively mare and at the head of a company of friends and relatives who were to herd to Connecticut several hundred head of cattle belonging to his father, Heman Oviatt, Seth Thompson, and others, he had every reason to be filled with foreboding. His need of money was so overwhelming that he could not conceive his not getting it. Suit after suit had been recently filed against him and there were more to come. The first was in 1837, when the Western Reserve Bank of Warren had sued for the $6,000 he had borrowed from it on a promissory note in 1836. When he could not pay, judgment was obtained against Captain Heman Oviatt, of Richfield, for $5,260, one of the six endorsers of his note and the only one who proved vulnerable to the bank's judgment.[2] John Brown assured Captain Oviatt, whom he had known since he was a boy in Hudson where Oviatt had opened the first store and made a fortune in trading with the Indians, that no one would lose money because of him. He would hand over to him his Westlands farm in Twinsburg, if he could not otherwise raise the $5,260. As an indication of good faith he signed over to Oviatt the penal bond of conveyance which was his contract to buy the property, and which stipulated certain monetary penalties to be paid Brown by the owner if he did not carry out the agreement. It was all he had to give since he did not yet have a deed, still owing some $5,000 on the farm.*

A few of the smaller suits John Brown would win, or the judgment against him would be less than asked, or they would be settled out of court, but he could not know this as he left for Connecticut in 1838. Moreover, he could see other troubles coming up. He had passed on to Haymaker little of the $5,866 in notes given him by Thompson in 1836 for the undivided half of the 95½ acres forming most of the Brown & Thompson Addition. He had sold most of them for cash, signing them over at a discount, and now he was threatened with suits not only by Haymaker for recovery of his farm, for which payment had not been completed, but by those to whom he had sold the notes which Seth had been unable to redeem. He had probably thought that he would pay Haymaker, who had handed over the deed to his property to Brown & Thompson, the remainder of what was due him, perhaps as much as $5,000, from the fabulous profits he had expected from the sale of his industrial lots.

He was still sure he could do this since the price of land had again shot upward after the resumption of the canal's construction. Yet his cheerfulness as he left for the East may not have been entirely due to any lack of knowledge of approaching danger. It was more that he did not believe in dwelling on it until it was inescapable, and he did believe in putting up a front. But the body has its own knowledge of impending peril and present strain, and however much he tried to convince himself that Providence would save him again, there were lines of worry about his face that had not been there before, while the first streaks of gray were appearing in his reddish brown hair.

---

* In addition to the suit of the Western Reserve Bank, a Milo Hudson was suing him for a $500 note on which $72.08 was still due. Alpheus Hoskins entered a claim in the Court of Common Pleas on a note of $600. As an official of the Cuyahoga Falls Real Estate Association, he, with others, was being sued for $264. Daniel Gaylord was demanding $1,445.50 on a Seth Thompson note that Brown had signed over to him. Valentine S. Nuckins was threatening suit on an alleged note of $3,400. William Astromo was suing for a due bill of $1,120 which Brown had given to William Folger, Sr., who had endorsed it to Ogden Wetmore who had signed it over to Astromo. B. W. and J. Alexander had declared they would sue on a note of $50 and later did so. The Bank of Wooster was preparing a suit on a draft for $3,479.90 which it had been unable to collect and for which it was soon to sue Brown and several of his associates. (From the Records of the Court of Common Pleas at Ravenna, Ohio.)

2

On both his trips East John Brown carried his Bible in his saddlebags.[3] On each of his journeys, as his prospects for a loan grew more dim while Captain Oviatt pressed for his $5,260, and as other judgments were entered against him in the Portage County Court of Common Pleas, he sought solace each night in Scripture. "Ask, and it shall be given you," he read, "seek, and ye shall find. . . . For every one that asketh receiveth; and he that seeketh findeth." He did not read narrowly or think he was being assured of a loan by such words as these. He knew, as he frequently said, that he must be prepared, as must all men, to smart under the rod of the Heavenly Father. But he sought mercy and a humble spirit, and unlikely as it was that he would ever receive either, he could not help being comforted.[4]

On his first trip East in 1838–9, he wrote his family from Erie, Pennsylvania, on November 26, 1838. "Say to my little folks I want very much to see them," he said, "and tell Ruth and Fred not to forget the verse their father taught them last." [5] One verse he taught them was:

> *Count that day lost*
> *Whose low descending sun*
> *Views from thy hand,*
> *No worthy action done.*[6]

He arrived in New York City on December 1, probably by way of the Erie Canal and the Hudson River, for he has been in western Pennsylvania five days before. He left his herd of some two hundred cattle near West Hartford, Connecticut, with the firm of Wadsworth & Wells, which bought and sold cattle although they had not as yet agreed on price. There was nothing of impending bankruptcy or failure in his air as he met Tertius Wadsworth and Joseph Wells. Rather, he seemed to them a saviour, his manner suggesting nothing but the quiet confidence of success. Cattle had been scarce and prices high. When he assured them that each year or oftener he could drive a herd from Ohio of two hundred or more they were sufficiently impressed both by the promised cattle and John Brown, himself, to suggest a partnership in the firm, which he was glad to accept. In the law of supply and demand he was to furnish much of the supply.

Upon his arrival on Broadway he may have exuded something of the bucolic, faintly redolent as he was of horses, leather, and steers, but one can be sure that he did not gawk or turn to stare in wide-eyed wonder at Broadway's crowds or thousand-hoofed traffic. He had a presence that did not go with gawking, preferring to be the observed rather than the observer. He was once seen walking down a busy city street, oblivious to everything but the apple he was paring with his jack knife and cutting into sections which he ate as he strode along. If his face was red and weather-beaten, his apparel was probably neat enough, for he undoubtedly carried his Sunday best from Ohio by a baggage wagon that contained, among other treasures, his deaconish suit of snuff-colored brown.

Not long after his arrival in New York, and bearing in his hands his handsomely boxed surveyor's compass, he made his way to B. Pike & Son at 166 Broadway where he left the instrument for repair, calling for it and paying the bill on December 5. He apparently visited a Mr. Burr at 50 Wall Street and called at Houghton & Co. at Wall and Williams Streets. These names and addresses are recorded in the pocket-sized memorandum book which served him as an account book and a kind of rough diary until 1845, and which he bought in a stationery store at 108 Broadway on this trip to New York. On its flyleaf he wrote, "Memorandum Book of John Brown Franklin Portage Co Ohio bought Decem 3d, 1838 G and C. Carvill & Co Price $0.25." [7]

It is from this memorandum book that we learn that if John Brown was occasionally dismayed at the fate bearing down on him during these two trips to the East in 1838 and 1839, he also had a never failing appetite for the minutiae of life and for the pursuit of wisdom. He obtained surcease, too, from his love of sheep. He had long hoped that he could some day become, as he said, "a practical shepherd," [8] and could scarcely think of his debts as he traveled hundreds of miles, all over New York and New England, seeking out his favorite breed of Saxony sheep, some of which he bought for his Westlands farm. He loved the practical details of living, of process and management, of how to make a certain kind of butter, how to cure sheep of scabs or ticks, how to determine a superior fleece, how to season sausage with sifted sage, how to cure "galls or scratches upon Horses." And when people talked of such matters during these trips he was utterly and completely absorbed as he had them dictate recipes or formulas while he carefully wrote out their directions in his memorandum book. He also enjoyed the recording of occasional flashes of wisdom, or so he regarded them, as to right living and proper conduct, which he wrote in the form of Franklin-like maxims.

Typical of the directions he entered in his memorandum book in 1838-9 was a recipe for the making of what he called "Orang[e] Co. Butter." "Set the milk," it began, in large pans or vessels till it becomes thick in a cool place. The sweeter the vesels and cooler the place in summer the better, in winter warm the room with a stove. Churn the whole milk. Wash the butter in cold water until the water derives no milky appearance from the butter then salt it sufficiently for use. Within twenty-four hours after salting work out every drop of the pickle, then pack it away in tight sweet vessels covering the butter when the vessel is filled with fine dry salt. Butter should be packed tight in new well soaked sweet oaken firkins for market, or in stone jars. Butter prepared as before described will keep sweet for a year or more. Boiling water will aid in the churning but avoid useing too much. In summer add plenty of cold water to the milk before churning. The slower the churning the better. Rules given by a lady of Orange Co N Y A large sheep or large dog will churn for twenty cows.[9]

Another item observed, "To cure the scab or Ticks in Sheep tak[e] 4 lbs Tobacco for 100 Sheep with 1 pint Spirits Turpentine. For foot rot, take Blue Vitrol & vinegar & pare down the foot till it bleeds then apply it. If Sheep are lame examine their eyelet holes." Another directed, "To make ewes nurse their lambs well. Feed them with rowen hay, Oil cake, or Oats, for ten days before yeaning, or with Potatoes, other roots, or Apples." Still another recorded the "Rule for Measureing Hay in the Barn" and continued "Multiply the length by the breadth & that product by the depth Divide that product by 27 which will give the cubic yards. From 8 to 12 yds will make a Ton as the Hay may be coarse or fine, moist or dry."

More philosophical was the entry describing Deacon Abel Hinsdale's victory over tobacco at the age of sixty-six, making him wonder if a man ever becomes too old to overcome a bad habit. Beneath this notation as to the deacon he writes, "To revive Lambs or Sheep when chilled with cold, put them all into a bath except their heads that is of blood heat, then keep them warm till perfectly dry." Later he returned to moral philosophy with the observation, "That kind of news which we most like to hear of others, affords the best possible index to the true character of our own hearts." Not wishing it to be mistaken for a quotation, and perhaps with something of pride, he firmly signed the moral "John Brown."

But, as we know, the primary object of his trip East was not recipes or philosophy, nor even cattle or sheep, but a loan. He may have tried to negotiate one in New York, perhaps visiting the Wall Street addresses recorded in his book for that purpose, for on December 5 he wrote from there to his family, and he was not referring to his cattle dealings,

I have not yet succeded in my business, but think the prospect such that I do not by any means despair of final success. As to that, may God's holy will be done. My unceaseing and anxious care for the present and everlasting wellfare of evry [member] of my family seems to be threefold as I get seperated farther and farther from them. Forgive the many faults & foibles you have seen in me, and try to profit by anything good in either my example, or my council. Try and not any of you get weary of well doing. Should the older boys read and coppy my old letters as I proposed to them, I want to have them all preserved with care. . . .[10]

Before leaving New York he made an entry, "Power of Religion by Lind M[illegible]," apparently referring to Lindley Murray's *Power of Religion on the Mind*, recently published and highly regarded by the pious. A short time later he wrote in his memorandum book, "Get a good truss for Jason," his second eldest son, then about sixteen, and "Get some new Bibles." On the thirteenth of December, after returning to Connecticut, he wrote Seth Thompson from West Hartford a very optimistic letter about the chances of getting a loan. "Dear Friend," he wrote, in asking that Thompson send him a power of attorney, "I am useing every exertion to obtain a loan in this quarter and have considerable hope of final success. There is no want of money here, for good names, for any length of time, the only difficulty is in useing our Western securities." [11] John Brown's Western securities were not stocks or bonds but the title held with Thompson to the Brown & Thompson Addition as well—if they were believed—as his glowing accounts of the profits to be expected from the Addition.

But all of his activities did not concern business. Circumstances had forced him to backslide almost completely from his public pledge of dedicating his life to the destruction of slavery although he could oppose it in private conversations and increasingly did so. Thus when he visited his native Torrington as a figure of success from the West returning home, he did not hesitate to express himself against it forcefully enough to receive an invitation for a talk on abolition before a class at a boy's school there.

One of the students, Henry B. Carrington, later a general in the Civil War, recalled the scene:

When I was a boy and went to school in Torrington, there came into the school room one day a tall man, rather slender, with grayish hair, who said to the boys: "I want to ask you some questions in geography. Where is Africa?" "It is on the other side of the ocean, of course," said a boy. "Why 'of course,' " asked the man. The boy couldn't say why "of course."

Then the man proceeded to tell them something about Africa and the negroes, and the evil of the slave trade, and the wrongs and sufferings of the slaves, and then said, "How many of you boys will agree to use your influence, whatever it may be, against this great curse, when you grow up?" They held up their hands. He then said that he was afraid that some of them might forget it, and added,

"Now I want those who are *quite sure* that they will not forget it, who will promise to use their time and influence toward resisting this evil, to rise."

Another boy and I stood up. Then this man put his hands on our heads and said, "Now may my Father in Heaven, who is your Father, and who is the Father of the African; and Christ, who is my Master and Saviour, and your Master and Saviour, and the Master and Saviour of the African; and the Holy Spirit, which gives me strength and comfort, when I need it, and will give you strength and comfort when you need it, and which gives strength and comfort to the African, enable you to keep this resolution which you have now taken." And that man was John Brown.[12]

3

Unable to negotiate a loan in or about West Hartford despite there being no want of money there for good names, Brown left for Boston on December 26, 1838, still seeking the relief that only money could give. In his memorandum book were the names Henry Hubbard, a wealthy Bostonian whose son he had known in Ohio, and George D. and Edmund Munroe, the latter the Boston capitalist who had founded Munroe Falls on the Western Reserve with the same kind of hopes that had possessed John Brown when he acquired the Haymaker farm. Before the end of December he had visited Mr. Hubbard in his home on Louisburg Square, presumably asking him for a loan, the deed for the Brown & Thompson Addition the security offered. He impressed the Hubbard family as "rather a strange character,"[13] but his proposition did not attract the head of the family. Later, Mr. Hubbard received from him what were described as "very wooley letters"[14] and which probably asked for money to invest in sheep. He undoubtedly asked others in Boston for a loan and when he left that city early in January he seemed somewhat hopeful that he would soon receive money from a Boston source he never named.

He was not discouraged nor was he one to economize despite his growing financial peril. From boyhood he had seen himself as a keeper of sheep and now he set about buying pure bred Saxonys, triumphant at obtaining them and unbothered at the outlay. On January 18 at West Hartford he wrote in his little book: "Agreed to sell this day to John Brown ten of my best Saxony sheep for one hundred and thirty dollars, including my best Saxony Buck." He handed his pencil to the owner of the sheep, Samuel Whitman, who signed Brown's statement. Early in February there is the entry, "Bought eight full blood Saxony ewes at Walpole, N.H., exchanged one with Mr.

Whitman marked with a small round hole in left ears and halfpenny under right ears."

On February 7, he wrote,

Bought of Mr. Whitman (West Hartford) four full blood Saxony ewes marked with small round hole in left ears and slit in right ears. The said ewes were sired by Don Pedro, uppon his half sisters. He and his half sisters [were sired] by imported Nonesuch. Two of the ewes with lamb by half brother to Don Pedro, the other by Don Pedro, by accident.

Bought of Mr. Whitman nine full blood Saxony bucks, marked same as the Whitman ewes among them Don Pedro four years old past, the others yearlings, two years old, and lambs all by Don Pedro. Old Don and Buck No. 10 have the ends of their horns cut off.

Beneath this record of triumph, he had Mr. Whitman write and sign, "I hereby certify that the afore mentioned sheep bought of me are full blood saxon sheep."

4

This was the beginning of his career as a shepherd, and if he was soon to lose these blooded Saxonys, the gaining of them had been one of the most pleasant achievements of his life, for he had a fondness for sheep and everything pertaining to them. He did not know, of course, that they soon would not be his as he drove them west from Connecticut to Albany and the Erie Canal. From Buffalo, the western end of the canal, he herded them before him along the shore of Lake Erie and then inland until he finally arrived at Franklin Mills at the end of February. Glad to be home, he could not relax or take proper pleasure in it as he waited for the loan from Boston. When it did not arrive, he knew he would have to go East again to press his case for a considerable sum, probably as much as $20,000. Although it is not known how much he paid over to his father, Seth Thompson, Captain Oviatt, and others for the cattle sold on the first drive East, it must have been satisfactory for he immediately made up a second herd, owned by the same people, and before the end of March he was again on the road to Connecticut and Boston, this time without benefit of the Erie Canal.

His temper, his letters indicate, as he began his second journey, was composed of opposites, his belief that he could not possibly fail of achieving his loan and a fear that he would never obtain it. It was clear by now to most, and perhaps even to John Brown, that if he did not get a considerable sum, bankruptcy would result; that his farms would be sold for his creditors, that his sheep, his farm implements, his horses, his houses, and even the Brown & Thompson Addition would go under the hammer at public auction. But there was also a certain resentment rising in him. Almost despite himself he found present in his mind ideas that may have shocked him.

Increasingly he could see neither justice nor equity in a system that took his land from him. It had been his work and sweat that had gained the farms, that had acquired the Brown & Thompson Addition; it was his industry that had surveyed and improved them and as law-abiding as he felt himself to be, there were times when he could not admit the justice of having them taken from him by legal writ, although there were other times when he would say that he meant to honor every cent of his indebtedness. But even as a young man in Pennsylvania, it will be recalled, he advised squatters not to give up their farms simply because a land company had a legal title to them.

It may have been about this time he began to think that land should properly belong to those who worked it, that in an ideal society production should be cooperative for the joint use of the producers, and that the profit system left much to be desired, for the ideas were common enough and advanced by many of the utopian communities. He became, over the years, what his son John described as a Christian Socialist, although it is doubtful if John Brown would have ever called himself that. It was not a sudden conviction but a process that probably began around 1840 and was completed by 1854. At any rate it was during these years, his son said, that "Father's favorite theme was that of the *Community plan of cooperative industry*, in which all should labor for the common good; 'having all things in common' as did the disciples of Jesus in his day. This has been, and still is," John Brown's eldest son added, "my Communistic or Socialist faith." [15]

But on this second trip East in 1839 such theories were scarcely in their inception, even if he was beginning to acquire the emotional basis for them. He only felt then that somehow he had to retain what was his. If he did not his family would not have a roof over their heads and how he would feed and clothe them he did not know. His first letters to his family are optimistic as to the loan but later letters warn that he may not succeed in obtaining it and yet still imply that he will. In the end, his hope and need were always sufficiently desperate to overcome any sense of reality.

On May 28, 1839, he wrote Seth Thompson from West Hartford,

Dear Friend   I suppose you will again fault me for neglect, & the only excuse I have is that I have not as yet been able to get away from the drove to go & attend to other matters. I can only say that I still expect to obtain money at Boston, & that I expect to start for that place this week, or within a day or two. We have sold about 100 of our Cattle & sold them pretty well You shall get the first deffinite information that I can give in regard to the money matter. . . .[16]

He did go to Boston early in June and this time he was convinced beyond doubt that he had obtained a loan. It was not turned over to him in Boston but in the fortnight immediately following he expected to receive it at West Hartford any day, any hour. No doubt he haunted the post office, present at the arrival of every mail. It did not come, but during the first half of June he alternated between despair and certainty that it would arrive.

Something of his mood is revealed in his letter to "My dear wife and children," written at New Hartford on June 12. "I write to let you know," he began,

that I am in comfortable health, and that I expect to be on my way home in the course of a week, should nothing befal me. . . . The cattle business has succeeded about as I expected, but I am now somewhat in fear that I shall fail of getting the money I expected on the loan. Should that be the will of Providence, I know of no other way but we must consider ourselves very poor; for our debts must be paid, if paid at a sacrifice. Should that happen (though it may not) I hope God, who is rich in mercy, will grant us grace to conform to our circumstances with cheerfulness and true resignation. I want to see each of my dear family very much, but must wait God's time. Try all of you to do the best you can, and do not one of you be discouraged; tomorrow may be a much brighter day. Cease not to ask God's blessing on yourselves and me. . . . I am not without great hopes of getting relief. I would . . . have you understand, but things have looked more unfavorable for a few days. . . .[17]

By now he needed money desperately if he was to retain his favorite farm, Westlands. He owed $5,000 more on it, and although he had promised the farm to Captain Oviatt in payment of his loan of 1836, he decided as he waited in West Hartford for the money from Boston, that he must save it from Oviatt or anyone else.

When the money from Boston did not come, he decided to use the funds of Wadsworth & Wells to save his Westlands farm. We do not know how he did it since his later admissions did not detail the method of his theft. Perhaps he had $5,500 of the firm's money from the sale of cattle and simply held on to it, not turning it over. Perhaps he entered the firm's office and took the money from the firm's cash box. In either event he was doubtless convinced that it was only a technical defalcation since he was certain he could replace it in a matter of hours, or days, at most, when the loan arrived from Boston. In addition, as he said later in a suit, he was a partner in the company and an accounting would show, he was sure, that the firm owed a considerable amount to him.[18]

Still, he may have scarcely understood himself, as he, the Sunday school teacher and lover of the Bible and virtue, either withheld money he had collected for the firm or put his hand into the box and withdrew it with $5,500.[19] It was not this that he had envisioned when he embarked on his career of borrowing with his purchase of the Haymaker farm, which was to lead him to certain wealth. Some men might have excused themselves by recalling the panic that had forced thousands into bankruptcy and the juggling of accounts; but not John Brown, whose acts were not governed by the economic but by obeying God—or as he now was doing, acting as if mesmerized—by disobeying Him.

A few days later the two partners found out that he had taken the money and threatened him with arrest.[20] He had apparently already sent it back to Ohio in making his final payment on Westlands. At the same time, George Kellogg, agent for the New England Woolen Company of Rockville, Connecticut, had advanced him $2,800 to buy wool for the company. To avoid arrest he gave this money to Wadsworth & Wells, thinking he could redeem it within thirty days when the money from Boston would surely have arrived. After paying the remainder due on his Westlands farm, he registered the deed in his own name, at the County Recorder's office, not informing Captain Oviatt of his action.

His troubles and his needs may have made him almost hallucinatory since he still hoped for the loan from Boston even as he began his journey home on or about June 18. He was certain at times that it would be at Franklin Mills when he arrived but there were other moments when he doubted it would ever come. At this juncture he did not seem to feel that he had committed a crime but that rather he had nobly sacrificed himself in an attempt to save his family from poverty. He suggested as much in a letter to "My Dear Wife and Children," on June 19, 1839, from Winchester, Connecticut:

"Through the great goodness of God," he wrote,

I am once more on my way home and should nothing befall me, I hope to see you all by the 1st. of July. I expect to return by way of our place in Pa. [Randolph]

I have left no stone unturned to place my affairs in a more settled and comfortable shape, and now should I, after all my sacrifice of body and mind, be compelled to return a very poor man, how would my family receive me? I do not say that such will be the fact, but such may be the fact.

Then, referring to the new Bibles he had bought, he wrote, "I expect at any rate to bring all of you that can read, a book that has afforded me great support and comfort during my long absence." [21]

When he arrived home early in July, he found that Daniel C. Gaylord

had obtained a judgment against him on the Seth Thompson note he had
endorsed over to Gaylord for $1,202.28, and within a short time Gaylord
had received a court order directing that Westlands be sold to satisfy his
judgment; but Brown appealed the order to the State Supreme Court. He
wrote Thompson a letter about it on July 10, 1839, also giving him the news
about the Boston loan which he said he still expected.

"I returned by way of the Lake three or four days ago," he said.

I found myself disappointed of the money I had engaged & returned moneyless,
but not in despair of final success. The prospect is rather dark however. We had
not sold much over half of the drove when I left, but our sales had been so far
pretty good. I did not give up the expectation of effecting the desired loan untill
the verry hour I started for home, & was then in hope I should get some good news
from it, when I should arrive. I have received a line from Boston since my return
giving me some encouragement, but nothing positive. I was sore disapointed for
I had every assureance from one man that . . . he had the money but before I got
on, he paid it out for land. Some persons can easily forget or dispence with their
engagements. . . . I do not yet give up. . . . We have been sustained wonderfully, & it
may be the will of Providence still to sustain us, & let us try to trust in him . . .
I feel rather more depressed than usual.[22]

By August 2, Mr. Kellogg had found out that the $2,800 he had advanced
Brown to buy wool for the New England Woolen Company had been
handed over to Wadsworth & Wells. On that day he wrote him asking for an
explanation, perhaps thinking of his letter as a preliminary to prosecution.
John Brown did not reply until August 27 when he wrote, and not unskill-
fully, confessing to his misappropriation with a melancholy, manly dignity
that sought not to excuse but only to repay.

"Yours of the 2nd was received in season, & I have no excuse for not
answering it promptly," he wrote,

except that I have found it hard to take up my pen to record, & to publish, my
own shame, & abuse of the confidence of those whom I esteem, & who have
treated me as a friend, & as a brother. I flattered myself till now, with the hope
that I might be able to render a more favorable account of myself, but the truth,
& the whole truth, shall be told. When I saw you at Vernon [Connecticut], I was
in dayly expectation of receiving a number of thousands of dollars from Boston,
something over five of which I owed for money I had used belonging to our cattle
company (viz Wadsworth, Wells & myself). On the day I was to set out for home,
as I was disappointed of the money I expected, I found no alternative but to go to
jail, or to pledge the money the money [sic] you had confided to my trust, & in
my extremity I did so with the most of it, pledging it for thirty days, believing
that in less than that I could certainly redeem it, as I expected a large amount from

a source I did believe I could depend uppon. Though I have been waiting in painful anxiety I have been disappointed still, & as the best course I could take, I have made an assignment of all my real & personal property for the benefit of my creditors generally, as our laws forbid any preference. I think my property much more than sufficient to satisfy all demands, & that I shall not have to subject you to anything worse in the end than disappointment & delay. I am determined that shall be all, if I & my family work out by the month, & by the day to make up a full return. I have yet hopes of relief from Boston, & should that be, it will set matters in measure to right again. . . .

Unworthily yours,
John Brown [23]

Mr. Kellogg, upon receipt of this letter, felt he could not prosecute so honest a thief, so penitent, so unflinching in facing his own wrongdoing, so strong in his indictment of it, so determined on restitution whatever the sacrifice. Under all the circumstances, he was inclined to believe, the dereliction might have happened to anyone as it had happened to many following the panic of 1837 when they tried desperately to raise sufficient money to avoid ruin. He did, however, venture a word of rebuke when he wrote again to Brown on September 12. One so ardent for the abolition of slavery, he said, and so free in expressing his opinions in opposition to it, could not indulge in wrongdoing without damaging the cause he professed to champion. He hoped, too, that a merciful God would enable John Brown to reform and pay to all their due. In answering this letter on September 20, Brown said that he couldn't agree with him more.

"Your kind letter of the 12th Inst I have just read," he wrote,

and I feel grateful to learn that you have feelings of tenderness towards one that has abused (I do not say with fraudulent intent) your confidence, injured your business and what is worse than all wounded a holy and greatly suffering cause. I think I can cordially join you in hopeing that a merciful God will give me wisdom, firmness, a propper sense of duty and ability to render speedily to all their due. That I ever had a fraudulent or trickish design, I utterly deny but that I in my distress to meet punctually my engagements, foolishly and wickedly presumed, relying on the engagements of others in a sorrowful truth to me & my much injured friends. The assignment of my property has been made to a trustee who thereby becomes an officer of the Court for the settlement of my business and who has since I wrote you before made a contract to sell a farm I had for seven thousand dollars, payable as follows (viz four thousand in four months from date of contract the balance in one year from date[)]. The name of the trustee is George B. De Peyster—[he] is one of the former associate judges of our court, is empowered either to sell at private sale, or to put any or all my lands and other property under the Hammer as he may deem propper. He resides in this place and the assignment is a matter of record in the recorders office of the county.

Brown concluded by urging Kellogg "to present a claim of sufficient amount abundantly to cover interest and every species of damage and disappointment" Kellogg had suffered, and signed himself, "Respectfully your unworthy friend, John Brown." [24]

However unworthy a friend John Brown was, Kellogg was now certain that he was an honest man who through lack of judgment had suffered misfortune. Most agreed with him. There was integrity in his very gait; probity was written large on his strongly marked features, in the direct and independent gaze of his clear blue eyes, in the bluntness of his words which contained nothing of concealment. Even Captain Oviatt agreed although at first he was inclined to charge John Brown with double-dealing in otherwise disposing of the farm he had promised to him in payment of the $5,260 judgment he had been forced to pay on John Brown's note. But a few months later Captain Oviatt, too, concluded that if John Brown was a thief he was an honest one, and made so only by circumstance. In 1841 he proved his faith in John Brown's integrity by making him his partner.

A FAMILY VOW

I

As Judge De Peyster proceeded, slowly enough, to liquidate John Brown's estate for the benefit of his creditors in 1839, while Brown looked on grimly trying to approve of the legal processes impoverishing him, his mind slowly began to shift to more important matters. If he was a man of many backslidings, he was also one of many returnings. An idea once lodged in his brain might descend for a time from immediate consciousness but it was never entirely forgotten or permanently abandoned. It may be, too, that his own increasing poverty gave him a new appreciation of the slaves he sometimes called "God's poor." His own sufferings in the shackles of the law may have given him a new sympathy with those suffering in the shackles of bondage, or perhaps a more sensitive moral climate may have returned his attention to the pledge he had given in 1837 to dedicate his life to the destruction of slavery.

If the public consciousness of slavery in the North was more sensitive in 1839 to the horrors of that institution, it was undoubtedly partly because of the publication in that year of the most successful and widely read abolitionist pamphlet ever issued, the most powerful indictment of American slavery in the country's history. It was called *American Slavery as It Is: Testimony of a Thousand Witnesses*. It was edited in the New York office of the American Anti-Slavery Society by Theodore Weld, whose voice had rebelled and almost vanished after years of beating against the catcalls and taunts of those trying to break up the hundreds of riotous meetings he had addressed. Its 224 pages were largely made up of testimony as to slavery gathered from Southern newspapers and first-person reports of travelers in the South as well as former residents of that section. Read by thousands in the North, most of its readers agreed that it documented fully the indictment which was returned against slavery in the introduction. It read:

We will prove that the slaves in the United States are treated with barbarous inhumanity; that they are overworked, underfed, wretchedly clad and lodged, and have insufficient sleep; that they are often made to wear round their necks iron collars armed with prongs, to drag heavy chains and weights at their feet while working in the field, and to wear yokes, and bells, and iron horns; that they are often kept confined in the stocks day and night for weeks together, made to wear gags in their mouths for hours or days, have some of their front teeth torn out or broken off, that they may be easily detected when they run away; that they are frequently flogged with terrible severity, have red pepper rubbed into their lacerated flesh, and hot brine, spirits of turpentine, &c., poured over the gashes to increase the torture; that they are often stripped naked, their backs and limbs cut with knives, bruised and mangled by scores and hundreds of blows with the paddle, and terribly torn by the claws of cats, drawn over them by their tormentors; that they are often hunted with blood hounds and shot down like beasts, or torn in pieces by dogs; that they are often suspended by the arms and whipped and beaten until they faint, and when revived by restoratives, beaten again until they faint, and sometimes till they die; that their ears are often cut off, their eyes knocked out, their bones broken, their flesh branded with red hot irons; that they are maimed, mutilated and burned to death over slow fires.[25]

2

If John Brown read *American Slavery as It Is* (there is no evidence that he did nor any that he did not), it might account for the renascence of his concern in 1839 to his pledge two years before to devote his life to the destruction of slavery. Its bloody details of floggings and torture and maimings might account too, in part, for the choking excitement with which he began discussing slavery on occasion at about this time when it seemed to some as if John Brown saw and felt each lash as one who had personally suffered it. Beneath his usual matter-of-fact attitude, his frequent absorption in himself and his family, there was increasingly a simmering, incredulous indignation that such things could be in the United States and the growing conviction that if they long endured there would ultimately be no liberty for white or black, North or South.

Yet it makes little difference if he did or did not read the pamphlet, for material similar to its contents, if not always so well documented, was the very stuff of abolitionist agitation and a thousand posters, handbills, engravings, articles, almanacs, speeches, magazines, and newspapers concentrated on the details of the tortures and floggings that were part of slavery, woven into its inevitable fabric and impossible to change to any widespread degree by the individual benevolence of specific slaveholders. It was this ever-greater flood of unceasing agitation that was more sharply penetrating the consciousness of John Brown as well as that of most others even slightly interested in the abolition of slavery. It is true that Weld's indictment of 1839 was an important historical event, and as such a part of our story of the time. But we use it here in a speculative effort to account for John Brown's decision in that year, to which we have referred in an earlier chapter, that he must act to destroy slavery by force of arms. Perhaps he had implied it in 1837 in Hudson; now, for the first time, he solemnly declared it his purpose.

His eldest son and namesake told years later how his father revealed that decision and purpose to his family. Declaring that it "was certainly as early as 1839," John Brown, Jr., wrote,

The place and the circumstances where he informed us of that purpose are as perfectly in my memory as any other event of my life. Father, mother, Jason, Owen, and I were, late in the evening, seated around the fire in the open fire-place in the kitchen, in the old Haymaker house, where we then lived; and there he first informed us of his determination to make war on slavery—not such war as Mr. Garrison informs us "was equally the purpose of the non-resistant abolitionists," [26]—but war by force and arms.

He said that he had long entertained such a purpose, that he believed it his duty to devote his life, if need be, to this object, which he made us fully to understand. After spending considerable time in setting forth, in most impressive language, the hopeless condition of the slave, he asked *who* of us were willing to make common cause with him, in doing all in our power to "break the jaws of the wicked, and pluck the spoil out of his teeth."

Naming each of us in succession, "Are you, Mary, John, Jason and Owen?" Receiving an affirmative answer from each, he kneeled in prayer, and all did the same. This position in prayer impressed me greatly, as it was the first time I had ever known him to assume it. After prayer, he asked us to raise our right hands, and he then administered to us an oath, the exact terms of which I cannot recall, but in substance it bound us to secrecy and devotion to the purpose of fighting slavery, by force and arms, to the extent of our ability.

According to Jason's recollection, Mr. Fayette, a colored theological student at Western Reserve College (Hudson, Ohio), was with us at the time, but of this I am not certain—he was often at our house. As to the others, I know they were present; and if my affidavit would add strength to my statement, I am ready to make it. At that time Jason was about sixteen years old, Owen between fourteen and fifteen, and I was between eighteen and nineteen years of age.[27]

But like the pledge at Hudson, the family vow in the old Haymaker house was to seem for many years to be only words, an intention which could not be carried out until national crisis made some such occurrence possible and even probable. It was not in John Brown's power effectively to assault slavery until events made such an attack—if not by him then by others— almost inevitable.

THE BITTER CUP

I

Whatever John Brown's desire to fight slavery, the reality was that he could fight nothing but his increasing poverty. He was the captive of his business reverses. They continued to go from bad to worse and he continued to hope for a loan that would rescue his property from his creditors and Judge De Peyster, who was proceeding very slowly in his attempts to liquidate Brown's debts. Brown was still unable to accept defeat, although thousands had had to accept it because of the long-lasting business depression. He still believed that Providence would somehow save him, still had faith in the Brown & Thompson Addition which was still in his possession, although the Franklin Land Company and the Franklin Silk Company were no more. The combination of the panic of 1837 and the cold of the Western Reserve that had made it impossible for the silk worm to flourish, as well as the silk industry to prosper, had done them in.

But John Brown perceived that the rushing waters of the Cuyahoga still supplied power for potential flour and woolen mills, saw that the Pennsylvania-Ohio Canal, now almost completed, would supply transportation for the products that could be produced through the Cuyahoga's abundant flow. All he had to do was to hang onto the Brown & Thompson Addition long enough to profit from the sale of industrial lots before they were sold beneath his feet for the benefit of his creditors, or were taken from him by judgment or suit.

Living in the center of his enterprise in the old Haymaker farmhouse, he emerged early each day to sample the weather and cast a proprietary eye at the fast-running Cuyahoga, a little to the north and west, at the canal not far to the south. They were cheering, irreversible facts and he, an optimist in the very midst of failure, may have still indulged himself in fancies in which he saw himself rich and his land the site of smoking industry. He was partly right. His land would contain factories and a railroad shop, be crossed by a railroad running between St. Louis and New York, and be worth hundreds of thousands of dollars. But it would come about between 1860 and 1880 when it could not contribute to the profit of John Brown.

If he still stubbornly dreamed of wealth almost within hearing of the auctioneer's hammer, he also had to support his family. For some time he had been breeding racehorses, among a good many other activities. There was a racing course at nearby Warren and it was there he went to sell his yearlings and two-year-olds. He trained them as colts and later broke them to the saddle. He had ideas about the handling of horses, as on most other matters, and liked to talk, particularly to his sons, about how a colt should never, never be frightened, recommending that the foal should be taught very early the uses of a halter and how one should only very gradually break in a colt to lines or reins. He had ideas, too, about the use of the bit and the extreme importance of a good mouth in a horse.

He liked to lecture his sons on the fine points of a racer, running his hands over the withers and back, over the barrel and gaskin, calling attention to the powerful chest and the slim, strong legs, stooping to lift a foot, pointing at fetlock and pastern, and speaking of the proper care of the hoof. He instructed them in riding, too, particularly on how to bring their horses to a jump over a fence or ditch. Later they credited their father with being indirectly responsible for narrow escapes in Kansas when they leaped their horses over obstacles that baffled their pursuers.[28]

But John Brown was soon to abandon the breeding and training of racehorses in the face of an unbelievable fact. It is not known when he first realized that the abundant power of the Cuyahoga River was no more. It is known that the directors of the Pennsylvania-Ohio Canal Company, most of whose officers were heavily involved in the ownership and development of Akron industry, diverted much of the water of the Cuyahoga at Franklin and Franklin Mills to their canal, fearful that the two communities if they had the Cuyahoga's power might develop as John Brown hoped into industrial rivals of Akron.[29] Whether the water gradually diminished or whether John Brown one day walked to the Cuyahoga's banks and saw it astonishingly reduced is not known. It is known that the Brown & Thompson Addition was nearly worthless for a time as industrial property, after the running off of much of Cuyahoga's power.

Whenever or however he perceived the diminished Cuyahoga, John Brown could not believe it; or more properly, he still could not give up. He preferred to think that the water would be restored. His personal property was auctioned off on June 23, 1840, his farm implements, his furniture, his Saxony sheep. It was the loss of the last that gave him the severest pang. To see his sheep, which were to have been the beginning of a great flock, become the property of another, his nine full-blooded Saxony bucks, the four ewes and even the great Don Pedro, may have made his face more stern and frozen as he tried not to show the wrench it cost him. But it was his personal property rather than his land which had been auctioned off. His farm in the northeast corner of Hudson township, three miles from the village of Hudson, still was his, as was Westlands in the adjoining township of Twinsburg, the farm for which he had so peculiar an affection. Even though it, too, was soon to be scheduled for public sale, he meant somehow to hang onto it.

"Notwithstanding all our difficulties," he wrote Seth Thompson, "let us trust in him who hears the young Ravens when they cry."[30] As for the Cuyahoga's vanished power, he had been told "that when they get the canal completed and the Reservoir in order, there will be as much water as formerly."[31]

He was mistaken. The diverted water was never returned to the Cuyahoga—or at least not in John Brown's time. From the very first and to the very last on this venture as to the Brown & Thompson Addition, he had hoped that Providence would save him. Even when it had sent the panic of 1837, sent the cold that had destroyed the silk worms which so many, including John Brown, thought would result in riches, he had believed in the benevolence of Providence because the Cuyahoga's power had still been there, as the stars were there, because both had been made by Almighty God. The land remained, panic or no panic, because He had created it. Now the power was gone, the land nearly worthless. Providence had not saved him. Rather, it had permitted wicked men to succeed in a wicked design. He who had heard the young ravens when they cry had not heard John Brown. With the Brown & Thompson Addition to Franklin Village now one with Nineveh and Tyre, Brown moved back to Hudson in 1840 and never saw again the Haymaker acres he had believed so long were to make him rich.

2

For the next few years it may have seemed to John Brown as if the blight of God Almighty were upon him. He tried to feel, as he said, "Though He slay me, yet will I trust in Him and bless His name forever." But it was a struggle. He fought hard to accept God's decrees, even when his children died, seeking to regain the faith that had once been his and which he dared to hope he had never really lost. But he was smitten hard and he was smitten often before his pride was humbled. He had to suffer jail before he would submit to the law, and it was painful for him to think that the law's judgment might have been Heaven's also.

For almost the first time his spirit was curdled, although he tried to overcome his sourness. Until now he had been able to convince himself of his inherent benevolence and he still tried to do so, even when filled with hot aggression and a burning sense of the world's injustice. But he was changed. He was bitter. He thought men were saying, "Now that he lieth he shall rise up no more," [32] and fancied everyone gloried in his misfortune. It was as if all his past months, however harried, were sheer contentment compared to the present, which he later described as the time of "my extreme calamity," [33] a calamity continuing in various forms for more than three years.

When he returned to Hudson in 1840, he apparently thought his failure too humiliating for him to stay on the Western Reserve where his reputation as a businessman had considerably depreciated. He must begin again and at a point far removed from his misfortunes. Consulting his father, he decided that it might be best for him to move to western Virginia, even though it was a land of slavery, legally if not actually, since most of its farmers were too impoverished to own slaves. Oberlin Collegiate Institute owned a huge tract there, the gift of Gerrit Smith, and Owen Brown felt that as a trustee of Oberlin he might gain access to the land for his sorely pressed elder son. It was agreed by the Board of Trustees that John Brown would survey a part of the land, particularly where titles were in dispute, and as recompense receive a dollar a day and expenses, as well as the privilege of buying one thousand acres at a nominal sum and with adequate time to pay.

In April of 1840, John Brown began his survey and thought for a time he would settle in western Virginia. He wrote home that he had "seen the spot where if it be the will of Providence, I hope one day to live with my family."[34] It was not the will of Providence. Upon his return to Hudson he alternated so long between thinking that he would move and deciding that he would not, that Oberlin finally revoked the agreement to sell him land. Long before it did so Brown had "commenced tanning at the old stand" in Hudson, he wrote Seth Thompson, adding that he seemed "to be getting along pretty well so far."[35]

His mild contentment was short-lived. Within three days of his writing Thompson, the Supreme Court of the State of Ohio joined with one he was beginning to consider as his arch enemy, Daniel C. Gaylord, and ordered Westlands sold to satisfy Gaylord's judgment against Brown of $1,202.28. Brown had appealed to the Supreme Court, charging fraud, but instead of protecting him the court, or so it seemed to him, collaborated in the fraud by helping Gaylord rob him of his favorite farm. A public auction was set for October 12, 1840.[36] John Brown convinced himself that no friend of his would bid on the farm. When a Hudson neighbor, Amos Chamberlain, a friend whom he had liked particularly and had known since youth, bought it for $1,681, the price unusually low because there were no other bidders, Brown was outraged. In the long series of his misfortunes he had reached a breaking point, and his actions for some months had a quality of defiant aggression they had never shown before. Brown was still convinced that the farm was morally his, that he was holding it in trust for the ultimate benefit of "all my honest creditors." When Chamberlain tried to take possession, John Brown had him arrested for trespass on a warrant issued by one of Brown's friends who was a justice of the peace.

All winter he smoldered with indignation, no matter how hard he tried to reason with himself or recover the benign feelings he had once had for his old friend and neighbor. It was no use to think of former days of friendship. Instead, he made plans for what he himself called war. He resolved to hold Westlands by using an old log house on it as a fort in which he and his sons, armed with some ancient muskets, would repel Chamberlain or anyone else who tried to seize the farm. He seemed to conceive of himself as a sovereign state with every right to make war if he was invaded. In April, one of his sons told him of some conciliating statement that Chamberlain had addressed to him and he resolved to make one more effort for peace. He wrote Mr. Chamberlain on April 27:

I was yesterday makeing preparation for the commencement and vigorous prosecution of a tedious, distressing, wasteing and long protracted war, but after hearing by my son of some remarks you made to him, I am induced before I proceed any further in the way of hostile preparation: to stop and make one more earnest effort for Peace. And let me begin by assureing you that notwithstanding I feel myself to be deeply and sorely injured by you (without even the shadow of a provocation on my part to tempt you to begin as you did last October;) I have no consciousness of wish to injure either yourself or any of your family nor to interfere with your happiness, no not even to value of one hair of your head. I perfectly well remember the uniform good understanding which had ever (previous to last fall) existed between us from our youth. I have not forgotten the days of cheerful labour which we have performed together, nor the acts of mutual kindness and accomodation which have passed between us. I can assure you that I ever have been and still am your honest, hearty friend. I have looked with sincere gratification uppon your steady growing prosperity, and flattering prospects of your young family. I have made your happiness and prosperity my own instead of feeling envious at your success. When I antisipated a return to Hudson with my family I expected great satisfaction from again haveing you for a neighbor. . . .

And now I ask you why will you trample on the rights of your friend and of his numerous family? Is it because he is poor? Why will you kneedlessly make yourself the means of depriveing all my honest creditors of their Just due? [He ignored the fact that the proceeds of the sale went to one creditor, Gaylord, not counting him as an honest creditor.] Ought not my property if it must be sacrifised to fall into the hands of honest and some of them poor and suffering Creditors? Will God smile on the gains which you may acquire at the expence of suffering families deprived of their honest dues? And let me here ask Have you since you bid off that farm felt the same inward peace and consciousness of right you had before felt? I do not believe you have, and for this plain reason that you have been industrious in circulateing evil reports of me (as I believe) in order to prevent the community from enquiring into your motives and conduct. This is perfectly natural, and no new thing under the sun. If it could be made to appear that Naboth the Jezreelite had blasphemed God and the King, then it would be perfectly right for Ahab to possess his vineyard. So reasoned wicked men thousands of years ago. I ask my old friend again is your path a path of peace? does it promise peace? I have two definite things to offer you once and for all. One is that you take ample security of Seth Thompson for what you have paid and for what you may have to pay (which D. C. Gaylord has ever wickedly refused) and release my farm and thereby provide for yourself an honorable and secure retreat out of the strife and perplexity and restore you to peace with your friends and with yourself. The other is if you do not like that offer, that you submit the matter to disinterested, discreet and good men to say what is just and honest between us. . . .[37]

When Chamberlain did not avail himself of this "honorable and secure retreat," John Brown and three of his sons, John, Jr., Jason, and Owen, then nineteen, seventeen, and sixteen respectively, took "some old fashioned muskets" and stayed in the log cabin "night and day." Once Chamberlain and his sons approached the cabin and John Brown called out to his sons, referring to Amos, "Shoot him if he puts his head inside!" [38]

"Then Amos Chamberlain," said Jason years later, "sued father and sent the constable and his posse to drive us out. We showed them our guns." The constable and his posse retreated. The sheriff of Portage County and his posse came a few days later, while the Brown boys were alone in the cabin, to the tannery where their father was at work. Their father had no shirt on, only his red undershirt. He did not resist and it was with some pleasure that Mrs. Chamberlain saw that the sheriff refused Brown permission to go inside and put on a proper shirt or at least get his coat.[39] With their father under arrest and in the hands of the sheriff, the boys in the log house surrendered and were arrested, except for Jason, who afterwards said, "being the family coward I ran into the brush and escaped." [40]

The two Brown boys and their father, still in his red undershirt and rather distressed by it, were taken to the Akron jail and locked in a cell. But somehow it didn't seem right to the sheriff to have John Brown in a cell. He felt he was an honest man who had committed no offense except to fight for property he honestly thought was his. Almost with the same motion that he had locked the cell door, he unlocked it and waved the Browns out, telling them that he would trust them to appear for their trial. But Chamberlain refused to prosecute. While the Browns were in Akron he and his sons tore down the log cabin and John Brown never again tried to hold what he called his farm. He brooded a long time over the humiliation of being locked up in the Akron jail, writing of it almost three years later.[41] He did not mention his red undershirt but it does seem as if the sheriff might have waited at least until he got a coat from the house.

3

"Oh, we were poor!" Jason once exclaimed in describing those days.[42] It was fast becoming apparent, and even to John Brown, that his liabilities far exceeded his assets and that after his farms were sold at public auction and the Brown & Thompson Addition disposed of he would still owe several thousands of dollars. Nevertheless, he continued trying to pay something, however little, on the $2,800 he had promised to restore to Mr. Kellogg. In 1840 he was forced to write Kellogg that often he did not even have money for postage, explaining that the reason his means were

so very limited is in consequence of my being left penyless for the time being, by the assignment and disposal of my property with no less than a family of ten children to provide for, the sickness of my wife and three of my eldest children since that time, and the most severe pressure generally for want of money ever known in this Country. Specie is almost out of the question and nothing but specie will pay our postage. . . . I most earnestly hope to make amends for all the wrong I have done.[43]

Somehow during the first days of August 1841, probably from the sale of wool, he acquired a draft from Lawrence, Stone and Company of Boston for $56.64. Although there may have been many contestants for the money, as well as many family needs, he sent the draft on to Mr. Kellogg, writing him on November 15, "Please let me know if the draft was received & paid over small as it was," and signed himself again, "your unworthy friend." [44] If it was unusual for Mr. Kellogg to treat him with "tenderness," as John Brown described it, it was even more unusual for Captain Heman Oviatt, of Richfield, to whom Brown still owed $5,667.96 and who could also charge him with shady dealing in failing to hand over Westlands as he had promised, to make Brown his partner in two enterprises, the first a tannery, the second involving a large herd of sheep for which John Brown would care and Oviatt put up the capital.[45]

In 1841 he began sheep herding as Captain Oviatt's partner in Richfield. But he did not move his family there until 1842, when the Hudson farmhouse was sold over the family's heads at a public auction, disposing of his last farm. He no longer had a financial interest in the Brown & Thompson Addition for which two of his creditors were contesting in court. On September 28, 1842, he availed himself of the new federal bankruptcy law and was officially declared a bankrupt without assets of any kind while at the same time he was legally cleared of any obligation to pay his outstanding debts. His creditors appear to have thought he had suffered enough, or to have agreed that he was a pauper from whom nothing could be gained, for none raised any objection to his legal discharge from debt.

Judge De Peyster was named federal assignee for the settlement of his estate. He was particularly generous in exempting from public auction the little remaining of John Brown's property. Something of the time and the Browns's manner of living may be gained from the articles they were allowed to keep: "10 Dining Plates, 1 set of Cups and Saucers, 1 set Teaspoons, 2 Earthen Crocks, 1 Pepper Mill, 1 Cider Barrel, 4 Wooden Pails, 6 Bedsteads old, 1 Writing Desk, 4 Blankets, 1 Wash Tub," and "1 pr flat Irons." Provisions granted the family included "1 Bushel Dryed Apples, 20 Bushels corn, 15 Galls Vinegar, 8 Bushels Potatoes, 1 Bushel Beans, 20 Galls Soap, 150 lbs. Pork" and "10 lbs Sugar."

Books exempted from auction included "11 Bibles & Testaments, 1 Vol Beauties of the Bible, 1 do [ditto] Flints Surveying, 1 Vol, Dicks Works, 1 do Rush, 1 do Church Members Guide, and about 36 Miscellaneous books." He was also allowed to keep among "other articles and necessaries, 2 Mares, 2 Halters, 2 Hogs, 19 Hens, 1 Mattock, 1 Pitchfork, 1 Branding Iron, 1 Handsaw, 4 Old Axes, 2 Beaming Knives, 2 Roping Knives, 2 Ink Stands, 4 Slates, 4 Cords of Bark, 2 Saddles, 1 Ton of Hay, 19 Sheep Pledged to H. Oviatt, 1 Shovel, 1 Harrow, 1 plane, 1 Log Chain, 1 Crow Bar, 2 Cows, 2 Hoes, 1 Iron Wedge, 1 pr. Sheep Shears" and "3 Pocket Knives."

Clothing allowed to the family consisted of "2 overcoats—5 coats—10 vests—12 pairs pantaloons—26 shirts—10 Women's and Girl's Dresses—3 Skirts—2 cloaks—4 Shawls—8 Women's and children's aprons—5 pairs boots —3 pairs of Shoes—13 pairs of Socks & Stockings—7 Stocks and Handkerchiefs—4 Bonnets—1 Hat—5 Palmleaf Hats—8 Men's and Boys Cloth Caps— 1 Fur Cap & 1 Wool Cap." [46]

This was all of John Brown's worldly goods, and all of his family's worldly goods, when they began their new life at Richfield. But if John Brown was a bankrupt he meant to be an honest one. Among his first actions after being discharged from the legal necessity of paying his debts was the swearing of affidavits to pay two of the largest. On October 17 he appeared before a justice of the peace in Richfield before whom he admitted his $2,800 misappropriation from the New England Woolen Company, pledging to pay it in view of the "great kindness and tenderness of said Company toward me in my calamity, and more particularly because of the moral obligation I am under to render all their due."

He said he would pay "from time to time as Divine Providence shall enable me to do." [47] Divine Providence never enabled him to pay much of it and just before he was hanged he turned the whole affair into a moral triumph by showing that he had not forgotten it, that he still acknowledged his debt, and by leaving a bequest in his will of $50 to Mr. Kellogg's company. The second affidavit was made on October 29, 1842, pledging to pay as Divine Providence enabled him to do so $5,667.96 to his new partner, Captain Oviatt, who had lost that sum on John Brown's promissory note of 1836. [48]

By 1843 twelve Brown children were sitting around the family table, eating their suppers of porridge and Johnny-cake in a log cabin at the center of Richfield. Supper began, of course, with the saying of grace by the children's father. As he sat at the head of the table keeping order and quiet with stern benevolence, he may have thought his troubles were over for a time. But his bitter cup was not yet drained.

4

John Brown always said that if a man retained the affection of his family at home almost anything could be endured from the world outside.[49] He always retained it. When his boys grew older he was gratified that they still enjoyed his company [50] and perhaps did not know that when together they sometimes laughed, perhaps a little painfully, as they recalled the peculiarities incidental to being John Brown's sons, such as his whippings, and the agonizing Sabbaths when a child was not encouraged to move or speak. As for his wife, according to a visitor, she not only loved but revered him. When she had a scissors handy when his letters arrived, she occasionally cut from them sentences praising her or expressing regard, putting them away among her keepsakes as if they were a special treasure.[51]

She was a calm woman and John Brown always seemed more worried than his wife when there was sickness in the family. If he was frightened when his children became ill it might be because first and last ten of them died, or exactly half of the twenty born to him. It seemed sometimes as if he liked the last-born best and he once said that although the numbers of the Brown family were large, they could not afford to lose any and particularly the one just born. He was a hard man, who expected the world to be hard, and although he was stony in feature and all his attitudes, it did not seem to help much when one of his little ones died. To show this side of his nature let us skip ahead for an instant to April of 1849 in Springfield, Massachusetts, before returning to events in Richfield. In that month, his little daughter Ellen, not yet a year old, was dying.

"The time that he could be at home was mostly spent in caring for her," Ruth, his eldest daughter, later recalled.

He sat up nights to keep an even temperature in the room, and to relieve mother from the constant care which she had through the day. He used to walk with the child and sing to her so much that she soon learned his step. When she heard him coming up the steps to the door, she would reach out her hands and cry for him to take her. When his business at the wool store crowded him so much that he did not have time to take her, he would steal around through the wood-shed into the kitchen to eat his dinner, and not go into the dining room where she could see or hear him. . . .

He noticed a change in her one morning, and told us he thought she would not live through the day, and came home several times to see her. A little before noon he came home, and looked at her and said, "She is almost gone." She heard him speak, opened her eyes, and put up her little wasted hands with such a pleading look for him to take her that he lifted her from the cradle, with the pillows she was lying on, and carried her until she died. He was very calm, closed her eyes, folded her hands, and laid her in her cradle. When she was buried father broke down completely and sobbed like a child. . . .[52]

Yet in the summer of 1843 in Richfield all was well as John Brown reported, changing the tense and repeating the fact, "But all is well, all is well."[53] If he had failed in the outside world he had not failed at home, knowing his wife, as the Bible says ("and Adam knew Eve his wife; and she conceived") with regularity and frequency. He was at the very peak of his replenishment of the earth at this time, his dozen children, the most ever alive at any one time, ranging from grown men to a year-old infant. They were his namesake, John, twenty-two; Jason, twenty; Owen, eighteen; Ruth, fourteen; Frederick, twelve; Sarah, nine; Watson, nearly eight; Salmon, nearly seven; Charles, five; Oliver, four; Peter, two; and Austin, nearly one.

He may have been apprehensive when Charles, five, became ill on September 4, and more frightened when Sarah, nine, took to her bed, rapidly followed by the smaller children, Peter and Austin. No one believed more firmly than he that the world contained no accidents, believed more fully that not even an acorn fell without the Lord's willing it. He may have wondered if his were the sins that were, in Jason's words, bringing these days of God's rebuke. The children rapidly grew more ill as he sat up each night, passing swiftly from bed to bed as if he sought to hold at bay the predestination all were powerless to avert. By September 22, all four of John Brown's children were dead, and like Cain, he may have murmured to the Lord, if only for an instant, "My punishment is greater than I can bear." It may have seemed hard, even to Brown, who accepted God's judgments, that He would strike at the guilty by slaying his innocent children.

XVII

Wool and the

Great Design

THERE IS LITTLE more certain in life than that change is the only constant, at least until that final change of which John Brown thought so often, knowing as he did that this world is not the home of man. Wherever man's final home, however, earthly troubles are usually cyclical and even tragedy cannot torment forever. John Brown himself had predicted, when his worldly fortunes were near their lowest ebb, that "Tomorrow may be a much brighter day,"[1] and he meant here on earth. It was, and the reason for it was that John Brown proved a genius in the raising and breeding of sheep, in judging and buying them, and in growing a fleece of unusual quality.

He seemed born to his task for every aspect of sheep behavior intrigued him. To some they were the most provoking of animals but he delighted to tell of the acuteness of their hearing, of how in a flock of a thousand making a terrible din with their bleating, the youngest ewe could pick out the voice of its mother and run unerringly to her. He maintained, too, that they had about as much individuality as men, declaring that in a flock of hundreds he could recognize a particular dam or buck as easily as recognizing a friend in a crowd.

Apparently he seldom felt so fulfilled as when on a frosty morning he found a lamb near dead from a night's cold and succeeded in reviving it. He began by bringing it into the kitchen in his arms, sometimes elbowing his wife

344

and daughter, Ruth, out of the way and commandeering the water they were heating on the wood stove. Pouring it into a tub he would immerse the lamb very slowly and gradually, dipping it in and out until it could take the heat, and after it began to show signs of life carefully drying it with a flannel cloth before feeding it hot milk with a teaspoon as he held it in his arms with a blanket wrapped around it as if it were a baby. When at last it was revived he would fairly shine with satisfaction as the lamb, so near death an hour before, now scampered and capered about the kitchen floor. That such satisfaction was not always wholly disinterested was indicated in 1844 when he recalled to his daughter how he had irritated her the year before by seizing the hot water she was about to use for washing clothes. "Ruth," he said, "that lamb I hindered you with when you were washing, I have just sold for one hundred dollars." [2]

But his feelings for sheep, as we know, included a great deal more than the mercenary. As he himself wrote in his autobiographical letter on July 15, 1857, using, it will be remembered, the third person in describing himself: ". . . as soon as circumstances would enable him he began to be a practical *Shepherd*: it being a calling for which in early life he had a kind of *enthusiastic longing*: together with the idea that as a business it bid fair to afford him the means of carrying out his greatest or principal object." [3]

By his "greatest or principal object," John Brown meant his plan for the freeing of the slave. He may have fancied that as a buyer of sheep, and later as a broker in the purchase of wool, he could penetrate the area of slavery and there observe conditions at first hand. It may be that he was already thinking of recruiting brave black men for his army of liberation, a plan which was growing more definite in his mind, and perhaps he even dreamed of secretly accosting slaves and enlisting them as he traveled in Virginia seeking wool to sell on commission and sheep for the flock at Akron.

When he read, as he did, of Cinque, the young and handsome African chieftain who had led a revolt in 1839 of captured African slaves on the schooner *Amistad*, killing most of the crew, he did not doubt that he was right in believing slaves would fight. When he read of Washington Madison, the slave who had led a similar revolt on the slave ship *Creole*, taking her and 133 of his fellow revolting slaves who had overcome the crew in a fierce battle for liberty to the British Bahamas, he felt additionally certain that blacks were brave and valued their freedom as much as any white. [4]

These cases shocked and divided the whole country, particularly when the national government proposed to return Cinque and his fellow slaves, who had been captured by American naval forces in Long Island Sound, to slavery in Cuba. In addition, the government demanded that the British return Madison and his colleagues so that they might be punished for mutiny and murder. The British refused and J. Q. Adams won the freedom of Cinque and the mutineers of the *Amistad* by his argument before the Supreme Court in 1841, after a long and complicated political struggle while the Africans remained in a Connecticut jail. John Brown's representative in the Congress, Joshua R. Giddings of the Western Reserve, was censured by a vote of the House on March 23, 1842, for his defense of the revolting slaves of the *Creole*. He said that the laws of slavery and the slave states did not reach beyond their confines and that once on the Atlantic, slaves had the right to revolt and kill those who were illegally holding them in slavery. Upon receiving congressional censure, Giddings immediately resigned and at a special election on the Western Reserve was overwhelmingly vindicated and re-elected to Congress.

John Brown, occasionally thinking of such matters, and speaking of them, too, repeatedly traveled as a buyer of sheep and a broker in the sale of wool in northern Virginia, in the Ohio Valley region, as well as southwest Pennsylvania, also in that valley, and there is reason to believe, as we shall see, that he helped a good many fugitive slaves across the Ohio while on these trips. The times were propitious for such actions and more than a few participated in them on a wider scale than John Brown. He read of their feats and admired them [5] although they made his own efforts seem small, but he had hopes of ultimately outdoing those he admired. If it was a much brighter day, perhaps it was partly because John Brown felt that the temper of the times was bringing nearer the "carrying out of his greatest or principal object." If he had not tried to free the wool growers of the country from the economic bondage of the Eastern wool manufacturers at the same time he was trying to advance his plan to free the slaves, it is possible, although not likely, he might have sooner mounted his drive against slavery. The real point is that he was always overconfident, always overextended as to his resources, always trying too much with too little. But he did try.

MUTTON HILL

I

After two and a half years of partnership with Captain Oviatt, Brown's success in managing their flock attracted the attention of Colonel Simon Perkins of Akron. Perkins, one of the richest men on the Western Reserve, wanted John Brown as a partner in the care and management of a large flock "to share equally in the gain or loss yearly." Perkins agreed to furnish food and shelter for the sheep during the winter, and pasturage in summer while, according to the contract, "Said Brown agrees on his part to furnish throughout the year all the care and attention of every description which the good of the flock may require." In addition, said Brown agreed to "wash the sheep, shear the wool, sack and ship the same for market in the neatest and best possible manner, an equal set-off against the food etc. necessary for the wintering of the flock," which was to be improved and increased "from time to time as the business will justify" and as the partners "may agree." [6]

The contract also provided that Brown should have an attractive cottage on Mutton Hill, not far from Akron and the white-columned Perkins Mansion built of stone and still one of the most imposing homes in Ohio.[7] The cottage overlooked the rolling countryside. Its rent was $30 a year, which included the use of a vegetable garden and the privilege of wood for fuel. John Brown was delighted. He regarded it as not only an advance in the world but in view of the distinction of his partner a vindication of his business past with all its misadventures.

On January 11, 1844, three days after signing the agreement, he wrote a triumphant letter to his eldest son at the Grand River Institute in Ashtabula County, Ohio, characteristically delaying his good news until he had indulged himself in some casual small talk. "Dear Son," he wrote. "Your letter dated 21st Dec was received some days ago but I have purposely delayed till now in order to comply the better with your request that I should write you about everything. We are all in health; amongst the number is a new sister [8] about three weeks old." After detailing news about others of the family and declaring "I have gone to sleep a great many times while writing the above," he at last arrived at his climax.

"I have lately entered," he wrote,

into a copartnership with Simon Perkins Jr. of Akron with a view to carry on the sheep business extensively He is to furnish all the feed, & shelters for wintering as a set off against our taking all the care of the flock. . . . I think this is the most comfortable and the most favourable arrangement of my worldly concerns that I ever had, and calculated to afford us more leisure for improvement, by day, & by Night, than any other. I do hope that God has enabled us to make it in mercy to us, & not that he should send leanness into our soul. . . .

This I think will be considered no mean alliance for our family & I most earnestly hope that they will have wisdom given to make the most of it. It is certainly endorseing the poor Bankrupt & his family three of whom were but recently in

Akron jail in a manner quite unexpected, & proves that notwithstanding we have [not] been a company of Belted Knights, our industrious & steady endeavours to maintain our integrity & our character have not been wholly overlooked. Mr. P[erkins] is perfectly advised of our poverty, & the times that have passed over us. Perhaps you may think best to have some connection with this business. . . .[9]

Colonel Perkins, a mild little man with a goatee, a dominating wife, and as deficient in business sense as John Brown, had inherited his position of wealth and influence from his father, General Simon Perkins, a founder of Akron and a general in the War of 1812. Politically conservative and always proper through the influence of a powerful and conventional wife, a sister of Governor Tod of Ohio, the colonel's title was as completely honorary as if he had been a wealthy man of position in Kentucky. Nevertheless, John Brown always seemed somewhat in awe of him, once describing him as "a most noble-spirited man," [10] and always almost pitifully anxious to please him. He seemed impressed, too, by the handsome and elegant mansion nearby which all of the Browns, just like the slaves and poor whites of the South when speaking of the master's house on a plantation, were in the habit of referring to as "the big house."

But whatever his admiration for the colonel, a title that John Brown at least never used when addressing him, he had no doubt of the identity of the principal partner. It was, of course, himself, the practical shepherd, not because he wished to lord it over Perkins but because the assumption of authority was as natural to him as breathing. He even tried to overcome the tendency, feeling an almost involuntary respect for a man so favored by Providence, but it was no use. What else could he do but make the decisions when he knew so much more than Perkins, particularly about sheep? As for the colonel, poor man, he said, a little plaintively, "I had no controversy with John Brown for it would have done no good." [11]

For almost ten years the Perkins & Brown flock was considered one of the best in the country. The journalists and writers who described it in agricultural books and magazines knew who to see and who was responsible for the flock's excellence. In neither case was it the colonel. They always interviewed John Brown upon their arrival in Akron, and in 1845 when the flock contained 1,300 sheep, Saxonys and mix-blooded Saxonys and Merinos, the editor of the *Ohio Cultivator*, M. B. Bateham, who had inspected the sheep, wrote in his publication, "Too much cannot be said in praise of these sheep, and especially in praise of the care and skill displayed by Mr. Brown." [12] In the same year Brown's words were quoted with respect in a book, *The American Shepherd*, published in New York by Harper's.[13] In still another book, this one widely circulated and published in 1852, the Perkins & Brown flock was listed as one of the finest in the United States.[14]

None of this praise or attention to John Brown particularly endeared him to Mrs. Perkins. She said he was a rough and violent man and her oldest daughter, Anna, agreed, adding that perhaps he had to be to control his sons, who she maintained were wild and rebellious. About the only compliment either ever gave John Brown was a bit backhanded when Anna said, years later, "Mrs. Brown was a good ordinary soul, by no means John Brown's equal."[15] They said he had once shot a dog that persisted in straying, and had forced his wife to remount behind him when she had been thrown from a horse on the way to church.

Usually Mrs. Perkins called him "that man" and when he returned from Kansas in 1857, visiting the Perkinses for an evening, Mrs. Perkins excused herself at a certain point in the conversation and hurried upstairs where her children had already gone to bed. They were in the habit of leaving their bedroom doors ajar and it was this that worried her. "Children," she said, "close and lock your doors. That man carries bowie knives in his boots!"[16]

Anna Perkins in recalling the Browns said that her grandmother had called on the family after the death of an infant[17] and found John Brown

making the coffin in the room in which his wife lay in bed. He would have no help, but finished the box, put the baby in, carried it out in the yard and buried it. . . . He belonged to no church while in Akron because he could not accept the creed. But he used to go down to prayer meetings sometimes and would argue with the elders there as long as they would go on or listen. He was faithful to his own conscience.

On Saturday nights at sundown his Sunday began and all his children had to come indoors and spend the evening in absolute quiet. On Sunday evenings at sundown Sunday was over. The doors opened and the children came rushing out perfectly wild.[18]

These long Sabbaths were so excruciating in their silence, and in the complete lack of activity imposed, that once the older boys decided to escape from the second floor by sliding down a rain pipe. Owen and Frederick got away but Jason slipped and broke an arm. His father heard him fall and ran out, finding him on the ground, writhing in pain. "Well, Jason," he said, "I think I will not punish you for this. You have had punishment enough."[19]

The younger boys, too, were a sore trial to him as he was to them. In 1845 they had a short fierce feud with two of the Perkins's hired girls. The girls reported to Mrs. Perkins that Watson, nine, Salmon, eight, and Oliver, six, had stolen some cherries from the Perkins orchard. The boys, determined on revenge, got some "cow-itch" from a drugstore, a substance that was almost unendurable when it came into contact with the skin. They put it on the seats of the outhouse used by the girls who, suspecting the identity of their tormentors, again complained to Mrs. Perkins. When she hotly protested to John Brown, he promised to punish his boys if they were guilty.

"Father could get nothing out of us by questions," Salmon recalled. "That night, he came out to the barn—for we were sleeping in the hay-mow —thinking, probably, that we might talk it over alone, and listened at the scuttle," which was the opening leading to the hay-mow. The boys could hear him breathing below in the dark, and occasionally shifting a little as he listened. The younger boys had with them their fourteen-year-old brother Frederick, who sympathized with their plight. "Fred got up," Salmon resumed, "and said, in a good clear voice, 'if Dad's down that scuttle-hole, I'm going to hit him with this stick of wood' and picking up a heavy stick, he tossed it down the scuttle. If it had hit father it would have killed him," Salmon said, but it did not hit him, and he tiptoed out of the barn.

He finally found out that the boys had spread the "cow-itch" in the outhouse. "He didn't whip us," Salmon remembered, "but he gave mother a new dress to go over and tell Mrs. Perkins that his boys did the deed. We younger boys respected Father, but we didn't respect him so much but what we'd fight when it came to a question like that with him." Salmon fought so hard when eleven as his father tried to whip him that he never tried again.[20]

Salmon was particularly indignant and sorrowful with the results of a deal his father made with him and Watson that summer of 1845. He offered the two little boys 10 cents for every fly they caught of a special kind, called by John Brown, and no doubt correctly, the *Oestris Ovis*, which was believed responsible for a disease of sheep known as worm in the head. "We went at it with a vim," Salmon recalled, "and soon presented a considerable bill, laying great plans as to how we should spend the money."[21]

But they never received any. Just as they were about to be paid, a book agent came along. John Brown used Salmon's money to buy Doddridge's *Rise and Progress of Religion in the Soul*, presenting it to the eight-year-old boy, who burst into tears. He bought a copy of Baxter's *Saints' Rest*, that ponderous tome which he so liked, for Watson and with Watson's money. Perhaps he later understood their disappointment. Only a few days had passed when he bought for Salmon, with the remainder of the money due him, a pocket knife for which Salmon had long yearned. But he broke off the points of the blades of the knife in the interest of safety. It was the second tragedy Salmon suffered in the affair of the *Oestris Ovis*.

2

The most basic reason for the strain between the Perkins and Brown families was abolition and the Underground Railroad. The Perkinses did not approve of either, being law-abiding, conventional folk who did not enjoy having their property the scene of crime. They were often shocked and startled by suddenly glimpsing the faces and forms of strange black men and women about John Brown's house and barn. A few days would pass and they would disappear, soon to be replaced by other escaping slaves.[22] New fugitives almost always appeared after his return from the Ohio Valley region of Pennsylvania and Virginia.

He enjoyed these trips, which he had made repeatedly since 1842, combining as they did sheep and abolition, and even contributing, at least in his own mind and however indirectly, to "his greatest or principal object." He usually went first, sometimes on horseback, sometimes with a wagon, to Columbiana and Stark Counties in northeast Ohio near the Pennsylvania border, after 1844 seeking superior sheep for the Perkins-Brown flock, then to Brooke and Ohio Counties in northern Virginia before proceeding to the adjacent Washington and Beaver Counties in southwest Pennsylvania. The whole country was dominated by the Ohio River, which gave the states of Ohio and Virginia a common boundary for some 275 miles before proceeding upstream into Pennsylvania and flowing on to Pittsburgh and its source. Much of the countryside along the river, at least on the Ohio side, was punctuated with crossings of the Underground Railroad, usually houses in towns or on farms whose occupants would take in slaves before helping them on to the next station. Most of the crossings from Marietta, northeast up the river to Pennsylvania and the northern Virginia counties, were of easy access to John Brown on these trips.

He had been immensely impressed with the feats of those who actually went into the South to rescue slaves, later mentioning in his writing the Reverend Charles T. Torrey, who on December 30, 1843, was sentenced to six years in prison for attempting to break jail after he had been convicted in Maryland for rescuing slaves.[23] While awaiting trial, Torrey wrote Henry B. Stanton, the abolitionist leader, "If I am a guilty man, I am a very guilty one; for I have aided nearly four hundred slaves to escape to freedom, the greater part of whom would probably, but for my exertions, have died in slavery." Torrey died in prison on May 9, 1846.[24]

John Brown also admired Captain Jonathan Walker, a Massachusetts skipper, who had impressed him by rescuing slaves from the South. Captain Walker, while on the northwest coast of Florida near Pensacola, in 1844, granted the pleas of seven slaves to aid them in escaping to the Bahamas where they would be free under British law. After doubling the capes of Florida in an open boat Walker was drawing near the Bahamas off the southeast coast of Florida when he suffered a sunstroke. With the black men unable to navigate the vessel, they were overtaken and captured.

The slaves were returned to their masters, their fates otherwise unknown. Captain Walker was taken to Key West and kept in irons until he was sent in chains by ship to Pensacola where he was secured by iron links to the floor of a cell. He was tried in federal court and sentenced to be branded on the right hand with a redhot iron which would burn into his flesh the letters "S.S." for Slave Stealer. In addition, he was sentenced to stand in the pillory for an hour and to pay fines for each of the seven slaves he had attempted to rescue, or, failing that, to serve a prison term until the fines were paid. A United States marshal branded his palm with the letters and while standing in the pillory with his mutilated hand, he was pelted with rotten eggs by a pro-slavery Northerner. Subscriptions were widely taken in the North to pay his fines and after eleven months in prison with a chain on his leg, he was liberated. Thereafter he gave his testimony at scores of anti-slavery meetings.[25]

John Brown was to write, as we shall see, of "the Branded Hand." So did Whittier in words quoted at many an abolitionist meeting and often sung with thrilling effect, sometimes by George W. Clark, who had set them to music. They included the stanzas:

> *Then lift that manly right hand, bold ploughman of the wave,*
> *Its branded palm shall prophesy, "*SALVATION TO THE SLAVE*":*
> *Hold up its fire-wrought language, that whoso reads may feel*
> *His heart swell strong within him, his sinews change to steel.*
>
> *Hold it up before our sunshine, up against our Northern air.*
> *Ho! men of Massachusetts, for the love of God, look there!*
> *Take it henceforth for your standard, like the Bruce's heart of yore:*
> *In the dark strife closing round ye, let that hand be seen before.*[26]

It was of such matters, of "the dark strife closing round" and other aspects of slavery, that John Brown often talked when he arrived on his journey in Washington County, a center of the Underground in southwest Pennsylvania. Sometimes he stayed at the home of a wool farmer named McElroy near West Middletown, and often, too, at the home of Mathew

McKeever, whose residence west of town was a well-frequented station on the Underground.

He visited these men at intervals for almost a decade, at first buying sheep but later contracting for wool which he sold at a commission from his depot at Springfield, Massachusetts. Many of the leading wool farmers of the county would turn up in the evenings at either McElroy's or McKeever's to meet with Brown, for his opinions both as to wool and slavery were provocative. General talk might begin with the grievances of the growers of wool, of how manufacturers refused to classify or grade wool but paid instead a price as if the poorest wool in a farmer's clip represented the quality of the entire amount sold and of how some wool farmers depressed the price of wool by failing to remove the grass, burrs, twigs, and dirt from the fleeces they sold.

But almost always the talk would finally turn to the fight against slavery. "Brown was an earnest enthusiastic advocate of the abolition of slavery as was also my father," McElroy's son recalled.

Both were well informed on all subjects of the day and interesting talkers. I well remember that Brown would come over to our house in the evening [when he was not staying there] after hard riding all day in the neighborhood buying wool. Our men neighbors would gather in, mainly to listen to the talk between Brown and my father on the abolition of slavery. Brown was desperately in earnest and very bitter in his denunciation of slavery and the apologizers for it.

My father, in one of these talks, even now . . . well remembered, declared his belief . . . [that] slavery was becoming stronger and more defiant instead of weaker and less aggressive and that in the providence of God it would go down in blood before the end came.

Perhaps John Brown nodded gravely before seconding the prediction, but Mr. McElroy might have been surprised if he had known he was addressing one who would make certain, as far as one man could, that slavery "would go down in blood."

"In those days," the younger McElroy later wrote,

many escaped slaves found their way to West Middletown. That generally meant safety and freedom for they found helping hands in Judge Thomas McKeever and Mathew McKeever, his brother, near the town, food and raiment and a hiding place from which at night they would be taken to another station on the underground railroad in the northern part of the country, and on and on to other stations, on the same road until they reached Canada in safety.[27]

It would not be strange if John Brown escorted some of these slaves from the house of his friend, Mathew McKeever, where he himself so often stayed,[28] across the Ohio River and even to his cottage on Mutton Hill before passing them on toward Lake Erie and Canada. In considering the likelihood of this, the testimony of Charles S. S. Griffing, whose honesty and rectitude have been generally recognized, about John Brown's activities on the Ohio Underground may be relevant. His memories of the Underground went back to 1844. Mr. Griffing in an interview in the Cincinnati *Enquirer* of June 18, 1879, was discussing the men on the Western Reserve who "helped manage the underground railroad between slavery and freedom, or geographically speaking between Kentucky and Virginia soil and Canada." Referring to John Brown, he said,

He was one of our band long before he went to Kansas. . . . He had a consuming idea in life, and that was to free the black man. He had no other aim. . . . John Brown was a man of action; no one would brave greater perils, or incur more risks to lead a black man from slavery to freedom than he. I've seen him come in at night with [a] gang of five or six blacks that he had piloted all the way from the river . . . and if anybody was following he would keep them stowed away for weeks. He would appear on the streets without saying a word to anyone about it. But let any slaveholder discover the whereabouts of his charges and attempt to take them back, and he would fight like a lion.[29]

If he did guide slaves to freedom from the Ohio River region after his trips to Pennsylvania and Virginia that would explain Anna Perkins's complaint that "He was always concerning himself with Negroes, often having several hidden at once about his place." [30]

WATERSHED

I

John Brown moved to Springfield in June of 1846 to embark on a grandiose plan to capture the market in fine wool for the benefit of the American wool farmer and the profit of Perkins & Brown. As he opened a wool depot for sorting, storing, and the sale of wool, he may have had trouble in keeping his mind on his business. Just the month before, American armies had invaded Mexico when that country refused to acquiesce to the annexation of Texas, a Mexican province in which slavery had been abolished, until its latest settlers, chiefly from the American South, revolted and established a new slaveholding nation.

The resulting war against Mexico, brought about by the seizure of what had been Mexican territory, was one of the great watersheds of American history, laying the basis to a large degree for the Civil War; but it was so predatory in nature that more than one American Army officer thought he should resign his commission rather than fight in it. Captain Ulysses S. Grant, for example, wrote, "I had a horror of the Mexican War . . . only I had not moral courage enough to resign. . . ." Grant as long as he lived would never forgive himself for not having resigned his commission rather than participate in an unjust war against an unoffending people. Lieutenant Colonel Ethan Allen Hitchcock, commander of the Third United States Infantry, thought the war "monstrous and abominable" and also thought he should resign his commission and "abandon a government corrupted by both ambition and avarice to the last degree." [31]

The Mexican War had the racist overtones not unknown in later American adventures abroad. "Six-sevenths of the people of Mexico were said to be Indians, half-breeds and negroes—'mere slaves' and the rest degenerate Spaniards who 'would be scattered like chaff by the first volley from the Anglo-Saxon rifle, the first charge of the Anglo-Saxon bayonet.' " [32] But Senator Thomas Corwin, Whig of Ohio, hoped not. On February 11, 1847, he declared to the Senate, "If I were a Mexican, I would tell you, 'Have you not room in your own country to bury your dead men? If you come into mine, we will greet you with bloody hands and welcome you to hospitable graves.' " [33] And Joshua R. Giddings, representative from the Western Reserve and John Brown's favorite politician, told the House, "If I were a Mexican, as I am an American, I would never sheathe my sword while an enemy remained upon my native soil." [34] Theodore Parker, no pacifist, called on Americans to refuse to serve in the war. "Men will call us traitors," he said, and asked, "What then? That hurt nobody in '76. We are a rebellious nation; our whole history is treason; our blood was attainted before we were born. . . ." [35]

Abraham Lincoln, a young Whig from Illinois serving his first term in the House, also raised his voice against the war with the result that he failed of re-election. James Russell Lowell, the Cambridge poet, had his Yankee farmer observing in the dialect verse of *The Bigelow Papers* that the war was for more slave territory, for "Bigger pens to cram with slaves." Thousands of Whigs and Democrats in the North were angry with the Polk administration for moving, as they thought, to increase slave territory through war with Mexico while refusing to gain more free territory in the Pacific Northwest, surrendering to British opposition the American claim to an Oregon reaching to Alaska. Scores of abolitionist meetings, and later Free Soil meetings, in all parts of the North condemned the war as a plot to expand the area of bondage. Henry Thoreau went to jail, if only for a single night, as his protest against the war, declaring it was time for honest men "to rebel and revolutionize," but there were others who suffered death for opposing it.

These were the American soldiers who, in a little-known episode that may have had its own grim glory, rebelled and revolutionized against the war after they had seen something of the invasion of Mexico. Some 260 deserted from the American forces, forming the San Patricio contingent of the Mexican Army. Some said that all were Irish and all were Catholics, deserting only because of their abhorrence of the invasion of a Catholic country; but if they were in fact Irish and Catholic they had been so when they enlisted in the American Army for its invasion of Mexico. It may be that there were more rational reasons for opposing the invasion which ripped away half the territory of a conquered and weaker country. Whatever the real truth, these ex-American soldiers fought with gallantry against the invaders at the battles of Monterey and Buena Vista, also distinguishing themselves for their bravery at the Battle of Churubusco in August of 1847. Some eighty were captured by American forces at Churubusco and fifty were summarily executed after the battle.[36]

2

Believing that it was largely the South's blood and treasure that was defeating Mexico, its leaders were humiliated, infuriated, and ready for almost any reprisal against the North when the Wilmot Proviso was introduced before the House on August 6, 1846, providing that slavery should be forever barred from territory conquered from Mexico. Sentiment in the free states was so strong for the proposal, although the slave states were unanimous against it, that even some hitherto pro-slavery Democrats of the North voted for it. It was passed in the House by a vote of 87 to 64, only to be later defeated in both House and Senate.

But the battle as to whether slavery had the right of entry and existence into the Western territories did not subside after the defeat of the proviso. Rather, it rose in fury. Every Northern legislature save Iowa passed resolutions demanding that slavery be excluded from the territories by act of Congress. Seventy Southern members of Congress addressed a resolution to their constituents in 1849 urging the South to unite in defense of slavery's right to expand. The Virginia legislature passed a resolution declaring that the banning of slavery from the new territories of the West would force Virginians to "abject submission and outrage" or "determined resistance at all hazards and to the last extremity."

As the slaveholders became more aggressive in the realization that if the program of no expansion became fact slavery might be threatened with ultimate extinction, the industrial North was becoming more restive under the brakes put on its development by the pro-slavery Democratic Party. The Chicago *Daily Journal*, in a statement increasingly typical of much of the North's press, addressing itself to the South's opposition to a protective tariff and internal improvements wrote editorially on August 14, 1846:

> The North can and will be no longer hoodwinked. If no measures for protection and improvement of anything North or West are to be suffered by our Southern masters, if we are to be downtrodden, and all our cherished interests crushed by them, a signal revolution will inevitably ensue. The same spirit and energy that forced emancipation for the whole country from Great Britain will throw off the Southern yoke. The North and West will look to and take care of their own interests henceforth. They will . . . see . . . that the power to oppress shall not again be entrusted to men who have shown themselves slave-holders but not Americans. . . . The fiat has gone forth—Southern rule is at an end.[37]

3

It was these slow-moving, but diametrically opposed economic interests, gradually inching toward a catastrophic collision, that forced the men on either side—the Northern manufacturer, for example, who gave not a damn in any humanitarian sense whether blacks were slave or free, the occasionally benevolent Southern plantation owner, who loved the Union and who could not help but sometimes think that slavery was a great wrong—almost against their will toward hostility and war. Many in each section tried desperately to avoid the Civil War, particularly in the immediate months before it began; but the economic forces upon which they were borne were moving toward conflict, regardless of their wishes or their will.

But because of this one must not conclude too swiftly, at least in this writer's opinion, that the clash of economic systems was primary in bringing the war. There cannot be an economic system without people to carry it out although they are often forgotten in tables of production or export. In the South's case, the people carrying out its production were slaves and as Dumond has written, "All historians are agreed there would have been no civil war if there had been no American slavery."[38] If this is true it may be possible that the actual fact of slavery, the actual fact of people suffering under forced and unpaid labor, may have preceded sectional economic rivalry as a cause of war, that it may even have been primary, for without slaves there could not have been the South's particular and specific plantation system, the demands of which clashed with those of the North and its growing industry, increasingly tied to the farmers of the Northwest (now the Middle West).

We can measure cotton production or an increase in horse power but it is still difficult to measure a great moral wrong even though it is dynamite beneath a social system. The activities of the abolitionists had long attested to that and yet not many have been attracted to the question whether white abolitionists would have ever moved without millions of black slaves, some protesting but all a disturbing and ever-present ferment within the body politic. If slaves had acquiesced in the peculiar institution, insisted that it was right and just within the American framework because they were not men as defined by the Declaration of Independence, it is doubtful if Americans in the North would have suffered to prove them wrong. Their protest, however limited and aborted in some cases, but however direct, too, through revolt and thousands of individual flights from slavery, was primary in the fight against it. It may be that the black men and women in slavery will finally be seen as the prime movers of the period's history, as unlikely as that seems now to most white scholars, and as later the anonymous inhabitants of ghettoes were an admittedly explosive force—how explosive we do not yet know.

As far as Southerners themselves were concerned it was not economic differences with the North, not the tariff nor internal improvements, that sent them into their most violent paroxysms of resentment. It was slavery, and any moral condemnation of it, any reference to its abolition, or any criticism of it as an institution, which brought defiance and hostility, particularly in Congress, where shrieks of protest and outrage came as quickly with its adverse mention as if some raw nerve had been deliberately jabbed.

Even as the Mexican War approached, Giddings, to give an instance, was confronted as he was speaking against slavery on the floor of the House of Representatives by Dawson of Louisiana, who, putting his hand on his pistol and cocking it, shouted as he stood before him, "I'll shoot him, by God, I'll shoot him!" [39] Four of Giddings's friends leaped to his side, their hands in their pockets as if they, too, were armed while four of Dawson's colleagues ranged themselves beside him, their hands also threateningly poised. As the two groups confronted each other, Giddings resumed speaking and Dawson did not shoot. During the same debate about Congress voting appropriations to indemnify slaveholders whose slaves had fled to the Seminoles in Florida, another Southern congressman, Black of Georgia, charged Giddings with a

sword cane and lifting it as if to strike, roared, referring to Giddings's condemnation of slavery, "If you repeat those words, I'll knock you down." [40]
Giddings, 6 feet 2 inches in height, with a silver mane of hair and something
slow and benign about him until aroused, repeated the words and then cried
out, "Come on! The people of Ohio don't send cowards here!" [41]

All of this, particularly in view of his special interest in Giddings whom
he would soon try to help, may have been somewhat unsettling to John
Brown as he tried to keep his mind on wool. More slaves were escaping the
South than ever before, a matter of concern to Brown and in a different way
to Representative Thomas L. Clingman of North Carolina, who estimated
at about this time that the total monetary loss to slaveholders as a result of
fugitives escaping from bondage was $15 million, while Senator Butler of
South Carolina said in 1848 that slaves were escaping at a rate of a $200,000
annual loss to their owners.

With the European revolutions of 1848 there were increasing exhortations for armed slave insurrections. In 1849, Ohio Negroes meeting in state
convention cited the revolutions abroad, which most Americans hailed joy-
fully, declaring in a resolution that he "who would be free himself must
strike the blow." [42] During the same year, and also pointing to the enthusiasm
with which even Southerners greeted the European revolutions, the *Ram's
Horn*, the Negro newspaper in New York to which John Brown contributed,
issued a call for a slave rebellion.[43] As early as 1843 the twenty-seven-year-
old black leader, the Reverend Henry Highland Garnet, himself an escaped
slave whom John Brown would meet in 1846, had called for a slave rebellion
before a National Negro Convention in Buffalo.

"Brethren," he said,

arise, arise! Strike for your lives and liberty. Now is the day and the hour. Let
every slave throughout the land do this, and the days of slavery are numbered.
You cannot be oppressed more than you have been—you cannot suffer greater
cruelties than you have already. *Rather die freemen than live to be slaves*. Remember that you are FOUR MILLIONS![44]

SPRINGFIELD

I

This growing social upheaval was the framework of John Brown's life, as
it was of the lives of all Americans, and within its brackets he tried to find

the time for both his adventure in wool and his plan for the destruction of slavery. At first the difficulty of combining his two objectives did not dismay him. As he opened his wool depot, he was at a height of confidence, certain that he could advance his plan for the liberation of the country's wool growers from the domination of the manufacturers while he established communication with black men bold enough to enlist in his greater plan for their freedom.

As an example of his procedure, he was sorting wool in his warehouse shortly after he had opened the Springfield operation when his sons, John and Jason, who had accompanied their father to the Massachusetts city while the remainder of the family stayed for a time in Akron, told him they had met an enterprising black of the right stamp by the name of Thomas Thomas. He was a fugitive from a Maryland plantation and they had been much impressed with him. Brown told them to ask if Thomas would see him and when the former slave presented himself he was offered and accepted a job as a porter.

"How early shall I come tomorrow?" Thomas asked.

"We begin work at seven," Brown said, "but I wish you would come around earlier, so that I can talk with you." [45] Thomas came between five and six and found Brown waiting for him. After a few preliminary questions, Brown outlined his plan for using the Appalachians as a means of invading the South and asked Thomas if he would join him. If Thomas was surprised there is no record of it. He said he would. As for John Brown, he had apparently determined that he must speak of his plan if he was ever to enlist men for his band and he seems to have determined, too, that black men were the safest to approach. Even as he spoke to Thomas, he was trying to get in touch with Garnet, the black Patrick Henry, who had cried for liberty or death, for insurrection by the country's slaves before the National Negro Convention in Buffalo. He was also seeking an interview with the Reverend J. W. Loguen, Negro pastor of Syracuse, active in the Underground and who had escaped from slavery (as had Garnet). Above all, he wanted to meet the fast-rising young Negro leader, Frederick Douglass, who had also broken free from slavery. [46] All three were young, all three were fighters. But it was Douglass whom John Brown most wished to meet. Even when one only read of him, or heard others speak of him, he conveyed challenge, impact, stature. As an orator he was overwhelming. He was a personality who from the first had outshone his peers and he was growing daily as a public figure. John Brown wanted him for a very special role.

2

If John Brown had more than usual confidence in himself that summer of 1846 he had some reason for it. He was accomplishing a difficult feat, one never accomplished before. The wool farmers of eastern Ohio, the panhandle of Virginia, and western Pennsylvania, particularly—although to a lesser extent farmers of New York and New England—thought they were being exploited by the wool manufacturers who, they said, were paying less for their wool than it was worth. He was organizing these highly individualistic farmers, who had always acted on their own, competing against each other, into a united group with common policies. Many had agreed to his program for selling their wool, a program that had something of the aspect of a cooperative, and had decided to send their wool to the Perkins & Brown depot at Springfield where John Brown would sell it for them, holding it in the warehouse when prices were low, selling when they were high but not at so fast a rate as to lower prices by flooding the market.

Since 1845, meetings of wool farmers in Ohio, New England, and Pennsylvania had heard his plan. Stubborn and independent as they were, there was something compelling in his presentation, not only because his auditors were troubled about a serious problem requiring solution, but because of John Brown himself. Standing on the platform before them, he radiated a restrained energy, completely certain that he and his plan were right, slim, sinewy, and farmer-like, but dignified and proper in his snuff-colored frock coat, its tails dangling behind nearly to his knees. It was not his eloquence that convinced but rather some force or conviction or vitality within him. He was not a phrasemonger. He talked plainly of plain matters to the farmers crowded before him, emphasizing, for example, that if the price of wool was to go up, the product must be better, and sent to the market in better shape, washed and clean of grass, twigs, and burrs.

Another reason that made his colleagues listen with respect was that the Perkins & Brown flock was widely conceded to be about the best in the United States while the firm's clip each year brought the highest prices from manufacturers. Again and again the widely read *Ohio Cultivator* had described his methods, his cures for sheep disease, particularly for bots or grubs in the head, and the prizes his fleeces had won, as at the exhibition of the American Institute in New York City and the Massachusetts Mechanics Association in Boston. Samuel Lawrence, manufacturer of Lowell, and one of the great textile dynasty, was quoted as saying, "Mr. Brown's wool has ever been of the highest quality since he first brought it here, but this year it amazes us." [47] In a letter to Brown, quoted in the *Cultivator*, Mr. Lawrence wrote, "Your flock is now superior to any in old Spain"—one of the foremost sheep-raising countries in the world and famous for its Merinos. He added, "There is no reason why it should not be superior to the Germans," [48] also pre-eminent in the raising of fine wool, particularly from Saxony sheep.

The crux of John Brown's proposal for the sale of wool so as to receive better prices was its classification into nine grades, selling the highest grade for the highest price and the lower grades at gradually descending prices. He claimed, as did many other farmers, that manufacturers buying a clip in its entirety without classification, as was the rule, denied the farmer adequate compensation for the finer wools. In 1846, his first year in business, his prices ranged from 75 cents a pound for the finest wool to 25 cents for the lowest grade.[49]

Understandably morbid on the subject of credit and promissory notes, he proposed to sell wool for cash only.[50] This was virtually unprecedented, manufacturers usually buying on credit and paying the farmers ninety days after receipt of their wool. One of his plan's cooperative features provided that while each farmer would be paid for his own clip, as to number of pounds and classification, the price would not be what it actually brought on the market but an average figured from the whole season in each of the various classifications. In addition, and from the very first, John Brown hoped to advance the price of fine wool by opening a competing market for it abroad, particularly in England, France, and Belgium.

He had not envisioned himself, when he began advocating these reforms before wool growers' meetings, as the man who would head up the venture. But to his surprise, or so he said, "they pitched on him as their agent. I understood," said a friend, "that he was finally persuaded to take the agency with considerable difficulty, but at last, consented and went into it with his usual energy." [51] If he was at first unwilling, it may have been because he still smarted from the failures and humiliations that had begun with the Brown & Thompson Addition. He had just regained his standing, attained some eminence in his new career. He felt, as he frequently wrote, that he could not bear to bring any loss to Colonel Perkins nor to forfeit his trust.

On the other hand he could not forego advocacy of his plan of a central depot near the New England manufacturers where wool farmers would send their product. He continued arguing so stubbornly for his proposal that he himself at last was the only logical candidate and the only available one, for the position he had so long persisted in declaring necessary to the welfare of all wool farmers. He convinced Colonel Perkins of the proposal's worth to the wool farmers if not to his own profit. They would continue the flock at Akron, under the care and supervision of John Brown's sons, Jason and Owen, while opening the Springfield depot or warehouse where John Brown would store, sort, and sell wool at a commission of 2 cents a pound and one mill a pound for insurance. Without counting overhead and other business expenses such as freight and rent, their commissions would total only about $2,600 annually on 130,000 pounds of wool, which was about the average received yearly.

When Brown inaugurated the wool depot, twenty of the foremost wool growers of eastern Ohio, northern Virginia, and western Pennsylvania had publicly endorsed his venture. But John Brown wanted a wider, more formal endorsement and immediately began working for it. As he sorted the wool into nine classifications, new shipments arrived periodically, often containing as much as 2,000, 3,000, and 5,000 pounds. Up to his knees in wool and choked by dust, a judgment to be made on every fleece classified that would gain or cost a farmer money, with scores of letters being received weekly, each one requiring an answer, and while trying to attract hostile wool manufacturers to his new method, John Brown at the same time began to organize further meetings of wool growers whose formal endorsement he hoped to obtain. As early as the end of 1846, he was charging "that some of the principal manufacturers are leagued together to break us down, as we have offered them wool at their own price & they refuse to buy." [52] Only the unity of wool growers, he said, could overcome the opposition of manufacturers.

Others also were eager for conventions at which wool farmers would adopt such cooperative policies as were being advocated by Brown. The first meeting to consider such plans was held on July 1, at Lowell, Massachusetts, with wool growers from eight states present. But both John Brown and the meeting were diverted from their purpose when he precipitated a bitter argument about the relative merits of Saxony and Merino sheep, he himself arguing with considerable heat that the Saxony was much the superior. The argument consumed the entire time of the one-day meeting and John Brown was somewhat embarrassed.[53] The second assembly was held at Springfield in August, its purpose to organize a larger meeting of wool growers at Steubenville, Ohio, on February 10, 1847.[54] Brown promised, in a letter to the *Cultivator*, that he would not bring up any "Saxony or Merino disputes" at the Steubenville meeting.[55]

It was this meeting, a large and representative assembly of wool farmers, that formally endorsed by resolution the wool depot of Perkins & Brown. Equally important to Brown, his policies as to classification, the necessity of opening new markets in Europe for finer American wools, and the proper cleaning of wool before sending it to market were also endorsed by the convention after he read a written report on "preparing wool for market and kindred subjects." [56] Its sober, specific language, its detailed directions give a good example of his manner of speech when such provocative subjects as slavery or Merinos as compared with Saxonys did not intrude. It reveals, too, the substance of many of his work days, and much of his routine as a keeper of sheep.

"The best mode of preparing wool for market," he began,

is as follows: First, before washing, remove carefully with the shears all locks containing dirt in a hardened state. Then wet the sheep in every part, and let them stand crowded together for an hour or two. They should be taken out of the water, (when first put in for wetting,) as quickly as may be after the wool is fairly wet, in order to retain a soapy substance the fleece contains, which acts upon the dirt and gum in the wool while the sheep stand before washing. The soapy substance is the first thing to escape as washing is commonly done.

The best mode of washing is to use a [water] fall of three feet or over, turning the sheep in different ways under the fall, till the action of the water brings every part of the fleece to an almost snowy whiteness. A much less fall will answer as well if the sheet of water is 8 or 10 inches deep.

If the water under the fall is not deep enough to remain clear while the sheep are in, a plank bottom should be provided to prevent any sand or earthy substance from getting into the wool by stirring up the water. A clear rock bottom is just as good.

When a fall cannot be had, a clear running stream should be found, and the dirt worked out perfectly from all parts of the fleece with the hands after first soaking the sheep as before mentioned.

To wash sheep immediately after a soaking rain will answer very well, instead of soaking as above. The sheep when washed should be driven to a clean grassy field, free from bare spots of earth, and avoiding muddy and dusty roads on the way after washing. The shearing should be done as soon after the washing as the wool is dry, which will be in two or three days. When confined for shearing, the flock should be kept well littered, and the floors or tables, or whatever place they are sheared upon, should be kept thoroughly clean. The fleeces must be kept whole by the shearers, or they [the shearers] are wholly unfit for their business.

After the fleeces are taken off, they should be placed on a smooth, clean floor, or table with the outer end upwards, and be carefully examined all over by patting with the hands to find every *burr*, which should be taken out without fail. The fleece should then be rolled up snugly and tied with a small twine. If farmers would not suffer a burr-bearing plant to live in their sight, it would be vastly better, and would cost but little yearly. Of this we speak from experience.[57]

If John Brown's words had authority it was because all of his auditors knew he spoke from practice, knew that he himself had stood beneath a waterfall, its flow splashing over his head and back, his drenched clothes clinging to his gnarled body, his hair splattered flat to his skull as he turned and twisted his sheep, hundreds of them and hour after hour, until their fleeces were of an almost snowy whiteness. His audience undoubtedly had a sense, as he spoke, that he more than once had knocked together a plank bottom when the surface water had become too muddy, perhaps could almost see him anxiously searching for roads or detours without mud or dust down which he could herd his sheep after washing, see him shearing the sheep, beginning with the rump, advancing to the brisket and neck, then down the shoulders and to the belly and then the left side and after that the right, shearing steadily on until the sheep was naked and the fleece intact, for those who did not keep it so were "wholly unfit for their business." When he spoke of "patting with the hands to find every burr," there was no question but that his hands had patted searchingly over thousands of fleeces. His words were prosaic but he was describing his art, his work, and even his life as far as it pertained to work. One knew that he had never suffered a burr-bearing plant to live in his presence, that on the contrary, he had pounced on every thistle, on every obnoxious bush in sight, bending to pull it from the earth by the roots.

For a moment he passed from instruction to ethics, indicting those who followed "the shameful, dishonest practice . . . of wrapping up coarse and unwashed wool inside of some of the finest fleeces, putting in dirt balls, dirty sweepings of barn floors, doing up their fleeces wet, so that they often mould," all in an effort to increase the size and weight of a bale so as to get a better price. It was this practice, he said, that was closing foreign markets to American wool and forcing the farmer to sell his product, no matter what the price, to manufacturers at home.

"The laws of England are said," he continued,

to make such things a penal offence, and would our farmers put their wool in such a condition yearly, as some now do, and as a good farmer would be proud of doing with his wheat, pork, butter, &c we should soon have enough of English and French competitors in our wool market, which would do much more for the trade than any protective measures we can hope for. Our slovenly, dishonest habits deprive us of foreign competition, and leave us entirely at the mercy of our large manufacturing companies,—bodies without souls.[58]

The convention passed a resolution condemning the practices the speaker had indicted but without too much effect. John Brown was later to suffer humiliation in England when American bales, the contents of which he had neither sorted nor graded in the hurry of getting the shipments off, were opened for sale. Many fleeces had dirt and other impurities concealed within them,[59] and John Brown could not look in the eye the Englishmen who had come to buy but remained to scorn.

DOUGLASS

I

By 1846 John Brown had succeeded in meeting, among other Negro leaders, Garnet and Loguen, telling them both of his plan for attacking slavery and impressing both with the likelihood that the proposal might be more than the idle talk of an eccentric farmer turned wool merchant. As a matter of fact, twelve years later they were both still helping him in carrying it out, by raising money and recruiting members for John Brown's private army. In 1858, Loguen went with Brown to Canada where he introduced him to Harriet Tubman, that indomitable little black woman whom John Brown desired as a co-worker in his plan and who had penetrated the South on innumerable occasions, armed and ready to fight if she had to, while rescuing whole parties whom she conducted to freedom, often through miles of swamp and forest.

When Loguen and Garnet first heard of John Brown's plan from John Brown's lips, they were impressed and excited enough to pass their knowledge on to other Negro leaders, among them Frederick Douglass. He was soon to find that Brown's "character and conversation made a very deep impression upon my mind and heart." "His name," Douglass wrote, "had been mentioned to me by several prominent colored men. . . . In speaking of him their voices would drop to a whisper, and what they said of him made me very eager to know and see him." [60]

Brown was equally eager to know Douglass, who had just returned from a tour of Great Britain in which his personality and words against slavery drew tremendous audiences and made a profound impression. Although in England members of Parliament, including Richard Cobden and John Bright, stage and literary celebrities, had hailed Douglass, his progress for the past five years in the United States as an abolitionist had been almost as remarkable as his triumph in England. There his admirers had subscribed $700 to buy him from his Maryland master, from whom he had escaped when twenty-one in 1838, so that he would not be menaced by attempts to recapture him.

He was a phenomenon, looming head and shoulders over most of his contemporaries, literally as well as figuratively. After his escape from slavery he read everything upon which he could lay his hands, until his growth and many-sidedness seemed almost visible and as if increasing day by day. If he had a powerful mind, he also had an inherent eloquence that could clothe his perceptions in language that was irresistible. But he had more than eloquence. He was an actor, he had humor, a change of pace, an easy narrative style, sometimes alternating with a regal wrath that almost frightened his auditors. His voice was a vibrant, living instrument that answered to his will whether it called for ridicule, pathos, or anger. He could make his auditors laugh when mimicking a man of God addressing the slaves, unctuously preaching to them from the biblical text, "Servants, obey thy masters"; or weep when he told of a fellow slave being shot and killed when he failed to obey an order.

He had such vividness of feeling and of word that sometimes his audience felt as if he had summoned slavery before him and was about to destroy it by the sheer force of his exposure of it. "It was not what you could describe as oratory, or eloquence," wrote one reporter, describing a Douglass appearance in New Hampshire.

It was sterner, darker, deeper than these. It was a volcanic outbreak of human nature, long pent-up in slavery and at last bursting its imprisonment. It was the storm of insurrection; and I could not but think as he stalked to and fro upon the platform, roused up like the Numidian lion, how that terrible voice of his would ring through the pine glades of the South, in the day of her visitation, calling the insurgents to battle, and striking terror to the hearts of the dismayed and despairing mastery. He reminded me of Toussaint among the plantations of Haiti. There was great oratory in his speech, but more of dignity and earnestness than what we call eloquence. He was not up as a speaker, performing. He was an insurgent slave, taking hold on the right of speech, and charging on his tyrants the bondage of his race.[61]

He was handsome and had presence, being 6 feet in height, his nose large and commanding, his hair long and extending nearly to his broad shoulders, his features strong and the color of bronze. His father, he thought, had been a white slaveholder.

Above all he was believable. White abolitionists were charged with exaggeration, with the authorship of spurious atrocities. The whole movement was attacked by thousands who believed their stories of slavery only fabrications. But Douglass had felt the lash on his own back. He had seen his aunts and cousins and friends flogged until they could not stand, their backs open bloody wounds, and when he told of it, it took a brazen soul to doubt him.

There were endless arguments as to the adequacy of food given slaves, but when Douglass told of fighting with dogs for scraps from his master's table, that argument was resolved for his auditors. There were similar debates about the adequacy of slave clothing, but when Douglass spoke of freezing as a child in a single coarse tow-linen shirt, without trousers and without shoes even in winter, without bed or without blanket, he himself sleeping in a closet off a kitchen in a bag he drew over his head for warmth on cold January nights, this argument, too, seemed resolved.

Nor did he stress suffering alone. He told of kind slaveholders, of a mistress who had helped teach him to read, but he insisted that kindness was no cure for slavery, however welcome to the slave, and that a benevolent slaveholder was only an irrelevancy as far as providing a solution for slavery.

He was so overwhelming in his impact, so entirely convincing in his words concerning slavery, that the only possible attack against him was to say that he was an imposter. "People doubted if I had ever been a slave," Douglass wrote. "They said I did not talk like a slave, look like a slave, nor act like a slave, and that they believed I had never been south of Mason and Dixon's line." [62] It was a natural mistake, it being almost universally believed then that a slave was a thing, little more human than a cow or horse, devoid of feeling and impossible to educate.

On Douglass's first appearance on the platform in 1841 at Nantucket he so moved an abolitionist audience of five hundred that Garrison leaped to the stage after his address and called out, "Have we been listening to a thing, a piece of property, or to a man?" "A man! A man!" the audience clamored. "Will you allow him to be carried back into slavery?" Garrison cried. "No!" the audience thundered with one strong shout.[63] It was after this that Douglass was engaged by the Garrisonians as an anti-slavery lecturer and organizer.

2

On May 15, 1847, John Brown wrote his eldest son, "I'm expecting Fred Douglas[s] within the hour." [64] It is not likely that he arrived on that day for about that time Douglass was being welcomed home from his tour of Great Britain at a series of triumphal banquets and meetings in Boston, New York, and New Bedford. It may be wondered why John Brown was so intent on meeting the young Negro leader, thirty years old in 1847. He was known then as a Garrisonian, a nonresistant and presumably against the kind of invasion of the South that Brown envisioned. Perhaps Brown had heard Douglass speak; assuredly he had followed his course, as he himself told Douglass, "at home and abroad." [65]

It may be that he had read Douglass's first book, *Narrative of the Life of Frederick Douglass*, published in 1845 when its author was only twenty-eight and seven years out of slavery. Eleven thousand copies were sold in the United States by 1848 when nine editions had been published in England. It was also translated into German and French. It was a story of struggle and it is possible that John Brown perceived in it the leader described by the reporter who wrote of Douglass's speech, in New Hampshire; perceived something of one "calling the insurgents to battle" in "the pine glades of the South," saw a potential "Toussaint" not among the plantations of Haiti, but rallying the slaves of Virginia.

If Brown was disappointed that May 15, as he impatiently waited for Douglass's appearance, he repeated his request for an interview. Sometime in 1847, according to Douglass, "I was invited to see him in his own house." [66] By that time the Brown family, with the exception of Jason, Owen, and Frederick, who remained in Akron as the guardians of the Perkins-Brown flock, had moved to Springfield. Years later Douglass wrote of the meeting.

"At the time to which I now refer this man [Brown] was a respectable merchant in a populous and thriving city, and our first place of meeting was at his store," Douglass wrote in his autobiography of 1882.

This was a substantial brick building, on a prominent, busy street. A glance at the interior, as well as at the massive walls without, gave me the impression that the owner must be a man of considerable wealth. From this store I was conducted to his house, where I was kindly received as an expected guest. My welcome was all that I could have asked. Every member of the family, young and old, seemed glad to see me, and I was made much at home in a very little while.

I was, however, a little disappointed with the appearance of the house and with its location. After seeing the fine store I was prepared to see a fine residence, in an eligible locality, but this conclusion was completely dispelled by actual observation. In fact, the house was neither commodious nor elegant, nor its situation desirable. It was a small wooden building, on a back street, in a neighborhood chiefly occupied by laboring men and mechanics; respectable enough to be sure, but not quite the place, I thought, where one would look for the residence of a flourishing and successful merchant.

Plain as was the outside of this man's house, the inside was plainer. Its furniture would have satisfied a Spartan. It would take longer to tell what was not in this house than what was in it. There was an air of plainness about it which almost suggested destitution. My first meal passed under the misnomer of tea, though there was nothing about it resembling the usual significance of that term. It consisted of beef soup, cabbage, and potatoes; a meal such as a man might relish after following the plow all day, or performing a forced march of a dozen miles over a rough road in frosty weather. Innocent of paint, veneering, varnish, or table-cloth, the table announced itself unmistakably of pine and of the plainest workmanship. There was no hired help visible. The mother, daughters, and sons did the serving and did it well. They were evidently used to it, and had no thought of any impropriety or degradation in being their own servants. It is said that a house in some measure reflects the character of its occupants; this one certainly did. In it there were no disguises, no illusions, no make believes. Everything implied stern truth, solid purpose, and rigid economy.

I was not long in company with the master of this house before I discovered that he was indeed the master of it, and was likely to become mine too if I stayed long enough with him. He fulfilled St. Paul's idea of the head of the family. His wife believed in him, and his children observed him with reverence. Whenever he spoke his words commanded earnest attention. His arguments, which I ventured at some points to oppose, seemed to convince all; his appeals touched all, and his will impressed all. Certainly I never felt myself in the presence of a stronger religious influence than while in this man's house.

In person he was lean, strong and sinewy, of the best New England mould, built for times of trouble, fitted to grapple with the flintiest hardships. Clad in plain American woolen, shod in boots of cowhide leather, and wearing a cravat of the same substantial material, under six feet high, less than 150 pounds in weight, aged about fifty [he was forty-seven but appeared older], he presented a figure, straight and symmetrical as a mountain pine. His bearing was singularly impressive. His head was not large, but compact and high. His hair was coarse, strong, slightly gray and closely trimmed, and grew low on his forehead. His face was smoothly shaved and revealed a strong square mouth, supported by a broad and prominent chin. His eyes were bluish gray, and in conversation they were full of light and fire. When on the street, he moved with a long, springing race horse step, absorbed by his own reflections, neither seeking or shunning observation. Such was the man, whose name I had heard in whispers, such was the spirit of his house and family, such was the house in which he lived, and such was Captain John Brown, whose name has now passed into history, as one of the most marked characters, and greatest heroes known to American fame.

After the strong meal already described, Captain Brown cautiously approached the subject which he wished to bring to my attention; for he seemed to apprehend opposition to his views. He denounced slavery in look and language fierce and bitter, thought that slaveholders had forfeited their right to live, that the slaves had the right to gain their liberty in any way they could, did not believe that moral suasion would ever liberate the slave, or that political action would abolish the system. He said he had long had a plan which could accomplish this end, and he had invited me to his house to lay that plan before me. He said he had been for some time looking for colored men to whom he could safely reveal his secret, and at times he had almost despaired of finding such men, but that now he was encouraged, for he saw heads of such rising up in all directions. He had observed my course at home and abroad, and he wanted my cooperation.

His plan as it then lay in his mind, had much to commend it. It did not, as some suppose, contemplate a general rising among the slaves, and a general slaughter of the slave masters. An insurrection he thought would only defeat the object, but his plan did contemplate the creating of an armed force which should act in the very heart of the south. He was not averse to the shedding of blood, and thought the practice of carrying arms would be a good one for the colored people to adopt, as it would give them a sense of their manhood. No people he said could have self respect, or be respected, who would not fight for their freedom.

He called my attention to a map of the United States, and pointed out to me the far-reaching Alleghanies, which stretch away from the borders of New York, into the Southern States. "These mountains," he said, "are the basis of my plan. God has given the strength of the hills to freedom, they were placed there for the emancipation of the negro race; they are full of natural forts, where one man for defense will be equal to a hundred for attack; they are full also of good hiding places, where large numbers of brave men could be concealed, and baffle and elude pursuit for a long time. I know these mountains well, and could take a body of men into them and keep them there despite of all the efforts of Virginia to dislodge them. The true object to be sought is first of all to destroy the money value of slave property; and that can only be done by rendering such property insecure." [67]

It was then, according to Douglass, that he recalled the example of Nat Turner, declaring that his revolt had shaken slavery to its foundation.[68]

"My plan then," Brown continued,

"is to take at first about twenty-five picked men, and begin on a small scale; supply them arms and ammunition, post them in squads of fives on a line of twenty-five miles, the most persuasive and judicious of whom shall go down into the fields from time to time, as opportunity offers, and induce the slaves to join them, seeking and selecting the most restless and daring."

He saw that in this part of the work the utmost care must be used to avoid treachery and disclosure. Only the most conscientious and skillful should be sent to this perilous duty; with care and enterprise he thought he could soon gather a force of one hundred hardy men, men who would be content to lead the free and adventurous life to which he proposed to train them, when these were properly drilled, and each man had found the place for which he was best suited, they would begin work in earnest; they would run off the slaves in large numbers, retain the brave and strong ones in the mountains, and send the weak and timid to the north by the underground railroad; his operations would be enlarged with increasing numbers, and would not be confined to one locality.[69]

Brown had said he knew the Alleghenies well but where and how and when had he known them? Had it been on his expedition in 1840 to the Oberlin lands in Virginia or had it been when buying sheep in the Virginia panhandle? But both of these areas are somewhat west of the mountains. Had he taken time out to explore them, or had he surveyed them on some expedition unknown to history of which there is no record? Douglass did not ask him how or when he came to know the Alleghenies well, but he did ask how he expected to support his men and Brown replied, "He would subsist them upon the enemy. Slavery was a state of war, he said, and the slave had a right to anything necessary to his freedom."

In resuming his account, Douglass wrote,

But said I, "suppose you succeed in running off a few slaves, and thus impress the Virginia slaveholder with a sense of insecurity in their slaves, the effect will be only to make them sell their slaves further south." "That," said he, "will be first what I want to do; then I would follow them up. If we could drive slavery out of *one county*, it would be a great gain; it would weaken the system throughout the state." "But they would employ bloodhounds to hunt you out of the mountains." "That they might attempt," said he, "but the chances are, we should whip them, and when we should have whipt one squad, they would be careful how they pursued." "But you might be surrounded and cut off from your provisions or means of subsistence."

He thought that could not be done so they could not cut their way out, but even if the worst came, he could but be killed, and he had no better use for his life than to lay it down in the cause of the slave. When I suggested that we might convert the slaveholders, he became much excited, and said that could never be, "he knew their proud hearts and that they would never be induced to give up their slaves, until they felt a big stick about their heads."

He observed that I might have noticed the simple manner in which he lived, adding that he had adopted this method in order to save money to carry out his purposes. This was said in no boastful tone, for he felt that he had delayed already too long and had no room to boast either his zeal or his self denial. Had some men made such display of rigid virtue, I should have rejected it, as affected, false, and hypocritical, but in John Brown, I felt it to be real as iron or granite.[70]

3

As Douglass left John Brown's home after spending the night he was half convinced that his host had been right, that only blood and force would loose the slaveholder's grip on the millions he held in bondage, that profitable property, human or otherwise, would never be relinquished without a struggle. Occasionally he felt, but only occasionally, that over long years persuasion had failed, moral appeal had been fruitless, political effort without result, and that it was possible that only John Brown's plan offered a chance for freedom. "While I continued to write and speak against slavery," he reported, "I became all the same less hopeful of its peaceful abolition. My utterances became more and more tinged by the color of this man's strong impressions." Not long after visiting Brown, Douglass shocked a convention of Garrisonians at Salem, Ohio, by declaring that "slavery could only be destroyed by bloodshed." [71]

If the effect of the visit was great on Douglass, it was probably equally great on Brown. His plan may have seemed to him to be emerging at last toward some semblance of reality now that he had disclosed it not only to Douglass, but to Garnet and Loguen, apparently impressing them all as a serious proposal. Hitherto it had been virtually the secret of his family, with one or two exceptions, since he had divulged his purpose to his wife and children in 1839.

Since then there have been writers who doubted that Brown had his idea so early, that he held it to him for so long, "sleeping and waking upon it, summering and wintering the thought," in Thoreau's words, and they have somehow made of their doubt an impeachment of John Brown's character and aspirations.[72] Only his family knew of it that early, they write, as if that were an indictment. But Douglass's account of John Brown's disclosure of his plan in 1847 and the fact that he actually carried it out in 1859 might offer presumptive evidence that he may indeed have thought of it as early as his eldest son said he did. It is not as if it had been said that he thought of a plan in 1839 that remained only a fancy, that never became reality. It became reality enough to shake the country and take the lives of Brown and sixteen of the young men who followed him.

To return to the Douglass visit, the young black leader influenced Brown in many ways. If the future was to show he misunderstood Douglass, it is true nevertheless that he saw before him an individual whose abilities were equal to those of any white man and this was important to him since from the very first he knew he could not lead an insurrection in the South, however controlled and restricted, without the cooperation of black people and their leaders. But Douglass may have made a lasting impression on him in yet another way, namely, as an editor and writer whose thoughts he must have read for years.

At the time he met Brown, Douglass was at the point of breaking with Garrison, over the Garrisonian refusal to take political action against slavery, among other reasons, and establishing his newspaper, *The North Star*, later *Frederick Douglass' Paper*, in Rochester in upstate New York. Brown was an early advocate of the paper, subscribing to it himself, as well as for his daughter Ruth and her husband, Henry Thompson.[73] Later he thanked his son John for sending it to him while he was in London. He read Douglass faithfully over the years, pondering his words on a wide variety of subjects, such as the Mexican War, the revolutions of 1848 in Europe, the Free Soil Party and its convention in Buffalo in 1848 which Douglass attended. He followed his articles on the rights of women, the responsibility of the North for slavery and anti-Negro legislation and discrimination there; on the Wilmot Proviso, the Fugitive Slave Act, and the Constitution as a basically anti-slavery charter, despite Garrison's belief that it was "a covenant with death and an agreement with hell"; on slaveholder plans for conquering Cuba and Central America; on Harriet Beecher Stowe's *Uncle Tom's Cabin*; on meetings of the National Negro Convention, as well as articles on the Kansas-Nebraska Act. He read Douglass on the propriety and justice of killing those who attempted to return a fugitive to slavery, on the hopelessness of abolishing slavery without force, on the aspirations and abilities of the black people, on the subservience of most Northern Whigs and Democrats to slavery, and on scores of other subjects. The articles were as vigorous and well written as anything in American journalism and doubtless deepened and broadened John Brown's convictions.

From the first meeting the two men remained firm friends, no matter how strange the association might have seemed to some, the copper-colored former slave who was handsome and gifted and young, the thin, sinewy merchant-farmer, already gauntly patriarchal although he was not fifty, a trifle bleak and narrow yet somehow attractive and compelling. From the first, too, it would seem that John Brown saw Douglass as a partner, a vital and necessary figure for his coming invasion of the South. If Douglass never agreed to such a role, John Brown knew he sympathized with his plan and had no doubt that he would ultimately be able to convince him of the necessity of his participation.

They were very different kinds of men, however much each admired the other. John Brown was as capable of guile as the next man but on occasion he was as direct as a bullet and scarcely more subtle. Every act and every thought, no matter what his delay or backsliding, finally narrowed to his single-minded goal. Douglass was infinitely broader and more complicated, and to him there was more than one way of accomplishing a given end, the best way not necessarily violent. Moreover, as a leader of the Negro people he could not indulge himself in possible mistakes, particularly violent mistakes, without bringing tragedy to the people he led. Nor did he favor death and failure as a method of liberation, yet there came a time when both seemed to lie in the path he was being urged to take.

XVIII

The Trials
of Commerce

JOHN BROWN was a skillful juggler, often maintaining in addition to the wool business three or four anti-slavery projects in being at the same time, dashing here and there in his effort to keep them going, and if now and again one slipped from his grasp, it was small wonder. As in any juggling act, each object was synchronized and connected with the others and when all were circling about him it was sometimes difficult to separate wool from abolition or clearly define one project from another.

When he was rushing over Europe, as he soon would be, trying to rescue the affairs of the American wool farmer by gaining for him an export market, as he studied military affairs and the battlefield at Waterloo in preparation for his coming invasion, it might have been difficult to tell where the wool broker ended and the militant abolitionist began. When he moved most of his family to the wilderness of New York's Adirondacks in Essex County, he himself shuttling between the wool business in Springfield and the forested mountains near the Canadian border to help the colony of black farmers which had settled there, he was certainly aiding the Negro people. On the other hand, he liked to think he had made this move as preparation for his trip to Europe and partly in an effort to reduce the expense of maintaining his family while he was away.

When he wrote an article posing as a Negro counseling his fellow blacks against "tamely submitting to every species of contempt and wrong instead of nobly resisting," [1] he was, in his own view at any rate, furthering the cause of black liberation. Yet he was also obtaining surcease from the painful problems of the wool business. For it was clear that his plans for liberation liberated him and that he turned to them most frequently when harried most by the trials of commerce.

The wool business was so exhausting that he had sore need of a change of pace. It was an overwhelming and even passionate experience, testing him in every fiber, calling into question his ability if not his integrity, ranging in space from Akron to Brussels to Hamburg, from Springfield to London and Paris and a good many points in between. It involved some of the largest wool manufacturers in the United States as well as the owners of the finest flocks of the Union.

John Brown regarded himself as the guardian of these flocks, the one who would determine if they grew and prospered or vanished because they could not be made to pay. He was, too, or so he thought, the tactician and strategist of the American wool farmers, and as later in the Kansas civil war he was to advocate opening up a second front against slavery in the South, so he tried in this fight to open up a second front in Europe. For weeks and months at a time he forced himself to forego all thoughts of slavery and devote himself entirely to the American wool farmer whose problems he had somehow taken on his back. That it had come about through his own dominating character, inducing others to accept his solutions, did not lessen but rather increased the weight of his responsibility. It was a burden almost too heavy to bear and there was no denying that when harassed beyond endurance by demands for money for wool he had not sold, when charged by farmers with incompetence or worse, when confused by the complications of insurance, freight charges, notes due, rates of exchange, and an endless correspondence, he was inclined to seek relief through escape to the countryside and the more congenial problems of abolition. It was his weakness, at least as far as business was concerned, that he always knew there was a larger world than wool, a greater necessity than raising its price.

THE BARGAINER

I

John Brown's confidence in his ability to combine wool and abolition never did quite vanish but it did fluctuate in intensity. Often he was sure while pressing his anti-slavery plans that he was going to best the wool manufacturers and drive up the price of wool, writing one with cheerful insolence, "I expect to blow all you poor famished wool manufacturers sky low." [2] With equal cheer he wrote another, "We are classing some wool today that would make you whistle." [3]

Occasionally he assuaged his political conscience by using business letters to write mockingly of the "doughfaces"—the Northern congressmen with Southern principles—who had aided in bringing the annexation of Texas, the Mexican War, and the Walker Tariff, nonprotectionist and for revenue only, which had depressed the price of wool.[4] He was convinced at times, even as late as 1849, that he was a cunning bargainer and, in an excess of confidence and good spirits, he once called himself in a letter to Colonel Perkins "Yankee Brown," to indicate his shrewdness as a trader.[5]

During these periods of near joviality, he addressed, whether in speech or letter, the dignified and wealthy Lowell wool manufacturer, Samuel Lawrence, as "Lawrence, the Just." [6] The appellation could be used as praise when Lawrence's price for wool was satisfactory and as derision when John Brown thought it unconscionably low. "Lawrence the Just was in a desperate rage, & foam, with Yankee Brown," he wrote Perkins, in telling how he was forcing Lawrence to buy wool at a high price. "He says," he continued with satisfaction, "that I am a disgrace to humanity." * [7]

---

* Some, including members of a Massachusetts legislative committee, thought that Samuel Lawrence was himself "a disgrace to humanity," guilty of graft and corruption. It was charged before the committee that Lawrence was responsible for the failure of the Middlesex Mills in Lawrence and the Bay State Mills in Lowell, partly as a result of a witness who testified before the committee that "the Middlesex books had been falsified by $103,000 and that $89,000 had been spent by the corporation presumably to bribe members of Congress. Sam Lawrence had also forfeited bonds of $25,000 each to the Middlesex Mills and Lawrence, Stone & Company but had never been obliged to make good on his bonds because his friends took over the companies and never pressed him for payment." Hannah Josephson, *The Golden Threads, New England's Mill Girls and Magnates*, New York, 1949, pp. 298-9.

Some wool farmers thought he was too aggressive and "too loud" in dealing with manufacturers, but he wrote, referring to himself in the third person, "The manufacturers would not care *a straw* how loud our Mr. Brown, *talked*, if in the meantime he would sell the wool at prices that would tickle, & that on a long credit without interest." [8] He often described publicly those to whom he was trying to sell as predatory profiteers, members of selfish corporations which, he said, as he had before a wool growers association in 1847, were "bodies without souls." * [9]

He was one of the first Americans to challenge the modern corporation, already embarked on the course that would finally result in its domination of American economic life. The refusal to pay an adequate price for wool, he thought, was based on the manufacturers' lie that they could not make a fair profit if they did so. He knew to the contrary. He had launched a variety of investigations into their ability to pay. Near the beginning of his venture, describing Perkins & Brown as "we wool growing Green Horns," he said that the firm "had been probed to the verry bottom by manufacturers and this year prices offered us for fine wool have been so unreasonably low as to lead us to enquire after their [the manufacturers'] health somewhat particularly." Declaring it only just that if the manufacturers investigated Perkins & Brown that firm should be allowed to investigate manufacturers, he sent the latter a series of questions, two of them being "Is your manufacturing business prosperous?" and "How much wool do you work yearly?" [10]

If questions, asking manufacturers to document his case against them, revealed a certain innocence, innocence at the beginning was Brown's chief stock in trade. It had to be since he and his partner had had no experience in the business in which they were engaged. In his earliest letters to both American firms and those abroad, he occasionally said that Perkins & Brown were properly only wool growers, only wool farmers selling the product of their flocks and that of their "Brother wool growers in different parts of the country." [11] Since they were not regular wool merchants, they did not know

---

* Theodore Parker agreed. The officials of the textile corporations, the Lawrences, the Appletons, and the Lowells, still called themselves and were described as merchants. In speaking of such Parker said, "The bad merchant still lives. He cheats in his trade sometimes against the law commonly with it. . . . He over-reaches the ignorant; makes hard bargains with them in their trouble, for he knows that a falling man will catch at a red-hot iron. . . . No interest is illegal if he can get it. He cheats the nation with false invoices, and swears lies at the customhouse." Josephson, *The Golden Threads*, p. 110. Francis Cabot Lowell and Nathan Appleton were pioneers in the establishment of the modern corporation.

enough to set a price per pound on the fine wool they wished to sell at home or to export to Europe. They would let the buyer set the price, he wrote in letters to manufacturers in England and France and Belgium, or to their representatives in New York City. In a typical letter to Messrs. Thirion Maillard & Company, agents for French manufacturers, he said, "We do not know what this wool is worth but we mean to sell to those who will pay us most for it." To an American manufacturer he wrote, after describing some wool on hand, "Please say what such a lot of wool would be worth to you. We are wool growers and not wool buyers." [12]

2

Perhaps such expressions of ignorance were only ploys to begin negotiations, but whatever they were, John Brown's confidence in the shrewdness of "Yankee Brown" as a bargainer was misplaced. He was more generous than shrewd, at least with the wool farmers, and more stubborn than cunning in his dealings with the manufacturers. He was consistently sympathetic with the farmers when they asked for advances on their as yet unsold wool. "Their calls [for advances] are incessant, & how to avoid sacrificing their wool, & yet relieve them, calls for all the tact I am master of," he wrote Colonel Perkins.[13] His solution was to advance, first and last and with his partner's consent, thousands of dollars on wool still to be sold, while stoutly refusing to sell it at prices he thought would sacrifice the farmers' interest. He always saw a peculiar virtue in not selling. He felt that a manufacturer refused was a kind of asset who would return at last when he learned he could not cheat the poor wool farmer. As a result of this asset, he did not sell out in 1847 or in 1848, and by 1848 he needed increased space to store his wool. Another result of not selling was that the longer farmers waited for their returns the more imperious they became in demanding advances and Brown was sore pressed to keep the firm's advances less than the total received by Perkins & Brown for wool sold.

Some said that in grading his wool, he overpriced the best wool and underpriced the lower grades with the result that manufacturers snapped up the last while refusing to buy the first. This was serious since the essential purpose of the wool growers was to force up the price of the finer wools to be used in the manufacture of broadcloths, doeskins, cashmeres, and satin-ettes. From the first he was caught between two fires, from the farmers on the one hand, who had to sell their wool at last no matter the price because of their need for cash, and from the wool manufacturers on the other, some of whom may have hoped, as he thought, that they could finally force him out of business by refusing to meet his prices.

It hurt him that farmers were often pressing him to sell their wool at less than what he deemed its worth and blaming him for delay in doing what he could not conscientiously do. He could accept the opposition of the wool manufacturers, but to be criticized by those he was trying to help aroused his temper and a testy sense of grievance. The first criticism came when he sold his own clip, or his firm's clip, some 2,300 pounds, at an average price of 69 cents a pound immediately after the opening of Perkins & Brown in Springfield, and thereafter was unable to sell much for some weeks for any- one at any price. The reason was the passage of the Walker Tariff, which, as we have seen, depressed the sale and price of wool for a time; but some wool farmers gave a less charitable construction to the incident. "Unchristian and ungentlemanly insinuations," Brown wrote to one complaining farmer, "are the kind of return we may always expect from a certain class of persons." [14] And to another, he wrote near the end of 1846, "After spending months of painful anxiety, doing our utmost to dispose of the wool entrusted to us by our friends, we are still obliged to report it unsold, & we find there has existed a determination on the part of some of the principle manufacturers to smother us out effectually." [15]

"Uncle John was no *trader*," said E. C. Leonard, a business acquaintance of John Brown's.

He waited until his wools were graded, and then fixed a price; if this suited the manufacturers they took the fleeces; if not they bought elsewhere, and Uncle John had to submit finally to a much less price than he could have got. Yet he was a scrupulously honest and upright man,—hard and inflexible, but everybody had just what belonged to him. Brown was in a position to make a fortune, and a regular-bred merchant would have done so,—benefiting the wool growers and the manufacturers mutually. . . .[16]

He had other critics, the foremost being Aaron Erickson, a wool dealer of western New York, who had for some months been suspicious of him and his plan to classify wool. He felt that the method by which the manufacturers purchased ungraded wool from single farmers was eminently just and he expected to find when he arrived at Springfield a sharper and a crook, using wool farmers for his own profit. Instead, he wrote, he found a frank and simple man of "an almost childlike ignorance of the great enterprise in which he was embarking," selling his lower grades for much less than they were worth while pricing his finer grades infinitely higher than manufacturers would pay.

He had, said Erickson, an inflexible confidence in himself and his classifications, willing enough to listen courteously to Erickson's many objections but completely and utterly unimpressed. Even when Erickson switched fleeces from one classification to another when Brown's back was turned, the latter refused to take notice and insisted as they continued arguing that the fleeces were still correctly classified. Erickson was convinced that John Brown was as innocent of any intent to defraud as he was opinionated and wrongheaded, but destined for ruin, a sacrifice and "a victim of his own delusions."[17]

"... LET OUR MOTTO STILL BE ACTION, ACTION ..."

I

If John Brown had the weight of wool upon him he also had the weight of his own character, predominantly somber, however streaked with spells of optimism and romantic dreams of some magnificent future triumph. During his first year in Springfield, when most of his family was still back in Akron, he spent his nights in the loneliness of a room at the Massasoit Inn, poring over his Bible and doubtless wondering, as he did more and more, why his elder children were beginning to doubt its incontrovertible truth, yet freely taking to himself the blame.

At such times he almost basked in self-recrimination,[18] dwelling on "the follies and faults" with which he was "justly chargeable," and blaming himself not only for his children's failures but for his unfeelingness in leaving his family alone and untended far away in Ohio. During these spells, he felt that even though absent he must be the guardian of his family's morals, felt the necessity to advise its members on how to carry out every duty, every day. But letters, no matter how frequent, were a poor substitute for the actual presence of a husband and father who, for whatever reason and however unwillingly, had, in effect, or so he accused himself, abandoned his family.

Strange, unreasoning fears and apprehensions always filled his mind about what his family was undergoing during his absence. Once he was so obsessed with the fear that the house back home would or already had burst into flames that he finally had to write, asking if there had been a fire and also pleading with the boys that they be careful in disposing of the ashes from the fireplace, certain that they did not contain live embers. At the same time he was troubled with a persistent fear that "the snow will be left to pile on the roof of the shed till it breaks down, & kills the Cattle or some person." [19]

He certainly would have endured his trials more serenely if he had had his family with him during that first year in Springfield. Despite an effort to retain a certain jauntiness, writing hearty letters of encouragement to "Friend MacFarland" and "Friend Blanchard," making the most of such sales as he did bring off, and telling them, as well as other wool farmers, to hang on in the struggle against the heartless manufacturers, he felt that the complications tearing at him were ruining his health. He was sure that if he could just get back home to Akron and his family for a time all would be well.

After a short period of illness, he wrote his wife on October 19, 1846:

My Dear Mary. I have but little to say at this time save that I am not verry stout yet, and quite homesick; and hope to get a discharge sometime before spring. Our sales seem to be a little more brisk which gives some encouragement. . . .
I send 2 or 3 Tracts, & I am about to send some Fish, Sugar, Cloth &. . . . Say to the boys to make ample provision for keeping the house warm during the fall & winter, & to be kind to each other. . . . I shall feel like one out of Jail when I can get ready to come home again. You must get some raisins or something on my account for Anne, & Kitty [his baby girls] to make them a small payment; & I do not forget that I shall owe Oliver [seven years old] a good deal when he gets done talking loud in the house. I want Ruth and the older boys to write me often. . . . I may think not best to buy Sugar here.[20]

Braced as he always was for news of tragedy or disaster from home he was shocked, he said, to the point of speechlessness when he received word from Akron that his youngest child, a baby daughter whose name was Amelia and whom he called Kitty, had been accidentally scalded to death by her sister Ruth, then seventeen years old. On November 8, 1846, he wrote from Springfield:

Sabbath evening
MY DEAR AFFLICTED WIFE & CHILDREN
I yesterday at night returned after an absence of several days from this place & am utterly unable to give any expression of my feelings on hearing of the dreadful news contained in Owens letter of the 30th & Mr. Perkins of the 31st Oct. I seem to be struck almost dumb.
One more dear little feeble child I am to meet no more till the dead small & great shall stand before God. This is a bitter cup indeed but blessed be God: a brighter

day shall dawn; & let us not sorrow as those that have no hope. Oh that we that remain, had wisdom wisely to consider; & to keep in view our latter end. Divine Providence seems to lay a heavy burden; & responsibility on you *my dear Mary;* but I trust you will be enabled to bear it in some measure as you ought. I exceedingly regret that I am unable to return, & be *present* to share your trials with you: but anxious as I am to be once more at home I do not feel at liberty to return yet. I hope to be able to get away before verry long; but cannot say when. I trust that none of you will feel disposed to cast an unreasonable blame on my dear Ruth on account of the dreadful trial we are called [to] suffer; for if the want of proper care in each, & all of us has not been attended with fatal consequences, it is no thanks to us.

If I had a right sence of my habitual neglect of my familys Eternal interests; I should probably go crazy. I humbly hope this dreadful afflictive Providence will lead us all more properly to appreciate the amazeing, unforseen, untold, consequences; that hang upon the right or wrong doing of things seemingly of trifling account. Who can tell or comprehend the vast results for good or for evil; that are to follow the saying of one little word. Everything worthy of being done *at all;* is worthy of being done in *good earnest,* & in the best possible manner. We are in midling health & expect to write some of you again soon. Our warmest thanks to our kind friends Mr. & Mrs. Perkins & family. From your affectionate husband, & father

JOHN BROWN.[21]

More than a fortnight later he was still thinking of the dead child and wondering if a father should absent himself from his family even if he did so in order to advance the fortunes of the country's wool growers. "Of the motives that lead one into such business as will, or does deprive me of the society of my family I will say nothing," he wrote his wife,

but any ideas that to me the separation is not a painful one are wholly mistaken ones. I have sailed over a somewhat stormy sea for nearly half a century, & have experienced enough to teach me thoroughly that I may most reasonably buckle up & be prepared for the tempest. Mary let us try to maintain a cheerful self-command while we are tossing up & down, & let our motto still be Action, Action, as we have but one life to live.[22]

He mentioned his homesickness repeatedly in his letters from Springfield to his family in Akron and as he suffered his separation he often thought of the Negro slaves sold away and separated forever from their parents or children. His own plight, he wrote, should make him "feel the more for vast numbers who are forced away from their dearest relatives with little if any hope of ever meeting them again on this side [of] the grave." [23] While thinking of his Akron home, and of how his wife maintained it, he wrote from Springfield what for him was an ardent love letter:

"It is once more Sabbath evening," he began,

& nothing so much accords with my feelings as to spend a portion of it converse-ing with the partner of my own choice, & the sharer of my poverty, trials, dis-credit, & sore afflictions; as well as what of comfort, & seeming prosperity has fallen to my lot. . . . I would you should realize that notwithstanding I am absent in boddy I am verry much of the time present in spirit. I do not forget the firm attachment of her who has remained my fast, & faithful affectionate friend, when others said of me (now that he lieth he shall rise up no more.)

When I reflect on these things together with the verry considerable difference in our age, as well as all the follies, & faults with which I am justly chargeable, I really admire at your constancy; & I really feel notwithstanding I sometimes chide you severely that you ar[e] *really* my better half.

I now feel encouraged to believe that my absence will not be verry long. After being so much away, it seems as if I knew pretty well how to appreciate the quiet of home. There is a peculiar music in the word which a half years absence in a distant country would enable you to understand. Millions there are who have no such thing to lay claim to.

I feel considerable regret by turns that I have lived so many years, & have in reality done so verry little to increase the amount of human happiness. I often regret that my manner is no more kind & affectionate to those I really love, & esteem; but I trust my friends will overlook my harsh rough ways when I cease to be in their way as an occasion of pain, & unhappiness.

In immagaination I often see you in your room with Little Chick [the baby daughter, Sarah], & that strange Anna [four years old]. You must say to her that Father means to come home before long, & kiss someboddy. I will close for this time by saying what is my growing resolution to endeavour to promote my *own* happiness by doing what I can to render those around me more so.

If the large boys do wrong call them alone into your rooms, & expostulate with them kindly, & see if you cannot reach them by a kind but powerful appeal to their honor. I do not claim that such a theory accords verry much with *my prac-tice. I frankly confess it does not;* but I want *your face* to shine even if my own should be dark, & cloudy.[24]

But usually his letters contain less of affection and more of practical affairs. "It will be best for Owen," he writes from Springfield, "to take the 2nd. thickest calf skin to the shoemaker, so that the little boys may have their boots made up early, & be sure to have the boots made uncommon large to meet the growth of their feet. . . . Skins in the closet where flour is kept if not moved." [25]

2

It was a poor thing after the excitement of Frederick Douglass's visit to be forced to return to the prosaic business of wool. At least he had his family with him again, for they moved to Springfield in the summer of 1847; but the manufacturers were pressing him hard, some continuing to boycott his wool and refusing to buy his finer grades even when in desperation he finally priced them lower than they were bringing on the market.

For at least twelve hours every day, save for the Sabbath, he graded wool, answered letters, and then copied them into his Business Letter Book, dealing a little frostily with those manufacturers or their representatives who continued to examine his wool, his manner a rebuke yet always civil and sometimes rather casual as he explained to them their iniquities.

Sometimes Brown feared that one of his assistant sorters, who had always before worked for manufacturers, was still in the employ of one of them, surreptitiously throwing his finest and most expensive wools into the bins reserved for the lowest and cheapest grades. He had found fine wool mixed with his lower grades. But he was afraid of doing an injustice and never fired the sorter he suspected.[26]

But at night with wool forgotten, insofar as it could be, he could ponder the subject his days often prevented him from facing. Sometime in 1847 or 1848 he escaped from business long enough to take upon himself a new role, that of writer, a role in which he rather fancied himself and which he would enjoy periodically in the future when a few of his productions, mostly about his own exploits against slavery, appeared in the newspapers or were found later in his papers. This initial effort at literary creation concerned the black man, of whom he thought so obsessively, and was intended for the *Ram's Horn,* the anti-slavery newspaper of New York edited by Negroes from January 1847 to June 1848. It was one of his most ambitious works, entitled "Sambo's Mistakes," and labeled on the upper left hand corner of the first page, "For the Rams Horn." The purported autobiography of a black man, it ran to three chapters in length.

It is a peculiar production, but in reading it one must remember that most of those whom John Brown admired were blacks, whether Cinque or Nat Turner, Frederick Douglass or Garnet or Loguen, or those whom he expected some day to enlist with him in his attack against slavery. His essay is addressed, by implication at least, to the rank and file of free Negroes in the North who he seemed to feel could conquer their shortcomings if they could just become as John Brown was, or as he thought himself to be, never borrowing money or wasting it on foolish ventures. Neither did he smoke nor join secret societies (although he once joined the Masons), nor treat himself to fine dinners and fine clothes, nor spend his money at livery stables, as he wrote that Sambo did.

It was the best compliment he could pay Sambo, this asking him to be as John Brown. There was nothing of discrimination in it since he had labored even as a young man to make his white neighbors as he was himself, never hesitating to speak as uncompromisingly of their faults as he wrote of the shortcomings of Sambo. A prime tenet of Christianity then was to deal faithfully with the weaknesses of those one loved and valued. Could he do less for the black man than he had always done for the white? Yet he saw the delicacy of his position, a white man lecturing those of another race, but thought it could be overcome by becoming a black himself, at least for the purpose of composition.

The sentences of his creation are rather breathless and long, as if he were being carried forward as fast as he could write by the momentum of inspiration. But they have force behind them, too, the vigor that comes from one who knows exactly what he thinks and is pleased by his own shrewdness. They also contain as apt an expression of John Brown's philosophy and his own peculiar humor as anything he ever wrote. They have a beat and cadence, not uncommon in his writing, while plunging headlong into a recitation of Sambo's faults, and even contain a refrain, a regular repetition of thought that he may have believed rather fine.

"Chapter 1st," he wrote, in an effort that reveals more of John Brown than it does of Sambo, and then began:

Notwithstanding I may have committed a few mistakes in the course of a long life like others of my colored brethren yet you will perceive at a glance that I have always been remarkable for a seasonable discovery of my errors & quick perception of the true course. I propose to give you a few illustrations in this & the following chapters. For instance when I was a boy I learned to read but instead of giving my attention to sacred & profane history by which I might have become acquainted with the true character of God & of man, learned the true course for individuals, societies, & nations to pursue, stored my mind with an endless variety of rational and practical ideas, profited by the experience of millions of others of all ages, fitted myself for the most important stations in life & fortified my mind with the best & wisest resolutions, & noblest sentiments & motives, I have spent my whole life in devouring silly novels & other miserable trash such as most newspapers of the day & other popular writings are filled with, thereby unfitting myself for the realities of life & acquiring a taste for nonsense & low wit, so that I have no rellish for sober truth, useful knowledge or practical wisdom.

John Brown felt that he himself was widely read in sacred and profane history and had fortified his mind with the best and wisest resolutions, the noblest sentiments and motives. Continuing in the knowledge of his own accomplishments and the liabilities of those who had not acted similarly, he went on:

By this means I have passed through life without proffit to myself or others, a mere blank on which nothing worth peruseing is written. But I can see in a twink where I missed it.

Another error into [which] I fell in early life was the notion that chewing & smoking tobacco would make a man of me but little inferior to some of the whites. The money I spent in this way would with the interest of it have enabled me to have relieved a great many sufferers, supplyed me with a well selected interesting library, & pa[i]d for a good farm for the support and comfort of my old age; whereas I have now neith[er] books, clothing, the satisfaction of having benefited others, nor where to lay my hoary head. But I can see in a moment where I missed it. . . .

In "Chapter 3d" he wrote,

Another small mistake which I have made is that I could never bring myself to practice any present self denial although my theories have been excellent. For instance I have bought expensive gay clothing, nice Canes, Watches, Safety Chains, Finger rings, Breast Pins, & many other things of a like nature, thinking I might by that means distinguish myself from the vulgar as some of the better class of whites do. I have always been of the foremost in getting up expensive parties, & running after fashionable amusements, have indulged my appetite freely whenever I had the means (& even with borro[w]ed means) have patronized the dealers in Nuts, Candy, &c freely & have sometimes bought good suppers & was always a regular customer at Livery stables. By these & many other means I have been unable to benefit my suffering Brethren, & am now but poorly able to keep my own Soul and boddy together; but do not think me thoughtless or dull of appre[he]ntion for I can see at once where I missed it.

Another trifling error of my life has been that I have always expected to secure the favour of the whites by tamely submitting to every species of indignity, contempt & wrong instead of nobly resisting their brutal aggressions from principle . . . but I find that I get for all my submission about the same reward that the Southern Slavocrats render to the Dough faced Statesmen of the North for being bribed & browbeat, & fooled & cheated, as the Whigs and Democrats love to be, & think themselves highly honored if they may be allowed to lick up the spittle of a Southerner.

But I am uncomm[only] quick sighted, I can see in a moment where I missed it. Another little blunder which I made *is*, that while I have always been a most zealous Abolitionist I have been constantly at war with my friends about certain religious tenets. I was first a Presbyterian but I could never think of acting with my Quaker friends for they were the rankest heretiks & the Baptists would be in the water, & the Methodists denied the doctrine of Election, & of later years since becoming enlightened by Garrison, Abby Kelley [a woman abolitionist and lecturer and follower of Garrison] & other really benevolent persons I have been spending all my force on my friends who love the Sabbath & have felt that all was at stake on that point. . . .[27]

This was a reference to Garrison's introduction of an anti-Sabbath campaign into abolitionist ranks, which offended many anti-slavery adherents. Although Brown loved the Sabbath it is evident that he did not believe the campaign against its observance should be allowed to divide abolitionists.

If the pen is more powerful than the sword, as it was finally to become in John Brown's case, it was evidently not so at this juncture of his life. Nevertheless, he continued to use it occasionally, hoping that through it he could combine the selling of wool with something that might help the anti-slavery crusade. It grieved him that abolitionists were charged with being un-American for he felt that those who loved their country well enough to oppose it when wrong, no matter the penalties received, were the true patriots. It was with this feeling that he wrote Giddings from Springfield on June 22, 1848:

Dear Sir
    I have at my command a fund of One Thousand Dollars & some thing over to be expended in premiums from Three to Ten Eagles each [from $30 to $100] on the best cases of American Woolen goods manufactured from American grown wools *exclusively*. I wish to manage the business in such a way as to benefit the abolitionist cause to which I am most thoroughly devoted; whilst at the same time I wish to encourage American tallent, & industry. I have thought that were this fund or these premiums to be offered by you in some way as an encouragement to American Tallent, & industry, it might do a two fold good by showing that you are an *American* to the *core;* as well as an abolitionist. It seems to me that it might be so used at this time to secure favour to the cause of humanity which you have *nobly* defended often.
    I know perfectly well that I am not the man to offer them but I feel so deeply interested in having the thing done *right* that I will go to Washington if need be to consult about it. Now sir you will see at once that some of the strong interests of the country are to be both *flattered*, & *benefited*, by the encouragement these premiums offer. All the controll I wish over the matter is to advise as to the kinds of goods that may compete, & who are to be the Judges to award the premiums; & at what time the exhibition shall come off. . . .

He appended a postscript to his letter remarking, "Mr. H. Clay has been called an *American*. Why may not Abolitionists?" [28]

    The proposal never came to fruition although further correspondence seemed to indicate that Giddings was willing enough. Why it was dropped is not known. One might think that the reason was that the affairs of Perkins & Brown were nearing crisis were it not that Brown became more determined and intent on all his plans, including those against slavery, the nearer his affairs approached ruin. He found it unusually difficult to change from any policy upon which he had once determined. He might have succeeded as to

Perkins & Brown had he priced his fine wools a little lower, or dropped the cooperative elements of his program, or agreed to sell on credit, as most others did, instead of cash, but that was nearly an impossibility. "It was always difficult for him to fit himself into circumstances," a son wrote. "He wanted conditions to change for him." [29]

XIX

Timbucto
and Waterloo

No MATTER how hard John Brown tried he could not give his whole mind to wool. It was, to be sure, a nagging and a worry and a vexation forever flowing beneath the larger plans that he could not bring himself to forego. It was as if, despite himself, he agreed with his father and Ecclesiastes that the mere making of money was "vanity and a great evil." Always he felt, as he had written his wife, "considerable regret . . . that I have lived so many years, & have in reality done so verry little to increase the amount of human happiness."[1] As if it were becoming a matter of habit or a compulsion he could not avoid, his mind ever more frequently turned to the plight of the country's blacks, apparently becoming more occupied with the problem the worse affairs became with Perkins & Brown.

As early as 1846 he had planned to make his counter-move to American manufacturers by traveling to Europe to sell his wool there for a higher price than he could get at home, writing one Hamilton Gay in that year that he would have already embarked "but for unforeseen hindrances."[2] Such hindrances continued to delay his departure year after year and often they were real enough, sickness in his family, or the necessity of his presence at the Springfield wool depot. But often he was diverted from wool by some happening or idea that he fancied he might somehow use in his plan for black liberation. So it was, for example, after Gerrit Smith's announcement on August 1, 1846, that he was giving three thousand farms in eight counties in New York State to three thousand black men, many of whom were escaped slaves and some of whom would soon be trying to farm rocky acres of the Adirondacks in Essex and Franklin counties.

It was not long, particularly when he was suffering acutely from what he called "a most wearing, perplexing, & harrassing business,"[3] before Brown was imagining himself living among these blacks, many of whom had never farmed before. He liked to fancy himself far from the city of Springfield, pioneering as when a youth, showing Mr. Smith's settlers how to clear land, fell trees, burn brush, build cabins, plant, cultivate, and harvest, while helping them gain pure-bred cattle, hogs, and sheep.

After all he was a farmer, not a businessman. He had always disliked cities and he disliked them more now that he was being accused while working in Springfield of every kind of incompetence, delay, and mistake in the handling of the farmers' wool—and often correctly. How much more pleasant it would be in New York's Adirondacks, leading the black farmers in prayer, preaching to them on the Sabbath, protecting them from predatory whites, and perhaps even recruiting some of them for that visionary army which existed thus far only in his own mind. He always saw himself as the patriarch, the good shepherd, and it quickened his pulse even to think of farming again instead of being imprisoned in a warehouse, sentenced to an endless round of letters, complaints, fleeces, and haggling over prices.

TIMBUCTO

☆

It would be some time before he lived among New York's black farmers amid the mountain peaks of Essex County. In the meantime he had other dreams which lightened his burdens in wool. In 1847, when wool sold for a better price than it had in years, his chief interest for a time was the possibility of establishing a black high school in Canada where thousands of fugitives had fled from slavery. Writing about his plan to his oldest son, he said, "I would like to know if George Delamater would feel disposed to go to Canada in order to commence an Affrican high school provided he can be properly supported."[4] Delamater, now a young man, was the boy who had lived and attended school in John Brown's home in Randolph, Pennsylvania.

In 1848, Perkins & Brown apparently suffered a loss for the year of almost $8,000, but that seemed to increase rather than decrease John Brown's interest in Gerrit Smith's settlers. On April 8 of that year he deserted his business cares long enough to visit Smith at his imposing estate in Peterboro in Madison County, New York, meeting for the first time the large and lordly philanthropist who was to play as important a part in Brown's life as Brown did in his.

Professionally benevolent, a writer of doggerel verse celebrating birthdays and other family festivals, often trying for the gay and nonsensical if it did not war with his strong sense of propriety and religion, Smith was also a professional host. It was against his principles to turn any man from his door, with the result that he had at all times as large and queer an assortment of guests as any man in history, and his ingenuity was frequently taxed to make some move on so others could take their place. In at least one instance he resorted to prayer, publicly imploring God before the guest who had stayed for days and weeks that Providence protect him as he left the Smith roof and proceeded on his way. Through the divine intervention, or Smith's pointed prayer, the long-staying guest left immediately.[5]

Smith was immensely impressed by John Brown. A large, soft man himself, he could not help but admire the hard angularity of Brown and all that it implied of self-reliance and initiative. He was pleased not only by Brown's knowledge of farming, and his obvious interest in the black farmers, but by his rectitude so plainly based on Scripture. Thus it was natural that Smith welcomed John Brown's offer of help for his colony in Essex County near the Canadian border. Brown apparently said nothing of his burdens in wool. Rather, he said he would settle among Smith's colonists, clearing land of his own and farming it as a demonstration of how it should be done. "I will also employ some of them on my land," he told Smith, "and look after them in all ways and be a kind of father to them."[6] Smith was delighted. It was the beginning of a relationship that would cost Smith a good deal, including his reason.

In the fall of 1848 Brown took time out from the affairs of Perkins & Brown, despite the firm's deepening crisis, to visit the black farmers in a colony called Timbucto in the township of North Elba in Essex County. All about him were the peaks of the Adirondacks, the northern beginning of that Appalachian range which he felt had been created by God at the beginning of time as a refuge and field of operations for the slaves when they should strike for liberty under John Brown. He had never liked any country so well, as he wrote to his family in many subsequent letters, feeling a natural

affinity for the wilderness grandeur. He was, a friend wrote, "keenly alive
to the attractions of the wild and sublime in Nature," adding, "Had he been
born among these mountains he could not have felt their beauty more
deeply." [7]

Perhaps the painful complications of the wool business dropped from
him for a time as he went from family to family and from cabin to cabin in
the little settlement of Timbucto, telling all he met to be of good cheer for
he was determined to help them. They had need of encouragement for their
presence was not welcome to the few white residents of the area. There were
ten families in the colony, each with a grant of forty rocky, forested acres.
They worked their farms by day but left each night, huddling together for
company in their minute community beneath the stern and unfamiliar mountains. A tattered red flag fluttered from a staff in the center of the colony
bearing the legend "Timbucto." Its inhabitants may have been startled by the
sudden appearance of a strange white man who for some reason seemed
almost more determined than they were themselves that they should succeed.
To some, Timbucto with its shanties "built of logs with flat roofs out of
which little stove pipes protruded at varrying angles" [8] might have seemed
a tawdry and minor scene but to John Brown, one can be certain, it had immense significance. If he did not view it as a kind of prologue to liberty, he
at the very least saw it as a scene where he might "increase the amount of
human happiness."

Yet when he wrote his father some months later about his visit, his
words had their usual understated temperance. "I was on some of the Gerrit
Smith lands lying opposite Burlington Vt. last fall that he has given away to
the blacks & found no objection to them but the high Northern latitude in
which they lie," he wrote.

They are indeed rather inviting on many accounts. There are a number of good
colored families on the ground; most of whom I visited. I can think of no place
where I think I would sooner go, *all things considered* than to live with those
poor despised Africans to try, & encourage them; & show them a little so far as I
am capable how to manage. You kneed not be surprised if at some future time I
should do so. [9]

The mere contemplation of moving to Essex County stimulated him to
further planning. Even before he visited Timbucto, he was writing his son
John, suggesting that he might be able "to get some colored men of the right
stamp for colonists. I have thought should you find George Delamater at
rights you might do well to find out how he would like to go on the Smith

lands immediately," he continued, "& take a general look after the welfare of the colony, & see to making some beginnings." [10]

In a mood almost gay, he expressed enthusiasm in this same letter for the Revolution of 1848, declaring that it might extend to all Europe. "The slave case at Washington," he continued, "seems likely to set the Pot aboiling again in Congress. Ireland arming, &c. &c. Let us hear from you often, Your Affectionate Father." [11] The world seemed to him to be going well despite his own difficulties. The slave case in Washington concerned the escape and later capture of some seventy slaves on the schooner *Pearl*. Giddings defended their right to liberty in Congress and, as Brown predicted, "set the Pot aboiling again."

But for all his preoccupation with Gerrit Smith's colonists, the firm of Perkins & Brown still demanded his attention and still was going from bad to worse. Just how bad is indicated by some undated calculations in John Brown's handwriting which probably refer to the year 1848. The notation reads:

FREIGHT	$ 1,000.52
INSURANCE	140.76
COMMISSIONS	2,598.49
POSTAGE	1.10
CASH	52,701.33
INTEREST TO 7TH. AUG.	1,332.21
SUNDRIES	110.07
TOTAL PAID	57,884.48
TOTAL RECEIVED	49,902.67
	7,981.81

The last figure of nearly $8,000 represents the firm's loss for a year. The cash paid out of $52,701.33 is probably the total paid to farmers for wool, while the total received is the sum paid in by wool manufacturers. The calculation indicates that the firm received some 130,000 pounds of wool during the year and that the average price was less than 39 cents a pound. [12]

This was far beneath what John Brown believed the true worth of the wool. It must have brought to his mind again his old plan to best the wool manufacturers by taking the fleeces to Europe, although he made no mention of this for a time either to his partner, Mr. Perkins, or to any of the wool farmers with whom he was in constant correspondence. As a matter of fact, he seemed increasingly reluctant to go abroad. It was almost as if in his own mind he was counterposing the necessary trip to Europe, for so he thought it, with his desire to be among the blacks and mountains of Essex County.

His continuing preoccupation with the Negro community was revealed on October 28, 1848, when he wrote of buying five barrels of pork and five barrels of flour for the black farmers. The letter was addressed to Willis A. Hodges, another white man passionately concerned with the welfare of the new farmers and trying to help another colony called Blacksville in Franklin County which bordered Essex. Brown said in his letter that he had three barrels of pork and three of flour sent to Hodges at Blacksville, the remainder being sent to Timbucto. "You must try and make your money reach now until Spring," Brown wrote Hodges, "as I have now paid out quite a sum in different ways. I shall expect to hear from you soon; and whether you get the provisions all safe. Yours in truth, John Brown." [13]

He wrote a good many other letters in similar vein after sending shipments of food. His motto continued to be "Action, Action," but it concerned Mr. Smith's colonists in the Adirondacks rather than wool and Europe.

"OUR MR. BROWN" AND MR. McKIM

I

At the beginning of 1849 John Brown found himself experiencing an unexpected surge of optimism. All reports indicated, at least to him, that wool was scarce and that its price was bound to rise. He felt it probable that he would not have to go to Europe after all, the difficulties of Perkins & Brown now being only a part of the past. Again and again he wrote farmers that wool would sell quickly and easily for a high price. He would soon be proved right but in a way he had not expected.

At the end of January his prediction of high prices and quick sales seemed on the way to being fulfilled. He sold, or thought he had sold, 41,000 pounds of wool for cash at prices ranging from 34 cents a pound for his No. 3 grade to 84 cents for his highest grade, Triple X, or "Threble X," as he always wrote it. [14] This was about the best price he had ever obtained. From that time on for some months he would not think of selling lower, or selling on credit, and when farmers wrote asking for what price he could sell their wool he unfailingly replied that their best wool would bring 84 cents a pound, [15] although he was to sell little for that price or any other. He was not weakened in his policy by the fact that manufacturers' agents were traveling the countryside buying unclassified wool from individual farmers, some of whom included his own clients, at prices considerably lower than his and buying on credit. His former clients apparently believed that it was better to get something for their wool, however low, than to get only promises from Brown, who would not sell until he got his price and who seldom got it. Neither did it shake Brown nor his price when the 41,000 pounds he thought he had sold was ultimately neither paid for nor removed from his depot at Springfield.[16]

When he later substantially lowered his prices, out of pride formally keeping them on his 84 cent scale, he obtained his lower price by giving large discounts on each classification while stubbornly maintaining that the real price, and the usual price, was the higher level.[17] But even when his actual prices were lower than his competitors, buyers were not interested. It seemed clear to John Brown then, when manufacturers would not buy his wool for prices either high or low, that he was the victim of a conspiracy by those who resented his attempts to increase the price of wool by organizing its growers.

Writing Bishop Alexander Campbell, a sheep farmer of western Virginia and the founder of the Campbellite sect, he said, "Manufacturers are obstinately holding back notwithstanding our prices are decidedly below European prices. They are evidently making an effort to get rid of us permanently; & get the wool again under their own absolute controll." [18] And to J. J. Abbott, he wrote in April, "The difficulty has not been so much to get our prices for the wool as to effect cash sales at any price." [19] On April 14, he wrote to Samuel McFarland, "We have not the shadow of a doubt but that manufacturers can richly afford to pay our prices at this moment, & even *more* but they appear determined to rule *as formerly* cost what it may." [20]

By the middle of April it was clear that he would have to go to Europe and sell his wool there as he had so long planned to do, or surrender to the American manufacturers. He began writing scores of letters to wool farmers, asking, for example, "Will Washington County submit" to the conspiracy of the manufacturers or will they fight and stand together "like brothers" [21] by exporting their wool to Europe? Sometimes, despite his arguments for exporting the wool, he did not see how he could possibly leave either his family or the business.

His wife was ill. His youngest child was dying. His chief clerk on hearing rumors that Perkins & Brown was about to fail suddenly quit and took a job as a train conductor. He was drowning in a correspondence that he could not keep his head above, already weeks and months behind in answering vital mail. He was failing to sort and classify fleeces which soon would be shipped to London. The money necessary to operate the business was becoming daily more difficult to come by as rumors of the firm's impending failure spread. Who would tend to the business if he left? What would become of his family while he was away? Who would look after the blacks of Timbucto?

He was in a dilemma that was making him physically ill. Under the increasing pressures, necessitating quick trips to Washington County, western Virginia, and Ohio, urging meetings of farmers to send their wool abroad for him to sell, he fell sick. For a time it was thought he had contracted cholera but it proved to be only the ague, or malaria, from which he was a periodic sufferer. His shoulders were becoming more stooped as if he had been carrying too heavy a burden too long and his usual expression was one of resigned endurance.

He was becoming convinced by his own exhortations to growers that the export of wool would be successful, and yet he must have known that his plan defying all the usual laws of trade was a great gamble. American wool had never been sold in any quantity in Europe, while despite the tariff British wool products were imported here. It was true that trade papers reported wool was being sold in England for almost twice the price it brought in the United States, but it was also true that British manufacturers had an invincible prejudice against Yankee wool.

It was generally thought that the United States did not grow fine wool, that the farmers there habitually placed burrs and mud and unwashed wool in the fleeces they sent to market, partly out of ignorance and partly out of dishonesty in an effort to increase the weight. As a matter of fact he was told all this by Thomas Musgrave, an Englishman with a woolen mill at Northampton, Massachusetts, who offered to buy Brown's own clip from Akron for 60 cents a pound, a handsome price as wool was then selling.

If John Brown refused it may have been because he hoped to get between 15 and 40 cents more per pound in England. But it may have been also because he could not urge others to send their wool abroad while refusing to do it himself. If he knew the risks of going abroad he also felt he had no other alternative. If he did not go, the cause of fine wool was dead in the United States without a final fight. If he did not succeed in Europe, the flocks of the country would vanish because they could not be made to pay.

On April 30, his baby daughter, Ellen, died after a long illness. Whatever his grief, and we may recall that he "broke down completely and sobbed like a child," he was back at the wool depot the next day. Part of it was spent in writing of his coming voyage to the Ladd brothers, sheep farmers, who had telegraphed—a rather startling procedure then—asking when, if ever, their wool would be sold. "Your Tellegraphic dispatch received a day or two since," he wrote them,

> & by its contents we should judge you must have the Hysterics midling bad . . . J. Brown of the firm intends to go to Europe to attend to the sale of wool sent & to make acquaintance for the fine wools of this country as the best & almost the only chance of saving the fine flocks of the Union. We have no doubt of being able to make permanent, & advantageous arangements by so doing. The great press in the matter at this moment is that we are continually harrassed by our customers for money.[22]

In this letter, as in most others concerning business, John Brown referred to himself as "J. Brown of the firm," although occasionally he varied the designation to "our Mr. Brown." In writing his partner, Colonel Perkins at Akron, on the same day he had written the Ladd brothers, however, he used the first person singular: "I am thinking *hard*," he wrote, although in reality he had already made up his mind,

> of taking the fine wool of such as are willing to send it at their own risk, & going over with it . . . I have done *all*, *& everything* I could consistently do to get off the fine wools, but when I see manufacturers go elsewhere, & pay from 25 to 75 pr cent more than we ask rather than buy of us *in order to get back the full controll of the market* it looks dark.[23]

The partners decided not to receive any more wool for sale during the 1849 season. In addition, they decided they might liquidate their firm unless Brown made a profitable coup through the sale of wool in Europe. Naturally they did not wish this news to become general for it would make it much harder for them to sell at a fair price the large amount of fleeces still on hand. To keep the wool farmers in some state of contentment, Brown hoped to receive an advance from William C. Pickersgill & Company, British wool brokers with offices in London and New York, of half the value of the wool shipped. He did not receive that much but did collect some $35,000 on 690 bales, or about 200,000 pounds of wool, shipped by the Pickersgill Company. Most of it was disbursed in advances to the individual wool farmers who had sent their wool abroad, the remainder being used to pay Brown's expenses on his trip to Europe as well as to support his family while he was away.

2

If Perkins & Brown was nearing its end, there would be no reason for the presence of Brown and his family in Springfield, nor any financial basis of maintaining them there. The possibility of the firm's demise made Brown still more eager to move his family to the township of North Elba in Essex County near the black farmers of Timbucto. He made the move, among other reasons, for the sake of economy and because he felt they would be safer there during his absence, there being a smallpox epidemic in Springfield. With a small farm rented in Essex County from one Cone Flanders for $50 a year, he had driven to Springfield from Ohio, on an earlier journey there, a large two-wheeled wagon, each wheel 5 feet in diameter, and drawn by a single ox. About the middle of May he loaded aboard this wagon all his household goods, placing his wife, still in poor health, and the little girls, Anne, five, and Sarah, two, in chairs near the front. He guided the ox on foot, Ruth, twenty, and Oliver, ten, often walking beside him.

John Brown was elated as he guided his ox, wagon, and family up the Connecticut Valley, a pioneer again as he had been when a boy; if he was not traveling west as he had then he was at least moving toward a wilderness perhaps even more remote than the Western Reserve had been in 1805. Within ten days, near the end of May, they had arrived at Burlington, Vermont, crossing Lake Champlain on a ferry to Westport, New York.

His sons, Owen, twenty-four, Watson, thirteen, and Salmon, twelve, had driven a small herd of Devon cattle he had bought in Connecticut from there to Essex County and were already at the rented farm. As for the rest of the family, John, Jr., now twenty-eight, who had married Wealthy Hotchkiss, a classmate at Grand River Institute in Ohio, was acting as chief clerk for Perkins & Brown in Springfield; Jason, twenty-six years old, married to Ellen Sherbondy, was in Akron caring for the sheep of Perkins & Brown, aided by his brother Frederick, eighteen.

On his arrival at Westport, John Brown was afraid that the trip over the mountains to his rented farm might be too much for his lone ox, hauling furniture as well as a part of the family. He "bought a span of good horses and hired Thomas Jefferson (a colored man who with his family was moving to North Elba from Troy) to drive them" [24] and his ox cart through the mountains to their destination. John Brown was in high spirits, his years and cares seeming to drop from him as he plodded along beside the wagon. The fact that he was in the mountains, God's bastion of liberty, and approaching the blacks, God's poor, quite apparently made him happy. From the first he had a special feeling for the Adirondack countryside and now he kept demanding that his children appreciate its beauties.

"The day we crossed the mountain from Keene was rainy and dreary," Ruth said,

but father kept our spirits up by pointing out something new and interesting all the way. . . . We never tired of looking at the mountain scenery, which seemed awfully grand. Father wanted us to notice how fragrant the air was, filled with the perfume of spruce, hemlock, and balsams.

The little house of Mr. Flanders, which was to be our home, was the second house we came to after crossing the mountain from Keene. It had one good-sized room below, which answered pretty well for kitchen, dining room and parlor; also a pantry and two bedrooms; and the chamber [upstairs] furnished space for four beds—so that whenever "a stranger or a wayfaring man" entered our gates, he was not turned away. We all slept soundly and the next morning the sun rose bright and made our little home quite cheerful.

Before noon a bright, pleasant colored boy came to our gate (or rather our bars) and enquired if John Brown lived there. "Here is where he stays," was father's reply. The boy had been a slave in Virginia, and was sold and sent to St. Augustine, Fla. From there he ran away, and came to Springfield, where by his industry and good habits he acquired some property. Father hired him to help carry on the farm, so there were ten of us in the little house. . . . As soon as father could go around among the colored families, he employed Mrs. Reed, a widow, to be our housekeeper and cook; for mother was very much out of health.[25]

With eleven in the tiny house, Brown said to his family, "It is small but the main thing is, *all* keep good natured." [26] He set the example with a cheerful burst of activity which included frequent visits with the black farmers whom he found unusually industrious and intelligent, as well as almost daily surveying to locate some of the farmers on the lands their deeds called for and for which they had been given inferior sites. Although he was trying to economize, "He bought a quantity of provisions" for the black farmers and their families and "some cloth to be made up into garments." [27] In addition, according to his daughter Ruth, "He saw in Mr. Smith's proposal" of giving land to the blacks "an opening through which he thought he might carry out his cherished scheme" [28] of liberating the slaves and, at least later, tried to recruit some of the blacks of Timbucto, including a Mr. Epps to whom he explained his plans for special fortifications in the Southern mountains, laying out representations of the forts on a drawing board.[29] None of the black farmers was impressed by his invitation but Mr. Epps recalled that John Brown "though about the farm like any other pioneer of the wilderness," always wore fine clean linen shirts and a brown frock coat, "never descending to the usual flannel shirt," [30] or divesting himself of his frock coat when he worked.

Among his other activities, it is likely that he gave attention to the Underground Railroad whose passengers had been seeking Timbucto ever since the black farmers established it.[31] If John Brown impressed his black colleagues, he impressed the whites of the district, too, and before June had passed he was being called "a kind of king" of the region, an abolitionist king who aided black fugitives and black farmers impartially, at least according to a Mr. Aikens.

Mr. Aikens knew the country well although he became lost, as has been told, near John Brown's wilderness home about June 27, 1849, with Richard Henry Dana, the Boston attorney and author of *Two Years Before the Mast*. It may be recalled that when Dana and Aikens met Brown after a hungry night in the mountains, Dana had the strong impression that Brown was at the moment of their meeting engaged in the act of forwarding two passengers on the Underground Railroad.[32] At any rate, John Brown was active and happy in the Adirondacks and reluctant to leave. He did not do so until the middle of July, when he returned to Springfield and the troubles of wool before sailing for Europe.

3

If John Brown was active on the Underground Railroad within a month after his arrival in the Adirondacks, as Dana thought, it cannot be overemphasized that his activity was not unusual. Rather, it was a common experience, a development which included an ever-increasing number of men and women, occasionally even in the South. For example, at about the time Brown was engaged in this activity in Essex County, J. Miller McKim, who was to become a part of the John Brown story at its most agonizing hour, was having his own peculiar adventures on the Underground in Philadelphia.

Mr. McKim, a former Presbyterian minister, was thirty-nine years old in 1849, a slim man with the sensitive, apprehensive face of one given to worry, if engravings of him are any indication, and a goatee so firmly and thickly jutting from his chin that it almost seemed like a handle by which to seize him. For more than twenty years he had been a member of the Pennsylvania Underground, as well as an abolitionist organizer and editor; but in the spring of 1849 he found himself involved in a stranger form of Underground activity than he had yet experienced.

He had been persuaded into his queer adventure by a Richmond merchant, Samuel A. Smith, thought to be a loyal Virginian and a staunch advocate of slavery. Instead, he was an important member of the Underground, traveling all over the South as if on business but in reality helping slaves escape. He had always worked with consummate caution until he became obsessed with the notion that he could ship slaves North packed into crates or boxes as he almost daily shipped more orthodox freight. All he needed to do this, at least for the initial venture, was three brave and reckless men: the first, himself, who would nail up and address the human baggage, risking imprisonment or worse as he did so; second, a man who would receive the shipment in the North where the freight might turn out to be only a body rather hard to account for; and above all, as far as bravery was concerned, the escaping slave.

As a matter of fact he had the first and last of these (himself and the slave) and it was the slave, a Henry Clark, who had suggested the method in the first place. Smith when he was approached had been reluctant. It was not only that any white man implicated might be lynched or imprisoned. More than that, he was convinced that the human cargo would either suffocate or suffer multiple fractures as the box was banged about from wagon to station to train to ferry, when crossing the Delaware, back into a train, and then to a wagon in Philadelphia where Clark proposed he be delivered. But Clark, an athletic, closely knit Negro of middle age, said he would rather die than continue as a slave, that he was willing to take the risk, and even that he would pay $100, money he had saved over a lifetime through extra work, to anyone who would consent to receive the shipment that would be himself in Philadelphia.

Once persuaded, Smith became an enthusiast for the procedure. He could see himself shipping North slave after slave, particularly after Clark told him that he knew of two other slaves who were eager to try the method. Smith's first move was to go to Philadelphia, where he promptly reported at the office of the Anti-Slavery Society. Smith talked to McKim, an essentially timid man, who if it had not been for the grip of a Puritan conscience might have been a conservative in a less compelling age.

At first he demurred, as Smith himself had, and when he at last consented his days and his nights were filled with visions of a dead body in the Anti-Slavery office for which he could give the police no adequate explanation. He, of course, refused the $100 that Clark was prepared to pay. As McKim wrote in a letter from the "Anti-Slavery Office, Phila March 28/49," when he described his adventure in the detail of one attempting to recall a nightmare:

The following Tuesday was fixed upon as the time when the box should be shipped and with this understanding the man [Smith] left and returned to Richmond. On his arrival there he wrote me back that for certain causes the box would not be shipped before the following week. This was quite a relief to me, as I had been in mortal fear for the previous day or two, lest the man should die of suffocation in the box, & we should be compelled on his arrival to submit to the exposure of a coroners inquest.

I wrote to the man [Smith] that on reconsideration the risk seemed to me so great that I must withdraw my consent to be a party to the scheme. He replied that the risk was not great, & that the man was determined to take it & that therefore he should on the following Tuesday morning put the box on board the cars & that I might look for him in due course of Express the next morning—directed to James Johnson—a fictitious address—31 N. 5th A. I replied that my mind had undergone no change as to the risk, but that if he was determined to send the box on his own responsibility—I of course wd make no objection.

An acquaintance of mine would take measures to see the box safely delivered. Having thus extenuated myself & this office from all legal responsibility, and as much moral responsibility as I felt bound to, I had things put in train to receive the box on its arrival; which in due course would be 3 o'clock next morning.[33]

At that time, McKim, who had not been able to sleep during the night, was on hand with an express driver he had employed to help him. It was the custom not to open or unload express cars bearing freight until ten in the morning, but they succeeded in gaining entry to the cars. They "were disappointed to find no box." "A letter, however came by mail," McKim continued in his account,

informing us that Wednesday was to be the day. So we were on hand the next morning with like result. But by this time I became so nervous from loss of sleep and apprehensions that the man would come to us dead that I [again] wrote to him [Smith] declining to accept the consignment.

This was Thursday evening but on Friday forenoon came a telegraphic dispatch saying, "Those foods were shipped this morning and will be in Phil[a] tomorrow morning." There was now no backing out. The services of the express porter were again put in requisition. This express man suspected, I suppose, what was going on but he had sense enough to *know* nothing. The next morning a little before 6 the box was set down "this side up" inside of the office door of the Philadelphia Anti-Slavery headquarters. It was just barely daylight and no one was yet moving on the streets.

The express wagon had left & I curtained the office, dreading that I should find the man inside dead. You can better imagine than I describe my feelings when tapping on the box & calling out "All right?" the prompt reply came from within— "All right Sir." I never felt happier in my life hardly. It was an immense burden off my mind.[34]

At this point he was joined by a friend and by William Still, a young black man who was the real head of the eastern Pennsylvania Underground and who would also help John Brown in 1859. "We opened the box," McKim continued in his letter, "and up rose—with a face radiant with joy and gratitude—one of the finest looking men you ever saw in your life." Clark, who never used that name again for fear of detection by his owner but who was henceforth known as "Box Brown," a name he carried with a good deal of pride, stood upward in his crate, extending his hand and saying a little formally, "How do you do, gentlemen?" With the same grave air, and before climbing out of the box, he said that he had promised the Lord that if he arrived safely, he would sing a hymn of thanksgiving. He then sang a hymn that began with the words "I waited patiently for the Lord and He heard my prayer." [35]

"He had a fine voice and understood music," McKim said in his letter. "It was impossible to listen to him without tears." Amid the tears Clark told those who had freed him from the box that he had worked for years in a Richmond tobacco factory, turning over to his owners the $21 he earned each week until his wife and four children were sold South in August 1848. Then "he resolved . . . he would be free or die in the attempt." [36]

He almost had died. He had begun his journey of twenty-one hours between Richmond and Philadelphia by sitting down in the box, which was 3 feet in length, 2 feet wide, and 2 feet 8 inches deep, with his back pressed against the latter side and his feet braced against the opposite end. The box had been moved six times during the journey from dray to train to ferry to wagon, and several other times, but never gently and seldom with any attention to the signs tacked on one surface proclaiming, "This side up" and "Handle with care." Twice the box was upside down with Clark on his head, his feet above him, once for 20 miles until "the veins in his temples were swollen to the thickness of his finger & beat like hammers." [37] He had a bladder of water to drink, a few biscuits, and a gimlet with which he was prepared to try to make a hole if he was actually suffocating. Sometimes, buried deep beneath other crates, he thought he would suffocate but was afraid to attempt to use the gimlet for fear someone would hear him.

McKim thought it a miracle Clark had lived and vowed he would never be involved in any similar effort. In making his vow he had reckoned without Smith, who was jubilant on receipt of the news of the successful escape. He immediately wrote McKim that he was sending him another box containing the same kind of shipment. McKim wrote back on April 8, 1849, "I must positively decline receiving any consignments and I advise you for your own sake not to send any. The thing is known to multitudes in this city & there is every reason to believe it will reach Richmond. You must not send any more of these foods, till you know all the circumstances." [38]

Smith was unimpressed, writing on April 11 that he was sending more merchandise. The next day a frantic McKim wrote, "You say there is no danger. I tell you you know nothing about it. It was a miracle your friend did not lose his life. . . . I cannot allow you to compell me against my will to be a party to what I so strongly disapprove." [39]

But Smith was not to be deterred. Two slaves were willing to take the risk and he shipped two more boxes to Philadelphia at the same time. They never arrived. The news of the first successful shipment had spread to Richmond and someone suspected Smith. Perhaps a spy had watched him packing the slaves into the boxes and noted the route they would take to Philadelphia. Both boxes were intercepted and the slaves within returned to their masters and whatever other punishment awaited them. Smith was sentenced to eight years in the penitentiary. While he was serving his term he was stabbed five times near the heart by a hired assailant and for a long time was near death. When he was discharged from prison, he emigrated to the North, arriving there penniless but still strong in the faith that a box, if a brave man were within, could be an effective weapon for freedom.[40]

As for McKim it was by such experiences that he was sufficiently hardened by 1859 to advance on a violently hostile Harper's Ferry just before John Brown was hanged. On his arm was Mrs. Brown, intent on seeing her husband once more before he died, and around him were hundreds who hungered to assault or kill him. Later, one shot was fired by an unseen sniper at him and a friend who accompanied him. But by then McKim had been trained to face such dangers with calm, if not with eagerness.

WOOL AND WATERLOO

I

Recently returned from Timbucto and its black refugees from slavery, John Brown, as we shall see, had much on his mind when he embarked for Europe later that summer. He followed his 200,000 pounds of wool—which had been shipped in 690 bales to London during May, June, and July—on August 15, leaving Boston on that date by the steamer *Cambria*. Although he was, as he wrote shortly after his arrival in Liverpool, "a debtor to Grace for health and a very pleasant and quick voyage," [41] adversity pursued him even while he was on the Atlantic. As he left Boston, the *Dry Goods Reporter*, a trade paper published in New York, was charging in an article that Brown's wool in London had already been sold to American manufacturers for ruinous prices to the sheep farmers, greatly below what wool was selling for in the United States, and was already on the way back to this country.[42]

Although the report was false, perhaps it contained some intimation of what Brown's opponents hoped to do. In any case, it was widely accepted in the United States as the truth. Immediately there came a flood of bitterly protesting letters to Springfield from outraged farmers who had sent their wool to London. Representative was the letter of Samuel McFarland, who said that American wool growers had been victimized in one of the greatest swindles known to man. Presumably he fancied that John Brown, still on the Atlantic as McFarland wrote, had profited from a kickback because the wool had been sold so low.

In replying to McFarland's letter, John Brown, Jr., said in part:

Your favor of August 18 is at hand. We are astounded that a man of Sam'l McFarland's judgment should so far lose his balance as to accuse us who have labored might and main for his interest as well as that of wool growers generally, of "practicing upon the wool growers one of the most stupendous frauds ever perpetrated upon men."

Now for the facts. 1st. There has not been a pound of that wool sold in Europe. 2nd A evaluation of about 200 bales of first invoice was made by a London broker. As follows:

Average rate for no.	2	.30 [cents a lb.]
" " " "	1	.33
" " " "	X	.36
" " " "	XX	.38
" " " "	XXX	.40

From that the Dry Goods Reporter made a statement which is of a nature grossly to mislead, as none of our wool has been sold. 3rd Our Mr. Brown sailed for Europe on the 15th and will be on the ground himself within 4 or 5 days more. Sickness in his family had prevented him from leaving sooner: but as it is he will be there before a sale of any portion of the wool can take place, in accordance with our agreement with our consignees in London.[43]

Although young Brown had disavowed the exaggeration, the reality was bad enough. The very low evaluation of Brown's wool by a respected London authority made it unlikely that he could sell it for higher prices. He had hoped to get between $1 and 74 cents a pound, the price being paid by British manufacturers for fine wool,[44] but his best grade had been valued before his arrival at 60 cents below the best British price.

Worse than that, at least from the standpoint of John Brown and the farmers who had exported their wool to England under his persuasion, the price of fine wool had begun to rise in the United States. Even before his arrival in England, his eldest son had succeeded in selling a quantity of wool, the first sold by Perkins & Brown in months, at prices a good deal higher than usual and much higher than John Brown was likely to get for his wool in London.[45] By August 31 the price had advanced so sharply, probably to about 60 cents a pound, that John Brown, Jr., proposed shipping the exported wool immediately back to the United States without even trying to sell it in England. He feared that the American manufacturers John Brown was fighting would score a decisive victory over him by buying his wool in England at the low London evaluation while prices were rising in the United States.[46]

2

The irony was that John Brown had been right. There *was* a scarcity of wool in the United States and the price had been destined to rise, although not as high as he hoped, just as he had predicted back in January and February. But neither he nor anyone else had thought that he himself would help create both the price rise and the shortage. He had contributed to both by his withdrawal of 200,000 pounds of the finest American wool from the domestic market.

But knowing none of this as yet, John Brown was blithe and cheerful as he arrived in Liverpool "on Sabbath Day," as he noted, August 26, after an eleven-day voyage. On Wednesday, August 29, he wrote his eldest son, John, from London, describing England almost as if it were some large farm, impressive on the whole but with some shortcomings. "England is a fine country, so far as I have seen," he said,

but nothing so very wonderful as yet appeared to me. Their farming and stone-masonry are very good; cattle, generally more than middling good. Horses, as seen at Liverpool and London, and through the fine country betwixt these places, will bear no comparison with those of our Northern States, as they average.

I am here [London] told that I must go to the Park to see the fine horses of England, and I suppose I must; for the streets of London and Liverpool do not exhibit half the display of fine horses as do those of our cities. But what I judge from more than anything is the numerous breeding mares and colts among the growers. Their hogs are generally good, and mutton-sheep are almost everywhere as fat as pork.

Thinking of one of his employees, a wool sorter for Perkins & Brown, he concluded, "Tell my friend Middleton and wife that England affords me plenty of roast beef and mutton of the finest water, and done up in a style not to be exceeded." [47]

Although John Brown's wool was not thought remarkable by the English, he was. The English wool buyers gathered around him at later sales as interested as if he were Leatherstocking or some frontiersman, but it seemed even more quaint and primitive to them that he actually thought Americans could grow wool worthy of sale to a British manufacturer. They may have been particularly interested, too, in the strip of leather this queer old pioneer from Timbucto and places equally foreign and remote wore around his throat instead of a silk cravat and in his outmoded, long-tailed suit of brown, as peculiar to the English as if it had been some strange national costume. His dress, however, was no more outlandish to the English than his Yankee twang, which made him difficult to understand. Although he clearly had a sense of his own worth and dignity he did not seem averse to the attention he was attracting, his bright blue eyes gleaming shrewdly over his great nose as the English gathered around him, intent on having a little fun with the provincial from across the sea.

They were convinced that he could not possibly know much about wool, at least with anything of the subtlety of a British expert, although the fact was that he could stand in the dark, a bit of wool in his hand, and by his sense of touch alone tell from what breed of sheep the wool came and often in what part of the country it had been raised. One of the men crowding about him gave him some hair from a poodle and asked what he thought of that kind of wool. Brown passed his fingers over it and immediately knew that it did not have the minute hooks, common to all wool, by which the fibers are bound together. "Gentlemen," he said after a moment, "if you have any machinery that will work up dogs' hair, I would advise you to put this into it." After that, a contemporary account says, Brown "in spite of some peculiarities of dress and manners, soon won the respect of all whom he met." [48]

However, those whom he met might have been surprised if they had known that the rustic wool dealer from across the sea was even stranger than they thought, that he regarded himself not only as an authority on wool but as a secret agent for abolition. At times wool was only his cover for more important business. Even in England and Europe he was to seesaw between abolition and wool as he had at home between Timbucto and Springfield. After a day on the wool market he would prowl about London seeking out wealthy abolitionists and asking their support for his plan to invade the South.

He did not get it.[49] In addition, as we shall see, he was to become a kind of amateur and thoroughly innocent espionage agent, dropping his business in wool for days at a time and seeking out all the military parades and maneuvers he could, as well as battlefields, convinced that he was ferreting out military knowledge that would later be useful to him.

Still ignorant of the situation in wool at home, he left for France on August 29, two days after arriving in London, where members of the Pickersgill firm told him that his wool would not be sold until the middle of September. He spent his first night in France at the Hotel Meurice in Calais, perhaps articulating more loudly and distinctly than was his habit in an effort to overcome the difficulty the French might have had in understanding him. The next morning he paid 7½ francs for his night's lodging and *petit déjeuner*[50] and took the train for Paris. There he met officials of Messrs. Thirion Maillard & Company, the representatives of French wool manufacturers with whose New York agents he had already dealt. They said they would send an agent to London to examine his wool.

The next day he started for Brussels and Hamburg. It was a five-day journey with a stopover in Brussels. John Brown, as ignorant of French, Flemish, or German as a Neanderthal man, had to make his way about Europe by sheer force of character and perhaps an occasional meeting with someone who could understand him. He must have traveled by something resembling instinct, like some latter-day Daniel Boone tracing his way through this wilderness of strangeness, not by deer paths or disturbed leaves on the forest floor, but rather by the direction people were rushing for a train, or by the wild motions and unintelligible cries of an official trying to help him, or by catching a glimpse of a sign that he thought indicated Brussels or Hamburg, and at last, seated on some train with his baggage at his feet, glancing anxiously about not entirely certain whether he was bound for Belgium or Italy. Whatever his difficulties, neither Paris nor Brussels, London nor Hamburg, nor anything else he saw in Europe, impressed him much. As with the horses in England, he had seen better in the United States. "He thought," said a friend, "that no American could visit Europe without coming home more in love with our country." [51]

It was on this trip to Brussels and Hamburg that he ceased being a wool merchant for a time and assumed the more congenial role of military abolitionist. After arriving in Brussels he traveled to the battlefield at Waterloo, paying particular attention to its contours as any surveyor might, and concluding, he later said, that Napoleon had made a good many mistakes, particularly in his choice of position.[52] If wool brought him little but vexation, one can be sure he enjoyed his role at Waterloo, disguised as an elderly provincial tourist, although as unmistakably American as an Iroquois, no one but himself knowing that he was in reality a warrior studying another warrior's mistakes.

His investigations into military science on this trip must have been remarkably brief for on September 5 he was in Hamburg at the Hotel de l'Europe, according to his bill, where he stayed but a single night. There he had a breakfast of "1 Rosstboeuf," after enjoying "Logis mit Bett." [53] He also hired a horse and buggy, or a "Droschke," for 26 pfennigs, but whether it was used in an effort to sell wool or in pursuit of military knowledge is not known. Here he drops from sight, as far as any documentation is concerned, appearing again in England about ten days later. His friends thought, and he implied that it was true, that he had doubled on his tracks, journeying back through Germany and thence to Austria and France, tracking down any military maneuvers, drills, parades, or exhibitions that he heard of. In addition, it is said that he visited more of Napoleon's battlefields.[54]

However brief his military researches, their significance grew in his own mind, and more importantly in the minds of others, until by 1858 when he was collecting money in Boston for his projected invasion, some of that city's foremost citizens thought his strategical and tactical studies abroad, to which he alluded on fitting occasions, one reason for making substantial contributions. When telling Sanborn—his fellow conspirator, future biographer, and extravagant admirer—about his investigations, he seemed to that young man quite a military authority.

"I have heard from him an account of his travels in Europe, and his experiences as a wool-grower," Sanborn told Redpath. "He had chiefly noticed in Europe," Sanborn said admiringly, as if proving Brown's Yankee sagacity,

the agricultural and military equipment of the several countries he visited. He watched reviews of the French, English, and German armies and made his own comments on their military systems. He thought a standing army the greatest curse to a country, because it drained off the best of the young men and left farming and the industrial arts to be managed by inferior men. The German armies he thought slow and unwieldy; the German farming was bad husbandry, because there the farmers did not live on their land, but in towns, and so wasted the natural manures which should go back to the soil.[55]

And in his own book on John Brown Sanborn writes:

He had followed the military career of Napoleon with great interest, and visited some of his battle-fields. We talked of such things while driving from Concord to Medford one Sunday in April, 1857. He then told me that he had kept the contest against slavery in mind while travelling on the Continent, and made a special study of the European armies and battle-fields. He had examined Napoleon's positions, and assured me that the common military theory of strong places was unsound; that a ravine was in truth more defensible than a hill-top. . . . Brown often witnessed the evolutions of the Austrian troops, and declared that they could always be defeated (as they have since been in Italy and elsewhere) by soldiers who should manoeuvre more rapidly. The French soldiers he thought well drilled, but lacking individual prowess; for that he gave the palm to our own countrymen.[56]

3

John Brown was back in England by September 17 when a part of his wool was put up for sale. About 150 bales of his No. 2 grade were sold at from 26 to 29 cents a pound, the same grade selling in the United States for 35 cents a pound. "This is a bad sale & I have withdrawn all the other wools from public sales," he wrote his son John, on September 21. "I have a great deal of stupid, obstinate prejudice to contend with as well as conflicting interests; both in this country and the United States." He was beginning to suspect that the Pickersgills were in league with American manufacturers, fearing that some of his wool would be sold to their representatives at rates below those it would bring in the United States. However, he did not think it had happened in this sale. "I can only say," he continued, "that I have exerted myself to the utmost and that if I cannot effect a better sale of the other wools privately; I shall start them back. I believe that not a pound of No. 2 wool was bought for the United States. I believe that the general feeling now is that it was quite undersold." [57]

It was at this sale that John Brown was publicly humiliated. He was astounded at the way in which British buyers ripped into his bales. They pawed over every fleece, examining each one so roughly that he was afraid he would never be able to sell at another sale the wool that was being examined and rejected. "It is very much injured for selling again," [58] he wrote his son John.

But this was not the humiliation he suffered. In examining the fleeces, the British buyers found folded in them unwashed wool, twigs, mud, and other impurities, placed in them by farmers who hoped to be paid by the weight of the bale after a superficial examination of the outer fleeces, which were much superior to any in the interior. But the British had not been superficial. John Brown usually went over every fleece as he sorted and graded but in the rush for shipment he had apparently dispatched some of the bales without opening them.

However it was, he did not blame himself but the wool farmers who had inserted the filth. British wool manufacturers and buyers, he wrote, had

always heard the worst accounts from American wools as to the dishonest manner in which they are put up, prove, &c. During the examinations of some wool we offered at public & private sale made by many hundreds of persons search was made in the inside of fleeces, & coarse unwashed wool, & various kinds of filth, & waste matter found concealed in them. Such things were shown up as much as possible in proof of our character for honesty in the U States, & we did not fail of our own personal share in the compliment.[59]

The picture of John Brown receiving his "personal share in the compliment" is only implied. Yet it is not difficult to fill out the scene. In hundreds of conversations and letters he had pledged his professional reputation that the quality of his wool was equal to any grown by the British or anyone else. We can picture him standing there, increasingly embarrassed as the British shook out each fleece, occasionally accompanying their examination with exclamations of scorn and disgust. We can envisage some Englishman, a fleece in his hand which had sandwiched filth, publicly charging John Brown with dishonesty while Yankee Brown's florid face flushed a deeper red. We can see him as he attempted excuses or explanations only to fall painfully silent in the realization that there were no excuses or explanations for the discoveries of the English buyers. "Had no such Penny wise & Pound foolish thing been detected in our shipment of wool," he wrote, "not only could we have realised Thousands of Dollars more on that shipment, but another shipment would have been received with an increased confidence, & favour. Nothing will enable American wools to compete successfully in that market but the opening & removing from every fleece whatever may be in the least degree objectionable." [60]

At a second sale he sold some of his highest grades at from 30 to 46 cents a pound,[61] this probably resulting in a loss of between $17\frac{1}{2}$ and 6 cents a pound when compared with what the wool would have brought in the United States. Fortunately, he had only sold about twelve bales of the higher grades, much of it his own clip from Akron, when he halted the sales, directing the Pickersgills to sell no more of the wool unless they could get a price of 30 cents on grade No. 2, 36 cents on grade No. 1, 42 cents on grade X, 48 cents on XX, and 52 cents on XXX,[62] the two lower grades 5 cents and 3 cents a pound lower than they were being sold for in New York. As a result, American firms were anxious to get John Brown's No. 2 and No. 1 grades at the lower English prices and he charged that, even after he had countermanded the order to sell at these prices, the Pickersgills loaned money to a New York firm permitting it to buy for the countermanded prices a quantity of wool at a substantial saving to American manufacturers and a substantial loss to John Brown and his wool growers.[63]

By this time Brown should have shipped his wool home but we have seen that his weakness was not only stubbornness but an innate difficulty in the changing of plans once formulated. Instead of returning his unsold wool, he decided he would try to sell it himself, without benefit of the Pickersgills or public sale. He made a quick trip to the mill towns of "Leeds, Wortley, Branley, Bradford & other places," [64] between September 28 and October 5. Just before he left London on the twenty-eighth he wrote his son John, thanking him for sending him an issue of Frederick Douglass's *The North Star*.[65] On this trip to the English mill towns he sold no wool. Perhaps it was the discouragement of rejection that caused him to take some ale on October 2 while at the Scarborough House in Leeds,[66] for in the United States he usually stopped at temperance hotels and was regarded by most as a teetotaler. One can hope that it cheered the lonely American as he sat in the taproom of the Scarborough, perhaps following events far removed from Leeds and wool in *The North Star*.

On October 5 he wrote his son John from London that he expected to "close up the sale of wool here today," and he added, "It is impossible to sell the wool for near its value compared with other wools. . . . I have at any rate done my utmost, & can do no more. . . ." [67] On or about October 15 he sailed for home, all his No. 1 and No. 2 wool sold in London for a loss, the remainder, probably more than half of that shipped, still in London and not selling at all under the higher prices he had placed on it.

4

It may be that John Brown's business failures were as important to American history, at least to a limited extent, as whatever success he later won, in that the last might never have been possible without the first. If he had become the wealthy man he sometimes hoped to be, a merchant prince in wool, the liberator of the wool grower, or if even earlier in Ohio he had become rich through the sale of industrial lots, it is almost certain that he would never have gone to Kansas or headed his expedition to Harper's Ferry. Great wealth, fulfilling success, and the continuing effort to retain both, have not often made for insurrectionists or emigrants to far away places and there is little reason to believe that the case would have been otherwise with John Brown.

His failures and their ensuing humiliations, even including jail and his own self-indictment for theft, quickened his sympathy for others who were humiliated, poor, and in the prison of slavery. But more than that, his failures closed business as a field of activity and opened to possibility that other activity of fighting slavery which had been only a hope, or at best a part-time pursuit, until his grievous mishaps in commerce turned him entirely to the great question before the nation. American history may have been changed in its details if not in its essential direction by John Brown's failure in wool.

And yet even with the great good fortune of failure, which he emphatically did not recognize as such, it seemed for a time in John Brown's case as if he would insist on avoiding the grim triumphs awaiting him.

He certainly saw nothing to cheer as he boarded the steamer at Liverpool that was to take him back to the United States. Sea changes are often referred to, however figuratively, in accounting for transformations in climate or spirit. Perhaps John Brown suffered one as he stood in the stern of his returning ship and stared at the tumbling wake for hours on end, enveloped in the trembling of the deck from the ship's engines and the strangeness of the all-encompassing sea. He had much fermenting within him that might have made for change whether on the ocean or on land. He had been defeated, humiliated, every aspect of his policies in wool a failure, involving not only himself but scores of farmers on the distant American hills and pastures toward which he was returning. He knew he would be subject to recrimination and accusation upon his arrival but was resolved not to reply in kind. He would not return insult for insult as he had done all too often in the past.

Perhaps his Bible, read between glimpses through his porthole of the rolling waves, helped him toward the humility he had always sought but seldom found. Yet if anyone could appreciate the wool farmer's desperate need for income, the long tension of waiting day after day, week after week, and month after month for news that his wool had been sold for prices that would enable him to survive, it should be John Brown, a wool farmer himself. He would try to make the growers understand how and why he had failed and it might be that some good would come from it after all.

Upon arriving in Boston on October 27, he might well have yearned to flee to the seclusion of the Adirondacks and the comfort of his family, but instead went immediately to Springfield. In the ensuing weeks he received, as he had expected, an avalanche of criticism in the form of protesting letters. He was the target, he declared sadly, of "the most bitter reproaches and injurious insinuations." [68] He was accused, he said, of "unfaithfulness or incapacity or both." [69] He was regarded, he wrote, "as unfaithful, incapable and unworthy of confidence." [70] He admitted, humbly enough, that "our exporting fine wool has greatly relieved and stiffened the market," [71] resulting in good sales for all those who had failed to follow his advice and ship abroad. He confessed that the criticism of farmers, complaining that he was not selling their wool fast enough, had "litterally goaded" him "to desperation" while he was "contending with all the obstacles that human ingenuity could place before us," and that this criticism was one of the reasons he had sent the wool abroad.[72] He frankly admitted that he "never was so much in the dark as to what could be done in this country with wool" [73] as when he recommended the export of the wool entrusted to him.

His answers to the letters attacking him reveal honesty and a certain wry pain. He did not spare himself, his only defense being patient summaries of the manufacturers' opposition to the collective sale of wool and its classification at a depot, and a description of himself as one increasingly puzzled when the manufacturers would not buy at a proper price and when the wool farmers demanded that he sell and that quickly. After cataloguing his troubles, the illness in his family, the desertion of his chief clerk, the necessity of his often being in the field while unanswered correspondence mounted, he said in one instance, "Now it *may be* that many others in the same circumstances would have done vastly better. Do not pretend to say as to that: but did as well as we could, & did all in our power." [74]

Such concessions, even when qualified, were not easy for him. He had pride and did not know for a time how badly he was being hurt as he swallowed every accusation, making it his policy to turn the other cheek, a practice in which he was not well versed. Only once or twice did he flare up when accused, but with little of his old fire. Upon receipt of "a very insulting letter," he was tempted to a hot reply but instead he *"copied it & returned it unanswered."* [75] Proud of this victory over himself, he reported it to Colonel Perkins, emphasizing his spiritual triumph by underlining. On another occasion he indulged himself in mild retort with the remark to an abusive correspondent, "Your communication, seems a little uncourteous . . . but we conclude you are quite young." [76]

Shortly after his arrival in the United States he contracted to sell the remainder of his wool still in London and ordered that it be returned to New York. His highest grade brought 52½ cents a pound, not a high price but a good deal better than having the wool stored unsold in London. Even some of the wool he had sold in London, however, including his own clip from Akron, had gone so cheaply that it was to return to the United States where it was to continue to goad him and remind him of his folly. Not long after his return from England, E. C. Leonard, the Springfield businessman who had offices in the same building that contained the activities of Uncle John, as he called Brown, received a visit from Thomas Musgrave. He was the Englishman, now a woolen manufacturer of Northampton, Massachusetts, who had advised Brown against his London venture and offered 60 cents a pound for his Akron clip just before he had exported it to London where he had inadvertently sold it for from 30 to 46 cents a pound, stopping the public sale as soon as he clearly realized the price at which the wool was selling.

"Musgrave came into my counting-room one forenoon all aglow, and said he wanted me to go with him,—he was going to have some fun," Leonard said.

Then he went to the stairs and called Uncle John, and told him he wanted him to go over to the Hartford depot and see a lot of wool he had bought. So Uncle John put on his coat, and we started. When we arrived at the depot, and just as we were going into the freight-house, Musgrave says: "Mr. Brune, I want you to tell me what you think of this lot of wull that stands me in just fifty-two cents a pund."

At a glance, Leonard said, Uncle John took in the whole situation. He recognized his wool. He said not a word but wheeled and walked rapidly away. "I can see him now," Leonard recalled,

as he "put back" to the lofts, his brown coat-tails floating behind him, and the nervous strides fairly devouring the way. It was his own clip, for which Musgrave, some three months before, had offered him sixty cents a pound as it lay in the loft. It had been graded, new-bagged, shipped by steamer to London, sold and reshipped, and was in Springfield at eight cents in the pound less than Musgrave offered.[77]

John Brown accepted such hazing as best he could, trying for a spirit of Christian resignation. There were some, particularly those who remembered his Ohio fiasco, who were beginning to believe that he was one of the time's foremost successes at failure. It was possible that even he himself took some grim pride in his adventure in that he had played out his hand to the very end. He had not surrendered; he had only been defeated and that after opening a second front that leaped the Atlantic and stretched from London to Hamburg to Leeds. In a collateral sense, at any rate, it had also stretched from Timbucto to Waterloo.

Moreover, there was no moral collapse as there had been in his other failure in Ohio. He had not been an honest thief or any other kind of thief. Whatever the charges against him, it seems certain that in his venture in wool he was completely honest if also frequently incompetent. If his letters reveal a spirit of concession and confession, they also display a quiet pride in the faithfulness of his effort. Sometimes they almost openly ask for sympathy and clearly portray his feeling that few had ever suffered so much or worked so loyally in the interest of others. If he had failed, he had failed greatly. He had challenged the powerful profiteers, the manufacturers who were refusing to pay a proper price for wool, by organizing farmers into a plan for coopera-tive selling. In sickness and in health, in Springfield and in Paris, he had fought only, in his own view, for the prosperity of others. With these feelings, it might be possible that all his displays of humility were only the facade of a proud man who could see no other way to conceal an injury to his image of himself from which it might be difficult to recover.

Nevertheless he believed himself content and at peace after he had con-ferred with his partner Colonel Perkins. The colonel, at least, did not blame him. He understood the incredible complexity of what had faced him. As long as that was the case, he felt, he could take the accusations of others. Writing his son John about his confrontation with Mr. Perkins, which he had dreaded, he said:

Our meeting together was one of the most cordial, & pleasant, I ever experienced. He met a full history of our difficulties, & *probable losses* without a frown on his countenance, or One sylable of reflection, but on the contrary with words of com-fort, & encouragement. He is wholly averse to any separation of our business or interests, & gave me the fullest assurance of his undiminished confidence, & per-sonal regard. He expressed a strong desire to have our flock of sheep remain un-divided to become the joint possession of our families when we have gone off the Stage. Such a meeting I had not dared to expect, & I most heartily wish each of my family could have shared in the comfort of it. Mr. Perkins has in this whole business from first to last set an example worthy of a Philosopher, or of a *Chris-tian*. I am meeting with a good deal of trouble from those to whom we have *over advanced* but feel nerved to face any difficulty while God continues me such a partner.[78]

But however he rationalized his second and largest failure, or Colonel Perkins's acceptance of it, it was a fact from which he could not escape. His partner's kindness could salve his wounds but not heal them. Instead, they festered and their effects, however slow in arriving, were prolonged and painful.

PART THREE

FREE AT LAST

1850–1855

XX

On the Illness
of Indecision

IT ALWAYS TOOK John Brown some time to know that he had been hurt. By now he expected adversity and when he met it, it was only something to overcome. Perhaps that was the reason he could not quite recognize that adversity at length was slowly overcoming him. While his second failure was not fatal, it was almost so in a psychic sense, and for a space he might have reminded an imaginative onlooker of some gaunt old moose, still charging ahead, crashing blindly against all obstacles, after receiving a mortal wound. It is true that he recovered at last but he apparently went through a crisis, or so the evidence indicates, that even caused him to doubt for a time his ability to carry through his long-cherished plan for destroying slavery. It might be that it was only the foolish fancy of an aging and habitual failure.

But this was a slow culmination. When he first returned from Europe he had felt that however great his reversal he had resources within to accept and encompass it; and he felt so more strongly after receiving the understanding and encouragement of Colonel Perkins. He laughed as often as usual, which was not very often, although it sometimes seemed to hurt his face. He still called upon God with all his customary vehemence while likening himself to Job whose friends, he recalled, were as unmoved by his sufferings as John Brown's friends were by his failure in wool.[1] He still governed his family with as firm a hand as ever but his letters indicate a new tendency to lean on its members for sympathy, support, and even advice.[2] Sometimes he was extraordinarily cheerful and one son wondered how he could possibly be so in the face of his ever-mounting troubles.[3]

During all this time he never flinched from the consequences of his business reverses nor did he falter until near their end. It required four years in fact, and the dragging, seemingly almost endless suspense of the damage suits against Perkins & Brown, the resulting trials being postponed and adjourned and recessed and delayed again over weeks and months, before the crippling severity of John Brown's financial and psychic wounds became fully apparent. In the meantime he went about his business and his pleasure, or so it seemed to the casual observer, much as usual. He regarded slavery with an undiminished hatred and after the passage of the Fugitive Slave Law in 1850 he helped organize the blacks of Springfield into a system of armed resistance so militant that it somehow suggested that his old plan for invading the South was at that point, at least, still high in his consciousness.

It would not be so for long. He had been hurt, and hurt badly, and he was to be hurt more.

RESPITE

I

A man such as John Brown tries to heal his wounds by never acknowledging them. It was not, of course, that he did not know that he had failed in wool. But his troubles not yet having spiraled to a dismaying climax, John Brown tried for a calm exterior upon his return to Springfield from Europe late in October 1849, and usually succeeded in attaining it. He retreated from Springfield as soon as he could to the comfort of his family in the Adirondacks. On November 9 he bought a farm of 244 acres for $244 from Gerrit Smith in Essex County at North Elba township near the Cone Flanders farm which he still rented, his sons Owen and Jason helping him pay for the new farm and each having a one-third title to the land.* He had never liked North Elba so well. It was a refuge in time of trouble, a retreat so remote that here

---

* The deed was registered by the Essex County Clerk on December 13, 1849. Later, the land was conveyed on April 10, 1852, to John Brown and his wife after Jason and Owen had been paid $85 each by their father.

he was safe from possible process servers and the threats of attorneys preparing to sue.

His hiatus from distress was short-lived. He spent most of the ensuing year of 1850 in weary travel, chiefly to northwest Virginia, southwestern Pennsylvania, and the Western Reserve, meeting scores of hostile wool farmers and trying to persuade some to accept without complaint the little money he had received from the sale of their wool, others to return that part of advances which had exceeded the amount brought in by their wool. In either event, he had to beg and wheedle and justify himself and he found the business both demeaning and exhausting. He was so short of funds that he had to borrow, perhaps as much as $80, from his young black farm hand, Cyrus, the thrifty escaped slave now working for him at North Elba. On July 3, still on the road, he sent a draft for $80 to Owen at North Elba, so, he said, "that Cyrus might get back what he had lent us." [4]

In August he went back to the wool farmers of Virginia, Pennsylvania, and Ohio, spending three weeks in trying to settle up accounts. "I have now got nearly through settling with those who have money coming to them," he wrote his wife, "but do not know when I shall be done with some that owe us. . . . I now hope to be on my way home about the first of September, & after I get on the way do not expect to be many days on the road." [5]

He was unusually eager to get back to North Elba because his daughter Ruth was to be married on September 26 to Henry Thompson, a young farmer who lived nearby. In addition, he hoped to show some of his Devon cattle at the Essex County Fair which would also be held during that month. Moreover, he always longed to see his black neighbors again, worrying that he was not helping them to the extent that he had promised Gerrit Smith, and he liked, too, preaching to them on an occasional Sunday. [6] He loved the region, [7] particularly in autumn, enjoying driving his "long buckboard wagon" [8] into Keene for supplies, on a route described by a son as "the most grand and beautiful that I ever saw in my life," [9] his team jogging along while he listened, perhaps, to the rhythm of his rig's revolving wheels, occasionally looking back at the dust settling on goldenrod and asters.

Since he agreed with his son about the extraordinary beauty of the route to Keene, it may well be that on such a trip he pulled up now and again at the side of the road, lifting his hawk nose upward as his eyes, startlingly blue in the red of his face, searched the mountains, noting, perhaps, the wreaths of fog which sometimes shrouded their tops, or regarding an expanse of cliff ascending upward from a pond, the silver green of spruce, the scarlet of maple, the yellow of birch climbing unaccountably up the sheerness, their roots in ledges so narrow that their appearance in the upward thrust of wall seemed almost a miracle. All about him on such trips in and about Keene were peaks and valleys, Iron Mountain, Bald Peak, Limekiln Mountain, Tripod, Noble, Nob Look, Pitchoff, Saddleback, Hurricane, and, as he returned home, Old White Face rising at the head of Lake Placid.

When he looked at them or spoke of them he was at times seized by some strange repressed excitement. "He seemed to think there was something romantic in that kind of scenery," his wife said, who herself saw only a lonely wilderness with arctic winters. "There was indeed," a friend recalled, "always a sort of thrill in John Brown's voice when he spoke of mountains. I shall never forget the quiet way in which he once told me that 'God had established the Alleghany Mountains from the foundation of the world that they might one day be a refuge for fugitive slaves.' " [10]

2

It was in a rickety little church not far from Timbucto in North Elba township that John Brown preached to his Negro neighbors on the Sabbath. Usually this was in the afternoon, for in the morning there was customarily a service for whites which John Brown did not attend since he thought the preacher lukewarm as to abolition. Often his sermon was preceded by hymns and occasionally the Epps family, whose voices were moving and even thrilling, pleased him by singing as a special part of the service his favorite:

> *Blow ye the trumpet, blow*
> *The gladly solemn sound;*

Then, the black faces looking up at him as serious as his own, he would begin his sermon. No one could have been more intent on his words, more certain of their truth, more anxious that his thoughts become the property of those to whom he preached and so little equipped, it sometimes seemed, to make them so. Yet the thin, gaunt face projecting from the little pulpit with a remarkable earnestness had its own power and did something to overcome his limitations as a preacher. His text on at least one Sabbath was from Micah, Chapter 6, verse 8: "He hath shewed thee, O man, what *is* good; and what doth the LORD require of thee, but to do justly, and to love mercy, and to walk humbly with thy God?"

We still have John Brown's notes for this sermon, and although they are undated, it is very probable that the sermon was delivered before his black friends of Timbucto.[11] After repeating the verse, he told his audience, or so his notes indicate, that it was his object not only to make them understand in their minds but to feel in their hearts. Who that understands the requirements of loving justice and mercy and walking humbly with God, he said, and "does not live in thoughtless disregard of the course they pursue, like 'beasts that perish,'" can possibly avoid mentally saying "Amen!" to these injunctions of God? "Our reason will tell us in a moment," he continued,

that these are just the requirements we might expect from the *true* God, were we now for the first time in our lives, called into his awful presence to learn our duty.

Nothing but an incomprehensible stupidity on our part can keep us from breaking out at once in strains of the most exalted praise when we reflect that God is ever reasonable. His language to erring man is, "Come and let us reason together." What possible character could a fellowman possess, that would in our eyes be so befitting, as the character that God requires of us? Let us for a moment in our imagination look at the man who does justly, loves mercy and walks humbly. It would seem that the bare contemplation were of itself sufficient to awaken in us the most powerful hungering and thirsting after righteousness. . . .[12]

John Brown on occasion and in his own severe style verged on the eloquent. But as a preacher he was not always effective. He was obsessed by a kind of scriptural legalism and was intent on proving, at least in this sermon, that "the attributes of the One only living and True God" were mercy, justice, and reason. His black congregation may have listened to him more than to his words, apprehended his strange compelling personality more than the message of his sermon. However, if he himself received pleasure from this effort, it was but a part of the general satisfaction he experienced from this visit to his family in Essex County. He spent most of his days surveying, "working early and late," as he said, "tracing out old lost boundaries," always dressed a little formally in his frock coat with its tails; he was paid $2 a day, probably by the county or Gerrit Smith.[13] He exhibited, as he had planned, choice specimens of his Devon cattle at the Essex County Fair where they won an award and attracted much attention.* He was pleased with Ruth's marriage to Henry Thompson, writing his son John that he thought Ruth had done well.[14] He liked Thompson and the young man thought John

---

* The report of the county agricultural society said: "The appearance on the grounds of a number of very choice and beautiful Devons, from the herd of Mr. John Brown, residing in one of the most remote and secluded towns, attracted great attention and added much to the interest of the fair. The interest and admiration they excited have attracted public attention to the subject, and have already resulted in the introduction of several choice animals into this region. We have no doubt that this influence upon the character of the stock in our county will be permanent and decisive." Quoted from Redpath, *John Brown*, p. 74. Everywhere John Brown lived—with the exception of Springfield, and even there he bought prize bulls for Colonel Perkins—he introduced blooded stock.

Brown about the most impressive individual he had ever met. He was one of eleven brothers who between them, with their father, owned some thousand acres in Essex County.

Perhaps it was by candlelight, or from a whale oil lamp, and after a day's work of surveying, that John Brown read his newspapers, *The Liberator*, *The Anti-Slavery Standard*, and *The North Star*, later to become *Frederick Douglass' Paper*.[15] From the first agitation in Congress for the passage of the Compromise of 1850, which included the Fugitive Slave Act, all three papers opposed it as an essentially pro-slavery measure, condemning its failure to prohibit the entry of slavery into the Territories of New Mexico and Utah, but condemning particularly the provision for the capture and return of blacks in the North to slavery, without trial by jury or the opportunity of testifying in their own behalf.

The Fugitive Slave Act became law on September 18, while John Brown was still at North Elba. Before he left for Springfield almost a month later the North was at a higher crescendo of fury, as we have seen, than it had ever been before, a fury so intense that it would not be long until some Northern cities were on the verge of civil war.[16] The most reserved and temperate of men, such as Emerson, were soon to be writing in their journals with the desperate indignation of those who had lost their country and had been personally betrayed by those they had elected and entrusted with their honor. "This filthy enactment," Emerson was to write of the Fugitive Slave Law, "was made in the Nineteenth century by people who could read and write. I will not obey it, by God." [17] And Henry Thoreau, writing on the same subject in his journal, declared, "I hear a good deal said about trampling this law under foot. Why, one need not go out of his way to do that. This law lies not at the level of the head or the reason. Its natural habitat is the dirt." [18]

3

The conflict as it began in the Senate during the debate over what was later the Compromise of 1850, seemed to some, at least in the North, to be exemplified by two personalities, the unpretentiously drab Senator William H. Seward of New York, and the majestically imposing Daniel Webster of Massachusetts. Seward had a weak voice sometimes difficult to hear, Webster great organ tones that seemed to reverberate through the Senate even when he whispered. Seward, we will recall, was against any compromise, any concession to slavery, any admission of it into the West, and in opposing the Fugitive Slave Act he quoted that Higher Law stemming from God Almighty which would negate and defeat the act if the people of the North acted on their consciences and not on the fear of authority as Seward predicted they would. This was anathema to any man of business, to any conservative fearing the anarchy of conscience, fearing the people's selective judgment on what was law and what was legislative crime.

Webster, the matchless Webster of Massachusetts, pride of the Commonwealth, whose mighty brow, great domelike head, and cavernous black eyes, whose power and dignity and aplomb had made him the idol of his state, admired by all whether abolitionist or financier, Webster who had always spoken for liberty, who had even defended, in 1837, the abolitionists as a movement that could not be "trifled with or despised," who had favored the Wilmot Proviso, prohibiting the introduction of slavery in any territory conquered from Mexico, spoke not for liberty on March 7, 1850. Instead, he defended the compromise measures which had been offered by Senator Henry Clay of Kentucky in the belief they might avert an imminent civil war, precipitated by the contest for the West. Webster reversed himself completely as to the Wilmot Proviso, ignoring well-publicized plans by Southern senators and representatives for colonizing slaves in New Mexico and California.[19]

To many, Webster's stand on March 7 was his finest hour when he rose above faction and risked his entire career to speak for the whole nation instead of section. Some saw it as a vulgar courting of the South, the result of his inordinate desire to win the Whig nomination for President for which he needed slaveholder support. To others it was a fall from virtue as sudden and unexpected as an archangel's fall from Heaven. But his great and unforgivable apostasy, particularly to the Free Soilers, the Conscience Whigs, abolitionists, and transcendentalists of Massachusetts, as well as to a growing number who simply could not stomach the new law, was his advocacy of the Fugitive Slave Act.

His admirers in the anti-slavery ranks were those hurt most by his action. They had known of his ambition, of his indulgence in amiable and expensive weaknesses that required purses to be made up for him by the State Street constituents whom he had served. But the grace and power of the man, the force of his intellect, the sheer dominating presence of him, which had something lordly and seignorial about it, had always held them in thrall. If his dominating qualities, and even his weaknesses, were used for liberty, as in the opinion of many they always had been before March 7, they could forgive his shortcomings which had, as did all the rest of him, something of attraction. Perhaps the general admiration flowed from a parochial pride. Webster looked like a senator, looked as a great man should. No other state but Massachusetts had in the Senate any who even faintly equaled him either in appearance or ability. Calhoun was a strait-laced Calvinist, a logician clad in black, arguing for slavery like a medieval Thomist expounding an ecclesiastical theorem proving the necessity of God. He was cold, legalistic, rationalizing astutely for what most of the world knew by then was wrong. Clay compared with Webster was only an adroit red-faced politician, a bluff and hearty slaveholder of some skill, but who could not hold his liquor as impressively as the darkly noble Daniel.

Emerson's reaction to Webster's stand on the Fugitive Slave Act was representative of the reaction in Massachusetts among virtually everyone even faintly concerned with the slave's liberty. He had been enamored of Webster much of his life. All that he lacked, Webster had. Emerson was a little prim and rarefied but Webster was hearty and had substance whether before the bar of a tavern or a court. He could make men laugh and do it carelessly as if, out of his good nature, he were throwing them a bone. Everything of attractive genius, particularly as it concerned the wonderfully appropriate phrase and sound and homely reason, everything of an oaklike seasoned manliness, and all effortless and natural, were to be found in Webster, in Emerson's opinion.

Every time he appeared at Concord courthouse, Emerson, in common with most of his townsmen, would go to worship and admire. After seeing Webster at some ordinary Concord trial, Emerson could not write for a week. He had seen what he so longed to be—at least with half of him—but could never, never achieve. It upset him. His only composition was in his journal and it concerned Webster; in feeling thus and writing thus, he was at one with most of the citizens of Massachusetts. It was not that he did not see Webster's failings but that they drew him, too.

On August 17, 1843, with Webster at Concord, he wrote in his journal of the great man:

His wonderful organization, the perfection of his elocution, and all that thereto belongs,—voice, accent, intonation, attitude, manner, are such as one cannot hope to see again in a century. . . . What is small, he shows as small, and makes the great, great. In speech he sometimes roars, and his words are like blows of an axe. His force of personal attack is terrible, he lays out his strength so directly in honest blows, and all his powers of voice, arm, eye, and the whole man are so heartily united and bestowed on the adversary that he cannot fail to be felt. . . .

His splendid wrath, when his eyes became fires, is as good to see, so intellectual it is, and the wrath of the fact and cause he espouses, and not at all personal to himself. Rockwood Hoar said, nothing amused him more than to see Mr. Webster

adjourn the Court every day, which he did by rising, and taking his hat and looking the Judge cooly in the face; who then bade the Crier adjourn. . . .

Webster quite fills our little town, and I doubt if I shall get settled down to
writing until he is well gone from the county. He is a natural Emperor of men;
they remark in him the kingly talent of remembering persons accurately, and
knowing at once to whom he had been introduced, and to whom not. . . . Elizabeth Hoar says she talked with him, as one likes to go behind the Niagara Falls,
so she tried to look into those famed caverns of eyes, and see how deep they were,
and the whole man was magnificent. . . .[20]

This was the man who, in Emerson's view, had suddenly and without
warning cast his prestige and power behind the perpetuation of slavery. The
unexpected revulsion to his hero had something of agony as well as anger for
Emerson. It was in May of 1851, after the fugitive Shadrach [Frederick
Williams] had been delivered from the Fugitive Slave Act by the blacks who
rescued him and after Boston had been given over to military control in the
sending of Thomas Sims, a seventeen-year-old fugitive, back to slavery in
Georgia, that Emerson shuddered with shame when contemplating the condition to which the citizens of Massachusetts had been reduced. All those,
and there had been thousands, who had demonstrated, protested, and even
tried to rescue Sims had been cowed by the military and the police. Emerson
felt that Massachusetts had been transformed into what was tantamount to a
slave state by the actions of Webster and his powerful friends. It was then
that he wrote, commenting on a recent Websterian apostrophe to liberty,
"The word *liberty* in the mouth of Mr. Webster sounds like the word *love*
in the mouth of a courtezan." [21]

It was to Webster and his Fugitive Slave Act that he ascribed the fact that

We wake up with painful auguring, and, after exploring a little to know the cause,
find it is the odious news in each day's paper, the infamy that has fallen on Massachusetts, that clouds the daylight and takes away the comfort out of every hour.
We shall never feel well again until that detestable law is nullified in Massachusetts and until the Government is assured that once and for all it cannot and shall
not be executed here. All I have and all I can do shall be given and done in opposition to the execution of the law. . . .

Mr. Hoar [an aged and honored Concord citizen] has never raised his head
since Webster's speech in last March, and all the interim has really been a period
of calamity to New England. . . . Mr. Webster has deliberately taken out his name
from all the files of honour in which he had enrolled it,—from all association with
liberal, virtuous, and philanthropic men, and read his recantation on his knees at
Richmond and Charleston. . . . He has taught us the ghastly meaning of liberty in
his mouth. It is kidnapping and hunting to death men and women. . . .[22]

If Emerson was representative of a sizable segment of Massachusetts public opinion, it must not be thought that he or the segment for which he spoke was a majority although they might not have been so far from it. Boston's State Street with its millions of dollars of investments, Boston's leading families and leading bankers and clerics—the Lawrences and the Curtises, the Perkinses and Appletons and Everetts, the Prescotts and Eliots—backed Webster and the Fugitive Slave Law, organized huge mass meetings, dinners, and memorials for him, and had probably persuaded the majority of the prosperous, at least, and perhaps more than the prosperous, to support both Webster and the law for the capture of fugitives. But Emerson was typical enough of the intellectuals, the poets, the abolitionists, the Free Soilers. Longfellow, for example, wrote of Webster, "Fallen, fallen from his high esteem," and Horace Mann, the Massachusetts educator and congressman, exclaimed, "Webster is a fallen star! Lucifer descended from Heaven." [23] Whittier, the abolitionist poet, wrote of Webster in lines that are still remembered:

> *Of all we loved and honored, naught*
> *Save power remains,*
> *A fallen angel's pride of thought,*
> *Still strong in chains.*
>
> *All else is gone, from those great eyes*
> *The soul has fled;*
> *When faith is lost, when honor dies,*
> *The man is dead!*

4

John Brown knew all of this, or the most important part of it—Webster's apostasy and the Fugitive Slave Act—from his newspapers. It is a mistake to regard him as a creature solely of emotion or instinct. He was instead, up to a certain point, a deliberate and slow-moving man. He knew what was happening. His outrage was not like Emerson's. He was indignant but it was a permanent indignation as if it derived from his genes, a more modern determinism than Calvinism, as if it came from his most fundamental nature rather than from anything new like the Fugitive Slave Act. There was no astonishment at the law's passage if there was indignation, nor was such likely in one who thought that all events were only the working out of God's purpose, a purpose determined before the creation of the world. Neither was there hurry in him to return to Springfield, in order to protect his black friends from capture under the new law. Why should there be hurry in one who answers to the decrees of the Omnipotent, for early or late he will, as all must, fulfill the predetermined will. Under such cosmic circumstance a man can be deliberate and methodical or even indulge his own caprice, since even caprice is determined.

Probably it was there at North Elba during that fall after the Fugitive Slave Act was passed, reading his Bible in candlelight before he went to bed or in the dusk of early morning, that he began to see more clearly that Judges, Chapter 7, verse 3, and Deuteronomy, Chapter 20, verse 8, held wisdom that might be of service to the blacks of Springfield in fighting the Fugitive Slave Act. He hated to leave North Elba and did not depart for Springfield until November 15, two months after the act was passed.

It was with real regret that he left the Adirondacks, for he was beginning to think that it might be long before his return and that he ought to move himself and his family back to Akron, however unwillingly he made the change. He still had his partnership with Colonel Perkins in the flock of sheep there, which continued as one of the most notable flocks of the country; but more than helping with the sheep he believed he should be near Colonel Perkins so that he could confer with him at every step as to the upcoming law suits. His trip to Essex, he wrote, had "almost entirely diverted my mind from its burdens,"[24] but now he felt he should face them. On a comparatively short trip to see his brother-in-law Orson Day at Whitehall, New York, near Lake George, he concentrated on the difficulties facing him long enough to write his son John: "We have trouble with Pickersgills, McDonald, Jones, Warren, Burlington, & Patterson, & Ewing. These different claims amount to some $40 M [$40,000] & if [I] lose will leave me nice & flat."[25]

After his return to Springfield, despite exciting and significant activity to which we shall soon refer, he could not forget his visit to Essex County. Somehow, even though he was considering moving with his family to Akron, he meant later to return permanently to North Elba and "rest at evening" in its peaceful precincts. In a letter to "Dear Sons John, Jason, & Frederick & Daughters," the brothers now being in charge of the flock at Akron, he wrote:

John asks me about Essex. I will say that the family were living upon the Bread, Milk, Butter, Pork, Chickens, Potatoes, Turnips, Carrots &c of their own raising; & the most of them abundant in quantity, & of superior quality. I have no where seen such Potatoes. Essex Co so abounds in Hay, Grain, Potatoes, Rutabaga, &c that I find unexpected difficulty in selling for cash Oats, & some other things we have to spare. . . . The weather was charming up to the 15th Nov when I left, & never before did the country seem to hold out so many things to entice me to stay on its soil. *Nothing* but the strong sence of duty, Obligation and propriety, would keep me from laying my bones to rest there; but I shall cheerfully endeavour to make that sense my guide; God always helping.[26]

In writing of the strong sense of obligation that might prevent him from spending his final days at North Elba, he was not referring to his desire to fight slavery. He was alluding to his feeling that it was his duty to return to Akron that he might confer almost daily with Colonel Perkins about the forthcoming law suits. But his son John strongly advised against such a return. Mrs. Perkins, he said, held John Brown solely responsible for the reversals in wool and felt that he alone should meet all the losses resulting from them. She was a strong woman, he wrote, and "a talking woman," of such persistence that John Brown, Jr., was sure she would convince her husband that since the fault was John Brown's alone the penalties should also be his alone. He pointed out that as Perkins & Brown was a partnership, the two men should share all losses. If his father returned to Akron, he continued, he would be a kind of vassal to the Perkinses and both he and his family would be living in an atmosphere of blame and recrimination. "The self Esteem, manliness and *real* dignity of the family," he concluded, "can never be secured where a burden such as I have been describing must inevitably rest on them." [27]

For several months John Brown did not know exactly what he should do in regard to Colonel Perkins and the suits nor where his family would live. He only knew that the vision of that talking woman, Mrs. Perkins, greatly increased the attractions of North Elba. It was so far away from any number of vexations that he thought more and more that only the peaks of Essex County could bring him peace.

5

If John Brown helped rescue the blacks of Springfield from the menace of the Fugitive Slave Law, they rescued him from the loneliness of being away from his family and his foreboding thoughts about the impending law suits. They did more than that. In his effort to help them, Brown revealed abilities he had never displayed before. It was as if in working with them, he approached the reality of himself more closely than he ever had before. As he had written to his wife, and as we shall remember, he had always lamented that he had lived so long and done so little to help mankind. Now in helping it he had a liberation and growth, however brief it was to be before business, and its dismal results, captured him again.

As always his methods were entirely his own, even revealing something of the implacable foe of slavery that he was later to exemplify in Kansas, something of his desire, first effected there, to engage the enemy at close quarters, the better to destroy him. While in other cities—Boston, New York, Philadelphia, Cleveland, and Syracuse, for example—great mass meetings of white citizens were held, passing resolutions, forming Vigilance Committees, often composed of a hundred or so white men and perhaps four or five Negroes, John Brown in Springfield worked with no white man and organized no meetings save those attended by the threatened blacks. No resolutions were passed petitioning repeal of the Fugitive Slave Act, no addresses concerning its constitutionality were delivered. The only talk at John Brown's meetings, attended by scores of black men and women, concerned how to defeat and kill, if necessary, any band of slaveholders, or group of federal officers, or anyone else who attempted to return Springfield fugitives to slavery. His meetings had on their agenda such practical matters as the necessity of executing any traitors or informers, after they had been found guilty, and of what to do and where to go after engaging pro-slavery forces in battle.

In many Northern cities there were plans to spirit away to Canada on the Underground any Negroes threatened with seizure, and while John Brown agreed with this tactic to a limited extent—he opened an Underground station in his warehouse for this purpose—his main advice to the fugitives was to arm themselves in Springfield where they would stay and fight. Theodore Parker in Boston was already talking of the necessity of killing, if necessary, any who tried to return men and women to slavery and the Reverend Thomas Wentworth Higginson was not slow in agreeing with him. None but John Brown, however, planned the matter, that is, the killing, if it came to that, of those attempting the capture of fugitives, with such thoroughgoing, practical detail. He did not favor wanton violence. He favored only enough to liberate any escaped slaves who had been captured. The slaveholders were the aggressors; they were waging war and if they suffered casualties the fault was theirs.

John Brown's activities with the blacks of Springfield revealed another aspect of his peculiar character, practical as well as mystical, revealed how to him the Bible he read daily was as much a guide to militant action as it was to holiness. His Bible was to him what theory was to the later Marxist. It is probable that he had long mulled over the use in conflict of Judges, Chapter 7, verse 3, and Deuteronomy, Chapter 20, verse 8, which advised never going into battle until all cowards were given full and free opportunity to absent themselves. The Lord's advice to Gideon for weeding out cowards might have seemed to many only an Old Testament story but to John Brown it was a plan for battle, for an actual battle in which he would participate, and in which he would be as much a part of the eternal purpose as was Gideon at an earlier date.

> AND THE LORD SAID UNTO GIDEON, THE PEOPLE THAT ARE WITH THEE ARE TOO MANY FOR ME TO GIVE THE MIDIANITES INTO THEIR HANDS, LEST ISRAEL VAUNT THEMSELVES AGAINST ME, SAYING, MINE OWN HAND HATH SAVED ME.
> NOW THEREFORE GO TO, PROCLAIM IN THE EARS OF THE PEOPLE, SAYING, WHOSOEVER IS FEARFUL AND AFRAID, LET HIM RETURN AND DEPART EARLY FROM MOUNT GILEAD. AND THERE RETURNED OF THE PEOPLE TWENTY AND TWO THOUSAND; AND THERE REMAINED TEN THOUSAND.
> AND THE LORD SAID UNTO GIDEON, THE PEOPLE ARE YET TOO MANY; BRING THEM DOWN UNTO THE WATER, AND I WILL TRY THEM FOR THEE THERE: AND IT SHALL BE, THAT OF WHOM I SAY UNTO THEE, THIS SHALL GO WITH THEE, THE SAME SHALL GO WITH THEE; AND OF WHOMSOEVER I SAY UNTO THEE, THIS SHALL NOT GO WITH THEE, THE SAME SHALL NOT GO.

And the Lord reduced the thirty-two thousand who first had been under Gideon to only three hundred, knowing that all the rest were cowards. And that seemed very astute to John Brown.

6

Black Americans, for reasons that may be historically evident, do not often like to serve under white leadership. That they did so in Springfield was unusual and it was only because they knew John Brown as a rare and extraordinary being who did not much resemble most white men. In the first place he had circulated now and again among them since his arrival in 1846, searching for blacks of the right stamp to enlist in his great plan. In the next place he had attended the Zion Methodist Church, an abolitionist dissident church which may have had as many blacks as whites among its members, and they heard him pray and preach, and knew, really knew, that he was not a fake in his deep hatred of slavery. Finally, he had talked to many and there was a soberness, a respect, and a receptivity in his attitude that told them he was listening to them, rather than talking at them, and something else that told them, too, that he expected to find heroes among their number. That was a great relief and a great attraction to those who could not find many who knew that they were men. Moreover, he did not flatter them. His manner was often stern as he said they themselves must win their liberty.

Within a little more than a fortnight after his return from North Elba to Springfield, he began his effort to help the city's blacks. On November 28, 1850, he wrote his wife,

It now seems that the fugitive slave law was to be the means of making more abolitionists than all the lectures we have had for years. It really looks as if God had his hand in this wickedness also. I, of course keep encouraging my friends to "trust in God and keep their powder dry." I did so today at thanksgiving meeting publicly.[28]

This Thanksgiving Day meeting was probably held at the Zion Methodist Church.

Not much later he was writing his wife,

Since the sending off to slavery of Long [a captured fugitive] from New York, I have improved my leisure hours quite busily with the colored people here, in advising them how to act, and in giving them all the encouragement in my power. They very much need encouragement and advice; and some of them are so alarmed that they tell me they cannot sleep on account of either themselves or their wives and children. I can only say that I think I have been enabled to do something to revive their broken spirits. I want all my family to imagine themselves in the same dreadful condition. My only spare time being taken up (often till late hours at night) in the way I speak of, has prevented me from the gloomy homesick feelings which had before so much oppressed me; not that I forget my family at all.[29]

In mentioning his busy hours, often extending until late at night, spent in working with the colored people, he was referring to his action in organizing the branch of the United States League of Gileadites, an organization for resistance by black fugitives to any effort to return them to slavery and referring, also, to the "Words of Advice" and "Agreement" which he had written and they had adopted. This document from his pen revealed even if indirectly, not only his past, his long admiration of Cinque of the *Amistad*, of Lovejoy and Torrey and Walker, of the branded hand, but showed, too, if also indirectly, the nature of his future in every word and every emphasis. His words show, too, his continuing concern with the revolutions abroad, his abiding devotion "to the great family of man." It is a crucial document in John Brown's life, one of the best things he ever wrote, more to the point than most of his words as to the actual business of fighting slavery. It included a kind of codicil more specifically outlining a program of resistance, and was signed by forty-four black men and women. It is worth quoting in full:

Branch of the United States League of Gileadites.
Adopted Jan. 15, 1851, as written and
recommended by John Brown.
"Union is Strength."

Nothing so charms the American people as personal bravery. Witness the case of Cinques, of everlasting memory, on Board the "Amistad." The trial for life of one bold and to some extent successful man, for defending his rights in good earnest, would arouse more sympathy throughout the nation than the accumulated wrongs and sufferings of more than three millions of our submissive colored population. We need not mention the Greeks struggling against the oppressive Turks, the Poles against Russia, nor the Hungarians against Austria and Russia combined, to prove this. *No jury can be found in the Northern States that would convict a man for defending his rights to the last extremity. This is well understood by Southern Congressmen, who insisted that the right of trial by jury should not be granted to the fugitive.* Colored people have ten times the number of fast friends among the whites than they suppose, and would have ten times the number they now have were they but half as much in earnest to secure their dearest rights as they are to ape the follies and extravagances of their white neighbors, and to indulge in idle show, in ease, and in luxury. Just think of the money expended by individuals in your behalf in the past twenty years! Think of the number who have been mobbed and imprisoned on your account! Have any of you seen the Branded Hand? Do you remember the names of Lovejoy and Torrey?

Should one of your number be arrested, you must collect together as quickly as possible, so as to outnumber your adversaries who are taking an active part against you. Let no able-bodied man appear on the ground unequipped, or with his weapons exposed to view: let that be understood beforehand. Your plans must be known only to yourself, and with the understanding that all traitors must die, wherever caught and proven to be guilty. "Whosoever is fearful or afraid, let him return and part early from Mount Gilead" (Judges, vii, 3; Deut. xx, 8). Give all cowards an opportunity to show it on condition of holding their peace. *Do not delay one moment after you are ready; you will lose all your resolution if you do. Let the first blow be the signal for all to engage; and when engaged do not do your work by halves, but make clean work with your enemies,—and be sure you meddle not with any others.* By going about your business quietly, you will get the job disposed of before the number that an uproar would bring together can collect; and you will have the advantage of those who come out against you, for they will be wholly unprepared with either equipments or matured plans; all with them will be confusion and terror. Your enemies will be slow to attack you after you have done up the work nicely; and if they should, they will have to encounter your white friends as well as you; for you may safely calculate on a division of the whites, and may by that means get to an honorable parley.

Be firm, determined, and cool; but let it be understood that you are not to be driven to desperation without making it an awful job to others as well as you.

Give them to know distinctly that those who live in wooden houses should not throw fire, and that you are just as able to suffer as your white neighbors. *After effecting a rescue, if you are assailed, go into the houses of your most prominent and influential white friends with your wives; and that will effectually fasten upon them the suspicion of being connected with you, and will compel them to make a common cause with you, whether they would otherwise live up to their profession or not. This would leave them no choice in the matter.* Some would doubtless prove themselves true of their own choice; others would flinch. That would be taking them at their own words. You may make a tumult in the courtroom where a trial is going on, by burning gunpowder freely in paper packages, if you cannot think of any better way to create a momentary alarm, and might possibly give one or more of your enemies a hoist. But in such a case the prisoner will need to take the hint at once, and bestir himself; and so should his friends improve the opportunity of a general rush. [As Shadrach's black friends four months later rescued him from the courtroom at Boston.]

A lasso might possibly be applied to a slave catcher for once with good effect. Hold on to your weapons, and never be persuaded to leave them, part with them, or have them far away from you. *Stand by one another and by your friends, while a drop of blood remains; and be hanged, if you must, but tell no tales out of school. Make no confession.*

Union is strength. Without some well-digested arrangements nothing to any good purpose is likely to be done, let the demand be never so great. Witness the case of Hamlet and Long in New York [fugitives captured there and returned to slavery], when there was no well-defined plan of operations or suitable preparation beforehand.

The desired end may be effectually secured by the means proposed; namely the enjoyment of our inalienable rights.

Then John Brown, wanting to be even more practical than he had been in his "Words of Advice," added a portion that he called "Agreement," in which he displayed his own old-fashioned patriotism and his love for the American flag. This read:

As citizens of the United States of America [it was a considerable conclusion that these fugitives were citizens but they were so in his mind], trusting in a just and merciful God, whose spirit and all-powerful aid we humbly implore, *we will ever be true to the flag of our beloved country, always acting under it.* We, whose names are hereunto affixed, do constitute ourselves a branch of the United States League of Gileadites. That we will provide ourselves at once with suitable implements, and will aid those who do not possess the means, if any such are disposed to join us. We invite every colored person whose heart is engaged in the performance of our business, whether male or female, old or young. The duty of the aged, infirm and young members of the League shall be to give instant notice to all members in case of an attack upon any of our people. [Our people apparently included John Brown.] We agree to have no officers except a treasurer and secretary *pro tem.*, until some trial of courage and talent of able-bodied members shall enable us to elect officers from those who have rendered the most important services. Nothing but wisdom and undaunted courage, efficiency, and general good conduct shall in any way influence us in electing our officers.* [30]

All of the names of the forty-four adhering to the agreement are in the handwriting of John Brown, as if each individual had advanced to a table where he was sitting and recited his or her name for Brown to affix to the document.[31] The League did efficient service; its guns, organization, and spirit were impressive enough that few, if any, fugitives were returned to slavery from Springfield. William Wells Brown, the well-known Negro writer, visited Springfield in June of 1854, a week after state and federal military forces had been called out to assure the return to slavery of Anthony Burns in Boston, and found the Springfield organization mobilized and ready to repel a group of slaveholders and their agents supposed to be in Springfield. Armed sentries were posted everywhere in the black section of town. The women had organized a boiling water brigade to scald any slave catchers who ventured near or into a central building.

"Returning to the depot," William Wells Brown writes,

to take the train for Boston, we found there some ten or fifteen blacks all armed to the teeth and swearing vengeance upon the heads of any who should attempt to take them.

True, the slave-catchers had been there. But the authorities, foreseeing a serious outbreak, advised them to leave, and feeling alarmed for their personal safety, these disturbers of the peace had left in the evening train for New York. No fugitive slave was ever afterwards disturbed at Springfield.[32]

ORDEAL BY LAW

I

John Brown's brief respite from trouble was over with his organization of the League of Gileadites. By the time the blacks of Springfield had overawed the slave catchers in 1854 he was, and long had been, in the straitjacket of the law suits against Perkins & Brown. He could help neither his Springfield friends nor himself for he was imprisoned in courtrooms and law offices, by writs and motions and hearings and trials, almost as effectively as if he had

---

* Since there are no misspellings it is possible that someone helped in the composition of this document. Its style and phraseology are clearly that of John Brown.

been in jail. He was not the master of his own time or his own actions, nor had he been since the spring of 1851 when most of the law actions against him and his partner began. He had moved, and moved his family, too, from his beloved mountains in Essex County back to Akron, which was to be his headquarters as he traveled the East as a kind of circuit defendant, revolving from court to court.

His most troublesome cases were a suit at Troy, New York, brought against him by Henry Warren, a New York wool farmer, alleging that he had been paid several thousand dollars less than the worth of his wool; a suit in Boston filed by the Burlington Mills Company of Burlington, Vermont, for a $60,000 loss allegedly suffered when the company paid John Brown for a higher grade of wool than he delivered to the firm; a suit in New York City in which the Pickersgill Company alleged it had advanced John Brown some thousands of dollars more for shipping his wool to London than it had ever received from him after the sale of his wool in England; and a suit brought by a Pittsburgh party, to which John Brown alludes in his letters but does not name, but which was probably Patterson and Ewing, sheep farmers of Burgettstown, Washington County, Pennsylvania, to whose claim he referred in his letter to his son John of November 4, 1850.

It is probable, or so John Brown's correspondence indicates, that the Pittsburgh case and the Pickersgill claim were settled out of court after trials had begun. But for a long time he regularly revolved between Troy and Vernon, New York, where his attorney in the Warren case had his office, and New York City, Boston, and Pittsburgh, going back and forth between varying combinations of these towns as the caprice of the law dictated. His attorney in the Warren case, until the litigation lasted so long that he died, was J. Whipple Jenkins, of Vernon, who was succeeded by Ralph McIntosh of the same town. His attorney in Boston in the Burlington case was A. B. Ely, who assisted Joshua V. Spencer, a leading lawyer of New York City. His attorneys in the Pickersgill case were Cleveland & Titus of New York City.

These lawyers are mentioned because for four years John Brown spent much of his time in one or another of their offices when not at Akron or on the witness stand undergoing direct examination, cross-examination, re-direct examination, and re-cross-examination at the trials in which he was involved. Whether he was in his lawyers' offices or in the courtroom, his efforts were expended in defending again and again his own alleged mistakes, inadequacies, inaccuracies, and inefficiencies.[33] He could not escape this most painful part of his life but instead had to relive for months at a time the irreversible failures of his past.

He found this constant concern, day after day, week after week, month after month, and even year after year, with his own derelictions an exhausting and distressing experience. He said as much to Colonel Perkins, complaining that "too much responsibility" was being put upon him. There was "no doubt" in the Burlington case, being tried at Boston, he wrote Perkins, "that all that perjury & bribery can do, will be done in order to best us." [34]

Feeling inadequate to the task before him, he pleaded with Colonel Perkins to come to Boston and help him. Still profoundly grateful to Perkins for understanding and forgiving his failure in London, and afterwards continuing their partnership in the sheep business at Akron, he found it distressing that every mistake he made in the trials was liable to cost Perkins additional thousands of dollars. He had done badly enough by failing in the wool business and now he feared he was failing in defending his failures. Moreover, he was broke, without money or assets that did not derive from his sheep partnership with Perkins and that was enough only to maintain himself and his family. He could not share in the payment of any damages his own mistakes had brought upon Perkins. Fearing a loss in the Boston trial, he wrote Perkins with evident chagrin, "I have no means to divide the loss with you." [35]

In the main he did not complain but plodded through his legal ordeal as if suffering it as stoically as possible were the only payment he could make to Colonel Perkins. His long, uncomfortable absences from Akron made the farm when he returned to it seem a paradise. His letters are almost sensuous as he describes a stand of golden wheat, just about to be harvested, and which may go as high as 30 bushels an acre. He writes with such appreciation of growing things, whether bleating lambs, bawling calves, or hay, corn, wheat, and potatoes, that we can almost see the grain being tested between his fingers, the dirt-encrusted potatoes being weighed and judged in his hand, almost feel the weight of the timothy or clover on his fork as he thrusts it upward to the hay rack. "We are getting along very well," he continues, in a letter typical of many others, "in raising Calves, Lambs, Pigs, Turkeys, & Chickens. Have the finest lot of Calves I ever saw together." [36]

But these intervals at the Akron farm were mere recesses in the grinding, seemingly never-ending business of the suits. He spent a great deal of time in locating witnesses to testify in his behalf, traveling far in his searches for those who had moved from Springfield since 1849, and in calculating their witness fees and other expenses due them for journeying from their homes to testify, particularly to Troy and Boston. Not a deposition was drawn up without consulting him on preliminary drafts, usually as to the questions asked, many of which he framed. He was the sole repository of all the information needed for the defense of Perkins & Brown in the various suits against them, with the result that his attorneys could scarce make a move without him, and preferred having him present in their offices during preparation of the cases. Even when an answer to an appeal was being drafted, his lawyers found it helpful to have him beside them as they wrote.

It is not through any written lament, specifically referring to the trials, other than the letter to Perkins, that we can perceive their effect upon him. But more frequently than ever before he writes that he is "not very stout"— his frequent phrase for some generalized and unidentified malady—complains about weakness and lack of energy as well as of the ague and the shakes, says his eyesight is failing, and makes prediction of his own early demise.[37] It is during this period that he becomes worried almost to the point of obsession about the religious failings of his children.[38] If he made no complaint as he alternated between Akron, Troy, Boston, and New York, particularly during the three years beginning in 1851, his appearance testified to the debilitating effects of the law. He seemed more frail, his hair more gray, although still predominantly reddish brown, his whole aspect suggesting a man at least five years older than his years. He was described in 1854 as "a . . . quiet old gentleman." [39]

If he seemed to talk and write more often of his own approaching death, of "the incredible amount of sin and folly" [40] of which he was guilty, that was, at any rate, in the Puritan tradition. His father, Owen, had written and spoken so all his life and so had John Brown if not as feelingly as he did now. The big difference within him seemed to be his conviction that life was done, that from now on the years would hold no surprise. If he talked more frequently of death, he also spoke more often of the peace he hoped to gain at last on his farm in New York's Adirondacks at North Elba.[41]

The refuge he hoped to achieve there seemed at times the only constant in his plans, even when the chance came to fight slavery with bullets instead of words. As a matter of fact, it is likely that he was suffering a weakening and a slow attrition, a diminution of will and purpose as if his vital forces were being squeezed gradually from him by the sterile and endless intricacies of the law. If one loses faith in oneself in one realm, the doubt may extend until it includes the whole personality. In letters to his children, he did not cease to oppose slavery, condemning the churches which still approved it. But seldom did he discuss with them or anyone else, as far as the evidence indicates, his plans for invading the South, nor was he active now, although thousands were, in opposing the Fugitive Slave Act.

Instead he had been brought, as we shall see, to a painful state of indecision, making it almost impossible for him to decide where and how he would play his part in the struggle against slavery or if he would indeed play any effective role at all.

2

But this state of indecision, as we have said, was a gradual development. When he first heard of the first suit, that of the Pickersgill concern, he was sanguine of winning and thought if he could only give a puppy to his attorneys it would help in victory. In a letter to his sons at Akron, he said,

I want you to *save* or *secure* the first real prompt fine looking Black, Shepherd Puppy whose ears stand erect that you can get. I do not care about his training at all further than to have him learned to come to you when bid, to set down & lie down when told; or something in the way of play. Messrs. Cleveland & Titus our lawyers in New York are very anxious to get one for a play thing & I am well satisfied that should I give them one as a matter of friendship it would be more appreciated by them, & do more to secure their best service in our suit with Pickersgill than would a hundred dollars paid them in the way of Fees.[42]

Whether the gift of a puppy secured the best services of Cleveland & Titus is not known. It is known, however, that Brown was equally optimistic that he would win when Henry Warren filed his suit at Troy. He became increasingly annoyed at the frequent postponements of the trial all through 1851 which more than once necessitated his own presence, and the presence of his witnesses at Troy, for no purpose, it turned out, when the trial was postponed. It came up at last in January of 1852, but dragged interminably on with frequent recesses until early 1853 when decision went in favor of Perkins & Brown.[43] Warren immediately appealed and so the case dragged on into 1854. John Brown was so angry at what he considered unconscionable skullduggery on Warren's part that he wrote a letter to the church of one of Warren's witnesses, asking that it expel him for perjury at the trial.[44]

All during 1852 the Boston trial of the Burlington Mills was repeatedly delayed, the concern's lawyers desiring a thorough familiarity with the testimony in the Warren case before they tried their own, the Warren testimony indicating, they apparently thought, John Brown's sloppy way of doing business. In November, the Burlington suit was called for trial but postponed. In December, it was again scheduled but postponed until January 14, 1853, when it went to trial before a jury in the courtroom of Caleb Cushing, soon to be appointed Attorney General of the United States in the pro-slavery administration of President Pierce. He was a close friend of Jefferson Davis, Secretary of War, having served with him in the Mexican War, and as John Brown looked up at him from the floor of the courtroom, he could not have been reassured. Chief counsel for the Burlington Mills was Rufus Choate, the leading light of the Boston bar, and a Webster Whig.

However, John Brown had one pleasant experience in Boston, if he was to have no other, when he heard Theodore Parker. "I have a very distinct memory," his son John said in writing of this time in Boston, "of going with Father one Sunday to Music Hall to hear Theodore Parker for the first time. Though Father did not consider Mr. Parker's theology as sound, he was wonderfully taken up with the discourse and from that time on had a liking for Mr. Parker which constantly increased during the remainder of his life." [45]

As to the Burlington trial, John Brown quickly concluded that it was going against Perkins & Brown. It seemed probable to him that his benefactor, Mr. Perkins, might have to pay the full $60,000 claimed by the Burlington Mills if the case went to the jury. He instructed his attorneys to seek a settlement out of court. On February 3 they succeeded in arranging one and the case was dismissed. It is probable that Colonel Perkins had to pay at least $40,000 to the Burlington Mills. His total losses in the cases tried or settled out of court are believed to have been about $60,000.

3

In his reaction to such disasters, perhaps trying to sublimate his concern for mere transient earthly reverses into a regard for the everlasting, John Brown turned more strongly to religion. While he still hoped, despite his confessed record of sin and folly, for salvation for himself, it was about his children's salvation that he worried particularly, feeling that if they suffered eternal torment it could be justly chargeable to him and to his example. All during the period of the suits he wrote letters pleading with them to return to the faith of their fathers.

While suffering through the Warren trial in January 1852, his mind turned to the spiritual state of Ruth and Henry Thompson. "I really hope," he wrote them,

some of my family may understand that this world is not the *Home* of man; & act in accordance. *Why* may I not hope this of you? When I look forward as regards the religious prospects of my numerous family (the most of them) I am forced to say, & to feel too, that I have *little, very little* to cheer. That this should be so, is

I perfectly well understand the legitimate fruit of my own planting; & that only increases my punishment. Some Ten or Twelve years *ago*, I was cheered with the belief that my elder children had chosen the *Lord*, to be their *God;* & I valued much on their influence & example in attoning for my deficiency & bad example with the younger children. But; *where are we now?* Several have gone to where neither a good or bad example from me will better their condition or prospects, or make them the worse. . . . God grant you *thorough* conversion from sin, & full purpose of heart to continue steadfast in his ways through the *very short* season of trial you will have to pass. . . .[46]

In a letter to John, Jr., and his wife, Wealthy, he seems a little skeptical about the conversion of Henry Thompson at a revival in Essex County, as he observes, "My earnest, & only wish is that those seeming conversions may prove genuine; as I doubt not 'there is joy in Heaven over One sinner that repenteth.' "[47] In another letter to his eldest son, he says,

I forgot to say that my younger sons (as is common in this "progressive Age") appear to be a *little in advance* of my older ones; & have thrown off the *old Shackles* entirely after *thorough & candid* investigation. They have discovered the Bible to be *all* a fiction. Shall I add? that a letter received from *you* some time since; gave me little else than pain & sorrow. . . .[48]

His determination to return to North Elba seemed to increase all during the trials, as well as later, and to be almost as strong as his hope of attaining Heaven. He wrote some seventeen letters between 1852 and 1855, most of them to Henry and Ruth Thompson but to others of his family as well, concerning his plans and his hopes of returning to Essex County.[49] One typical of this period gives Henry Thompson instructions on how to construct a log house on Brown's farm at North Elba but expresses a fear that "I may never live to occupy it." This is the letter in which he speaks of his sin and folly, announcing "Yesterday I began my 54th year; & I am surprised that one guilty of such an incredible amount of sin & folly should be spared so long; & I certainly have reason to be surprised. I still keep hopeing to do better hereafter." Although he felt that he had been reduced by time and fate to a point where it was unlikely that he would ever have the pleasure of living in the house Henry Thompson was to build for him, his passion for giving detailed instructions overcame his pessimism and he wrote of its construction:

I am not able to pay for anything better than a good Log House hewed inside, of peeled logs, (with a good Cellar under it,) House to be about Two feet longer inside than the old one we lived in on the Flanders place, & done off below on the same plan; but so as to make the Bed rooms larger. I would wish it to stand square with the world; longest East & West: with doors opening North & South. I would place it as near the water as I could, & have a dry Cellar; & if any way consistent (with other things;) so as to avoid having to carry water *up* hill; as I have done a great deal at that. . . . I would be at a good deal of pains to avoid luging water up a steep place. I would like a strong tight roof, would carry the boddy up pretty well, & run a tie across from Plate to Plate so as to keep the roof from sagging & spreading the building. I think it the best way to Saddle & notch the logs at the corners instead of laying them over each other flat. These are my general ideas of a Log House. . . .[50]

4

But this retreat to North Elba, if at this point only in desire, as well as his retreat from the fight against slavery, for it was that too, was not serving him well. When working with the blacks of Springfield against the Fugitive Slave Law he had a vigor both of mind and body that was not his now. Then the whole world was his vista and in the political movements for liberty, in Europe as well as in America, he saw the working out of God's purpose. For example, he wrote to his wife shortly after his efforts with the fugitives of Springfield,

There is an unusual amount of very interesting things happening in this and other countries at present and no one can foresee what is yet to follow. The great excitement produced by the coming of Kossuth [the Hungarian patriot seeking aid for his country's liberation from Austria], and the last news of a new revolution in France with the prospect that all Europe may soon be in a blaze seem to have taken all by surprise. I will only say in regard to these things that I rejoice in them from the full belief that God is carrying out his eternal purpose in them all. . . .[51]

Without such struggles for liberation in his mind he was a diminished man. Perhaps he was conscious of this, for on at least one occasion he tried hard to resume his activity against slavery. In June of 1854 he was in the office of his attorney at Vernon, New York, helping him prepare an answer to the appeal in the Warren case. He seemed restless. Presently he rose from his chair and paced back and forth across the office. Suddenly he said, "I am going to Boston."

"Why do you want to go to Boston?" his lawyer asked.

"Anthony Burns must be released, or I will die in the attempt."

The counsel dropped his pen in consternation; then he began to remonstrate; told him that the suit had been in progress a long time, and a verdict just gained; it was appealed from, and that appeal must be answered in so many days, or the whole labor would be lost; and no one was sufficiently familiar with the whole case except himself.[52]

If he went to Boston it would probably cost Mr. Perkins thousands of dollars.

John Brown glared a moment and then slowly sank into a chair beside his counsel. It was as if his sitting down was a gesture of formal surrender. He was the prisoner of his failures and without his own liberty he could not fight for the liberty of others. To some at the time, and even to himself, his impulse to aid Anthony Burns might have seemed the last flare of his old fire.

SONS AND BROTHERS

I

Later in the summer of 1854 John Brown learned that Warren had won his appeal, that his only victory as to both claims and suits had been reversed by a higher court. He had other troubles, however, that took his mind from his legal defeats. Northern Ohio was suffering from the most severe drought "ever experienced during this nineteenth century." [53] The temperature was hot and stifling and a clear blue sky and constant sun, usually so desired by men, had become an affliction. There was scarcely a drop of rain through June, July, August, and September. The crops were virtually a complete loss, the corn sere, its ears scrawny and undeveloped, the wheat stunted, little more than dried-up stubble, the fruit trees barren, most gardens only parched soil, the grass that was to have been hay nonexistent, the sheep and cattle lean and poorly. America's evil, John Brown said, had brought the Lord's punishment.

The two oldest Brown boys, John and Jason, owned Ohio farms by 1854, while the younger brothers worked on farms, sometimes those of their older brothers, sometimes elsewhere. As the sun ruined crops, making certain that farmers could not meet payments due, the Brown brothers were seized with restlessness. All of the country, it sometimes seemed, was on the move. The gold fever that had drawn thousands to California had made the Pacific coast almost as familiar as the Atlantic. The full continental United States was in the minds of land-hungry men, drawing them particularly to California and the Pacific Northwest, making them eager for the opening of new Territories such as Kansas and Nebraska. The constant talk of a Homestead Law, balked for years by the plantation owners, had whetted appetites for rich new soil in the West which a man would only have to improve, only have to build a cabin on, and let his plow bite into the virgin land for a number of seasons in order to own it.*

If northern Ohio was a desert without water, and so it seemed in the summer of 1854, only those without spine or initiative would want to remain in that drought-ruined land. This seemed more emphatically true after the passage of the Kansas-Nebraska Act, when many Northern newspapers "were not only full of glowing accounts of the extraordinary fertility, health and beauty of the Territory of Kansas . . . but of urgent appeals to all lovers of freedom . . . to go there as settlers and . . . save Kansas from the curse of slavery." [54]

The Brown boys were sufficiently sons of their father to be attracted by both riches and liberty. In fact, one could not have the first without securing the latter. If Kansas became a slave state—and adjacent Missouri, with much the same climate and soil in its western portions as eastern Kansas, was such a state—there would be no opportunity for the Browns, and thousands like them, to be independent freeholders in Kansas, or so the current belief went in the North and probably correctly. The brothers seemed to have expected that their father would emigrate to Kansas with them. His partnership with Perkins was to expire at last at the end of 1854. He would have to move somewhere and they expected, hoped, and urged that he move to the Territory of Kansas, now widely recognized as the decisive center in the fight against slavery.

2

The sons and brothers of the Brown family were at once a representative product of the Western Reserve and the peculiar result of being John Brown's sons. They all resembled him in appearance, their hair auburn, their noses prominent, but, for example, where John Brown's nose had a predatory slant, his eldest son's was finely formed and Roman. All of them had marked variations, of course, from their progenitor, whether it was an increased delicacy, a decreased hardihood, an added softness, a larger perception into a newer world, or a more excessive wildness than he ever had, as was the case with poor Frederick, his fifth son (twenty-four years old in 1854), who suf-

---

* A Homestead Law was passed May 20, 1862, Southern opposition no longer present in Congress due to secession. It offered any citizen, or prospective citizen, 160 acres of public domain after five years of continuous residence and payment of a registration fee ranging from $26 to $34. Land could also be acquired after six months residence and payment of $1.25 an acre.

fered from some unidentifiable periodic illness during which he was almost beyond control, his own or that of anyone else. But however the brothers were, they were all peculiarly the sons of John Brown rather than of their mothers, in appearance and in temperament, with the possible exception of Jason, a very gentle man, who in later years often called himself "the family coward."

They all admired their father, laughed at him at times, when he was not present, recalling such incidents as when he underwent a strange torment, as we shall presently see, in trying to prove that a hypnotist appearing in Springfield was a fraud or how he was chased out of Meadville by Masons after exposing their order, or how he had once inadvertently intoned during family prayers, "Oh Lord, we are all sinful from the soles of our heads to the crowns of our feet." [55] They even opposed him at rare intervals when they thought they could get away with it. Often the brothers thought their father outrageously old-fashioned, particularly over the Bible, but they had to admit that on questions such as Christian socialism and common owner-ship of the land, the production for use and not for profit, he was rather advanced.

He had worked all of them hard from the time of childhood and they never grew too old for him to give them minute instructions on how to bed down the cattle or dole out the feed and hay. They sometimes resented his iron discipline, most of them having memories of whippings he had inflicted; resented his never-ending overseeing of all the details of their lives; resented the constant imposition of Bible readings and prayers forced upon them daily even when they were adults and only visiting him. It was all a little oppressive and one of the sons, probably Salmon, said after his father's death, "We boys felt a little pleased sometimes, after all when father left the farm for a few days."

"We girls never did," Ruth said on this occasion.

"Well," said her brother, repenting, "we were always glad to see the old man come back again; for if we did get more holidays in his absence we always missed him." [56]

It is evident that their father had an irresistible attraction to his children, a capability for dramatizing every reverse and every aspect of his and their lives, a kind of loneliness in the stands he took and the person he was that somehow drew endlessly on their sympathy. He was such an overwhelming fact that he could not be forgotten and abandoned by his sons, even when they grew older and had their own families; and yet they did not think that he had forced on them his own conceptions as to slavery and the necessity to fight it. To their minds any man who breathed and had the slightest concept of justice had to be against slavery.

Their sister Sarah, in speaking of her brothers and her father, but of her father most, once said long after he was dead,

He did not "sacrifice" his boys and their wives and little children, nor "drag" them with him. His boys felt as he did. Read their letters. His boys went of themselves, both to Kansas and to Harper's Ferry. John Brown had no need to urge them. Where their wives wished to hold them back, and could, they did so.

You do not know the time and the great impulse there was in the air. Everything was black. The fugitive slave law had been passed, the Squatter Sovereignty bill [the Kansas-Nebraska Act]. Everything stood as a bulwark in defense of slavery. Abolition seemed a hopeless cause. Those were times to nerve every man to act. All the Brown boys were ready for something desperate. Their father gave them cohesion. He coerced them in no way. They had all the passion to act of themselves.[57]

He did not even give them cohesion initially. They pressed him to go to Kansas, not he them.

3

In 1854 John Brown, Jr., was thirty-three years old, the favorite of his father, despite his unorthodox views of life, being old enough to have had knowledge of, and sympathy for, many of John Brown's misfortunes. A handsome and imposing man, about 6 feet in height, he was also a little plump, ambrotints and other pictures indicating that his heft sometimes pressed and strained against his clothing. Yet he had a certain air as of one not to be trifled with. He thought well of himself, perhaps too well, of his bravery, his dignity, his essential worth as a man and a gentleman, and if he went to Kansas he did not propose to let any Southern slaveholder run over him or any other Brown.

He had, too, a fascinating authority, a kind of bedside manner, almost as if he were a physician, the result of his studying phrenology, which essayed not only to diagnose the character through the contours of the head but also to improve the health, particularly through cold water therapy and a thorough knowledge of physiology and diet. He had studied in 1850 with the firm of Fowler and Wells in New York City, who had made a big business of phrenology and various other nostrums, teaching the young as at a medical school and sending out lecturers over the land, their authenticity guaranteed as graduates of Fowler and Wells. In addition they owned a publishing house, printing books and pamphlets on various aspects of phrenology and health as well as promoting and selling the first edition of Whitman's *Leaves of Grass* in 1855.[58]

John Brown, Jr., was in the vanguard of his time, a member of a rather esoteric but widespread movement of the 1840's and 1850's as representative, if not as important, as the abolitionists. There was scarcely a great man of the period, including Horace Greeley, Horace Mann, Charles Sumner, Walt Whitman, Charles A. Dana, Dr. Samuel Gridley Howe, and William Cullen Bryant, who had not had his cranium read and his personality expounded after a phrenological examination.* In addition to phrenology the oldest Brown son believed, as did many others, in hypnotism, now established as a fact but then regarded with suspicion and particularly by his father. He believed in spiritualism, as did thousands of other men (including, for example, William Lloyd Garrison) and was passionately interested for a time in any evidence of rappings and tappings and mediums giving voice to the departed. He believed in mental telepathy and in the possibility of specially gifted persons knowing of one's future as well as past through some kind of sympathetic vibration, even though the medium had never seen the person to whom he was directing his attention until the occasion of their meeting in seance or session. Even in provincial Springfield there were those who swore of miracles of revelation about their own lives performed by those they had never seen before.[59]

But during his studies at Fowler and Wells in New York, where he also became a part-time employee in 1850, it seems likely that young Mr. Brown was particularly interested in that part of the curriculum described as "Health —Its Value, Conditions and Restoration." [60] When he heard, for example, that his little nephew, the son of Ruth and Henry Thompson, had been seriously ill from the croup, he gave them medical advice gained from his studies.

"Should he be taken in that way again," he wrote,

I will give you some rules to guide you in treating him yourselves. Ist. in all cases of colds croup and the like the system is first thrown into an *Electrical* or *negative* state this then is the first form of disease—The surface and extremities have been unduly chilled the consequence of this is that the blood is thrown in too great

---

* What was called the science of phrenology was as popular in England and France as it was in the United States, perhaps more so since it originated in Europe with the empirical system of psychology formulated by F. J. Gall and developed by J. K. Spurzheim and George Combe. Such intellectuals as Herbert Spencer and George Eliot believed in phrenology, having their own craniums read and using its principles to study the characters of others. It was a part of the vocabulary of most intellectuals, as current as Freudianism was to become later, although there was always strong opposition to it.

quantities upon the *internal* organs. This constitutes what is termed congestion; if the throat and lungs are most *susceptible* or have been most *exposed* they will be most *effected*. Remember that there is a *congestion* (ie) an *under quantity* of *blood* or obstructed action in the throat and lungs in these cases. The remedy consists in withdrawing this *accumulation* by *warm* applications to the body and extremities *generally*, and to the most effected parts in *particular*. The use of water in these cases is excellent but it should be *warm* or at least tepid and the wet cloth should be instantly covered by several thicknesses of woolen in order that it may produce a sweating or drawing effect. The application of Goose-oil externally, also swallowed, when mixed with honey is a most superior remedy.

If this obstruction or congestion is not removed then follows the magnetic state or stage of fever. Now, you may safely apply cold water and so long as the fevered state continues you cover the wet cloth, only up to such time as it becomes warm by the heat of the body when it should again be wet with cold water and applied until a temperate or natural warmth is restored and the fever is subdued. These rules apply both to the general applications or to parts of the body.

Two illustrations: if your hands are cold you can apply warmth, if on the other hand you have burned them, what is there so refreshing as to apply cold. But I need not enlarge, these simple rules are worthy your careful thought for they contain a great secret of success, in treating disease. . . .[61]

As a result of his study at Fowler and Wells, John Brown, Jr., was further qualified to reveal the potentialities and tendencies of any individual by running his large probing hands over the skull of whoever was being diagnosed. The head's various bumps and declivities, its valleys and ridges, corresponded with every individual's traits, and a specific sinking in the skull, or a specific largeness at various precise points, revealed that its owner possessed more or less what Orson Squire Fowler had classified as "Cautiousness, Amativeness, Conjugality, Self-Esteem, Benevolence, Veneration, Firmness, Hope, Mirthfulness," and many other characteristics which could be scientifically indicated by the topography of the cranium.

In addition, young Mr. Brown was trained at Fowler and Wells to lecture on phrenology, and after his return to Ohio where he bought a small farm early in 1850 from the estate of his wife's father near Vernon in Trumbull County he occasionally went about the Western Reserve lecturing on his subject until his voice failed him in December of 1850.[62] The content of his talks might seem little more than nonsense to a later age but at the time phrenology, hypnotism, spiritualism, and associated enthusiasms were seen by many as liberation from dogma and superstition. The very idea that one's destiny was not controlled, determined, and predestined by an invisible Almighty but physically determined by the body and its health, which of course, one could improve—and self-improvement of the mind and body was an integral part of Fowler's program—was to many raised on Genesis and a vengeful God an incredible relief.

But Old John Brown continued, of course, to prefer "Rock of Ages" to rappings on a table. He saw nothing in the ridges and valleys of the cranium to impeach his belief in predestination or in the validity of each and every word of the Bible. Perhaps he yearned to understand and sympathize with his eldest son, to talk easily and familiarly in the new language of the new sciences even while refuting them; but as he said, while he did not feel estranged from his children, he could not flatter them, nor cry peace when there was no peace.[63] He later learned, perhaps through the example of the young, that spiritualism might be combined, however briefly, with his own beliefs. During the last year of his life, he told his oldest son that he had received comfort and support from the spirit of Dianthe, the wife of his youth, as he dreamed of her one night not long before Harper's Ferry.[64]

But in 1847 he deemed most of these developments from spiritualism to hypnotism a fraud and a deception. He may, however, have been persuaded to phrenology by O. S. Fowler's reading of his character on February 27, 1847, in New York although it was not entirely flattering. "You have a pretty good opinion of yourself," the diagnosis read in part, and "would rather lead than be led. You might be persuaded but to drive you would be impossible. You like your own way, and to think and act for yourself—are quite independent and dignified, open and plain, say just what you think, and most heartily despise hypocrisy and artificiality. . . ."[65]

While Mr. Fowler may have derived his knowledge more from talking with John Brown than from the bumps on his head, nevertheless he seemed to have described John Brown's traits accurately enough when the latter rose at a public demonstration of hypnotism, and said openly and plainly that the demonstration he was witnessing was a fraud. La Roy Sunderland, the hypnotist in this Springfield performance in 1847, had put a young lady to sleep and rendered her, he said, insensible to pain. John Brown, who had consulted with skeptical local physicians, shouted out from his place on the floor of a theater that he could render her sensible to pain. La Sunderland said he would permit the young lady to undergo any tests John Brown wished to perform provided he underwent the same tests himself.

This idea, Sunderland reported, seemed unexpected to Brown but he could not or would not retreat and advanced to the stage with a vial of concentrated ammonia and a handful of *Dolichos Pruriens* or cowhage. "This 'cow itch,' as it is sometimes called," Sunderland explained, "is the sharp hair of the plant, and when applied to the skin, it acts mechanically for a long time, tormenting the sufferer like so many thistles or needles constantly thrust into the nerves." Brown administered the ammonia to the nose of the hypnotized young woman. She did not move. He applied the cow itch to her neck. She neither flinched nor gave the slightest indication of feeling it.

Now it was Brown's turn to submit to the test. He "bore it like a hero," Sunderland said.

But then he had the advantage of the entranced lady—the skin of his neck looking like sole leather; it was tanned by the sun, and looked as if it were impervious. Not so, however, when the ammonia was held to his nose; for then, by a sudden *jerk* of his head, it became manifest that he could not, by his own volition, screw up his nervous system to endure what I had rendered a timid lady able to bear without any manifestation of pain. The infliction upon Brown [Sunderland was referring particularly to the cowhage] was a terrible one. . . .[66]

With what must have been an excruciating effort at self-control, John Brown bore the pain until he was out of the theater and into the night. Then, according to his son Salmon, he clawed at his neck in a frenzy and even rubbed up against poles in an effort to relieve his torment. Sunderland reported that "he confessed three days afterwards, that he had not been able to sleep at all since the cowhage was rubbed into his neck." [67] So science advances, convincing skeptics from personal experience.

4

It was probably late in August 1854 that the four oldest Brown sons, John, Jr., Jason, Owen, and Frederick, decided that they would emigrate to Kansas. The two youngest, Owen and Frederick, would herd the cattle and the horses to southwestern Illinois in the fall of 1854, winter them there, and start for Kansas early in the spring. John and Jason would leave Ohio at about the same time, the spring of 1855, with their wives and children, Jason and his wife Ellen having a son Austin about four years old, and John and Wealthy a boy named John of about three. They would raise the necessary capital by selling their farms. They would go by boat, or so it was planned, down the Ohio and up the Mississippi to St. Louis. There, after buying tents and a plow, they would embark for Kansas via the Missouri River, which formed the northeastern boundary of Kansas on the way to its source in Montana's Rockies.

Jason had a small farm near Akron in Summit County which his father liked to refer to as "The Rock," perhaps indicating something of its fertility.

Thirty-one, tall and scrawny, Jason was a plain young farmer without pose or flourish. He had a strangely thin and narrow face, so narrow that when he became older it appeared as if its sides had been forcibly and unaccountably pressed together. He shared none of his brother John's aplomb or magisterial manner, perhaps the partial result of John's having been a justice of the peace in Trumbull County, nor could Jason make a graceful speech as could his brother.

He had scarcely been off an Ohio farm in all his years except for a short time in Springfield when he helped his father in the wool business. A little offended when his brother John wrote warning him against marrying Ellen Sherbondy, predicting that if he did so he would have "an unhappy and miserable life," he quietly ignored the advice and married her. He put the letter "into the fire," he wrote his brother, adding, "but remember I did not burn my affection for you with it." [68]

"I never knew him to engage in a fight," his brother Salmon observed of Jason, writing of their boyhood and of Jason's "love for peace" and aversion to bloodshed. Once in Kansas when Jason and all the Browns were very hungry, almost in a state of semi-starvation, Salmon "trapped a bunch of quail in a cornfield" and "killed and dressed them," but "Jason would not touch them" despite his hunger pangs. "He had seen the birds flutter as they were dying," Salmon continued, "and it so worked on his sympathies he could not eat them. He . . . could never endure the sight of suffering in either man or beast." [69]

Jason was as against slavery as his father but he could not think of it constantly, being given to dreams about such strange things as machines that flew through the air. He knew even less of money than did his father, a good deal less as a matter of fact, for it was his inclination to give it no mind at all, particularly when he had borrowed it. Jason was a tinkerer and a horticulturist rather than a general farmer. He experimented on "The Rock" in raising rare grapes and fine fruit, rather than in raising a money crop such as wheat or corn. He had, according to his father, "a very valuable collection of Grape vines: & also of choice fruit trees which [he] took up and shipped in boxes [to Kansas] at a heavy cost." [70]

Jason was proficient at repairing farm machinery and would later spend years in trying to construct a heavier-than-air flying machine. He always had a special fondness for children, his son Austin above all, whom he once described when the boy was about three pretending to write a letter and looking, he said, as "honest as an old deacon." [71] He often carried cheese in his pockets which he fed to any stray and hungry dog he happened to meet.

If he tried hard to be a nonresistant during the Kansas civil war, not quite successfully for all his efforts, he always spoke his mind fearlessly and even to his father whom he condemned for the Pottawatomie executions. If he hated bloodshed he was also a brave man, as he proved at the Battle of Osawatomie.

Owen Brown, the third son, was thirty years old in 1854. He had a weakened right arm, the result of an injury in his boyhood, and his father always tried to protect him from hardship or overwork because of this liability. In addition, his father listened to him more than he did to some of his sons for, as a friend said, "Owen's calm, philosophical way of thinking and speaking did not permit him to be imperatively brushed aside." [72] His hair was tawnier, containing more of yellow than the reddish brown of his brothers and father, and he wore a beard before any of them. He occasionally liked to think of himself as a humorist and sometimes couched his letters in the "Wal, I rekon pertickerly" school then and later favored by certain American humorists. He was sentimental, too, once falling in love with a girl in Iowa but too timid or too uncertain of his own future under his father, to whom he was very loyal, ever to tell her so. Neat and methodical, he liked to mend his own clothing and darn his own socks, sewing on his clothing the initials O.X. to distinguish them from those of his large younger brother Oliver, who marked his clothing O.B. His brothers said that O.X. stood for Old Xcentricity. [73]

Frederick, of whom his father repeatedly wrote, "Frederick has been very wild again," [74] was twenty-three when he left for Illinois with Owen on the first leg of their journey to Kansas. In love when he left Ohio, he expected to return later and marry. Perhaps striving for an unattainable purity (unattainable at any rate for a lusty, exceedingly emotional young man), he seems to have become stricken with a sense of his own utter sinfulness while undergoing one of the spells of wildness he periodically experienced. While suffering so he "subjected himself to a most dreadful surgical operation," according to his father, "but a short time before starting for Kansas which well might have cost him his life; & was but just through with his confinement when he started on his journey pale & weak." [75] He had attempted to emasculate himself.

His father wrote of him, "Frederick though a very stout man was subject to periodical sickness for many years attended with insanity. It has been publicly stated that he was idiotic. Nothing could be more false." [76] Whether he was in fact medically insane at times is difficult to tell from this distance. But it is certain that the bouts were periodic, for in Kansas he gave repeated proofs of his bravery and integrity, participating effectively there in both politics and war.

Salmon, now eighteen years of age, was sent forward early in 1855 to assist his brothers in Illinois.[77] He was of tougher fiber than either John or Jason, and as time was to prove, not overly troubled by bloodshed and strife. Salmon was, his sister Sarah said, "the sanest minded, level headedest one of the family." [78] Oliver, the youngest of the Brown sons, was sixteen in 1855, eager to go to Kansas and soon to succeed in doing so. Of all his brothers he most enjoyed reading—liking Theodore Parker's books particularly—and when intent on a book one could speak to him and he would not hear, push him and he would not feel. Such absorption seemed to his brothers to indicate a lack of intelligence and during his early teens they called him "Brown's fool." [79] Both he and Watson, twenty in 1855, when the latter would return with his father and others of the family to North Elba, had handsome and sensitive faces, or so their daguerreotypes indicate, each with the suggestion of somber shadow across their features as if they half suspected their ends would be bloody and tragic.

The Brown brothers were very human, all of them having their share of frailty. Yet they also had a certain generosity, a willingness to give of themselves for what they deemed their country's welfare. They even rose at times to a kind of nobility however difficult it was for them to achieve.

ON NOT GOING TO KANSAS

I

John Brown very nearly avoided the scaffold on which Edmund Ruffin, moved by a sudden unwanted respect, saw him hanged. The route to it began in Kansas and he almost refused to take that path. When the civil war broke out there in 1854 he decided not to accompany his sons to Kansas. Instead, he would return to the secluded peace of the Adirondacks at North Elba as he had yearned to do ever since he had been forced to leave in the spring of 1851.

One might have thought that after fifteen years of talking about attacking slavery he would have jumped at whatever chance to do so Kansas offered. Several times he almost did jump but then pulled himself back, however reluctantly, to his determination to retire to North Elba. For almost

eleven months he was manifestly in a misery of indecision, repeatedly deciding to join his sons and repeatedly deciding not to. It was not that he did not
know the importance of Kansas, later declaring of the slaveholders that "had
they succeeded in Kansas they would have gained a power that would have
given them permanently the upper hand, and it would have been the death
knell of republicanism in America." [80]

Even the Missouri invasions of Kansas did not move him, at least until
the news festered within him for a time. He remained the epitome of uncertainty while the so-called Border Ruffians, the pro-slavery cohorts of Missouri's slaveholders, invaded Kansas on November 29, 1854, seizing an election by force and violence and illegally electing a pro-slavery candidate as
the Territory's representative in Congress. He was shaken by the second
attack on Kansas and almost decided to go there when some 5,000 Missourians, armed with all the implements of war, again invaded the Territory on
March 30, 1855, again seized an election by force and, while preventing Free
State settlers from voting, themselves voted in an entirely pro-slavery territorial legislature.[81]

His listless behavior may have been because he still felt old and tired, as
he had described himself in letters to his children in 1852 and 1853, because
he was still eager for the security of the Adirondacks after his exhaustion
resulting from his second failure and the long-drawn-out law suits. It may be
that he had further lost confidence in himself, the fact that Colonel Perkins,
whom he so ardently admired, had at last terminated their partnership at the
end of 1854 not adding to it. He no longer had a half interest in the famous
flock of Perkins & Brown, all title reverting to the richer partner, an occurrence which could not have cheered the poorer. But he was more than a
prisoner of his own indecision. He was again a captive of economic circumstance. The only property he owned now was the farm at North Elba. It was
the only remaining home available for himself and his family and if he occasionally longed to escape to Kansas, the practicality of North Elba consistently canceled all such impulses.

In addition he also felt strongly his obligation to Gerrit Smith, having
promised him in 1849 that he would teach the black farmers of Timbucto
the ways of husbandry and thrift. He had not carried out his pledge at all as
he should have, due to the pressure of the wool business and the suits which
forced him to desert entirely, for a time, Essex County and its Negro farmers.
Perhaps he feared, too, that his projects had always been too grandiose—his
plan for wool indicated that this was so—too complex and lofty for reality,
particularly his dream of invading the South, and that at long last he must

abandon the impossible and carry into reality the only practical plan remaining before him which involved his promise to Gerrit Smith. He would have been on his way to North Elba already, he wrote on January 23, 1855, from a farm called the Ward place near Akron, which he rented after the termination of the Perkins partnership, had he not been almost penniless or "moneybound" as he phrased it. Before he could move to North Elba, he said, he would have to sell his cattle that he might have funds to move.[82]

How much his desire to return to North Elba was to some extent a rationalization, at least after the beginning of the Kansas civil war, is difficult to determine. Any other course, including Kansas, may have seemed to him almost an impossibility because of his impoverishment. But surely he must have felt at times the urge to escape, as he finally did escape, the humdrum ways of a backwoods farm, the anonymous labor of caring for his family, the conscious acceptance of old age, all striving gone. Surely as the conflict over slavery began in Kansas, he recalled his old plan of war against it. How many years had he planned attacking it? Enough to make him only an eccentric to those who like Douglass might recall his bold talk of years before. But it was still impossible to do. He had to return to North Elba. It was the only resource, the only move left to him, and no doubt the best move for an elderly man who had seen his share of failure.

So he thought during the last five months of 1854 and the first months of 1855, in the latter period still money-bound on the Ward place. If his sons were eager for the ardors of Kansas he wished them well but he would not accompany them. Doubtless out of pride—he had talked too often to his sons of attacking slavery—he said nothing to them of his problems. Rather, he implied that he had as important a venture against slavery under way as they would have in going to Kansas. He dignified his retreat with something of the heroic if only in words. On August 21, 1854, he wrote his son John:

> If you or any of my family are disposed to go to Kansas or Nebraska to help defeat *Satan* and his legions in that direction, I have not a word to say *but I feel committed to operate in another part of the field*. If I were not so committed, I would be on my way this fall. Mr. Adair [John Brown's brother-in-law, who had married his half sister, Florilla] is fixing to go and wants to find "good men and true" to go along. I would be glad if Jason would give away his Rock and go. Owen is fixing for some move; I can hardly say what.[83]

Most historians have thought that John Brown was referring in his grandiloquent phrase about operating in "another part of the field" to his coming attack on Virginia, but he himself is explicit enough in this correspondence with his children in stating that he is referring to North Elba and its black farmers. Despite the bold resonance of his words, it is not likely that he was trying seriously to recruit the Negro farmers for his attack, since there were only ten families there, most of the men elderly or middle-aged, and most also so demoralized by the hardships of Essex County that they needed John Brown's help not for an expedition far away, but to survive where they were.

This is of some importance in our estimate of John Brown. His earliest admirers always stated that his hatred of slavery was inborn, immanent, constant, and never-changing, and that his plan to attack slavery was as unvarying as he was unfaltering in its pursuit.* He, himself, when at last his decision to remain at North Elba was reversed and when he was enjoying that renascence of vitality, that vigor of one almost born again which came with the reversal, once said, with something of a flourish, that he had ordered his affairs for twenty years so that at any time he could leave within two weeks to answer "the call of the Lord" by attacking slavery in the South.[84] But as a matter of fact he hesitated, retreated, and backslid over the years, his plan often becoming little more than a memory of an ancient resolve, on the whole moving no faster, and sometimes not as fast as other men, responding to the same pressures at the same time and in the same way as those who had never vowed to attack slavery by force of arms.

---

* Both the transcendentalists and the Calvinists who included Brown's first biographers and panegyrists preferred to think of human character as something innate and unchangeable, rather than the product of environment or development. The transcendentalists believed that character rather than a progression came from the immanent perception of that eternal truth of which each individual was a part and which Emerson called the Oversoul. The Calvinists believed every attribute and every act the predetermined will of God, from whose amplitude came all things and all events to the last exactitude. Thus Sanborn found Brown "a predestined hero," a "prophetic, Heaven-appointed" figure, and Redpath discerned "A Warrior saint," a "warrior of the Lord and Gideon," while even Thoreau and Emerson saw a greatness in Brown that was inborn.

Even the later Villard saw Brown's character if not as Providential, then as a mysterious and unsolvable riddle. "From what midnight star," he asks, "did this shepherd draw his inspiration to go forth and kill? What was there in the process of tanning to make a man who had never seen blood spilt in anger ready to blot out the lives of other human beings whose chief crime was that they differed with him as to the righteousness of human bondage?" (Villard, *John Brown*, p. 42.)

While a difference as to the justice of human slavery is in truth quite a difference, there was of course nothing in the process of tanning that drove John Brown to Kansas and Harper's Ferry. The force that drove him was the dynamics of that national struggle, the increasing crisis concerning the gigantic, material fact of chattel slavery, which drove hundreds of men to participation in the Kansas civil war and which finally involved all Americans everywhere.

2

In a letter of September 30, 1854, John Brown reveals both his urge to go to Kansas and his inability to make the decision to go, even suggesting that others should make the decision for him and making it abundantly clear what he meant by the phrase "to operate in another part of the field." Writing his daughter Ruth and her husband Henry Thompson, he indicates he cannot and should not make the decision himself between Kansas and North Elba. Rather, he proposes a vote by the black farmers of Essex County on the question. In addition, he wants the advice of Ruth and Henry Thompson, Gerrit Smith, Frederick Douglass, and Dr. J. McCune Smith, a leading Negro of the time and a trustee of the organization that Smith had set up for his distribution of land, as to what he should do. Here is no fanatic pressing recklessly forward to destruction.

"Dear Children," he writes.

After being hard pressed to go with my family to Kansas as more likely to benefit the colored people *on the whole* than to return with them to North Elba; I have consented to ask your *advice & feeling* in the matter; & also to ask you to learn from Mr. Epps & all the colored people (so far as you can) how they would wish and advise me to act in the case all things considered. As I volunteered in their service; (or in the service of the colored people); they have a right to vote as to the course I take. I have just written Gerrit Smith, Fredk Douglas[s], & Dr. Mc-Cune Smith for their advice. We have a new daughter now Five days old.* Mother & child are doing well to appearance.[85]

On November 2, 1854, he wrote Ruth and Henry Thompson from Akron,

I still feel pretty much determined to go back to North Elba; but expect Owen and Fredk will set out for Kansas on Monday next with cattle belonging to John Jason & themselves, intending to winter somewhere in Illinois. . . . Gerrit Smith wishes me to go back to North Elba; from Douglass and Dr. McCune Smith I have not heard. . . .[86]

His vacillation between North Elba and Kansas remained academic for he had no money to go anywhere until early June 1855. But that did not stay his torment as to what he should do or where he should go. On February 13, 1855, he wrote that he had undertaken to direct the operations of a surveying and exploring party to be employed in Kansas,[87] but he never went on such a party and insofar as is known never referred to it again.

---

* Ellen, his twentieth and last child.

Even as he prepared to depart from Akron for Essex County he was uncertain of his course, but increasingly shaken by events in Kansas. Failure and adversity had dimmed his senses until he could not hear the call of the Lord for which he was waiting. But others were hearing it, if that was what was sending thousands to Kansas. Perhaps there were other reasons for their going which would even at last move John Brown.

XXI

On the Dynamics

of Change

THE YEARS 1854–5 might sometimes have seemed as if designed for the proof that man proposes but crisis disposes. From the public occurrences of these months stemmed the personal history of thousands. As event followed event and one bold project after another was launched for slavery's expansion, it might have seemed as if the period beginning in January 1854 was, among other things, a demonstration that while a man may plan to buy the east 20 acres adjacent to his farm, or move to town, or go to college, or get married, or retire to the peace of North Elba, all such personal hopes may be uprooted and nullified when public crisis makes private desire only the caprice of national emergency.

The lives of thousands of Americans, even to the point of being a factor as to whether some would have any or not, were changed during these years by the oratory and votes of congressmen in distant Washington, by the actions of American diplomats in the little Belgian town of Ostend where they issued a manifesto, in staging areas for filibusters near Mobile in Alabama, by the ardent love of a Massachusetts schoolteacher for free enterprise, and the consuming desire of a diminutive and self-proclaimed general by the name of Walker for conquest and glory in Central America. As a result of these and related maneuvers, some young men were drilling for the seizure of Cuba while others were bound for battle in Kansas, and still others were charging on Grenada in Nicaragua with its avenues of palms, its orange trees and gold-tinted Cathedral of Guadeloupe.

Nor were the stratagems of these years unrelated to the massive blood-shed of the next decade in which 617,528 young Americans were killed at Bull Run and the Wilderness, Antietam, Chancellorsville, Gettysburg, Vicksburg, and Cold Harbor, in 2,400 battles which have received the honor of names, and thousands of crossroads skirmishes and chance encounters which never received the recognition of designation.

"THE SKY WAS NEVER SO DARK"

I

The Kansas-Nebraska Bill was signed into law by President Franklin Pierce on May 30, 1854. In the same year, the pro-slavery administration of President Pierce, dominated, so many thought, by Jefferson Davis, his Secretary of War and one of the South's most powerful advocates of slavery's expansion,* issued the Ostend Manifesto. Believing Cuba indispensable to the security of American slavery, and fearing that slavery might be abolished there with dire effect on the institution in the United States, the American pro-slavery ministers to Spain, France, and Great Britain proclaimed at Ostend, at the instigation of the administration, that Cuba "by every law human and divine" should be ours, by purchase if possible, by force if necessary.

Giving substance to such threats and many others less explicit were thousands of Southern filibusters, mobilizing during 1854 and 1855 in staging areas in the Gulf States, their object the conquest of Cuba. Jefferson Davis himself had been offered command of a similar expedition and payment of $200,000 in 1849, but thinking it improper for one serving in the United States Senate, as he then was, to invade Cuba he had recommended Major Robert E. Lee of the United States Army as the commander of the expedition.[1] Lee, too, had refused. But now the Secretary of War's political associate and old comrade-in-arms during the Mexican War, former Governor John A. Quitman of Mississippi, who was to receive $1 million from a Cuban junta to finance the attack, agreed to head the expedition.[2]

---

* Caleb Cushing, of Massachusetts, and as pro-slavery and expansionist in his views as Davis, was Attorney General in the Pierce cabinet, and also influential with the President.

It was proposed to annex the island by way of Quitman's conquest and admit it into the Union as a slave state, using much the same procedure as had been used to gain Texas.[3] As plans to seize or purchase more of Mexico for more slave territory, forming more slave states, were being covertly advocated, William Walker was sailing from San Francisco in May of 1855 with a rag-tailed army of fifty-eight, soon to be known as the Immortals and to conquer and take over Nicaragua as a first step in attempting to reduce all of Central America.[4] His plans had the sympathy and tacit backing of Secretary Davis,[5] who felt that an invasion of Nicaragua might help in the seizure of Cuba, outflanking it to the south and providing another base for invasion secret and secure from the prying eyes of anti-slavery Americans as well as without the jurisdiction of American law forbidding filibustering. Walker was eager to try for Cuba's conquest. In fact, it was part of his plan from the first. After all, Quitman might fail, and it was well, Davis apparently thought, to have other insurance.

Such failure, for a time, seemed unlikely. Some 50,000 men were reported to have joined Quitman, most from the Gulf States, but reinforced by a contingent of 1,000 from Kentucky.[6] Many of those enlisting were members of the "Order of the Lone Star," only one of several secret organizations, accompanied by lurid ritual, which were formed for political purposes in the 1850's. As Quitman rounded up transport and ammunition, chartering eight steamers and four sailing vessels, buying ninety field pieces and an immense quantity of small arms, he was cheered in the difficult business by his belief that he was carrying out the cherished aim of the administration. His belief stemmed from a series of discussions with "distinguished persons at the seat of government." He did not specifically mention his friend, the Secretary of War, but most felt that Davis was included in Quitman's "distinguished persons," and perhaps even the President himself, to whom Quitman had written more than once on the necessity of annexing Cuba. After his conference with leading officials, he had left Washington "with the distinct impression . . . not only that he had their sympathies, but that there could be no pretext for an intervention by federal authorities." [7]

And there probably would have been none had it not been for the great cry of protest that had gone up in the North against the Kansas-Nebraska Act specifically and against slavery's further expansion generally. The President had also decided that it might be safer to buy Cuba than invade it or at least to try to do so before the possible seizure announced at Ostend. It was clear to him, moreover, that if thousands above the Ohio were revolting against slavery's possible expansion at home, they were not likely to favor slavery's extension by armed conquest in the Caribbean. He could afford to wait out the protest—there were two more years of his term—before proceeding on his announced program of expansion into foreign fields, which he had vowed to carry out in his inaugural.[8]

Poor Quitman, assured and reassured by the administration, or so he thought, was the first victim of the North's clamor. He was cited before a federal grand jury in New Orleans for the violation of the neutrality laws that he thought Davis and Pierce had desired him to violate. Instead of wishing him Godspeed they had broken up and abandoned the expedition which their advice and consent had called into being.

But Quitman did not give up, despite the fact that he had been placed under bond not to violate the neutrality laws by engaging in his own private war against Spain, a sovereign state and the owner of Cuba. He felt that his support in both North and South, and in Cuba itself, was too influential to admit of surrender. He had no faith in the proclamation at Ostend as a means of actually acquiring Cuba, attacked as it was by anti-slavery forces at home as well as by Spain, France, and England abroad. If it was to be done, Quitman would have to do it. Slowly and with difficulty he organized another army, this one not as blatant in its presence and far more secretive than his first, divided up among a number of staging areas in and about New Orleans where support for him and his filibusters was as widespread as it was ardent. In this expedition, as in his first, he had the support of certain Northern commercial interests as well as widespread support throughout the South, save for the most conservative of its citizens.[9] He had, for example, as he had in his first attempt, the financial aid of "Live Oaks" George Law, a New York shipping magnate, president of the United States Mail Steamship Company, with interests in Havana and as passionate an advocate of the annexation of Cuba as Quitman himself.

By early 1855, he had ten thousand volunteers and Alexander H. Stephens, future Vice President of the Confederacy, urged Quitman to embark immediately and invade. By that time, however, it was impossible. The Cuban junta, which had backed Quitman, suddenly demanded to know, and with a good deal of publicity, where and how the $1 million it had paid him had been spent. Its members inferred he was only a crook, ignoring whatever were the higher aspects of his nature as he sought to spread the area of slavery. A splinter faction of the junta began not only to oppose him but to expose his plans for invasion.

At the same time, and perhaps as no coincidence, the Spanish Governor General came into possession of all of Quitman's plans of invasion. He posted Spanish military forces around the perimeter of the island in such a way that invasion would have been suicide. Quitman called off his invasion, scarcely having any other recourse. Later he was elected to Congress, where he still diverted and justified himself by periodically calling for the invasion and annexation of Cuba. He was as eager for the conquest of all of Mexico, a not uncommon demand in the South, although some favored acquiring only Sonora or Yucatan. But few paid much attention to an aging failure, however much they agreed with his goal.[10] Young William Walker seemed to have that destiny of success that made it almost inevitable, his admirers believed, that he could succeed where Quitman had failed.

2

A more important result of the Kansas-Nebraska Act agitation, much more important than the thwarting of Quitman, was the organization of the Republican Party at Ripon, Wisconsin, in the spring of 1854, its central tenet opposition to the extension of slavery. More than anything else, this was an indication of the deep and passionate feeling slavery's attempts at expansion were finally beginning to arouse. It takes a massive upheaval, a giant reversal of sentiment, a political tidal wave to sweep most Americans from party affiliations and party beliefs long held. It takes work by thousands and work by professionals to form a new party and it requires an almost universal sense of outrage to animate people into this kind of action. The new organization was launched as a popular movement at Jackson, Michigan, on July 6. Although the Democratic Party was still strong in the North, with the Cotton Whigs, the Hunker Whigs fighting for their lives, the Republicans from the first had the potential of a real mass party. They were a factor that could not be ignored, only six years removed from presidential victory. From almost the first, too, slaveholders branded it a sectional party whose victory in a national election would result in the South's secession.

In the fall elections of 1854, two years after the landslide victory of Pierce on a pro-slavery Democratic platform, the Republicans and their Free Soil allies, including increasing numbers of erstwhile Whigs and Democrats, scored notable advances in Iowa, Michigan, Wisconsin, Vermont, and Maine, as well as gains in New York and Massachusetts, although the presence of the Know-Nothings in the last two states served somewhat to obscure the anti-slavery advances. The next year the Republicans elected Salmon P. Chase, United States senator from 1849 to 1855 and a foremost opponent of the Kansas-Nebraska Bill, Governor of Ohio where the party also carried the legislature.

Yet it must be remembered that the Republican Party was formed to an extent on alarm, on fear that the South was winning and that if not stopped slavery might be triumphant in the whole country. The ballots of a new party sometimes seemed a frail response to the guns and expansionist threats of the South being directed against more places than Kansas. If the North, in the months and years immediately ensuing, had a new sense of urgency demanding new and independent political action, the South was winning in Kansas, its repeated armed invasions during 1854 and 1855 still almost unresisted, transforming a vital Territory in the center of the country that had once been free into a slave area where even verbal opposition to slavery might result in a prison sentence as provided by the force-imposed territorial code of law.

Nor was that the South's only victory. Young General Walker, now President of Nicaragua, was soon to overcome his alleged prejudice against slavery and—after allying himself with the most expansionist of Southern slaveholders as well as with Northern expansionist interests—was to impose slavery on that conquered country by decree.[11] Many Northerners feared that despite Quitman's failure they would soon hear news of the seizure of Cuba, of further forays into Mexico and Central America. If the slaveholders won in Kansas, and it seemed as if they would, the same procedures would be used in Utah, New Mexico, and Nebraska, where slaves and slaveholders were legally entitled to admission and where the contest would be decided by the same so-called squatter sovereignty now apparently winning for slavery in Kansas. Many Northerners felt that the Supreme Court, as eager to help slaveholders as was the President, might soon declare, as it did in 1857, that slavery was legal in all the territories of the United States.

"Never was the Slave Power more insolent in its consciousness of strength, or wilder in its delirium of empire," it was later said of this surge of 1854–5.[12] In addition to its other designs for foreign conquest, the Pierce administration had plans to acquire Samana Bay in Santo Domingo with its accompanying menace to neighboring Haiti, while an American naval expedition was exploring the valley of the Amazon with a "distinct reference to a pro-slavery colonization" and "an ultimate view to annexation," according to *The Liberator*.[13] Senator Sumner of Massachusetts said that when the Senate was in executive session he felt as if he were in a council of pirates. "They speak of getting Cuba and getting the Amazon and getting this and that," he said, "and that in disregard of all principles of the law of nations." [14]

It was at this apogee of success, more illusory than real and perhaps given more credence in the North than in the South, that even as optimistic a battler against slavery as Wendell Phillips declared that the struggle to abolish it had been defeated by Southern victory. Under indictment in Boston for his part in the Burns rescue attempt, he wrote in August of 1854 to a friend in England:

Indeed the *Government* has fallen into the hands of the Slave Power completely. So far as national politics are concerned we are beaten—there's no hope. We shall have Cuba in a year or two Mexico in five. . . . The future seems to unfold a vast slave empire united with Brazil, and darkening the whole west. I hope I may be a false prophet but the sky was never so dark. Our Union, all confess, must sever finally on this question. It is now with nine-tenths only a question of time.[15]

Nor was Phillips's estimate unusual. Similar statements were made by some of the bravest fighters against slavery, although in emphasizing despair they were often trying to arouse the North to greater efforts toward reversing the tide of events. Senator Wade of Ohio said, "The humiliation of the North is complete and overwhelming. No Southern enemy of hers can wish her deeper degradation." [16] And Giddings, who not many years hence would contribute to John Brown's cause, asked:

Who does not know that Southern and servile presses are already proclaiming . . . that slavery shall next be admitted into Minnesota, Washington and Oregon? Who does not know that the President and Cabinet are laboring . . . for a war on Spain with the undisguised purpose of maintaining slavery in Cuba? That Southern papers insist that we also conquer St. Domingo and restore slavery there? Then form an alliance with slaveholding Brazil as the only nation besides ours that legalizes the crimes of the peculiar institution? [17]

Even John Brown was suffering from a kind of angry despair as he surveyed the scene from Akron in January of 1854, expecting then to return to North Elba in the spring. As he read his newspapers he could see little that would save the nation from destruction. On January 9 he addressed a letter to Frederick Douglass expressing his fears.[18] He foresaw, unless the course of events was reversed, an utter breakdown in law, complete anarchy, followed by complete despotism in which the nation would be the captive of "fallen men," who would place the weight of slavery upon the entire country.

3

Yet the dismay experienced by John Brown, Wendell Phillips, Senator Wade, Giddings, and others was comparatively transient, a prelude to hard resolve, an essentially constructive recognition of the mounting peril facing the country. They could sense, as could most who felt or thought at all, the approach of a qualitative change in the spreading conflict. It was difficult in 1854 to foresee the development of the newly founded Republican Party, although for the next years it would grow by the week and month from the North's outrage over "Bleeding Kansas" into a great new revolutionary force that would harness the North's superiority in population, agriculture, transportation, and industry in opposition to the spread of slavery and profoundly change the balance of the contending forces struggling for control of the continental United States. It was easier for abolitionists and others to see—indeed, quite impossible not to—the mounting Southern victories.

Often recalled in anti-slavery circles was the alleged threat of Senator Robert Tombs of Georgia that "Before long the master will sit down with his slaves at the foot of Bunker Hill Monument." [19] Often emphasized was the belief that the South had enjoyed nothing but victory for thirty years with a resulting momentum that might prove irresistible, while in the North many leading citizens were themselves a part of "the Slave Power." [20] So, in a different way, were many of the North's rank and file, members of the Democratic Party, and no more eager for black liberation than some more wealthy. More anti-slavery adherents were beginning to fear that instead of slavery being abolished in the South, it might be established in the North.[21] It was increasingly being described in the South as "a moral good," "the least objectionable form of labour," "fit for Northern whites not less than African negroes." [22] Many in the free states were beginning to feel that the question was not so much the abolition of slavery as the abolition of the nation itself, that they were engaged in a struggle not only to eliminate or contain slavery but for the very life of democratic government.[23]

Garrison's formula in the face of the new and more dangerous situation was for the North to secede from the Union, to wash its hands of the South's slavery and the South's federal government, the identical policy of the South, if for very different reasons, when the North later controlled the federal power. (By 1857 Garrison would organize a Disunion Convention.) Theodore Parker, often called a traitor * and at this point about to be tried in federal court for his part in the Burns rescue attempt, was all for

---

* Garrison introduced Parker before an anti-slavery convention in New York in 1856 with the words: "Ladies and Gentlemen, the fanaticism and infidelity and treason which are hateful to traffickers in slaves and the souls of men must be well pleasing to God and are indications of true loyalty to the cause of liberty. I have the pleasure of introducing to you a very excellent fanatic, a very good infidel, and a first rate traitor, in the person of Theodore Parker of Boston."

fighting, if it came to that, without deserting the Union or the slaves within its precincts. He was trying to organize a convention of the Free States at Buffalo or Pittsburgh in 1854 to formulate measures for defeating the South's aggression while abolishing slavery.[24] Presently he was declaring that while he ordinarily spent $1,500 a year for books, he now intended to spend $1,300 of that sum for cannon to be used in Kansas and perhaps a larger war. "I make all my pecuniary arrangements," he wrote, "with the expectation of civil war." [25]

Parker's expectation was becoming a norm among militants both above and below the Ohio as both sides organized for war in Kansas. Leaders of each believed that if Kansas were won permanently other victories in the West would follow and through them they might attain such a decisive position as to take over the national government in near perpetuity or at the very least gain a victory putting them in a more favorable position to win a greater civil war if and when it came. Each side feared that the loss of Kansas, then extending to the Rockies, might be fatal, a Southerner writing in *DeBow's Review*, "If Kansas is not secured, there will never be another slave state, and the abolitionists will rule the nation; the Union will then become a curse rather than a blessing." [26] In the North it was believed that if Kansas was won for slavery all the territory south of the old Missouri Compromise line to the Pacific, including the southern half of California, would be divided into slave states with enough representation to dominate the North. As for predictions of a country-wide civil war, even President Pierce by the end of 1855 was warning of that danger as the result, he said, of "a fanatical devotion" in the North to "a relatively few Africans"—his description of the almost four million black Americans held in slavery.[27]

In the South there were those speaking more stridently and more frequently for war if necessary in defense of secession, although one of the earliest advocates of separatism and independence said, and others believed it, that the Yankees were "too discreet and careful of their own interests to sacrifice millions of treasure and many thousands of lives" in a war they were bound to lose.[28] Some restless and energetic spirits, as we shall soon see, were planning war on the high northern plains of Mexico, on the Spanish main, and in Cuba, Ecuador, and Columbia, as well as at home, if required, the common denominator of all the projects being the defense and extension of slavery.

These organizers and proponents of war, whether in Kansas or in defense of secession or further afield, were a strange lot, as diverse in their personalities as they were different in their plans, and including the noble and the raffish, the confidence man and the demagogue, the adventurer and the martyr. President Pierce perceived, however, in those planning private fili- bustering invasions abroad "the courageous and self-reliant spirit of our people" and saw their plans as "hardy enterprises."[29] Perhaps none of these organizers for war—whether North or South, approved or disapproved by President Pierce—was stranger than a bald-headed Massachusetts school- teacher of thirty-five who had undergone an almost religious experience when it was suddenly revealed to him how the power of a growing Northern capitalism, profits and dividends, might be used to defeat slavery in Kansas and everywhere else. President Pierce was to say that such as he were revolutionaries[30] and perhaps he was right. But one would have had to search far and wide for another revolutionary as openly admiring of corporate re- ports, the sale of stock, and the payment of dividends to those investing in liberty.

PATRIOTISM AND PROFIT

I

Few were transformed more swiftly or more completely by the furore in the North over the Kansas-Nebraska Bill than Eli Thayer, the shrewd and plausible schoolteacher in Massachusetts, already moderately wealthy at thirty-five because of his unfailing eye for the main chance and the available dollar. As some young men dreamed of noble service, he dreamed inces- santly of moneymaking schemes. Capitalization, amortization, incorporation were his poetry, and while he had nothing against noble service (in fact he rather aspired to it), he saw no reason why it should not be accompanied by profit and advancement to himself.[31]

He came to maturity with mortgages and interest rates at the center of his being. He periodically experienced visions of epic sweep but they had to deal with real estate and promotions and all the grand opportunities everywhere present for profit, a word he used frequently and rolled lovingly over the tongue. The census report of 1850 became his Bible and there was not a statistic in it showing the phenomenal growth of population, land values, industry, and railroads in the North generally, but in Massachusetts specifically, that he could not, and did not, endow with a kind of lyric grandeur, particularly during his great crusade to save Kansas from slavery.[32]

He used these glowing figures when electioneering and did so effectively enough to be chosen representative for Worcester in the state legislature in 1852. It should be said immediately, however, that as the self-appointed poet laureate of the North's growing industrial capitalism he was much more interested in the manifest destiny of its advance than his own personal profit. He would rather be right than rich but saw no reason why he could not be both. There was no illness of the body politic, he knew, that could not be cured by a strong unadulterated dose of *laissez faire* in the form of the money-making, dividend-declaring corporation.

Even as a young man he had that reassuring maturity that comes from a truly noble beard, betrayed only by his eager eyes, a little too feverish perhaps, peeking out above it. He was still in his twenties when he became obsessed with the potential value of Goat Hill, a rugged ascent on the edge of Worcester. Borrowing enough for a down payment, he sold most of it for a handsome profit and with the proceeds built on the remainder a large and fantastic castle, complete with turrets and towers and containing everything but a moat and drawbridge. Into a section of it he moved his family, for he was already married and had several children, using the rest of his castle to go into business for himself. His business was education, having worked his way through the Worcester County Manual Labor High School and Brown University by teaching school and later becoming principal of the Worcester Academy. In his castle on Goat Hill he established the Oread Collegiate Institute, one of the first women's colleges. While he administered it, teaching several classes himself as he pursued options on neighboring land, he also ran for office, being elected first to the school board and then to the board of aldermen before rising to the state legislature.[33]

His panegyrics to New England enterprise, particularly to that of Worcester, where new factories were rising fast and which contained in and about its environs an extraordinary group of inventors and mechanics, did not harm him in his quest for office.* A descendant of John and Priscilla

---

* "The mechanics of Worcester were unsurpassed for their ingenuity anywhere on the face of the earth. Worcester was the center and home of invention. Within a circle of twelve miles radius, was the home of Blanchard, the inventor of the machine for turning irregular forms; of Elias Howe, the inventor of the sewing machine; of Eli Whitney, the inventor of the cotton gin, which doubled the value of every acre of cotton-producing land in the country; of Erastus B. Bigelow, the inventor of the carpet machine; of Hawes, the inventor of the envelope machine; of Crompton and Knowles, Nourse and Mason, in whose establishment the modern plow was brought to perfection, and a great variety of other agricultural implements invented and improved. There were many other men whose inventive genius and public usefulness was entitled to rank with these. The first housewarming furnace was introduced here, and the second cupola furnace was set up near by. These inventors and mechanics were all men of

Alden, he was as parochially patriotic as the narrowest South Carolinian, believing that all ability (including his own) originated in the Bay State, that Plymouth Rock was the beginning of history and Bunker Hill its height, until a more significant event occurred that had sprung full-blown from his own brain while musing over the power and glory of an expanding capitalism.

If the idea changed Thayer, transforming him in his own view into the generalissimo of anti-slavery forces, it also transformed the North, particularly in those higher echelons of commerce and industry which had never before moved against slavery. If he was "teched" a trifle by his great idea, presently feeling that it could replace filibustering and peacefully conquer Central America, he was at the same time so overwhelmingly representative of all that his section contained in the way of commercial and industrial aspiration that when he spoke to the North's conservative wealthy it was as deep calling unto deep.

2

The great idea came to him while the Kansas-Nebraska Bill was still being debated in the Senate and weeks before it was passed. Heretofore he had been little concerned with slavery. It offended his aesthetic sense—he liked to say that one $10 steam engine could perform more work for $5 a year than a Negro slave costing $1,000 and $150 a year to feed and clothe—but he was more against those trying to abolish slavery than he was against slavery itself. He had always held, and continued to hold, that slavery was a greater wrong to the white than the black since it impoverished the whole South, and put a brake on the North's development.[34] Moreover, slavery had brought into being the country's chief curse, the Garrisonians who, in his view, would destroy the country before they abolished slavery. They were the main menace, he seemed to feel, not slavery.[35]

But within days of the introduction of the Kansas-Nebraska Bill into Congress, he had experienced a striking change. Thayer provides added proof that 1854 was the year of decision in American life before the Civil War. It symbolized the high-water mark of the Southern pro-slavery offensive, although few knew it then, the beginning of effective Northern resistance.

---

great public spirit, proud of Worcester, of its great achievements, and its great hope. They got rich rapidly." George F. Hoar, *Autobiography of Seventy Years*, New York, 1903, vol. I, p. 159. Corporations for the development and manufacture of these inventions were soon formed, and their return in dividends was part of the process that gave Eli Thayer his great faith in corporations and profit as an engine of progress.

Protest meetings were so numerous and so belligerent in temper that it would have taken a less intelligent politician than Eli Thayer not to see that he could never again be indifferent to slavery if re-election or political advancement was his goal. He already had his eyes on the congressional seat to which he was elected in 1856. Still, he was not a man to surrender entirely. If he was willing to join the protest it was on his own terms, particularly when he knew that the wealthy and conservative, without whom nothing could be won, had yet to enlist in the battle. If he was astonished at the depth and feeling of the protest, he was even more astounded that most above the Ohio were opposing the squatter sovereignty provisions of the bill in the apparent belief that in a contest at the ballot box between free enterprise and slavery, free labor and slave labor, slavery was bound to win. Thayer did not agree. He welcomed the contest, knowing as he knew that there were one hundred cents in every dollar, that nothing could stand before the power of profit and dividends in an expanding industrial capitalism.[36]

To most, including himself for a time, this knowledge seemed a non sequitur to the looming battle of gun and bowie knife for the possession of Kansas. But Thayer, hurt by the North's lack of faith in the system he celebrated almost daily, could think of nothing else but the coming struggle and how the drive for profits might be harnessed to it. Day and night, he said, in his dreams and while at work, the question dogged him. Where the solution came to him, whether in bed staring at the ceiling or listening to but not hearing the chatter of his wife, he never revealed. But he did say that when the vision came, it came complete and whole and long before the debate on the Kansas-Nebraska Bill was over, weeks before it became law. "Suddenly it came upon me like a revelation," [37] he said, and in an instant the North's plight as to Kansas and his own penchant for moneymaking, his own tendency to the fond contemplation of stocks, capitalization, and dividends all meshed together and he had the invention, for so he always regarded it, that would save the country.

His plan involved a $5 million corporation, called the Massachusetts Emigrant Aid Company, which would defeat the South in Kansas while earning "a profitable dividend in cash" for its stockholders by the export to the Territory of the Northern system of free labor and free enterprise. He proposed to send whole communities entire and all at once to Kansas, recruited and organized by his Emigrant Aid Company, where churches, schools, hotels, newspapers, and sawmills, owned by the company, along with choice land sites, would steadily increase in value as the company sent more and more emigrants in. The more people the company sent, the more the value of its land, hotels, and sawmills would increase while the greater dividends became, the more certain would be the victory of Free State forces. In selling his stock in $100 shares with only $5 immediately payable and promising dividends he was like a medicine man selling a cure-all. He said there was no greater happiness in the world than in uniting patriotism with profit. "When a man can do a magnanimous act, when he can do a decidedly good thing, and at the same time make money by it, all his faculties are in harmony," he said.[38]

For a time Thayer was irresistible. He had all the energy and dogmatic certainty of a man possessed and the great and wealthy who ordinarily might have paid him little heed were as putty in the young man's hands. He was convinced that the North was demoralized and waiting for a practical plan and he had it. He was certain that merchants who wanted larger sales, that investors who planned on a transcontinental railroad running through Kansas, that thousands of land-hungry farmers and laborers were dismayed at the possibility that slavery might own the West unless it was defeated by popular sovereignty. He was sure that those wealthy men in the North who heretofore had been regarded as pro-slavery Whigs and loyal Democrats had had enough. They were only waiting, he believed, for a legal and peaceful plan to oppose slavery's expansion, a plan thoroughly divorced from the Garrisonians advocating disunion.

Within a matter of hours after receiving his vision, he had forced through the Massachusetts legislature, of which he was still a member, a vote authorizing the charter for his company. One of the first he chose for his board of directors was Dr. Samuel Gridley Howe and one of the first who bought his stock was Charles Francis Adams, who subscribed $25,000, while Theodore Parker called together a congregation of ministers to preach the virtues of Thayer's plan.

Thayer acted at the beginning as president *pro tem*. Within a space of days he had convinced Horace Greeley, owner and editor of the *New York Tribune* and a power in the Whig Party, of the worth of his plan. Greeley called for subscriptions to the stock in a series of editorial articles called "The Plan of Freedom." Not long later Thayer had converted William Cullen Bryant, editor of the *New York Evening Post*, who was soon to leave the Democratic Party because of its support of slavery. In Boston, the *Daily Advertiser*, leading Whig organ of New England, advocated the Emigrant Aid Company and soon much of the Whig press in the North, most of it vacillating in its loyalty to the Whig Party, was writing editorials urging young men to enlist in the companies for Kansas and older men to subscribe to stock.

Before speaking to Horace Greeley, Thayer had hired Chapman Hall in Boston where he spoke twice daily, at one meeting gaining pledges for stock from businessmen, at the other seeking enlistments for emigration to Kansas. Although he had never been to Kansas he described its beauties and opportunities for wealth with so much eloquence—not at Chapman Hall alone, but soon all over the North from Bangor to Cleveland to Buffalo, and at a hundred whistle stops in between—that presently parties and individuals were leaving for Kansas from New Haven and Providence, from Albany and Detroit and Milwaukee, often expecting to find in the wilderness all the comforts of home as supplied by the Emigrant Aid Company.*

3

From the first Thayer said firmly he wanted no abolitionists either to subscribe to his stock or enlist in his companies. Not only were they defeatists, he said, believing Kansas already lost, but they would alienate the kind of solid Whig and loyal Democrat, hitherto either pro-slavery or silent on the subject, that he wanted as the basis of his organization.[39] The kind of men he desired as directors were such as Reuben A. Chapman, of Springfield, who had supported the Fugitive Slave Act and was generally regarded in Springfield as pro-slavery, as he himself proudly reported during a speech in that city in behalf of the Emigrant Aid Company.†[40] The type whose sub-

---

* Thayer had been a factor, if only indirectly, in sending the Brown brothers to Kansas. He had asked the Reverend Edward Everett Hale—a young neighbor in Worcester who later wrote *The Man Without a Country* and always described himself as "Thayer's man Friday" in the Kansas crusade—to write a book encouraging emigration to Kansas and implying that such was the fertility of its soil and the salubrity of its climate that a man, particularly if he was a farmer, could scarcely avoid becoming rich if he settled there. The book, 247 pages in length and called *Kansas and Nebraska: An Account of the Emigrant Aid Companies and Directions to Emigrants,* was published in August of 1854 and widely distributed. In December a copy of it was bought in Akron by the two elder Brown brothers. The book with their names and the date written in it, apparently in Jason's handwriting, "Jason Brown and John Brown, Akron, Dec 20th 1854," is now in the Sol Feinstone Collection at the Syracuse University Library. Its descriptions of streams and rivers, of forested land along their banks, of thriving wheat, corn, oats, and cattle on the few farms already in the Territory, could not have discouraged the brothers in their intent to emigrate as they looked about drought-stricken Ohio.

† Chapman was the first lawyer John Brown asked for after his defeat and capture at Harper's Ferry because, he said, he did not want an abolitionist lawyer who would only antagonize the local citizens. Chapman refused to represent Brown.

scription Thayer valued was exemplified by the New York merchants who later pledged $100,000 after he asked them to compare their sales in the free state of Ohio with the slave state of Kentucky and said they had a stronger pecuniary interest in keeping Kansas free than "any other people in the Union." [41] The kind of backing that he wanted was such as that of John Murray Forbes, Emerson's friend, whose son married Emerson's daughter, and who in 1854 took one hundred shares at a price of $1,000, perhaps not entirely unmindful of the injustice of slavery or of the fact that he was involved in the financing and building of the Hannibal and St. Joseph Railroad, which must seek an outlet across the Territory of Kansas if it were to become a transcontinental route, as it did become.[42]

Thayer may have been jubilant when another loyal Whig joined his cause. He was Amos Adams Lawrence, scion of the Massachusetts textile dynasty, with wide interests in railroads, textiles, and Western lands, one of the wealthiest of Americans and one of the country's most generous philanthropists. He liked to describe himself as a Hunker against all Higher Law but for the observance of any and every law on the statute books. He was not only against the abolitionists, but against the Free Soil Party and the Republican Party as sectional disrupters of the Union, although he saw the expansion of slavery as a menace even though his textile interests depended on the South for cotton.[43]

Lawrence was a strange man, as bold as brass one day and the next almost obsequious toward any authority, particularly that of the federal government. He had offered the federal government his personal help in returning the fugitive Sims but a few years later was grief-stricken at the return of Burns. It sometimes seemed as if he was brave enough concerning Kansas when he thought in the light of his Western interests and conservative when he thought of his mammoth textile holdings. But it went deeper than that. He had an extraordinary reverence for his father, Amos Lawrence, and his uncle, Abbott Lawrence, the founders and owners of the Atlantic Cotton Mills and the Pacific Mills at Lawrence, where the brothers owned the water power. They had worshipped Whiggism as the Covenant of the Ark, as the holy of holies, the sole advocate of a protective tariff, the sole friend of business, and it had been a family policy never to offend the tenets of the Whig Party, the authority in power, or the slaveholders who controlled cotton.

It was this policy, bred into him with his mother's milk and his father's money, that caused Lawrence to vacillate so widely after he decided to fight for a free Kansas; and there would come a time when he would whine miserably to Jefferson Davis that he had always been a friend to any and all laws, including those which authorized slavery.[44] Even a Lawrence is swayed by a tidal wave of opinion such as arose in the North after the introduction of the Kansas-Nebraska Bill and increased after its passage, and even a Lawrence may retreat if he is later menaced by a country-wide civil war.

But Lawrence, whatever his vacillations, always took charge of any venture in which he was intimately concerned. From the first he downgraded Thayer and from the beginning of his association he insisted that there would have to be a new charter. Under it he was named treasurer of what was called the New England Emigrant Aid Company. This provided for a capitalization of $1 million instead of $5 million, which had only been a device on Thayer's part, or so some said, to frighten the South rather than an amount which he had any real hope of obtaining through his sale of stock. But what hurt Thayer most was that Lawrence said he would have to desist in speaking so grandiloquently and constantly about profit and dividends as if that, instead of liberty, was the sole desire of the Emigrant Aid Company.

For the fact was that Thayer's unabashed love of money and profit embarrassed many who loved them as much as he did. He was so frank about it. He admired both so much he could not conceive of not declaring it. It was often apparent, a little too plainly for some, that he did not so much hate slavery as hate a system which denied to capitalism its fullest development. He was so ardent in his love for dividends, so evangelical in his certainty that the colonization of capitalism in Kansas would result in profit, that he was furnishing ammunition both to Southern opponents and to those in the North who thought there was a higher principle involved as to slavery than money.

He was bitter when Lawrence reorganized the company as well as checking him in his tactics. It was not that Lawrence did not want the company to make money. He just wanted less talk about it. Thereafter, Thayer always referred to the new company as operating on "the charity plan," although it also sold stock and bought property in Kansas but while emphasizing a free Kansas rather than dividends.

"My original plan," wrote Thayer years later, his bitterness still unabated,

was to form a business company, to be conducted upon business principles, able to make good dividends to its stockholders annually, and at its close, a full return of the money originally invested. To have done this would have required no marvelous financial skill. We should have had the power to build cities and towns wherever we might please to locate them and could invest money in western Missouri land as well as in Kansas. Twelve acres of land, now in the very center of Kansas City, were offered to us for $3000. The same tract is now worth several millions. I urged the purchase of this and other land in that place, but my associates opposed my views and the purchases were not made. The main objection of my associates to the original plan of a money-making company, was a fear that people might say we were influenced by pecuniary considerations in our patriotic work for Kansas.[45]

4

Months before the reorganization under Lawrence, Thayer had recruited and sent off from Boston the first pioneer colony for Kansas on July 17. It consisted of only twenty-seven men. "Immense crowds had gathered about the station to wish them godspeed," Thayer wrote. "They moved out of the station amid the cheering crowds who lined the tracks for several blocks."[46]

Thayer accompanied this first company through the state of New York. It was as near as he would ever get to Kansas, although as early as June he had sent ahead Dr. Charles Robinson, an adventurous and ambitious physician-journalist of Fitchburg, Massachusetts, who had engaged in a shooting affray during the California gold rush, as well as Charles H. Branscomb, as agents of the company to the Territory. They had selected the present site of Lawrence, then but an empty rolling prairie, beneath a hill near the Kansas River, for the initial settlement, it being the first desirable location in southeastern Kansas to which the Indians had ceded their rights.

Thayer left this first party of emigrants at Buffalo, turning back to organize more companies for Kansas and to sell more stock in the Emigrant Aid Company. If he was successful in both it was not entirely because of his own abilities. Resentment, instead of subsiding with the passage of the Kansas-Nebraska Act in the spring, seemed to be increasing weekly. The growing Republican Party, facing an election in the fall, was determined to win on the charge, agitated ceaselessly, that the administration was plotting to make Kansas slave territory, that the destiny of the nation would turn on its success or failure. The clergy, for the first time in the anti-slavery conflict, was almost a unit behind the crusade to make Kansas a free state.

Everywhere above the Ohio, and without assistance from Thayer or the New England Emigrant Aid Company, state and county and regional Kansas

Leagues or Aid Societies or Emigration Associations were being formed to recruit and aid emigrants. Thousands in the next months left from Ohio, Indiana, and Illinois, and many from Virginia and Kentucky, without benefit of organization or aid societies, in ox- or horse-drawn wagons containing their wives, children, and household goods, and driving a few cattle before them. Most of them, even those from such border states as Kentucky and Virginia, were anti-slavery not for the sake of the black but because they did not intend to compete with slave labor in the new Territory. Those going to Kansas were not primarily animated by anger over efforts to make Kansas slave territory; that was secondary to their hunger for the rich cheap land Kansas contained, some 126,000 square miles of unclaimed territory, going at $1.25 an acre for a quarter section, 160 acres, for those who lived upon and improved their claims. They would not have to pay when the land was bought from the federal government until the Territory was organized and the land surveyed.

As Thayer continued his organizing, aided by his assistant, the Reverend Edward Everett Hale, and by Dr. Thomas Webb, secretary of the Emigrant Aid Company, it sometimes seemed that despite his unusual success more Kansas organizations were being formed outside of New England than he and his assistants were organizing there. Many associations, Thayer reported, were being organized in 1854 "in Pennsylvania, New Jersey, southern New York, southern Ohio and Indiana," which sent companies of men and women to the Territory.[47] In Oberlin, the Kansas Emigrant Aid Association of Northern Ohio was organized. In Albany, a Kansas League was established at about the same time one was formed in Covington, Kentucky. The Union Emigration Society was founded at Washington, D.C. A New York Kansas League was established and later in that state an American Settlement Company. Vegetarians in New York were leaving the East to settle in an octagon-shaped colony in Kansas whose eight segments were to be divided into two farms of 102 acres each, all of the sixteen farms fronting upon a central octagon which was to be used for a common pasture. It would be a Utopia having all the advantages of a proper diet, the wilderness, and a rich community life.* Two emigrant aid societies were organized in Cincinnati, one of Germans called the Kansas Ansiedlungs-

---

* Almost one hundred vegetarians established such a colony on the western bank of the Neosho River, west of Fort Scott and six miles south of the present site of Humboldt, Kansas. By 1857 it had reverted to prairie and there was not a vegetarian or anyone else remaining in what had been the octagon settlement. See Russell Hickman, "The Vegetarian and Octagon Settlement Companies," *The Kansas Historical Quarterly*, November 1933.

verein.[48] By February 1855, 8,501 men, women, and children had emigrated to Kansas.[49]

Thayer later said that these companies of men, women, and children, unarmed save for an occasional squirrel rifle or some other weapon any ordinary farmer might have for hunting, were braver than the soldiers who enlisted in the Union Army during the Civil War.[50] They did not have a government to care for them. They had to supply their own food both on the way to Kansas and after they got there. They had to pay for their own transportation whether they went with an organized company or as a single family in a covered wagon as most went from Ohio, Kentucky, Indiana, and Illinois. They knew they were going into hostile territory from which the Indians were being ejected for land farther west, just as they had been previously forced from land east of the Mississippi River, after being solemnly promised the Kansas land from which they were again being expelled. But it was not the Indians they feared. It was the white inhabitants of the Missouri border, aroused by pro-slavery leaders to the point that they regarded every Free State settler as an invader hired to steal Missouri's slaves, and already known in the North as Border Ruffians.

5

The first party of settlers, twenty-nine in number, for they had gained two during their journey, arrived at what was later Lawrence on August 1, 1854, after traveling by ox teams from the village of Kansas City along the south bank of the Kansas River. They pitched their tents, supplied by the Emigrant Aid Company, on a hill beside the river which they called Mount Oread in honor of Thayer and his women's college on Goat Hill in Worcester. Two of the arrivals looked about the immense wilderness before darkness closed down on the little party, hearing the coyotes howl in the lonely distance, and deciding that this was not for them departed on the morrow for Kansas City and their homes in Massachusetts.[51]

Most of the men among this and later companies were farmers, hard men who had lived hard lives. But this company as well as subsequent ones had its share of entrepreneurs, speculators who hoped to buy town lots cheap and sell them dear when a growing population increased their value. There were tough and hardy men in this first company, such as Dr. John Doy and D. R. Anthony, earnest abolitionists, who would fight for Kansas with outstanding daring; but the company, and later ones as well, had its quota of men on the make uninterested in slavery or anything else that did not increase their profit. Thayer and Lawrence had stamped their identity and their policies on the emigrants and their leaders and there were few crusaders among them.

One who gave some evidence of their choice was Dr. Robinson, the Massachusetts physician employed by the Emigrant Aid Company, who led a larger party from Boston of about seventy men into the camp on Mount Oread two weeks later. He was a brave and able man but his great asset in the eyes of Lawrence and Thayer was his appearance of caution and judgment. He was anti-slavery, once describing himself as "in theory a non-resistant and an abolitionist," [52] but he never permitted theory to interfere with practice. Thus in California as a Forty-niner he led a group of squatters, whom he believed were being cheated of their land, into battle against the authorities of Sacramento, himself being seriously wounded, jailed, and charged with murder, the case later quashed. Two others were killed. He was elected to the territorial legislature of California where he was active in opposing a plot to make the southern half of California a slave state. But if he could act he could also compromise when that seemed to benefit him most. All in all he was just the man for Thayer and Lawrence.

In his middle thirties, sturdy and stocky, his expressionless face partly hidden by a beard, he had eyes as cold as ice. He was not an impulsive man and neither was he one to push around. To see him standing before a camp-fire under the stars of Mount Oread, keeping his own counsel and talking little, one might not have suspected that he would sometime be the very wealthy Governor of Kansas under unsuccessful impeachment proceedings, charged with illegally profiting from a state bond issue.

Near him was the young and jovial Samuel Pomeroy, also from Massachusetts, who had attended Amherst College as had Robinson. He was also an agent of the New England Emigrant Aid Company, and perhaps more positively anti-slavery than Robinson, having been a member of the abolitionist Liberty Party, somehow acceptable to Thayer, perhaps because he was not a Garrisonian. A born politician, often acting as a lobbyist before Congress for the New England Emigrant Aid Company, he too would do well in Kansas, being one of its first members in the United States Senate.

Within a short time of Robinson's arrival, it was found that he was a handy man to have around. Eighteen pro-slavery men, mounted and armed, alleging they had a prior claim to most of Lawrence, suddenly appeared in that little village of tents and announced they would attack its Free State settlers if they did not immediately remove a certain tent on one of their alleged claims. Thirty Free State men, led by that theoretical non-resister Dr. Robinson, immediately armed themselves, drawing themselves up in what they hoped was a military formation about 20 rods from the so-called Missourians.* As the two groups confronted each other, one of the Free Staters asked Dr. Robinson if he should fire to hit the Missourians or over their heads. Dr. Robinson replied that he "would be ashamed to fire at a man and not hit him." A man thought to be a spy left the Free State group "and went over to the other party which soon dispersed." It was thought that Dr. Robinson's remark had contributed to their departure.[53]

In the next weeks during the fall of 1854 four more parties left Boston, totaling, when their numbers were combined with the first two parties and with additions gained on the way, about 650 settlers. During the spring and summer of the following year, twelve companies left Boston containing 835 emigrants. They were joined by others as they proceeded west, at stopovers in Rochester, Buffalo, Detroit, Chicago, and St. Louis, Thayer declaring that the parties en route to Kansas often doubled and quadrupled in size but others believing that the increase was only about a quarter of their original number.[54]

It was men in these companies, or those immediately following, not interested in farming but in acquiring town sites, who founded the Free State communities of Lawrence, Topeka, Osawatomie, Manhattan, Wabaunsee, Hampden, Zeandale, Humboldt, Clafflin, Batcheller, and others. Kansas was founded on speculations in town sites, by pro-slavery entrepreneurs no less than Free State men, the former founding their towns in the northeast corner of the Territory where the Missouri, just before turning east for the Mississippi, formed the boundary between Kansas and its eastern slaveholding neighbor.

The wealthiest moving to the little settlements sometimes combined together to acquire a town site, occasionally as few as four men staking out claims to a quarter section each under the federal Pre-emption Act of 1841. Under this act, land was sold at $1.25 an acre to any settling on it and improving it before the area in which the claim was located was put up for public auction by order of the President. Combining their claims they would divide their town site of 640 acres into town lots, selling them for a handsome profit to those coming later, often at the same time deeding over property to the New England Emigrant Aid Company in return for a grist or sawmill or a building temporarily to house newly arriving settlers, or help in constructing a school or church. The company by 1855 owned a good deal of

---

* Several of the so-called Missourians were said to have come from the free states and to be more interested in obtaining certain claims in Lawrence than in the defense of slavery.

property in Kansas, hoping not so much for the dividends for which Thayer yearned but for a means of financing its operations.

Another means of acquiring a town site was by buying from the Indians what was called a "Wyandotte float." A good many leaders of the Wyandotte tribe had been given a section of public land, 640 acres, to induce them to move years before from Ohio and Michigan to Kansas. Now they were under the severest pressure to sell, usually at the rate of $1.25 an acre or $800 for a section. It was these sections which were called "Wyandotte floats," and many towns were founded on such a purchase.* Often a company was formed to undertake such a transaction, sometimes by as few as three men who owned the town and sold lots in it, sometimes by a few more who formed an association and sold shares in it, each buyer thereby owning a part of the town.

Osawatomie, for example, was owned by three men, O. C. Brown, William Ward, and S. C. Pomeroy as trustee of the Emigrant Aid Company, each holding a third interest, the share to the Emigrant Aid Company being in return for a sawmill and other improvements. The ownership of Topeka was divided into fifty shares in an association formed by nine men, the Emigrant Aid Company being given one-sixth of the shares after agreeing to build a sawmill, a schoolhouse, and a building for the receiving of emigrants.[55]

It was around these towns, virtually all in eastern Kansas and near the Missouri border, that most Free State farmers staked out their claims. Until surveyed, the claims could not be secure, and they could not be registered until surveyed, which was not done until the spring of 1856. The Pre-emption Law of 1841 stipulated that land did not have to be paid for until three months after its survey; in fact, it was almost impossible to pay the $1.25 an acre required until the location of a claimant's land could be determined. In the meantime, only strength could hold the land from marauders from Missouri, or from any group, Free State or otherwise, who could bring superior force against a claimant. As a result, groups of neighbors formed squatters associations to protect their claims and for at least two years these associations were about the only law in Kansas. In addition, most squatters wanted rights to a half section, 320 acres, instead of being held to the 160 provided in the pre-emption law. Often they used their squatters associations to enforce this extra-legal provision.

---

* As early as 1853 the government forced treaties on the Indian tribes north of the Kansas River, ceding 11,500,000 acres to the United States for pre-emption by settlers. The money from the sale of 634,000 acres to settlers was to go to the Indians. Other treaties were made with Indians south of the Kansas River, adding 2 million acres, most of it eligible for pre-emption by settlers.

It was the general practice in Missouri to regard all Free State settlers, however indifferent as to slavery, as abolitionists, come to steal their slaves. Yet the first fights between Free State men and pro-slavery settlers were not over slavery but over rival claims to the same land. Cole McCrea, a Free State farmer, shot and killed Malcolm Clark, a pro-slavery squatter, in a quarrel that broke out at a meeting of the Delaware Squatters Association on April 30, 1855. A little later F. N. Coleman, a pro-slavery settler, shot and killed Charles M. Dow, an anti-slavery man, in a murder precipitating the so-called Wakarusa War between Free Staters and pro-slavery Missourians.[56] If it seems a small matter, this quarrel over a few empty acres of wilderness, to be the partial cause of a civil war, it may be true that larger wars are often at bottom only the result of larger differences about larger property.

6

Whatever the immediate and partial cause, the long cold war over slavery, beginning with the birth of the nation, was about to change into hot, into a war in which bullets rather than words were decisive. Under the dynamics of events—the Kansas-Nebraska Act, the filibustering attempts against Cuba, the invasion by Walker of Nicaragua, the predominance and power of the Pierce pro-slavery administration, the formation and phenomenal growth of the Republican Party, the general feeling that as Kansas went as to slavery so would the nation go—more men than John Brown were beginning to show some evidence of change. By May of 1855 he was thinking again that perhaps he must go to Kansas and many others were thinking similarly.[57] A great American transformation, swelling as quickly and unexpectedly as a flash flood, was under way above the Ohio and would be followed soon enough in the South.

XXII

Slavery

Conquers Kansas

THE HAIR on the backs of the necks of most western Missourians rose in-stinctively upon hearing the word "abolitionist." No word in their lexicon indicated more strongly a foreign subversive, "a nigger stealer," a traitor to everything sacred and American. In the summer of 1854, rumors spread along the Missouri border that an army of 20,000 abolitionists, the spawn of far-away Yankee cities, Bibles in one hand and guns in the other, as Senator Douglas later said, was advancing on Missouri and Kansas. They were the hired mercenaries, so the report went, of a gigantic Eastern cor-poration, the New England Emigrant Aid Company, capitalized at the phe-nomenal sum of $5 million, paid to make Kansas free before they moved on to another territory to make it also free soil. It was probable, it was also said, that this army of abolitionists would invade Missouri, too, or at least make raids into it to free Missouri's slaves.*

---

* The source of the rumors was a rather flamboyant pamphlet written by Thayer and Hale about the Emigrant Aid Company and called the "Plan of Operations." To Missouri editors who read a Summary of the plan in the weekly edition of the *New York Tribune*, the pamphlet seemed to say that both the $5 million sought and the 20,000 emigrants to be recruited had already been raised and that the latter were about to start from Boston. Thayer and Hale had also written enthusiastically about planting Free State settlements throughout the Southwest from Kansas to New Mexico to Texas. Missourians felt that this same army, reported to be

If western Missouri ever was a monolithic unit, nearly one in its opposition to the alleged invaders whose advance guard, it was said, was already in Lawrence and other Kansas Free State settlements, it was so during 1854 and 1855. Almost everywhere it was believed, whether by poor farmers or prominent slaveholders or by the unemployed white supremacist riffraff of Missouri's border, that the Yankee "nigger stealers" were settling in a Kansas forbidden them and given to Missouri and slavery by a solemn if unofficial agreement supplementary to the passage of the Kansas-Nebraska Act. That agreement, they said, provided that Kansas would be made slave territory in return for the South's concession in surrendering Nebraska to free soil. Now these "foreigners," as Free State settlers were often described, were "intermeddling" in affairs that did not concern them by locating in a Kansas which had already been ceded to Missouri and slavery.[1]

SENATOR ATCHISON STARTS A WAR

I

The slaveholders of the Missouri border, owning (as we know) some fifty thousand slaves valued at about $25 million,[2] were the leading citizens of the western portions of the state, of Holt, Andrew, Buchanan, Platte, Clay, and Ray counties in the north, of Jackson, Cass, and Bates in the center of the Missouri-Kansas border, and Jasper, Barton, and Vernon counties in the south. They had considerable strength north and south of the Missouri River bisecting the state, in Lafayette and Saline counties to the south, in Carroll, Howard, Boone, and Macon counties to the north, the last three a hundred miles removed from the Kansas border. That the Free State settlers in Kansas were a menace they had no doubt. Slavery in Missouri was already hemmed in on the north by the free soil of Iowa, on the east by the Free State of Illinois, and many slaves were escaping in both directions. Neither did they doubt that a free Kansas to the west would mean the virtual end of slavery in Missouri, passing a resolution to that effect at a large and representative pro-slavery convention in July of 1855 at Lexington, Missouri.*[3]

---

embarking from Boston, would be used in all the operations. At about the same time, Horace Greeley had written editorially about carrying the war into Africa and some western Missourians interpreted this as a disclosure that their state was to be invaded. See Johnson, *Battle Cry of Freedom*, p. 95.

* However preponderant pro-slavery sentiment was in western Missouri, there were exceptions, decent, middle-class farmers, often from the South, who had moved West to avoid the compe-

Hundreds of land-hungry Missouri farmers, many of whom had already staked out claims in Kansas, were anxious for help from Missouri in protecting their land which they believed was being stolen from them by foreign intruders. If most of them were not slaveholders (and some were even opposed to slavery), many hoped to become so right there in Kansas. Thousands on the border of western Missouri, not many years removed from the frontier and including ex-buffalo hunters, former teamsters on the Santa Fe trail, broken-down fur-trappers back from the Rockies, disappointed gold miners returned from California and Colorado, restless veterans of the Mexican War, young bucks who admired them and wanted to prove themselves as devil-may-care, had a simple and direct solution for the Free State settlers in Kansas. It was to string them up, burn them out, kill as many as possible, and subjugate the rest by gun and bowie knife. Simple, uncomplicated souls who believed that the amount of whiskey a man could drink and his proficiency in personal combat were the gauge of manhood, they did not propose to allow foreign abolitionists, city people from New York and Boston, to take over a Kansas they knew should be theirs. It is doubtful if they knew that their program was not entirely their own. However naturally they came by their beliefs, United States Senator David R. Atchison, a slaveholder of Platte City, Platte County, Missouri, had done his best to encourage them in their proposals, aided and abetted by his many henchmen.

As early as 1853, when the opening of the Nebraska Territory was only a vague idea, before there was a Kansas (which only came with the division of Nebraska and the Kansas-Nebraska Act), Senator Atchison was thundering at Westport, Missouri, that he would see Nebraska in Hell before agreeing to its admission into the Union as a free state. As if suffering some premonition of the emigrants that would later arrive from the North, he said that if these foreign vermin did come in to "take up those fertile prairies, run off your Negroes, and depreciate the value of your slaves here, you will know how to protect your own interests; your rifles will free you from such neighbors. . . . You will go there if necessary with the *bayonet* and with *blood*." [4]

The senator spoke more often of bayonets and blood after the passage of the Kansas-Nebraska Act. A large, noisy, and effective defender of slavery,

tition of the plantation economies of their native states. Some of them moved from Missouri into Kansas, anti-slavery but also suspicious of Free State settlers and against the civil war that developed there. See William John Meredith, "The Old Plum Grove Colony," *The Kansas Historical Quarterly*, November 1938.

1. Daniel Webster of Massachusetts

2. William H. Seward of New York

3. Salmon P. Chase of Ohio

*PARTISANS,
NORTH
AND SOUTH*

4. John P. Hale
of New Hampshire

5. William Lowndes Yancey
of Alabama

6. Franklin Pierce
of New Hampshire

7. Henry A. Wise of Virginia

8. Jefferson Davis
of Mississippi

9. Maria Weston Chapman
of Boston

10. Angelina Emily Grimké,
Charleston aristocrat and
abolitionist

11. Charles Sumner of Massachusetts. He was 42.
An engraving from an 1853 daguerreotype

12. *J. Miller McKim*
of Pennsylvania

13. *William Walker,*
Tennessee filibuster

14. *John A. Quitman of Mississippi,*
who attempted to conquer Cuba

*15. Henry Wilson
of Massachusetts*

*16. Edmund Ruffin,
Virginia secessionist*

17. *Horace Greeley*

18. *Sojourner Truth*

The
just man shall
be in eternal
remembrance

Went to Prison for
Teaching
Colored Children.

19. *Prudence Crandall
of Connecticut*

Atchison was a native of Kentucky, forty-seven years old in 1854, 6 feet 2 inches in height and 200 pounds in weight. Affectionately known as "Old Bourbon," he did have a capacity for whiskey that matched his size. He was described by his enemies as "a boozy backwoods speaker"[5] and called by his admirers the Vice President of the United States. Both were wrong. As a stump speaker he could not be matched in western Missouri; profane, dominating, tough, he favored hanging without trial any and every abolitionist in Kansas but would not go so far as to hang all who called a cow a "keow"—thought by some to be the infallible mark of "a nigger stealer" from New England.[6]

As for being the Vice President of the United States, he was often described as such, if incorrectly by those who wished to flatter him, because as president and presiding officer of the Senate he was fulfilling the duties of William R. King, of Alabama, the elected Vice President on the Pierce ticket, who had died before he could assume office. Atchison had considerable prestige, too, both on the Missouri border and throughout the nation, as one of those who had induced Senator Stephen A. Douglas of Illinois to incorporate in his Kansas-Nebraska Bill the provision repealing the Missouri Compromise which had barred slavery from Kansas and Nebraska.

Despite his prestige he was faced with the most threatening crisis of his political career. In working to repeal the Missouri Compromise he had counted on Kansas becoming slave territory and he feared if it did not both the days of slavery in Missouri and his own political life would be numbered. For the fact was, he was engaged in a battle for political survival with the great Thomas Hart Benton, for thirty years senator from Missouri, who, although a slaveholder himself, was against the extension of slavery into Kansas and the West and had fought against the repeal of the Missouri Compromise and passage of the Kansas-Nebraska Act. No puller of punches, he regarded Atchison as a Catiline, willing to plunge his country into civil war if he could only save his political neck. The two men were engaged in a battle not only over slavery but for the control of the Democratic Party in Missouri. Benton had his followers even in western Missouri, opposed to slavery, however outnumbered and however dangerous it was for them to say so publicly.

Atchison, in the Senate since 1849, had succeeded in ousting Benton from the Senate in 1851 by running one Henry S. Geyer against him. But Benton was elected to the House of Representatives by his anti-slavery St. Louis constituency in 1852 and was expected to run against Atchison for the Senate in 1855. If Atchison could not rally the slave interests of Missouri behind him—

and he could not rally them if he could not save Kansas for slavery—it was doubtful if he could save his seat in the Senate from Thomas Hart Benton.

Benton, a great hulk of a man, occasionally liked to refer to himself in the third person as if he were describing some great natural force with rules of its own. "Nobody opposes Benton, sir," he said. "Nobody but a few blackjack prairie lawyers . . . Benton and the people, Benton and Democracy are one and the same, sir; synonymous terms, sir, synonymous terms." Once addressing the Senate, after a colleague had charged him with being quarrelsome, he said, "Mr. President, sir . . . I never quarrel, sir. But sometimes I fight, sir, and whenever I fight, sir, a funeral follows, sir." * He scourged his hide each morning while bathing with a brutal, bristly brush and when asked if the brush was really tough, he roared, "Why, sir, if I would touch you with that brush, sir, you would cry murder, sir!" [7]

Atchison liked to think that he was as tough. A general as well as a senator (his commission came from the Missouri militia) and also on occasion called Vice President, he was well supplied with titles. A brash and blustery man, often a little overbearing, he could not conceive of any being his superior. He was apt to address the stateliest figure, if not with condescension, then as if he were a chum, draping a large arm over the shoulders of those who were sometimes the unwilling recipients of his expansiveness. Senator Douglas, the Little Giant from Illinois, was reputed to be the most doughty fighter in the history of the Senate. But Atchison said he gave him an ultimatum: twenty-four hours to insert the repeal of the Missouri Compromise into the Kansas-Nebraska Act or take the consequences. Douglas had introduced the act as chairman of the Senate Committee on Territories, but Atchison reported that he told Douglas he personally would see that he was removed from the chairmanship, that in fact he would take the chairmanship himself, if Douglas did not immediately include in the bill the elimination of the Compromise. [8]

His influence in the Senate was such that he might have been able to make good the threat. Most liked his rough-and-ready bonhomie but it is doubtful if Jefferson Davis enjoyed it. He made a pal and almost a fellow conspirator of the soldierly and reserved Davis, who as Pierce's Secretary of War may not have wanted prior knowledge of Atchison's plans of killing and burning out Free State settlers in Kansas. As part of the executive, as head of the Army under President Pierce, and the reputed chief adviser of the Presi-

---

* President Jackson, as we have seen, could have attested were he alive to the truth of these words, even if a little exaggerated.

dent, Davis's public role was that of the neutral enforcer of the law who would use the Army if necessary to put down large-scale violence no matter from what quarter it came, including Missouri.

But Atchison would not permit him his official pose. Knowing that underneath the Secretary's pretended neutrality was a rabid partisan of slavery and its expansion, he made Davis his partner in crime by indicating how he intended to carry it out before he did so. Referring to the Kansas Free State settlers as "Negro Heroes," he wrote Davis from his home at Platte City on September 24, 1854:

> We will have difficulty with the Negro Heroes in Kansas. They are resolved to keep the Slave holder out, and our people are resolved to go in and take their *"Niggers"* with them. Now the men who are hired by the Boston Abolitionists to settle and abolitionize Kansas will not hesitate to steal our slaves. Taking this for granted, I on the 21st of this month advised in a public speech the Squatters in Kansas and the people of Missouri, to give a horse thief, robber or homicide a fair trial, but . . . to hang a Negro thief and Abolitionist without judge or jury. This sentiment met with almost universal applause, and I could with difficulty keep the "plebs" from hanging two gentlemen who called a cow, *"keow."*
>
> We will before six months rolls round, have the Devil to pay in Kansas and in this State. We are organizing, to meet their organization. We will be compelled to shoot, burn & hang, but the thing will be soon over. We intend to "Mormonise" the Abolitionists.* [9]

2

It might be difficult to determine who was the most bloody in threat and pose, Atchison or those of his constituents he called the "plebs" and whom the Northern press called Border Ruffians. These last were the stuff of Missouri's armies, soon to invade Kansas and seize its elections, at present being organized by the Atchison political machine. Often local bullies and loafers, the unemployed of the Missouri border, assorted alcoholics and political hangers-on, always ready for a drink or a dog fight, the more daring of them were blood brothers to the frontiersman who after wrestling with a trained bear came up with a bloody mess in his hand and the appreciative exclamation, "Why the cute little son-of-a-bitch chawed off my ear!" As champions of slavery, they aspired to the code of the Southern Chivalry and however raggedy-assed their appearance they liked to think of themselves as those who would fight to the death any slur on their manhood.

---

* Twenty Mormons were killed in the so-called "massacre at Haun's Mill," in Missouri in 1838 when their leaders were arrested and imprisoned and fifteen thousand Mormons driven out of Missouri into Illinois.

Their heroes were such fighting men as Alexander Keith McClung, the Black Knight of the South who once killed seven members of a family which had annoyed him,[10] and the Speaker of the Arkansas House of Representatives, who interrupted legislative debate on bounties given for wolves' tails by drawing his bowie knife and fatally impaling to his desk a legislator who had offended him.[11] Suffering the gibes of those who thought them underbred, Missouri's western frontiersmen admired the punctilio and high-toned decorum of the Old Dominion, as when Thomas Ritchie, son of the editor of the Richmond *Enquirer*, killed and terribly mangled a rival editor, J. H. Pleasants, in an affair of honor with eight shots, each one true.[12] Feeling the impoverishment of their rude surroundings, they admired the delicate sensitivity of the South Carolinian Louis T. Wigfall, who met a friend in the street, was invited to his wedding, strolled on for a few yards, then suddenly shot and killed the scheduled bridegroom for a word, perhaps accidental, that Wigfall felt reflected on his gentility.[13] The loafers of the border—often reduced to mere tavern brawls, tarring and feathering some lonely dissenter, or tying a tin can to a dog's tail—were impressed by the class of the young Kentuckian who shot and killed a stranger because he did not like the way the man had looked at him.[14] And it was men of this heroic mold from Alabama, Georgia, and South Carolina, as eager to defend slavery as their honor, who were said to be on the way to join Missouri's men of mettle in the war over Kansas.

Regarding all northeast of the western Missouri border as naturally effete, the Border Ruffians were somewhat surprised when they later found men from New York and Wisconsin, Massachusetts, Ohio, and Indiana as reckless in assault and raid, in ambush and bushwhacking, in burning out and running off their enemies, in stealing cattle and horses, as they were themselves. The Northern press was always prone to describe Free Staters from Michigan and Illinois and everywhere else as clean-limbed, clear-eyed idealists who neither cursed nor drank. But as a matter of fact, most had little more idealism than their opponents with whom they could hold their own in cursing and drinking as well as fighting.

Those of the Free States, including their leaders back home, Lawrence and Thayer, were as indignant when called abolitionists as if they had been Missourians.* They wanted, as did the Missourians, the land of Kansas. But

---

* From an Atchison letter to Amos A. Lawrence on April 15, 1855, it appears that Lawrence had written Atchison saying, "neither is there any truth in the assertion that those who go from New England to Kansas are abolitionists. No person of that stamp is known to have gone from here." Atchison replied that any man who had gone to Kansas to make it free was an abolitionist

they did not want either slavery or free Negroes upon that land and they took measures, as we shall later see, to prevent any black man, however free, from settling on Kansas soil. Most of them, although against slavery in Kansas, were as white supremacist as if they had been raised in the slave states, as a good many had been.

But this discovery of the toughness of their enemies was some time away. Early in November 1854, the Missourians, through Senator Atchison and his allies, had arrived at a policy as to their coming invasions of Kansas. They would invade only to seize the Kansas elections and through taking them over transform Kansas into slave territory. They would shoot or hang only those Free Staters who opposed their capture of the Kansas elections, for these clearly would be abolitionists.

Before the Kansas election for a territorial representative to Congress on November 29, 1854, Senator Atchison gave some directives to his constituents in an address at Liberty, Missouri. "Now if a set of fanatics and demagogues a thousand miles off," he said, referring to the New England Emigrant Aid Company,

can afford to advance the money and extend every nerve to abolitionize the Territory and exclude the slaveholder, when they have not the least personal interest, what is your duty? When you reside in one day's journey to the Territory, and when your peace and quiet and your property depend upon your action, you can, without exertion, send five hundred of your young men who will vote in favor of your institutions.[15]

If every county in Missouri would do the same, he said, Kansas would be saved for slavery.

It was Atchison's contention, and the firm belief of most western Missourians, that if a man could travel 1,500 miles under the auspices of the New England Emigrant Aid Company from Bangor, Maine, for example, to vote in Kansas elections, then Missourians only a few miles away had an equal right to do so. The proclamation of Andrew H. Reeder, first Governor of the

---

to him. In a bluffly insolent manner, he advised Lawrence to straighten himself out by becoming a slaveowner and emigrating with his slaves to Kansas.

He wrote: "I have been informed that you have an income of $100,000. Let me suggest that you purchase $90,000 worth of negroes, come out to Kansas, feed and clothe your slaves well, give them employment, build for them and yourself good houses; improve their condition, build for yourself fine barns and stables; cover the prairie with wheat, hemp, and corn; feed your cattle on a thousand hills; assist your poor white neighbor; and my word for it, you will do more good for your race, both white and black, than you are doing or can do in Boston." He began his letter by implying that if he had black slaves, Lawrence had white, saying, "I live within a few miles of Kansas, and have a few slaves; you have none,—at least no black ones." From an undated lecture on Kansas by F. B. Sanborn, Stutler Collection.

Territory, appointed by the President, that only residents of the Territory could vote in a Kansas election, was nonsense according to Atchison. Any man present on the day of an election was a resident by the mere fact of his being in Kansas.[16] If an election judge appointed by Reeder challenged his vote on the grounds that he lived in Missouri, that judge should be removed by bowie knife and revolver, as was later done with some frequency, and another designated who would permit all Missourians to vote.

Despite his "pacific views," as Atchison described them, he declared at Liberty that he favored hanging all "negro thieves," a description he seemed to think fitted most Free State settlers. As a matter of fact, however, he was downright temperate compared to his neighbor and ally, B. F. Stringfellow, who in a speech at St. Joseph, Missouri, directly across the river from Kansas, advised a group of Missourians crossing to Kansas to vote: "I tell you to mark every scoundrel . . . who is in the least tainted with free soilism or abolitionism and exterminate him.

"Neither give nor take quarter from the damned rascals," he continued.

To those who have qualms of conscience as to violating laws, State or national, the time has come when such impositions must be disregarded, as your rights and property are in danger; and I advise you, one and all, to enter every election district in Kansas, in defiance of Reeder and his vile myrmidons, and vote at the point of the bowie-knife and revolver. Neither give nor take quarter, as our cause demands it. It is enough that the slave-holding interest wills it, from which there is no appeal.[17]

THE ELECTION

I

Secret societies in the 1850's were occasionally the facades for political conspiracies, particularly when they involved large numbers. The solemn folderol, the midnight oaths of eternal silence, the ritual involving skulls or other paraphernalia indicating the fate of traitors, not only gave the conspirators a certain amount of entertainment but afforded them as much protection as they could contrive for their plots. So they were used to shield filibustering expeditions, to conspire toward gaining control of the federal government as with the Know-Nothings, and in the case of Senator Atchison and his slave-holder allies to plan and carry out the raising of armies to invade Kansas for the purpose of making it a slave territory. For all the alleged confidence of

Senator Atchison and others that Missourians in invading Kansas to vote were acting entirely legally, they did not wish their planning to be open even though there was no way to conceal its results.*

The Missouri secret society was formed in the fall of 1854, giving great delight to those who joined it. At last they had a function in life and a noble purpose, the routing of the foreign agitators. While it was one organization with one purpose, its chapters in different parts of western Missouri were variously known as "The Sons of the South," the "Social Band," the "Friends' Society," and the "Blue Lodge." [18]

The day before the Kansas election of March 30, 1855, when the first territorial legislature of Kansas was to be chosen, an eager thrill of anticipation ran along the Missouri border and for that matter penetrated deep into the state's interior. Men were up early, for this was the grand day for which they had been trained, to be exceeded in excitement only on the morrow when the election took place. Companies gathered in courthouse squares in Andrew, Buchanan, Platte, and Clay counties on the Missouri side of the Kansas-Missouri border in the north; in Jackson, Cass, and Bates counties in the center; and in Jasper County at the southernmost end of the border. At an even earlier hour men were mobilizing in counties more distant, in Lafayette and Ray, in Carroll and Saline, in Howard, Boone, Randolph, and Macon counties, every man with a bowie knife, revolver, or shotgun, and a few with all three, most with a bottle of whiskey in hip pocket or coat, reinforced by barrels of whiskey being hauled in wagons also containing ammunition, tents, food for the men, and fodder for the horses, as well as in a few instances small brass howitzers. Many of those mobilizing were on horseback, some were in buggies and buckboards, and all were gay. They planned to arrive in the Territory the night before the election and make camp near the polling places to be on hand early in the morning.

The expedition was a great jubilee, a riotous holiday, a grand adventure, and laughter and threats of what they would do when they entered Kansas were common. Now and again someone would discharge a revolver out of sheer good spirits. Men called from wagon to wagon and there was exuberance and even awe as they entered Kansas and looking back saw wagons and men on horseback still far in the distance following for miles behind them in a great invasion. The guzzling of whiskey, the tooting of horns, the beating of drums, the waving of flags bearing such designations as "Clay County Boys"

---

* Subsequently the Free State settlers formed a secret organization known as the Kansas Legion, to be described later.

or "Saline Friends' Society" were a constant accompaniment to their jogging progress into Kansas; and sometimes when a contingent paused for a final briefing, someone got out a fiddle and went to it as the men leaped and hollered, jumping, twisting, and cavorting with wild shrill shrieks to "Turkey in the Straw" or some other favorite. Some of the older men were pretty well tuckered before noon.[19]

At such briefings, necessary to direct the companies to specific polling places, it may have been emphasized once more that if the Missourians elected a pro-slavery legislature to rule Kansas the battle would be won. Kansas would become slave territory, for the legislators would pass a slave code not only authorizing slavery but preventing any man from holding office who did not swear loyalty to it. To do this, the invaders would have to control the elections in the majority of the election districts, in each of which, usually through the machinations of the secret society and Missourians who had settled in Kansas, there was a pro-slavery candidate. If every Missourian voted, they were bound to win since there were an estimated 5,000 in the invading army and there were only 2,905 voters in the Territory of Kansas according to a census ordered by Governor Reeder and just completed.

Violence was discouraged unless someone prevented or attempted to prevent a Missourian from voting. That could not be endured and whatever violence was necessary to see that all voted was approved policy. Despite this policy, the Missourians upon arriving at the polls sometimes could not forgo a little bullying, pressing around men who had incurred their disfavor while shouting "Shoot him!" "Cut his guts out!" "Kill the damned nigger thief!" "Cut his throat!" "Tear his heart out!" At Lawrence, where about a thousand Missourians were deployed, they fired a few shots at a Lawrence voter, a Mr. Bond, who objected to their presence. Bond had scarcely opened his mouth when strangers snatched out bowie knives and revolvers, pushing and grabbing at him, as they shouted "Shoot the damned abolitionist! Shoot the damned bully!" while Bond, wrenching free, fled for the Kansas River, diving over its bank for protection as bullets kicked up the dust in his wake.* [20]

In the excitement, some of the Missourians said "they must drive all the damned abolitionists off the ground," [21] meaning every Free Soil advocate. Many citizens of Lawrence did not vote, fearing assault or injury, but a Mr. Willis was approaching the polls to vote when

---

* The quotations above and in the next pages are taken from the report of the Howard Congressional Committee, appointed to investigate the elections in Kansas, as well as from testimony before it.

a cry was raised that he was one of the men concerned in abducting a black woman. . . . Several men raised a cry to hang him. Some were on horseback and some were on foot. Movements were made towards him by strangers armed with rifles and smaller arms. The cry was repeated by a large number of persons to "hang him," "get a rope," &c. At the suggestion of some friends he left the ground.[22]

While all this was going on, hundreds of Missourians were pressing into the polling place, most armed with bowie knives and revolvers and some carrying shotguns. There were three election judges appointed by Governor Reeder, with instructions to permit none to vote who would not swear, taking a formal oath to the effect that they were permanent residents of Kansas intending to remain in the Territory. One of the judges, N. B. Blanton, resigned even before the polls opened after having met a large company of armed Missourians the night before.

"They argued," Blanton testified before the congressional committee,

that all the citizens of the United States had a right to come here and vote if they wanted to; they got to trying to persuade me to let them vote without swearing, saying the oath the governor had prescribed was not right and legal. After a while one of these men—an old man—said to me: "Go on, son, and act as judge, and let us vote, and we will pay you for it." Two or three more spoke up and said, if I did not let them vote without swearing that their men would get enraged and maybe hang me; and that I had better resign.[23]

Blanton took their advice. He did not even appear at the polls the next morning.

At the end of the day as the invaders mounted horses and wagons to return to Missouri, many were saying they intended to hang Governor Reeder if he did not officially approve of the election. But they made the threat with great good nature, in the natural exuberance of those returning home after work well done. A good many remained overnight in their Lawrence encampment, Gaius Jenkins meeting them the next day as they returned home and as he was driving toward Lawrence from Kansas City. "I was frequently detained," he testified, "as much as fifteen minutes, allowing them to pass in the road; a good many of them were quite wild and uproarious, and seemed to enjoy themselves, frequently asking if I had seen Governor Reeder." The Governor was then at Shawnee Mission, a little settlement near Missouri in the northeast corner of the Territory that he was using as his headquarters, and some of the returning men who had been drinking, according to Jenkins, said they were going to the Mission and that if the Governor "did not sanction the election they would run him up to the first tree, God damn him!" [24]

2

The election at Bloomington in the second election district was a remarkable affair, with more bellowing and threats of death, more cocking of revolvers and more pressing of bowie knives against Free State throats, and more galloping around on horseback in pursuit of recalcitrant election judges than occurred that day in any other district of the Territory. This was undoubtedly because of the presence of Samuel J. Jones, an excitable, large, and violent man, then the postmaster of Westport, Missouri, but soon to be pro-slavery sheriff of Douglas County in Kansas. In command of "some 500 or 600" Missourians, he hated Free Staters with so implacable a malignancy that it was to become historic. Jones demanded that two of three election judges appointed by Governor Reeder for the Bloomington district resign or take the consequences which, he said, might involve their lives. The election judges appointed by Governor Reeder were Harrison Burson, Nathaniel Ramsay, and Parris Ellison, the last pro-slavery in sentiment and willing to permit the Missourians to vote. His two colleagues were resolved to require those voting to take the oath ordered by the Governor and these were the two Jones was determined to depose.

"The invaders tied white tape or ribbons in their button-holes, so as to distinguish them from the 'abolitionists,'" according to the congressional report, which continued:

They again demanded that the judges should resign; and upon their refusing to do so, smashed in the window, sash and all, and presented their pistols and guns to them, threatening to shoot them. Someone on the outside cried out not to shoot as there were pro-slavery men in the house with the judges. They then put a pry under the corner of the house, which was a log-house and lifted it up a few inches and let it fall again, but desisted upon being told there were pro-slavery men in the house.

During this time the crowd repeatedly demanded to be allowed to vote without being sworn, and Mr. Ellison, one of the judges, expressed himself willing, but the other two judges refused; thereupon a body of men, headed by sheriff Jones,* rushed into the judges' room with cocked pistols and drawn bowie-knives in their hands, and approached Burson and Ramsay. Jones pulled out his watch and said he would give them five minutes to resign in, or die. When the five minutes had

---

* By the time of the Howard Report, Jones had been appointed sheriff of Douglas County in which Lawrence, Kansas, is situated.

expired and the judges did not resign, Jones said he would give them another minute and no more. Ellison, the pro-slavery election judge, told his associates that if they did not resign there would be one hundred shots fired in the room in less than fifteen minutes, and then snatching up the ballot-box ran out into the crowd, holding up the ballot-box and hurrahing for Missouri. About that time Burson and Ramsay were called out by their friends, and not suffered to return.

As Mr. Burson went out he put the ballot poll-books in his pocket and took them with him, and as he was going out Jones snatched some papers away from him, and shortly afterwards came out himself, holding them up, crying "Hurrah for Missouri!" After he discovered they were not the poll-books, he took a party of men with him and started off to take the poll-books from Burson. [It was apparently thought that the election could not be held without the poll books.] When Mr. Burson saw them coming, he gave the books to Mr. Umberger and told him to start off in another direction, so as to mislead Jones and his party. Jones and his party caught Mr. Umberger, took the poll-books away from him, and Jones took him up behind him on a horse and carried him back a prisoner.

After Jones and his party had taken Umberger back, they went to the house of Mr. Ramsay and took Judge John A. Wakefield prisoner, and carried him to the place of election, and made him get up on a wagon and there make a speech; after which they put a white ribbon in his button-hole and let him go.

They then chose two new judges and proceeded with the election. They also threatened to kill the judges if they did not receive their votes without swearing them, or else resign. They said no man should vote who would submit to be sworn; that they would kill any man who would offer to do so, "Shoot him!" "Cut his guts out," &c. They said no man should vote this day unless he voted an open ticket and was all right on the goose; * and that if they could not vote by fair means, they would by foul means.

Some of the citizens [of the Bloomington election district] . . . who had not voted . . . upon attempting to vote were driven back by the mob or driven off. . . .[25]

It was after the Free State men had been driven from the polls that J. N. Mace, an unusually stubborn resident of the election district, decided that come hell or high water he was going to vote. Tucking a small American flag under his arm, which he thought might somehow protect him, he pushed through the crowd of Missourians and was just about to vote when, as he said in his testimony before the Howard Committee,

I was seized by the people in the crowd, and dragged from the polls through the entire crowd. They made shouts of "Kill the damned nigger-thief," "Cut his throat," and many cries of that kind.

---

* Being "right on the goose" in the parlance of Missourians meant favoring slavery in Kansas. A good many were killed in Kansas when asked "How are you on the goose?" and replying in a way that did not satisfy their interrogators.

I saw revolvers cocked and bowie-knives drawn, all around me, at that time. After I had been dragged out of the crowd I regained my feet. I had a small American flag under my arm. When I got to my feet, I unfurled it and held it over my head. I told them that we were here, and had no law to protect us, and I sought protection under the American flag. . . . I heard some voices say that flag was false, and pointed to a flag waving over one of their wagons with one star in it and said that was the true flag. I then said, "Who calls this flag false are traitors." One man who had a large cloak on, threw it off and came up to me, and, thrusting his fist in my face, asked me if I called him a traitor. . . . Then another man stepped up to me, and told me to take that back, at the same time opening a clasp knife, and put it so it touched the breast of my coat. Another man had a revolver, which he held close to my ear. Another man struck at me with a club, and a friend of mine turned it off with his arm, and it struck somebody else. At this instant, a fight, or row of some kind, was got up at some distance, which attracted their attention, and they left me.[26]

3

At about the time Mr. Mace was standing with his small American flag over his head, a knife at his breast and a revolver at his ear, Judge Wakefield, a stout old man but a brave one, was being captured. Outraged at the Missourians' seizure of the polling place, he had retired to the house of Mr. Ramsay, one of the deposed election judges, where he and others were drafting a petition to Governor Reeder asking that the election be set aside as illegal. Just as they finished it they saw "a large number mounted on horses" led by Jones galloping toward the Ramsay house. Judge Wakefield, a Free State candidate for the legislature, walked out on the steps to confront them.

"As they came," Judge Wakefield testified,

they cried out, "Take Wakefield, dead or alive—damn him, take him!" I then ran into the house, and told Mr. Ramsay to give me his double-barreled shot-gun, he having taken it down and cocked both barrels when the mob first came to the house. [The mob had been there earlier before galloping away in pursuit of Mr. Umberger.] The mob rode up, and I should think a dozen or more presented their pistols to me. I drew up the gun at Jones, the leader. We stood that way perhaps for a minute.

A man professing to be my friend undertook to take the gun from me, saying, "If you shoot we will all be killed; we can't fight this army." My reply was, to stand off, or I would shoot him, which he did. Then one of my friends spoke in a very calm manner, and said, "Judge, you had better surrender; we cannot fight this army without arms." I then said I must know the conditions, and remarked to the mob, "Gentlemen, what do you want with me?"

Some one said, "We want you to go back to the polls, and state whether it was not you who persuaded the judges to take away the poll-books." I said I could easily do that, as I could not get in hearing of the judges; but if I could have got in their hearing, I should have done it. "But," said I, "if I go back, what security have I that I will not be mobbed or maltreated on the way?" Some two or three of them spoke, and said they would go my security; that I should not be hurt. I said I would go, but go alone.

I went back with them, and got up in a wagon and made them a short speech, stating to them that I had been an old soldier, and had fought through two wars for the rights of my country; and I thought I had a privilege there that day. I then went on to state that they were in the wrong; that we were not the abolitionists they represented us to be, but were free-State men, and that they were abusing us unjustly, and that their acts were contrary to the organic law of the constitution of the United States.

A man cried out while I was speaking, several times, "Shoot him! He is too saucy." I then made an effort to those who gave their security that I should not be hurt. When I had done speaking, and got off the wagon, a man came up to me and told me he wanted to tie a white ribbon in my button-hole, or the boys would kill me. I first refused, but he insisted, and I let him do it; and then I turned round and cut it out with my knife. I then made an attempt to leave, and they cried out, "Stay with us and vote; we don't want you to leave." I thanked them and told them they could have it to themselves. I then left them.[27]

As a result of similar activities in other election districts, all but seven of the thirty-nine members of the territorial legislature elected on March 30 were pro-slavery. "Old Davy" Atchison, as his followers sometimes called him, led a band of eighty heavily armed Missourians from Platte County to the Wolf River precinct in Kansas on the day of the election where, it was testified by Dr. G. A. Cutler, "There was considerable whiskey demolished."

According to Dr. Cutler, General Atchison made a speech in which he said, "There are 1,100 coming over from Platte county and if that ain't enough we can send you 5,000 more. We came to vote, and we are going to vote or kill every God-damned abolitionist in the Territory." [28] Later Dr. Cutler in questioning a Missourian as to why he had voted in Kansas where he did not live, received the reply that "he had not violated the organic law; that Atchison had helped to make the bill [the Kansas-Nebraska Act] and had told them they had a right to vote, and he knew a God-damned sight better than I did." * [29]

There were 5,427 pro-slavery votes cast at the election, of which 4,908

* Atchison despite his efforts to make Kansas a slave state was never re-elected to the United States Senate. Election for the Senate in Missouri was through the vote of the state legislature and neither in 1855 nor later could he get the necessary majority in the Missouri legislature (nor could Benton). Atchison's continued activities to make Kansas a slave state, his enemies said, stemmed partly from his desire to represent Kansas in the Senate since he could not represent Missouri.

were later declared illegal by the Howard Committee, and 791 Free State votes.[30] Governor Reeder considered throwing out the whole election as a gigantic fraud but in the end he only set aside the votes in six districts, five of the contests being won by Free State candidates to the legislature in later elections but without practical result. The "bogus legislature," as it was called by Free State settlers, promptly expelled them, declaring their opponents victors. When two other Free State members resigned, the legislature was unanimously pro-slavery.

It immediately passed a slave code by which it was a penitentiary offense even to speak against slavery or to be in possession of literature which condemned it. It provided the death penalty for any who should aid an escaping slave. In addition, it passed laws preventing any man from voting or serving as an official or a judge of election or as a juror or lawyer who would not swear to uphold the Fugitive Slave Act.[31] At the same time it made provision that any native-born, white American twenty-one or over, from Missouri or anywhere else, could vote in any Kansas election merely by appearing at the polls, swearing to uphold the Fugitive Slave Act, and paying a $1 poll tax. Finally, it empowered the legislature to appoint all local county sheriffs, deputies, constables, tax collectors, and assessors.[32] The judiciary and executive were appointed, of course, by the pro-slavery Pierce administration under federal territorial law.

Governor Reeder, a stout man of middle age with goggle eyes and a magnificent gray mustache, was an individual of more than ordinary courage, as he later proved, but if in this instance he had been intimidated by frequent threats of hanging it would have been understandable. Almost daily his office was invaded by gun-brandishing Missourians threatening his life if he did not approve the March 30 election, one of whom shoved him off a couch on which he had been lying and then kicked him. Before announcing his decision on the election, he armed himself and asked Robinson and a Free State group to ride over to the Shawnee Mission from Lawrence to give him protection. As he sat at his desk before giving his decision the tension grew almost unbearable, a large crowd of Missourians before him glaring at him and the Free Staters behind him, both groups armed and ready for battle. Governor Reeder, a revolver on the desk before him, expected the worst but apparently his invalidating the vote in only six districts prevented any attempt to kill him. Most of the Free Staters were sorry they had come to give Reeder protection for they had hoped he would declare the entire election illegal.

An administration Democrat from Pennsylvania, Reeder at the time of his appointment by the President had tried to placate Southern congressmen by declaring that he had as little against buying a slave as buying a horse. He had changed considerably under the outrages perpetrated in the Kansas elections as well as against himself. Immediately after the special elections in May, he returned East knowing that Missourians, and particularly Atchison and String-fellow, were pressing President Pierce to demand his resignation.

At his home in Easton, Pennsylvania, he gave a speech in which he said that "the territory of Kansas has been invaded by an organized army, armed to the teeth, who took possession of the ballot-boxes and made a legislature to suit themselves."

He told his hearers, according to the Boston *Atlas*,

that the solemn duty involved on the North was "to vindicate and sustain the rights of her sons. . . ." He also declared that "accounts of the fierce outrage and wild violence perpetrated at the election, and published in the Northern papers, were in nowise exaggerated." He concluded by saying that Kansas was now a conquered country—conquered by force of arms, but that the citizens were resolved never to yield, and relied upon the North to aid them. . . .[33]

He had come to Kansas as its Governor in the fall of 1854 as an administration, pro-slavery Democrat. Soon he would be transformed into an associate of John Brown and others almost as militant.

4

The press of western Missouri proclaimed a complete and definitive victory for slavery in Kansas following the March 30 invasion and election. The Richfield *Enterprise* was typical of the public prints of the whole border in its issue of April 2 as it declared, "Come on, Southern men, bring your slaves and fill up the Territory. Kansas is saved! Abolition is rebuked, her fortress stormed, her flag is dragging in the dust!" [34]

The Kansas *Herald*, the pro-slavery newspaper published at Leavenworth, described, "The brilliant and glorious triumph achieved by the noble and unaided efforts of the gallant and chivalrous sons of the South over the combined forces of the abolitionists, free-soilers and Emigrant Aid Societies in our late territorial election. . . ." Thousands of families with slaves from the old Southern states, the *Herald* said, could now come without fear of "the hordes of paupers, hirelings and convicts" sent by the defeated "Emigrant Aid societies to abolitionize our Territory." [35]

But they were a little premature. It was really the prelude to civil war in Kansas and there were editors sufficiently prescient to fear that it was also leading to civil war between North and South. The St. Louis *Intelligencer*, for example, declared that if the Atchison forces succeeded in Kansas, then Missouri, most of its central and eastern portions anti-slavery, "will soon be in a flame. It will spread to the South; the Union itself will perish thus. . . . We warn our friends throughout the State that a volcano will speedily burst under their feet and destroy the State and the Union. . . ." [36]

The *New York Tribune* said, "The appeal is now made to arms" and predicted that the North when mobilized and determined would "scatter its enemies like chaff." [37] Even as he wrote the editorial Horace Greeley was buying arms for Free State forces.[38] The New Haven *Palladium* said that it favored resisting the making of Kansas a slave state "though it costs rivers of blood and a hundred millions of treasure." [39] The *Mercury*, of Charleston, South Carolina, was equally aggressive, if from an opposing viewpoint, declaring,

Had the South in its past contest exhibited half the courage and promptness of Atchison and his true men, abolitionism would have long since been a harmless thing. It is also a timely lesson to the North, yet which will scarcely be heeded in its present fierce and aggressive mood, that there is a point at which the South will rise and wipe out, with deeds worthy of her hope and destiny, the wrongs and shame of the past.

The operative clause was, of course, "there is a point at which the South will rise. . . ." [40]

The *Mercury* wrote of the North's "present fierce and aggressive mood." It was accurate in its description and as the months went by it would become more so. Robinson, the Emigrant Aid Company's agent at Lawrence, was forming two military companies and asking for two hundred Sharps rifles and two field guns, while threatening to give freedom to such of Missouri's slaves as could be reached by the Underground Railroad if that state's depredations against Kansas did not cease.[41] But the Sharps rifles may have impressed Missourians more than Robinson's rhetoric. They were among the earliest breech loaders, firing at a rate of ten shots a minute, and had a far greater range than any similar weapon. The carbine was invented by Christian Sharps, who had worked at the arsenal at Harper's Ferry, and after its patenting in 1848 it "appeared to take its place among the world's great firearms." * [42]

---

* In 1859 a good many Sharps rifles were found in the armory at Harper's Ferry after the John Brown Raid as well as at a schoolhouse nearby. They were the models of 1852 and 1853, with "the slanted breech and brass mountings," and have since been known to gun collectors as the "John Brown Sharps." Harold L. Peterson, *The Treasury of the Gun*, New York, 1962, p. 174.

So began the great era of the Sharps rifle in the North, where for two years there was scarcely a meeting in church or convention that someone did not arise to make a plea for subscriptions for the weapons. From Brooklyn to Boston to Syracuse to Chicago, men of the cloth took to the pulpit, their Bibles before them, some calling out like auctioneers, "Who else will contribute to the rifle fund? Who will subscribe fifty dollars for Sharps rifles? Do I hear a hundred? Can I get a hundred and fifty for liberty?" Henry Ward Beecher, using the phrases and the chant of an auctioneer, raised so much money for rifles that his Plymouth Church in Brooklyn was known to the irreligious as "the Church of the Holy Rifles." [43] He even auctioned off escaped slave girls from the pulpit, or those he said were such, the money to be used to buy them from their masters, but the emotion to be used to buy more Sharps rifles.[44]

Even Lawrence and Thayer, cautious men whose central policy was to avoid violence, to take every precaution to prevent a clash between the Free State settlers and the Pierce administration (already backing the Missourians and their "bogus" legislature), contributed money for rifles. In fact they sent the first one hundred, costing with ammunition $2,670.[45] First and last, officials of the New England Emigrant Aid Company raised some $12,500 for rifles, which, after some of the money was returned to Amos Lawrence who had put up his own to buy the first weapons, bought about 325 Sharps rifles.[46] However closely officials of the Emigrant Aid Company had been involved in the purchase, they always denied that the company had the slightest part in buying them, feeling perhaps, as the battle became more desperate against the Missourians and the federal government, that they might be charged with treason if Free State settlers, armed through them, clashed with United States troops.[47]

If Lawrence and Thayer were worried about raising money for Sharps rifles, it was becoming the chief activity for many. Within a year, Theodore Parker, himself a valiant raiser of funds for weapons, was writing, "Dr. Howe and others raised five thousand dollars one day last week to buy Sharps rifles. We want a thousand rifles, and got two hundred in one day." [48]

At about the same time, Parker went down to the Boston railroad station to see another group depart, writing in his journal:

Saw the Kansas party go off, Dr. Charles H. Sanborn at their head—*nearly half of them women and children*. There were twenty copies of "Sharp's Rights of the People" in their hands, of the new and improved edition, and divers Colt's six shooters also. As the bell rang for the train to move (at five and a half, Providence Railroad), they were singing—

"When I can read my title clear."

But what a comment were the weapons of that company on the boasted democracy of America! Those rifles and pistols were to defend their soil from the American Government, which wishes to plant slavery in Kansas! [49]

THE PATH TO WAR

I

Atchison, his illegal legislature, and his Border Ruffians were still in control of Kansas as the Brown brothers advanced toward the Territory in the spring of 1855. John and Jason, their wives, and two little boys boarded an Ohio riverboat on or about April 10 at Wellesville in northeastern Ohio, only a little below where the river passes from Pennsylvania on its 981 mile journey to the Mississippi.[50] It was an unusually mild spring.

They may have climbed to the hurricane deck where the river doubtless seemed to them as broad and endless as the ocean, forever disappearing behind some far bend, forever resuming when the bend was rounded and another point loomed faint and far ahead. Across the wide river was the state of Virginia, slave soil, but the Browns may have had to admit that it appeared little different from the familiar free soil of Ohio on the right bank. Forward was the pilot house and above it two tall twin stacks, a scroll between, the smoke tumbling from them and blowing aft, thick with ash and grit that filled the ears and stung the eyes and probably soon forced the Browns to retreat to a lower deck.

As day followed day on their journey, the everlasting pulsing of the boat became as unremarked and unfelt as the flow of their own blood. Before they arrived at Louisville they must have known every inch of every deck, trooping periodically about, careful that Jason and Ellen's boy, Austin, four years old, did not climb too high on the white rail fencings that edged the decks, holding Jonny, John and Wealthy's boy, about three, very tightly by the hand as they passed the boilers aft on the lowest deck with their open doors and their great hot glow of red.

After supper, if the evening was pleasant, the two brothers may have sought the stern, watching the tumbling wake in the half-light. Perhaps they saw in a clearing on the Kentucky shore a little country church, horses and wagons hitched before it, heard, the exaltation still strong for all the distance, the singing of a hymn ". . . Jesus loves me . . ." so far away but borne by the wind and suddenly clear. They may have heard, too, on rare occasions, other voices traveling from the river's slave shore far over the water, so wild and lonely and sad and yet exultant, too, in some strange way, that they somehow knew the singers were slaves. Occasionally from the Ohio shore when the boat was tied up, its engines still, there was the long-drawn wail of a locomotive and sometimes they could hear, if only for an instant, dogs barking distantly or even the rumbling of far-away freight cars. As the dusk deepened into night the reflection of the fire from the boilers crimsoned the waters at the sides of the boat, the glow in the river continuing as ceaselessly as that in the boiler until the break of day.

Every five or six hours the steamer made for the shore and some wood yard at the edge of a forest, placed there to supply boats with fuel, the matter usually a spot transaction in cash. If it was dark several hoarse blasts would thrill out over the river, making spines tingle wherever they were heard, their purpose the warning of those in the wood yard of the craft's approach. At the very end of the stage, slanting out and up over the river from the side of the bow, stood a deck hand, a pine torch held above him illuminating his figure, a rope at his feet which he threw to those on shore who made it fast to a tree on the bank. As the vessel neared the bank there was the delicate urgency of the bells, the paddle wheels stopped, there was another melodic tinkle in the night signaling them into reverse, and with a great foaming of water they back-pedaled and brought the steamer to a standstill.

If the wood yard was on the Virginia or Kentucky side, a flood of slaves might clamber up the stage, heavy loads of logs on their backs, and with great cackles of laughter and uproarious shouting they would have four or five cords of wood stored before the boilers in a matter of minutes. We can picture John looking down on them from forward on the passenger deck, it may be, seeing slaves in any number for the first time and wondering at their vigor and their spirit.

Perhaps as he stood on the deck while the boat gained the channel again, a spread of stars over his head if the night was clear, he may have thought a little of where the great river was bearing him and his family and to what. The flow of the Ohio, mile after mile, the dark forest a shadow on either side, may have mesmerized him into thinking of it, of the vast network of which it was a part, of the Mississippi into which it would presently roll, of the Missouri which would take him to Kansas, and even of the continental extent of this arterial flow stretching from the Appalachians to the Rockies, from

Montana to Virginia, from Minnesota's forests to the bayous of Louisiana, various segments of which would bring, and were bringing, others than the Browns to Kansas.

Even as he thought, men with opinions differing from his own were traveling from the South, up the Cumberland and Tennessee, both of which flowed into the Ohio, some determined to make Kansas a slave state, an astonishing number favoring a free state even if against abolition. A few frontier fire-eaters may have been coming down the Arkansas and the Red River west of the Mississippi but eager to gain it so as to travel to St. Louis and on to Kansas via the Missouri. Some were traveling from New Orleans, but if that city did not send its share of fighters to Kansas it was because its citizens were more interested in Walker's expedition to Nicaragua. Some young men, revolvers in shoulder holsters, occasionally came aboard at Natchez and Vicksburg, for the lower Mississippi above New Orleans carried its share of Southern warriors toward the conflict in Kansas. It was in truth a large and violent land that spring of 1855.

At Eufalia, Alabama, one Jefferson Buford was raising a company of three hundred to fight for slavery in Kansas, opening offices and establishing organizing committees in South Carolina, Georgia, and Florida, in addition to Alabama, to recruit the men. Some four hundred responded. Soon Major Buford, as he was called, was raising money for this expedition by auctioning off his forty slaves as a patriotic service, perhaps disturbed by the sorrow of old family servants being sold to points far and wide but gratified by the price they brought, averaging $700 apiece, whether man, woman, or child. After all, it was the only way the poor creatures could contribute to the Southern way of life.[51]

His regiment, as he called it, was organized into four companies with himself as colonel although for some reason he was still called "Major." After a gala send-off in Montgomery where the warriors were given food, drink, and Bibles, they made their way across Alabama and Mississippi to the river, probably embarking from Natchez.

John Brown, Jr., did not know, of course, as he stood on the deck of the boat moving down the Ohio that the Browns would meet Buford and his four hundred in warfare in Kansas. He was not even certain there would be war and preferred to think of his wide and peaceful acres, lush with prairie grass and thick with cattle, every steer, bull, and cow belonging to him. As he mused in the night on what might be coming, perhaps stretching before turning in, and looking all around, at the wide expanse of starry sky above, at the dark river ahead and behind, he might have seen the dim lights of a steamer on the Kentucky side and heard its whistle, faint and lonely from the further shore. There was an answering blast near him, rolling and reverberating across the river, soon peaceful and serene and quiet again, but nevertheless the path to war.

2

As John and Jason and their families were approaching St. Louis on the Mississippi on April 20, their three younger brothers (Owen, Frederick, and Salmon) were arriving in Kansas. Two had ridden on horseback across Missouri, driving eleven head of cattle before them,[52] the third driving a covered wagon. They had wintered the stock at Meredosia, Illinois, west of Springfield, on the farm of their Uncle Frederick and had started on their journey through the slave state early in March. They passed their nights in the wagon while waiting for their older brothers 10 miles west of Osawatomie, about halfway down the Missouri-Kansas border and some 25 miles from Missouri. Their uncle, the Reverend Samuel Adair, lived near Osawatomie, between the juncture of the Osage and Pottawatomie rivers, with his wife Florilla (half sister of John Brown).

"During their slow journey with their stock across the entire width of Missouri," their father later wrote of his three sons, "they heard much from her people of the stores of wrath & vengeance which were then & there gathering for Free State men & abolitionists gone or going to Kansas; & were themselves often admonished in no very mild language to stop before it should be 'too late.' "[53]

"The stores of wrath & vengeance" threatened against the brothers only made them more hostile to the Missourians, who were themselves aroused to a fighting pitch by their preparations for their invasion of Kansas on March 30 and their mood following it. The Browns camped out each night in their wagon, seeking places where they would not attract visitors. Owen with his tawny beard and crippled right arm was not very well, having experienced, according to his father, "no little suffering" from the exposure incidental to wintering the cattle. Frederick, jogging along on his horse, his golden auburn hair bright above his face, was probably still "pale and weak," as his father described him when he left for Illinois after his self-inflicted operation. Salmon, characterized by his father as "a very strong minor son," who would be nineteen on October 2, was the only one of the brothers in perfect health, exuberant at being embarked on his first adventure into the world.[54]

Yet they were in no mood to take any harangues from Missourians about their beliefs or about the wisdom of turning back before it should be too late. After all, they had been raised on plans of striking against slavery and now it seemed to them as if such an opportunity was soon to come. Salmon told his father in his first letter from Kansas that as a result of the trip across Missouri, "The boys have their feelings well worked up so I think they will fight. There is a lack of arms here in Brownsville," he continued, apparently referring to their camp, which the brothers sometimes called "Brown's Station."

Then, as if trying to revive his father's old interest in his plan to invade the South by way of the Appalachians, or at least reinvigorate his former fighting spirit, he wrote, "I feel more like fighting now than I ever did before and would be glad to go to Alabama." [55] That state must have been named in the many discussions John Brown had had with his sons about his plan for penetrating the South through the mountains leading into Alabama and Georgia. John Brown was in Rockford, Illinois, when Salmon wrote to him, trying to sell his cattle so he could use the proceeds to move himself and his family to North Elba. If he was growing more restive as he read of the outrages in Kansas so were thousands in the North. Whatever his outrage, he did not see how he could abandon his family after moving them to the Adirondack wilderness with its days of 30° below zero when the winters were severe.

The two older Brown brothers, their wives, and little sons probably left St. Louis on the night of April 22 after buying two small tents, a prairie plow, and a hand-mill for grinding corn. These were loaded on the *New Lucy*, a Missouri river steamer, which would take the Browns through the slave state on the swift but often shallow river. Boats, particularly when traveling upstream, were frequently stranded on sandbanks and damaged by snags, often giant trees embedded in the sand beneath the surface of the water after the banks in which they grew had caved in. The Browns regarded the coming trip up the Missouri with dread, thoroughly tired of steamers after their long journey from Ohio. Their money was running out and the fares and freight charges seemed to them exorbitant. They had been cut off from news of Kansas since their departure when the first news of the Missouri invasion on March 30 began to appear in the North's press.

"At this period," John, Jr., said, in recalling their experience years later,

there were no railroads west of St. Louis; our journey must be continued by boat on the Missouri at a time of extremely low water, or by stage at great expense. We chose the river route, taking passage on the steamer, "New Lucy," which too late we found crowded with passengers, mostly men from the South bound for Kansas. That they were from the South was plainly indicated by their language and their dress; while their drinking, profanity, and display of revolvers and bowie-knives—openly worn as an essential part of their make-up—clearly showed the class to which they belonged, and that their mission was to aid in establishing slavery in Kansas.

A box of fruit-trees and grape-vines which my brother Jason had brought from Ohio, our plough and the few agricultural implements we had on the deck of that steamer looked lonesome; for these were all we could see which were adapted to the occupations of peace. Then for the first time rose in our minds the query: Must the fertile prairies of Kansas, through a struggle at arms, be first secured to freedom before free men can sow and reap? If so, how poorly we were prepared for such work will be seen when I say that, for arms, five of us brothers had only two small squirrel rifles and one revolver.

But before we reached our destination other matters claimed our attention. Cholera, which then prevailed to some extent at St. Louis, broke out among our passengers, a number of whom died. Among these brother Jason's son Austin, aged four years . . . fell a victim to this scourge; and while our boat lay by for the repair of a broken rudder at Waverley, Mo., we buried him at night near that panic-stricken town, our lonely way illuminated only by the lightning of a furious thunder storm.

True to his spirit of hatred of Northern people, our captain, without warning to us on shore, cast off his lines and left us to make our way by stage to Kansas City, to which place we had already paid our fare by boat. Before we reached there, however, we became very hungry, and endeavored to buy food at various farm-houses on the way; but the occupants, judging from our speech that we were not from the South, always denied us, saying, "We have nothing for you." The only exception to this answer was at the stage-house at Independence, Mo.

Arrived in Kansas, her lovely prairies and wooded streams seemed to us indeed like a haven of rest. Here in prospect we saw our cattle increased to hundreds, and possibly thousands, fields of corn, orchards and vineyards. At once we set about the work through which only our visions of prosperity could be realized. Our tents would suffice for shelter until we could plough our land, plant corn and other crops, fruit trees, and vines, cut and secure as hay enough of the waving grass to supply our stock the coming winter. . . .[56]

Owen, Frederick, and Salmon, after exploring the vicinity, had chosen possible claims for the Brown family all immediately east of Middle Creek between the Pottawatomie and Osage rivers, the land high and rolling with plenty of water and timber on the various claims, which amounted to 160 acres for each of the five brothers. The claims were about ten miles west of Osawatomie and less than that from the cabin of the Adairs. Now on the arrival of John and Jason, they were asking the approval of the oldest of their brothers of the tentative choices of claims. He thought they had chosen well. Already his tall form, his handsome face, were becoming a little leaner and there was a tension in his movements that had not been present in Ohio. His career in Kansas for the next year was the high point of his life. He became a political leader of the Free State movement, not of the stature of Robinson or Pomeroy or James H. Lane, soon to arrive on the scene, but one who performed important tasks against the bogus legislature, rallying Free State settlers as best he could to defy it and playing his part in the organization and election of the rival Free State government which opposed the bogus legislature of the Missourians and President Pierce.

From the first hour of their life in Kansas, John took charge, directing where the tents should be erected, supervising the digging of trenches around them, the erection of a corral for the cattle at night, the plowing of 10 virgin acres of prairie for corn, another acre for a garden in which they planted "onions, cabbages, peas, squash, corn, garden beans, lettuce, cucumbers, water and musk mellons, potatoes, early turnips and sweet potatoes." By May 24 "almost everything in the garden" was "up and ready to hoe," and they were "chopping in sod corn," and had about 1 acre planted in the 10 acre plot.[57]

Poor Jason was not good for much in all this labor. He and Ellen were so grief-stricken by the death of Austin that they could work with little vigor and from the first spoke of returning to Ohio as soon as possible. The brothers soon knew that they faced danger because of their views. "A few days after our arrival," Jason recalled years later,

we were at our dinner when a squad of Missourians rode up. All were heavily armed. They numbered six or eight. Martin White, as we afterwards knew, was their leader. They pretended to be looking for stray cattle and after asking if we had seen any, inquired how we were on the goose. "We are Free State," we answered, "and more than that we are Abolitionists." They rode away at once, and from that moment on we were marked for destruction. Before we had been in the Territory a month, we found we had to go armed, and to be prepared to defend our lives.[58]

It was probably John who made the reply to the Missourians. He meant from the first to be a marked man if that was necessary to win freedom for Kansas, although he could not have known that Martin White, leader of the Missourians and a pro-slavery preacher of the region, would soon kill one of his brothers.

John recognized at once, after this confrontation with the well-armed Missourians and a few other events, that their big need was for weapons if they were not to be overrun. On May 20 he began a long letter to his father about their need, continuing his writing on May 24 and 26. He was apparently convinced by then that John Brown was not coming to Kansas for he did not visualize him delivering the weapons in person. Instead, he asked if his father could get them by borrowing money from Gerrit Smith, or elsewhere, which the brothers pledged to repay, and ship them in a box "to one of us, Kansas City, care of Walker & Chick and care of B. Slater. no. 19 Levee St., St. Louis, Mo." He sent the letter to his father at North Elba, care of Ruth and Henry Thompson, adding in a note to the latter under the date of May 26, "If Father has not yet moved to North Elba, or is not going there this season, we wish this letter *immediately* forwarded to him if you know where he is." [59]

As early as June, John and Frederick were going to Lawrence, some 35 miles away, joining in the conventions planning the Free State Party and the Free State government. John was a vice-president and a member of the committee on resolutions of the Free State Convention, meeting in Lawrence on June 25, which resolved concerning Missouri's reputed plans for another invasion, "That in reply to the threats of war so frequently made in our neighbor state, our answer is 'WE ARE READY.' " [60]

If Kansas had been conquered for slavery by Atchison and his legions, John Brown, Jr., and thousands of others both in Kansas and elsewhere meant to reverse that conquest. His attitude may be further judged from an incident which was soon to occur when the law of the bogus legislature went into effect which provided two years in prison for any who said slavery in Kansas was illegal. He immediately sought out a slaveholder who lived near Osawatomie and told him that slavery was illegal in Kansas. "I called on him to witness that I had broken the law," he wrote a day later, "and that I still intended to do so at all times and places, and further that if any officer attempted to arrest me for violation of this law and should put his villanous hand on me, I would surely kill him so help me God." [61]

But he was not as deadly a man as he thought he was and his efforts to be so would soon strain him beyond endurance. He could strike an attitude but he could not hold it.

And during all this time John Brown, the Old Man, was not in Kansas.

XXIII

The Stakes
Are Raised

THE LEGEND of John Brown in its narrowest sense has a sharp duality, an inherent contradiction. But both aspects of the legend have this in common—they have served to obscure the reality of John Brown's life. Both try to strip him of himself. Those who called him saint, sent by God to perform the quintessential American deed and to become an American martyr, could not have him as he was. They could not or would not accept his hesitations and retreats, his doubts and sweatings, his backslidings and collapses from virtue and purpose. To them he was the same at the beginning as he was at the end, a constant in virtue with little more of change or development than a straight line aimed always and forever at slavery. They could not have him learning from Lovejoy's slaying, pushed forward by Nat Turner and Cinque and Torrey and Walker of the branded hand, developing no faster or not as fast as many of his countrymen, the product of his time and place and the fierce currents that finally eventuated in a war abolishing slavery.

Nor would those who called him devil, as consistent a part of this narrowed legend as its opposite, give him any share of humanity. To them he was innate evil, primal and unalloyed, his battles and slayings having little to do with the slavery that he felt, and thousands felt, was killing the country. And to them his violence came only from his own nature, a thing apart from the growing national convulsion. Neither side of those promulgating opposing versions of this simplistic legend was interested in any theory of development. To both John Brown was full-born, the same at the beginning as he was at the end, now and forever, whether devil or saint.

The legend so conceived not only conceals the reality of his years but obliterates the nature of his personality, replacing an intensely human and many-troubled man with a symbol. In neither aspect of it is there anything to suggest John Brown in his overwhelming and unexpected reality, as, for example, when a little tipsy after repeated nips from a jug of whiskey as he clatters along behind his team, standing upright in his open wagon, he suddenly hurls and smashes the jug against a roadside rock with the equally sudden and permanent resolve never again to touch whiskey. Nor is there anything to suggest the ordinary routines and triumphs of his days, as when he won prizes for sheep and cattle at state and county fairs or stood for hours beneath a waterfall, his clothing clinging wetly to him as he washed hundreds of bawling, protesting sheep.

Neither version of the legend suggests much of his lifelong panting after holiness and money nor prepares one for the picture of his sitting before a roaring fire in his home, one of his children on his lap, as he sings "Blow Ye the Trumpet, Blow." There is little in the legend, presented so, to suggest the quality in him that made him so delighted with the games and debates he organized in his home or of the man who liked to watch the clouds moving over the spruce-covered slopes of the Adirondacks with strange thoughts welling in him of why God had placed the mountains there.

Nor is there much suggestion in either aspect of the legend of the promoter and Sunday school teacher driving for the success which eluded him so thoroughly that he, the honest thief, as he was conceived to be, stole thousands in his effort to avoid bankruptcy and save his family from hardship. There is little of the lover of *Aesop's Fables* and *Plutarch's Lives*, or of the Calvinistic adventurer with his muted swagger, or of the man who so closely followed Garrison's *Liberator* and *Frederick Douglass' Paper*. There is little in the legend suggesting that individual who took such delight in Durham cattle and Saxony sheep and fine swine, who preached sermons in a tannery and to the blacks of Timbucto and pitched hay in distant fields, his mind alternating, perhaps, between the problems of gaining loans for a failing company and liberty for a captive people. Nor is there much to indicate the expert tanner, the acute judge of leather, the best, or one of the best, breeders and raisers of sheep in the country, or the man who traveled the ocean sea to Europe and ruin through challenging the country's largest wool corporations, nor of how he had studied astronomy and liked to stand in the night pointing out the constellations. "Everything moves in sublime harmony," he said once, indicating the stars above him, "in the government of God. Not so with us poor creatures. If one star is more brilliant than the others, it is continually shooting in some erratic way into space."[1]

THE UNTOLD STORY

I

The impact of John Brown's bloody deeds in Kansas and particularly at Harper's Ferry was so overwhelming, so tremendous in its shock and significance, that few were able to regard the perpetrator other than in stereotypes of hero or villain largely, although not entirely, geographic in their origin. These nation-shaking episodes, which helped to precipitate civil war and change the life and history of a country, playing their part in sending many to war and even to death, were John Brown's story and story enough. For the most part this has remained true, both as to stereotypes and in confining the story to Kansas and Virginia, with the result that the first fifty-five years of John Brown's life—that is, all of his years save four—have seldom been told in any detail although they may shed vital light on the last four. Particularly when a man has been reduced to devil or saint, when his life has become a caricature because of the fierce division between North and South, it is more than ever necessary, if we care to understand him or his time, that we should have available to us not only his four final years but all of them.

In addition, it may have been felt that this many-peopled story of a country being torn apart, and containing characters as disparate and necessary to its development as Douglass and Thoreau, Emerson and Edmund Ruffin, Governor Wise and Theodore Parker, Dr. Howe, Thomas Wentworth Higginson, Gerrit Smith, and Jefferson Davis, as well as many others, was a little too massive to encompass. Consequently, much central to the story has never been recounted in the context of the time that made John Brown and the crisis which gave him power. It was enough to tell of Kansas and Harper's Ferry, too much to reveal their genesis.

With the time and its temper stripped away—its duels and shootings and assaults, its go-to-hell bravado, its frequent persistence in bringing almost any dispute to mortal encounter, its readiness for martyrdom and pistols at twenty paces, its long cold war over slavery, its private armies and filibustering—with all this gone, John Brown's acts may seem strange to the point of psychosis. With this framing them, however, they are distressingly representative of a tragic and violent age. If the time and its temperament were seldom indicated in accounts of John Brown, neither was the quality of slavery, nor the black man's valiant and repeated attempts for freedom, nor the long and excruciating tension within the lives of many Americans, from Washington to Lincoln, committed to the founding premise that all men were created equal while enslaving millions of their fellow countrymen. Thus the basic social dynamic thrusting John Brown, his associates, and opponents into history has seldom been emphasized in the story of that long-maturing crisis that he and his famous colleagues, black and white, brought to explosion. Prominent and successful men do not enter such a plot as John Brown's without a social and national history impelling them to it.

Nor has the road West in a covered wagon, breaking camp at dawn, the long day's journey, the campfire leaping in the darkness, the wolf's howl far away, the stir of the wind in the night, been much more than indicated in the story of John Brown, although it was almost his earliest experience as well as the transcendent American experience for the legions who made the West for which Free Soil and slavery would fight. That transient log cabin society of Hudson and its Indians, a society wrought from the wilderness and a replica of many others like it, with its hymn-singing and its revivals, its honor for learning, for holiness and money, has never been closely examined in the context of which we write; nor has the later Hudson, with its feuds and cleavages and the triumph of the Oberlin Collegiate Institute, which finally gave a common cause and an anti-slavery ideology to most on the Western Reserve, the birthplace of the Higher Law beyond the Alleghenies. Yet this was the culture which bred John Brown, and such societies and such experience, whatever their variation, were the background of most Americans above the Ohio in that predominantly rural age before the Civil War. It was in them that the extra-legal Underground may have reached its greatest strength and from them that young men marched to war by the thousands in 1861.

John Brown has usually been extracted from the time that formed him, almost divorced from the great struggle that made him no less than Garrison and Weld, Ruffin and Wise. The narrative to this point has tried to tell something of this largely untold story.

2

A later time with a broader perspective saw John Brown's legend as being essentially the story of a nation in crisis, involving, as John Jay Chapman wrote, "everyone living at the time" and encompassing "an epoch . . . the whole of a society . . . a national and religious birthpang." [2] Yet there must have been some who saw the legend as having wider aspects than saint or devil even as it was being formed. John Brown, of course, played a part in forming the legend, both through his deeds and his fondness for the public eye; but he was not its creator. The thousands of Americans who gave it currency, who, hating slavery, saw something of themselves as they would like to be in John Brown, or at least found sympathy for him, were its real creators, building so firmly that it has impact still not only in this country but all around the world.* Knowing themselves and their own inner struggles in accepting the

---

* From China to Africa John Brown's legend still lives. Before the United Nations on April 7, 1965, Achkar Marof, Guinea's chief delegate and chairman of the UN's eleven-nation committee inquiring into South Africa's apartheid, likened opposition to that policy in South Africa to John Brown's attack at Harper's Ferry, to his "giving his life because of his passionate hatred of slavery." R. H. Amonoo of Ghana in speaking before the United Nations on October 9, 1963, against South Africa's policy of apartheid, said of John Brown: "It was in another context that he spoke but it is nevertheless as applicable today as then when John Brown, that great American whose soul still goes marching on throughout the world, was taken prisoner at Harper's Ferry over 100 years ago and said to his captors, 'You may dispose of me very easily; I am nearly disposed of now; but this question—this negro question I mean—the end of that is not yet.' Mr. Chairman, John Brown's soul still goes marching on in South Africa today. It will find no rest until it has seen justice done."

In February 1953, a great crowd of Chinese at Peking greeted the arriving Dr. W. E. B. Du Bois, pre-eminent black American scholar, pioneer Pan-African, and a founder of the National Association for the Advancement of Colored People. They sang "John Brown's Body," with its chorus of "Glory, glory, hallelujah . . . his soul goes marching on. . . ." It was fitting enough in that Du Bois was one of Brown's biographers and spiritual descendants, founding the Niagara Movement, predecessor of the N.A.A.C.P., at Harper's Ferry.

The vitality of John Brown's legend from 1859 to the present in the United States is attested by the literally thousands of poems, plays, pageants, odes, novels, biographies, short stories, paintings, engravings, radio scripts, songs, movie scenarios, essays, addresses, ballads, lectures, newspaper and magazine articles concerning him listed in the collection of Boyd B. Stutler, Charleston, West Virginia. The Stutler collection chiefly reveals the popular response to the legend over all the years since Brown's hanging, but for better-known writers and poets see Ruchames, *A John Brown Reader,* "The Literary Heritage," ranging from Edmund Clarence Stedman, Theodore Parker, William Dean Howell, A. Bronson Alcott, and Victor Hugo to Louisa May Alcott, Oliver Wendell Holmes, Theodore Tilton, Wendell Phillips, Herman Melville, Walt Whitman, Whittier, Emerson, Thoreau, and Douglass; from James Whitcomb Riley, W. E. B. DuBois, and John Jay Chapman to Carl Sandburg, Gamaliel Bradford, and Clarence Darrow; from Stephen Vincent Benet and John Cournos to David Karsner and Truman Nelson. There have been other scholars, it should be said, who have described John Brown as only a bloodthirsty marauder, and who believe that it is only the people's credulity that still gives life the world around to his legend as a fighter for freedom.

real risks of fighting slavery, their retreats and their surges forward, some of these men and women surely knew, despite the conventional simplifications of the legend, that John Brown was never an unchanging monolith.

In reality he was a battleground, a microcosm of the wider one shaking the nation and even reflecting to an extent the advances and defeats of the anti-slavery crusade. And this being so, it must seem strange that virtually everything written about John Brown has ignored the inner struggle that dogged his years. After his initial fever for wealth, his frantic scrambling for success through the promotion and sale of the Brown & Thompson Addition, he made his first public declaration against slavery as a result of Lovejoy's murder, developed further with the growth of the Underground Railroad, made his own portentous pledge to his family to attack slavery by force at about the time J. Q. Adams was declaring that only civil war might abolish it, and expanded his doctrine of force with his organization of the League of Gileadites after the passage of the Fugitive Slave Act.

Yet during most of this time, and again not unconnected with the North's dominant currents, he fluctuated constantly between his desire to give his whole life to the struggle against slavery and his ache to dominate in the world of business. However much he tried to be faithful to each of his goals, business and anti-slavery, he found that the pursuit of one negated success in the other and that in trying to accomplish both he could be successful in neither.

Yet this dichotomy is not the sole reason for his delay in fighting slavery, remarked upon by Frederick Douglass, one of his closest associates, long years after the Civil War. "Like Moses," Douglass said, as we may recall, John Brown made excuses as to why he should not attack slavery, "but like Moses he was overruled," [3] presumably by the Lord God Almighty who finally would not stand for delay. In telling Douglass in 1847 of his plan for invading the South, John Brown admitted that he might be killed in carrying it out. It was never and is not now the fashion to give John Brown any capability for fear and yet, despite this idealization, he may have had some normal human reluctance to being killed, some hesitation in leaving the family for which he was responsible and plunging into an unknown which might include death and death for more than himself. The dark of night, which arrived as regularly for John Brown as others, may give strangely accurate foresights.

And yet his plan for invading the South may have also, in a queer way, been somewhat responsible for his indecision over Kansas. After all, he had his share of idiosyncrasy and even after he had apparently abandoned his plan for attacking slavery below the Ohio in favor of returning to North Elba, he may have found it hard to abandon it utterly. There are even stories that in 1854 or 1855 he approached a relative, a Colonel Daniel Woodruff, with the proposal that they immediately assault Harper's Ferry; but since he had no money, no supporters, no recruits for the attack, the story is probably apocryphal. Nevertheless, it may indicate some casual conversation, may reveal that the plan was still in his mind.[4] It was exceedingly difficult, as we have seen, for him to change his plans in accordance with new circumstances and his almost involuntary reluctance to relinquish his long-held dream may have contributed to his painful indecision as to joining his sons.

For all his periodic depressions he loved life, loved his family, however stern at times his method of expression, loved farming and the peace and beauty of the Adirondacks. There were other reasons, more shadowy and difficult of explication, perhaps, than commerce for his reluctance to move toward war whether in Virginia or Kansas. But the dilemma pressing him would not let him be, continuing to itch and plague even after he thought he had firmly decided to return to Essex County.

Something of his misery may be indicated by the letter he wrote to Sanborn in 1858. Before he had been wholly committed to the fight against slavery, he wrote, as we may remember, "I felt for a number of years in earlier life a steady strong desire to die," but since he had joined the struggle, or as he put it, "since I saw any prospect of becoming a 'reaper' in the great harvest, I have not only felt quite willing to live, but have enjoyed life much." [5] Yet he was not enjoying life much in June of 1855 as he prepared to move at last with his family to North Elba. The struggle within him was still unresolved. He had written, on May 24 from Rockford, Illinois, where he later sold his cattle, to his sons in Kansas that he "still intended to come on," but again he changed his mind, or so he later indicated.[6]

THE DECISION

I

The stress and strain of John Brown's long indecision, as well as the other vicissitudes that had marked his years, were revealed by his appearance as the family left for North Elba, his shoulders permanently stooped, his mouth a wide bitter line framed by parentheses of crevice-like wrinkles, his brown hair increasingly streaked with gray, the word "old" being the first that leaped to mind in any who saw him. If his attitude had little of contentment as he herded his family before him when they boarded the train at Hudson, it may have been because he was hovering on the very edge of change, everything he had read or heard pushing him toward Kansas while he was in the very act of retreating from it, embarking in the opposite direction to the North Elba he had so long tried to gain.

He may have wondered a little, as he, his wife, and four children began their railroad trip to Cleveland, why he did not feel more of triumph. After all, he had worked for this moment for a year and a half, trying to raise the money to take them all to North Elba where he had fancied himself enjoying at last a hard-won peace. Perhaps he knew his dissatisfaction derived, at least in part, from the fact that every newspaper he took up seemed to have the quality of personal indictment.

If he had been following his *Liberator,* for example, he may have discerned a personal reflection against him in a story telling of those who did go to Kansas,[7] and in another declaring that Kansas had already been won by slavery;[8] and while it did not add that John Brown had made no move to prevent it, he may have thought of that. His comfort would not have been increased by the article asserting that now that Kansas was won for slavery Cuba was about to be seized to extend slavery's area again[9] or by the account of how Colonel H. L. Kinney, a Texas adventurer, was preparing to seize the Atlantic coast of Nicaragua while Walker was planning to invade its Pacific littoral, both threatening Costa Rica to the south as well as Nicaragua, both in *The Liberator*'s view advances for slavery.[10] But the most personal indictment of all, aimed directly at John Brown, or so it may have seemed to him, was carried in an article from the *New York Tribune* and quoted in *The Liberator* of May 11, 1855, reading in part:

Slavery is to be extended indefinitely over this Continent. . . . If it can be allowed to spread peaceably, very well. If not the purpose is clear to force it at the point of the bayonet. It [slavery] buckles on its armor and declares itself ready to fight for supremacy and for the humiliation and subjection of the free States. . . . The vital question is, what will the people of the free States do? Are they to prove cowards and poltroons, or will they show the mettle of free men?

With such a question, or questions like it, within him, John Brown may have been no lively companion on the train to Cleveland. All his letters to Ruth and Henry Thompson at North Elba had indicated that he expected to stay there permanently and as far as is known his wife also expected him to do so. Sixteen years younger than he, thirty-nine to his fifty-five, she carried a baby in her arms as the family left for North Elba, a practice with which she was familiar, this one Ellen, not yet a year old. Often silent, and knowing, it may be, that John Brown's friends and relatives almost always said she was not his equal in intellect or background, she was perhaps a little resentful of her husband for all her loyalty to him. In poor health for some years, she had written John, Jr., while her husband was in Europe that "he never believed there was any disease about me." During his absence she escaped North Elba for several weeks for the water cure at a sanitarium at Northampton, Massachusetts, for an illness she did not specify in her letter to John. But she evidently enjoyed her brief escape from the burdens upon her, resting in the morning and taking carriage rides in the afternoon.[11]

Also on the train to Cleveland was the dutiful Watson, nearly twenty years old, and careful and judicious enough to have taken the family to North Elba without his father's aid had the latter wished to leave for Kansas before the family left Ohio. There were in addition the two little girls, Anne, eleven, and Sarah, eight, who were young enough to enjoy the steady clackety-clack of the speeding train, watching their father and mother as they bounced up and down in steady but minute rhythm with the motion of the train. Soon it gathered speed, achieving the phenomenal rate of 20 miles an hour, the whistle reaching into the sky with long exciting blasts as they approached road crossings where horses reared in terror, sometimes trying to bolt, their drivers standing erect in their wagons, seesawing back and forth on their reins as they tried to bring their horses under control. Even John Brown, a traveled man who knew the cars, as they were called, may have been pleasantly thrilled by the rock and roll of the train as it sped by farmhouse and village, recalling how often he had walked that route, or ridden it on horseback, and how very slow it had been in the old times.

The family may have proceeded by the cars, rocketing forward through day and night, the whistle thrilling its warning up ahead, straight across the state of New York to Albany, thence north to Westport near North Elba. It is more likely, however, that after arriving at Cleveland, they went by Lake Erie and Lake Ontario. In a letter to Henry and Ruth Thompson from Hudson on June 18, John Brown said,

I write to say that we are (after so long a time) on our way to North Elba, with our freight delivered at the Akron depot; we look for it here tonight. If this reaches you before we get on, I would like to have someone with a good team to go out to Westport on next Tuesday or Wednesday forenoon, to take us out or a load of our stuff. We have some little thought now of going with our freight by the Welland Canal and by Ogdensburgh to Westport, in which case we may not get around until after you get this.[12]

Since the Browns probably did not arrive at North Elba until June 24 or 25,[13] it is likely that they took the longer water route from Cleveland and Lake Erie through the Welland Canal west of Buffalo and Niagara Falls into Lake Ontario, traversing its whole length and then up the St. Lawrence to Ogdensburg. There they would have taken a train again to Champlain on the Quebec border and down the shore of Lake Champlain to Westport, John Brown increasingly fidgety and on edge.

2

No doubt someone met them with a wagon and team at Westport, as John Brown had requested. The family with their furniture and goods moved off through the wilderness on the rocky ascending road leading to the township of North Elba which seemed, to most outsiders at any rate, almost as remote as Africa. The sheer cliffs that periodically loomed high above them and the road, the mountains covered with spruce, pine, fir, maple, and birch, emphasized their retirement to a place as removed from the country's troubles as could possibly be found; yet it is unlikely that John Brown's spirits rose as he penetrated deeper into that wilderness he had sought so long.

After some eight hours of jolting progress, through Elizabethtown and Keene and on a course generally westward, they arrived late in the day, at the farm of 244 acres that John Brown had bought from Gerrit Smith for $244 in 1849. They turned from the road into a bare and rocky pasture. Some hundred yards or more beyond the turn-in was the plain little house that Henry Thompson had built for them, not the log cabin that John Brown had suggested, but of unpainted yellow lumber, cut in a nearby sawmill. If the tiny house with its pitched roof, its two rooms on the ground floor, kitchen and parlor, an unpartitioned attic above, a cellar below, was unimpressive, the surroundings were grand enough. The mountain called Whiteface rose to the north, a ridge of low mountains was just visible to the east, as well as Mount Marcy to the south, the highest peak of the Adirondacks. Their farm formed a kind of plateau, 2,000 feet above sea level, rimmed by distant ranges that dipped and curved over the line of the encircling forest.

John Brown and his arriving family were probably met at the new house, still unplastered, by Ruth and Henry Thompson. Perhaps he scarcely looked at the new abode, at the great outcropping of rock near the house, occupied as he was with helping move in the furniture, setting up the beds and the stoves, connecting them with two red brick chimneys. It was during this work that Ruth or Henry may have handed over the letter his eldest son had written him on May 20, 24, and 26 from "Brownsville Kanzas Territory" asking for arms.*

It may have been nearly dark by then, the end of a long and arduous day, and we can imagine him straining over the letter in the flickering light of candles, the little girls and the baby already asleep in the beds just erected in the attic, Ruth and Mrs. Brown struggling to get supper in the unfamiliar surroundings. The letter, the first from John in far-away Kansas, began quietly enough:

Dear Father

I am seated in one of our tents upon a bedstead of poles and covered with brush, to say we are all well, and with the exception of Jason & Ellen, are in very good spirits. Our situation is about 10 miles west of Osawatomie, where Mr. Adair lives and upon an elevation I should judge of fully 300 feet above that place.

We have made 5 claims here,—Salmon having one with the rest—these claims we have not yet had time to divide, when they are divided each one will be amply supplied with living water, with timber enough for firewood; and if judiciously used, for building purposes, besides having stone enough to make good substantial walls around each 160 acres, these too being the very best for buildings and then there will be enough of these left for succeeding generations.

Our timber is principally in a ravine putting into Middle Creek, a "Right-smart" tributary of the Osage River and which has its mouth about 1½ miles North East of our camp which is at the head of S^d [Said] Ravine. Our water both for drinking and for stock is supplied from springs in this ravine. The stone lies on each side of it, forming the sides, and what is peculiar all the stone is flat or nearly so. . . .

The prairie lies in every direction, rich as the bottom lands of the Scioto [an Ohio River], yet high, and in vast, gently rounded waves, as though the Ocean once were here, and before retiring had taken pains to smooth her bed that not a rough spot might be seen. . . .

After declaring that Jason and Ellen were incurably melancholy because of the death of their little boy, Austin, and wanted to return to Ohio, John continued,

Salmon, Fred^k and Owen say that they never was in a country that begun to please them as well and I will say that the present prospect for health, wealth and usefulness much exceeds even my most sanguine anticipations. I know of no country where a poor man endowed with a share of common sense & with health can get a start so easy. If we can succeed in making this a *free* state, a great work will be accomplished for *mankind*.

And now I come to the matter, that more than all else I intended should be the principal subject of this letter. I tell you the truth when I say that while the

---

* For a short time "Kanzas" was an acceptable variant.

interest of despotism has secured to its cause hundreds of thousands of the meanest and most desperate of men, armed to the teeth with Revolvers, Bowie Knives, Rifles & Cannon—while they are not only thoroughly organized, but under pay from Slaveholders—the friends of freedom are *not one fourth* of them *half armed*, and as to *military organization* among them *it no where exists in this territory* unless they have recently done something in Lawrence. The result of this is that the people here exhibit the most abject and cowardly spirit, whenever their dearest rights are invaded and trampled down by the lawless band of miscreants which Missouri has ready at a moments call to pour in upon them. This is the *general* effect upon the people here so far as I have noticed; there are a few, and but a few exceptions. . . .

John Brown may have looked more grim than usual as he read this.

Now Missouri is not alone in the undertaking to make this a Slave State. Every Slave holding State from Virginia to Texas is furnishing men and money to fasten Slavery upon this glorious land by means no matter how foul. . . . From the statement of the Rev. Mr. Finch of Osawatomie who was here but a short time since on his way home from Lawrence, (a distance of 35 miles from here,)—the people of that place are at this time thrown into a great excitement owing to a report having reached there from, as they told him, an authentic source, that there was organized and organizing, a force in Missouri of 3000 men whose purpose is to drive out from the Territory every Anti Slavery man they can find in it—that they intend to do so *now* while they can nip their opponents in the bud as it respects numbers and strength. . . .

Now the remedy we propose is that the Anti-Slavery portion of the inhabitants should *immediately, thoroughly arm*, and *organize themselves* in *military companies*. In order to effect this, some persons must begin and lead off in the matter. Here are 5 men of us who are not only anxious to fully prepare, but are thoroughly determined to fight. . . .

The old apostle of military action, of organized force against slavery, may have felt a quickening of spirit and pride at this evidence of his sons' resolve. Continuing, he read:

We have among us 5, 1 Revolver, 1 Bowie Knife, 1 middling good Rifle, 1 poor Rifle, 1 small pocket pistol and 2 sling shot. What we want in order to be thoroughly armed for each man, is 1 *Colts* large sized Revolver, 1 "Allen & Thurbers" large sized Revolver . . . 1 *Minnie Rifle* . . . and 1 heavy Bowie Knife. [That is, five of each of the weapons named.] With these we could compete with men who even possessed Cannon. The real Minnie Rifle has a killing range almost equal to cannon and of course is more easily handled. Now we want you to get for us these arms. We need them more than we do bread. . . .

Some half-formed resolve was rising within the Old Man at North Elba. It was not a change. It was more as if the aspirations of a lifetime had come alive again, had fallen into place once more, as if the division in himself had suddenly snapped shut. His son suggested, as we have seen, that his father ship the arms by freight. "Would not Gerrit Smith, or someone," the letter continued,

furnish the money and loan it to us for one, two or three years, for this purpose, until we can raise enough to refund it from the *Free* soil of Kanzas? We must have them. We pledge ourselves jointly and severally to pay for these arms as soon as we can raise the means from our labor, and the prospect of doing this was to us never so bright before. If we begin in this matter others here will at once take hold. Then Kansas may have a chance for freedom.[14]

John Brown himself is explicit in declaring that he did not fully determine to go to Kansas until he had read John's letter. "On receipt of that letter," he later wrote, in an account that he thought might be published, "the elder Brown fully resolved to proceed at once to Kansas & join his children." [15] But first he must get the arms his sons needed more than bread. There was an excitement in him that had long been absent. He must have left the next morning, after only a single night at North Elba. On June 26 he was at a convention of political abolitionists at Syracuse of which Gerrit Smith was a leader and where Old Brown, as he would soon call himself, revealed nothing of indecision. His address to the convention was as fiery as if he had been young again and he did not only ask funds for arms for his sons but spoke of the necessity of arming all the Free State settlers of Kansas.

Frederick Douglass, who was there, later said of the convention at which he spoke supporting John Brown's plea that some were unwilling to contribute because of their peace principles. "The collection was taken up," he said, "with much spirit, nevertheless, for Capt. Brown was present and spoke for himself; and when he spoke men believed in the man." [16] Brown was delighted with his reception and the convention and wrote to his wife and children from Syracuse on June 28:

I reached here on the first day of the convention [June 26], and I have reason to bless God that I came; for I have met with a most warm reception from all, so far as I know, and—except by a few sincere, honest peace friends—a most hearty approval of my intention of arming my sons and other friends in Kansas. I received today donations amounting to a little over sixty dollars—twenty from Gerrit Smith, five from an old British Officer; * others giving smaller sums with such earnest and affectionate expressions of their good wishes as did me more good than money even. John's two letters † were introduced, and read with

---

* Charles Stuart, the closest and most intimate friend of Theodore Weld, and also a friend of Smith.

† It is not known to what second letter John Brown referred, unless he counted the one begun on May 20 as two. The most important part was under date of May 24.

such effect by Gerrit Smith as to draw tears from numerous eyes in the great collection of people present. The convention has been one of the most interesting meetings I ever attended in my life; and I have made a great addition to the number of warm-hearted and honest friends.[17]

John Brown was at last fully committed to Kansas. For the first time in years he was at one with himself. He had arrived at his career, although it had taken him fifty-five years to do so. Perhaps he felt young again even though he had only four more years to live. He spent the month of July working on the house at North Elba, although it was never entirely completed, laying in supplies for his family, and making final preparations for his departure. He planned to stop at Akron, where he knew a good many people, in an effort to raise more arms and money. Henry Thompson, his son-in-law, decided to accompany him to Kansas.

The Browns, for all of their efforts at the stoic and their usual absence of demonstration, had their share of emotion. Apparently all of them were weeping as the two men left North Elba for the dangers of Kansas. At the door John Brown turned again to his family and said, "If it is so painful for us to part with the hope of meeting again, how of poor slaves?" [18]

A DIVERSITY OF WARRIORS

I

The great American transformation, changing brothers into enemies, the peaceful into killers, the quick into the dead, was almost completed. There would be further hesitations, retreats, maneuvers, but essentially the sides had been chosen, the battle lines had been drawn. If John Brown was transformed at last after many failures, irrelevancies, and defeats it was as a part of this larger transformation.

By 1855 there were other men than John Brown in both South and North beginning to flirt, however distantly, with charges of treason and a possible prison sentence, or even a noose. The halter was already being advocated for some by Senator Douglas of Illinois while he lamented the failure of the federal government to use it on those he considered traitors.[19] The stakes had been raised since the clash in Kansas with the Pierce administration's determination that the Free State leaders, to whom Douglas referred in his grim suggestion, were revolutionaries plotting treason, a concept that might be extended to include those who supplied them with weapons, Theodore Parker, for example, and his friend Dr. Samuel Gridley Howe.[20]

As a matter of fact, Benjamin F. Hallett, federal district attorney and a leader of Massachusetts administration Democrats, had already urged that such as Parker and Howe be charged with treason for violations of the Fugitive Slave Act, adding that he who violated it "must risk hanging for it."[21] As for the likelihood of his hanging, Parker occasionally agreed in transient moments of discouragement that such might be his fate. By the next year, when considering the situation between the North and South, he was writing, "Of course *we shall fight*. I have expected civil war for months. . . . Nay, I think affairs may come to such a pass, that my own property may be confiscated; for who knows that we shall [be] beat at the beginning—and I be hung as a traitor!" [22]

But Parker, whatever the risk, was continuing to use his own money for guns instead of books, while preparing his defense to the indictment charging him with obstructing federal authority in the attempt to rescue Anthony Burns in which a federal deputy had been killed. In the intervals of preparation for his trial he was carrying out his customary pastoral duties, comforting the sick, visiting the dying, counseling the desperate young on how to survive a broken heart; he was serving on the Vigilance Committee, traveling by foot and by coach all over the Boston area, warning specific fugitives that they were being pursued by masters or their agents who had arrived in Boston; he was stumping the free states, living on railroads and cold sandwiches as he tried to study and write while his train bumped along, each night warning his countrymen of the impending test, of his certainty that either slavery or freedom would soon control the whole country through war or some other overwhelming political victory. Possibly freedom would win through a Republican triumph in the presidential election of 1856.

Always he tried to arrange his speaking so as to be back in Boston for his Sunday sermon, where three thousand continued to hear him weekly at the Music Hall and usually succeeded in doing so save when he ranged as far as Ohio and Illinois. While he expected war, he did not forget politics, feeling that there was more than one way to beat slavery and that before it was abolished all of them would doubtless have to be tried. Almost daily he wrote a half dozen letters to Senators Seward, Hale, Sumner, Wilson, Chase, and others, telling them in his programmatic way exactly what the situation had come to, and exactly what he expected of them, numbering his points 1, 2, 3, and so on. They always replied in equal detail, for there were none in the

North then, particularly politicians, who did not regard Parker as a power to be reckoned with. Almost daily in times of public tumult in Boston he wrote or conferred with Dr. Howe. If no man is a hero to his valet, sometimes he is not so either to his friend. At any rate, Parker was not to Howe, who criticized him constantly, saying he was too dogmatic or too given to windy generalizations or too secular in manner when in the pulpit.

Although Parker liked to say that he was the best-hated man in all New England, speaking airily as if it were a matter of no consequence, he was in reality as sensitive as he was combative. He was as tender-hearted as he was unsparing. It was an unfortunate combination as painful to himself as to his victims. He did not just attack wrong, he conscientiously tried to execute its perpetrators, verbally, of course, sparing neither himself nor them. He sought to be just, too, and that often made some wince the more when he slew the victims he had made so attractive. All of this gave him pain and he sometimes wept, as when preparing his sermon attacking Webster.[23]

But if he could be terrible in indictment, he could also show something of poetry in his fairness, as in this of the dead Webster he had condemned:

He was a farmer, and took a countryman's delight in country things, in loads of hay, in trees, in turnips, and the noble Indian corn, in monstrous swine. He had a patriarch's love of sheep, choice breeds thereof he had. He took delight in cows, short-horned Durhams, Herefordshires, Ayrshires, Alderneys. He tilled paternal acres with his own oxen. He loved to give the kine fodder. It was pleasant to hear his talk of oxen. And but three days before he left the earth, too ill to visit them, his cattle, lowing, came to see their sick lord; and, as he stood in his door, his great oxen were driven up, that he might smell their healthy breath, and look his last on those broad, generous faces, that were never false to him.[24]

In speaking so, Parker was describing himself as well as Webster. He never lost his wistfulness for a rural past. No one ever longed more for friends in the crowded city of Boston, which was always a little unfamiliar no matter how well he knew it. He had them but he could never get enough of them and although a coterie of cultured and cultivated women was always about him who adored him, he yearned for more substantial fare, yearned for membership in a men's club with billiards and singing and easy good fellowship. He craved affection as insatiably as he craved the children he never was to have. He could stand the attacks of his enemies, he said, and even asked his friends to criticize him, "Faithful are the wounds of a friend; but the kisses of an enemy are deceitful." Yet Dr. Howe's harsh complaints made him wince. "This is, in reality," he wrote, when Howe said his preaching was not religious enough, "the most painful criticism I ever heard made on my ministry." [25]

His friend did not mean to hurt him any more than was necessary to rid him of his faults. A strait-laced man with everyone but himself, rather conservative in matters of religion, Dr. Howe was now almost as busy as Parker. He continued to collect money for Sharps rifles while running chores for his friend Senator Sumner, editing the *Commonwealth*, and administering the involved and exhausting business of the Perkins Institute and Massachusetts Asylum for the Blind, as well as a school for the feeble-minded; in addition, he served on the executive committee of the New England Emigrant Aid Company, presiding frequently at public meetings and appearing often before state legislatures in behalf of the blind. Yet he might have been surprised had he known that he was already embarked on the course which would later put him into the leadership of an armed column advancing through Iowa to the relief of Kansas Free State forces.

Howe, as we have seen, was a man in conflict with himself. He did not like the compromises of politics, the flouting of the law by abolitionists, the illegal strategems of the Underground Railroad, although he participated in all three activities. When he succumbed to one of his severe attacks of migraine, he seemed to be drained of all blood until he appeared a corpse to those who glimpsed him in bed. Once a visitor at the Howe home, "Green Peace," witnessed an attack and spread the report in Boston that Howe was dying. The next morning he was approaching the Howe home, prepared to present his condolences, when he was startled by the sight of an intensely vigorous man galloping by on a black mare. It was Dr. Howe, "a trifle pale, but holding his head high, ready for the day's work." [26]

2

If the stakes had been raised for such as Parker and Howe, they had also been raised, as time would prove, for those advocating secession in the South. The threat had long been a political pastime for the more reckless of that section's fire-eaters. It was often easy enough to make when the Democrats, largely controlled by slaveholders, were in power but it might be altogether another matter if the Republicans, pledged to opposition to slavery and to its containment, won in 1856, only a year away. Then what had sometimes been merely rhetoric might result, if not in the rough reality of a rope, at least in the confiscation of property, as it later did. This increased risk, however, did not discourage some in the South any more than similar risks did others in the North. Treason, both sides knew, is only a synonym for an opposing view and the action supporting it when the stakes of conflict have become high enough to kill the opposition.

Robert Barnwell Rhett, former senator from South Carolina whose newspaper, the *Mercury* of Charleston, threatened secession if a Republican were elected the following year, gloried in any possible charge of treason, as he had since 1828 and the beginning of the crisis over South Carolina's effort to nullify federal acts and secede during the Jackson administration. " But let it be that I am a Traitor," he had said in 1850, and would say again in some form or other. "The word has no terrors for me. . . . I have been born of Traitors, but thank God they have ever been Traitors in the great cause of liberty, fighting against tyranny and oppression. Such treason will ever be mine whilst true to my lineage. . . ." [27] Theodore Parker could not have phrased it better; but there was some difference of opinion between Rhett and Parker, and increasingly between many others in the South and North, as to what constituted liberty, tyranny, and oppression.

The stakes were being raised for many others but not all took it as blithely as Robert Barnwell Rhett. They were being raised, for example, for little William Walker in Nicaragua, soon to be forced to choose between being his own man, an Emperor or a King perhaps, or becoming the paid servant of leading Southern expansionists who would raise the money to buy him; they were being raised for Gerrit Smith, the wealthy New York abolitionist, faced with the demands of the Kansas war, while yearning only for peace and quiet after collapsing upon his unexpected election to Congress where he had found the vulgarity, the whiskey-drinking, and tobacco-spitting too much for his sensitive nature and had resigned; and they were being raised for Henry S. Wise, running for Governor of Virginia in 1855 but torn between his bellicosity for the South's independence and his yearning to be President of the United States.

Others felt the increased pressure, responding to it with various degrees of grace or caution, testy Edmund Ruffin of Virginia, and that golden voice of the Southland, William Lowndes Yancey, as well as James H. Lane, the black-eyed Free State soldier-orator of Kansas, whose thrilling periods could make men weep or fight and who was having a difficult time during the first months of 1855 in deciding whether he should favor Free State forces or the administration of President Pierce. There were some, of course, who saw the increasing crisis as opportunity: as did the Cincinnati physician, or alleged physician, who was to become known as General George Washington Lafayette Bickley and who had at one and the same time all the allure of a snake-oil salesman and the sincerity of the true believer.

Bickley, a shrewd and handsome man with few principles beyond his belief in slavery and its extension by conquest, perceived that the time was ripe for a mass approach to filibustering. He saw, as did many others, that the Kansas civil war had changed the political climate of the country. Most knew that Kansas was only a crisis within a larger one, due to explode if the collision course of the sections was not changed. Thomas Hart Benton, in addition to Parker, was stumping the North in 1855 proclaiming that the Union was in danger of dissolution and quoting J. Q. Adams, who had said in 1843, "I am satisfied slavery will not go down until it goes down in blood." [28] As Parker, Benton, and others in the North or border states warned of possible war, Southern apostles of secession were beginning to raise their voices again after being temporarily silenced by the Compromise of 1850.

At the same time a vague unease, a restless tension was seizing many far removed from Kansas or politics, as in the case of Bickley intent on transforming himself from a doctor to a general. Their accustomed occupations seemed as confining as straitjackets but what they should do they did not quite know. They only knew they were tired of clerking or the law or farming or selling town lots or running a livery stable or getting drunk or trying for constable of the township. Something was in the air of great events shortly to explode. Many wanted to be in on whatever of adventure was soon to transpire but they were often more attracted to Walker than to Kansas; or if not to Walker, to some other filibustering adventure in the softness of the tropics, amid the whispering of a night containing music and maidens of a kind not likely to be found in Kansas.

Walker's was a great name. The press was filled with accounts of his Immortals, of his brave yellow-haired Anglo-Saxons charging with cold steel into the ineffectual fire of the little brown men of Nicaragua, so ignorant that they fought those who came to help them. Parker devoted part of a speech to him,[29] and while he was opposed to his reinstitution of slavery, even he could not quite forgo some admiration for the Anglo-Saxon bringing order, commerce, and law to the superstitious, ineffectual, Pope-ridden impoverished of the tropics. His only caveat was that Walker should bring liberty instead of slavery and that not by force. But he predicted that benevolence would one day bring the United States an empire reaching from the southernmost Andes to the Arctic.[30]

Few whether North or South could remain entirely unmoved when they read such stuff as this—and it was everywhere—which appeared in *Harper's Weekly*:

We have again and again called Walker a hero. . . . We are obliged to recognize a persistence, an endurance, a resolute heroism which merit a higher place in human esteem than can be ceded to all the knights errant of history and Faëry-dom. . . . The difference is that ours is a nineteenth century hero. . . . Who knows how soon he may replace the laurel of the hero with the diadem of a king? [31]

Beginning in 1855 this kind of bilge was a commonplace. It did its share in attracting first and last 2,500 men, who sailed from New York, San Francisco, Mobile, and New Orleans to the gallant Walker in Nicaragua. His conquest of that country, his threats against Cuba and the four other Central American republics, seemed to fill some deep psychic need in the American people, some wistful yearning to overcome more and more of the benighted natives below the Rio Grande. Such feelings were not common solely to Northern shipping interests or Southern proponents of slavery's expansion. They were more general, as if the conquest of Mexico had left many Americans unsated and as if they felt the acquisition of an empire was a rite of manhood which should be enjoyed by any self-respecting and rising nation.

Walker's career tallied roughly in time with that of John Brown. While Walker fought to extend slavery and John Brown to defeat it, Walker was wildly popular in more areas than below the Ohio and in a manner entirely different from any regard ever won by the dour Old Man. Although Walker executed many more than Old Brown ever did, some twelve in all—including the head of the Nicaraguan army, whom he charged with treason for opposing him—he was always widely regarded as the reincarnation of a knight of old. Although he killed scores in battle, razing the city of Granada, he was always seen as a chivalrous warrior. Although he accepted thousands of dollars from the Accessory Transit Company of Commodore Cornelius Vanderbilt—which supplied transportation at a handsome profit across Walker's Nicaragua for those traveling between New York and San Francisco—before confiscating it and turning it over to Vanderbilt's enemies from whom he received additional thousands, he was always pictured as the soul of honesty. Only after a terrible inner struggle, or so it is said, did he restore slavery to Nicaragua, embracing it only because he needed money and the backing of American slaveholders. In his heart, or so the story goes, he was against slavery and besides he preferred to be his own Napoleon rather than the purchased vassal of slaveholders.

Yet none of these contradictions, at least during his days of triumph, diminished the romance and glory of his name. He was a 5 foot 5 Galahad, a 120 pound protector of womanhood, always executing any of his soldiers who insulted it. In his early thirties while conquering Nicaragua, he was boyish, almost immature, in his slight and undersized appearance until one looked into his hard eyes or glanced at his pugnacious slant of jaw. He himself favored his eyes, liked being called "the gray-eyed man of destiny," a phrase perhaps written by himself and appearing in the newspaper he published in Nicaragua. Born in Nashville, Tennessee, he graduated from college at the age of fourteen, studying medicine in Pennsylvania and in Paris before he was out of his teens. A doctor, a lawyer, a newspaper editor in New Orleans before he was twenty-seven, it was said that a broken heart, shattered when his fiancée died, spurred him to his career of conqueror.[32]

There was other news from Nicaragua in 1855 than that of Walker's military deeds: reports of lovely nymphs swimming nude in a river overhung by palms, all curves and a gleaming sinuosity in the sunlight,[33] and the restless back home at the livery stable knew how attracted the voluptuous beauties would be to the blue-eyed conquerors of the North. It was this restlessness and these longings that Bickley was trying to satisfy by forming a secret organization known as the Knights of the Golden Circle, which would supply for a fee all the delights of filibustering at a half-dozen lovely sites in Mexico, Cuba, Central America, northern South America, and various isles of the Caribbean. Those unable to depart their native shores to extend slavery would protect it in their homeland while participating in a fascinating pageant provided by the secret society for domestic use.

By 1855 Bickley had formed two castles, as the local lodges of his order were known, in Cincinnati and Covington, Kentucky, across the Ohio River. Within several years he and his associates had castles all over the South, numbering thousands in their membership and said to include many of that section's quality, as well as enough in Ohio and Indiana to give the North cause for alarm after the Civil War began.[34] The first project of the Knights, however, was an invasion of Mexico, which they designated in their code as number 2.[35] The invasion remained designation rather than reality.

If one wonders how Bickley changed so quickly from doctor to general, it is no great mystery given the prevailing mores of the country. Most titles in those days were of free and easy access, depending more on the gall of the user than any special training or experience. A man might become a doctor, if he were brazen enough and Bickley was, by sweeping out a physician's office, listening attentively to his triumphs and fatalities, and looking over the five or six medical books his employer owned. A professor might possibly have taught briefly in some semi-literate academy even if his designation was everlasting. A judge was sometimes any portly or elderly lawyer whose character seemed judicial to his associates and who had perhaps once been for a fortnight or so an acting justice of the peace. Military titles were as swiftly come by as a man could acquire the brass to use them. Sometimes it was a fine point whether one should prefix Major or Colonel to his name, depending in the last analysis on his own vanity and how much his friends could take without laughing or how well and dangerously he could confront or challenge those who laughed. Doctor and Professor Bickley—he was a professor of materia medica in the Eclectic Medical Institute of Cincinnati—esteemed himself enough when he turned to the military to take the title of general.

He came by it as honestly as he did the title of doctor. He said that his military title was somehow justified because he was a graduate of West Point. He was a physician, or so he said, through the medical degree he had won from the University of London. He had attended neither institution, nor had he received any title from either.[36] But a man so impressive, so impregnated with sincerity, did not need to fear any doubt of whatever he said he was. "Gen. Bickley," said the Houston *Telegraph*, reflecting the general impression, "is a tall, fine looking middle aged gentleman, having an uncommonly fine expression of countenance, and a high intellectual forehead."[37] He even changed his name after embarking on his new career from George William Lamb Bickley to the more euphonious and patriotic George Washington Lafayette Bickley.[38]

A native of Virginia, he had been a novelist, an editor, a contributor to medical magazines, and now as he went South to organize more castles he was only resuming the military career that he had not begun at West Point. Several times the members of the Knights of the Golden Circle, a large and important organization by the late 1850's, asked for an accounting and an explanation of where all the money the general had received had gone. But Bickley, if he never accounted satisfactorily for the money, was more than a mountebank or fake. The North, after the Civil War began, attested to his sincerity and worth by arresting him as a spy after he had appeared in Ohio and Indiana to activate castles of the Knights of the Golden Circle, urging its members to aid the Confederate cavalry raid into these states by Confederate General John Hunt Morgan.[39]

3

The possibility of a charge of treason did not deter sixty-one-year-old Edmund Ruffin from retiring from his various pursuits in 1855 to devote all his time to the cause of secession, although he was beginning a course that would ultimately take his life. He was a farmer but a literary one in his own highly individual manner. He preferred working in his study to politics, writing on hour after hour, sometimes for as many as twelve, on the drainage of fields and marl, a calcareous fertilizer which he believed would restore (and it did to a certain extent) the tired acres of Virginia and South Carolina to something approaching their pristine vigor.

Whatever his topic when writing, however—and it included first and last the recording of almost everything that ever happened to him, subject to the laws of Southern propriety, noting every slight received, every injury suffered, every triumph of a worthless rival, every doubt of an all-wise Creator, every idiocy of white manhood suffrage—the emotion accompanying his words was usually a simmering bitterness directed against a world which would not answer to his will. Of all the professions he hated, and he hated them all save the art and science of farming, he hated bankers most and when he had been the editor and founder of an agricultural weekly his greatest pleasure had been in making them howl. If he received an outraged letter from a Virginia banker, that was a happy day. For all of the hate and impatience within him, he was a conscientious and a loving father, although he had been forced as a matter of principle to disinherit a wayward son, and he was, too, an agronomist of an ability not excelled in his time.[40]

Now in 1855, retired from the quest of his Holy Grail, his everlasting search for marl which had led him thousands of miles hunting for its traces in riverbanks, stone quarries, hillsides, and gravel pits, as well as from the management of his estates, he was trying to bring together and unite the secessionist forces in the various Southern states. His entrance into combat, into the fight for war, if necessary, made him a new man. He had never felt so well and friends remarked on his new appearance. This release to the open advocacy of secession or war commonly had a rejuvenating effect on its proponents, North and South, and Ruffin was no exception. Yet he was a poor, halting, and unconvincing speaker, aching for the eloquence of cheap orators he hated. He was not a politician, having the failing of speaking his mind, and as for bringing men together he was more likely to force them apart. But he was a strong-willed and utterly honest man and he had a slow impact. When at first Virginians seemed to him as wrong-headed and self-seeking as bankers, almost all of them spurning secession, he retreated to his beloved state of South Carolina. Although he was a Virginian, South Carolina had honored him richly for his services in discovering marl deposits during the 1840's within the state which had reinvigorated its soil, increasing agricultural production and land prices as his demonstration of the efficacy of marl had done already in Virginia. South Carolina had been for secession, or powerful forces within it had been, since 1828. But even there the cause was having a hard time. Although there were Union men in South Carolina such as B. F. Perry and his adherents, the state would be essentially divided between those who had long called for immediate secession, alone if need be, and those who were for secession only when South Carolina could declare against the Union in company with other Southern states.

As his first move Ruffin formed his own lobby, consisting entirely of himself, going frequently to Washington, living and dining with Southern congressmen in their messes and boardinghouses, in the very capital of the nation he sought to undermine, always keeping before them the advantages of revolt and secession. But it was a hard, tough fight, for there were Southern politicians other than Wise with a real love for the Union and who hoped for their own progress as well as slavery's within the status quo.

Like Antaios, the Greek god who could be defeated only when lifted from the ground, Ruffin returned to the soil for strength, returned either to Beechwood, his mansion and farm overlooking the James, or to Marlbourne, with its beautiful prospect over the Pamunkey, when he was bedeviled beyond endurance by those who could not perceive the self-evident truth that the South must be independent if slavery were to survive. As he surveyed his acres on such an occasion, worrying about a foal or a sick calf or the vexing ways of his slaves, or mourning as he constantly did the death of his two daughters, or the suicide of a friend that remained in his mind like a prediction or a nightmare, he did not seem like a warrior.

One might not have guessed that this little jockey of a man, aging and with long silver ringlets hanging to his shoulders, was a one-man army. There was nothing to suggest in his endless pages on drainage, in the voluminous recording of his pursuit of marl deposits that occupied months and years of his time, in his disquisitions on chess and novel reading, that here was a man who at sixty-eight would go into battle on his own, fighting in an army in which he had neither rank nor membership, fighting as a civilian under his own command because no authority on earth could stop him from fighting Yankees whenever they were within a hundred miles of him. Perched unaccountably on a caisson, the old man would appear, equally unaccountably, on a battlefield, and seizing a musket and the ammunition of a dead soldier charge into battle, advancing and retreating with the battle's roll, until he collapsed exhausted.[41] He was, in a way, as time was to prove, John Brown's opposite number in the South, and if John Brown hated slavery, Edmund Ruffin hated Yankees more.

4

Presently Ruffin was writing William Lowndes Yancey of Alabama, whose henchmen believed his eloquence one of the great natural wonders of America, and who was returning from political retirement in 1855 in the belief that the times were sharp enough to make propitious a new planting of the seed of secession. His eloquence was such that it could even overcome Ruffin's prejudice against orators, although Ruffin complained on one occasion that Yancey spoke too long, for four hours, and was a trifle drunk.[42] His admirers never felt so. They were overcome by his brilliance, drunk or sober. They said that when he spoke such was the projection of his personality that a halo appeared around his head as if from the magic or electricity of his overwhelming belief in secession and himself. His voice was like the sea, they added, sometimes thundering, sometimes whispering, sometimes like "the burst of a hurricane, tearing, uprooting, demolishing and scattering all in its path." It had a peculiar "ventriloquial property," so filling any space in which he threw it that some said it seemed to come from the rafters and others that it came from beneath the platform but that everywhere it was equally audible, as strong a quarter mile away as it was immediately before the rostrum.[43]

A man pudgy in form, his face the color of dough, his constituents believed that whatever his appearance, forgotten as soon as he began to speak, he had the heart of a lion. Ruined as a young man and a planter by the accidental but fatal poisoning of his slaves, he revealed no pain nor did he ever complain. Moving himself and his family to Wetumpka, Alabama, he began all over again, this time as a lawyer and the editor of the town's weekly, the *Argus*.[44] Similarly, when he was forced to shoot and kill his wife's uncle in a family quarrel he raised no outcry but waited with uncomplaining self-possession until fined $1,500 for manslaughter and sentenced to a year in jail. He was released after paying two-thirds of the fine.[45]

Upon being elected to Congress in 1844 as a Democrat, his maiden speech favoring the annexation of Texas was so fierce in invective—in which he was particularly skilled—against Thomas L. Clingman, Whig, of North Carolina and opposed to the annexation, that Clingman was forced to challenge him. In explaining his acceptance of the challenge, Yancey revealed his religious, law-abiding, and chivalrous nature when he wrote to a friend, "The laws of God, the laws of my state, the solemn obligations due to that young wife, the mother of my children, to whom you so feelingly and chastely allude, were all considered." [46] Neither congressman was touched in an exchange of shots in which nothing was gained but honor.

He loved dogs, horses, food, poetry, and the sound of his own voice. As for his dogs, of which he had scores, he carefully trained them to come running toward him whenever he returned home so that as far as the eye could see dogs were leaping fences and creeks, running pell-mell from every direction until they converged in a circle of frantic canine affection around the beaming Yancey. "At the table he was a trencherman of no mean capacity," said an admiring friend, suggesting with some awe the amounts of corn on the cob, fried chicken and gravy, mashed potatoes, hot biscuits, fried fritters, squash, black-eyed peas, yams, lima beans, and apple pie he could consume, always talking as he chewed, occasionally quoting poetry, some of it his own, and all with so much unction and culture that everyone around the board was impressed and improved. No matter how hungry he was, admirers said, and they knew how sharp were his pangs, he would not approach the table until he had seen that his horses were well put up and fed. [47]

Although the canebrake region of Alabama, in which Yancey lived and grew steadily more rich, owning as the years went by more slaves and more plantations, was described by its inhabitants as a singular combination of culture and refinement, it did have its ruder aspects. Yancey, for example, first won his fame as an orator in prosecuting for damages an aristocratic lady of the region who had ordered her servant to throw a lady caller, equally aristocratic, over the railing of a second-story portico. The slave had the visitor in his arms and was about to drop her when a gentleman intervened. The youthful Yancey won substantial damages for his client and a reputation as a new Patrick Henry. "To say that his speech was powerful," said the presiding judge, "is meager praise. His voice was music's self." [48]

It was this voice which was returning to the wars in the belief that the time was ripe for a new drive for secession. It was a great institution in the South, particularly in Alabama and Georgia, inhabited by connoisseurs of oratory. If Emerson went to the Concord courthouse to hear Webster, thousands, particularly in the lower South, drove into the county seat from isolated farms to hear contesting attorneys as often as possible. With the court-house square and every hitching post thick with buggies and farm wagons, the horses waiting patiently through long hours of oratory, men and women savored the sob that could be implied by a tremolo passage in a lawyer's voice, judged the effectiveness of voice and gesture as he went through customary ceremonial tributes to flag and mother, had a nice ear for that poignant question, always asked in murder trials, if the jury would cut off forever from this unfortunate young man, who had killed only for his honor, all sight of the blue sky, all sound of the singing birds and that sweeter sound of a mother's voice, deny him forever any glimpse of the sun, yea, even of the very stars, eternally bringing hope because they spoke of God. Would they be so heartless as to immure him in total darkness, sentence him to prison walls, to death in life? Oh! better then the gallows! Better some foreign strand for all Americans if this beloved land had become so base as to punish an American whose only offense was that he had defended his honor!

No one could execute this indigenous American art form in better style than Yancey. He had not only won an acquittal for a young man who had killed an Irishman in a tavern brawl but won him an ovation as a patriot who had maintained the rights of an American against a foreigner. He could speak as convincingly for secession, and war if it came to that, although that was usually implied rather than stated. No one could be more incendiary while seemingly only chatting in all innocence as he gave his views to some huge crowd.

His first speech on his return to public life in 1855 was at Columbus, Georgia, before passing on to Macon and a series of other Georgia towns. He was only, he said, his voice the essence of forbearance, for the protection of the South whether in the Union or out of it. It was true that the grasping Yankee was the inveterate foe of all for which the South stood. "It is folly to blind ourselves to our true condition," he said. "We are in the midst of a mighty sectional contest." [49] It was a contest that was inevitable, decreed by the Creator from the beginning of time when he formed the earth.

"The Creator," he said, and his voice was music's self,

has beautified the face of this Union with sectional features. . . . He has made the North and South; the one the region of frost, ribbed in with ice and granite; the other baring its generous bosom to the sun and ever smiling under its influence. The climate, soil and productions of these two grand divisions of the land, have made the character of their inhabitants. Those who occupy the one are cool, cal-culating, enterprising, selfish and grasping; the inhabitants of the other are ardent, brave and magnanimous, more disposed to give than to accumulate, to enjoy ease rather than to labor.[50]

No one doubted which section contained the ardent, brave, and magnanimous.

Yancey could make a closely reasoned constitutional argument as exciting as the defense of some lurid crime. His thesis was simple enough. The Constitution made slaves property. The Constitution protected property from illegal confiscation or from discrimination or restriction in moving from one place to another within the territory of the United States. The West, won by the South's valor, was being denied to slavery. Popular sovereignty was even an unconstitutional infringement on the rights of slavery, for no territorial legislature had the right to ban it. Senator Douglas of Illinois, hated by many in the North as a servant of slavery, was only a disguised abolitionist, according to Yancey. It was this fundamental right of property that had been nullified by the North and the only remedy for the South as to the Union, he thundered, was "withdraw from it!"[51]

He had a magnificent change of pace. While he could thunder with the best of them, whisper with a solemn sibilance that carried a quarter of a mile, he also often spoke with sweet reasonableness until his voice suddenly swelled with an anger pulling men screaming to their feet. He was capable of magnificent non sequiturs in his climaxes, their object not logic but a mind-blowing finale.

Thus in one speech that had nothing to do with the Napoleonic wars, but tried to suggest the South closing ranks, he told of Marshal Macdonald rallying the French at the Battle of Wagram. A contemporary describes his peroration. "The battlefield," through Yancey's words, he says, "loomed up to view; banners waved before men's eyes; bloody gaps in the advancing column opened and the very notes of martial music seemed audible. Now the orator [Yancey] firm and erect, his countenance stern, stood upon the edge of the stage." He was now Macdonald on the battlefield and

seeing his line disordered by the impetus of the charge, rushed to the front, crying out in thunder tones: "Keep time, my men! Keep time!" A wilder frenzy could not be conceived than the audience fell into. Men leaped upon their seats and threw their hats and waved their canes, while the ladies were overcome. . . . The orator resumed his seat, his work was over, while yet the confusion reigned supreme.[52]

Such drama was irresistible in the South, or so it proved in the end, although a good deal more than Yancey's eloquence was involved. The grievances he made sting were real enough to those who heard them, particularly to the owners of slaves who would not forgo their property without fighting to the death. Yet even with this reality backing him, Yancey was the Pied Piper of the South, his golden notes more responsible for luring it into secession than the words of any other single man. Now that he was back from retirement he was beginning a crusade that would have no end until the halo appeared, perhaps, above his head for one last time and his great voice led the Southern delegates out of the Democratic National Convention at Baltimore five years later and into secession and a resulting civil war.

THE ACCUSER

I

As crisis and tension increase so does the cost in human life. A man may be killed when fighting for a cause in other places than the battlefield or on the scaffold, as Theodore Parker was demonstrating in 1855 although he did not know it yet, or at least did not admit it, despite a collapse that sent him to his bed. Neither did he know, although he soon would, that tuberculosis was eating out his lungs, sapping his strength, transforming him into a hollow shell in which the homely Socratic face shone more wanly, the farmer's shoulders outlined more gauntly over his sunken chest.

He was fighting for his life in more ways than one at the beginning of 1855. Soon he was to go before his accusers on the charge of obstructing federal justice by "force and arms" in connection with the attempted rescue of Anthony Burns. But it was not that which worried him. It was more the fact that he could not fight without hating, for he was convinced that the men who had indicted him and would try him for his liberty were the center of the slave power in Boston, as guilty and as responsible for slavery through their alliances, connections, and support of the South as any Virginia slaveholder.

He abhorred them so intensely for their unfeelingness for humanity if its skin was black, for their willingness to kill American liberty by adhering to the letter of the law, his aggressiveness was so high, he was so completely engulfed by his opposition to slavery, that he was having to fight to retain his identity, to keep his personality intact. He was afraid that hate was shrinking him. It was an effort to continue with the kindness and the love he tried to live by, to pursue the scholarship and reading that gave a man perspective, to cultivate the friendship of men and women, as creative an act, in his view, as composing music or poetry, and without which an individual was dead even while he lived. He was afraid that he was being transformed into only a hater and he tried to resist but there were times when his success in doing so was questionable.

Something of his temper and the temper of the time may be gained from his cry when he was told that a black assaulter of the courthouse trying to rescue Anthony Burns had shot at Federal Marshal Freeman and missed him. "Why didn't he hit him?" he cried. "Why didn't he hit him?"[53] Something, too, of his ambivalence, and perhaps the ambivalence of every exhausted man when caught in a mortal fight, was expressed in his hope, confided only to his diary and that by implication, that he might be removed from the struggle by being sent to the peace of prison. There in the clean and whitewashed cell, or so he imagined it, he could see himself pursuing the study of languages, particularly Russian, and writing on and on without the constant interruptions of a trying time, writing at last on his long-deferred history of religion. But the writing of only one book would not be nearly enough for him. He would also write his autobiography there and would write his sermons, too, to be delivered by one still out of jail. In fact, he noted a little hopefully in his journal immediately after the assault on the courthouse:

> What shall I do if I am sent to gaol?
>
> 1. Write one sermon a week and have it read at Music Hall, and printed the next morning. Who can read it? Write also a prayer, &c. (Prayer, Saturday night)
> 2. Prepare a volume of sermons from old MSS.
> 3. Write Memoirs of Life &c.
> 4. Vol I of "Historical Development of Religion," i.e. The Metaphysics of Religion.
> 5. Pursue the Russian studies.[54]

2

Parker meant in his trial to reach an apex in the long history of the accused becoming the accuser. He did not doubt that he would. All of the right was on his side, all iniquity on the other, and the fact that his prosecutors believed the same made not a whit of difference to him. Any thought possessed by his antagonists only proved it evil. The near civil war in Boston had progressed to the point where high principle and personal enmity were one and the same, completely inseparable by the beginning of 1855. Through the Shadrach rescue and the Sims case and the Burns rendition, and indeed starting long before, as far back as 1836 and progressing through the Webster apostasy and the passage of the Fugitive Slave Act, Boston had become increasingly divided into warring camps whose members did not speak or nod in greeting or have any special relationship whatever, each side feeling that the members of the other camp were traitors.

As the trial neared and the division between North and South reached a new height with the Kansas invasions, Parker found he had less and less trouble with such concepts as returning good for evil. Even Jesus Christ, only a man to Parker and other Unitarians but nevertheless a great one, had said, "I come not to send peace, but a sword," and that was a text that Parker could understand. As he felt the power within him rising, swelling over the fatal illness in his body, he was certain he could use the trial to shake slavery in Boston to its very foundations and in so doing make the Curtis family quail. Its members were and long had been one of slavery's chief supports in Boston. Theirs was a "private personal malice, deep, long cherished rancorous" against Parker, to which he intended to call the attention of the jury.

One of them, Judge Benjamin R. Curtis, of the United States Circuit Court, would try him on the charge of obstructing federal justice in the case of Anthony Burns. Another member of the family had been a member of the grand jury which had indicted him. A third, George T. Curtis, Benjamin's brother, was a United States Commissioner who, Parker said, "had the glory of kidnapping Mr. Sims" [55] and returning him from Boston into slavery. Still another member of the family, Edward G. Loring, had been the United States Commissioner who had issued the warrant for the Burns arrest and then the order for his return to slavery. He was a judge of probate in the Massachusetts courts and a teacher at Harvard College, but he would be neither for much longer, nor would he be a United States Commissioner after Parker had finished with him. Soon the women of Woburn would be sending him thirty pieces of silver.

Parker recalled his last confrontation with one of the family with satisfaction. It had been at his arraignment before Judge Benjamin R. Curtis of the United States Circuit Court on November 29, 1854. When he came into court, Parker reported, "the Hon. Judge Curtis sat on the bench and determined the amount of my bail, and the same eye which had frowned with such baleful aspect on the rescuers of Shadrach, quailed down underneath my look and sought the ground." [56]

The Curtis family had long been political enemies of Parker. They became personal enemies also when he charged Commissioner Loring in a sermon attended by thousands with being guilty of the murder of the federal deputy who had been killed during the assault on the courthouse to free Burns. "Edward Greeley Loring," Parker had intoned at the Music Hall on May 28 just after the killing,

Judge of Probate for the County of Suffolk, in the State of Massachusetts, fugitive slave bill Commissioner of the United States, before these citizens of Boston, on Ascension Sunday, assembled to worship God, I charge you with the death of that man who was killed on last Friday night. He was your fellow-servant in kidnapping. He dies at your hand. You fired the shot which makes his wife a widow, his child an orphan. . . . I charge you with filling the Court House with one hundred and eighty-four hired ruffians of the United States [the Marshal's guard], and alarming not only this city for her liberties that are in peril, but stirring up the whole Commonwealth of Massachusetts with indignation which no man knows how to stop—which no man can stop. You have done it all! [57]

3

Often during the winter of 1855 Parker gained his study, where he was preparing his defense in the Burns case, only after a four- or five-day interruption caused by a lecture tour, sometimes returning a little depressed at the way hours on cold trains with poor sleep and worse food sapped his strength. As early as August 24, 1853, his forty-third birthday, he was worrying about his health, writing, "I used to think I would live as long as my fathers; but certain admonitions of late warn me that I am not to live to be an old man." [58]

Something of his activities during 1855 and later are indicated in a letter to Edward Desor, a German naturalist and one of his dearest friends, who had lived in Boston for a time before returning to Europe. Writing to Desor in August of 1856, he reports, "I have lectured more than 110 times since October 1855." [59] And again on his forty-sixth birthday a few days later he wrote Desor, reporting on the physical results of a situation in which the stakes were daily being raised, "I fear you would hardly know me, I am grown so old in look. My head is bald and my beard is gray. . . . I have grown very old within the last three years; too much work and too many cares have done this to me." [60] He was always pretending that soon he would take an extended holiday in which he and Decor would have great adventure in South America or perhaps Norway, and now he added, "But I shall mend one day when I take a little leisure, and you and I run down to the tropics and see the Orinoco; I shall recruit straightway and become young once more." [61]

He never recruited his health on the Orinoco but the security of his study on his return from lecturing was medicine to his tired body that winter of 1855. It was his books which were his solace in hours of trial. They did not turn on him as Howe repeatedly did, charging him with being vengeful and harsh and refusing to have anything to do with the petition Parker was circulating for the removal of Loring, who had returned Burns to slavery as United States Commissioner.[62] As for books he had twelve thousand of them, filling each of the four walls of his study on shelves stretching from floor to ceiling, overflowing into stacks on the floor and on a great oak table in the middle of the study and then stealing down the staircase, shelves on either side, into rooms on the third floor before descending into rooms on the second and first floors, the staircases to each lined with yet more books.

Almost every volume was a triumph of pursuit and desire, sometimes sought for years half around the world, occasionally run down by him while on a trip to Europe in the bookstalls along the Seine or in London, more often found by his agents in Warsaw, Leipzig, Prague, or Rome, or even in provincial villages of the Ukraine or Catalonia. To some the library seemed an intellectual portrait of Parker, revealing his astonishing diversity, his ubiquity in virtually every field of knowledge. As a matter of fact, it was nothing so esoteric. It was merely Parker's workshop. It contained the bases of his sermons, his reviews of books, his historical articles, his essays on philosophy, religion, and science, his letters on the Homeric question, or on botany, or on Descartes, Bacon, Leibnitz, Newton, and Hegel, or Goethe, Coleridge, Carlyle, and Heine, the source of the translations, usually poetry, from Greek, Latin, and German that he made for his own amusement. It was the source of all he wrote, but the genius and ferment of his own personality transformed the old into something new and alive.

He loved books, yet he was never obsequious with them, not even with the greatest. He approached a book as he would a man, without awe whatever its reputation, and determined to judge it out of his own self and not out of its past and prestige. It was a dull work to which he did not give the honor of written summary. Now as he began more fully formulating his defense, probably early in February after a lecture tour ending in Chicopee, he may have gone at once to that long stretch of volumes labeled *English State Trials*, to his multiple-volumed *History of the British Parliament*, to his extensive accounts of Star Chamber sessions in which arbitrary judges had sentenced good and pure men to the ax for their political or religious ideas, to sections containing histories of revolutions that ensued when wicked laws enforced by venal judges forced men to burst the laws asunder, to great tomes describing the evolution and the virtues of untrammeled juries, unafraid of the corrupt judges who instructed them, to shelf after shelf containing accounts of British tyranny in America and how it was overthrown by American revolutionaries. And he may, too, have taken a reassuring glance at his vast collection of pamphlets, books, reports, newspaper clippings, speeches, protests, petitions, and debates concerning the struggle against American slavery that he had collected over the years with no little labor.

Once before his desk and under way in the writing of his defense, no one could have written the sentences he was framing without some excitement, without getting up and now and then pacing the floor, whispering the words he would soon transfer to the paper on his desk, seeing himself, an arm raised in gesture, pressing the mighty truths he was writing on the jury. He could not have written long without realizing that he was fashioning a massive edifice; it would run to 125,000 words, and prove perhaps the best production of its kind in all American literature.

It was his purpose to summarize the struggle over American slavery from its beginning to its latest hour, from the American Revolution to the last outrages of Atchison and Stringfellow in Kansas, always warning of the danger of war if slavery was to be stopped from taking over the whole country. It was equally his aim to show how oppression had always found venal judges to accomplish its design and their own advance, from James I and Charles I to George III in the American Revolution and on into the nineteenth century when the American slave state had found no difficulty in finding reactionary judges to enforce the Fugitive Slave Act.

Judges, he said, were almost never principals; they were artificers, technicians, servants, bending the law to policy's needs, that policy given to them from above. Few judicial despots escaped his notice, starting with Francis Bacon, Sir Edward Coke, and Chief Justice Ley presiding over the Court of the King's Bench. This was only the beginning, of course, vile and servile magistrates following in steady array for more than two hundred years ever willing to sell out to power for hoped-for promotion or benefit. In this long list he gave prominent attention to Judge Curtis, who was trying him, as well as to other members of his family, the bastion of slavery, he said, in Boston.

4

Tears may well have been in his eyes as he reached his conclusion, it touching him, his life, and family and everything he held dear so closely. As he bent over his desk, he may have been breathing quickly as he penned his words following both them and the picture of himself addressing the jury. In his mind's eye, he paced up and down, solemnly pausing before the jury rail as he reached his peroration.

"I drew my first breath," he said,

in a little town not far off, a poor little town where the farmers and mechanics first unsheathed that Revolutionary sword which, after eight years of hewing, clove asunder the Gordian knot that bound America to the British yoke. One raw morning in spring—it will be eighty years the 19th of this month—Hancock and Adams, the Moses and Aaron of that Great Deliverance, were both at Lexington; they also had "obstructed an officer" with brave words. British soldiers, a thousand strong, came to seize them and carry them over sea for trial, and so nip the bud of Freedom auspiciously opening in that early spring.

The town militia came together before daylight "for training." A great, tall man, with a large head and a high, wide brow, their Captain,—one who "had seen service,"—marshalled them into line, numbering but seventy, and bade "every man load his piece with powder and ball." "I will order the first man shot that runs away," said he, when some faltered; "Don't fire unless fired upon, but if they want to have a war,—let it begin here."

Gentlemen, you know what followed: those farmers and mechanics "fired the shot heard round the world." A little monument covers the bones of such as before had pledged their fortune and their sacred honor to the Freedom of America, and that day gave it also their lives. I was born in that little town, and bred up amid the memories of that day. When a boy my mother lifted me up, one Sunday, in her religious, patriotic arms, and held me while I read the first monumental line I ever saw:—

"SACRED TO LIBERTY AND THE RIGHTS OF MANKIND."

Since then I have studied the memorial marbles of Greece and Rome in many an ancient town; nay, on Egyptian Obelisks have read what was written before the Eternal roused up Moses to lead Israel out of Egypt, but no chiselled stone has ever stirred me to such emotions as those rustic names of men who fell

"IN THE SACRED CAUSE OF GOD AND THEIR COUNTRY."

Gentlemen, the Spirit of Liberty, the Love of Justice, was early fanned into a flame in my boyish heart. That monument covers the bones of my own kinsfolk; it was their blood which reddened the long, green grass at Lexington. It is my own name which stands chiselled on that stone; the tall Captain who marshalled his fellow farmers and mechanics into stern array and spoke such brave and dangerous words as opened the War of American Independence,—the last to leave the field,—was my father's father. I learned to read out of his Bible, and with a musket he that day captured from the foe, I learned also another religious lesson, that

"REBELLION TO TYRANTS IS OBEDIENCE TO GOD."

I keep them both, "Sacred to Liberty and the Rights of Mankind," to use them both "In the Sacred Cause of God and my Country."

Gentlemen of the Jury, and you my fellow-countrymen of the North, I leave the matter with you. Say "Guilty!" You cannot do it. "Not Guilty." I know you will, for you remember there is another Court, not of fugitive slave bill law, where we shall all be tried by the Justice of the Infinite God. Hearken to the last verdict, "INASMUCH AS YE HAVE DONE IT UNTO ONE OF THE LEAST OF THESE MY BRETHREN, YE HAVE DONE IT UNTO ME." [63]

5

Although Parker is the favorite character in all American history to some of his aficionados, it is not because he was without faults. He was not a modest man. Although he wrote and spoke of as varied a group of issues and subjects as any man of his generation, he never wrote, in a sense, of anything but himself. Everything from Newton to Hegel, to a flower in the woods, or a tree on a hillside, or his association with John Brown was a fascinating personal experience. Every aspect of the knowledge he acquired was an exciting part of his autobiography. He could not conceive of the trial before Judge Curtis without regarding himself as the central figure. His belief that he was the center of that proceeding was so overwhelming that it made others believe so too, so that to the Reverend Thomas Wentworth Higginson, himself a defendant, Parker, "busy with his terrible notebook . . . seemed as important a figure in the scene as the presiding judge, himself." [64]

If activity in the attempted rescue of Burns was a criterion, Parker was the least important figure. All he had done, although he was not charged with that, was to run a few steps toward the courthouse after the speeches at Faneuil Hall that night. All activity was over before he arrived, the attempted attack repulsed, the deputy marshal slain, the wounded Higginson long gone, Martin Stowell who had been prominent in the attack fled and disappeared, a man named Kemp also active in the assault gone, as was Lewis Hayden, the black leader who later aided John Brown and who fired a shot during the melee in the courthouse to cover Higginson's retreat.

Of this number only Stowell, later to fight in Kansas and be killed in the Civil War, and Higginson were arrested and indicted, charged as was Parker with obstructing federal justice by force and arms. John Morrison, Samuel T. Proudman, and John C. Cluer were also arrested in connection with the assaulting mob and were similarly charged, as was Wendell Phillips who, like Parker, had spoken at Faneuil Hall before the attack.

Of these seven defendants Parker had no doubt who was the most important. Only he was prepared to address the jury, intent on tearing apart as far as words could do it the whole edifice of slavery as well as its main buttress in Boston, the Curtis family, including the judge who was trying him.

As he arrived in the courtroom on the opening day, he was determined, as he had said, to "give them their bellyful." [65] Surrounded by the notable men being tried with him and an equally notable battery of lawyers, he seemed, at least to Higginson, to be the outstanding figure. His lawyers were Senator John P. Hale of New Hampshire and Charles M. Ellis of Boston. Lawyers for the other defendants were William L. Burt, H. F. Durant, and John A. Andrews, soon to be Governor of Massachusetts and a leading member of its bar. As the trial began with the reading of the indictments and a series of motions to dismiss them, Parker took notes so copiously, scowling at Judge Curtis as he did so, that one might have thought he was reporting impeachment proceedings against the court instead of making notations on his own trial. He was apprehensive from the very beginning that he would be denied the chance to give his forensic masterpiece.

It was not only that "the great political revolution," [66] as he called it, was still advancing, making the time unpropitious for conviction. It was also that his attorneys felt that the indictment was so defective that they should move for its dismissal. It was a great sacrifice his attorneys were asking of him when they recommended attacking the indictment as faulty, thus quashing the case if their pleas were granted, and also quashing any necessity for Parker's speech. He had pride of authorship. He knew how well he could deliver his plea to the jury and that during the time he stood before it he would be the center of the country's attention in what he felt was its most historic case. But since all the indictments were being tried jointly, he had some responsibility to his fellow defendants. They apparently did not savor the privacy of a cell as a refuge for writing with the same ardor he did.

After five days of argument the court, evidently with considerable relief, dismissed the indictments on the ground that Edward G. Loring, the United States Commissioner who had issued the warrant for Burns and then returned him to slavery, was not properly described as such in the indictments and that therefore the indictments were void. Benjamin F. Hallett, United States Attorney, who had once threatened to hang for treason all who violated the Fugitive Slave Act, immediately moved to enter a *nolle prosequi* in all the cases, thus disposing of them and setting the defendants free without penalty. As Parker was leaving the court, "Mr. Hallet who had rather a squeaky voice said to him, 'You have crawled out of a very small hole this time, Mr. Parker,' to which Parker replied in a deep bass voice: 'I will make a larger hole next time, Mr. Hallet.' " *

---

* Stearns, *George Luther Stearns*, p. 90. The author spells Mr. Hallett's name incorrectly.

As for his *Defence,* Parker decided to publish it, presenting it to the whole American people instead of only to a jury of twelve. In so doing he could neither be interrupted by the court nor sentenced for contempt. He worked on it that summer in Dublin, New Hampshire, polishing it up and even adding to it. It came out in November 1855 and was immediately recognized as unique. He received an unusual amount of praise, letters from Senator Sumner and Herndon, Lincoln's partner, among others, but the one he prized most was from the man who was his sternest critic. "It is a wonderful monument of power, learning, wisdom, labour, zeal and humanity," wrote Howe.[67]

That winter Parker went back to work, stumping the free states again, lecturing on the crisis confronting the country in a series of one-night stands that were almost as cold and arduous as an Arctic expedition. In April he almost fainted while lecturing. "Last night," he wrote in his journal,

I was to lecture at New Bedford and tried to speak; but was so ill, that I could not hear or see or speak well. I left the room, and went out with Mr. Robeson and walked a few minutes. Went to an apothecary's and took about a spoonful and a half of sherry wine, which helped me. Spoke but with great difficulty. Am better today, but slenderly and meanly. *I take this as a warning,*—not the first.[68]

Sometimes on returning from a lecturing expedition in the winter cold of upstate New York, virtually always on trains and seldom with proper food or sleep, he was so exhausted he craved nothing so much as rest. "I don't know what is to come of it," he wrote. "Sometimes I think of knocking at earth's gate with my staff, saying, 'Liebe Mutter, let me in.' "[69]

But given a little rest and he was determined not to die until the death of slavery. He would play his part in further harrying it until it received a mortal wound.

PART-TIME HEROES

I

Most of these men, North and South, were not always heroes although the role was more highly prized then than later and men tried harder to fill it. Many found, however, that the private self also needs nourishment and is liable to satiation with too much of high purpose. Theodore Weld, it may be recalled, had to yip and contort and leap about during each day's dawn as relief from his own nobility and the constant facing of mobs. Knowing the absolute necessity for a change of pace where a constant loftiness is required, he had firmly declared "I must cut capers."

Sergeant S. Prentiss, the Mississippi congressman, friend of Henry Wise, and prototype of all that was gallant in the Southern legend, often went out and got drunk after a four-hour speech on Southern Chivalry. Roistering around was Prentiss's relief and if his capers were different from Weld's, every man to his taste. Wise, who loved Prentiss in the manly sentimental manner of the age and exchanged bits of jewelry with him as a pledge of their eternal regard, also enjoyed escaping periodically from his own and the time's tensions to the peace of Chesapeake Bay where the only sound was the flap of the sail, the only pressure that of the tiller in his hand.[70]

Even little William Walker, who perhaps tried harder than any to be the flawless hero, had peculiarities from which he may have sought escape, including some flaw that made him a trifle too eager (some thought psychopathically so) to execute those who stood in his way or offended his strong, chaste sense of propriety.[71] Dr. Howe of Boston, also a professional hero and seen by many as the finest example of Chivalry above or below the Ohio, had his despairs as when he cried out to his wife in 1854, the famous but aging Julia Ward Howe, that he was tired of her and what he needed "was some young girl who would love him supremely."[72]

Perhaps he found some solace in attaining this youthful and beautiful love, or at least Julia believed he had.[73] More certainly he found escape and comfort during most of his adult life by almost daily visits to Laura Bridgman, the blind and deaf mute he had restored to life, intelligence, and quick communication with the world. Her fingers would fly as she spelled out her thoughts to Dr. Howe and then her sensitive hand would delicately and loosely enfold his while he spelled out words often having to do with God and virtue.[74]

Although Yancey was gallant enough to accept a challenge, spirited enough to blast into eternity an offensive relative, he was not always heroic and found his rest in pleasant ways. As he chomped on an ear of corn, whirling it circularly in his hands, his teeth close and eager, the golden buttered grains scattering wetly about, raising his head occasionally to speak, he was not an heroic figure but he was relaxed and enjoying both the taste of the food and the sound of his own voice, among his greatest pleasures.

Gerrit Smith found refuge from the great battles in which he was a participant in writing poetry, celebrating his griefs and antic humors, singing pretty ballads for his friends, and cataloguing the many ailments that were his and which he found so painfully fascinating.[75]

Edmund Ruffin often found his release in a careful enumeration in his diary of the slights and insults he had received, their pressure receding as he recorded them in a kind of pre-Freudian, self-applied therapy.

Theodore Parker had more escapes and needed more than most, and one of them was bears. He had always been infatuated by ursine characteristics, finding them simultaneously wise and droll, and once while on a holiday he went to New Hampshire to make "the acquaintance of two half-domesticated bears. . . . In a week," he wrote, "they became much attached to me. I put my hand in their mouths and played with them a good deal every day." They clearly admired each other, Parker and the bears, enjoying a perfect rapport.[76]

He liked bears so much that he collected statues of them, usually small figurines in clay, from all over the world and any friend anywhere who found a representation of a bear wearing a hat, or smoking a pipe, or climbing a tree, or just standing on his hind legs, would send it on to Parker. He even called his wife "Bearsie," or sometimes "Bear," and had a little verbal game he played with her which may have given both more pain than pleasure.

"What are you?" he would ask.

"A bear," she would reply.

"What must this bear do to be saved?"

"Have pups." [77]

She never had any and Parker never ceased to mourn. Even in public he sometimes remarked, parenthetically but compulsively, when speaking of the good that posterity would enjoy from the removal of some evil, that he would have no posterity of his own for he had no children. A romantic and sentimental man, when his eyes met those of a young girl as both walked a Boston street, he imagined some instant perfect communication in the swift exchange of glances by strangers. His whole being vibrated for hours afterwards. "I felt an unspeakable delight," he wrote, in describing the experience, "which lasted all the morning." [78]

Parker's admiration for his friend Dr. Howe was almost unbounded, a common phenomenon in Boston to all who knew him. The youthful warrior who had fought with Byron for the freedom of Greece, the gentle healer of Laura Bridgman, no wonder they called him "The Chevalier," or "Chev," if one knew him well, all unmindful of his miseries. Parker's friends called him "Parkie." But Parker envied Howe most not for his adventures in Greece or the miracle of Laura Bridgman but for his children and Julia Ward Howe. Not that he loved Mrs. Howe in any romantic sense. He only envied her fertility and her facility in bringing forth babies. Howe had four children in 1853 and Parker begged to be given the next for adoption. Howe, perhaps because he pitied the urgency of his friend's need, did not at first refuse him.

All during that miserable year of 1854 Parker waited, eyeing Mrs. Howe with eager anticipation. Although it was the year of Anthony Burns and his own indictment, he may have been almost as concerned with Mrs. Howe and her pregnancy of that year as with his possible sentencing to prison. He planned to name the child Theodora if a girl, Theodore if a boy. It was a girl. She was named Maud, for neither Dr. Howe nor Julia Ward could conceive of giving her to Parker or anyone else.[79]

2

Most of this disparate aggregation of warriors, as we shall see, had a consummate ability for facing the ultimate—whether on the battlefield, as did Wise, who lost in one bitterly contested field a life more precious than his own; or alone and with a shotgun in his mouth, as was Ruffin's end; or before a firing squad, as was Walker's fate; or awaiting death patiently and bravely, propped up in bed in Italy and writing a final justification, as Parker did, of the use of force by Americans opposed to slavery.

Men seemed to savor themselves more fiercely than at a later time, to be more concerned with the flair of their own personalities, more determined that at some point of peril they found themselves capable of a go-to-hell gesture. Even the scholar, the bookman, the churchman, Theodore Parker, was as capable of all this as any Southern fire-eater, as he demonstrated when threatened with murder by the criminals, informers, pimps, jailbirds, and gamblers who formed the marshal's guard, hired and deputized by the government for the rendition of Anthony Burns. This was no idle threat, as they proved when one of their number assaulted and injured Richard Henry Dana, one of Burns's attorneys.

When Parker heard of the threat he immediately went and sat among those who had made it at the Burns hearing. "I sat between men who had newly sworn to kill me, my garments touching theirs," he wrote, with something of the bravado we are considering. "The malaria of their rum and tobacco was an offense in my face. I saw their weapons and laughed as I looked at these drunken rowdies in their coward eye. They touch me!"[80]

Yet they all had their share of frailty, these fallible warriors of whom we write, and not all were able to manage the grand gesture when faced with imminent peril. All of them were part-time heroes, the bravest having their moments of weakness, even including John Brown. But being a hero at all, part-time or otherwise, is so unusual a distinction that once gained its resonance never quite fades from history.

3

Whatever these men were or were not, they all had one attribute in common. All expected a civil war soon over slavery. One would like to say they feared it, but the seconds had been ticking away toward explosion for so long over the years and even the generations that men's nerves demanded the relief of fact. As early as Jefferson's time, many agreed with his words: "I tremble for my country when I consider that God is just; that His justice cannot sleep forever. . . . The Almighty has no attribute which can take sides with us," he said, if it came to a contest between masters and slaves.[81]

Jefferson had almost despaired of his country, the fight over the Missouri Compromise, "like a firebell in the night," [82] threatening the country he had helped found with destruction over slavery. J. Q. Adams spoke similarly in 1820 when he said that he believed that slavery might "be the destined sword in the hand of the destroying angel which is to destroy the ties of this union," adding that if such a conflict abolished slavery, "as God shall judge me, I dare not say that it is not to be desired." [83]

Such perceptions were not peculiar to Jefferson and Adams. They continued and deepened year by year in their posterity. That so many men and women saw for so long the deadly course of events, and as if mesmerized by some inevitability pursued, and knowingly pursued, the fatal path to catastrophe, has in itself that peculiarly human tragedy found so often in history. One sees the ultimate ruin, thousands see it, but it cannot be avoided although there seem to be such rational escapes as freeing the slaves through federal bonds issued to their owners or a gradual emancipation like that used after the Revolution in the Middle Atlantic States and New England. Such measures were proposed but refused by North and South. It is as if the genes of men bear within them a massive urge toward self-destruction and also, though perhaps less certainly, an infinite ability to rise again from the ashes.

But men then neither spoke nor knew of genes. Theirs was another determinism. From Jefferson to Adams, from Garrison to Weld and Nat Turner, anti-slavery Americans spoke of a righteous God whose wrath must consume slavery and punish the nation which had nurtured it.

XXIV

Zero Hour

IF, IN THE LAST AND ULTIMATE CONSIDERATION, all of history is a whole from atoms to empires, from the further reaches of endless space to the smallest rabbit warren on the earth's prairies, most anti-slavery Americans of John Brown's day had a way of saying so and believing so, a spiritual cosmology that gave meaning and direction to their lives. They believed so, not because they considered history causal in any scientific sense but because of their faith that all, the greatest event, the smallest sparrow's fall, came from the Lord God Jehovah, who always was and always will be.

If this theological cosmology was based on what seemed to them the clear coherence and final unity of a moral universe governed by God, that should not extract from it, even to modern eyes, the human wisdom and experience that may adhere in some degree to any substantial accretion of man's thought. They had a sense of the present mortgaging the future, of the remoteness in time of any beginning, and if they fixed both in God's Providence, that did not diminish their sense of endless cause and consequence.

Particularly when condemning slavery did they emphasize the penalty that might be exacted for that national sin, this the theological perception perhaps of the historical truth that payment is always exacted if persistent error and long inequity are not corrected. It was something of this deeply held and quite general feeling that shaped Lincoln's words when, referring to the raging Civil War, he said in his last inaugural:

Yet if God wills that it continue until all the wealth piled up by the bondsman's two hundred years of unrequited toil shall be sunk, and until every drop drawn with the lash shall be paid by another drawn with the sword, as was said two thousand years ago, still must it be said that the judgments of the Lord are true and righteous altogether.[1]

Even yet it may occasionally seem as if Lincoln's words have a continuing relevancy of a kind, the lash having been exchanged for other cruelties, particularly when we recall that a continuing and enduring problem of the American nation still stems from the enslavement of the descendants of the black African kingdoms of Ghana and Melle and Songhay, beginning some four centuries ago. For it is strange, as only history and truth are strange, that the penalties and inequities still inflicted against black Americans, the bloody carnage of the Wilderness and Gettysburg and Shiloh, and our foreign relations with the two-thirds of the world whose inhabitants are colored, should all have a connection far back in time and far over the Atlantic on a steaming West African coast in the fifteenth century.

John Brown thought of these matters, or matters much like them, as he left for Kansas to do his part in denying that Territory to the bloody iniquity that was to make Lincoln's just equation of bloody war. If he was a product of his time, he was not just any product. He was more strongly buttressed than most men by an ideology, however theological, that would give him strength and perspective and boundless confidence in the developing struggle. All the liberating verses of the Bible, his private converse with himself for years, may have sung within him with a new fervor as he paced toward Kansas: "Remember them that are in bonds, as bound with them"; "And ye shall . . . proclaim liberty throughout *all* the land unto all the inhabitants thereof"; and "The Spirit of the Lord God *is* upon me; . . . he hath sent me to bind up the brokenhearted, to proclaim liberty to the captives, and the opening of the prison to *them that are* bound."

These were John Brown's politics or at least one form of their expression. Seeing, it may be remembered, the Declaration of Independence and the Golden Rule as one and the same thing, he was as enamored of the American Revolution as he was of the Bible, believing it to be the working out of God's will. And this being so, the counterrevolution of slavery could never triumph. That was the rock sustaining his every thought about the developing struggle.

And yet he sometimes thought that God might punish a guilty people, and experienced something of the feeling that Lincoln and many others expressed. He wrote not long before he left for Kansas: "Should God send famin[e], pestilence & war uppon this guilty hypocritical nation to destroy it, we need not be surprised. Never before did a people so mock & despise him. There seems to be no sign of repentance amongst us."[2] If the Marxist feels that history is his ally, John Brown felt that he and his cause had one more certain.

ARMS AND THE MAN

I

In the long history of religion and the shorter history of psychiatry, which may ultimately include the first in part, there are repeated instances of men and women being born again, as the expression is, from Saul becoming Paul at the beginning of the Christian era, to those ascending into sainthood all during the Middle Ages, to Americans being reborn in great bursts of holy light and weeping during the protracted meetings and revivals of the nineteenth century. If such phenomena did nothing else they at least attested to the belief that there was always the possibility of change. It was never too late to mend. The crabbed old man could change more quickly than the youth if he apprehended truth more quickly.

Yet if John Brown was reborn in 1855 we need seek nothing of the miraculous in explaining it. There can be no doubt that in that year he did become a new man, but his rebirth came from giving reality to the thoughts and resolves that had simmered within him for years. He had been maimed by his own most ardent desires, by denying himself any real effort to fulfill his strongest ambitions. He had romanced about them; he had not acted. Now the time and place and a special point in history had enabled him after long years to break through to the essential John Brown. The fact that he was acting on his convictions, not as a sideline or an occasional foray on the Underground Railroad but as a professional, as a man whose whole activity would thenceforth be toward the destruction of slavery, gave him a unity and strength he had never enjoyed before. Constantly increasing pressure over the years, even if it is only the pressure of desire, forever sharpened by the special circumstance of time and place, will finally and suddenly explode and it was this explosion within that had liberated John Brown.

There was a new vigor in all his movements. If he did not seem younger in appearance, he did seem as one who had experienced deliverance. He was free at last. For nearly twenty years he had been cheated of the greatness he felt within him, held to the small and shoddy ways of commerce, escaping as often as he could to farming. But he had been called to more than that. Never again would he engage in business for profit. Henceforth he would be about his Father's business, the freeing of a people. He was no longer "our Mr. Brown," the property of Perkins & Brown whose days were spent haggling over the price of wool. Neither was he the Brown of the Brown & Thompson Addition to Franklin Village, panting for riches, as he desperately tried to avoid bankruptcy by buying and selling town lots for worthless promissory notes.

He was now, although few but himself knew it as yet, the historic John Brown, the John Brown whose sense of mission would combine with increasing crisis to make him irresistible. This was the Brown whom Emerson would celebrate, whom Theodore Parker, the greatest preacher of the North, would be glad to follow, the Brown who would inspire Thoreau and change his life, his most fundamental thought, the Brown who would lead Howe and Higginson and Wendell Phillips and Gerrit Smith, as well as making many others, old and young, black and white, answer to his will no matter how great the danger of destruction and disgrace.

It was not that he did not progress after 1855 nor that the imperatives of a terrible time did not force upon him further development. It was that he took the basic and necessary step in that year, that he broke through to his desire and to himself, that he enlisted fully then in the cause of battling slavery and with a purity, ardor, self-sacrifice, and determination that few ever achieved. The thousands who had gone to Kansas before him, including his own sons, the particular political situation in which slavery seemed about to triumph in Central America, Cuba, and Kansas, perhaps in the whole West, suddenly meshed with his own life in a way that gave him a liberty he had never been able to achieve by his own efforts.

The change in him was evident to most. He had a power he had never had before. When he arrived in Akron on August 13 on his way to Kansas, there was absolutely nothing in his aspect to remind his friends of the business failures with which they had associated him. He immediately called for a mass meeting and one was almost instantly arranged with the help of former Mayor Lucius V. Bierce and Samuel A. Lane, soon to be Sheriff of Summit County, two of Akron's foremost citizens. The meeting was packed and John Brown could scarcely have been more militant in his appeal for arms for those fighting slavery in Kansas. Nor could his auditors have been more enthusiastic in their response.

The fact was that if John Brown had changed so had the people of Akron, as susceptible as any to the great American transformation that had made conservative merchants, hidebound farmers, and cautious bankers eager to give money and arms for the conflict in Kansas. As a matter of fact they were eager to stretch the law, or even break it, in their determination adequately to equip one going to Kansas with the avowed purpose of fighting and arming its Free Soil citizens. At the mass meeting where John Brown's speech aroused those attending "to the highest pitch of indignation and enthusiasm,"[3] various committees were formed to help him in canvassing the town for weapons as well as for money with which to buy them.

"Among the various committees appointed," Lane later recalled, "I was selected to accompany Brown among the stores, shops, offices, etc., of the village in a personal canvas for contributions. Besides considerable money, guns, pistols, swords, butcher knives, powder, shot, lead and other warlike materials" were contributed, "together with boots, shoes, clothing—anything in fact which could be of use to the struggling free staters. . . ."[4] It was not an everyday occurrence for the inhabitants of an Ohio town to gather together all the lethal weapons they possessed to be used against their fellow countrymen and this fact in itself indicates something of the great American transformation of which we write.

As Lane and John Brown were canvassing the community, one Dick Smetts, otherwise unknown to history, was "spiriting away several cases of guns belonging to the state of Ohio which were being gathered in from the disbanded independent military companies of Akron and Tallmadge."[5] This was Mr. Smetts's contribution to John Brown's plea for the fight against slavery. Meanwhile Mayor Bierce (usually called General Bierce, perhaps because he had headed an unsuccessful filibustering expedition to seize Canada in 1838) was renewing his youth, as far as memory could do it, by prowling through a dark and musty storeroom in which the weapons used by his expedition had been hidden long years ago. With some help he gathered together the guns, ammunition, and "some artillery short swords," on each of which was emblazoned an American eagle, which had been intended for the purpose of detaching Canada from the British Empire. He gave them to John Brown, who used the swords in the terrible work at Pottawatomie.[6]

If John Brown was a more compelling figure at Akron than he had ever been before, it was because his own desire tallied with a swell of public sentiment. That was the real cause of his success. He had planned to stay only one day in Akron but he stayed two days longer as arms and money continued to roll in and as he crated and boxed the supplies he had received, preparatory to sending them by railroad to Chicago. While Brown, and perhaps General Bierce and others, was waiting for the train upon which to ship the weapons, Milton Lusk, the brother of Dianthe and John Brown's brother-in-law, drove up in a buggy from Hudson. With him was a friend, thirty-seven-year-old Benjamin Kent Waite who also knew John Brown, having been a member of his Sunday school class in Hudson.

"Milton Lusk and John Brown had a long conversation there at the station," Waite recalled. "John had made his brag that he was armed from head to foot, with everything from a Sharps rifle to a gimlet.

" 'Now, John, you look out,' said Milton. 'You'll be coming into collision with the Government.' "

John Brown seemed impatient at the warning.

" 'I'm going to Kansas,' " he said, slowly emphasizing his words, as if Milton somehow lacked good sense, " *'to make it a Free State.'* " [7]

Brown was delighted with his success in Akron, writing his wife from there on August 15, "I expect to leave here for Hudson today & shall probably be on my way to Cleveland tomorrow. I should have been off before; but I have met with such good encouragement from the people here in the way of contributions in Guns, Revolvers, Swords, Powder Caps, & money that I thought it best to detain a day or two longer on that account. . . ." [8]

2

If John Brown believed in the God of Battles, he also, at least sporadically, believed in political activity as an effective means of aiding Providence. His first move, when he had at last decided to act, was to attend a political convention, that at Syracuse, to publicize his cause and obtain its aid. His second was his appeal to the people of Akron, whom he had mobilized so effectively in his behalf and that of Kansas that even the guns of an ancient filibustering expedition against Canada as well as those of the State of Ohio were contributed to the cause.

But now his task was to get his heavy load of arms as swiftly as possible to Kansas. By August 21 he and his son-in-law, Henry Thompson, were in Chicago where they were met by sixteen-year-old Oliver Brown, the Old Man's youngest son, who had been working for some months on a farm near Rock Island, Illinois. Before picking up the boxes of weapons at the freight depot they bought a canvas-covered wagon and "a nice young horse" for $120, but found that stout as their horse was he had difficulty in hauling the weapons. In addition the wagon contained, prominently displayed, John Brown's theodolite and other surveying instruments, a kind of passport, or so Brown hoped, through the slave state of Missouri, since most surveyors bound for Kansas were government men and regarded as pro-slavery. "We have so much of a load," John Brown wrote to North Elba, "that we shall probably have to walk a good deal, enough probably to give us an opportunity to supply ourselves with game." [9]

On August 23 they began their journey from Chicago to Kansas, which consisted mostly, as John Brown predicted, of walking a distance of some 550 miles. They must have made a queer trio as they pushed on beside their wagon, one of them with the reins in his hands leading the horse: Oliver with as much youngness upon him as if he were a colt; Henry, a tightly trim young man of thirty; but strangest of all the Old Man. Lean and dour but with dignity enough, he plodded through the dust probably wearing the rusty frock coat he wore even when doing farm work at North Elba, its claw-hammer tails dangling behind him. Perhaps it was the only coat he had now. He usually also wore a hard-boiled stiff collar, its points shooting upward and grazing his considerable chin, his leather strap sometimes serving as a cravat, his gold collar button sometimes nude and uncovered. There is no reason to believe that he had removed either the coat or the collar because of the hot sun as he paced ahead, his sharp blue eyes darting to the left and right as if he were determined neither to miss anything nor to be taken by surprise.

However he appeared we can be certain that no emigrant to Kansas, of all the thousands who had preceded him, was ever more determined than he. He was a man who, when he made up his mind, went at once the full length. The guns and swords in his wagon attested to that. They were not for show but for use. He meant to fight. He meant from the beginning to raid Missouri and rescue slaves. He himself wrote later that it had been his "deliberate judgment since 1855 that the most ready and effectual way to retrieve Kansas would be to meddle directly with the peculiar institution." [10] The most direct way to meddle with that institution was to free slaves in Missouri and perhaps elsewhere also.

From his first arrival in Kansas, if we may anticipate a little, John Brown was regarded as an original, a leader, stern and strange, so redolent of the Old Testament that he was quite different from any other Free State leader in the Territory. He did not want to run for office, neither for Congress nor the Senate, nor did he plan to develop a town and become rich through the sale of town lots. He had been through all that and he was grateful that it was over. He had only one idea, one purpose, one passion: to defeat slavery by voting it out or running it out, by pursuing the conflict Missourians had initiated in Missouri into that state and freeing their slaves if it were necessary and could be done.

If the defeat of slavery required him to kill its defenders he was ready.

If it required near starvation while "dwelling like David of Old . . . with the serpents of the rocks and the wild beasts of the wilderness," [11] as exposed to the rain and snow as an aging wolf, he was prepared to endure. He had crossed the Rubicon in deciding to arm his sons and he was ready for its most ultimate consequence. If his past life had taught him anything, it was the evil of delay, rationalization, the compromise of principle. He did not intend to make that mistake again.

3

From Scott County, Iowa, John Brown informed his wife and children on September 4,

I am writing "in our Tent" about twenty miles west of the Mississippi to let you know we are in good health, & how we get along. . . . Our load is hevy so that we have to walk most of the time; indeed all the time the last day. The Roads are mostly very good & we can make some progress if our Horse does not fail us. We fare very well on Crackers, Herring, boiled Eggs, Prairie Chickens, Tea, and sometimes a little Milk. Have 3 Chickens now cooking for our Breakfast. We shoot enough of them on the wing as we go along to supply us with fresh meat. Oliver succeeds in bringing them down quite as well as any of us.

Our expences before we got away from Chicago had been very heavy; since then very light; so that we hope our money will not entirely fail us. . . . We expect to go direct through Missouri. . . .

He then added a rather apologetic sentence, saying, "I think could I hope in any other way to answer the end of my being, I would be quite content to be at North Elba." [12]

The next letter was from Adair County, Missouri, about two days after crossing the Iowa-Missouri border. Henry was threatened with the ague but they had "plenty of Quinine Bark," if he proved to really have it. They were almost out of money but John Brown added, "We are not however disheartened: and we shall make some shift to get along we trust." [13]

Apparently they saw few on the road from the free states emigrating to Kansas, most settlers still going by boat by way of St. Louis and the Missouri River. But there were frequent stories of river boats being halted and Free State passengers being mistreated while their arms were confiscated and that, John Brown said in a later account, was the primary reason for their traveling by land with their stout little horse instead of by boat on the Missouri.

"Oweing to the hostile attitude of the people of Missouri & their treatment of Free State men, & companies on the river," John Brown wrote in his account, in which he used the third person, it was decided the Three [himself, Oliver, and Henry] should make their way overland through Missouri to Kansas camping out all the way from Chicago. As their load was all that a stout horse could move at all; their progress was extremely slow, & just before getting into Missouri their horse got the distemper: after which for most of the journey they could only gain some Six to Eight miles a day. This however gave them great opportunity for seeing & hearing in Missouri.

Companies of armed men, & individuals [from Missouri] were constantly passing & repassing Kansaswise continually boasting of what feats of patriotism & chivalry they had performed in Kansas: & of the still more mighty deeds they were yet to do. No man of them would blush when telling of their cruel treading down & terrifying of defenceless Free State men: they seemed to take peculiar satisfaction in telling of the fine horses, & mules they had many of them killed in their numerous expeditions against the d——d abolitionists. The coarse, vulgar and profane jests & the blood thirsty brutal feelings to which they were giving vent continually would have been a most exquisite treat to the Ears, & their general appearance to the Ey[e]s of the past & the present Administration. . . .[14]

Going through the little Missouri towns and villages, feeling as if they were scouts in an enemy country, they may have been a trifle annoyed by attention they occasionally attracted. If they stopped near a town square to buy provisions, a small crowd might gather around them and their wagon, the curiosity of its members as strong as their hostility upon suspecting that the three were from the North. The Old Man's surveying instruments were not always the passport he had hoped they would be. If anyone had succeeded in prying into one of the boxes in the wagon, or had in any other way found out that these Yankees were carrying arms to Kansas, death might have resulted for someone.

At Brunswick, a village on the Missouri River, John Brown and his companions were waiting for a ferry when an old man began prowling around their wagon.

"Where you going?" he demanded.

"Kansas," John Brown answered.

"You'll never live to get there."

"We are prepared," John Brown said, in words that italicized themselves and routed their interrogator, "*not to die alone.*" [15]

About two or three days further on they arrived at the village of Waverly on the Missouri River where little Austin, dead of the cholera, had been buried by Jason and his wife and by John and Wealthy and their boy, during the thunder and lightning of a fearful night storm (their boat, the *New Lucy*, putting off without them). Since then Jason and Ellen had been disconsolate. "On the way at Waverly," John Brown wrote of himself (in the account to which we have referred), "he took up the body of his little grandson . . . thinking it would afford some relief to the broken hearted Father and Mother, they having been obliged to leave him amidst the ruffian like people by whom (for the most part) they themselves were so inhumanly treated in their distress." [16]

This, at least to the Brown sons, was an example of their father's tenderness. They always said that he was very severe but in the same sentence they almost always spoke of his tenderness and sympathy. Occasionally, they did not know which to dread most, his stern rebuke or the tears that often welled in his eyes as he gave it. It had been so since their childhood when he flogged them, the tears streaming down his cheeks and proving to them that the punishment hurt him more than it hurt them. They were individuals in their own right, strong as most and even rebellious at times, but the Old Man because of his long domination over them from their earliest consciousness could usually make them do what he wanted them to do.

JOURNEY'S END—AND BEGINNING

I

If John Brown had any misconception about Kansas as he journeyed toward it, it lay in the belief that most Free Staters thought as he did. Nor did he know that life at Brown's Station, as his sons sometimes called their camp, had deteriorated as much or more than Free State politics. The two were not unconnected, the Brown brothers having been so concerned with rescuing the Territory from slavery and the bogus legislature that they spent most of their time going to meetings in Lawrence and Pottawatomie, with the result that they were still living in tents in the ravine that John had described in the May 24 letter to his father. Rains had made it damp and muddy.

If John's morale was low, it may have been partly because he feared that the great crusade to save Kansas from slavery had abandoned all principle and degenerated into the most gross opportunism. When the movement began to form a Free State Party which would completely defy and reject the pro-slavery government foisted upon it by Missouri while asking for admission into the Union as a free state, even the cautious Robinson had threatened raids into Missouri for the liberation of its slaves if Missourians continued their invasions and seizures of elections.[17]

By August such talk was regarded as incendiary. The great majority of

Free State settlers had been stung by the charges of Missourians that they were "abolitionists and nigger stealers." They were not, and yearned for a chance to prove their political respectability. Most favored the banning of all blacks, slave or free, from entry or residence in the state or Territory of Kansas. Kansas was to be made free but a free *white* state. White supremacy was to be made as complete in Kansas as it was in Missouri, even if it took a different form.

It was this widespread sentiment that James H. Lane capitalized upon in marking his entry into Free State politics. When he came to Kansas from Indiana in the spring of 1855 he had been an administration Democrat, a former lieutenant governor of that state, an officer of the Mexican War, and a former congressman when he had voted for and backed the Kansas-Nebraska Act. His purpose had been to organize what he called a National Democratic Party in Kansas, but his convention on June 27 which repudiated neither the pro-slavery legislature nor its laws had been so sparsely attended that he immediately decided to join Free State forces. He could stand anything but defeat.

He was a man usually without principle, although unpredictable enough occasionally to show flashes of it; but with or without it, he was irresistible if he had a chance to speak. He was a demagogue possessed of no emotion so strong as his own ambition, but when he spoke he exuded a sincerity that convinced. More than that he was entertaining, a thin and lanky mountebank who could make men roar with laughter, a tragedian, a two-bit Hamlet who could make them weep, a hero who could make them hysterical with the demand that he lead them into battle and death. Even John Brown came to like him, if failing to trust him, after the Kansas civil war broke out, for Lane would fight or give such a good imitation of it that he often routed the Border Ruffians. He killed a man for drilling a well on property he claimed and when he was jailed before his acquittal John Brown called on him in his cell, lecturing him against his ungovernable temper. Salmon Brown, writing about his father's admonition to Lane, observed, "I thought that was the case of the pot calling the kettle black as my father was very high strung himself." [18]

Lane has been described by an admirer as a

strange magnetic man in his middle forties, six feet tall, slender, wiry, nervous, tremendously alive. He burst with vitality—his voice was hypnotic. His hair was long and reckless, and above his ears black locks curled like horns. There was always the hint of Mephistopheles about him—or of Dionysus, the god of revelry. . . . He had a wide, loose mouth, as mobile as that of a Shakesperian "ham" actor. He was indeed an actor, an artist—perhaps a great artist. [19]

It was this man who took over the Free State Big Springs Convention on September 5. John Brown, Jr., was there, if not as a delegate as a member of the Free State Executive Committee which had planned the convention and the general strategy of calling a later constitutional convention. But neither he nor anyone else could break Lane's control of the convention. With the majority of the convention agreeing with him that all blacks should be barred from Kansas, and that abolitionists and "nigger stealing" should be condemned, it did not take him long to succeed in inserting the following resolutions in the Free State platform:

Resolved, That the best interests of Kansas require a population of free white men, and that in the organization we are in favor of stringent laws, excluding all negroes, bond or free, from the Territory; that nevertheless such measures shall not be regarded as a test of party orthodoxy.

Resolved, That the stale and ridiculous charge of Abolitionism, so industriously imputed to the Free-State party, and so persistently adhered to in spite of all the evidence to the contrary, is without a shadow of a truth to support it, and that it is not more appropriate to ourselves than it is to our opponents, who use it as a term of reproach, to bring odium upon us, pretending to believe in its truth, and hoping to frighten from our ranks the weak and the timid, who are more willing to desert their principles than they are to stand up under persecution and abuse, with the consciousness of right.

Resolved, That we will discountenance and denounce any attempt to encroach upon the constitutional rights of the people of any State, or to interfere with their slaves; conceding to their citizens the right to regulate their own institutions, and to hold and recover their slaves, without any molestation or obstruction from the people of Kansas.[20]

Probably as part of a deal, Charles Robinson and his allies, who were against these lily-white provisions, finally agreed to them with the understanding that Lane would permit them to name the Free State candidate for congressional representative from the Territory. That election would take place in complete defiance of the territorial pro-slavery government on October 9, when delegates would also be elected to the Free State constitutional convention to be held at Topeka on October 23. It was this convention as well as that at Big Springs that were regarded as treasonous and revolutionary by the Pierce administration.

The Free State candidate for Congress endorsed by the Big Springs Convention was ex-Governor Andrew H. Reeder, who had been removed as Governor of the Territory by President Pierce on trumped-up charges of illegal land speculation. Wilson Shannon, a pro-slavery Democrat from Ohio, had been appointed Governor of the Territory in his place. The real reason for Reeder's removal was the demand by Missourians and other pro-slavery men who had concluded that they could not control him. Their continual threats to "string him up, by God," in addition to other offenses less personal, had converted a pro-slavery Governor into a rabidly anti-slavery Free State candidate for Congress. At the Big Springs Convention which nominated him, Reeder introduced fiery resolutions, unanimously adopted, defying the pro-slavery legislature and its laws as illegal, the result of violence and fraud, and threatening war if any attempt was made to enforce the so-called bogus laws. One of the resolutions passed by the convention and offered by Reeder said:

> *Resolved,* That we will endure and submit to these laws no longer than the best interests of the Territory require, as the least of two evils, and will resist them to a bloody issue as soon as we ascertain that peaceable remedies shall fail, and forcible resistance shall furnish any reasonable prospect of success, and that in the meantime we recommend to our friends throughout the Territory the organization and descipline of volunteer companies and the procurement and preparation of arms.[21]

2

John Brown, Jr., probably became a part of the Big Springs wheeling and dealing as a member of the Free State Executive Committee,[22] the highest body of the party, although he reported that Lane had said, "So far as the rights of property are concerned I know of no difference between the negro and the mule."[23] Although not a delegate to the convention he undoubtedly attended, favoring Reeder, and liking his tone of defiance to the pro-slavery territorial government, but abhorring Lane's resolutions. He had probably gone along for the sake of unity. He had not resigned from the Executive Committee however much he may have protested, when the abolitionists were condemned, when all blacks were excluded from Kansas, as far as the Free State platform could do it, and when all efforts to free slaves in Missouri were rejected by the Free State Party.

Only one member of the Big Springs Convention, Charles Stearns of Lawrence and a Garrisonian, condemned the platform scorning abolitionists and banning blacks from the Territory's precincts, writing that he spat upon it.[24] John Brown, Jr., did not spit upon it and in failing to do so he may have felt that he not only betrayed himself but his father, still on the way with guns and the intent of using them whether in Kansas or Missouri and who would soon declare himself at a time of crisis in Kansas as an "abolitionist, dyed in the wool."[25]

The various conflicting pressures may have made John Brown, Jr., ill although there was enough illness around to make it unnecessary to attribute conflict within as a contributing factor. It was probably after returning from the Big Springs Convention that he collapsed into chills and fever. He was placed in the largest of the Brown tents in the ravine where his brothers were lying in moldy hay, prairie grass cut long before, their teeth clicking convulsively, their faces flushed with fever, occasionally vomiting, so weak they could scarcely rise even though the stench around them was enough to make a dead man take up his bed and walk. The Brown brothers, all of them ill with malaria which periodically brought spells of chills and fever, were so sick that they wished they were dead. Only Wealthy and her little boy Jonny were up and about, sometimes assisted by Ellen, Jason's wife, who was not as ill as all the men.

Most of them had been sick for some weeks. The garden had gone to ruin, the cows had eaten the half-grown corn the Browns had planted weeks before, and they were almost without food save for some dried apples, a few potatoes, and a little milk. The camp was dirty and foul and some of the cattle had wandered away, sometimes pursued by the most healthy of the brothers, staggering and falling as he tried to herd the animals back. No cabins had been built and the winds already seemed piercing to the shivering and feverish sick. Often it rained, with the result that the ravine was a quagmire, the floors of the tents small swamps. The Brown brothers, alternately shaking with violent chills and burning with fever, were usually too weak to serve themselves, Wealthy washing their faces and bringing them water but that was all she could do. They knew their father was approaching and were half longing for his presence—that dominating will which could always organize and overcome, or so it seemed to his sons—half dreading his disapproval when he saw their helpless squalor.[26]

3

As he paced behind the stout young horse straining forward across Missouri bearing the heavy load of swords with American eagles emblazoned on their blades, muskets, revolvers, and ammunition, as well as the body of his grandson, each step toward Kansas brought John Brown nearer to that common climax which would involve so many lives in addition to his own. Each step brought him nearer to the bloody midnight executions at Pottawatomie, to the quest which enlisted behind his revolution some of the greatest Americans in history. Soon, very soon, as history goes, Thoreau would describe him as "an angel of light" and Emerson call him "a hero of simple artless goodness." If he had hitherto reacted to others for the most part, now others would react to him. If he had been at the periphery of events for most of his life, now he would be at their center. If he had been made by the time, now for a space he would make the time.

The wagon creaked endlessly on, its wheels sometimes shrieking against gravel, sometimes sinking to the hub in Missouri mud, sometimes pushing through a cloud of dust when the road was dry and the sun was hot. The interminable miles dragged on, each step followed by another until it sometimes seemed as if they were suspended in space and time, as if events themselves were standing still and awaiting their arrival in Kansas. As yet there had been no battles there although events trembled on the verge of armed hostilities. It was the calm before the storm, the pause before war with Americans everywhere, their sides chosen, waiting in tortured suspense. Most knew it was zero hour.

Mostly the weather in the journey across Missouri had been hot and clear. But now and again the sky would darken, the wind hushing and dying away as if listening in a profound silence for the coming storm. It would begin with a far-away mutter across a sky suddenly zigzagged with a flick of lightning. Then there was the deafness of a crashing smash shaking the very earth. The Old Man, his son, and son-in-law would often pitch their tent for shelter from the downpour but often too they would continue through the cloudburst until they emerged at length in sunshine. As John Brown later said, he could not remember "a storm so serious and dreadful as to prevent the return of warm sunshine and a cloudless sky." [27]

Finally, after forty-four days and nights on the road they arrived in Kansas near Brown's Station on October 6. The Old Man was tired but more than that it is probable that he thought it more delicate to give his sons a little warning before he appeared, give them a chance to neaten up and make things shipshape. At any rate within a mile of his sons' camp he instructed Oliver and Henry to go on ahead. He would keep the wagon and camp overnight almost within earshot of his family in Kansas.

4

They had apparently heard neither him nor his wagon when he pulled up at the Brown camp. He approached a tent. He drew open its flap and looked down on his sick sons, startled by his sudden appearance before them, but no more startled than he himself. As he stared down at them he said no word but slowly his eyes took on that expression his sons knew so well, composed of outrage and pity. He may have seemed immensely tall as he stood above them, his sons regarding him from their backs on the ground. If there were tears in his eyes, there was more of anger, and one by one the Brown brothers may have staggered to unsteady feet to greet him.

It was then that he told Jason and Ellen he had brought their son's body from Missouri. "The parents," John Brown wrote, "were almost frenzied with joy on being told that their dead child was again with them," and then added in the next sentence, "On his arrival at the place . . . he found all the company completely prostrate with sickness."[28] Yet as they staggered about they must have known that they would have to work now, ill or well. They knew, too, that whatever it might cost them they would soon have cabins.

As John Brown watched his sons attempt to work, no matter how unsteadily, he may have felt for a moment almost cheerful. Perhaps it was then that he climbed aboard the wagon, and with the help of his eldest son began unloading the guns that would be used at Black Jack, the swords that would swish through the night cleaving bone and gristle at Pottawatomie. The Old Man had arrived in Kansas and it would never be the same again, not for his sons or for anyone else. Nor would the country.

Notes

FOREWORD

1. John Jay Chapman, *Learning and Other Essays*, New York, 1910, p. 131.
2. Bradford Torrey and Francis H. Allen, eds., *The Journal of Henry D. Thoreau*, Boston, 1906, vol. XII, p. 436.
3. From a letter of John Brown to his wife and children from Charlestown Prison in Virginia, Nov. 30, 1859, in the Dreer Collection, Historical Society of Pennsylvania, Philadelphia, Pa. "Nothing," he wrote, "can so tend to make life a blessing as the consciousness that you *love: & are beloved:* & 'love ye the stranger' *still.* It is ground of the utmost comfort to *my mind:* to know that as many of you as have had *the opportunity;* have given full proof of your fidelity to the great family of man. Be faithful unto death."
4. From John Brown's speech on Nov. 2, 1859, before sentence of death by hanging, copy in the Dreer Collection. ". . . I believe that to have interfered as I have done—in behalf of His despised poor, was not wrong, but right. . . ."

I

*On the Success
of Being Hanged*

1. For John Brown's indecision at Harper's Ferry and his eagerness to justify his motives to the slaveholders he held captive, see Richard J. Hinton, *John Brown and His Men*, New York, 1894, pp. 296, 300, 302–5; also John E. P. Daingerfield, "John Brown at Harper's Ferry," the first-person narrative of one of his prisoners in *Century Magazine*, June, 1885; also Allan Keller, *Thunder at Harper's Ferry*, Englewood Cliffs, N.J., 1958, pp. 123, 127–8.
2. "In his habits he was jocuse and mirthful when the conversation did not turn on anything profane or vulgar and the Bible was almost at his tongues end from one end to the other," wrote James Foreman, a friend and employee of John Brown on Dec. 28, 1859, to James Redpath, Brown's first biographer. The original is in the Kansas State Historical Society, Topeka, Kansas.

The biographies of John Brown, arranged chronologically in order of publication, are: Redpath, *The Public Life of Captain John Brown*, Boston, 1860; Richard D. Webb, *Life and Letters of Captain John Brown*, London, 1861; F. B. Sanborn, *The Life and Letters of John Brown*, Boston, 1885; Herman von Holst, *John Brown*, ed. F. P. Stearns, Boston, 1889; Richard J. Hinton, *John Brown and his Men*, New York, 1894; J. E. Chamberlin, *John Brown*, Boston, 1899; William Elsey Connelley, *John Brown*, Topeka, Kansas, 1900; John Newton, *Captain John Brown of Harper's Ferry*, London, 1902; W. E. B. Du Bois, *John Brown*, Philadelphia, 1909; Oswald Garrison

Villard, *John Brown, 1800–1859: A Biography Fifty Years After*, Boston, 1910, revised edition: New York, 1943; Hill Peebles Wilson, *John Brown, Soldier of Fortune*, Boston, 1918; Robert Penn Warren, *John Brown, The Making of a Martyr*, New York, 1929; David Karsner, *John Brown, Terrible Saint*, New York, 1934. Other books about John Brown, although not formal biographies, include James C. Malin, *John Brown and the Legend of Fifty-Six*, Philadelphia, 1942; Allan Keller, *Thunder At Harper's Ferry*, Englewood Cliffs, N.J., 1958. There is also a valuable anthology of John Brown's letters and speeches, as well as selections from his associates and from writers with Brown as their theme, in *A John Brown Reader*, Louis Ruchames, ed., New York, 1959. In addition, there are two notable novels about John Brown: Leonard Ehrlich, *God's Angry Man*, New York, 1932; and Truman Nelson, *The Surveyor*, New York, 1960, a sometimes brilliant and always moving portrayal of John Brown in Kansas. And in 1970 appeared *John Brown: The Sword and the Word*, by Barrie Stavis, New York; Stephen B. Oates, *To Purge This Land with Blood*, New York; and in 1971, *Man on Fire*, by Jules Abels, New York.

3. Letter of Samuel Gridley Howe to Thomas Wentworth Higginson, Boston, Feb. 16, 1860, Higginson Collection, Boston Public Library, copy in Villard Collection, Columbia University, New York City; also Thomas Wentworth Higginson, *Cheerful Yesterdays*, Boston, 1898, pp. 222–3.

4. Annie Brown Adams, undated account of life at the Kennedy Farm House, Henry E. Huntington Library and Art Gallery, Department of Manuscripts, San Marino, Calif. John Brown's followers often called him the Old Man.

5. Katherine Mayo, interview with Mrs. Thomas Russell, at whose house in Boston John Brown was in hiding in April 1857 and in the spring of 1859. *New York Evening Post*, Oct. 13, 1909.

6. Quotations from John Brown letter from Kansas, April 7, 1856, to "Dear Wife & Children every One," Kansas State Historical Society, and John Brown letter from Kansas, June 1856, to "Dear Wife and Children Every One," F. B. Sanborn, *The Life and Letters of John Brown*, Boston, 1885, pp. 236–41.

7. Mrs. Stearns to Richard J. Hinton, undated MS., Hinton Papers, Kansas State Historical Society; also Hinton, *John Brown and His Men*, pp. 719–27.

8. Cleveland *Plain Dealer*, March 22, 1859.

9. *New York Tribune*, Oct. 19, 1859.

10. Report of the Select Committee of United States Senate inquiring into the Harper's Ferry Invasion, 36th Congress, 1st Session, hereinafter called the Mason Committee, Washington, D.C., 1860, p. 192. Mr. Andrews testified before the Mason Committee on Feb. 9, 1860.

11. Lincoln at Springfield, Ill., June 16, 1858, as reported in Paul M. Angle, ed., *Created Equal? The Complete Lincoln-Douglas Debates of 1858*, Chicago, 1958, p. 2.

12. William H. Seward at Rochester, N.Y., Oct. 25, 1858, *New York Tribune* pamphlet, 1860, p. 2. The pamphlets were issued for sale in bundle orders for the presidential campaign of 1860.

13. Letter of Theodore Parker to Francis Jackson, Rome, Nov. 24, 1859, Henry Steele Commager, ed., *Theodore Parker: An Anthology*, Boston, 1960, pp. 257–8. In this letter defending Brown, and saying that it might possibly be the duty of every American to use force in helping free the slaves, Parker also saw the issue, as had Lincoln and Seward, as "we must give up Democracy if we keep Slavery, or give up Slavery if we keep Democracy."

14. Thomas Wentworth Higginson, *Contemporaries*, Boston, 1899, pp. 294–5.

15. Ralph Volney Harlow, *Gerrit Smith*, New York, 1939, p. 357.

16. Ibid., pp. 260 and 305.

17. Syracuse *Journal*, May 31, 1856.

18. Higginson Collection, Boston Public Library. For an extended account of similar plans and sentiments, see Herbert Aptheker, *To Be Free*, New York, 1948, pp. 41–74.

19. John Brown himself described the affair at Black Jack as "the first regular battle fought between Free State and proslavery men in Kansas," Sanborn, *John Brown*, p. 241.

20. Ibid., p. 496, Sanborn writes, "There may have been a thousand men who knew he meant to harass the slaveholders in some part of the South with an armed force." The correspondence and memorandum books of John Brown, particularly Memorandum Book No. 2 at the Boston Public Library; the letters of his young men and the girls who replied to them; as well as many letters and statements of John Brown's associates, including testimony before the Mason Committee, indicate that literally scores of people in all parts of the North, from Kansas to Iowa to Ohio to New York to Massachusetts to Pennsylvania, knew something of his plan and that many helped forward it in one way or another. Those named in John Brown's Memorandum Book No. 2, in his letters and the letters of his associates, include the well-known and the nearly anonymous, Negro and white, men and women, many of whom have never been identified as having possible prior knowledge of the John Brown plot. The honor of knowing of the invasion before it was made has been reserved almost exclusively for the so-called Secret Six, the five prominent Bostonians and the wealthy Gerrit Smith. In a later section we shall recur to this evidence.

21. O. B. Frothingham, *Theodore Parker*, Boston, 1870, p. 455.

22. Mason Committee Hearings, pp. 148 and 153. The Mason Report, p. 11, refers to lectures "throughout the country" at which money was raised for Brown and which "appear to have been patronized by the principal men in the States where they were delivered." These lectures, the Report says, were not always made by Brown but sometimes by those who handed over the proceeds to him.

23. *The Liberator*, Oct. 28, 1859.

24. Odell Shepard, ed., *The Journals of Bronson Alcott*, Boston, 1938, p. 316.

25. "Speech on Affairs in Kansas," Cambridge, Mass., Sept. 10, 1856, James Elliot Cabot, ed., *The Works of Ralph Waldo Emerson*, Boston, 1883, vol. XI, *Miscellanies*, p. 248.

26. F. B. Sanborn to JB (John Brown), Concord, Mass., Sept. 14, 1857, Henry P. Slaughter Collection, Trevor Arnett Library, Atlanta University, Atlanta, Ga.

27. F. B. Sanborn to Higginson, Concord, Mass., Sept. 11, 1857, Kansas State Historical Society.

28. Brooks Atkinson, ed., *Walden and Other Writings of Henry David Thoreau*, 1937, New York, p. 639. The quotation is from "Civil Disobedience."

29. *The Journal of Henry D. Thoreau*, vol. XII, Oct. 22, 1859, p. 437.

30. W. P. and F. J. Garrison, *William Lloyd Garrison*, Boston, 1894, vol. III, pp. 453–7.

31. Official orders of Jefferson Davis, Secretary of War, to Col. E. V. Sumner and Lt. Col. Philip St. George, Washington, D.C., Feb. 15, 1856, War Department Records, National Archives. See also annual report for 1856 of Jefferson Davis, Secretary of War, p. 161.

32. President Pierce, May 27, 1854, to Watson Freeman, U. S. Marshal, Boston, Charles Emery Stevens, *Anthony Burns*, Boston, 1856, Appendix H, p. 273.

33. William H. Seward, "The Irrepressible Conflict," a speech delivered at Rochester, N.Y., Oct. 25, 1858, *New*

York Tribune pamphlet, 1860, p. 7. See also Frank Preston Stearns, *George Luther Stearns*, Philadelphia, 1907, on the widespread revolutionary resistance in the North to the Pierce administration, pp. 184–5, 190.

34. A number of American historians, such as Charles A. and Mary R. Beard and Louis M. Hacker, have held, whatever their own emphasis, that the American Civil War was the second American Revolution. Among the latest to take this view are William Appleman Williams, *The Contours of American History*, Cleveland and New York, 1961, pp. 296–303, and Barrington Moore, Jr., *Social Origins of Dictatorship and Democracy*, Boston, 1966, pp. 111–55. If the second Revolution had its Brumaire in the sellout of Reconstruction after 1876, even the French Revolution, one of the most thoroughgoing in history, had suffered that kind of reaction.

35. Cleveland *Plain Dealer*, March 22, 1859; Cleveland *Leader*, April 29, 1894, an article by J. W. Schuckers, who attended John Brown's lectures in Cleveland in 1859.

36. Collection of Boyd B. Stutler, Charleston, W. Va. Thoreau also saw Brown as a Cromwellian figure as he revealed in his "A Plea for Captain John Brown," Atkinson, ed., *Walden and Other Writings*, pp. 685–6. See also Katherine Mayo, *New York Evening Post*, Oct. 23, 1909, reprinted in Louis Ruchames, ed., *A John Brown Reader*, New York, 1959, p. 234.

37. Commager, ed., *Theodore Parker: An Anthology*, p. 310.

38. JB in a letter to his father from Springfield, Mass., April 2, 1847, denies Owen Brown has cause for the fear expressed in a previous letter, Stutler Collection.

39. JB to F. B. Sanborn, Peterboro, N.Y., Feb. 24, 1858, Sanborn, *John Brown*, pp. 444–5.

40. JB to Hon. D. R. Tilden, from Charlestown, Jefferson Co., Va., Nov. 28, 1859, James Redpath, *The Public Life of Captain John Brown*, Boston, 1860, p. 359.

41. JB to "Dear Wife & Children every One," Charlestown, Jefferson Co., Va., Nov. 8, 1859, Massachusetts Historical Society, Boston; also copies in Stutler Collection and Dreer Collection.

42. Higginson, *Cheerful Yesterdays*, pp. 226–34; *New York Tribune*, Nov. 9, 1858; MS. of interview with Higginson, by K. Mayo, Villard Collection; Oswald Garrison Villard, *John Brown, 1800–1859, A Biography Fifty Years After*, Boston, 1910, pp. 511–19.

43. John W. LeBarnes, Boston attorney, another leader in the rescue plans, in letters to Higginson, Nov. 14, 15, 22, and 27, 1859, and Spooner to Higginson, Nov. 20, 1859, all in the Higginson Collection, Boston Public Library.

44. Owen Brown, "Owen Brown's Escape From Harper's Ferry As Told . . . To A Well Known Friend," Ohio Historical Society, Columbus, Ohio.

45. *The Journal of Henry D. Thoreau*, vol. XIII, Dec. 3, 1859, pp. 3–4; Walter Harding, *The Days of Henry Thoreau*, New York, 1965, pp. 421–2.

46. Cleveland *Plain Dealer*, Oct. 8, 1899; Jefferson [Ohio] *Gazette*, Oct. 20, 1899; E. C. Lampson, "The Black String Society," E. C. Lampson Collection, Ohio Historical Society; E. C. Lampson, "John Brown and Ashtabula County," typescript, Western Reserve University Libraries, Cleveland; MS. of interviews with Charles D. Ainger, Andover, Ohio, and J. B. Noxon, of Wayne, Ohio, by K. Mayo, Jan. 3 and 4, 1909, Villard Collection.

47. Hinton, *John Brown*, pp. 539–41; C. B. Galbreath, "Barclay Coppoc," *Ohio Archeological and Historical Quarterly*, Columbus, Ohio, October 1921, pp. 469–77.

48. *New York Herald*, Nov. 2 and 12, 1859.

49. Stearns, *George Luther Stearns*, pp.

188 and 198; Harold Schwartz, *Samuel Gridley Howe*, Cambridge, Mass., 1956, pp. 238–9; Hinton, *John Brown*, an article in the appendix by Mrs. Mary E. Stearns, "George Luther Stearns and John Brown," pp. 726–7; Senator Charles Sumner, letters from Boston, Nov. 23, 1859, and from Senate Chamber, Dec. 8, 1859, to Howe refer to Howe's flight, Houghton Library, Harvard University.

50. James Redpath, ed., *Echoes of Harper's Ferry*, Boston, 1860, p. 68. The quotation is from a letter of Parker's of Nov. 24, 1859, to Francis Jackson of Boston.

51. F. B. Sanborn, *Recollections of Seventy Years*, Boston, 1909, vol. I, pp. 208–11.

52. Stearns, *George Luther Stearns*, p. 198.

53. Frederick Douglass, *Life and Times of Frederick Douglass*, Hartford, Conn., 1882, p. 326.

54. John W. LeBarnes in a letter to Higginson, Nov. 22, 1859, Higginson Collection, Boston Public Library.

55. Jennie Dunbar describes her trip to see the Governor at Richmond as well as her visit with Stevens just before he was hanged in a letter to James Redpath from Cherry Valley, Ohio, on May 7, 1860. Copy in the Villard Collection.

56. Reminiscences of James Hanway, Topeka *Commonwealth*, Jan. 31, 1878. The young woman from Kansas was Mary Partridge, whose brother George had been killed when fighting under Brown at the Battle of Osawatomie. She never went to Virginia because of John Brown's refusal to consent to rescue plans.

57. Hinton, *John Brown*, p. 366; Villard, *John Brown*, pp. 421–42.

58. MS. interview with Mrs. Russell, by K. Mayo, Jan. 11, 1908, Villard Collection.

59. To Samuel Pomeroy, later U. S. senator from Kansas, who visited Brown at the Charlestown jail where he proposed Brown's rescue, according to Pomeroy's story in the *Christian Cynosure*, March 31, 1887. John Brown greeted Pomeroy with the biblical quotation, " 'In prison ye came unto me.' " Villard, *John Brown*, p. 546.

60. Higginson, *Cheerful Yesterdays*, pp. 231–4; Hinton, *John Brown*, pp. 520–6. Hinton was also a leader and a participant in the rescue attempts.

61. Hinton, *John Brown*, pp. 396–7 and 401.

62. Higginson, *Cheerful Yesterdays*, pp. 233–4; Hinton, *John Brown*, pp. 501–2.

63. *New York Herald*, Nov. 16, 1859; Clement Eaton, *A History of the Southern Confederacy*, New York, 1954, pp. 1–3.

64. *New York Herald*, Oct. 27 and 29, 1859. See also Mason Committee Hearings for testimony of Seward, pp. 253–5, and Wilson, pp. 140–5, and Sanborn-Higginson correspondence, Boston Public Library.

65. Most of those mentioned are listed in John Brown's Memorandum Book No. 2, Boston Public Library. Sanborn in a letter to Higginson, June 4, 1859, indicates something of Harriet Tubman's part in the conspiracy, Higginson Collection; Lewis Hayden writing Mrs. Stearns, April 8, 1878, tells of recruiting Francis J. Meriam and others for John Brown's band, copy Villard Collection; John Brown writing to the Rev. J. W. Loguen, May 1859, asks him to be chaplain to the slaves he hoped to free in Virginia, J. W. Loguen, *As a Slave and a Freeman*, Syracuse, N.Y., 1859, p. 451; Sanborn, *John Brown*, p. 451; Hinton, *John Brown*, pp. 169 and 178.

66. Mason Report, testimony of John B. Floyd, Secretary of War, March 5, 1860, p. 251. The two brothers were David J. and Benjamin F. Gue. Their cousin was A. L. Smith. MS. interview with David J. Gue, by K. Mayo, November 1907, Villard Collection.

67. James Redpath, *The Roving Editor or*

Talks with Slaves in the Southern States, New York, 1859, pp. iii–vii.

68. Lydia Maria Child to "Dear Captain Brown," Wayland [Mass.], Oct. 26, 1859, *Letters of Lydia Maria Child*, with a biographical introduction by John G. Whittier and an appendix by Wendell Phillips, Boston, 1883, p. 118; JB to Mrs. L. Maria Child, Charlestown, Jefferson Co., Va., Nov. 4, 1859, Stutler Collection.

69. Sanborn, *John Brown*, p. 621; John Brown acknowledged Mrs. Spring's help in a letter to her from prison on Nov. 24, 1859, copy Stutler Collection.

70. *New York Evening Post*, Oct. 23, 1909, an interview with Mrs. Russell by K. Mayo.

71. Walt Whitman, *Leaves of Grass*, edited by his literary executors, New York, 1891, centenary edition, "Year of Meteors (1859–60)," pp. 291–2.

72. F. O. Matthiessen, ed., *The Oxford Book of American Verse*, New York, 1950, Herman Melville, "The Portent, (1859)," p. 396.

73. Ruchames, ed., *A John Brown Reader*, William Dean Howells, "Old Brown," pp. 266–8.

74. MS. interview with Brackett, by K. Mayo, Jan. 13, 1908, Villard Collection. Brackett also drew plans of the jail for a possible rescue attempt and went to Harrisburg, Pa., with those trying to liberate the last two of the prisoners to be hanged. Also Lydia Maria Child's MS. account of Brackett and his bust of John Brown, Stutler Collection.

75. Redpath, ed., *Echoes of Harper's Ferry*, p. 58.

76. Ibid., pp. 382–3.

77. Ralph L. Rusk, *The Life of Ralph Waldo Emerson*, New York, 1949, p. 402. Emerson made his declaration in a lecture on "Courage" given in Boston on Nov. 8, 1859.

78. Ruchames, ed., *A John Brown Reader*, p. 270.

79. Benjamin P. Thomas, *Theodore Weld,*

Crusader for Freedom, New Brunswick, N.J., 1950, p. 237. "Last night," wrote Sarah Grimké, "I went in spirit to the martyr."

80. Lydia Maria Child to "Dear Mary," Friday, Dec. 2, 1858, Stutler Collection.

81. *The Independent*, New York, Nov. 24, 1859.

82. Thoreau, "A Plea for Captain John Brown," delivered at Concord on Oct. 30, 1859, at a meeting called by Thoreau himself and one of the first public pleas for John Brown. Atkinson, ed., *Walden and Other Writings*, p. 689.

83. *The Journal of Henry D. Thoreau*, vol. XII, Oct. 22, 1859, p. 437.

84. *New York Herald*, Oct. 21, 1859.

85. *The Journal of Henry D. Thoreau*, Dec. 6, 1859, vol. XIII, p. 12.

86. Ibid., Dec. 5, 1859, p. 7.

87. "A Plea for Captain John Brown," from Atkinson, ed., *Walden and Other Writings*, p. 706. The plea was given while John Brown still lived.

88. *The Journal of Henry D. Thoreau*, Oct. 22, 1859, vol. XII, p. 426.

89. Thoreau, "The Last Days of John Brown," Ruchames, ed., *A John Brown Reader*, p. 304.

II
Dramatis Personae

1. Commager, ed., *Theodore Parker: An Anthology*, p. 4.

2. Ibid. From a Parker sermon to a Quaker congregation in Chester Co., Pa., 1858, p. 117.

3. Higginson, *Contemporaries*, "Theodore Parker," pp. 34–59.

4. John Weiss, *Life and Correspondence of Theodore Parker*, New York, 1864. "Experience as a Minister," vol. II, pp. 476–8.

5. Parker's own description of arming himself for defiance of the Fugitive Slave Act as contained in his book, *The Trial of Theodore Parker for the "Misdemeanor" of a Speech In Faneuil Hall against Kidnapping, Before the Circuit Court of The United States,*

at Boston, with the Defence, Boston, 1855, p. 187; a reference to his projected history of religion is in his letter to J. P. Hale, written from Boston, Jan. 9, 1858, Parker Letters, Massachusetts Historical Society.

6. Ralph Waldo Emerson, *Essays, First Series,* "Self-Reliance," new and revised edition Boston, 1884, p. 53.

7. Edward Waldo Emerson and Waldo Emerson Forbes, eds., *Journals of Ralph Waldo Emerson,* Boston, 1913, vol. IX, p. 305; Shepard, *The Journals of Bronson Alcott,* pp. 315–16.

8. *Journals of Emerson,* vol. VIII, p. 316.

9. Ibid., p. 469.

10. *The Trial of Theodore Parker,* p. 186.

11. Redpath, ed., *Echoes of Harper's Ferry,* p. 75.

12. Letters of Theodore Parker, Massachusetts Historical Society.

13. Commager, ed., *Theodore Parker: An Anthology,* p. 243.

14. *The Trial of Theodore Parker,* p. 187.

15. Higginson, *Cheerful Yesterdays,* pp. 4 and 7.

16. Tilden G. Eddelstein, *Strange Enthusiasm, A Life of Thomas Wentworth Higginson,* New Haven, Conn., 1968, pp. 41-2.

17. Higginson, *Cheerful Yesterdays,* pp. 152–3.

18. Ibid., pp. 153–8.

19. Letter of Edmund Quincy, Boston, to Mrs. L. P. Quincy, Aug. 10, 1841, Massachusetts Historical Society; also Harlow, *Gerrit Smith,* p. 45.

20. Samuel J. May, *Some Recollections of Our Anti-Slavery Conflict,* Boston, 1869, "The Rescue of Jerry," pp. 373–83.

21. Harlow, *Gerrit Smith,* p. 306.

22. Ibid., p. 308.

23. *New York Herald,* Nov. 12, 1859.

24. *Journal of Henry D. Thoreau,* vol. VI, pp. 355, 357, and 358.

25. *Frederick Douglass' Paper,* Rochester, June 2, 1854.

26. *Life and Times of Frederick Douglass, passim.*

27. Ibid., pp. 320–1.

28. Letters of Charles Sumner to Samuel Gridley Howe, Washington, D.C., Jan. 15 and 21, 1855, Howe-Sumner Correspondence, Houghton Library.

29. Higginson, *Contemporaries,* "Dr. Howe's Anti-Slavery Career," pp. 294–5.

30. Letter of Wendell Phillips to Elizabeth Pease, Boston, March 9, 1851, W. P. and F. J. Garrison, *W. L. Garrison,* vol. III, p. 324.

31. Copy of a letter by Samuel Gridley Howe, Sept. 26, 1835, to the Greek Secretary of State acknowledging receipt of the honor, Howe Papers, Houghton Library.

32. Laura E. Richards, *Letters and Journals of Samuel Gridley Howe,* Boston, 1909, quoting George P. Hoar, p. 350.

33. *New York Herald,* Oct. 27, 1859; letter of F. B. Sanborn to Thomas Wentworth Higginson, Concord, May 18, 1858, tells of Forbes's disclosures to "Wilson as well as Hale and Seward and God knows how many more. . . ." Higginson Collection, Boston Public Library.

III

The Cast in the South

1. Hudson Strode, *Jefferson Davis, American Patriot, 1808–1861,* New York, 1955, pp. 330 and 335.

2. Varina Howell Davis, *Jefferson Davis, Ex-President of the Confederate States of America, A Memoir,* by His Wife, New York, 1890, vol. I, p. 171.

3. Ibid., vol. I, pp. 169–70; Strode, *Jefferson Davis,* pp. 301-2; William E. Dodd, *Jefferson Davis,* Philadelphia, 1907, pp. 25-6 and 98-9; Burton J. Hendrick, *Statesmen of the Lost Cause,* "Jefferson Davis, Southern Nationalist," New York, 1939, pp. 12–56.

4. Davis, *Jefferson Davis,* vol. I, pp. 171–80; Dodd, *Jefferson Davis,* pp. 107-8.

5. Henry A. Wise, *Seven Decades of the Union,* Philadelphia, 1872, p. 115.

6. Kenneth M. Stampp, *The Peculiar Institution*, New York, 1956, p. 188.

7. Richard Hofstadter, "John C. Calhoun, the Marx of the Master Class," in *The American Political Tradition*, New York, 1954, p. 77.

8. The quotations in these paragraphs are, in order of appearance, from advertisements appearing in the following newspapers: Wilmington [N.C.] *Advertiser*, July 13, 1838; Raleigh [N.C.] *Standard*, July 18, 1838; *The Standard of Union*, Milledgeville [Ga.], Oct. 2, 1838.

9. Fayetteville [N.C.] *Observer*, June 20, 1838; Newborn [N.C.] *Spectator*, Dec. 2, 1836. All the advertisements cited were collected along with hundreds of others by Theodore Dwight Weld, editor of *American Slavery as It Is: Testimony of a Thousand Witnesses*, New York, 1839. "No apologist disputed the evidence published by Theodore Dwight Weld for he gathered it from newspapers and public records," writes Kenneth M. Stampp in *The Peculiar Institution*, p. 180, who lists many similar cases, pp. 109–32. "*American Slavery as It Is* is history well written and well documented," writes Dwight Lowell Dumond in *Anti-Slavery: The Crusade for Freedom in America*, Ann Arbor, Mich., 1961, pp. 249–50. "It is an encyclopedia of knowledge. It is a book of horrors. It is the greatest of the anti-slavery pamphlets. . . . Twenty thousand copies of such widely scattered and prominent papers as the New Orleans *Bee*, Charleston *Courier*, Charleston *Mercury*, Vicksburg *Sentinel*, Huntsville *Democrat*, Memphis *Enquirer*, Montgomery *Advertiser*, Raleigh *Standard*, and Mobile *Register* were searched for advertisements, speeches, court trials, and other evidence of the treatment of slaves."

10. Edward A. Pollard, *The Lost Cause, A New Southern History of the War of the Confederates*, New York, 1866, p. 49.

11. Daniel R. Hundley, *Social Relations in Our Southern States*, New York, 1860, as quoted by Kenneth M. Stampp, ed., *The Causes of the Civil War*, Englewood Cliffs, N.J., 1959, pp. 176–8.

12. *Southern Literary Messenger*, July 1860, from a poem, "The Southern Man," by W. H. Holcombe, and representative of a quantity of similar verses in that magazine during the twenty years before the Civil War. See John Hope Franklin, *The Militant South*, Cambridge, Mass., 1956, pp. 192–213.

13. *Southern Literary Messenger*, March 1847, from a poem signed "Je Reviendra," of Norfolk, Va.

14. Ibid., June 1860, from an unsigned article called "The Difference of Race Between the Northern and Southern People."

15. Muscogee [Ga.] *Herald*, reported in the *New York Tribune*, Sept. 10, 1856.

16. Pollard, *The Lost Cause*, p. 49.

17. W. J. Cash, *The Mind of the South*, New York, 1941, reissued 1954, pp. 18–34.

18. Wise, *Seven Decades of the Union*, p. 30.

19. Mary Boykin Chesnut, *A Diary from Dixie*, New York, 1905, reissued by Ben Ames Williams, ed., Boston, 1961, pp. 21–2.

20. Ibid., pp. 514–15.

21. Stampp, *The Peculiar Institution*, p. 182.

22. Aptheker, *To Be Free*, pp. 44–5.

23. James Grier Sellers, Jr., "The Travail of Slavery," in *The Southerner as American*, James Grier Sellers, Jr., ed., Chapel Hill, N.C., 1960, p. 54.

24. Frederick Law Olmsted, *The Cotton Kingdom*, New York, 1861, reissued New York, 1953, p. 14. The reference to ten bales meant that the man being sold was capable of raising and harvesting that much cotton a season.

25. Sellers, *The Southerner as American*, p. 49.

26. Wise, *Seven Decades*, pp. 27 and 28.

27. Ibid., p. 30.
28. Barton H. Wise, *The Life of Henry A. Wise of Virginia, 1806–1876*, New York, 1899, p. 402.
29. Ibid., p. 75.
30. John B. Jones, *A Rebel War Clerk's Diary*, New York, 1866, reissued New York, 1961, p. 3.
31. Wise, *Henry A. Wise*, pp. 40–1.
32. Don C. Seitz, *Famous American Duels*, New York, 1929, pp. 260–7; Samuel Flagg Bemis, *John Quincy Adams and the Union*, New York, 1956, pp. 377–8; Wise, *Henry A. Wise*, pp. 80–6.
33. Bemis, *John Quincy Adams*, p. 434.
34. Wise, *Henry A. Wise*, pp. 95–101, 206–8; John S. Wise, *The End of an Era*, Cambridge, Mass., 1899, p. 79.
35. Wise, *Henry A. Wise*, pp. 263, 267–8.
36. Avery Craven, *Edmund Ruffin, Southerner, A Study in Secession*, New York, 1932, p. 5.
37. Edmund Ruffin, Diary, Oct. 19 to Dec. 31, 1859, vol. III, from Ruffin's entry for Dec. 2, Library of Congress, Washington, D.C.
38. Ibid., entry for Oct. 26, 1859, Library of Congress.

IV
*Of Time and
Temperament*

1. JB to Theodore Parker, Boston, Mass., March 7, 1858, Sanborn, *John Brown*, p. 449.
2. Sanborn, *Recollections*, vol. I, p. 163, tells of John Brown weeping as he listened to Schubert's *Serenade*. Milton Lusk, John Brown's brother-in-law, related how Brown "prayed with me and shed tears," Sanborn, *John Brown*, p. 34.
3. Redpath, *John Brown*, pp. 111–14.
4. This description of Brown comes from Redpath's account of meeting him this day, May 30, 1856, *op. cit.*; from a daguerreotype taken of him in Kansas at about this time; from George B. Gill's description of him in Kansas in his MS. recollections, Hinton Collection, Kansas State Historical Society; from Salmon Brown, "My Father, John Brown," *The Outlook*, Jan. 25, 1913; and from reminiscences of life in the Brown camp on the Ottawa by August Bondi, typescript, Bondi Papers, Kansas State Historical Society.
5. Redpath, *John Brown*, p. 113.
6. JB to "Dear Wife & Children, Every one," near Brown's Station, Kansas Territory, June 1856, Sanborn, *John Brown*, pp. 236–41.
7. Bondi, Reminiscences, typescript, Kansas State Historical Society.
8. Villard, *John Brown*, p. 8.
9. MS. interview with Salmon Brown, by K. Mayo, Portland, Ore., Oct. 11, 12, and 13, 1908, Villard Collection.
10. Ibid.
11. Hinton, *John Brown*, p. 425.
12. Luke Parson's account of his participation in the Battle of Osawatomie, copy in Stutler Collection.
13. Sanborn in a lecture before the Concord school, March 1857, Stutler Collection.
14. *Emerson's Journals, 1856–1863*, p. 82.
15. Foreman in his letter to Redpath, Dec. 28, 1859, Kansas State Historical Society, writes ". . . for courage and determination Gen. Jackson was never more than his equal."
16. David Donald, *Lincoln Reconsidered*, New York, 1961 edition, Chapter 11, "An Excess of Democracy: The American Civil War and the Social Processes," pp. 209–35.
17. Letter of Charles Sumner to Samuel Gridley Howe, New York, Nov. 26, 1851, Howe-Sumner Correspondence, Houghton Library.
18. Letter of Samuel Gridley Howe to Charles Sumner, "My Well-Beloved Friend," Boston, Nov. 30, 1854. Richards, ed., *Letters of S. G. Howe*, pp. 407–8.
19. Rev. Edward Beecher, *Riots at Alton*, Alton, Ohio, 1838, pp. 91–2.
20. Charles G. Finney, *Lectures on Revivals of Religion*, New York, 1835,

p. 332. See also pp. 25–6 on weeping. In this handbook on revivals, Finney, who was the professor of theology at Oberlin and one of the great religious figures of his time, insists that a church must be four-square for the abolition of slavery before any of its members can gain salvation.

21. Edmund Ruffin, MS., "In Remembrance of Jane Dupuy, formerly Ruffin, Born, January 16th. 1829, Married January 26th, 1854, Died July 24th. 1855," handwritten account in the Edmund Ruffin Papers, Southern Historical Collection, University of North Carolina Library, Chapel Hill, N.C., vol. V.

22. Richard N. Current, *Daniel Webster and the Rise of National Conservatism*, Boston, 1955, p. 185.

23. See Jefferson's *Notes on Virginia*, in *The Writings of Thomas Jefferson*, Andrew A. Lipscomb and Albert E. Bergh, eds., 20 vols. vol. II, pp. 225–8.

24. Thomas, *Theodore Weld, passim*. Weld, who was born in upstate New York in 1803, doubtless influenced John Brown as he did thousands of other Americans. He spoke against slavery all over the Western Reserve, including Hudson, John Brown's home, and one of John Brown's most intimate friends, Augustus Wattles, was brought to abolition by Weld.

25. Theodore Dwight Weld to Angelina Grimké, Thursday, March 1, 1838, from *Letters of Theodore Dwight Weld, Angelina Grimké Weld and Sarah Grimké 1822–1844*, Gilbert H. Barnes and Dwight L. Dumond, eds., New York, 1934, vol. II, pp. 576–8.

26. Ibid., pp. 593–5 and 599.

27. All of the quotations concerning Prentiss are from his friend and contemporary, Joseph G. Baldwin, "Hon. S. S. Prentiss," from *The Flush Times of Alabama and Mississippi*, New York, 1853; reissued with an introduction by William A. Owens, New York, 1957, pp. 144–5, 156–7, and 159.

28. Wise, *The End of an Era*, pp. 94–7; Clement Eaton, *The Growth of Southern Civilization, 1790–1860*, New York, 1961, p. 276.

29. Seitz, *Famous American Duels*, pp. 324–30.

30. President Jackson's proposal was embodied in a bill which passed the Senate by a narrow vote but was defeated in the House of Representatives through crippling amendments.

31. W. P. and F. J. Garrison, *W. L. Garrison*, vol. I, p. 178.

32. Ibid., vol. II, pp. 23–4.

33. Parker Pillsbury, *Acts of the Anti-Slavery Apostles*, Concord, N.H., 1883, pp. 123–203.

34. Maria Weston Chapman, *Right and Wrong in Boston*, Boston, 1836, p. 32.

35. May, *Our Anti-Slavery Conflict*, p. 51. For an account of the Prudence Crandall story, see pp. 39–71. The school was closed in 1834 after an attempt to burn it down and a final attack by a mob which partially wrecked it. Miss Crandall's first trial for operating a school for Negro children resulted in a hung jury; her second in a conviction which was reversed by a higher court on a technicality.

36. Testimony of Mrs. Margaret Ann Caldwell, Jackson, Miss., Jan. 20, 1876, *Report of the Select Committee to Inquire into the Mississippi Election of 1875 . . .*, Report No. 527, 44th Congress, 1st Session, vol. I (serial no. 1669), pp. 435–40.

37. Aptheker, *To Be Free*, p. 204.

38. For additional poems and addresses current during the 1840's and 1850's see the centenary volume, Harvey C. Minnich, ed., *Old Favorites from the McGuffey Readers, 1836–1936*, New York, 1939.

v

The Large
and Varied Land

1. Ralph Waldo Emerson, in "Man, the Reformer," a lecture before the Me-

chanics' Apprentices' Library Association, Jan. 25, 1841, *Nature, Addresses and Lectures,* new and revised edition, Boston, 1884, p. 220.

2. Stampp, *Peculiar Institution,* pp. 29–33.

3. William E. Dodd, *The Cotton Kingdom,* New Haven, Conn., 1920, pp. 118–46.

4. Dwight Lowell Dumond, *Antislavery Origins of the Civil War in the United States,* Ann Arbor, Mich., 1939, reissued 1959, pp. 6–8.

5. Letter of John Brown to Editor of the *Summit Beacon,* Akron, Ohio, Osawatomie, Kansas Territory, Dec. 20, 1855, and printed in *Peterson Magazine,* March 1898. Photostat of magazine article in the Stutler Collection.

6. Hendrick, *Statesmen of the Lost Cause,* pp. 283–301.

7. Letter of Sergeant S. Prentiss to his mother in 1835 as quoted by Charles S. Sydnor, *Slavery in Mississippi,* New York, 1933, p. 146.

8. Thomas Hudson McKee, ed., *The National Platforms of all Political Parties, from 1789 to 1892,* Washington, D.C., 1892, pp. 24–68.

9. Charles Francis Adams, "What Makes Slavery a Matter of National Concern?", pamphlet containing lecture in New York, Jan. 30, 1855, New York, 1855.

10. Curtis B. Sutton to William H. Lyons, Sept. 25, 1853, as quoted in Eaton, *Growth of Southern Civilization,* p. 45; Dodd, *Cotton Kingdom,* pp. 1–10.

11. Letter of Lydia Maria Child to T. D. Weld, Northampton, Dec. 18, 1838, listing Northampton's connections with slavery, *Weld-Grimké Letters,* vol. II, p. 726.

12. From *DeBow's Review,* vol. XXIX, p. 318, as quoted in Philip S. Foner, *Business and Slavery,* Chapel Hill, N.C., 1941, p. 4.

13. Ibid., pp. 285–96.

14. May, *Antislavery Conflict,* pp. 127–8.

15. Robert Waters, *Career and Conversation of John Swinton, Journalist, Orator, Economist,* Chicago, 1902.

16. Something of the unusual extent of the Underground Railroad may be gained from the fact that more than thirty years after slavery, Wilbur Henry Siebert, associate professor of European history in Ohio State University, was able to list the names of some three thousand operators on the Railroad. See Wilbur Henry Siebert, *The Underground Railroad from Slavery to Freedom,* New York, 1898, Appendix E, "Directory of the names of Underground operators, arranged alphabetically by States and Counties," pp. 403–39.

17. JB to T. W. Higginson, Feb. 12, 1858, Higginson, *Cheerful Yesterdays,* p. 218.

18. *Journals of Bronson Alcott,* p. 190.

19. Franklin, *The Militant South,* pp. 96–128; Allan Nevins, *Ordeal of the Union,* New York, 1947, vol. II, pp. 347–79; Philip S. Foner, *A History of Cuba and Its Relations with the United States,* New York, 1963, vol. II, *passim.*

20. As in the case of Commodore Hiram Paulding, who broke up and interned the private army of William Walker in Nicaragua in 1857. See Albert Z. Carr, *The World of William Walker,* New York, 1963, pp. 233–9.

21. McKee, ed., *National Platforms of Political Parties,* p. 61.

22. Franklin, *The Militant South,* pp. 105–12; Foner, *History of Cuba,* vol. II, pp. 41–65. Narcisco Lopez, Cuban adventurer, enjoyed wide Southern support for his Cuban expeditions including that of Jefferson Davis and his friend John A. Quitman, Governor of Mississippi, who with other prominent Southerners hoped for Cuba's annexation as slave territory to the United States. As a result of Lopez's third effort in August 1851, Colonel William L. Crittenden of Kentucky and fifty other Southern volunteers were tried and executed after their Cuban defeat and Lopez was publicly garroted at

Havana on September 1. Later Quitman, as we shall see, organized an invasion but it never came off.

23. Ollinger Crenshaw, "The Knights of the Golden Circle," *American Historical Review*, October 1941, pp. 23–50; C. A. Bridges, "The Knights of the Golden Circle: A Filibustering Fantasy," *The Southwestern Historical Quarterly*, January 1941, pp. 287–302; for the activities of Bickley and the Knights of the Golden Circle in the North during the Civil War, see George Fort Milton, *Abraham Lincoln and the Fifth Column*, New York, 1942, pp. 66–71 and 84–6; for more on Bickley and summaries of Walker, Lopez, Quitman, and other filibusterers, see Franklin, *The Militant South*, pp. 96–128; also for more on Walker and slavery, William Walker, *The War in Nicaragua*, Mobile, Ala., 1860, pp. 272–80.

VI

The Great Transformer

1. Carr, *William Walker*, pp. 23 and 198–205.

2. Charles Francis Adams, *Memoir of John Quincy Adams, Comprising Portions of His Diary from 1795 to 1848*, 12 vols., Philadelphia, 1874–7, vol. IV, p. 531, Feb. 24, 1820.

3. James Ford Rhodes, *History of the United States from the Compromise of 1850*, 6 vols., New York, 1904, vol. I, p. 39. After a year's struggle, Missouri entered the Union as the first trans-Mississippi slave state. During congressional debate, 1820–1, over this expansion of slavery, civil war was frequently threatened.

4. Carl Van Doren, *Benjamin Franklin*, New York, 1941, p. 774.

5. Alice Felt Tyler, *Freedom's Ferment*, Minneapolis, 1944, p. 467.

6. J. Franklin Jameson, *The American Revolution as a Social Movement*, Boston, 1956, p. 23.

7. Bemis, *Adams and the Union, passim.*

8. Henry Steele Commager and Allan Nevins, eds., *The Heritage of America*, Boston, 1939, "The Reverend Mr. Walsh Inspects A Slave Ship," pp. 449–54; W. E. Burghardt DuBois, *The World and Africa*, New York, 1949, pp. 64–5, 56; John Hope Franklin, *From Slavery to Freedom, A History of American Negroes*, New York, 1949, pp. 56–8; Samuel Flagg Bemis, *John Quincy Adams and the Foundation of American Foreign Policy*, New York, 1941, p. 412; Basil Davidson, *Black Mother: The Years of the African Slave Trade*, Boston, 1961, *passim*; David Brion Davis, *The Problem of Slavery in Western Culture*, Ithaca, N.Y., 1966, pp. 181–96.

9. The first cargo of Africans was landed in Virginia in 1619, a year before the Pilgrims landed on Plymouth Rock. Some authorities have held that the Africans were used as indentured servants rather than slaves until about 1640, when the increasing tobacco crop gave slavery an economic and social *raison d'être*. However, the records of this twenty-one-year period are very scanty and if slavery was a development rather than a fact upon the arrival of the first African in Virginia it was a very swift development. See Winthrop P. Jordan, *White Over Black*, Chapel Hill, N.C., 1968, pp. 71–82.

10. Russell B. Nye, *Fettered Freedom*, East Lansing, Mich., 1949, *passim*.

11. Eleanor Flexnor, *Century of Struggle, The Woman's Rights Movement in the United States*, Cambridge, Mass., 1959, p. 41.

12. As in the case of John Humphrey Noyes, an important influence on Garrison and the founder of Oneida in upstate New York. W. P. and F. J. Garrison, *W. L. Garrison*, vol. II, pp. 204–7.

13. George Fitzhugh, who wrote these words in 1856, disclaimed any desire to enslave Northern white workers. He said they were already enslaved, save

for the legal determination of their status as slaves, by a Northern industrial system which he thought more rapacious than the South's slavery. Harvey Wish, *Ante-Bellum, Writings of George Fitzhugh and Hinton Rowan Helper on Slavery*, New York, 1960, pp. 43–156.

14. William H. Seward, *The Irrepressible Conflict,* a speech delivered at Rochester, N.Y., Oct. 25, 1858, and contained in a pamphlet published by the *New York Tribune,* 1860.

15. Letter of Lydia Maria Child to her husband, David Lee Child, Wayland, Mass., Jan. 7, 1857, describing a conversation with Senator Wilson at an anti-slavery fair, *Letters of Lydia Maria Child,* p. 88.

16. *New York Herald,* Oct. 30, 1859, quoting Joshua R. Giddings in a speech recalling Clingman's words in 1850.

17. W. A. Swanberg, *Sickles, The Incredible,* New York, 1956, paperback edition, pp. 21–2.

18. Henry J. Carman and Harold C. Syrett, *A History of the American People,* New York, 1957, vol. I, p. 590.

19. *New York Daily Tribune,* June 5, 1856.

20. Joshua R. Giddings, representative from Ohio, in a letter to Lyman Bryant, from Washington City, July 4, 1846, describes naming his weapons when challenged by a Southerner in the House as "green hydes" and stipulating that "our left hands be tied together to prevent either of us from running away," Western Reserve Historical Society, Cleveland.

21. May 31, 1851.

22. Franklin, *The Militant South,* pp. 88–90.

23. The Wilmot Proviso, the widely backed Northern effort to prohibit slavery in the territory acquired through the Mexican War, provided ample evidence of the North's fears. See Eugene D. Genovese, *The Political Economy of Slavery,* New York, 1965, pp. 243–70, for the forces which made many Southerners favor slavery's expansion in the West and elsewhere.

24. McKee, ed., *National Platforms of Political Parties,* p. 39.

25. See Dodd, *The Cotton Kingdom,* "The Planter in Politics," pp. 118–46, for an account of the South's political domination of the North; also Nevins, *Ordeal of the Union,* vol. II, pp. 194–300, for description of the North's preponderance in railroads, population growth, and immigration.

26. James N. Richardson, ed., *Messages and Papers of the Presidents,* Washington, D.C., 1896–9, vol. V, pp. 197–203.

27. Richard Hofstadter, ed., *Great Issues in American History,* New York, 1958, vol. I, pp. 354–9; Rhodes, *History of the United States,* vol. I, pp. 441–4. Senator Salmon P. Chase of Ohio wrote the protest from a draft prepared by Representative Giddings.

28. Ibid., p. 463.

29. As quoted in *The Liberator,* April 7, 1854.

30. Henry Wilson, *History of the Rise and Fall of the Slave Power in America,* Boston, 1874, vol. II, p. 388.

31. Leverett W. Spring, *Kansas, The Prelude to the War for the Union,* Boston, 1885, p. 24.

32. For a comprehensive contemporary account, much of it eyewitness testimony, of the violence and election-stealing of the Missouri invaders, see the 1,206-page *Report of the Special Committee Appointed to Investigate the Troubles in Kansas,* hereinafter called the *Howard Report,* 34th Congress, 1st Session (House Report No. 200), Washington, D.C., 1856. The congressional committee gained its name from its chairman, William A. Howard, of Michigan. The other members were John Sherman, of Ohio, and Mordecai Oliver, of Missouri.

33. Ibid., pp. 3–100.

34. Ibid., pp. 30–3, 357–8; Charles Robinson, *The Kansas Conflict,* New York,

1892, pp. 103–20; Spring, *Kansas*, pp. 43–50; *New York Tribune*, May 17, 1856.

35. *New York Tribune*, April 9, 1856.

36. The New York area around Oneida from Troy on the east to Auburn on the west was known as the Burned-Over Region because the great revivals there between 1825 and 1830 were said to have burned out sin in a great wave of repentance and regeneration.

37. Samuel A. Johnson, *The Battle Cry of Freedom, The New England Emigrant Aid Company in the Kansas Crusade*, Lawrence, Kan., 1954, *passim*, but particularly pp. 124–8.

38. David Donald, *Charles Sumner and the Coming of the Civil War*, New York, 1961, pp. 304–7.

39. *Alleged Assault Upon Senator Sumner*, 34th Congress, 1st session (House Report No. 182), Washington, D.C., 1856, pp. 23–4.

40. Massachusetts Historical Society *Proceedings, Boston*, 1927–8, LXI, p. 222.

41. *New York Tribune*, May 23, 24, and 25, 1856; Donald, *Charles Sumner*, pp. 288–311.

42. Everett to Horace Maynard, Oct. 3, 1857, as quoted by Donald, *Charles Sumner*, p. 300.

43. Speech of Hon. William H. Seward, of New York, in the Senate of the United States, April 9, 1856, *New York Tribune* pamphlet, 1856, p. 11.

44. *Howard Report*, p. 63. The slain man, captured by a pro-slavery militia company called the Kickapoo Rangers, was R. P. Brown. The Kickapoo Rangers wore hatchets as side arms.

45. Villard, *John Brown*, p. 201.

46. Owen Brown describes his father's costume and his demand for Pate's surrender in his eyewitness account of the Battle of Black Jack, dictated to his brother John, and in the latter's handwriting. John Brown, Jr., Papers, Ohio Historical Society.

VII

*Portrait of
the Old Man*

1. The *New York Tribune*, for example, on June 9, 11, 17, and 20, July 4, 8, and 11, 1856, carried descriptions of the battle and its aftermath, some fragmentary but most naming John Brown as the victor at Black Jack, sometimes called the Battle of Palmyra. On July 11, 1856, the *Tribune* published a long account of the battle written by John Brown himself, and sent by Brown to the New York newspaper from Kansas.

2. The Rev. Samuel Orcutt, *History of Torrington, Connecticut*, Albany, N.Y., 1878, p. 817. Torrington, John Brown's birthplace, was frequently visited by him since he had friends and relatives there. Orcutt writes, "He was remarkably clear-sighted and quick of ear and so acute of smell that he could perceive the frying of doughnuts at a distance of five miles as he once told me."

3. *Frederick Douglass' Paper*, Rochester, N.Y., Jan. 27, 1854, Spingarn Collection, Howard University, Washington, D.C.

4. From John Brown's *Words of Advice* to Branch of the United States League of Gileadites, Sanborn, *John Brown*, pp. 124–6.

5. Ibid., pp. 371–2. Sanborn himself used these words in introducing John Brown to a committee of the Massachusetts legislature.

6. JB to Henry L. Stearns, "My Dear Young Friend, Red Rock, Iowa, 15th. July, 1857," copy, Stutler Collection.

7. JB to John Brown, Jr., "Dear Son, Richfield 25th. Sept., 1843," Illinois State Historical Society, Springfield, Ill.

8. JB to Henry L. Stearns, July 15, 1857.

9. Ibid.

10. Ibid.

11. Salmon Brown, *The Outlook*, Jan. 25, 1913.

12. JB to John Brown, Jr., Sept. 25, 1843, Illinois State Historical Society.

13. JB to "Dear Children, Troy, N.Y., 23 Jany 1852," Chicago Historical Society.

14. JB to "Dear Father, Springfield, Mass. 16th. June, 1848," Sanborn, *John Brown*, pp. 24–5.

15. Foreman to Redpath, Dec. 28, 1859.

16. Douglass, *Frederick Douglass*, p. 279.

17. John Brown admitted the misuse of the money in a letter to "George Kellogg, Esqr. Dear Sir: Franklin Mills, 27th. Aug. 1839," Library of Congress.

18. John Brown, Jr., quoted his father as declaring he had lived under the weight of debt "like a toad under a harrow" in a letter to Sanborn, Sanborn, *John Brown*, p. 88.

19. Ibid., p. 122.

20. Villard, *John Brown*, p. 20.

21. Thoreau, *Journal*, vol. XII, Oct. 22, 1859, p. 420.

22. JB to Henry L. Stearns, July 15, 1857.

23. Ibid.

24. Ibid.

25. Interview with John Brown, Jr., *Cleveland Press*, May 3, 1895.

26. JB to his father, Owen Brown, "Dear Father: Randolph, Pa. Aug. 11, 1832," from copy owned by the Rev. Clarence S. Gee, Lockport, N.Y.

27. JB to "Dear Sons John, Jason, & Frederick, & Daughters, Springfield, Mass 4th. Decem 1850," Brown Papers, Ohio Historical Society.

28. Sanborn, *John Brown*, pp. 37, 39.

29. Ruth Brown Thompson, John Brown's daughter, as quoted in Sanborn, *John Brown*, p. 94.

30. Ibid.

31. Ibid.

32. Ibid.

33. MS. interview with Miss Sarah Brown, John Brown's daughter, by K. Mayo, at Saratoga, Calif., Sept. 16, 1908, Villard Collection. Miss Brown and others of the Brown children said their father read *The Liberator*, first in the home of his own father, Owen Brown, in Hudson, and then subscribing to it himself while it was still a young newspaper when he was living in Ohio and later at North Elba, New York. In addition, Miss Sarah Brown said her father read the *Anti-Slavery Standard* and *Frederick Douglass' Paper*.

34. Frederick Douglass, typescript of "A Lecture on John Brown, delivered at Harper's Ferry, May 30, 1882," p. 28, Douglass Papers, National Park Service, Washington, D.C.

35. MS. of interview with Benjamin Kent Waite, Columbus, Ohio, by K. Mayo, Dec. 26 and 27, 1908, Villard Collection. Waite knew Brown when both lived in Hudson.

36. Douglass, "A Lecture on John Brown," p. 28.

37. Louis Filler, ed., "John Brown in Ohio, An Interview with Charles S. S. Griffing," *Ohio State Archaeological and Historical Quarterly*, Columbus, Ohio, April 1849. This article describes some of John Brown's exploits on the Underground Railroad. See also Charles Francis Adams, *Richard Henry Dana, A Biography*, Boston, 1891, vol. I, p. 156, for some mention of his Underground Railroad activities in North Elba.

38. John Brown, Jr., to F. B. Sanborn, Put-in-Bay, Ohio, Dec. 12, 1890, Stutler Collection.

39. Douglass, "A Lecture on John Brown," pp. 27 and 28.

40. Thoreau, "The Last Days of John Brown," read at July 4, 1860, ceremony at John Brown's home, North Elba, New York. From *The Writings of Henry David Thoreau*, Boston, 1894, vol. X, pp. 237–8.

41. Wise, *Henry A. Wise*, pp. 246–7, 251–2.

42. JB to "My Dear Wife & Children Everyone, Hudson, Ohio, 27 May, 1857," Villard Collection.

43. Brooks Adams, *The Emancipation of Massachusetts*, Boston, 1887, reissued

Boston, 1962, with a new introduction by Perry Miller, Intro., p. xxx.

44. Extracts from an undated address delivered at Meadville, Pa., by George Delamater, who as a boy lived with John Brown, Villard Collection. The description below of a typical evening in John Brown's Randolph home also comes in part from Delamater's address.

45. Salmon Brown, *The Outlook*, Jan. 25, 1913.

46. Ibid.

47. George B. Delamater, *op. cit.*

48. Ibid.

49. Ibid.

50. John Brown described the use of the Duke of Argyle's name at moments of exasperation as an old Scottish custom, according to Owen Brown's journal for Monday, Dec. 8, 1857. Excerpts from this journal, incorrectly described as Jason Brown's, were carried in the *New York Times* of Oct. 24, 1859.

51. JB to "Dear Sons . . . and Daughters," etc., Dec. 4, 1850, Ohio Historical Society.

52. Sanborn, *John Brown*, p. 34.

53. Foreman to Redpath, Dec. 28, 1859.

54. Ibid.

55. Salmon Brown, *The Outlook*, Jan. 25, 1913.

56. Ruth Brown Thompson, John Brown's eldest daughter, to Sanborn, Sanborn, *John Brown*, p. 39.

VIII
The American Moses

1. JB to "Dear Mary, Springfield, 29th Nov 1846," Stutler Collection.

2. JB to "Dear Wife, Springfield, Mass 13th. Dec. 1849," Huntington Library.

3. JB to "Dear Wife, Akron, 22d. Aug 1850," Huntington Library.

4. Undated letter of JB, Slaughter Collection.

5. JB to "Dear Father, Centreville (Allegany Co N Y) 9th April 1839," copy in Villard Collection.

6. Ibid.

7. JB to "Dear Mary, Canal Boat, Union Mills, 4 miles from Buffalo Evening of 23d. Nov. 1845," Huntington Library.

8. JB to "Dear Son John. Hudson 18th Jany 1841," Ohio Historical Society.

9. JB to "Dear Son John, Richfield, Ohio, July 24, 1843," Sanborn, *John Brown*, pp. 58–9.

10. JB to "Dear Son John, Cleveland, June 22, 1844," Sanborn, *John Brown*, p. 61.

11. JB to "Dear Son, Richfield, 11th Jany 1844," Ohio Historical Society.

12. JB to "Dear Son John, Akron 23d May 1845," Massachusetts Historical Society.

13. JB to "Dear Son John, August 26, 1853, Akron, Ohio," Sanborn, *John Brown*, pp. 45–51. The original is in the Stutler Collection.

14. JB to "Dear Ruth, Akron, Ohio, 19th. Aug. 1852," Huntington Library.

15. C. F. Adams, *Richard Henry Dana*, vol. I, p. 146. Not much later John Brown built a house of his own near the cabin in which Dana met him.

16. Ibid., pp. 155–60.

17. JB to Henry L. Stearns, July 15, 1857.

18. JB to "My Dearly beloved Wife, Sons: & Daughters, *every one*, Charlestown Prison, Jefferson Co. Va. 30th Nov 1859," Dreer Collection.

19. JB to Henry L. Stearns, July 15, 1857.

20. "J.B.'s marked Bible texts in Charlestown prison," Villard Collection; also Ruth Brown Thompson's list of her father's favorite Bible passages, Sanborn, *John Brown*, p. 39. The Bible used by John Brown at Charlestown is owned by the Chicago Historical Society.

21. MS. of interview with Miss Sarah Brown, by K. Mayo, Sept. 16–20, 1908, Villard Collection.

22. W. A. Phillips, "Three Interviews with Old John Brown," *Atlantic Monthly*, XLIV, December 1879.

IX
In the Beginning

1. Henry Adams, *History of the United States of America During the First Ad-*

ministration of Thomas Jefferson, New York, 1889, the first six chapters of which were reissued as *The United States in 1800*, Ithaca, N.Y., 1955, p. 12.

2. Clarence S. Gee, ed., *Owen Brown's Autobiography*, Lockport, N.Y., 1960, an unpublished monograph of eight single-spaced pages, p. 3. The autobiographical material is taken from Owen Brown's letters to his children, partly printed in many biographies but assembled in their entirety here.

3. Ibid., p. 5.

4. Ibid., p. 1.

5. Herbert Aptheker, *American Negro Slave Revolts*, New York, 1943, pp. 219–20.

6. Ibid., pp. 223–4.

7. Dumas Malone, *Jefferson and the Ordeal of Liberty*, Boston, 1962, p. 480.

8. *The Writings of Thomas Jefferson*, vol. XVII, pp. 102–3; vol. II, pp. 225–8; vol. XV, p. 250.

9. Jefferson in his *Notes on Virginia* gives an eyewitness account of the scene at the meeting of the rivers. It is quoted in many places, including Claude G. Bowers, *The Young Jefferson*, Boston, 1945, pp. 291–2.

10. See Daniel J. Boorstein, *The Lost World of Thomas Jefferson*, New York, 1948, reissued Boston, 1960, pp. 194–8, for the degree to which slavery impeached Jefferson's philosophy of rights, and pp. 92–4, for the equivocation implanted by slavery in other of Jefferson's most basic ideas. See also Jordan, *White Over Black*, "Thomas Jefferson, Self and Society," pp. 429–81. See, too, Hofstadter, *The American Political Tradition*, "Thomas Jefferson: The Aristocrat as Democrat," particularly pp. 19, 21, 24, and 25, for the contradiction between Jefferson's views on all men being created equal and his role as slaveholder.

11. "But if something is not done, and soon done," Jefferson wrote in a typical passage, this one referring to a slave insurrection in Santo Domingo and a possible insurrection in Virginia, "we shall be murderers of our own children." Letter to St. George Tucker, Aug. 28, 1797, *The Writings of Thomas Jefferson*, vol. IX, pp. 417–18. Three years later he was involved with a Virginia insurrection, the Gabriel Rebellion.

12. Dreer Collection; also Hinton, *John Brown*, pp. 619, 637–43, "A Declaration of Liberty by the Representatives of the Slave Population of the United States." This document, described as "Brown's Declaration of Independence" by Hinton, is reported to have been among the documents seized near the Kennedy Farm House, gathering point of the John Brown forces before the Harper's Ferry raid. The document in the Dreer Collection purports to be a copy of the original draft by John Brown. It may have been written by one of his black followers for its language and spelling do not suggest John Brown's style. The last line comes from Shakespeare's *Henry VI, Part I*, Scene I, line 1: "Hung be the heavens with black, yield day to night." Preachers often used the quotation, which may have given the writer familiarity with it. His own initiative apparently was responsible for the change from black to scarlet.

13. JB to Henry L. Stearns, July 15, 1857.

14. Ibid.

15. Gee, *Owen Brown's Autobiography*, pp. 4–5.

16. Ibid., p. 5, for description of the route; see also Karl H. Grismer, *Akron and Summit County*, Akron, Ohio, n.d., pp. 45–6, for a description of the route and other aspects of the movement west from Connecticut to Ohio.

17. Lucius V. Bierce, *Historical Reminiscences of Summit County*, Akron, Ohio, 1854, p. 83.

18. Gee, *Owen Brown's Autobiography*, p. 5.

19. Christian Cackler, *Recollections of an Old Settler*, p. 9, undated pamphlet

containing reminiscences of a Hudson pioneer, Western Reserve Historical Society, Cleveland.

20. JB to Henry L. Stearns, July 15, 1857.
21. P. P. Cherry, *The Western Reserve and Early Ohio*, Akron, Ohio, 1921, pp. 76–9, and Lora Case, typescript, *Personal Reminiscences, of an Aged Pioneer*, Hudson Library and Historical Society, Hudson, Ohio. Mr. Case was a friend of the Browns. Both Mr. Cherry and Case describe the construction of cabins of the type in which the Browns lived, as well as details of the daily life within them.
22. Gee, *Owen Brown's Autobiography*, p. 5.
23. Case, *Reminiscences*.
24. Gee, *Owen Brown's Autobiography*, p. 5.
25. Ibid., p. 2.
26. Case, *Reminiscences*.
27. JB to Henry L. Stearns, July 15, 1857.
28. Case, *Reminiscences*.
29. JB to Henry L. Stearns, July 15, 1857.
30. Ibid.
31. Ibid.
32. Ibid.
33. Ibid.
34. Ibid.
35. Ibid.
36. Emily Metcalf, MS. history of *The First Congregational Church of Hudson, Ohio*, the Hudson Library and Historical Society.
37. Gee, *Owen Brown's Autobiography*, p. 5.
38. Ibid.
39. Metcalf, *First Congregational Church*; Bierce, *Historical Reminiscences*, pp. 87, 88; Cherry, *The Western Reserve*, p. 132; F. C. Waite, *Western Reserve University, The Hudson Era*, Cleveland, 1934, p. 19.
40. Metcalf, *First Congregational Church*; Villard, *John Brown*, p. 17.
41. Elizur Wright to Elizur Wright, Jr., Talmadge, Sept. 29, 1823, Wright Letters, Western Reserve Historical Society, Cleveland.
42. Metcalf, *First Congregational Church*.
43. JB to Henry L. Stearns, July 15, 1857.
44. Sanborn, *John Brown*, p. 38; Villard, *John Brown*, p. 16.
45. Gee, *Owen Brown's Autobiography*, p. 5.
46. Cherry, *The Western Reserve*, pp. 250–62.
47. Cackler, *Recollections*.
48. *Sesquicentennial of Hudson, Ohio*, June 17, 1950, pamphlet, *passim*.
49. JB to Henry L. Stearns, July 15, 1857.
50. Gee, *Owen Brown's Autobiography*, p. 5.
51. JB to Henry L. Stearns, July 15, 1857.
52. MS. interview with Mrs. Danley Hobart, Levi Blakeslee's daughter, by K. Mayo, December 1908, Villard Collection.
53. Cackler, *Recollections*, pp. 37, 38.
54. Sanborn, *John Brown*, p. 33.
55. JB to Henry L. Stearns, July 15, 1857.
56. Ibid.

X

*On Growing Older
and Eli Whitney*

1. Alfred A. Thomas tells of such an instance in his *Correspondence of Thomas Ebenezer Thomas: The Anti-Slavery Conflict in Ohio*, Dayton, Ohio, 1909, p. 6.
2. Cackler, *Recollections*, p. 7.
3. Ibid., p. 11.
4. Ibid., p. 2.
5. Ibid., p. 29.
6. Dumond, *Antislavery: The Crusade for Freedom in America*, pp. 50–1.
7. Sanborn, *John Brown*, pp. 10–11.
8. Gee, *Owen Brown's Autobiography*, p. 6. (War was declared June 18, 1812, but military action in the Northwest did not begin until July.)
9. Case, *Reminiscences*; Cackler, *Recollections*, p. 16; P. G. Wright and E. Q. Wright, *Elizur Wright, The Father of Life Insurance*, Chicago, 1937, pp. 8, 9.
10. JB to Henry L. Stearns, July 15, 1857.
11. Despite the Ordinance of 1787 prohibiting slavery in the Northwest and

Ohio, there were occasional slaves in the state, usually brought there by Southerners. Court action would have been necessary to free them, action not often taken until a much later time.

12. JB to Henry L. Stearns, July 15, 1857.

13. Ibid.

14. Sanborn, *John Brown*, pp. 19, 20 n.

15. A court-martial sentenced Hull to death for cowardice but the sentence was remitted because of his heroic record in the Revolutionary War.

16. Craven, *Edmund Ruffin*, p. 4.

17. JB to Henry L. Stearns, July 15, 1857.

18. Owen Brown in his first will drawn up in 1816 left his tannery to John Brown. Copy of will in Hudson Library and Historical Society.

19. JB to Henry L. Stearns, July 15, 1857.

20. Ibid.

21. Sanborn, *John Brown*, p. 34 n.

22. JB to Henry L. Stearns, July 15, 1857.

23. Metcalf, *First Congregational Church*.

24. The psalms and hymns whose first lines are quoted are from Isaac Watts, *Psalms of David, Hymns and Spiritual Songs*, Boston, 1791, pp. 217, 203, 11, 201, and 193. Familiarly known as *Watt's Hymnal*, this edition and later ones were widely used on the Western Reserve.

25. P. G. and E. Q. Wright, *Elizur Wright*, p. 16.

26. Elizur Wright to his son, August 4, 1823, Western Reserve Historical Society.

27. JB to Henry L. Stearns, July 15, 1857.

28. Ibid.

29. Redpath, *John Brown*, p. 36.

30. Sanborn, *John Brown*, p. 31 n.

31. Redpath, *Echoes of Harper's Ferry*, p. 388.

32. Foreman to Redpath, Dec. 28, 1859.

33. Ibid.

34. JB to Henry L. Stearns, July 15, 1857.

35. MS. interview with Mrs. Danley Hobart, by K. Mayo, 1908, Villard Collection.

36. JB to Henry L. Stearns, July 15, 1857.

37. Ibid.

38. Sanborn, *John Brown*, pp. 33-4.

39. Ibid., p. 32.

40. Phillips, *Atlantic Monthly*, XLIV, December 1879.

41. Metcalf, *First Congregational Church*.

42. Waite, *Western Reserve University*, p. 15.

43. A. S. Fletcher, *A History of Oberlin College*, Oberlin, Ohio, 1943, vol. I, p. 81.

44. Metcalf, *First Congregational Church*.

45. Grismer, *Akron and Summit County*, p. 110.

46. Ibid., pp. 108-9.

47. Theodore Weld to C. G. Finney, Cincinnati, Ohio, Feb. 28, 1832, *Weld-Grimké Letters*, vol. I, p. 66; J. J. Shipherd to Z. R. Shipherd, April 6, 1831; Fletcher, *History of Oberlin College*, vol. I, p. 76.

48. Foreman to Redpath, Dec. 28, 1859.

49. *California Christian Advocate*, July 18, 1894, Villard Collection.

50. MS. interview with Mrs. Danley Hobart, by K. Mayo, 1908, Villard Collection.

51. Foreman to Redpath, Dec. 28, 1859.

52. Ibid.

53. Ibid.

54. Ibid.

55. File on Hudson Pioneers, undated clippings from Hudson *Independent*, Hudson Library and Historical Society.

56. Jeanette Mirsky and Allan Nevins, *The World of Eli Whitney*, New York, 1962, p. 296.

57. Ibid., p. 296; Constance McL. Green, *Eli Whitney and the Birth of American Technology*, Boston, 1956, p. 185.

58. Frederic Bancroft, *Slave-Trading in the Old South*, Baltimore, 1931, as quoted in Eaton, *The Growth of Southern Civilization*, pp. 53-4.

59. The expression used by Joseph G. Baldwin to describe this period in the Gulf States and the title of his book on the subject published in 1853.

60. MS. interview with Miss Sarah Brown, John Brown's daughter, by K. Mayo, 1908, Villard Collection, in which she

said her father regularly read *The Liberator*, seeing it first in his father's home in Hudson. He apparently saw it infrequently during his ten years in Pennsylvania, except when visiting his father in Hudson, but upon his return to Ohio again read it regularly. A good many other of John Brown's relatives and friends also say he read *The Liberator* and other anti-slavery newspapers which not only told of the exploits of Weld, Garrison, and Wright but gave the widest news as to slavery, its proponents and opponents. Miss Sarah Brown in her interview in the Villard Collection said that her father also subscribed to the *Anti-Slavery Standard*, the *New York Tribune*, and *Frederick Douglass' Paper*.

XI
The Drama of Self

1. Waite, *Western Reserve University*, pp. 94–111; Fletcher, *History of Oberlin College*, vol. I, pp. 142–5; Wright, *Elizur Wright*, pp. 58–65; Case, *Reminiscences*.
2. Fletcher, *History of Oberlin College*, vol. I, Chap. XVIII, "Hotbed of Abolitionism," pp. 236–53.
3. Wright, *Elizur Wright*, p. 52.
4. Metcalf, *First Congregational Church*.
5. Waite, *Western Reserve University*, pp. 95–7.
6. Elizur Wright, Dec. 11, 1832, to Garrison, published in *The Liberator*, Jan. 5, 1833; also Beriah Green to Garrison, published in the same issue of *The Liberator*. Both the participants in the controversy and its later historians are unanimous in insisting that it was precipitated by reading *The Liberator*.
7. W. P. and F. J. Garrison, *W. L. Garrison*, vol. IV, p. 323.
8. Walter M. Merrill, ed., *Behold Me Once More*, Boston, 1954.
9. W. P. and F. J. Garrison, *W. L. Garrison*, vol. I, p. 76.
10. Ibid., vol. IV, p. 314.
11. Waite, *Western Reserve University*, p. 95.
12. *The Liberator*, March 30, 1833.
13. May, *Recollections*, pp. 36–7.
14. *The Liberator*, Jan. 1, 1831.
15. W. P. and F. J. Garrison, *W. L. Garrison*, vol. I, p. 297.
16. Ibid., pp. 299, 300 *n*.
17. Waite, *Western Reserve University*, pp. 96–7.
18. Ibid., pp. 92–100.
19. Ibid., p. 99.
20. *Weld-Grimké Letters*, vol. I, p. 95.
21. Thomas, *Theodore Weld*, p. 36.
22. Wright, *Elizur Wright*, p. 16.
23. Case, *Reminiscences*.
24. Waite, *Western Reserve University*, pp. 101–2.
25. Elizur Wright to his son, Jan. 25, 1829, Western Reserve Historical Society. Hudson was in Portage County until 1840, when it became a part of the newly created Summit County.
26. Elizur Wright to his son, June 24, 1836, Western Reserve Historical Society.
27. Case, *Reminiscences*.
28. Waite, *Western Reserve University*, p. 103.
29. Ibid.
30. MS. interview with John Brown's daughter, Miss Sarah Brown, by K. Mayo, Sept. 16, 1908, Villard Collection.
31. Foreman to Redpath, Dec. 28, 1859.
32. Fletcher, *Oberlin College*, vol. I, p. 145.
33. The communities listed are from the *Annual Report of the American Anti-Slavery Society*, New York, 1837, pp. 135–40, which listed anti-slavery societies organized since 1833. From the beginning of that year to the end of 1836, 213 local anti-slavery societies had been organized by residents of towns and villages.
34. JB to "My Dear Afflicted Wife & Children," Springfield, Mass., Nov. 8, 1846, Villard, *John Brown*, pp. 35–6.

35. Foreman to Redpath, Dec. 28, 1859.
36. Ibid.
37. Ibid.
38. Ibid.
39. Higginson, *Cheerful Yesterdays*, p. 219.
40. Adams, *R. H. Dana*, p. 157.
41. Ernest C. Miller, *John Brown, Pennsylvania Citizen*, Warren, Pa., 1952, p. 7.
42. Foreman to Redpath, Dec. 28, 1859.
43. MS. interview with George B. Gill, by K. Mayo, 1908, Villard Collection.
44. E. W. Emerson, Ralph Waldo Emerson's son, and the Rev. H. L. Wayland, as quoted in F. B. Sanborn, *Recollections*, vol. I, pp. 109 and 114.
45. MS. interview with Jason Brown, by K. Mayo, 1908, Villard Collection; Sanborn, *John Brown*, p. 94.
46. In his letter to "My Dear Afflicted Wife & Children," *op. cit.*, John Brown makes such a statement. It was a favorite admonition both to his children and employees, according to his daughter Ruth Brown Thompson.
47. Salmon Brown, *The Outlook*, Jan. 25, 1913.
48. Miller, *John Brown, Pennsylvania Citizen*, p. 17.
49. Stutler Collection.
50. Ibid.
51. JB to Seth Thompson, Randolph, Sept. 6, 1830, Slaughter Collection. All JB letters to Seth Thompson are in the Slaughter Collection unless otherwise designated.
52. JB to Seth Thompson, Randolph, Feb. 18, 1831.
53. Slaughter Collection.
54. Ibid.
55. Ibid.
56. Foreman to Redpath, Dec. 28, 1859. Foreman says these questions were two of a series debated with a Randolph preacher.
57. Mrs. Mary E. Stearns to Richard J. Hinton, undated MS., Kansas State Historical Society; Henry Thoreau suggests the similarity when he calls John Brown's Kansas military company "a perfect Cromwellian troop," in "A Plea for Captain John Brown," address delivered at Concord, Oct. 30, 1859; Thomas Wentworth Higginson, another friend of Brown's and a member of the so-called Secret Six, also suggests his Cromwellian impact when he calls him "a belated Covenanter" in *Cheerful Yesterdays*, p. 219.
58. *Journals of Emerson*, vol. IX, February 1857, p. 82.
59. John Brown memorandum Book No. 1, Boston Public Library.
60. Phillips, *Atlantic Monthly*, XLIV, December 1859, tells how John Brown recited the story of Spartacus in 1859 when telling of his forthcoming raid as proof that slaves would fight. The account of the slave revolt led by Spartacus in *Plutarch's Lives* is given in the biography of Crassus.
61. John Brown's Memorandum Book No. 2, Boston Public Library, contains a notation, probably entered in 1855, about the Spanish guerrillas in the Napoleonic wars.
62. John Brown may have read Rollin after leaving Randolph, since one of the first American editions of his work was published in New York by Harper & Brothers in 1846. There had been, however, many English translations published in London.
63. JB to the Rev. H. L. Vail, Charlestown, Jefferson Co., Va., Nov. 15, as quoted in Redpath, *John Brown*, pp. 354–5.
64. Ruth Brown Thompson to F. B. Sanborn in listing her father's favorite books, Sanborn, *John Brown*, p. 58. Since the evidence, particularly statements of James Foreman and George B. Delamater, indicates that John Brown may have read more widely and persistently in Randolph than he ever did again, most of the books he liked, insofar as they are known, are mentioned above.
65. JB to "Dear Children," Troy, N.Y.,

Jan. 23, 1852, Chicago Historical Society.

66. MS. interview with Salmon Brown, by K. Mayo, 1908, Villard Collection.

67. William Ellery Channing, *Thoreau, The Poet-Naturalist, With Memorial Verses,* Boston, 1903, p. 32. Authony Trollope in his *Autobiography,* Leipzig (Tauchnitz edition), 1883, p. 29, says that when he was going to school at Winchester in England in 1827, "It was just possible to obtain five scourgings in one day . . . and I have often boasted that I obtained them all."

68. JB to Henry L. Stearns, July 15, 1857.

69. MS. interview with Jason Brown, by K. Mayo, 1908, Villard Collection. The italics are Miss Mayo's.

70. Sanborn, *John Brown,* pp. 91–3.

71. John Brown, Jr., tells of his father shaving in an interview published May 3, 1895, in what apparently is the Boston *Herald.* The clipping with the name of the newspaper cut away is in the Rust Collection, Huntington Library. John Brown's shaving gear is in the Kansas State Historical Society. The strop bears the legend: "A. H. Ryder's Magnetic Strop"; the razor, imported from Sheffield, is of excellent workmanship; but the brush has only a brief unpainted wooden handle, its tough bristles fastened on, or reinforced, by string wound around the handle's top. There is also a black razor case with the name of "Jackson & Co."

72. Ibid.

73. Foreman to Redpath, Dec. 28, 1859.

74. Bemis, *John Quincy Adams and the Union,* p. 299.

75. *Crawford Messenger,* April 29 and May 20, 1830, as quoted in Miller, *John Brown, Pennsylvania Citizen,* p. 12.

76. JB to "Dear Father," Randolph, June 12, 1830, copy owned by Boyd B. Stutler and quoted in full by Miller, *John Brown, Pennsylvania Citizen,* pp. 10–11.

77. *Cleveland Press,* May 3, 1895.

XII
A Brief Calvinistic Euphoria

1. Frederick Douglass, describing his Springfield interview with John Brown in 1847. "He held," said Douglass, referring to Brown, "that there was need of something startling to prevent the agitation of the question from dying out; that slavery had come near being abolished in Virginia by the Nat Turner insurrection, and he thought his method would speedily put an end to it, both in Maryland and Virginia." Douglass, Lecture on John Brown, delivered at Harper's Ferry, May 30, 1882, typescript, National Park Service. See also John Brown's defense of the slave's ability to fight, Phillips, *Atlantic Monthly,* XLIV, December 1859.

2. "He admired Nat Turner, the negro patriot, equally with George Washington, the white deliverer," Redpath, *John Brown,* p. 105.

3. John Brown in his letter to the Stearns boy of July 15, 1857, said that the War of 1812 "was to so far disgust him with Military affairs that he would neither train, *or drill;* but paid fines; & got along like a Quaker untill his age has finally cleared him of Military duty." William F. M. Arny, testifying before the Mason Committee on Jan. 16, 1860, said that John Brown had told him "twenty years ago" that he was a nonresistant, p. 72, *Mason Report.* This, of course, is at variance with John Brown, Jr.'s, story of his father pledging war against slavery in 1839.

4. Louis Filler, *The Crusade Against Slavery, 1830–1860,* New York, 1960, p. 60.

5. Wilson, *Slave Power in America,* vol. I, pp. 189–207.

6. St. Louis *Republican* as quoted in the *New York Observer,* May 7, 1836; also quoted in Aptheker, *American Slave Revolts,* p. 329.

7. Herbert Aptheker, ed., "*One Continual Cry," David Walker's Appeal to*

the *Colored Citizens of the World*, New York, 1965, pp. 45–6.

8. A reward of $500 for Turner's capture, bearing the description, was published in the *National Intelligencer* of Washington, D.C., Sept. 24, 1831. Quoted in Aptheker, *American Negro Slave Revolts*, pp. 294–5. William Lloyd Garrison, in commenting on Turner's scars and injuries, suggested that they might have been one reason for Turner's actions.

9. Letter of Governor John Floyd of Virginia to Governor James Hamilton, Jr., of South Carolina, Nov. 19, 1831, Floyd Papers, Library of Congress.

10. Sanborn, *John Brown*, p. 34 *n.*

11. Thomas R. Gray, ed., *The Confessions of Nat Turner, the leader of the late insurrection in Southampton [County] Va.*, Baltimore, 1831, as quoted in Herbert Aptheker, *A Documentary History of the Negro People of the United States*, New York, 1951, vol. I, p. 120.

12. Ibid., p. 121.

13. Ibid., pp. 122–3.

14. Ibid., p. 124.

15. Ibid., p. 123.

16. Miller, *John Brown, Pennsylvania Citizen*, p. 17.

17. Foreman to Redpath, Dec. 28, 1859.

18. From a copy owned by the Rev. Clarence S. Gee, of Lockport, N.Y. Although John Brown occasionally wrote more correctly at this period of his life than he sometimes wrote later, copies of his letters often replace the ampersand with the word "and."

19. JB to Seth Thompson, Randolph, Aug. 13, 1832.

20. MS. interview with Mrs. Danley Hobart, by K. Mayo, 1908, Villard Collection.

21. JB to Seth Thompson, Aug. 13, 1832.

22. JB to Seth Thompson, Randolph, Nov. 3, 1832.

23. JB to Seth Thompson, Randolph, Dec. 24, 1832.

24. JB to Seth Thompson, Randolph, Jan. 11, 1833.

25. MS. interview with Miss Sarah Brown, by K. Mayo, 1908, Villard Collection.

26. Ibid.

27. Ibid.

28. Ibid.

29. Address delivered at Meadville, copy in the Villard Collection.

30. JB to his brother Frederick, of Hudson, Randolph, Nov. 21, 1834, Sanborn, *John Brown*, pp. 40–1.

31. Miller, *John Brown, Pennsylvania Citizen*, p. 6.

32. JB to Seth Thompson, Randolph, April 19, 1834.

33. JB to Seth Thompson, Randolph, March 1, 1834.

34. JB to brother Frederick, *op. cit.*

35. Fletcher, *History of Oberlin College*, vol. I, pp. 145–6.

36. Lydia Maria Child to Mrs. Ellis Gray Loring, New York, Aug. 15, 1835, Women's Archives, Radcliffe College, Cambridge, Mass.

37. Ibid.

38. W. P. and F. J. Garrison, *W. L. Garrison*, vol. I, pp. 247–8.

39. Ibid., p. 342.

40. Ibid., p. 343.

41. Ibid., p. 285.

42. Thomas, *Theodore Weld*, pp. 112–13.

43. *Weld-Grimké Letters*, vol. I, pp. 205–7.

44. Ibid.

45. Ibid.

46. Fletcher, *History of Oberlin College*, vol. I, p. 155.

47. Sanborn, *John Brown*, pp. 40–1. Sanborn always edited John Brown's letters, correcting the spelling, occasionally shortening the sentences and replacing the ampersand with "and," but he seldom altered the language or sequence. Since a good many letters used by him have apparently been lost or at any rate are not present in collections of historical societies or libraries, there are important letters for which Sanborn is the only available source. John Brown, Jr., sent an extensive collection of his father's correspondence to Sanborn during the 1870's and 1880's

when Sanborn was preparing his biography.

XIII
Case History

1. Kent [Ohio] *Courier*, Sept. 14, 1906. Interview with Marvin Kent, son of Zenas.
2. Foreman to Redpath, Dec. 28, 1859.
3. JB to Henry L. Stearns, July 15, 1857.
4. Kent *Courier*, Sept. 14, 1906.
5. Brown-Thompson Letters.
6. See Brown's Memorandum Book No. 1, Boston Public Library, and letter to Amos Chamberlain, Hudson, April 27, 1841, Villard, *John Brown*, pp. 40–1.
7. Kent *Courier*, Sept. 14, 1906.
8. JB to Henry L. Stearns, July 15, 1857.
9. Ibid.
10. JB to wife, Dec. 3, 1846, Stutler Collection.
11. Sanborn, *John Brown*, p. 88.
12. A photostat of a copy of John Brown's survey and map of the Addition is in the Stutler Collection.
13. Brown-Thompson Letters.
14. Ibid.
15. Sanborn, *John Brown*, p. 87.
16. Two suits in the Court of Common Pleas, Ravenna, Ohio, reveal that Brown was an officer of the Association.
17. JB to John Brown, Jr., Akron, Ohio, May 23, 1845, Massachusetts Historical Society.
18. Stutler Collection.
19. Grismer, *Akron and Summit County*, pp. 112–13.
20. Brown-Thompson Letters.
21. MS. interview with W. S. Kent, son of Marvin Kent, Dec. 23 and 24, 1908, Villard Collection; Kent *Courier*, Sept. 14, 1906. The village of Franklin was renamed Kent in honor of Marvin Kent.
22. John Brown, Jr., tells this story, Sanborn, *John Brown*, pp. 52–3, but dates it a year later than it happened.
23. Brown-Thompson Letters, July 23, 1836.

24. Ibid., Dec. 30, 1836.
25. Ibid.
26. Ibid., Feb. 24, 1837.
27. Grismer, *Akron and Summit County*, pp. 113–14.

XIV
An Increasing Commitment

1. Waite, *Western Reserve University*, p. 157.
2. Fletcher, *History of Oberlin College*, vol. I, p. 417.
3. Ibid.
4. From Finney's MS. Memoirs, as quoted in Fletcher, vol. I, p. 9.
5. "John Brown's Ohio Environment," by Mary Land, *Ohio State Archaeological and Historical Quarterly*, January 1948, p. 28.
6. Map of Hudson, showing its Underground stations, drawn by K. Mayo, Villard Collection.
7. Salmon Brown, *The Outlook*, Jan. 25, 1913.
8. Case, *Reminiscences*.
9. MS. interview with Miss Sarah Brown, by K. Mayo, Sept. 16–20, 1908, Villard Collection.
10. "John Brown in Ohio," an interview with Charles S. S. Griffing, ed. Louis Filler, *Ohio State Archaeological and Historical Quarterly*, April 1949, quoting the Cincinnati *Enquirer*, June 1879.
11. MS. interview with Salmon Brown, by K. Mayo, Oct. 11, 12, and 13, 1908, Villard Collection.
12. MS. interview with B. K. Waite, by K. Mayo, Dec. 26 and 27, 1908, Villard Collection.
13. Wilbur Henry Siebert, *Mysteries of Ohio's Underground Railroads*, Columbus, Ohio, 1951, and Siebert, *The Underground Railroad from Slavery to Freedom*. Also Henrietta Buckmaster, *Let My People Go*, New York, 1941.
14. "John Brown in Ohio," ed. Filler, *op. cit.* The article is based on an interview with Griffing in the Cincinnati *Enquirer* of June 18, 1879. Professor

Filler regarded it as substantial proof of "Brown's uprightness and disinterestedness in behalf of the Negro and antislavery."

15. Map of routes of Underground in Ohio in Siebert, *Mysteries of Ohio's Underground Railroads*.

16. Ibid., p. 15.

17. JB to his father, Springfield, Mass., April 2, 1847, Stutler Collection.

18. Owen Brown to his son, John, Nov. 26, 1855, and Jan. 26, 1856, Stutler Collection.

19. Foreman to Redpath, Dec. 28, 1859; Sanborn, *John Brown*, p. 40; Villard, *John Brown*, p. 23.

20. Adams, *R. H. Dana*, vol. I, p. 124.

21. *The Diary of John Quincy Adams*, Allan Nevins, ed., New York, 1928, p. 525.

22. Wise, *Henry A. Wise*, p. 78.

23. Adams, ed., *Memoir of John Quincy Adams*, vol. IV, p. 531. Also Bemis, *John Quincy Adams and the Foundation of American Foreign Policy*, pp. 417–18.

24. Nevins, ed., *Diary of John Quincy Adams*, pp. 246–7.

25. Bemis, *John Quincy Adams and the Union*, pp. 118–19.

26. Ibid., p. 321.

27. Bemis, *Adams and the Foundation of American Foreign Policy*, p. 180.

28. *Weld-Grimké Letters*, vol. II, pp. 899–900.

29. Bemis, *John Quincy Adams and the Union*, pp. 340, 437, and 447. Millions signed abolitionist petitions, many of the signers not previously concerned with anti-slavery. As a result of the new accessions, anti-slavery congressmen were elected in Ohio, Vermont, New York, and Massachusetts.

30. *Weld-Grimké Letters*, vol. II, pp. 905–6.

XV

Murder, the Converter

1. W. P. and F. J. Garrison, *W. L. Garrison*, vol. II, p. 183.

2. John Gill, *Tide Without Turning: Eli-jah P. Lovejoy and Freedom of the Press*, Boston, 1957, p. 125.

3. Joseph C. and Owen Lovejoy, *Memoir of the Rev. Elijah P. Lovejoy*, New York, 1838, pp. 257–8.

4. Beecher, *Alton Riots, passim*.

5. Ibid., p. 90.

6. Frank H. Dugan, "An Illinois Martyrdom," *Papers in Illinois History and Transactions for the Year, 1938*, Illinois State Historical Society, Springfield, Ill., 1939. Also Thomas Dimmock, *Lovejoy*, an Address at the Church of Unity, St. Louis, March 14, 1888, p. 16. Dimmock says that Lovejoy's attempt to resign came after the meeting in Alton on Nov. 3, 1837.

7. *Alton Riots*, p. 103.

8. Ibid., p. 54.

9. Ibid., p. 69–70.

10. J. C. and O. Lovejoy, *Memoir*, p. 268.

11. *Alton Riots*, pp. 86–90.

12. Ibid., p. 91.

13. Ibid., p. 92.

14. Adams, *Memoir*, Intro., p. 12.

15. In a letter to James Lemen, March 2, 1857, as quoted in Philip Van Doren Stern, *The Life and Writings of Abraham Lincoln*, New York, 1940, p. 236 n.

16. Bliss Perry, ed., *The Heart of Emerson's Journals*, Boston, 1926, p. 119.

17. *Weld-Grimké Letters*, vol. I., p. 481.

18. Phillips's so-called Alton Letter, printed in the Alton *Telegraph*, Nov. 12, 1897.

19. Wilson, *Slave Power in America*, vol. I, pp. 374, 382, and 387.

20. *The Liberator*, Dec. 1, 1837.

21. Ibid., Nov. 24, 1837. Garrison, while sympathizing with Lovejoy, asserted his regret that he had not died a nonresistant.

22. *The Liberator*, Dec. 8, 1837.

23. Gill, *Tide Without Turning*, pp. 206–7.

24. Rev. Edward Brown, "Pioneer Days in the Western Reserve: Beginning of John Brown's Career," *Northwestern Congregationalist*, Minneapolis, Oct. 21, 1892; Case, *Reminiscences*; Justus Newton Brown, "Lovejoy's Influence on John Brown," *The Magazine of His-*

tory, July–December 1916, Poughkeepsie and Tarrytown, N.Y.; J. N. Brown, letter, *The Nation*, Feb. 12, 1914; and Metcalf, *First Congregational Church*, p. 5.

25. Rev. Edward Brown, *op. cit.*
26. Ibid.
27. Ibid. The wording varies slightly in the various accounts. Lora Case, for example, recalls John Brown's words as "I pledge myself with God's help that I will devote my life to increasing hostility towards slavery."
28. Ibid.

XVI
The Backslider

1. JB to his father from Centreville, Allegheny County, N.Y., April 9, 1839.
2. From the Court of Common Pleas at Ravenna, Ohio.
3. JB to "My Dear Wife and Children, Winchester, Ct. 19 June 1839," in which he tells of the Bible affording him great support and comfort during his long absence, Sanborn Folder, Houghton Library.
4. Ibid.
5. Stutler Collection. Ruth, his eldest daughter, was almost nine; Frederick, his fourth surviving son, nearly eight. At this time Brown had nine children.
6. Letter of Annie Brown to Thomas Wentworth Higginson, Dec. 4, 1857. It was written from the family home at North Elba two days after her father's execution. Higginson Collection, Boston Public Library.
7. From John Brown's Memorandum Book No. 1, Boston Public Library. It is designated No. 1 to distinguish it from a similar record in a second memorandum book concerning his activities of the 1850's.
8. JB to Henry L. Stearns, July 15, 1857.
9. Memorandum Book No. 1, Boston Public Library. Few of the entries are dated, but often contain a date in the narrative which helps place them. Their position also indicates the time.

10. Stutler Collection.
11. Brown-Thompson Letters.
12. James Freeman Clarke, *Anti-Slavery Days*, New York, 1884, pp. 155–6. Carrington said the incident happened in 1836, but Villard, in *John Brown*, p. 47, placed the time as 1838 because John Brown had not been in Connecticut since his school days until that year.
13. Letter of Katharine D. Hubbard, granddaughter of Henry Hubbard, to Harriet Carpenter, Jan. 20, 1924, Chicago Historical Society.
14. Ibid.
15. John Brown, Jr., to F. B. Sanborn, Nov. 11, 1887, Stutler Collection.
16. Slaughter Collection.
17. From a copy in the Sanborn Folder, Houghton Library.
18. *Tertius Wadsworth and Joseph Wells vs. John Brown et al.*, Suit in Court of Common Pleas, Ravenna, Ohio, June 1842, for payment of a note of $5,500. The judgment was against Brown. It was in this suit that he alleged the firm owed him money.
19. JB to George Kellogg, Aug. 27, 1839. In this letter Brown admits taking the money. From a photostat in the Library of Congress.
20. Ibid.
21. Sanborn Folder, Houghton Library.
22. Slaughter Collection.
23. From a photostat of the letter, Library of Congress.
24. Chicago Historical Society.
25. Weld, ed., *American Slavery as It Is*, p. 9.
26. Wendell Phillips Garrison, the son of William Lloyd Garrison, wrote articles in *The Andover Review* of December 1890 and January 1891, in which he said that probably John Brown's 1839 vow to make war against slavery pledged him and his family to the same kind of war that was "equally the purpose of non-resistant abolitionists." He believed from an examination of John Brown's two memorandum books that their owner may not have been com-

mitted to attacking slavery by force of arms until the Kansas civil war.

27. John Brown, Jr., to F. B. Sanborn, Dec. 12, 1890, copy from the Stutler Collection.

28. Sanborn, *John Brown*, p. 69 *n.* Sanborn is wrong in his dates for Brown's horsebreeding at Franklin Mills. He was in Hudson during 1836–7.

29. Kent *Courier*, Sept. 14, 1906.

30. JB to Seth Thompson, July 21, 1840.

31. Ibid.

32. JB to his wife, March 7, 1844, Stutler Collection.

33. JB to his wife, Dec. 3, 1846, Stutler Collection.

34. Letter from "Tyler Co. Va., 27th. April, 1840," Huntington Library.

35. July 21, 1840, Slaughter Collection.

36. Copies of the Appeals from records in the Portage County Courthouse, Ravenna, Ohio, Villard Collection.

37. Villard, *John Brown*, pp. 40–1.

38. MS. interview with Mr. and Mrs. Sherman Thompson, by K. Mayo, Hudson, Dec. 20, 1908. Mrs. Thompson was the daughter of Amos Chamberlain.

39. Ibid.

40. MS. of interview with Jason Brown, by K. Mayo, Akron, Dec. 28, 1908, Villard Collection.

41. JB to his son, John, Jan. 11, 1844. Ohio Historical Society.

42. Ibid.

43. Villard, *John Brown*, p. 31.

44. JB to George Kellogg, Nov. 16, 1841, Stutler Collection.

45. The tanning partnership is dated Richfield, Jan. 3, 1842, Stutler Collection.

46. "Inventory and appraisement of the necessary and Kitchen Furniture and other articles and necessaries set off and allowed to John Brown . . ." signed Sept. 28, 1842, Richfield, Ohio, by George B. De Peyster, Assignee, Stutler Collection.

47. Sanborn, *John Brown*, pp. 55–6.

48. The affidavit is at the Western Reserve Historical Society, Cleveland.

49. An instance is in the letter of JB to "Dear Sons John, Jason, & Frederick & Daughters," Dec. 4, 1850, Ohio Historical Society.

50. Ibid.

51. The visitor was Levi Blakeslee's daughter, later Mrs. Danley Hobart, who told K. Mayo of Mrs. Brown's habit in December 1908 MS. interview, Villard Collection.

52. Sanborn, *John Brown*, p. 44.

53. JB to "Dear Son John," Richfield, Ohio, July 24, 1843, Sanborn, *John Brown*, pp. 58–9.

XVII
*Wool and
the Great Design*

1. JB to "My dear wife and children," New Hartford, Conn., June 12, 1839, copy in Sanborn Folder, Houghton Library.

2. Sanborn, *John Brown*, p. 95.

3. Stutler Collection.

4. For Brown's admiration of Cinque, see his "Words of Advice" to fugitive slaves given below, as well as in Sanborn, *John Brown*, pp. 124–6. For his admiration of Madison Washington, see Sanborn, p. 133, who reports that Brown sent a Negro friend to try to locate and recruit Washington.

5. See his "Words of Advice" to fugitive slaves for the names of some he admired for their rescue of slaves.

6. Copy of agreement in Sanborn Folder, Houghton Library.

7. The Perkins Mansion is now owned by the Summit County Historical Association.

8. Anne Brown, later the housekeeper at Kennedy Farm near Harper's Ferry just before the attack on that town.

9. Ohio Historical Society.

10. JB to children, Springfield, Dec. 1, 1850, Ohio Historical Society.

11. Sanborn, *John Brown*, p. 57.

12. *Ohio Cultivator*, Columbus, Aug. 15, 1845.

13. L. A. Morrell, *The American Shepherd*, New York, 1845, p. 422.

14. John L. Blake, *The Farm and the Fireside*, Auburn, and Buffalo, N.Y., 1855, p. 139.

15. MS. interview with Miss Anna Perkins of Perkins Hill, Akron, Ohio, by K. Mayo, Dec. 12, 1908, Villard Collection. Miss Perkins was about ten years old when John Brown entered into the partnership with her father in 1844 and about twenty when the partnership was dissolved in 1854.

16. Ibid.

17. This must have been an unnamed infant son, born April 26, 1852, at Akron and dying May 17, since he was the only child to die at Akron while John Brown was at home.

18. Interview with Miss Anna Perkins, Villard Collection.

19. MS. interview with Mrs. Charles P. Brown, by K. Mayo, Akron, Dec. 28, 1908, Villard Collection.

20. MS. interview with Salmon Brown at 24 Pearl Street, Portland, Ore., by K. Mayo, Oct. 11, 12, and 13, 1908, Villard Collection.

21. Portland [Ore.] *Telegram*, Oct. 20, 1906; also Kansas City *Star*, Oct. 21, 1906.

22. MS. interview with Miss Anna Perkins, Villard Collection.

23. See John Brown's "Words of Advice" to fugitive slaves, *John Brown*, Sanborn, pp. 124–6.

24. Wilson, *Rise and Fall of the Slave Power*, vol. II, p. 80.

25. Ibid., pp. 82–3; also Siebert, *The Underground Railroad*, pp. 170–1.

26. *The Liberator*, "The Branded Hand," Aug. 15, 1845.

27. From typescript reminiscences of James McElroy, Washington and Jefferson College, Washington, Pa.

28. Ibid.

29. Filler, ed., "John Brown in Ohio," *Ohio State Archaeological and Historical Quarterly*, April 1949.

30. MS. interview with Miss Anna Perkins, Villard Collection.

31. Lloyd Lewis, *Captain Sam Grant*, Boston, 1850, pp. 127, 136–7.

32. Justin H. Smith, *The War with Mexico*, New York, 1919, vol. I, pp. 125–6.

33. Joshua Morrow, *Life and Speeches of Thomas Corwin*, p. 49.

34. Walter Buell, *Joshua R. Giddings*, Cleveland, 1882, p. 165.

35. Henry Steele Commager, *Theodore Parker*, Boston, 1947, pp. 192–3.

36. Smith, *War with Mexico*, vol. I, pp. 391, 193, and 195; vol. II, pp. 111, 117, and 385.

37. As cited by Craven, *Edmund Ruffin*, notes, p. 265.

38. Dumond, *Anti-Slavery Origins of the Civil War*, p. 3.

39. George W. Julian, *The Life of Joshua R. Giddings*, Chicago, 1892, p. 174.

40. Ibid., 173.

41. *New York Weekly Tribune*, Feb. 26, 1859.

42. Aptheker, *Documentary History*, vol. I, pp. 278–9.

43. Ibid., pp. 290–1.

44. Ibid., p. 232.

45. Sanborn, "John Brown in Massachusetts," *Atlantic Monthly*, April 1872.

46. Douglass, *Life and Times*, p. 277.

47. *Ohio Cultivator*, Sept. 1, 1845.

48. Ibid. Other articles describing Brown's exploits in raising sheep and producing fine wool, or giving accounts of his efforts to unite wool growers, appeared in the *Ohio Cultivator* of Aug. 15, 1845; Nov. 1, 1845; Dec. 15, 1845; April 15, 1846; May 15, 1846; June 1, 1846; July 15, 1846; Sept. 1, 1846; Jan. 15, 1847; May 15, 1847; Oct. 15, 1847; March 15, 1848; and April 1, 1848. Some of the articles describe John Brown speaking before conventions of wool growers.

49. Perkins & Brown, Springfield, Mass., Aug. 18, 1846, to Charles Colt, from a Perkins & Brown Business Letter Book, Stutler Collection.

50. Perkins & Brown, Springfield, Mass., June 12, 1848, to Messrs. Kendall & Co., from Business Letter Book, Ohio Historical Society.

51. Sanborn, *John Brown*, pp. 64–5.

52. Brown to Benjamin W. Ladd, Dec. 14, 1846, Business Letter Book, p. 158.

53. *Ohio Cultivator*, July 15, 1846.

54. Cleveland *Weekly Herald*, March 17, 1847.

55. *Ohio Cultivator*, Feb. 1, 1847.

56. Cleveland *Weekly Herald*, March 17, 1847.

57. Ibid.

58. Ibid.

59. Perkins & Brown printed announcement to wool farmers, headed "Springfield, Mass," and sent out in December 1849, Ohio Historical Society.

60. Frederick Douglass, *Life and Times of Frederick Douglass*, 1882, p. 277. This was the third of his autobiographical works. The first was published in 1845, the second ten years later.

61. *The Liberator*, July 9, 1841.

62. Douglass, *Life and Times*, p. 219.

63. Philip S. Foner, *The Life and Writings of Frederick Douglass*, New York, 1950, vol. I, p. 27.

64. Copy in Huntington Library.

65. Douglass, *Life and Times*, p. 279.

66. Ibid., p. 277.

67. Ibid., pp. 277–80.

68. Commencement address at Storer College, May 30, 1882, by Frederick Douglass. Papers at Douglass's home in Anacostia, Va.

69. Douglass, *Life and Times*, pp. 280–1.

70. Ibid., pp. 281–2.

71. Ibid., p. 282.

72. For example, James C. Malin, *John Brown and the Legend of Fifty-Six*, Philadelphia, 1942, p. 507; and to a lesser extent, Wendell Phillips Garrison, "The Preludes of Harper's Ferry," *The Andover Review*, December 1890, and January 1891, *passim*.

73. JB to "Dear Children, Troy, N.Y. 19th Decem 1851," in which he tells Ruth and Henry Thompson, "I wrote Frederick Douglas[s] a few days since to direct his paper to Henry Thompson saying in case you did not promptly remit his Two Dollars in a few days for it; that *I would do so* by his advising me of the fact. . . ." Villard Collection.

XVIII
The Trials
of Commerce

1. John Brown, "Sambo's Mistakes," written in 1847 for the *Ram's Horn*, a New York anti-slavery magazine published and edited by Negroes. A copy of the article in Brown's handwriting was found by Maryland militia at the Kennedy Farm House near Harper's Ferry in 1859 at the time of the Raid. The copy is now in the Maryland Historical Society, Baltimore.

2. JB to Thomas Musgrave, Feb. 3, 1847, Business Letter Book, p. 199, Stutler Collection. Not all of John Brown's business letter books have survived. There are gaps in the record and therefore the books must be identified by the date of the letter, also giving the page number, rather than arbitrarily numbering the books 1, 2, etc.

3. JB to Samuel Lawrence, Sept. 1, 1846, Business Letter Book, p. 87.

4. JB to Messrs. Thomas Buchanan & Samuel Cowen, July 30, 1846, Business Letter Book, p. 49.

5. JB to Perkins, Springfield, Dec. 23, 1848, Dreer Collection.

6. JB to "Lawrence, the Just," Sept. 4, 1846, Business Letter Book, p. 94.

7. JB to Perkins, Dec. 29, 1848, Dreer Collection.

8. JB to Philo Buckingham, Dec. 29, 1849, Business Letter Book, p. 180.

9. Cleveland *Weekly Herald*, March 17, 1847.

10. JB to Ralph Smith, Jan. 27, 1847, Business Letter Book, p. 25.

11. JB to Messrs. Thirion Maillard & Co.,

July 21, 1846, Business Letter Book, p. 35.

12. To same, July 15, Business Letter Book, p. 34. Also July 15, 1846, to Messrs. W. & D. D. Farnum, Perkins & Brown Letter Book, p. 34.

13. JB to Perkins, Dec. 16, 1846, Stutler Collection.

14. Perkins & Brown to David Yant, Esq., Nov. 20, 1846, Business Letter Book, p. 145.

15. Perkins & Brown to Thomas More, Dec. 28, 1846, Business Letter Book, p. 167.

16. Sanborn, *John Brown*, p. 65.

17. Erickson to Henry A. Wise, Nov. 8, 1859, Library of Congress.

18. JB to "My Dear Mary," from Springfield, Mass., March 7, 1844, Stutler Collection. The letter is incorrectly dated. It is thought from its Springfield dateline and other circumstances that it should have been dated 1847.

19. JB to his wife, Jan. 22, 1850, Chicago Historical Society.

20. Huntington Library.

21. Villard, *John Brown*, pp. 35–6.

22. JB to "Dear Mary, Springfield 29th Nov 1846," Stutler Collection.

23. JB to "My Dear Wife, Springfield Mass 8th Jany 1847," Huntington Library.

24. JB to "My Dear Mary, Springfield, Mass. 7th. March 1844" (should be 1847, see note 18 above), Stutler Collection.

25. JB to "Dear Mary, Springfield Mass 29th. June 1846," Huntington Library.

26. John Brown, Jr., to F. B. Sanford, March 27, 1885, Stutler Collection.

27. John Brown, "Sambo's Mistakes," Maryland Historical Society.

28. Copy in Villard Collection. Senator Henry Clay of Kentucky, three times an unsuccessful candidate for President and the sponsor of the Compromise of 1850, was a proponent of the so-called American System, providing for a protective tariff and federal aid for internal improvements.

29. Salmon Brown, *The Outlook*, Jan. 25, 1913.

XIX
Timbucto and Waterloo

1. JB to his wife, March 7, 1847, Stutler Collection.

2. Business Letter Book, Nov. 27, 1846, p. 116.

3. JB to Thos. Lewis & Co., Dec. 26, 1849, Business Letter Book, pp. 171–2.

4. May 15, 1847, Huntington Library.

5. O. B. Frothingham, *Gerrit Smith*, New York, 1909, p. 142.

6. Redpath, *John Brown*, p. 59.

7. Sanborn, *John Brown*, p. 98.

8. Alfred L. Donaldson, *A History of the Adirondacks*, New York, 1921, vol. II, p. 6.

9. Jan. 10, 1849, Kansas State Historical Society.

10. April 24, 1848, Ohio Historical Society.

11. Ibid.

12. Sanborn, *John Brown*, pp. 65–6.

13. Copy in Villard Collection.

14. JB to J. W. and C. H. Buson, Jan. 30, 1849, Business Letter Book, p. 16.

15. JB to Abraham Miller, April 18, 1849, Business Letter Book, p. 108. There were similar letters.

16. JB to Lysander G. Perkins, April 17, 1849, Business Letter Book, p. 105; and to N. E. Austin, April 18, 1849, p. 106; and to Simon Gould, April 18, 1849, p. 107. In all of these letters, and others, he states that few of his supposed sales for cash were ever honored, declaring that "contracts that were made with us some months since have not been met by taking away the wool & paying the money."

17. JB to Samuel Slater & Sons, July 9, 1849, Business Letter Book, p. 41.

18. March 29, 1849, Business Letter Book, p. 68.

19. April 7, 1849, Business Letter Book, p. 89.

20. Business Letter Book of 1849, pp. 95–6.

21. JB to Mathew McKeever, April 16, 1849, Business Letter Book, pp. 99–100.

22. JB to James D. and William H. Ladd, Business Letter Book, pp. 117–18. May 1, 1849.

23. JB to Perkins, May 1, 1849, Boston Public Library.

24. Ruth Brown Thompson to F. B. Sanborn, Sanborn, *John Brown*, pp. 99–100.

25. Ibid.

26. Ibid., p. 99.

27. Ibid., p. 101.

28. Ibid.

29. MS. interview with Miss Sarah Brown, by K. Mayo, Sept. 16–20, 1908, Villard Collection.

30. *New York Tribune*, no date, Villard Collection.

31. Donaldson, *A History of the Adirondacks*, vol. II, p. 6.

32. Adams, *Richard Henry Dana*, vol. I, pp. 156–7.

33. J. Miller McKim to "Dear Friend, Anti-Slavery Office, Phila March 28/49," McKim Papers, Cornell University Library, Ithaca, N.Y. It is in McKim's handwriting and a copy of the letter sent.

34. Ibid.

35. William Still, *The Underground Railroad*, Philadelphia, 1872, p. 83. Still was the assistant to whom McKim referred.

36. McKim letter, March 28, 1849, McKim Papers, Cornell.

37. Ibid.

38. Copy of McKim's letter to S. A. Smith, April 8, 1849, McKim Papers, Cornell. The copy is in McKim's handwriting.

39. McKim to Smith, April 12, 1849, McKim Papers, Cornell.

40. Still, *Underground Railroad*, pp. 84–5.

41. JB to John Brown, Jr., London, Aug. 28, 1849, Sanborn, *John Brown*, p. 72.

42. John Brown, Jr., to Samuel McFarland, Aug. 21, 1849, Business Letter Book, p. 81.

43. Ibid.

44. JB to Perkins, October, 1849 (no further date), Yale University Library.

45. John Brown, Jr., to Perkins, Aug. 22, 1849, Business Letter Book, pp. 86–7.

46. John Brown, Jr., to Messrs. Patterson & Ewing, Aug. 31, 1849, Business Letter Book, pp. 102–3.

47. Sanborn, *John Brown*, p. 72.

48. Redpath, *John Brown*, p. 57.

49. Ibid.

50. Copy of bill, Villard Collection.

51. Redpath, *John Brown*, p. 57.

52. Ibid., pp. 56–7; Villard, *John Brown*, p. 62.

53. Copy of hotel bill, Villard Collection.

54. Sanborn, *John Brown*, p. 71.

55. Redpath, *John Brown*, p. 56. Redpath does not name Sanborn as his informant but Sanborn's book on John Brown, and other circumstances, indicate that he gave the information.

56. Sanborn, *John Brown*, p. 71.

57. Ohio Historical Society.

58. Ibid.

59. JB to Frederick Kinsman, Oct. 30, 1849, Business Letter Book, pp. 138–9.

60. Ibid., pp. 139–40.

61. JB to Philo Buckingham, Dec. 29, 1849, Business Letter Book, p. 180.

62. Ibid.

63. JB to Joseph Brownlee, Dec. 22, 1849, Business Letter Book, p. 167.

64. JB to John Brown, Jr., London, Oct. 5, 1849, Ohio Historical Society.

65. Syracuse University Library.

66. Copy of hotel bill, Villard Collection.

67. Ohio Historical Society.

68. JB to Philo Buckingham, Dec. 29, 1849, Business Letter Book, p. 180.

69. JB to Frederick Kinsman, Oct. 30, 1849, Business Letter Book, p. 139.

70. Ibid.

71. Ibid.

72. JB to Jacob Winter, Dec. 22, 1849, Business Letter Book, p. 166.

73. JB to Lysander Perkins, Jan. 21, 1850, Business Letter Book, p. 161.

74. Ibid.

75. JB to Simon Perkins, Feb. 20, 1850, Business Letter Book, p. 204.

76. JB to E. B. Beckwith, Dec. 29, 1849, Business Letter Book, p. 178.

77. Sanborn, *John Brown*, p. 68.
78. JB to "Dear Son John & Wife," Burgettstown, Pa., April 12, 1850, Ohio Historical Society.

XX
On the Illness
of Indecision

1. John Brown, Jr., to JB on Dec. 1, 1850, in which he quotes his father as having said his "friends and connections with few exceptions seem to be like those of Job," Ohio Historical Society.
2. JB to "Sons, John, Jason, Frederick & Daughters," Dec. 4, 1850, Ohio Historical Society.
3. Jason to John Brown, Jr., Feb. 8, 1853, Ohio Historical Society.
4. JB to his wife, July 3, 1850, Slaughter Collection.
5. JB to his wife, Aug. 22, 1850, Huntington Library.
6. Villard, *John Brown*, p. 73; Higginson, *Contemporaries*, p. 238.
7. Sanborn, *John Brown*, p. 98.
8. Dana as quoted in Adams, *Richard Henry Dana*, vol. I, p. 157.
9. Sanborn, *John Brown*, p. 105.
10. Higginson, *Contemporaries*, p. 242.
11. The notes for the undated sermon in the Stutler Collection do not contain the text but their content makes it certain that this verse from Micah, Chap. 6, is the one upon which he preached.
12. The words quoted are taken from JB's notes for his sermon.
13. JB to "Dear Sons John, Jason, Frederick & Daughters," Dec. 4, 1850, Ohio Historical Society.
14. Nov. 4, 1850, Ohio Historical Society.
15. MS. interview with Miss Sarah Brown, by K. Mayo, Sept. 16–20, 1908. Villard Collection.
16. In a sermon at the Free Church in Lynn, Mass., the Rev. Samuel Johnson reported on June 11, 1854, that Boston was at "the dizzy verge of a civil war." The situation was at times as serious at Syracuse and Cleveland.

17. Perry, *Heart of Emerson's Journals*, p. 256.
18. *The Journal of Henry D. Thoreau*, vol. II, p. 177.
19. *The Liberator*, April 5, 1850.
20. *Emerson's Journals, 1841–1844*, pp. 430–4.
21. Ibid., *1849–1855*, p. 182.
22. Ibid., pp. 179, 180, 184, 185.
23. Lawrence Lader, *The Bold Brahmins*, New York, 1961, p. 151.
24. JB to "Dear Sons John, Jason, Frederick & Daughters," Dec. 4, 1850, Ohio Historical Society.
25. JB to John Brown, Jr., Nov. 4, 1850, Ohio Historical Society.
26. Dec. 4, 1850, Ohio Historical Society.
27. John Brown, Jr., to father, Dec. 1, 1850, Ohio Historical Society.
28. Stutler Collection.
29. Sanborn, *John Brown*, p. 132.
30. William Wells Brown, the prominent Negro writer, in *The Independent*, New York, March 10, 1870; also Sanborn, *John Brown*, pp. 124–6. The two versions are identical with the exception that William Wells Brown's version does not contain the second sentence included in Sanborn's account. It is possible that William Wells Brown in copying the documents corrected the spelling and the grammar as Sanborn habitually did.
31. W. W. Brown, *The Independent*, March 10, 1870.
32. Ibid.
33. The best first-hand account of the trials and settlements resulting from them can be found in John Brown's letters, Part III, Brown & Perkins Letter Book fragments, 1851–1854, Stutler Collection.
34. JB to Perkins, Boston, Jan. 3, 1853, Stutler Collection.
35. Ibid.
36. JB to Ruth and Henry Thompson, July 20, 1852, Byron Reed Collection, Omaha, copy in Villard Collection.

37. JB to Ruth and Henry Thompson, Sept. 24, 1853, Sanborn, *John Brown*, p. 154; JB to John Brown, Jr., Aug. 26, 1853, in which he says "my own health has been poor," Stutler Collection; JB to Ruth, Aug. 10, 1852, in which he says, "I am pretty much laid up and not good for much anyway," Huntington Library; JB to Ruth and Henry Thompson, Sept. 24, 1852, in which he writes, "I am not strong," Stutler Collection; JB to his wife, Dec. 27, 1852, Sanborn, *John Brown*, p. 108; JB to Ruth and Henry Thompson, May 10, 1853, in which he says he may not live to return to North Elba, Stutler Collection.

38. JB to Ruth and Henry Thompson, Jan. 23, 1852, Chicago Historical Society; JB to Ruth Thompson, Aug. 10, 1852, Huntington Library; JB to John Brown, Jr., and his wife, Wealthy, Feb. 21, 1853, Ohio Historical Society; JB to John Brown, Jr., Aug. 26, 1853, Stutler Collection.

39. Sanborn, *John Brown*, pp. 80, 81.

40. JB to Ruth and Henry Thompson, May 10, 1853, Stutler Collection.

41. JB to Ruth and Henry Thompson, April 6, 1853; also letter to same June 30, 1853, Sanborn, *John Brown*, pp. 109, 110.

42. JB to sons, Dec. 4, 1850, Ohio Historical Society. He usually spelled "Cleveland," whether referring to the city or an individual, as "Cleaveland."

43. See JB letters to Perkins, Oct. 20, 1851, Dec. 1, 1851, Dec. 9, 1851, and Feb. 14, 1852, on Warren case, Stutler Collection. Also letter of JB to son, John Brown, Jr., Feb. 24, 1852, Syracuse University, and JB to Perkins, Jan. 26, 1852, Boston Public Library.

44. JB in an undated letter referring to Warren case and alleged perjury, Stutler Collection.

45. John Brown, Jr., to Sanborn, March 27, 1885, Stutler Collection.

46. JB to Ruth and Henry Thompson, Troy, N.Y., Jan. 23, 1852, Chicago Historical Society.

47. JB to John Brown, Jr., and Wealthy, Feb. 21, 1853, Ohio Historical Society.

48. JB to John Brown, Jr., Aug. 26, 1853, Stutler Collection.

49. "John Brown's Return to North Elba, 1855," typescript, Stutler Collection.

50. JB to Ruth and Henry Thompson, May 10, 1853, Stutler Collection.

51. Copy in Sanborn Folder, Houghton Library; also Ruchames, ed., *John Brown Reader*, pp. 78–9.

52. Sanborn, *John Brown*, p. 80.

53. JB to Ruth and Henry Thompson, Aug. 24, 1854, Byron Reed Collection, Omaha Public Library, copy in Villard Collection.

54. John Brown, Jr., to Sanborn, in Sanborn, *John Brown*, p. 188.

55. Salmon Brown in Portland [Ore.] *Telegram*, Oct. 20, 1906.

56. Higginson, *Contemporaries*, p. 235. In his story of "John Brown's Household," Higginson identified neither Salmon nor Ruth but other circumstances indicate their identity.

57. MS. interview with Miss Sarah Brown, by K. Mayo, Sept. 16–20, 1908, Villard Collection.

58. Andrew E. Norman, ed., *Phrenology: a Practical Guide to Your Head*, reprinted New York, 1969, Intro., p. x.

59. See letters concerning the marvelous divinations of mediums in Springfield of Thomas Middleton to John Brown, Jr., Jan. 19, and Feb. 4, 1850; and from W. Sizer, July 12, 1850, and July 18, 1851, on spiritualism and phrenology in general, Ohio Historical Society.

60. Norman, ed., *Phrenology*, pp. 6–11.

61. John Brown, Jr., to Ruth and Henry Thompson, Jan. 17, 1852, Chicago Historical Society.

62. Owen Brown, father of JB, writes him a letter on Dec. 10, 1850, in which he reports that John Brown, Jr., has quit lecturing "because of a difficulty in his throat," Stutler Collection.

63. JB to John Brown, Jr., and Wealthy, Sept. 13, 1853, Stutler Collection.

64. Interview with John Brown, Jr., Cleveland *Press*, May 3, 1895.

65. Redpath, *John Brown*, pp. 51–2.

66. *The Liberator*, Feb. 3, 1860.

67. Ibid.

68. Jason to John Brown, Jr., Sept. 9, 1847, Stutler Collection.

69. Salmon Brown, undated typescript dictated by Salmon shortly after Jason's death, Dec. 24, 1912, Stutler Collection.

70. JB, "A brief history of John Brown otherwise (old B) and his family: *as connected with Kansas: by one who knows.*" The MS. is in JB's handwriting and was written in 1858, Dreer Collection.

71. Jason to John Brown, Jr., Feb. 3, 1853, Ohio Historical Society.

72. MS. interview with George B. Gill, by K. Mayo, Nov. 12, 1908, Villard Collection.

73. Undated letter of Annie Brown Adams to Richard J. Hinton, Hinton Papers, Kansas State Historical Society.

74. As in JB's letter to John Brown, Jr., Dec. 1, 1851, Ohio Historical Society.

75. JB, "A brief history of John Brown," MS., Dreer Collection.

76. Ibid.

77. Ibid.

78. MS. interview with Miss Sarah Brown, by K. Mayo, Sept. 16–20, 1908, Villard Collection.

79. Ibid.

80. Phillips, *Atlantic Monthly*, XLIV, December 1879.

81. Howard Report, pp. 1–67.

82. JB to Ruth and Henry Thompson, Chicago Historical Society.

83. Sanborn, *John Brown*, p. 191.

84. Hinton, *John Brown*, p. 672; Redpath, *John Brown*, p. 203.

85. Western Reserve Historical Society.

86. Copy, Stutler Collection.

87. JB to John W. Cook, Akron, Torrington [Conn.] Public Library.

XXI

On the Dynamics of Change

1. Strode, *Jefferson Davis*, vol. I, pp. 211–12.

2. Nevins, *Ordeal of the Union*, vol. II, p. 371.

3. Foner, *History of Cuba*, vol. II, pp. 86–95.

4. For a summary of the expansionist schemes of the Pierce administration, see Nevins, *Ordeal of the Union*, vol. II, p. 379.

5. Carr, *William Walker*, pp. 110–11, 166.

6. Nevins, *Ordeal of the Union*, vol. II, p. 370.

7. John F. Claiborne, *Life and Correspondence of John A. Quitman*, New York, 1860, vol. II, p. 195. Claiborne was a friend and associate of Quitman.

8. Richardson, *Messages*, vol. V, p. 198. "The policy of my administration will not be controlled by any timid forebodings of evil from expansion," Pierce said. "Indeed it is not to be disguised that our attitude as a nation . . . render[s] the acquisition of certain possessions not within our jurisdiction eminently important."

9. Foner, *History of Cuba*, vol. II, pp. 86–95.

10. Ibid., pp. 91–5.

11. Carr, *William Walker*, pp. 198–205.

12. W. P. and F. J. Garrison, *W. L. Garrison*, vol. III, p. 411 *n*.

13. Ibid.

14. Adams, *R. H. Dana*, vol. I, pp. 288–9.

15. Wendell Phillips to Mrs. Elizabeth Pease Nicol, Aug. 7, 1854, as quoted in W. P. and F. J. Garrison, *W. L. Garrison*, vol. III, p. 411.

16. Eli Thayer, *A History of the Kansas Crusade*, New York, 1899, pp. 12–13.

17. Ibid., p. 11.

18. The letter was published in the Jan. 17, 1854, issue of *Frederick Douglass' Paper*. Copy from file in Spingarn Collection, Howard University. Prob-

ably Douglass removed the ampersands and corrected the punctuation and spelling.

19. *Trial of Theodore Parker*, p. 128.

20. Ibid., p. vi, preface, and pp. 12, 14.

21. Ibid., p. 15.

22. Commager, ed., *Theodore Parker: An Anthology*, p. 370.

23. See Thayer, *Kansas Crusade*, for demoralization of North in 1854; also *Trial of Theodore Parker*, pp. 12–18, 126–8.

24. Frothingham, *Parker*, letter to Senator W. H. Seward, N.Y., May 19, 1854, pp. 442–4; letter to Senator John P. Hale, N.H., May 23, 1854, pp. 444–5, advocating a Free State Convention at Buffalo "and measures (1) to *check* and (2) to *terminate* this matter of slavery," Massachusetts Historical Society.

25. Frothingham, *Parker*, pp. 439–40 and 448.

26. As quoted in Johnson, *The Battle Cry of Freedom*, pp. 5–6.

27. Richardson, *Messages*, Third Annual Message, Dec. 31, 1855, vol. V, pp. 349–50.

28. Edmund Ruffin Papers, University of North Carolina Library, Chapel Hill, N.C., vol. V, p. 250. Ruffin first made the statement, which was frequently repeated, in the Richmond *Enquirer* in 1850. It is pasted without date in one of his notebooks containing his written review of his activities for that year.

29. Richardson, *Messages*, vol. V, p. 371.

30. Ibid., p. 405.

31. Johnson, *The Battle Cry of Freedom*, p. 9.

32. Thayer, *The Kansas Crusade*, p. 32.

33. Allen Johnson and Dumas Malone, eds., *Dictionary of American Biography*, New York, 1928–44.

34. Thayer, *The Kansas Crusade*, p. 31.

35. Ibid., pp. 74–109.

36. Ibid., p. 283; also Johnson, *The Battle Cry of Freedom*, p. 7.

37. Ibid., p. 10.

38. Thayer, *The Kansas Crusade*, p. 282.

39. Ibid., pp. 89 and 96; Johnson, *The Battle Cry of Freedom*, p. 31.

40. Thayer, *The Kansas Crusade*, quoting Sumner in his speech, "The Crime against Kansas," pp. 118–19.

41. Ibid., p. 203; see also Foner, *Business and Slavery*, pp. 97–104.

42. Johnson, *The Battle Cry of Freedom*, p. 291.

43. Ibid., pp. 14, 15, and 16.

44. Ibid., p. 223 *n.*

45. Thayer, *The Kansas Crusade*, pp. 58–9.

46. Ibid., p. 69.

47. Ibid., p. 57.

48. Johnson, *The Battle Cry of Freedom*, pp. 67–9.

49. Daniel W. Wilder, *The Annals of Kansas*, Topeka, Kan., 1875, p. 44.

50. Thayer, *The Kansas Crusade*, pp. 68–9.

51. Johnson, *The Battle Cry of Freedom*, p. 78.

52. Robinson, *The Kansas Conflict*, p. 28.

53. Ibid., pp. 79–82.

54. Johnson, *The Battle Cry of Freedom*, pp. 75–6.

55. Ibid., pp. 80–6.

56. Malin, *John Brown*, p. 507.

57. According to a letter of his son in which JB is quoted as saying he is coming.

XXII
Slavery Conquers Kansas

1. *Howard Report*, pp. 926–7, 929.

2. Spring, *Kansas*, p. 24.

3. Ibid.

4. *Herald of Freedom*, Lawrence, Kan., Feb. 21, 1857.

5. St. Louis *News*, as quoted in the *Herald of Freedom*, Lawrence, Kan., June 16, 1855.

6. See Atchison's letter to Jefferson Davis, Sept. 24, 1854, quoted below, note 9.

7. John F. Kennedy, *Profiles in Courage*, New York, 1956, pp. 69, 70.

8. Nevins, *Ordeal of the Union*, vol. II, p. 95.

9. From a photostat of the original in the Stutler Collection. Atchison seldom capitalized the first letter of a new sentence; it has been done here for clarity.

10. Franklin, *The Militant South*, p. 39.

11. Knoxville [Tenn.] *Register*, July 4, 1838, as quoted in Weld, ed., *American Slavery as It Is*, pp. 188–90.

12. Nevins, *Ordeal of the Union*, vol. II, pp. 66–7.

13. Ibid., p. 67.

14. Eaton, *The Growth of Southern Civilization*, p. 278.

15. Boston, *Atlas*, Dec. 4, 1854, copied from Platte [Mo.] *Argus;* Robinson, *The Kansas Conflict*, pp. 93–4.

16. *Howard Report*, p. 358.

17. William Phillips, *The Conquest of Kansas*, Boston, 1856, p. 47.

18. *Howard Report*, p. 3.

19. Ibid., *passim.* This description of the Missourians is a compilation of many descriptions throughout the congressional report.

20. Ibid., p. 12; testimony of Dr. John Doy, p. 159.

21. Ibid., testimony of Samuel N. Wood, p. 141.

22. Ibid., testimony of Erastus D. Ladd, p. 116.

23. Ibid., Blanton's testimony, pp. 148–9.

24. Ibid., pp. 131–2.

25. Ibid., pp. 14, 15, and 16.

26. Ibid., p. 175.

27. Ibid., pp. 188–9.

28. Ibid., p. 357.

29. Ibid., p. 358.

30. Ibid., p. 30.

31. Ibid., p. 43.

32. Ibid., p. 43.

33. Boston *Atlas*, as quoted in the *Herald of Freedom*, Lawrence, Kan., May 26, 1855.

34. Robinson, *The Kansas Conflict*, p. 112.

35. Ibid., p. 113.

36. As quoted in the *Herald of Freedom*, Lawrence, Kan., June 16, 1855.

37. Robinson, *The Kansas Conflict*, pp. 115, 116.

38. Johnson, *The Battle Cry of Freedom*, p. 127.

39. Robinson, *The Kansas Conflict*, p. 115. All of these quotations from newspapers were published in the spring and early summer of 1855 but Robinson does not give the exact dates.

40. Ibid., pp. 133–4.

41. Ibid., p. 151.

42. Harold L. Peterson, *The Treasury of the Gun*, New York, 1962, p. 173.

43. Paxton Hibben, *Henry Ward Beecher, An American Portrait*, reprinted 1942, p. 134.

44. Ibid., pp. 110–12, 135–6, 142, and 150.

45. Johnson, *The Battle Cry of Freedom*, p. 125.

46. Ibid., pp. 127–8.

47. Ibid., p. 128; *Howard Report*, testimony of Amos A. Lawrence, p. 880.

48. Frothingham, *Parker*, p. 437.

49. Weiss, *Parker*, vol. II, p. 160.

50. JB, "A brief history of John Brown," MS., Dreer Collection.

51. Johnson, *The Battle Cry of Freedom*, pp. 208, 209, and 210.

52. JB to Ruth and Henry Thompson, Rockford, Ill., May 7, 1855, Sanborn, *John Brown*, p. 193; in the letter JB tells of receiving one from his son, John, in St. Louis, dated April 21; a letter from Salmon to his father, May 21, 1855, tells of arriving in Kansas on April 20. Copy in Villard Collection.

53. JB, "A brief history of John Brown," MS., Dreer Collection.

54. Ibid.

55. Salmon Brown, Brownsville, Kansas Territory, May 21, 1855, to JB, copy in Villard Collection.

56. Sanborn, *John Brown*, pp. 189–90.

57. John Brown, Jr., to his father, May 20 and 24, from "Brownsville, Kansas Territory," Dreer Collection.

58. MS. interview with Jason Brown, by K. Mayo, Dec. 13 and 14, 1908, Villard Collection.

59. Dreer Collection.

60. Kansas *Free State*, Lawrence, Kan., July 2, 1855.

61. John Brown, Jr., to the family in North Elba, Sept. 21, 1855, copy in Villard Collection. This was the way John Brown's sons talked before he ever arrived in Kansas.

XXIII
The Stakes Are Raised

1. Phillips, *Atlantic Monthly*, XLIV December 1879.

2. Chapman, *Learning and Other Essays*, p. 131.

3. Douglass, "A Lecture on John Brown," May 30, 1882, typescript, National Park Service, Washington, D.C.

4. Villard, *John Brown*, p. 54.

5. Sanborn, *John Brown*, pp. 444–5.

6. JB, "A brief history of John Brown," in which he says he did not make up his mind until the receipt of a letter from John Brown, Jr., of May 20. He continued writing the same letter on May 24 and 26. The letter was probably in North Elba when JB arrived near the end of June. Dreer Collection.

7. *The Liberator*, Feb. 23, 1855.

8. *The Liberator*, June 1, 1855.

9. *The Liberator*, April 13, 1855.

10. *The Liberator*, April 27, 1855.

11. Mrs. John Brown to John Brown, Jr., Sept. 25, 1849, copy, Villard Collection.

12. Sanborn, *John Brown*, p. 193.

13. Stutler, "John Brown's Return to North Elba, 1855," typescript, Stutler Collection, suggests that they did not arrive until June 26 or 27. It must have been a few days earlier, for John Brown, after arriving at North Elba, was at Syracuse on June 26.

14. Dreer Collection.

15. JB, "A brief history of John Brown," Dreer Collection.

16. Frederic May Holland, *Frederick Douglass, The Colored Orator*, New York, 1891, p. 247.

17. Sanborn, *John Brown*, pp. 193–4.

18. Statement of Annie Brown Adams to Oswald Garrison Villard, Villard, *John Brown*, p. 78.

19. Spring, *Kansas*, p. 68.

20. In reviewing Free State activities of 1855 in Kansas, President Pierce called them "treasonable insurrection," which he would suppress if necessary by use of the U. S. Army, Richardson, *Messages*, vol. V, p. 158.

21. As quoted in Parker, *Defence*, pp. 149–50.

22. Weiss, *Parker*, vol. II, p. 190.

23. Frothingham, *Parker*, p. 420.

24. Commager, ed., *Theodore Parker: An Anthology*, p. 8.

25. Frothingham, *Parker*, p. 344.

26. Richards, ed., *Letters and Journals of S. G. Howe*, p. 233.

27. Laura A. White, *Robert Barnwell: Father of Secession*, New York, 1931, p. 109.

28. Allan Nevins, *Fremont*, New York, 1955, pp. 422–3.

29. Weiss, *Parker*, vol. II, p. 194.

30. Parker, pamphlet of speech before American Anti-Slavery Society, New York, May 7, 1856.

31. *Harper's Weekly*, Jan. 31, 1857.

32. For Walker's complicated and ultimately disastrous career, see William Walker, *The War in Nicaragua*, Mobile, Ala., 1860; William O. Scroggs, *Filibusters and Financiers*, New York, 1916; Lawrence Greene, *The Filibuster, The Career of William Walker*, Indianapolis, 1937; and Albert Z. Carr, *The World and William Walker*, New York, 1963.

33. Carr, *Walker*, p. 115.

34. Milton, *Abraham Lincoln and the Fifth Column*, pp. 64–92.

35. Bridges, *The Southwestern Historical Quarterly*, January 1941, p. 297.

36. Crenshaw, *American Historical Review*, October 1941, pp. 24, 26.

37. As quoted by Crenshaw, ibid., p. 26.

38. The latter name is used by John Hope Franklin, *The Militant South*, pp. 124–8.

39. Milton, *Abraham Lincoln and the Fifth Column*, pp. 84–6.
40. Most of this section comes from information derived from Ruffin's writings, found in the Edmund Ruffin Papers, University of North Carolina Library, Chapel Hill, N.C., and the Diary of Edmund Ruffin, 14 MS. vols., Library of Congress.
41. Craven, *Ruffin*, pp. 226–32.
42. Ibid., p. 161.
43. John Witherspoon DuBose, *The Life and Times of William Lowndes Yancey*, reissued New York, 1942, vol. I, pp. 318, 351.
44. Ibid., p. 83.
45. Ibid., p. 75.
46. Ibid., p. 145.
47. Ibid., p. 401.
48. Ibid., p. 403.
49. Ibid., p. 300.
50. Ibid., p. 301.
51. Ibid., p. 302.
52. Ibid., pp. 331–2.
53. Frothingham, *Parker*, p. 426.
54. Weiss, *Parker*, vol. II, p. 140.
55. Parker, *Defence*, p. 6.
56. Ibid., p. 7.
57. Ibid., pp. 204, 203.
58. Frothingham, *Parker*, p. 481.
59. Weiss, *Parker*, vol. II, p. 188.
60. Ibid., vol. I, p. 330.
61. Ibid.
62. Parker to Howe, Chicopee, Feb. 6, 1855, a letter in which Parker chides Howe for his refusal to allow the circulation of the petition at a meeting. Parker protests Howe's constant criticism in letters to Howe of Nov. 29, 1854, Dec. 20, 1855, and Dec. 31, 1855, Howard University.
63. Parker, *Defence*, pp. 220–1.
64. Commager, *Theodore Parker*, p. 245.
65. Ellis, one of Parker's lawyers, quoting him, Weiss, *Parker*, vol. II, p. 147.
66. Parker, *Defence*, p. vi.
67. Commager, *Theodore Parker*, p. 247.
68. Frothingham, *Parker*, pp. 481–2.
69. Commager, *Theodore Parker*, p. 273.
70. Wise, *Wise*, pp. 75–8, 104.

71. Greene, *The Filibuster*, pp. 20–2.
72. Louise Hall Tharp, *Three Saints and a Sinner*, Boston, 1956, p. 233.
73. Ibid., p. 315.
74. Maud Howe and Florence Howe Hall, *Laura Bridgman*, London, 1904, *passim*.
75. MSS. of Smith's poetry from 1819 to 1864 can be found in the Smith Papers, Syracuse University; see also Frothingham, *Gerrit Smith*, p. 40, for his listing of ailments; also Harlow, *Gerrit Smith*, pp. 35–7 and 308, as to his singing.
76. Weiss, *Parker*, vol. I, pp. 326–7.
77. Maud Howe Elliott, *Three Generations*, Boston, 1923, p. 5, as quoted in Schwartz, *Howe*, p. 324.
78. Weiss, *Parker*, vol. I, p. 290.
79. Schwartz, *Howe*, pp. 323–4.
80. Parker, *Defence*, p. 6.
81. *The Writings of Thomas Jefferson*, vol. II, pp. 225–8.
82. Rhodes, *History of the United States*, vol. I, p. 39.
83. Nevins, ed., *The Diary of John Quincy Adams*, pp. 246–7.

XXIV
Zero Hour

1. Richardson, *Messages*, vol. VI, p. 276.
2. JB to "Dear Children," Jan. 23, 1855, Chicago Historical Society.
3. Akron, *Beacon-Journal*, Feb. 1, 1898. This consisted of an interview with Lane, who recalled Akron's efforts to help Brown.
4. Ibid.
5. Ibid.
6. MS. of interview with Jason Brown, by K. Mayo, at Akron, Dec. 28, 1908, Villard Collection.
7. MS. of interview with Benjamin Kent Waite, by K. Mayo, Dec. 26 and 27, 1908, Villard Collection. The emphasis is in the MS. of the interview.
8. Syracuse University Library.
9. JB to "Dear Wife & Children; every One," Aug. 23, 1855, Chicago Historical Society.
10. Villard, *John Brown*, p. 93.
11. Sanborn, *John Brown*, p. 240.

12. JB to "Dear Wife & Children All," Sept. 4, 1855, Kansas State Historical Society.

13. JB to "Dear Wife & Children All," Sept. 15, 1855, Stutler Collection.

14. JB, "A brief history of John Brown," Dreer Collection.

15. MS. interview with Henry Thompson, by K. Mayo, August 1908, Villard Collection; also Salmon Brown, *The Outlook*, Jan. 25, 1913.

16. JB, "A brief history of John Brown," Dreer Collection.

17. Robinson, *Kansas Conflict*, p. 151.

18. Salmon Brown to William E. Connelley, Sept. 14, 1913, Stutler Collection.

19. Lloyd Lewis, "The Man Historians Forgot," *Kansas Historical Quarterly*, February 1939.

20. Wilder, *Annals of Kansas*, pp. 60–1.

21. Ibid., p. 61.

22. Ibid., p. 55.

23. John Brown, Jr., in *Kansas Historical Publications*, vol. I, p. 272.

24. Robinson, *Kansas Conflict*, pp. 172–3.

25. Villard, *John Brown*, p. 123.

26. For the conditions at the Brown camp, see JB, "A brief history of John Brown," Dreer Collection; Wealthy Brown to Mrs. John Brown, Sept. 16, 1855, Villard Collection; JB to "Dear Wife, & Children every One," Oct. 13, 1855, Kansas State Historical Society; JB to "Dear Wife & Children every one," Nov. 2, 1855, Kansas State Historical Society; JB to "Dear Father," Nov. 9, 1855, copy, Villard Collection; and Salmon Brown to William E. Connelley, Aug. 4, 1913, in which he recalls his father reproving his sons for attending political meetings and not building cabins, Stutler Collection.

27. JB to "Dear Wife and Children Every one," Nov. 8, 1859, Massachusetts Historical Society.

28. John Brown, "A brief history of John Brown," Dreer Collection.

Manuscript Collections Consulted

OHIO HISTORICAL SOCIETY, Columbus: Although it is not generally known, this collection of John Brown letters is the largest held by any institution. It has more than ninety letters from John Brown, beginning in 1839, describing his life through specific events from his business failures of that year, through his venture in wool during the 1840's and 1850's, to his experiences in Kansas, and concluding with a photostat of his written prophecy of December 2, 1859, the day he was hanged. The collection, comprising some 382 pieces in all, includes letters of John Brown, Jr., Jason Brown, and Oliver Brown as well as Owen Brown's story of his escape from Harper's Ferry and his dictated account of the Battle of Black Jack in Kansas on June 2, 1856. Included also are two diaries of John Brown, Jr., from January 3 to December 27, 1858, and from January 1 to July 29, 1861. The collection includes a Business Letter Book of Perkins & Brown, Springfield, Mass., from March 13, 1847, to January 12, 1849, containing 632 letters written by John Brown. In addition, the Ohio Historical Society has a microfilm record of the Boyd B. Stutler Collection described below.

The Ohio Historical Society is unusually strong in other collections concerning the ante-bellum struggle against slavery. It has the Joshua R. Giddings Papers, letters, journals, and other material filling twenty-five boxes; the records of the Ripley (Ohio) Anti-Slavery Society; the Benjamin Lundy, Chester A. Lampson, John Rankin, Benjamin Tappan, and Charles Hammond Papers; as well as the Wilber H. Siebert notes and source material from which he wrote *The Underground Railroad from Slavery to Freedom*, New York, 1898, and perhaps still the most authoritative study of the subject. Its collection of Ohio newspapers of the period is unusually complete and its file of *The Ohio State Archaeological and Historical Quarterly* contains much useful material.

BOYD B. STUTLER COLLECTION, Charleston, West Virginia: For more than fifty years, Mr. Stutler, editor, author, and authority on John Brown, has been assembling the largest private collection of John Brown Papers, unrivaled in its depth and variety. It concerns the time almost as much as it does John Brown. It contains much on John Brown's contemporaries, whether in North or South. It has 104 letters and other manuscripts written by John Brown from the age of thirty-six to the day before his execution; three volumes of the Perkins & Brown Letter

Books; letters of members of the Brown family between 1850 and 1915; collected manuscripts between 1850 and 1920 relating to Brown, including eyewitness stories of the Raid at Harper's Ferry and the execution at Charlestown, Virginia; the correspondence of his early biographers, the undertaker's bill following Brown's hanging, as well as the hangman's letter of condolence to Mrs. Brown. Mr. Stutler's collection includes representative songs on John Brown as well as numerous variations of "John Brown's Body" or the "John Brown Song" as it was first called; broadsides, lithographs, and sketches of the Raid and the subsequent trial; a typescript bibliography of John Brown in periodical literature between 1845 and 1961, compiled by Mr. Stutler; the notes and scrapbooks of William E. Connelley used in the preparation of his biography of John Brown; numerous letters and scrapbooks of newspaper clippings gathered by Franklin B. Sanborn, adviser and biographer of Brown; newspaper clippings from the files of George Luther Stearns, like Sanborn, a member of Brown's so-called "Secret Six"; a bibliography of speeches, college papers, and theses on Brown, compiled by Stutler; a similar bibliography of radio scripts on Brown; and a bibliography of plays, movies, pageants, poems, novels, and short stories concerning John Brown between 1859 and 1950. This is the most summary outline of an extraordinarily rich collection.

KANSAS STATE HISTORICAL SOCIETY, Topeka, Kansas: Collections here, because they deal with the Kansas civil war, are in some ways more relevant to the historian of the period and the biographer of John Brown than any papers elsewhere. The papers include those of George Luther Stearns, Franklin B. Sanborn, Richard Hinton, W. R. L. Blackman, August Bondi, and the John Brown Collection presented by members of the Brown family, comprising some 135 items, including 32 letters either written or signed by Brown. In addition, the Kansas State Historical Society has the J. B. Abbott Papers, the Papers of James Blood, George Washington Brown, O. C. Brown, and George B. Gill, the letters of John and Sarah Everett from 1854 to 1864. Here also are the letters of Amos A. Lawrence on Kansas affairs, the Papers of Thomas A. Webb, the manuscripts of Thadeus Hyatt, the Papers of Augustus Wattles, as well as indispensable manuscript material on men and events, the Pottawatomie executions, the Battle of Osawatomie, the New England Emigrant Aid Society, Eli Thayer, James H. Lane, Charles Robinson, and Samuel C. Pomeroy. Perhaps as much as half of the extensive material in the Kansas State Historical Society concerns the period between 1850 and 1865. In addition, it has files, some of them virtually complete, of Territorial newspapers, Free State journals, as well as pro-slavery newspapers during the period of the Kansas civil war. Its files of *The Kansas Historical Quarterly* are invaluable. It is one of the most important collections available to the historian of the 1850's in the United States.

THE VILLARD COLLECTION, Columbia University Libraries, New York City: This is one of the most valuable and most neglected aggregations of John Brown material in existence; the neglect is apparently based on the theory that Oswald Garrison Villard used all of it in writing his masterly biography, *John Brown, 1800–*

1859: A Biography Fifty Years After, Boston, 1910. As a matter of fact he was forced to forgo, perhaps because of reasons of space, the full use of much important material gathered by his editorial assistant Katherine Mayo, the gifted newspaper reporter and later author, whose interviews of survivors of the John Brown story in 1908 and 1909 make up one of the most unusual accomplishments in American historiography. A pioneer in first-person verbal history, now accomplished through tapes, she interviewed Salmon Brown, Jason Brown, and Henry Thompson on their own lives and John Brown's in Kansas, on the Pottawatomie Execution, and the Battle of Black Jack, as well as interviewing Annie Brown Adams, John Brown's daughter, on life at the Kennedy Farm House, and the personalities of the young men comprising John Brown's minute army. Miss Mayo interviewed Sarah Brown on various aspects of her father's career and family life. It was not that Villard did not use Miss Mayo's facts. He did. But he had no space for the first-person accounts that she sought to reproduce as nearly as she could as they were spoken, some of her interviews running thirty pages or more, and the result of several days of interviews. More than that, she interviewed many who had known of Brown and his times in the Western Reserve, Kansas, Boston, and at Harper's Ferry and Charlestown in Virginia, recording the words of Wealthy Brown, the wife of John Brown, Jr., Thomas Wentworth Higginson, George B. Gill, Luke F. Parsons, Jennie Dunbar, Mrs. Rebecca Spring, F. B. Sanborn, and Horace White, among many other survivors of the time and the John Brown story. It is due to Katherine Mayo, also, that the collection contains copies of most letters and documents found in the other collections. It is a rich and rewarding collection of unusual diversity and magnitude.

HENRY P. SLAUGHTER COLLECTION, Trevor Arnett Library, Atlanta University, Atlanta, Georgia: The fifty-five letters of John Brown to his business partner, Seth Thompson of Hartford, Trumball County, Ohio, between 1826 and 1849 are in this collection. They form the best, indeed the only, real history of his financial difficulties and bankruptcy resulting from the depression of 1837 and his land speculations involving the Brown and Thompson Addition to Franklin Village in Ohio. They throw, too, a good deal of light on the background of the many civil suits brought against Brown at this time and reveal the pressure that led him to his misappropriations. The Slaughter Collection also contains seventeen letters to John Brown from Franklin B. Sanborn, his confederate and biographer, most of them written in 1857–8; a twelve-page handwritten eyewitness account of the Harper's Ferry Raid by D. E. Henderson; a written order by Colonel Robert E. Lee to place Brown and his surviving followers in jail; and miscellaneous papers of Richard Parker, the presiding judge at Brown's trial, who sentenced him to death.

BOSTON PUBLIC LIBRARY: This collection is crucial to the study of the time and of John Brown. It contains two of his memorandum books, the first from December 3, 1838, to February 1845, the second from early 1856 to mid-1859—the first revealing much of his character from the nature of his notations, the second from 1857 on revealing the day-to-day progress of his plan to invade the South, including the names and addresses of many associated in his effort but seldom named as participants in the plot. In addition, it contains notations of his reading on guerrilla warfare, including references to Mino, a Spanish guerrilla leader in the Peninsular War against Napoleon, from a two-volume *Life of Lord Wellington* by Joachim Hayward Stocqueler, London, 1852. Opposite there is a list of Southern towns—Little Rock, Charleston, San Antonio, St. Louis, Augusta, and others—as if he were considering possible operations in or about them. The collection contains the Thomas Wentworth Higginson Collection, including a series of telegrams and letters to B. F. Sanborn, Dr. Samuel Gridley Howe, his friend Theodore Parker, and others, before and after the Raid. Included also are the scrapbooks of Theodore Parker, dealing with fugitive slave cases, as well as the William Lloyd Garrison Collection, and the Papers of Lydia Maria Child, David Lee Child, Maria Weston Chapman, Henry Chapman, Amos Phelps, and Samuel J. May.

THE HISTORICAL SOCIETY OF PENNSYLVANIA, Philadelphia: The Collection of Ferdinand J. Dreer contains the original papers, and many of the letters or documents written by John Brown or his men, read into evidence at the trial of John Brown. Most of the material concerns the Harper's Ferry Raid or plans concerning it, and includes a copy of the Declaration of Independence thought to have been written by Brown or one of his followers, scheduled to be announced after Brown had freed a considerable area from slavery. It contains also an incomplete effort by John Brown called, "A brief history of John Brown otherwise (old B) and his family: as connected with Kansas; by one who knows." The documents in the Dreer Collection were liberated by Dreer, himself, either in Richmond or Charlestown, as a soldier in the Union Army. Most of them had been seized, at the time of the Raid on Harper's Ferry, at the nearby Kennedy Farm by Virginia militia. The collection also includes letters, from 1855 to 1858, exchanged between Henry A. Wise, Governor of Virginia, and President James Buchanan.

CHICAGO HISTORICAL SOCIETY: The Frank G. Logan Collection has twenty-seven letters and documents written by Brown, from 1842 to 1859; letters by members of his family including his eldest daughter, Ruth Brown Thompson, his son John Brown, Jr., and his brother Frederick Brown; letters expressing sympathy and esteem for Brown from O. P. Anderson, black survivor of the Raid, who wrote *A Voice from Harper's Ferry*, Boston, 1861; letters from F. B. Sanborn, William Lloyd Garrison, and John Henry Parr and others; letters of Henry A. Wise, Governor of Virginia, Thomas Hicks, Governor of Maryland, and Salmon P. Chase, Governor of Ohio, concerning the Raid on Harper's Ferry; a statement of Annie Brown Adams about her father and life at the Kennedy Farm, and also letters to Annie Brown from A. D. Stevens, W. H. Harrison, who was in reality Albert Hazlett, and Charles Plummer Tidd, all followers of Brown—the first two of whom were hanged.

The collection includes the Bible Brown used when in prison in Virginia before his execution; papers of Richard Parker, who presided at Brown's trial; and much collateral material concerning the anti-slavery movement in Illinois, as well as copies of newspapers and pamphlets of the period.

MASSACHUSETTS HISTORICAL SOCIETY, Boston: John Brown Papers, copies of the letters of Theodore Parker from June 22, 1854, to October 26, 1857; papers of Samuel Gridley Howe, Amos Adams Lawrence, treasurer of the New England Emigrant Aid Company, and John A. Andrews, abolitionist and Civil War Governor of Massachusetts, are to be found here. This society, founded in 1791, houses one of the most important collections of American historical manuscripts in existence, including the Adams Papers from 1639 to 1938, which contain the 14,898-page diary of John Quincy Adams from 1779 to 1848.

HOUGHTON LIBRARY, Harvard University, Cambridge, Massachusetts: The Sanborn Folder at this library includes copies of letters contained in Sanborn's biography of Brown. This library has letters and documents concerning many of the actors in the Brown story, including Emerson, Thoreau, Howe, Sumner, Parker, and Higginson. The writer was particularly interested in the 168 letters of Charles Sumner to Samuel Gridley Howe between 1843 and 1871, the letters before the Civil War, an unusual account of the stress and strain of anti-slavery politics in Massachusetts, referring to the assault on Sumner in 1856 and Howe's flight from Boston in 1859 at the time of the Harper's Ferry Raid.

THE WOMEN'S ARCHIVES, Radcliffe College, Cambridge, Massachusetts: The Ellis Gray Loring Collection is of unusual interest since it contains many letters by Lydia Maria Child from 1836 to 1864, which give a particularly vivid picture of the anti-slavery crusade in New York and Boston, particularly as it concerned women and more specifically as it concerned a sensitive and vigorous woman writer who was also editor of the *Anti-Slavery Standard*, New York City. In the Women's Archives are also letters of Abby Kelley Foster, Maria Weston Chapman, Anna Dickson, Eliza Lee Cabot Follen, all active in the anti-slavery cause as well as in the struggle for woman's rights. The May-Goddard Family Collection contains the papers of Abigail Williams May, one of the first women members of the Boston School Committee, and includes letters from Theodore Parker, Lydia Maria Child, William Lloyd Garrison, and Louisa May Alcott.

CORNELL UNIVERSITY LIBRARY, Department of Rare Books, Ithaca, New York: This library has the most extensive collection of anti-slavery literature in the East, as well as a complete file of *The Liberator*. It also includes an impressive variety of books, speeches, pamphlets, broadsides, journals, magazines, almanacs, memorials, and studies published by the abolitionist movement between 1831 and 1860, gathered by the prominent abolitionists Samuel J. May, of Boston, Connecticut, and central New York, and J. Miller McKim, of Philadelphia, as well as their letters and those addressed to them over nearly thirty years.

THE BOSTON ATHENAEUM: This distinguished library, visited by many of those mentioned in this book, such as Emerson, Sanborn, Howe, Parker, Higginson, and Alcott, has valuable material bearing on John Brown's visit to Boston in 1857, as well as material on most from Boston and vicinity prominent in the John Brown story. It has, too, an extraordinary collection of John Brown paintings and daguerreotypes, as well as many daguerreotypes or engravings of those prominent in planning and financing John Brown's invasion of Virginia.

THE LIBRARY OF CONGRESS, Washington, D.C.: The library has 300 items concerning John Brown, mostly having to do with the Harper's Ferry Raid and its consequences and including letters, telegrams, and documents, most of them from or to Governor Henry A. Wise of Virginia. In addition, it has nineteen affidavits, most from relatives and friends of John Brown, calling Brown innocent of his actions by reason of insanity—affidavits that Brown refused to use in his trial. There are also papers of Theodore Dwight Weld, consisting of correspondence with Wendell Phillips, Garrison, Giddings, Beriah Green, Gerrit Smith, and others. In addition, there is correspondence of Angelina Grimké Weld with L. L. Dodge, Anne R. Frost, George Thompson, Henry Wilson, Parker Pillsbury, Garrison, and others.

The library also contains the fourteen-volume *Diary of Edmund Ruffin*, from 1856 to 1865, one of the most fascinating accounts of a personality and secessionist in all American history, including his description of Harper's Ferry and the execution of John Brown, his glory in the Civil War and then his despair. The record ends on the day of his suicide.

THE UNIVERSITY OF NORTH CAROLINA LIBRARY, Chapel Hill: The library has in its Southern Historical Collection the voluminous papers of Edmund Ruffin, with the exception of the diaries in the Library of Congress and twenty-three manuscript letters from Virginians during the Revolutionary period, which had been collected by Ruffin and are at the Alderman Library of the University of Virginia, Charlottesville. The manuscript volumes in the Southern Historical Collection are six in number and include a farm journal kept at Ruthven by Julian Ruffin for 1843-7; a diary of Edmund Ruffin for 1843, dealing with his agricultural survey and soil analysis of South Carolina: "The Blackwater Guerilla," a forty-three-page manuscript of the Revolution written by Ruffin in 1851 for his children; "Incidents of my life, volume 2," autobiography covering years of 1823-51; "Incidents of my Life, volume 3," covering the years 1845 and 1852-3; "In Memoriam," Ruffin's tribute to his daughters, Jane Dupuy (1829-55) and Ella Ruffin (1832-55); and accounts of drainage in Marlbourne Farm, a ninety-seven-page manuscript with many diagrams.

NATIONAL ARCHIVES AND RECORD SERVICE, Washington, D.C.: The letters and records of Jefferson Davis as Secretary of War, 1852-6, are available here and show his part in directing the activities of the Army during the Kansas civil war. There are thousands of letters, orders, and memorandums, many directed against the Indians, enough to reveal something of the character of Davis (through his frequent quarrels with General Winfield Scott and others).

CLARENCE S. GEE, of Lockport, New York: The collection of the Reverend Gee concentrates chiefly on John Brown's genealogy and his life on the Western Reserve, particularly at Hudson. Gee has given his collection to the Hudson Library and Historical Society.

THE HUDSON LIBRARY AND HISTORICAL SOCIETY, Hudson, Ohio: This is a unique collection concentrating on the personal reminiscences of the friends, relatives, and neighbors of John Brown; it emphasizes the early days of Hudson—the first decade of the nineteenth century—and the struggle between militant abolitionists and conservatives for control of Western Reserve College. It has copies of the Hudson *Observer and Telegraph,* a weekly that carried detailed accounts of the college struggle in 1832 and 1833. Among its holdings are reminiscences in manuscript or from newspaper clippings of John Brown's friend Lora Case; of Zina Post, who arrived in Hudson in 1806; of Captain Amos Lusk, who came to Hudson in 1801, fought in the War of 1812, and was the father of Dianthe Lusk, John Brown's first wife; of Milton Lusk, John Brown's brother-in-law; of Asabiel Kilbourne, born in 1796 in Connecticut, who came with his parents to Hudson in about 1801 or 1802 and was a deacon in the Congregational Church, a strong anti-slavery man, and a member of the Underground; of Gideon Mills, John Brown's uncle; of Owen Brown, often called Squire Brown; and of Benjamin Wheedon, Heman Oviatt, Elizur Wright, and Elizur Wright, Jr., and many others. There is an excellent manuscript, "History of the First Congregational Church of Hudson, Ohio," by Emily Metcalf, which names the first missionaries to the Indians of the Western Reserve and tells of the early synods of the Congregationalists and Presbyterians and of the early ministers of Hudson's Congregational Church. The collection also contains a copy of the Journal of David Hudson, who left Goshen, Connecticut, on April 22, 1799, and arrived at what was later called Hudson on August 22, 1799.

THE HENRY E. HUNTINGTON LIBRARY, San Marino, California: The library has seventeen letters of John Brown, his Memorandum Book of 1843–6, and a large number of letters, newspaper clippings, and other material about him in the Rust and Eldridge Collections. The writer has some eighty-four Xerox copies of papers relating to John Brown, 1840–78, from these collections.

SYRACUSE UNIVERSITY LIBRARY, Syracuse, New York: The library here has a mammoth collection of Gerrit Smith Papers, unfortunately not entirely indexed or catalogued, but since Smith kept virtually everything he wrote—save any meaningful reference to John Brown—one may put his hand into almost any file and withdraw something of significance, including frequent references to Frederick Douglass, Theodore Dwight Weld, William Lloyd Garrison, Smith's career in Congress, his contributions to Kansas, his efforts for temperance, international peace, women's rights, and the Free Soil cause of Kansas, as well as records of his many benefactions totaling hundreds of thousands of dollars. He and his relatives, frenzied with panic after the John Brown Raid, went through his papers in an effort to destroy any written evidence of his close and intimate connection with it.

In addition, there is the Sol Feinstone Collection, containing a letter from John Brown, London, September 28, 1849; a diary of John Brown, Jr., in Kansas, January 1, 1856, to March 10 of that year, which details hardships and Free Soil political fortunes; an account book kept by John Brown, Jr., in Ashtabula County, Ohio, his father's staging center for Harper's Ferry for all of 1857 and part of 1858. It also contains an unidentified poem in this son's handwriting. There is also a Bible, which was owned by Wealthy Hotchkiss Brown, the wife of the eldest son of John Brown; it contains the Hotchkiss family ancestry, beginning with Charles Hotchkiss, born February 23, 1796, and records the births of the two children of John and Wealthy Brown and the marriage of one.

HOWARD UNIVERSITY, Washington, D.C.: The university has important material on Harriet Tubman, Sojourner Truth, and Frederick Douglass; on William Still, the Underground Railroad leader of Philadelphia; on Bishop J. W. Loguen, of Syracuse, New York; of Lewis Hayden, John Brown's black Boston aid; of the Reverend Henry Highland Garnet, of Troy, New York, and Washington, another of John Brown's black conspirators; and of Dr. J. N. Gloucester and his wife, of Brooklyn, New York, also contributors to John Brown's Virginia invasion. It also has other material in its Moorland-Spingarn Collection on Dr. Stephen Smith of Philadelphia and on Dr. Martin Robison Delany, the Civil War officer and African explorer who was a leader of the Chatham Convention in Canada, where black militants approved John Brown's plan for the invasion of Virginia and his Provisional Constitution setting up a non-slave state in the heart of the South.

In addition, the Howard Collection includes a valuable series of letters from Theodore Parker to Samuel Gridley Howe, 1851–6.

WESTERN RESERVE HISTORICAL SOCIETY, Cleveland, Ohio: The society includes in its collections a small number of John Brown letters; the original diary of David Hudson describing his exploratory trip to Ohio in 1799 and his later founding of Hudson, Ohio; copies of "Historical Reminiscences of Summit County" by General L. V. Bierce, Akron, Ohio, 1854, and Christian Cackler's pamphlet, "Recollections of an Old Settler," Ravenna, Ohio, 1872. Also included are letters and confidential reports of Joshua R. Giddings to I. A. Briggs, Ohio politician, from 1843 to 1848; a Giddings speech before the House against the annexation of Texas, as carried in the *Liberty Herald*, of Warren and Ashtabula, Ohio, March 27, 1845; the publications of the *Collections of the Western Reserve Historical Society*, particularly No. 101, issued in January 1920 on "The Western Reserve and the Fugitive Slave Law, A Prelude to the Civil War," by William C. Cochran, especially concerned with the Oberlin-Wellington Rescue Cases; and vital files of the Cleveland *Leader* and the Cleveland *Plain Dealer* on opposition to the Fugitive Slave Act in Ohio during the 1850's. In the Western Reserve University Libraries there is the fascinating story of "John Brown and Ashtabula County," in typescript, as well as newspaper articles written by Chester A. Lampson, editor of the Jefferson *Gazette*. They tell of the many citizens of Ashtabula who aided John Brown, knowing of his coming campaign against slavery in Virginia, and of the organization of a secret society, known as "The Black Strings," which protected from arrest John Brown, Jr., and guarded others who might have been sought by federal marshals in connection with John Brown's invasion. The same libraries contain an interesting unpublished doctoral thesis on "Early Slavery Controversy on the Western Reserve," 1940, by Edward C. Reilly.

UNIVERSITY OF AKRON, Akron, Ohio: The university has a small collection of the papers, books, and articles of General Lucius V. Bierce.

THE NEW YORK PUBLIC LIBRARY, New York City: The Rare Book Room contains copies of most of the books that John Brown read in the editions in which he probably read them. The Henry W. and Albert A. Berg Collection includes two letters by Thoreau to Isaiah Williams, while the Schomburg Collection, one of the chief records of black Americans, is particularly valuable for material on the insurrectionists Gabriel, Vesey, and Turner; on black women, including Harriet Tubman and Sojourner Truth; on John Brown's friends Frederick Douglass, Henry Highland Garnet, Bishop J. W. Loguen, Lewis Hayden, William Still, Dr. Stephen Smith, Dr. J. N. Gloucester and Mrs. Gloucester, Dr. Martin Robison Delany, Dr. James McCune Smith, and many others.

THE ADIRONDACK MUSEUM, Blue Mountain Lake, New York: The museum has material on John Brown's life in the Adirondacks, on the life and customs of the region—particularly of Essex County—and on John Brown's burial at North Elba.

THE NEW HAVEN COLONY HISTORICAL SOCIETY, New Haven, Connecticut: The society has materials on the revolt of the African chieftain Cinque and his followers on the schooner *Amistad* in 1839, on their jailing and trial in Connecticut, and on their freeing by the Supreme Court following the plea of John Quincy Adams. There is also a picture of Cinque.

VIRGINIA HISTORICAL SOCIETY, Richmond: The society has a sizable body of Henry Alexander Wise manuscripts, including the letters of Mrs. Ann (Jennings) Wise written between December 14, 1834, and April 28, 1836, while Wise was serving in Congress; and material concerning his eldest son, Jennings Wise, mortally wounded at the Battle of Roanoke on February 8, 1862. The society also has the manuscript account of David H. Strother (the artist known as Porte Crayon), which he called "The John Brown Raid: Notes by an Eye Witness and Citizen of the Invaded District," and which contains many details that have never been reported other than in the society's quarterly, *The Virginia Magazine of History and Biography*, vol. 73, No. 2. April 1965.

VIRGINIA STATE LIBRARY, Richmond: The library has a valuable collection of papers dealing with John Brown's Raid, trial, and execution, but has not any transcript of the trial proceedings apparently lost or destroyed during the Civil War.

THE PIERPONT MORGAN LIBRARY, New York City: The library has thirty-nine manuscript notebooks that form the Thoreau *Journal*—thirty-eight of them appeared in the Walden Edition of 1906 edited by Bradford Torrey and Francis H. Allen—which are used in the text on the assurance of Herbert Cahoon, Curator of Autograph Manuscripts, that they are reliable, "except for the deliberate omission of some classical quotations and references." Yet one volume was apparently missing from the wooden box containing the *Journal* by Thoreau when Torrey and Allen edited it, being later returned to the box before the *Journal* was transferred to the Morgan Library in 1956. It was this so-called "Lost Journal," volume 3, dated July 30, 1840, to January 22, 1841, that was edited and published by Perry Miller in Boston, 1958.

The most important Thoreau material connected with Brown possessed by the Morgan Library is the manuscript volume containing his handwritten autographed speech, as well as the written and signed speeches of Emerson, Alcott, and Sanborn delivered at the John Brown Memorial meeting. It was held at the Town Hall in Concord on the day of Brown's execution, 2 P.M., Friday, December 2, 1859.

There are small collections of material at the Omaha (Nebraska) Public Library; Torrington (Connecticut) Public Library; Yale University Library; Maryland Historical Society, which contains John Brown's manuscript entitled "Sambos Mistakes"; Illinois State Historical Library, Springfield; and Rochester University, New York; copies of virtually all of these materials are either in the Villard or Stutler Collections.

Acknowledgments

1

Few, I feel, have received more encouragement and help during a project such as this than the writer. The obligation I owe to Thomas Boylston Adams, President of the Massachusetts Historical Society, and Angus Cameron, Vice President and Senior Editor of Alfred A. Knopf, can scarcely be exaggerated. Both helped me not only as to the manuscript itself but in getting that support without which it could not have been completed.

It was Mr. Cameron's consistent encouragement and creative suggestion, nourishing this book through every vicissitude that did more than I can suggest to make it a reality. Mr. Adams not only read and criticized the first third of the manuscript but opened doors to sources and collections that were indispensable.

While these two have helped me most, many others have been uncommonly generous. Victor Rabinowitz, the New York attorney who directs the Louis M. Rabinowitz Foundation, supported this work with three successive grants. I am particularly grateful to two members of the Rabinowitz Foundation Board, Carey McWilliams, editor of *The Nation,* and Carl Marzani, New York writer and publisher, who read and praised the manuscript in reports which gained it further support. I take pleasure, too, in recording the help of the Chapelbrook Foundation of Boston for two grants that were crucial to the continuance of the project.

Of the many others who were helpful, I should like to mention Alfred A. Knopf, dean of American publishers and perhaps the first of their number, if the quality of the books published by him over a half century is a criterion. I should like to express my gratitude to Truman Nelson, the foremost American novelist writing of this period, whose letters over the years on John Brown and his time, and few know more of either, have been a sustaining force. Similarly, I cannot thank adequately Dr. Joseph Gennis of New Rochelle, New York; nor Boyd B. Stutler of Charleston, West Virginia, whose collection and writings on John Brown have made him the leading authority on this subject. Others who gave me important help were Robert H. Boyle, my friend and neighbor, writer on the Hudson and the Adirondacks, and the Reverend Clarence S. Gee, of Lockport, New York, who has spent a lifetime studying John Brown and collecting material concerning him.

Not all of those to whom I am indebted are still living. My friend, the late

Theodore McClintock, editor and writer, gave me help too many-sided to be easily reduced to words. Katherine Mayo, later the author of *Mother India*, and many other books, but at the time a reporter and an extraordinarily gifted one on the *New York Evening Post*, interviewed, in 1908 and 1909, many of the actors in the Brown story, and many were still living, recording their experiences as often as she could in their own words, frequently making the Western Reserve, Kansas, and Harper's Ferry live again as eyewitness, personal experience. Many of her interviews, only some of which are used in this book, will be contained in a second volume.

My gratitude to Milton Meltzer, an authority on the period, who helped me in the difficult business of obtaining illustrations and who loaned me a series of books about the time of John Brown, some of them out of print and all of them difficult to come by. The difference between having books in one's library and seeking them elsewhere is too great to need emphasis. I should like also to thank my friends Lloyd L. Brown of New York City; Beth Myers of Mill Valley, California; Albert E. Kahn of Glen Ellen, California; Richard Sasuly of Burlingame, California; Mr. and Mrs. Richard Stein and Mr. and Mrs. Cecil Lubell of Croton-on-Hudson, New York; as well as Lillian McClintock and Winifred and Denis A. Courtney, all of whom read the manuscript in whole or in part. My thanks also to Ben Botkin who has written so widely and authoritatively on American folklore and legend, and to Heman Chase of Alstead, New Hampshire, who wrote me at length on the science of surveying in John Brown's day and to Dan Botkin who photographed for me surveying equipment of that time. My thanks to Mr. and Mrs. Charlton M. Lewis, of Altadena, California, not only for their gracious hospitality but for introductions that helped me in my research. I should like to express my gratitude to Maxine Wood and Joan Terrall, of Cornwall Bridge, Connecticut, who gave the manuscript a careful and rigorous reading. I am indebted, too, to Harry Henderson, writer and editor, for photographs he took for me in eastern Kansas; and to Keith Irvine, then serving the Ghana Mission at the United Nations, for calling my attention to the tributes to John Brown made before that international organization (he is now an editor of the *Encyclopaedia Britannica*).

Those who have helped me most, of course, in the actual work of research are the staffs on those institutions that contain the great collections on John Brown and his time. Of these I should like particularly to thank the staff of the Hudson Library and Historical Society, Hudson, Ohio, for its aid in going over its unusual collection concerning the life and times of the village in which John Brown lived as a boy and a young man, as well as in his later years. I should like also to record my obligation to Kenneth A. Lhof of the Columbia University Libraries, New York City; Mrs. Elizabeth R. Martin, librarian of the Ohio Historical Society, Columbus, Ohio, and her former colleagues, Dr. James H. Rodabaugh, John Weatherford, and John H. Still. I am indebted to Nyle H. Miller, Executive Director of the Kansas State Historical Society, Topeka, Kansas, as well as to members of his staff, including Edgar Langsdorf, Robert W. Richmond, Kirke Mechem, Eugene D. Decker, Mrs. Lela Barnes, and Elsie Beine; to Norma Cuthbert of the Henry E. Huntington Library, San Marino, California; R. N. Williams, 2nd., Director of the Historical Society of Pennsylvania, Philadelphia; and Mrs. Maud D. Cole of the Rare Book Room and the staff of the Berg Collection of the New York Public Library. I am obligated to David C. Mearns, Chief of the Manuscript Division of the Library of Congress and to Leroy Bellamy of that library's Prints and Photograph Division, as well as to Elmer O. Parker of the National Archives and Records Service, and to Mrs. Dorothy Porter, Curator of the Moorland-Spingarn Collection, Howard University, all of Washington, D.C.

I am also indebted to Stephen T. Riley, Director of the Massachusetts Historical Society, as well as to Winifred Collins and Malcolm Freiberg of that society. I should like to thank Walter Muir Whitehill, Director of the Boston Athenaeum; W. H. Bond, Curator of Manuscripts, Houghton Library, Harvard University, Cambridge, Massachusetts; Barbara M. Solomon, Director of the Women's Archives, Radcliffe College, Cambridge, Massachusetts; Mrs. Arlene Lowe White, of the Western Reserve Historical Society, Cleveland, Ohio; the Trustees of the Summit County Historical Society, Akron, Ohio; and Miss Ellen Oldham of the Boston Public Library.

Others who gave generously of their time and knowledge include William W. Bennett, Librarian of the Trevor Arnett Library, Atlanta University, Atlanta, Georgia; Dr. Horace Mann Bond, and Dr. C. A. Bacote of Atlanta University. My thanks to Warren M. Robbins of the Frederick Douglass Institute and to Miss Elizabeth Albro and Steven A. Lewis of the National Park Service for access to the large collection of Douglass Papers which the Parks Department holds while the Douglass home at Anacostia is being repaired for use as a National Monument. I am grateful for the help of John Melville Jennings, Director of the Virginia Historical Society and William J. Van Schreeven, State Archivist of the Virginia State Library, both of Richmond.

I owe special thanks for the assistance of James W. Patton, Director of the Southern Historical Collection of the University of North Carolina, Chapel Hill, for aid in reproducing the papers of Edmund Ruffin; and also special thanks to Braden Vandeventer of Norfolk, Virginia, a descendant of Edmund Ruffin, for his kind permission to examine the papers. I am indebted to Miss Margaret Scriven, Librarian, and Archie Motley, Manuscripts Librarian, of the Chicago Historical Society; to Jean Hutson and Ernest Kaiser of the Schomburg Collection, New York City; to Donald D. Eddy and his staff of the Cornell University Library, Ithaca, New York, for skillful help over a prolonged period; to Howard L. Applegate, Administrator of Manuscripts, and David A. Fraser of the Carnegie Library, Syracuse University; to Herbert Cahoon, Curator of Autograph Manuscripts, the Pierpont Morgan Library, New York City, and Robert R. Macdonald, Executive Director of the New Haven Colony Historical Society, New Haven, Connecticut.

2

I wish also to indicate with more emphasis than can be given in footnotes my indebtedness to several scholars whose works have helped in shaping my thought as well as this book. Among this number is Kenneth M. Stampp, whose *The Peculiar Institution*, New York, 1956, has been a powerful force in combating that benign view of slavery presented in the works of Ulrich B. Phillips and so long accepted by many American scholars. I am indebted also to Herbert Aptheker whose *American Negro Slave Revolts*, published in 1943 by Columbia University Press, has exerted a truly pioneer influence in American scholarship, undenied by most however some may qualify his findings. His prolific later work has more than fulfilled the promise of his first. The writer has profited particularly from his *To Be Free: Studies in American Negro History*, New York, 1948, and his two volume *Documentary History of the Negro People in the United States*, New York, 1951.

I should like also to acknowledge my debt to Philip S. Foner not only for the ideas I have received from his four volume *Life and Writings of Frederick Douglass*, New York, 1950–2, but for the second volume of his *History of Cuba*, New York, 1963, which is of more than ordinary interest to any concerned, as I have been, with the American filibusters of the 1850's who tried to extend American slavery as John Brown was seeking to destroy it. Similarly, I am under obligation to John Hope Franklin for *The Militant South*, Cambridge, 1956, which contains much of value in itself while indicating further lines of inquiry.

However eclectic it may seem to those who view him as a Marxist Ulrich B. Phillips, I have profited from the books of Eugene D. Genovese who has proved once again, and with an impressive scholarship, that the slaveholders were in fact expansionist. This view was once a commonplace of political thought, particularly in the decades before and immediately after the Civil War, but with the rise of the so-called "revisionists" it was largely vitiated, at the very least becoming moot in the opinion of most scholars. I am grateful to Genovese for restoring the slaveholders' drive to extend their peculiar property and political influence to the realm of fact and the respectability of scholarship, particularly in his *The Political Economy of Slavery*, New York, 1965.

I should also like to record my obligation to Winthrop G. Jordan for his *White Over Black*, Chapel Hill, North Carolina, 1968, especially for his perceptive study of Thomas Jefferson, which includes a balanced discussion of much that has long been known of the great Virginian but censored on the grounds of policy and good taste—even though he emerges as a larger and more tragic figure and more attractive, too, when his dilemmas and ambiguities are added to the usual picture of classic serenity.

In singling out these scholars from the many I have consulted, I am perhaps being unjustly invidious. I have benefited more than I can say from the works of W. E. B. Du Bois, his novels and essays as well as his histories, and from the studies of Carter Godwin Woodson, the black scholar who was writing extensively and ably in American Negro history long before the present teachers of black studies were even born. I have consulted at every turn the works of the late Allan Nevins, in my opinion one of the most vivid and fascinating writers in the whole field of American historiography, as well as the many books of David Donald, so essential to an understanding of this period. I have gained much, I believe, from the studies, large and small, of Dwight Lowell Dumond, Clement W. Eaton, C. Vann Woodward, Henry Steele Commager, David Brion Davis, Stanley M. Elkins, Frank Tannenbaum, Oscar Handlin, Samuel Flagg Bemis, Roy F. Nichols, Alice Felt Tyler, James C. Malin, Avery O. Craven, W. J. Cash, William R. Taylor, Martin Duberman, Russel B. Nye, Bell Irvin Wiley, Benjamin Quarles,

Leon F. Litwack, Louis Ruchames, Staughton Lynd, Eric Foner, Frederick Merk, Charles Grier Sellers, Jr., John Hope Franklin, Fawn M. Brodie, Ray Allen Billington, James M. McPherson, Samuel A. Johnson, and Eleanor Flexner. I am indebted, too, to such historians, editors, critics, and biographers in the field of American literature as Edmund Wilson, Perry Miller, Walter Harding, Brooks Atkinson, Bradford Torrey, Francis H. Allen, Samuel Sillen, Henry Seidel Canby, Joseph Wood Krutch, Odell Shepard, Ralph L. Rusk, and F. O. Matthiessen.

Better scholars than I have concluded such a list without giving the titles of that written by those thanked, explaining that to do so would be supererogatory in view of the *Harvard Guide to American History*, Cambridge, 1954, as well as later readily available bibliographies. If I avail myself of this device it is not because of a lack of gratitude to the writers named but for lack of space.

Those who have written on John Brown, all of whose works I have, of course, read, are listed elsewhere.

3

I should also like to thank Alexander B. Boyer for calling to my attention a number of studies that I otherwise might have missed.

Lastly in this list of obligations, I come to one to whom I am most indebted and to whom this book is dedicated. She helped in the research. She typed and retyped a manuscript rewritten more times than either she or I like to remember. She checked references. She compiled the index. She went over the copyread manuscript and then over the proofs. I only hope that in her own work I may be as generous in helping her as she has been in helping me.

Index

A NOTE ABOUT THE AUTHOR

RICHARD O. BOYER was born in Chicago and received his primary and secondary education there before attending Washington University, St. Louis. Once named one of the three most outstanding reporters in the United States (by Frank Luther Mott and a board of cooperating editors), Mr. Boyer has reported for the St. Louis *Post-Dispatch*, the New York *Herald-Tribune*, the Boston *Herald*, and the Dallas *Times-Herald*, and during the Second World War as European war correspondent for *P.M.* Before and after serving abroad he worked for *The New Yorker*, where for twelve years he wrote Profiles and other articles. He is the author of three previous books: *Max Steuer* (1932), *The Dark Ship* (1947), and, with Herbert M. Morais, *Labor's Untold Story* (1955). Since 1955 he has been at work on the research (and the writing of this first volume) for his biography-history of John Brown and his times. Mr. Boyer lives with his wife, Sophia, in Croton-on-Hudson, New York. They have one grown son.

A NOTE ON THE TYPE

The text of this book was set on the Linotype in Janson, a recutting made directly from type cast from matrices long thought to have been made by the Dutchman Anton Janson, who was a practicing type founder in Leipzig during the years 1668–87. However, it has been conclusively demonstrated that these types are actually the work of Nicholas Kis (1650–1702), a Hungarian, who most probably learned his trade from the master Dutch type founder Dirk Voskens. The type is an excellent example of the influential and sturdy Dutch types that prevailed in England up to the time William Caslon developed his own incomparable designs from them.

This book was composed, printed, and bound
by the Haddon Craftsmen, Inc., Scranton, Pennsylvania.

Design by Philip Grushkin